THE REAL ECONOMY IN THE LONG RUN

12   Production and Growth

13   Saving, Investment, and the
Financial System

14   The Basic Tools of Finance

15   Unemployment and Its Natural Rate

These chapters describe the forces that in the long run determine key real variables, including growth in GDP, saving, investment, real interest rates, and unemployment.

MONEY AND PRICES IN THE LONG RUN

16   The Monetary System

17   Money Growth and Inflation

The monetary system is crucial in determining the long-run behavior of the price level, the inflation rate, and other nominal variables.

THE MACROECONOMICS OF OPEN ECONOMIES

18   Open-Economy Macroeconomics:
Basic Concepts

A nation's economic interactions with other nations are described by its trade balance, net foreign investment, and exchange rate.

19   A Macroeconomic Theory of the
Open Economy

A long-run model of the open economy explains the determinants of the trade balance, the real exchange rate, and other real variables.

SHORT-RUN ECONOMIC FLUCTUATIONS

20   Aggregate Demand and Aggregate Supply

21   The Influence of Monetary and Fiscal Policy
on Aggregate Demand

22   The Short-Run Tradeoff
between Inflation and Unemployment

The model of aggregate demand and aggregate supply explains short-run economic fluctuations, the short-run effects of monetary and fiscal policy, and the short-run linkage between real and nominal variables.

FINAL THOUGHTS

23   Five Debates over Macroeconomic Policy

A capstone chapter presents both sides of five major debates over economic policy.

THOMSON

SOUTH-WESTERN

Principles of Macroeconomics, 3e

N. Gregory Mankiw

Vice President, Editorial Director:
Jack W. Calhoun

Vice President, Editor-in-Chief:
Michael P. Roche

Publisher of Economics:
Michael B. Mercier

Senior Acquisitions Editor:
Peter Adams

Developmental Editor:
Jane Tufts

Contributing Editors:
Jeff Gilbreath
Sarah K. Dorger
Susanna C. Smart

Senior Marketing Manager:
Janet Hennies

Senior Marketing Coordinator:
Jenny Fruechtenicht

Production Editor:
Daniel C. Plofchan

Manufacturing Coordinator:
Sandee Milewski

Senior Media Technology Editor:
Vicky True

Media Developmental Editor:
Peggy Buskey

Media Production Editor:
Pam Wallace

Compositor:
Graphic Arts Center Indianapolis

Project Management:
Thistle Hill Publishing Services

Printer:
R.R. Donnelley
Willard, OH

Senior Design Project Manager:
Mike Stratton

Internal/Cover Designer:
Mike Stratton

Cover Illustration:
"Market Scene"
19th century French watercolor
Artist unknown
From a private collection

Cover Images:
PhotoDisc, Inc.

Internal Illustrator:
Roger Lundquist, AWS

Photography Manager:
John Hill

Photo Research:
Fred Middendorf
Marie LePage
Script Pict Ink, Ltd.

Library of Congress Control
Number: 2002111171

Package ISBN: 0-324-17189-7
Book ISBN: 0-324-26940-4

PRINCIPLES OF
MACROECONOMICS

THIRD EDITION

N. GREGORY MANKIW

HARVARD UNIVERSITY

THOMSON

SOUTH-WESTERN

Australia · Canada · Mexico · Singapore · Spain · United Kingdom · United States

ABOUT THE AUTHOR

N. Gregory Mankiw is Professor of Economics at Harvard University. As a student, he studied economics at Princeton University and MIT. As a teacher, he has taught macroeconomics, microeconomics, statistics, and principles of economics. He even spent one summer long ago as a sailing instructor on Long Beach Island.

Professor Mankiw is a prolific writer and a regular participant in academic and policy debates. His work has been published in scholarly journals, such as the *American Economic Review, Journal of Political Economy,* and *Quarterly Journal of Economics,* and in more popular forums, such as *The New York Times, The Financial Times, The Wall Street Journal,* and *Fortune.* He is also author of the best-selling intermediate-level textbook *Macroeconomics* (Worth Publishers). In addition to his teaching, research, and writing, Professor Mankiw is a research associate of the National Bureau of Economic Research, an adviser to the Federal Reserve Bank of Boston and the Congressional Budget Office, and a member of the ETS test development committee for the advanced placement exam in economics.

Professor Mankiw lives in Wellesley, Massachusetts, with his wife and three children.

To Catherine, Nicholas, and Peter,
my other contributions to the next generation

During my 20-year career as a student, the course that excited me most was the two-semester sequence on the principles of economics that I took during my freshman year in college. It is no exaggeration to say that it changed my life.

I had grown up in a family that often discussed politics over the dinner table. The pros and cons of various solutions to society's problems generated fervent debate. But, in school, I had been drawn to the sciences. Whereas politics seemed vague, rambling, and subjective, science was analytic, systematic, and objective. While political debate continued without end, science made progress.

My freshman course on the principles of economics opened my eyes to a new way of thinking. Economics combines the virtues of politics and science. It is, truly, a social science. Its subject matter is society—how people choose to lead their lives and how they interact with one another. But it approaches the subject with the dispassion of a science. By bringing the methods of science to the questions of politics, economics tries to make progress on the challenges that all societies face.

I was drawn to write this book in the hope that I could convey some of the excitement about economics that I felt as a student in my first economics course. Economics is a subject in which a little knowledge goes a long way. (The same cannot be said, for instance, of the study of physics or the Japanese language.) Economists have a unique way of viewing the world, much of which can be taught in one or two semesters. My goal in this book is to transmit this way of thinking to the widest possible audience and to convince readers that it illuminates much about the world around them.

I believe that everyone should study the fundamental ideas that economics has to offer. One purpose of general education is to inform people about the world and thereby make them better citizens. The study of economics, as much as any discipline, serves this goal. Writing an economics textbook is, therefore, a great honor and a great responsibility. It is one way that economists can help promote better government and a more prosperous future. As the great economist Paul Samuelson put it, "I don't care who writes a nation's laws, or crafts its advanced treaties, if I can write its economics textbooks."

For Whom Is This Book Written?

It is tempting for a professional economist writing a textbook to take the economist's point of view and to emphasize those topics that fascinate him and other economists. I have done my best to avoid that temptation. I have tried to put myself in the position of someone seeing economics for the first time. My goal is to emphasize the material that *students* should and do find interesting about the study of the economy.

One result is that this book is briefer than many books used to introduce students to economics. As a student, I was (and unfortunately still am) a slow reader. I groaned whenever a professor gave the class a 1,000-page tome to read. Of course, my reaction was not unique. The Greek poet Callimachus put it succinctly: "Big book, big bore." Callimachus made that observation in 250 B.C., so he was probably not referring to an economics textbook, but today his sentiment is echoed around the world every semester when students first see their economics assignments. My goal in this book is to avoid that reaction by skipping the bells, whistles, and extraneous details that distract students from the key lessons.

Another result of this student orientation is that more of this book is devoted to applications and policy—and less to formal economic theory—than is the case with many other books written for the principles course. Throughout this book I have tried to return to applications and policy questions as often as possible. Most chapters include case studies illustrating how the principles of economics are applied. In addition, "In the News" boxes (most of which are new to this edition) offer excerpts from newspaper articles showing how economic ideas shed light on current issues facing society. After students finish their first course in economics, they should think about news stories from a new perspective and with greater insight.

What's New in the Third Edition?

Much has happened in the world since I wrote the last edition of this book. Over the past few years, another U.S. recession, a new president, a tax cut, corporate accounting scandals, a new European currency, and terrorist attacks have all altered the economic landscape. Because the teaching of economics has to stay current with an ever changing world, this new edition includes dozens of new case studies and boxes.

In addition to updating the book, I have also refined its coverage and pedagogy with input from many users of the previous edition. There are many changes, both large and small. For example, the basic presentation of supply and demand in Chapter 4 has been rearranged and improved. More important, this new edition contains two new chapters. A new chapter on the "Frontiers of Microeconomics" introduces students to the economics of asymmetric information, political economy, and behavioral economics. A new chapter on "The Basic Tools of Finance" develops the concepts of present value, risk management, and asset valuation. (Only the complete 36-chapter version of this book includes both of these chapters. See below for outlines of each of the five available versions.) These new chapters are optional, and instructors can skip them without loss of continuity. But adding these topics should give students a greater appreciation of the use and scope of economics.

All the changes that I made, and the many others that I considered, were evaluated in light of the benefits of brevity. Like most things that we study in economics, a student's time is a scarce resource. I always keep in mind a dictum from the great novelist Robertson Davies: "One of the most important things about writing is to boil it down and not bore the hell out of everybody."

How Is This Book Organized?

To write a brief and student-friendly book, I had to consider new ways to organize familiar material. What follows is a whirlwind tour of this text. The tour will, I hope, give instructors some sense of how the pieces fit together.

Introductory Material

Chapter 1, "Ten Principles of Economics," introduces students to the economist's view of the world. It previews some of the big ideas that recur throughout economics, such as opportunity cost, marginal decisionmaking, the role of incentives, the gains from trade, and the efficiency of market allocations. Throughout the book, I refer regularly to the *Ten Principles of Economics* introduced in Chapter 1 to remind students that these ideas are the foundation for all economics. An icon in the margin calls attention to these key, interconnected principles.

Chapter 2, "Thinking Like an Economist," examines how economists approach their field of study. It discusses the role of assumptions in developing a theory and introduces the concept of an economic model. It also discusses the role of economists in making policy. The appendix to this chapter offers a brief refresher course on how graphs are used and how they can be abused.

Chapter 3, "Interdependence and the Gains from Trade," presents the theory of comparative advantage. This theory explains why individuals trade with their neighbors, as well as why nations trade with other nations. Much of economics is about how market forces coordinate many individual production and consumption decisions. As a starting point for this analysis, students see in this chapter why specialization, interdependence, and trade can benefit everyone.

The Fundamental Tools of Supply and Demand

The next three chapters introduce the basic tools of supply and demand. Chapter 4, "The Market Forces of Supply and Demand," develops the supply curve, the demand curve, and the notion of market equilibrium. Chapter 5, "Elasticity and Its Application," introduces the concept of elasticity and uses it to analyze events in three different markets. Chapter 6, "Supply, Demand, and Government Policies," uses these tools to examine price controls, such as rent-control and minimum-wage laws, and tax incidence.

Chapter 7, "Consumers, Producers, and the Efficiency of Markets," extends the analysis of supply and demand using the concepts of consumer surplus and producer surplus. It begins by developing the link between consumers' willingness to pay and the demand curve, and the link between producers' costs of production and the supply curve. It then shows that the market equilibrium maximizes the sum of the producer and consumer surplus. Thus, students learn early about the efficiency of market allocations.

The next two chapters apply the concepts of producer and consumer surplus to questions of policy. Chapter 8, "Application: The Costs of Taxation," shows why taxation results in deadweight losses and what determines the size of those losses. Chapter 9, "Application: International Trade," considers who wins and who loses from international trade and presents the debate over protectionist trade policies.

Macroeconomics

My overall approach to teaching macroeconomics is to examine the economy in the long run (when prices are flexible) before examining the economy in the short run (when prices are sticky). I believe that this organization simplifies learning macroeconomics for several reasons. First, the classical assumption of price flexibility is more closely linked to the basic lessons of supply and demand, which students have already mastered. Second, the classical dichotomy allows the study of the long run to be broken up in several, easily digested pieces. Third, because the business cycle represents a transitory deviation from the economy's long-run growth path, studying the transitory deviations is more natural after the long-run equilibrium is understood. Fourth, the macroeconomic theory of the short run is more controversial among economists than the macroeconomic theory of the long run. For these reasons, most upper-level courses in macroeconomics now follow this long-run-before-short-run approach; my goal is to offer introductory students the same advantage.

Returning to the detailed organization, I start the coverage of macroeconomics with issues of measurement. Chapter 10, "Measuring the Nation's Income," discusses the meaning of gross domestic product and related statistics from the national income accounts. Chapter 11, "Measuring the Cost of Living," discusses the measurement and use of the consumer price index.

The next four chapters describe the behavior of the real economy in the long run. Chapter 12, "Production and Growth," examines the determinants of the large variation in living standards over time and across countries. Chapter 13, "Saving, Investment, and the Financial System," discusses the types of financial institutions in our economy and examines their role in allocating resources. Chapter 14, "The Basic Tools of Finance," introduces present value, risk management, and asset pricing. Chapter 15, "Unemployment and Its Natural Rate," considers the long-run determinants of the unemployment rate, including job search, minimum-wage laws, the market power of unions, and efficiency wages.

Having described the long-run behavior of the real economy, the book then turns to the long-run behavior of money and prices. Chapter 16, "The Monetary System," introduces the economist's concept of money and the role of the central bank in controlling the quantity of money. Chapter 17, "Money Growth and Inflation," develops the classical theory of inflation and discusses the costs that inflation imposes on a society.

The next two chapters present the macroeconomics of open economies, maintaining the long-run assumptions of price flexibility and full employment. Chapter 18, "Open-Economy Macroeconomics: Basic Concepts," explains the relationship among saving, investment, and the trade balance, the distinction between the nominal and real exchange rate, and the theory of purchasing-power parity. Chapter 19, "A Macroeconomic Theory of the Open Economy," presents a classical model of the international flow of goods and capital. The model sheds light on various issues, including the link between budget deficits and trade deficits and the macroeconomic effects of trade policies. Because instructors differ in their emphasis on this material, these chapters are written so they can be used in different ways. Some may choose to cover Chapter 18 but not Chapter 19; others may skip both chapters; and still others may choose to defer the analysis of open-economy macroeconomics until the end of their courses.

After developing the long-run theory of the economy in Chapters 12 through 19, the book turns to explaining short-run fluctuations around the long-run trend. This organization simplifies teaching the theory of short-run fluctuations because, at this point in the course, students have a good grounding in many basic macroeconomic concepts. Chapter 20, "Aggregate Demand and Aggregate Supply," begins with some facts about the business cycle and then introduces the model of aggregate demand and aggregate supply. Chapter 21, "The Influence of Monetary and Fiscal Policy on Aggregate Demand," explains how policymakers can use the tools at their disposal to shift the aggregate-demand curve. Chapter 22, "The Short-Run Tradeoff between Inflation and Unemployment," explains why policymakers who control aggregate demand face a tradeoff between inflation and unemployment. It examines why this tradeoff exists in the short run, why it shifts over time, and why it does not exist in the long run.

The book concludes with Chapter 23, "Five Debates over Macroeconomic Policy." This capstone chapter considers five controversial issues facing policymakers: the proper degree of policy activism in response to the business cycle; the choice between rules and discretion in the conduct of monetary policy; the desirability of reaching zero inflation; the importance of balancing the government's budget; and the need for tax reform to encourage saving. For each issue, the chapter presents both sides of the debate and encourages students to make their own judgments.

Learning Tools

The purpose of this book is to help students learn the fundamental lessons of economics and to show how such lessons can be applied to the world in which they live. Toward that end, I have used various learning tools that recur throughout the book.

Case Studies   Economic theory is useful and interesting only if it can be applied to understanding actual events and policies. This book, therefore, contains numerous case studies that apply the theory that has just been developed.

"In the News" Boxes   One benefit that students gain from studying economics is a new perspective and greater understanding about news from around the world. To highlight this benefit, I have included excerpts from many newspaper articles, some of which are opinion columns written by prominent economists. These articles, together with my brief introductions, show how basic economic theory can be applied. Most of these boxes are new to this edition.

"FYI" Boxes   These boxes provide additional material "for your information." Some of them offer a glimpse into the history of economic thought. Others clarify technical issues. Still others discuss supplementary topics that instructors might choose either to discuss or skip in their lectures.

Definitions of Key Concepts   When key concepts are introduced in the chapter, they are presented in **bold** typeface. In addition, their definitions are placed in the margins. This treatment should aid students in learning and reviewing the material.

Quick Quizzes   After each major section, students are offered a "quick quiz" to check their comprehension of what they have just learned. If students cannot readily answer these quizzes, they should stop and reread material before continuing.

Chapter Summaries   Each chapter ends with a brief summary that reminds students of the most important lessons that they have just learned. Later in their study it offers an efficient way to review for exams.

List of Key Concepts   A list of key concepts at the end of each chapter offers students a way to test their understanding of the new terms that have been introduced. Page references are included so that students can review the terms they do not understand.

Questions for Review   At the end of each chapter are questions for review that cover the chapter's primary lessons. Students can use these questions to check their comprehension and to prepare for exams.

Problems and Applications   Each chapter also contains a variety of problems and applications that ask students to apply the material they have learned. Some professors may use these questions for homework assignments. Others may use them as a starting point for classroom discussions.

Alternative Versions of the Books

The book you are holding in your hand is one of five versions of this book that are available for introducing students to economics. South-Western and I offer this menu of books because instructors differ in how much time they have and what topics they choose to cover. Here is a brief description of each:

- *Principles of Economics:* This complete version of the book contains all 36 chapters. It is designed for a two-semester introductory course that covers both microeconomics and macroeconomics.
- *Principles of Microeconomics:* This version contains 22 chapters and is designed for one-semester courses in introductory microeconomics.
- *Principles of Macroeconomics:* This version contains 23 chapters and is designed for one-semester courses in introductory macroeconomics. It contains a full development of the theory of supply and demand.
- *Brief Principles of Macroeconomics:* This shortened macro version of 18 chapters contains only one chapter on the basics of supply and demand. It is designed for those instructors who want to jump to the core topics of macroeconomics more quickly.
- *Essentials of Economics:* This version of the book contains 24 chapters. It is designed for one-semester survey courses that cover the basics of both microeconomics and macroeconomics.

The table on the next page shows precisely which chapters are included in each book. Instructors who wish more information about these alternative versions should contact their local South-Western representative.

Wall Street Journal Edition

One goal in teaching the principles of economics is to provide students with a better understanding of the world around them. Many instructors, therefore, encourage students to read about economic issues in the newspaper as they take the course. Those instructors may want to consider the special *Wall Street Journal Edition* of this text. This version is the same as the standard edition but includes a 15-week subscription to both the print and interactive versions of *The Wall Street Journal*. Students can activate their subscriptions simply by completing and mailing a business reply card inserted in the back of the book. Instructors with at least ten students who activate their subscriptions will automatically receive their own free subscription. Talk to your South-Western representative or call 1-800-423-0563 for details.

Supplements

South-Western offers various supplements for instructors and students who use this book. These resources make teaching the principles of economics easy for the professor and learning them easy for the student. David R. Hakes of the University of Northern Iowa, a dedicated teacher and economist, supervised the development of the supplements for this edition.

South-Western will provide copies of these supplements free of charge to those instructors qualified under its adoption policy. Please contact your sales

AVAILABLE VERSIONS

The Five Versions of This Book

Principles of Economics	Principles of Microeconomics	Principles of Macroeconomics	Brief Principles of Macroeconomics	Essentials of Economics
1 Ten Principles of Economics	X	X	X	X
2 Thinking Like an Economist	X	X	X	X
3 Interdependence and the Gains from Trade	X	X	X	X
4 The Market Forces of Supply and Demand	X	X	X	X
5 Elasticity and Its Application	X	X		X
6 Supply, Demand, and Government Policies	X	X		X
7 Consumers, Producers and the Efficiency of Markets	X	X		X
8 Applications: The Costs of Taxation	X	X		X
9 Application: International Trade	X	X		X
10 Externalities	X			X
11 Public Goods and Common Resources	X			X
12 The Design of the Tax System	X			
13 The Costs of Production	X			X
14 Firms in Competitive Markets	X			X
15 Monopoly	X			X
16 Oligopoly	X			
17 Monopolistic Competition	X			
18 The Markets for the Factors of Production	X			
19 Earnings and Discrimination	X			
20 Income Inequality and Poverty	X			
21 The Theory of Consumer Choice	X			
22 Frontiers of Microeconomics	X			
23 Measuring a Nation's Income		X	X	X
24 Measuring the Cost of Living		X	X	X
25 Production and Growth		X	X	X
26 Saving, Investment, and the Financial System		X	X	X
27 The Basic Tools of Finance		X	X	X
28 Unemployment and Its Natural Rate		X	X	X
29 The Monetary System		X	X	X
30 Money Growth and Inflation		X	X	X
31 Open-Economy Macroeconomics: Basic Concepts		X	X	
32 A Macroeconomic Theory of the Open Economy		X	X	
33 Aggregate Demand and Aggregate Supply		X	X	X
34 The Influence of Monetary and Fiscal Policy on Aggregate Demand		X	X	X
35 The Short-Run Tradeoff between Inflation and Unemployment		X	X	
36 Five Debates over Macroeconomic Policy		X	X	

Note: Chapter numbers refer to the complete book, *Principles of Economics.*

representative to learn how you may qualify, or call the Academic Resource Center at 1-800-423-0563.

For the Instructor   Teaching the principles of economics can be a demanding job. Often, classes are large and teaching assistants in short supply. The supplements designed for the instructor make that job less difficult and more fun.

Instructor's Manual with Solutions Manual and Classroom Activities   For lecture preparation, the Instructor's Manual, written by Linda Ghent (Eastern Illinois University), offers a detailed outline for each chapter of the text that provides learning objectives, identifies stumbling blocks that students may face, offers helpful teaching tips, and provides suggested in-classroom activities for a more cooperative learning experience. The Instructor's Manual also includes solutions to all end-of-chapter exercises, Quick Quizzes, Questions for Review, and Problems and Applications found in the text.

Instructor's Resource CD   Included on this CD-ROM are the key supplements designed to aid instructors: Instructor's Integrated Resource Guide, Instructor's Manual with Solutions Manual and Classroom Activities, PowerPoint® Lecture and Exhibit Slides, Transparency Masters, and the Test Bank in both ExamView® Computerized Testing Software and Microsoft Word for ease of use.

Instructor's Integrated Resource Guide   Intended for use in planning instruction, this laminated guide provides a quick reference to all of South-Western's resources for teaching a course in economic principles and makes suggestions for incorporating them into all phases of instruction.

Test Bank   Daniel K. Biederman (University of North Dakota), Ken McCormick (University of Northern Iowa), Bryce Kanago (University of Northern Iowa), Penny Kugler (Central Missouri State University), and Andrew Parkes (University of Northern Iowa) have updated and revised the Test Bank. It consists of more than 200 questions per chapter. Every question has been checked to ensure the accuracy and clarity of the answers and painstakingly revised to address the main text revisions. Included are multiple-choice, true/false, and short-answer questions that assess students' critical thinking skills. Easy, medium, and difficult questions outline the process that students must use to arrive at their answers: recall, application, and integration. Questions are organized by text section to help instructors pick and choose their selections with ease.

Supplemental Test Banks   In order to keep the pool of Test Bank questions fresh and relevant, an additional testing resource will be published annually.

ExamView®   ExamView Computerized Testing Software contains all of the questions in the printed test bank. This program is an easy-to-use test creation software compatible with Microsoft Windows. Instructors can add or edit questions, instructions, and answers, and can select questions by previewing them on the screen, selecting them randomly, or selecting them by number. Instructors can also create and administer quizzes on-line, whether over the Internet, a local area network (LAN), or a wide area network (WAN).

The "Ten Principles" Video Set   Ken Witty, a talented documentary filmmaker, has produced a video series to illustrate the *Ten Principles of Economics* introduced in Chapter 1. Instructors can show these videos as an interesting and visually appealing introduction to topics discussed throughout the textbook.

PowerPoint Lecture and Exhibit Slides   Available only on the Web site and the IRCD are two versions of the PowerPoint presentation. Professors can save valuable time as they prepare for class using this comprehensive lecture presentation. This supplement covers all the essential topics presented in each chapter of the book. Graphs, tables, lists, and concepts are developed sequentially, much as one might develop them on a blackboard. Additional examples and applications are used to reinforce major lessons. The slides are crisp, clear, and colorful. Instructors may adapt or add slides to customize their lectures. A separate exhibit presentation provides instructors with all of the tables and graphs from the main text. The slides are all available for download at the support Web site: http://mankiw.swlearning.com.

Transparency Acetates   To help instructors build text images into their lectures, full-color transparency acetates for all important figures and tables in the third edition are available for use on an overhead projector. They are available to adopters upon request in both microeconomic and macroeconomic sets.

WebTutor   WebTutor is an interactive, Web-based, student supplement on WebCT and/or BlackBoard that harnesses the power of the Internet to deliver innovative learning aids that actively engage students. The instructor can incorporate WebTutor as an integral part of the course, or the students can use it on their own as a study guide. Benefits to students include automatic and immediate feedback from quizzes and exams; interactive, multimedia-rich explanation of concepts; on-line exercises that reinforce what they've learned; flashcards that include audio support; and greater interaction and involvement through on-line discussion forums.

WebTutor Advantage   More than just an interactive study guide, WebTutor Advantage delivers innovative learning aids that actively engage students. Benefits include automatic and immediate feedback from quizzes; interactive, multimedia-rich explanation of concepts, such as flash-animated graphing tutorials and graphing exercises that utilize an on-line graph-drawing tool; streaming video applications; on-line exercises; flashcards; and greater interaction and involvement through on-line discussion forums. Powerful instructor tools are also provided to assist communication and collaboration between students and faculty.

Instructor Resources on the Product Support Web Site   This password-protected Web site (http://mankiw.swlearning.com) features the essential resources for instructors in downloadable format: the Instructor's Manual in Word, the Test Bank in Word, and PowerPoint Lecture and Exhibit Slides.

TextChoice   TextChoice is the home of Thomson Learning's online digital content. It provides the fastest, easiest way for you to create your own learning materials. You may select content from hundreds of our best-selling titles, choose material from one of our databases, and add your own material. Contact your South-Western/Thomson Learning sales representative for more information.

Favorite Ways to Learn Economics: Instructor's Edition   Authors David Anderson of Centre College and Jim Chasey of Homewood Flossmoor High School use experiments to bring economic education to life. This is a lab manual for the classroom and for individual study that contains experiments and problem sets that reinforce key economic concepts.

Economics: HITS on the Web, *Mankiw Edition with InfoTrac*   This resource booklet supports students' research efforts on the World Wide Web. This manual includes an introduction to the World Wide Web, browsing the Web, finding information on the World Wide Web, e-mail, e-mail discussion groups and newsgroups, and documenting Internet sources for research. It also provides Internet activities for each chapter of the Mankiw text as well as a list of the hottest economic sites on the Web. Each booklet provides the student with an access code for InfoTrac College Edition, a fully searchable on-line university library containing complete articles and their images. Its database allows access to hundreds of scholarly and popular publications—all reliable sources, including magazines, journals, encyclopedias, and newsletters.

Turner Learning/CNN Economics Video with Integration Guide   Professors can bring the real world into the classroom by using the Turner Learning/CNN Economics Video. This video provides current stories of economic interest. The accompanying integration guide provides a summary and discussion questions for each clip. The video is produced in cooperation with Turner Learning, Inc. Contact your South-Western/Thomson Learning sales representative for ordering information.

For the Student   South-Western also offers supplements for students who are studying the principles of economics. These supplements reinforce the basic lessons taught in this book and offer opportunities for additional practice and feedback.

Study Guide   David R. Hakes (University of Northern Iowa) has prepared a study guide that will enhance student success. Each chapter of the study guide includes learning objectives, a description of the chapter's context and purpose, a chapter review, key terms and definitions, advanced critical thinking questions, and helpful hints for understanding difficult concepts. Students can develop their understanding by doing the practice problems and short-answer questions, then assess their mastery of the key concepts with the self-test, which includes true/false and multiple-choice questions. Solutions to all problems are included in the study guide.

Mankiw Xtra! Web Site   This site (http://mankiwxtra.swlearning.com) offers a robust set of on-line multimedia learning tools to help the student gain a deeper and richer understanding of economics, including:

- Diagnostic Pretests offer diagnostic self-assessment on student comprehension of each chapter and an individualized plan for directed study.
- The MAP (**M**ankiw **L**earning **A**ssistance **P**rogram) provides step-by-step instructions for each chapter's learning objectives to systematically guide the student to a deeper understanding of economic concepts.
- The Graphing Workshop is a one-stop learning resource for help in mastering the often difficult language of graphs. A unique learning system made up of graphing tutorials, interactive drawing tools, and exercises, it teaches the student how to interpret, reproduce, and explain graphs.
- CNN Video Clips and exercises let the student see economics in action in the real world, to help learn theoretical material by applying it to current events.
- Ask the Author Video Clips provide the student with an opportunity for review and clarification of difficult material.
- Xtra! Quizzing allows the student to create and to take randomly generated quizzes on the chapter of his or her choice.
- Economic Applications (e-con apps), including EconNews Online, EconDebate Online, and EconData Online, features help to deepen student understanding of theoretical concepts through hands-on exploration and analysis of the latest economic news stories, policy debates, and data.

PowerPoint Lecture Notes   A booklet is available that contains the Lecture Presentation in PowerPoint (both the notes and the graphics) with space next to each slide for taking notes during class. This supplement allows students to focus on classroom activities by providing them with the confident knowledge that they have an excellent set of notes for future reference. Instructors who choose to customize their PowerPoint presentations and would like to do the same with their accompanying customized printed lecture notes can do so via South-Western/Thomson Learning's custom publishing program.

Web Site   Valuable resources for students can be found on the Internet at the Mankiw textbook support site: http://mankiw.swlearning.com. Students will find links to economics-related Internet sites, PowerPoint slides for their review, and a sample chapter from the study guide. Also, career listings for students, leading economic indicator information, and an economic URL database can be found at http://economics.swlearning.com.

Economics Alive! CD-ROMS   These interactive multimedia study aids for economics are the high-tech, high-fun way to study economics. Through a combination of animated presentations, interactive graphing exercises, and simulations, the core principles of economics come to life and are driven home in an upbeat and entertaining way. This product is available in both micro and macro economics versions. Find out more at http://econalive.swlearning.com.

Favorite Ways to Learn Economics   Authors David Anderson of Centre College and Jim Chasey of Homewood Flossmoor High School use experiments to bring economic education to life. This is a lab manual for the classroom and for individual study that contains experiments and problem sets that reinforce key economic concepts.

9/11: Economic Viewpoints   The shape, pace, and spirit of the global economy has been greatly impacted by the events that occurred on September 11, 2001. South-Western now offers a new collection of essays that provides a variety of perspectives on the economic effects of these events. Each essay is written by one of South-Western's economics textbook authors, all of whom are highly regarded for both their academic and professional achievements. This unique collaboration results in one of the most cutting-edge resources available to help facilitate discussion of September 11th's impact within the context of economics courses.

Translations and Adaptations

I am delighted that versions of this book are (or will soon be) available in many of the world's languages. Currently scheduled translations include Chinese (in both standard and simple characters), Czech, French, Georgian, German, Greek, Indonesian, Italian, Japanese, Korean, Portuguese, Romanian, Russian, and Spanish. In addition, adaptations of the book for Canadian and Australian students are also available. Instructors who would like more information about these books should contact South-Western College Publishing.

Acknowledgments

In writing this book, I had the benefit of the input from many talented people. Let me begin by thanking those economics professors who read and commented on portions of the manuscript for this edition:

Uzo Agulefo,
 Northlake College
Josiah Baker,
 University of Central Florida
Charles A. Bennett,
 Gannon University
Joyce C. Bremer,
 Oakton Community College
Anne Bunton,
 Cottey College
Raymond L. Cohn,
 Illinois State University
Ron Cronovich,
 University of Nevada–Las Vegas
Susan Dadres,
 Southern Methodist University
Alan Deardorff,
 University of Michigan
Elizabeth Dickhaus,
 University of Missouri, St. Louis
Stratford M. Douglas,
 West Virginia University
Patricia J. Euzent,
 University of Central Florida

Ali Faegh,
 Houston Community College
Fred Foldvary,
 Santa Clara University
David Hakes,
 University of Northern Iowa
Andy Hanssen,
 Montana State University
Joseph Haslag,
 University of Missouri
F. Steb Hipple,
 East Tennessee State University
Brian T. Kench,
 University of New Hampshire
Jim Lee,
 Texas A&M University–Corpus Christi
Fiona C. Maclachlan,
 Manhattan College
Daniel R. Marburger,
 Arkansas State University
Pete Mavrokordatos,
 Tarrant County College–University of Phoenix
Carmen F. Menezes,
 University of Missouri

Thomas F. Pogue,
University of Iowa
Gyan Pradhan,
Westminster College
Ratha Ramoo,
Diablo Valley College
Marlene M. Reed,
Samford University
William Sander,
DePaul University
Jonathan Sandy,
University of San Diego

Sue Lynn Sasser,
University of Central Oklahoma
William Seyfried,
Winthrop University
Stanton Ullerich,
Buena Vista University
John Volpe,
Trinity College
William C. Wood,
James Madison University
Bassam Yousif,
California State University–Fullerton

Many professors contributed to the planning of this edition by reviewing the second edition. I am grateful for their suggestions and ideas:

James Q. Aylsworth,
Lakeland Community College
Laurence Ball,
Johns Hopkins University
James F. Booker,
Alfred University
Gerry Boyle,
National University of Ireland
Joyce C. Bremer,
Oakton Community College
Anne Bunton,
Cottey College
Catherine Carey,
Western Kentucky University
Christopher M. Cornell,
Fordham University
Dean Croushore,
Federal Reserve Bank of Philadelphia
Anna Della Vale,
Columbia University
Stratford Douglas,
West Virginia University
Gerard D'Souza,
West Virginia University
David A. Dyer,
University of Central Florida
Sally G. Finch,
The Westminster Schools
Eric Fisher,
The Ohio State University
Yee-Tien Fu,
National Chen-Chi University (Taiwan)
Sylvestre Gaudin,
Oberlin College
Tommy Georgiades,
DeVry Institute of Technology
Abhay Ghiara,
DeVry Institute of Technology
Douglas Irwin,
Dartmouth College

Brian T. Kench,
University of New Hampshire
Richard Lotspeich,
Indiana State University
Fiona Maclachlan,
Manhattan College
Rodney A. Madsen,
Long Beach City College
Daniel Marburger,
Arkansas State University
Marlene M. Reed,
Samford University
Stuart S. Rosenthal,
Syracuse University
June Roux,
Salem Community College
Juha Seppälä,
University of Illinois
Genevieve Signoret
University of Arkansas
Henry Siu,
Northwestern University
Dick Stanford,
Furman University
John J. Stevens,
University of Minnesota
Ginger H. Szabo,
DeVry Institute of Technology
Soumaya Tohamy,
Berry College
Randall E. Waldron,
University of South Dakota
Michael Welker,
Franciscan University (Ohio)
James D. Whitney,
Occidental College
Bonnie Wilson,
The University of Maryland, Baltimore County
Kathryn Wilson,
Kent State University

I appreciate the diligence of the diary reviewers. Their insights while using the second edition have contributed significantly to the third:

Ugur Aker,
Hiram College
Charles A. Bennett,
Gannon University
Elizabeth Dickhaus,
University of Missouri, St. Louis
Sharon Eicher,
Kansas State University

Chris Johnson,
Texas A&M University
Mark Karscig,
Central Missouri State University
Gary Lynch,
Indiana University, Northwest
Sharon Ryan,
University of Missouri–Columbia

The accuracy of a textbook is critically important. Although I am, of course, responsible for any remaining errors, I am grateful to the following professors for reading through final manuscript and page proof with me:

Tibor Besedes,
Rutgers University
Ronald Elkins,
Central Washington University

Marlene M. Reed,
Samford University
Thomas Rhoads,
Towson University

The following instructors participated in on-line surveys conducted during the revision process, contributing to the development of the text and the supplements:

Seemi Ahmad,
Dutchess County Community College
Gwendolyn Alexander,
Fordham University
Shahina Amin,
University of Northern Iowa
Cynthia Bansak,
San Diego State University
Gerald Baumgardner,
Gettysburg College
Doris Bennett,
Jacksonville State University
Ralph Brown,
University of South Dakota
David Carr,
American University
Byron Chapman,
University of Georgia
Raymond L. Cohn,
Illinois State University
Richard H. Courtney,
St Mary's College of California
Peter R. Crabb,
Northwest Nazarene College
Patrick Crowley,
Texas A&M University–Corpus Christi
Maria DaCosta,
University of Wisconsin–Eau Claire
Susan Dadres,
Southern Methodist University
Alan Deardorff,
University of Michigan
Stacy Dickert-Conlin,
Syracuse University

David Eaton,
Murray State University
Ronald Elkins,
Central Washington University
Zaki Eusufzai,
Loyola Marymount University
Patricia Euzent,
University of Central Florida
Ali Faegh,
Houston Community College
Donald Fagan,
Daniel Webster College
Daniel Flores-Guri,
Skidmore College
Fred Foldvary,
Santa Clara University
Robert Francis,
Shoreline Community College
Mark Frank,
Sam Houston State University
Rachel Friedberg,
Brown University
Lisa Geib-Gunderson,
University of Maryland
Jeffrey Gerlach,
The College of William and Mary
Mark Gius,
Quinnipiac University
Raj Goel,
Illinois State University
Lisa Grobar,
California State University–Long Beach
Barnali Gupta,
Miami University (Ohio)

Andy Hanssen,
  Montana State University
F. Steb Hipple,
  East Tennessee State University
Tom Hyclak,
  Lehigh University
Hans Isakson,
  University of Northern Iowa
Kristin Kucsma,
  Seton Hall University
Reuben Kyle,
  Middle Tennessee State University
Rose LaMont,
  Modesto Junior College
Jim Lee,
  Texas A&M University–Corpus Christi
Mary Lesser,
  Iona College
Martin Ludlum,
  Oklahoma City Community College
Ken McCormick,
  University of Northern Iowa
Khalid Mehtabdin,
  The College of Saint Rose
Kusum Mundra,
  San Diego State University

David O'Gorman,
  Santa Fe Community College
Darrell Parker,
  Georgia Southern University
Min Qi,
  Kent State University
William Sander,
  DePaul University
Robert Schwab,
  University of Maryland
William Seyfried,
  Winthrop University
David Sisk,
  San Francisco State University
Peter Thiel,
  Paradise Valley Community College
Stanton Ullerich,
  Buena Vista University
Sharmila Vishwasrao,
  Florida Atlantic University
Larry Wilson,
  Sandhills Community College
Jeff Yankow,
  Furman University
Bassam Yousif,
  California State University–Fullerton

Market surveys were conducted in preparation for this third edition of the textbook and its supplements. I appreciate the time taken by my colleagues to contribute their comments and am grateful for the useful information that they provided.

The success of the first two editions of this textbook was due in part to the many reviewers who helped me shape the manuscript. I continue to be grateful for their comments:

Kathleen S. Adler
Ashraf Afifi
Douglas Agbetsiafa
Seemin Ahmad
Rasheed Al-Hmoud
Terence Alexander
Neil O. Alper
Christine Amsler
Lisa Anderson
Kim Andrews
Okechukwu Dennis
  Anyamele
Clyde Arnold
Mahmoud P. Arya
Aliakbar Ataiifar
Leonardo Auernheimer
Paul Azrak
Kevin Baird
Stephen A. Baker
William Barber
Dru Barker
Daniel Barszcz
Klaus Becker
Doris Bennett
David Black

Peter Boettke
Michael Boyd
Chuck Britton
Robert Brooker
Oscar Brookins
Doug Brown
Mary Bumgarner
Robert J. Burrus, Jr.
Rebecca Campbell
Catherine Carey
Michael Carter
Thomas Cate
Subir Chakrabarti
Kenneth S. Chapman
John Chilton
Joy Clark
Howard Cochran
Paul Comolli
Joyce Cooper
Ron Cronovich
Dean Croushore
Susan Dadres
Doug Dalenberg
Patrick Dalendina
Justino De La Cruz

Alan Deardorff
Mary E. Deily
Stacy Dickert-Conlin
Elizabeth Dickhaus
Amy Diduch
Vern Dobis
Veda Doss
Mike Dowd
Richard Easterlin
James Eden
John Edgren
Ronald Elkins
Steffany Ellis
S. Kirk Elwood
Amy Farmer
Rick Fenner
David Figlio
Lehman Fletcher
Richard Fowles
Thomas Fox
Joseph W. Franklin
Jim Gapinski
Gay Garesche
Linda Ghent
Philip Gibbs

Kirk Gifford
J. Robert Gillette
Robert Gitter
Mark Paul Gius
Darrell Glenn
Robert Godby
Stephan F. Gohmann
Patrick Gormely
Randy Grant
Philip Gregorowicz
James Grisham
Lisa Grobar
Kwabena Gyimah-
   Brempong
R. W. Hafer
David R. Hakes
Arne Hallam
Andrew Hanssen
Mehdi Haririan
Richard Harper
Robert Harris
James Hartley
Jac C. Heckelman
Ron Heisner
James Henderson
Jannett Highfill
Daniel Himarios
Jane Himarios
Norman Hollingsworth
Thomas Husted
Beth Ingram
Darius Irani
Dwight Israelsen
A. Andrew John
Brenda Johnson
Stephen D. Joyce
Leo Kahane
Brad Kamp
Demetri Kantarelis
Mark Karscig
Alexander Katkov
Diane Keenan
Manfred Keil
George Kelley
Mark Killingsworth
Philip King
Linda Kinney
Peter Klein
Charles Klingensmith
Morris Knapp
Todd Knoop

James Knudson
Faik Koray
Patricia Koss
Marie Kratochvil
Rajaram Krishnan
Robert Krol
Penny Kugler
Mike Kupilik
Bob Lawson
Dan LeClair
Danielle Lewis
Stephen Lile
Luis Locay
Thomas Maloy
Neela Manage
Mike Marlow
Don Matthews
Cynthia McCarty
Bruce McClung
Rob Roy McGregor
Eugene McKibben
Thomas Means
Michael Meeropol
Deborah Merrigan
Charles Michalopoulos
Jeffrey Miron
Marie T. Mora
George Nagy
Farzeen Nasri
Walter Nicholson
Stephen Nord
Farrokh Nourzad
Tony O'Brien
John O'Connell
Peter K. Olson
Z. Edward O'Relley
Jack W. Osman
Jan Palmer
Ransford Palmer
Chris Papageorgiou
Tim Perri
Timothy Petry
Harmanna Poen
Naga Pulikonda
James Ragan
Reza Ramazani
Arnold H. Raphaelson
William Rawson
Francis E. Raymond III
Christine Rider
Steve Robinson

Christina Romer
S. Scanlon Romer
Joshua L. Rosenbloom
Leola Ross
Rose Rubin
Daniel Rupp
Fred J. Ruppel
Lynda Rush
Simran Sahi
Jolyne Sanjak
Rolando Santos
Sue Lynn Sasser
Edward Scahill
Torsten Schmidt
Bruce Seaman
Stanley Sedo
Michael Seelye
Linda Shaffer
Alden Shiers
David Shorow
Charles Sicotte
Mike Smitka
John Sondey
Kwang Soo Cheong
G.A. Spiva
Dennis Starleaf
William K. Steen
E. Frank Stephenson
Edward Stuart
Charles Stull
James L. Swofford
Bryan Taylor
James Thornton
Deborah Thorsen
Arthur Tobin
Naor Bich Tran
Tony Uremovic
Sharmila Vishwasrao
Joseph Walka
Harold Warren
Jack R. Wegman
Stephen Weiler
James Wetzel
Steven L. Widener
Joan Wiggenhorn
William Wood
Linus Yamane
Abdi Zahedani
Joachim Zietz

A special thanks go to Karen Dynan, Douglas Elmendorf, and Dean Croushore, who drafted many of the problems and applications presented at the end of each chapter. Yvonne Zinfon, my assistant at Harvard, as usual went beyond the call of duty as this edition was being prepared. I am also grateful to Fuad Faridi, a Harvard undergraduate, for assisting me in the final stages of this project.

The team of editors who worked on this book improved it tremendously. Jane Tufts, developmental editor, provided truly spectacular editing—as she always does. Peter Adams, senior economics acquisitions editor, did a splendid job of overseeing the many people involved in such a large project. Sarah Dorger, developmental editor, assembled an excellent team to write the supplements while managing thousands of related details. Dan Plofchan, production editor, along with the staff at Thistle Hill Publishing Services and GAC Indianapolis, had the patience and dedication necessary to turn my manuscript into this book. OffCenter Concept House professionally executed the production of the print supplements. Mike Stratton, senior designer, gave this book its clean, friendly look. Michele Gitlin, copyeditor, refined my prose, and Alexandra Nickerson, indexer, prepared a careful and thorough index. Janet Hennies, senior marketing manager, worked long hours getting the word out to potential users of this book, even as she gave birth to a future reader of it. Tom Gay, formerly of Harcourt, was instrumental in early stages of planning. Jeff Gilbreath worked as development editor until his untimely death; we will miss him. The rest of the South-Western team was also consistently professional, enthusiastic, and dedicated: Jon Schneider, Jenny Fruechtenicht, Terron Sanders, Carrie Hochstrasser, Vicky True, Peggy Buskey, Pam Wallace, and Sandee Milewski.

I must also thank my "in house" editor—Deborah Mankiw. As the first reader of almost everything I write, she continued to offer just the right mix of criticism and encouragement.

Finally, I am grateful to my children, Catherine, Nicholas, and Peter. Their unpredictable visits to my study offered welcome relief from long spans of writing and rewriting. Although now they are only ten, eight, and four years old, someday they will grow up and study the principles of economics. I hope this book provides its readers some of the education and enlightenment that I wish for my own children.

N. Gregory Mankiw
October 2002

PREFACE: TO THE STUDENT

"Economics is a study of mankind in the ordinary business of life." So wrote Alfred Marshall, the great nineteenth-century economist, in his textbook, *Principles of Economics*. Although we have learned much about the economy since Marshall's time, this definition of economics is as true today as it was in 1890, when the first edition of his text was published.

Why should you, as a student at the beginning of the twenty-first century, embark on the study of economics? There are three reasons.

The first reason to study economics is that it will help you understand the world in which you live. There are many questions about the economy that might spark your curiosity. Why are apartments so hard to find in New York City? Why do airlines charge less for a round-trip ticket if the traveler stays over a Saturday night? Why is Robin Williams paid so much to star in movies? Why are living standards so meager in many African countries? Why do some countries have high rates of inflation while others have stable prices? Why are jobs easy to find in some years and hard to find in others? These are just a few of the questions that a course in economics will help you answer.

The second reason to study economics is that it will make you a more astute participant in the economy. As you go about your life, you make many economic decisions. While you are a student, you decide how many years to stay in school. Once you take a job, you decide how much of your income to spend, how much to save, and how to invest your savings. Someday you may find yourself running a small business or a large corporation, and you will decide what prices to charge for your products. The insights developed in the coming chapters will give you a new perspective on how best to make these decisions. Studying economics will not by itself make you rich, but it will give you some tools that may help in that endeavor.

The third reason to study economics is that it will give you a better understanding of the potential and limits of economic policy. As a voter, you help choose the policies that guide the allocation of society's resources. When deciding which policies to support, you may find yourself asking various questions about economics. What are the burdens associated with alternative forms of taxation? What are the effects of free trade with other countries? What is the best way to protect the environment? How does a government budget deficit affect the economy? These and similar questions are always on the minds of policymakers in mayors' offices, governors' mansions, and the White House.

Thus the principles of economics can be applied in many of life's situations. Whether the future finds you reading the newspaper, running a business, or sitting in the Oval Office, you will be glad that you studied economics.

N. Gregory Mankiw
October 2002

BRIEF CONTENTS

TABLE OF CONTENTS

PART 1
INTRODUCTION   1

Mankiw

CONGRATULATIONS!

Your purchase of this new textbook includes complimentary access to the Mankiw Xtra! Web Site (http://mankiwxtra.swlearning.com). This site offers a robust set of online multimedia learning tools to help you gain a deeper and richer understanding of economics, including:

DIAGNOSTIC PRETESTS

Innovative quizzes that offer diagnostic self-assessment on your comprehension of each chapter and an individualized plan for directed study.

THE MAP (Mankiw Learning Assistance Program)

Provides step-by-step instructions for each chapter's learning objectives to systematically guide you through deepening your understanding of concepts.

THE GRAPHING WORKSHOP

A one-stop learning resource for help in mastering the often difficult language of graphs. A unique learning system made up of graphing tutorials, interactive drawing tools, and exercises that teaches you how to interpret, reproduce, and explain graphs.

CNN VIDEO CLIPS

CNN video segments and exercises let you see economics in action, in the real world, to help you learn theoretical material by applying it to current events.

ASK THE AUTHOR VIDEO CLIPS

These video clips, featuring N. Gregory Mankiw, are extremely helpful for review and clarification on material if you have trouble understanding an in-class lecture.

XTRA! QUIZZING

You can create and take randomly-generated quizzes on whichever chapter(s) you wish to test yourself, and endlessly practice for exams.

ECONOMIC APPLICATIONS

EconNews Online, EconDebate Online, and EconData Online features help to deepen your understanding of theoretical concepts through hands-on exploration and analysis of the latest economic news stories, policy debates, and data.

Tear Out Card Missing?

If you did not buy a new textbook, the tear-out portion of this card may be missing, or the Access Code may not be valid. Access Codes can be used only once to register for access to Mankiw Xtra!, and are not transferable. You can choose to either buy a new book or purchase access to the Mankiw Xtra! site at http://mankiwxtra.swlearning.com.

HOW TO REGISTER YOUR SERIAL NUMBER

STEP 1 Launch a Web browser and go to http://mankiwxtra.swlearning.com

STEP 2 Click the "Register" button to enter your serial number.

STEP 3 Enter your serial number exactly as it appears here and create a unique User ID, or enter an existing User ID if you have previously registered for a different product via a serial number.

SERIAL NUMBER: SC-00064QBU-NXTR

STEP 4 When prompted, create a password (or enter an existing password, if you have previously registered for a different product via a serial number). Submit the necessary information when prompted. Record your User ID and password in a secure location.

STEP 5 Once registered, follow the link to enter the product, or return to the URL above and select the "Enter" button. Note that the duration of your access to the product begins when registration is complete.

SOUTH-WESTERN

For technical support, contact
1-800-423-0563
or email
support@thomsonlearning.com.

PART 2
SUPPLY AND DEMAND I: HOW MARKETS WORK 61

CHAPTER 4
THE MARKET FORCES OF SUPPLY AND DEMAND 63

CHAPTER 5
ELASTICITY AND ITS APPLICATION 89

CHAPTER 6
SUPPLY, DEMAND, AND GOVERNMENT POLICIES 113

PART 3
SUPPLY AND DEMAND II: MARKETS AND WELFARE 135

PART 4
THE DATA OF MACROECONOMICS 201

CHAPTER 11
MEASURING THE COST OF LIVING   223

PART 5
THE REAL ECONOMY
IN THE LONG RUN   239

CHAPTER 12
PRODUCTION AND GROWTH   241

CHAPTER 13
SAVING, INVESTMENT, AND THE FINANCIAL SYSTEM   265

PART 6
**MONEY AND PRICES
IN THE LONG RUN** 329

PART 7
THE MACROECONOMICS
OF OPEN ECONOMIES 377

PART 8
SHORT-RUN ECONOMIC FLUCTUATIONS 425

1

INTRODUCTION

TEN PRINCIPLES OF ECONOMICS

The word *economy* comes from the Greek word for "one who manages a household." At first, this origin might seem peculiar. But, in fact, households and economies have much in common.

A household faces many decisions. It must decide which members of the household do which tasks and what each member gets in return: Who cooks dinner? Who does the laundry? Who gets the extra dessert at dinner? Who gets to choose what TV show to watch? In short, the household must allocate its scarce resources among its various members, taking into account each member's abilities, efforts, and desires.

Like a household, a society faces many decisions. A society must decide what jobs will be done and who will do them. It needs some people to grow food, other people to make clothing, and still others to design computer software. Once society has allocated people (as well as land, buildings, and machines) to various jobs, it must also allocate the output of goods and services that they produce. It must decide who will eat caviar and who will eat potatoes. It must decide who will drive a Ferrari and who will take the bus.

Kant is great

scarcity
the limited nature
of society's resources

economics
the study of how society
manages its scarce resources

The management of society's resources is important because resources are scarce. **Scarcity** means that society has limited resources and therefore cannot produce all the goods and services people wish to have. Just as a household cannot give every member everything he or she wants, a society cannot give every individual the highest standard of living to which he or she might aspire.

Economics is the study of how society manages its scarce resources. In most societies, resources are allocated not by a single central planner but through the combined actions of millions of households and firms. Economists therefore study how people make decisions: how much they work, what they buy, how much they save, and how they invest their savings. Economists also study how people interact with one another. For instance, they examine how the multitude of buyers and sellers of a good together determine the price at which the good is sold and the quantity that is sold. Finally, economists analyze forces and trends that affect the economy as a whole, including the growth in average income, the fraction of the population that cannot find work, and the rate at which prices are rising.

Although the study of economics has many facets, the field is unified by several central ideas. In the rest of this chapter, we look at *Ten Principles of Economics*. Don't worry if you don't understand them all at first, or if you don't find them completely convincing. In the coming chapters we will explore these ideas more fully. The ten principles are introduced here just to give you an overview of what economics is all about. You can think of this chapter as a "preview of coming attractions."

HOW PEOPLE MAKE DECISIONS

There is no mystery to what an "economy" is. Whether we are talking about the economy of Los Angeles, of the United States, or of the whole world, an economy is just a group of people interacting with one another as they go about their lives. Because the behavior of an economy reflects the behavior of the individuals who make up the economy, we start our study of economics with four principles of individual decisionmaking.

Principle #1: People Face Tradeoffs

The first lesson about making decisions is summarized in the adage: "There is no such thing as a free lunch." To get one thing that we like, we usually have to give up another thing that we like. Making decisions requires trading off one goal against another.

Consider a student who must decide how to allocate her most valuable resource—her time. She can spend all of her time studying economics; she can spend all of her time studying psychology; or she can divide her time between the two fields. For every hour she studies one subject, she gives up an hour she could have used studying the other. And for every hour she spends studying, she gives up an hour that she could have spent napping, bike riding, watching TV, or working at her part-time job for some extra spending money.

Or consider parents deciding how to spend their family income. They can buy food, clothing, or a family vacation. Or they can save some of the family income for retirement or the children's college education. When they choose to spend an extra dollar on one of these goods, they have one less dollar to spend on some other good.

When people are grouped into societies, they face different kinds of tradeoffs. The classic tradeoff is between "guns and butter." The more we spend on national defense (guns) to protect our shores from foreign aggressors, the less we can spend on consumer goods (butter) to raise our standard of living at home. Also important in modern society is the tradeoff between a clean environment and a high level of income. Laws that require firms to reduce pollution raise the cost of producing goods and services. Because of the higher costs, these firms end up earning smaller profits, paying lower wages, charging higher prices, or some combination of these three. Thus, while pollution regulations give us the benefit of a cleaner environment and the improved health that comes with it, they have the cost of reducing the incomes of the firms' owners, workers, and customers.

Another tradeoff society faces is between efficiency and equity. **Efficiency** means that society is getting the most it can from its scarce resources. **Equity** means that the benefits of those resources are distributed fairly among society's members. In other words, efficiency refers to the size of the economic pie, and equity refers to how the pie is divided. Often, when government policies are being designed, these two goals conflict.

efficiency
the property of society getting the most it can from its scarce resources

equity
the property of distributing economic prosperity fairly among the members of society

Consider, for instance, policies aimed at achieving a more equal distribution of economic well-being. Some of these policies, such as the welfare system or unemployment insurance, try to help those members of society who are most in need. Others, such as the individual income tax, ask the financially successful to contribute more than others to support the government. Although these policies have the benefit of achieving greater equity, they have a cost in terms of reduced efficiency. When the government redistributes income from the rich to the poor, it reduces the reward for working hard; as a result, people work less and produce fewer goods and services. In other words, when the government tries to cut the economic pie into more equal slices, the pie gets smaller.

Recognizing that people face tradeoffs does not by itself tell us what decisions they will or should make. A student should not abandon the study of psychology just because doing so would increase the time available for the study of economics. Society should not stop protecting the environment just because environmental regulations reduce our material standard of living. The poor should not be ignored just because helping them distorts work incentives. Nonetheless, acknowledging life's tradeoffs is important because people are likely to make good decisions only if they understand the options that they have available.

Principle #2: The Cost of Something Is What You Give Up to Get It

Because people face tradeoffs, making decisions requires comparing the costs and benefits of alternative courses of action. In many cases, however, the cost of some action is not as obvious as it might first appear.

Consider, for example, the decision whether to go to college. The benefit is intellectual enrichment and a lifetime of better job opportunities. But what is the cost? To answer this question, you might be tempted to add up the money you spend on tuition, books, room, and board. Yet this total does not truly represent what you give up to spend a year in college.

The first problem with this answer is that it includes some things that are not really costs of going to college. Even if you quit school, you would need a place to sleep and food to eat. Room and board are costs of going to college only to the extent that they are more expensive at college than elsewhere. Indeed, the cost of room and board at your school might be less than the rent and food expenses that you would pay living on your own. In this case, the savings on room and board are a benefit of going to college.

The second problem with this calculation of costs is that it ignores the largest cost of going to college—your time. When you spend a year listening to lectures, reading textbooks, and writing papers, you cannot spend that time working at a job. For most students, the wages given up to attend school are the largest single cost of their education.

The **opportunity cost** of an item is what you give up to get that item. When making any decision, such as whether to attend college, decisionmakers should be aware of the opportunity costs that accompany each possible action. In fact, they usually are. College-age athletes who can earn millions if they drop out of school and play professional sports are well aware that their opportunity cost of college is very high. It is not surprising that they often decide that the benefit is not worth the cost.

Principle #3: Rational People Think at the Margin

Decisions in life are rarely black and white but usually involve shades of gray. At dinnertime, the decision you face is not between fasting or eating like a pig, but whether to take that extra spoonful of mashed potatoes. When exams roll around, your decision is not between blowing them off or studying 24 hours a day, but whether to spend an extra hour reviewing your notes instead of watching TV.

Economists use the term **marginal changes** to describe small incremental adjustments to an existing plan of action. Keep in mind that "margin" means "edge," so marginal changes are adjustments around the edges of what you are doing.

In many situations, people make the best decisions by thinking at the margin. Suppose, for instance, that you asked a friend for advice about how many years to stay in school. If he were to compare for you the lifestyle of a person with a Ph.D. to that of a grade school dropout, you might complain that this comparison is not helpful for your decision. You have some education already and most likely are deciding whether to spend an extra year or two in school. To make this decision, you need to know the additional benefits that an extra year in school would offer (higher wages throughout life and the sheer joy of learning) and the additional costs that you would incur (tuition and the forgone wages while you're in school). By comparing these *marginal benefits* and *marginal costs,* you can evaluate whether the extra year is worthwhile.

As another example, consider an airline deciding how much to charge passengers who fly standby. Suppose that flying a 200-seat plane across the country costs the airline $100,000. In this case, the average cost of each seat is $100,000/200, which is $500. One might be tempted to conclude that the airline should never sell a ticket for less than $500. In fact, however, the airline can raise its profits by thinking at the margin. Imagine that a plane is about to take off with ten empty seats, and a standby passenger is waiting at the gate willing to pay $300 for a seat. Should the airline sell it to him? Of course it should. If the plane has empty seats, the cost of adding one more passenger is minuscule. Although the *average* cost of flying a passenger is $500, the *marginal* cost is merely the cost of the bag of peanuts and can of soda that the extra passenger will consume. As long as the standby passenger pays more than the marginal cost, selling him a ticket is profitable.

As these examples show, individuals and firms can make better decisions by thinking at the margin. A rational decisionmaker takes an action if and only if the marginal benefit of the action exceeds the marginal cost.

Principle #4: People Respond to Incentives

Because people make decisions by comparing costs and benefits, their behavior may change when the costs or benefits change. That is, people respond to incentives. When the price of an apple rises, for instance, people decide to eat more pears and fewer apples because the cost of buying an apple is higher. At the same time, apple orchards decide to hire more workers and harvest more apples, because the benefit of selling an apple is also higher. As we will see, the effect of price on the behavior of buyers and sellers in a market—in this case, the market for apples—is crucial for understanding how the economy works.

Public policymakers should never forget about incentives, for many policies change the costs or benefits that people face and, therefore, alter behavior. A tax on gasoline, for instance, encourages people to drive smaller, more fuel-efficient cars. It also encourages people to take public transportation rather than drive and to live closer to where they work. If the tax were large enough, people would start driving electric cars.

When policymakers fail to consider how their policies affect incentives, they often end up with results they did not intend. For example, consider public policy regarding auto safety. Today all cars have seat belts, but that was not true 50 years ago. In the 1960s, Ralph Nader's book *Unsafe at Any Speed* generated much public concern over auto safety. Congress responded with laws requiring seat belts as standard equipment on new cars.

How does a seat belt law affect auto safety? The direct effect is obvious: When a person wears a seat belt, the probability of surviving a major auto accident rises. But that's not the end of the story, for the law also affects behavior by altering incentives. The relevant behavior here is the speed and care with which drivers operate their cars. Driving slowly and carefully is costly because it uses the driver's time and energy. When deciding how safely to drive, rational people compare the marginal benefit from safer driving to the marginal cost. They drive more slowly and carefully when the benefit of increased safety is high. It is no surprise, for instance, that people drive more slowly and carefully when roads are icy than when roads are clear.

Consider how a seat belt law alters a driver's cost–benefit calculation. Seat belts make accidents less costly because they reduce the likelihood of injury or death. In other words, seat belts reduce the benefits to slow and careful driving. People respond to seat belts as they would to an improvement in road conditions—by faster and less careful driving. The end result of a seat belt law, therefore, is a larger number of accidents. The decline in safe driving has a clear, adverse impact on pedestrians, who are more likely to find themselves in an accident but (unlike the drivers) don't have the benefit of added protection.

At first, this discussion of incentives and seat belts might seem like idle speculation. Yet, in a 1975 study, economist Sam Peltzman showed that the auto-safety laws have had many of these effects. According to Peltzman's evidence, these laws

Basketball star Kobe Bryant understood opportunity cost and incentives. Despite good high school grades and SAT scores, he decided to skip college and go straight to the pros, where he has earned millions of dollars as one of the NBA's top players.

produce both fewer deaths per accident and more accidents. The net result is little change in the number of driver deaths and an increase in the number of pedestrian deaths.

Peltzman's analysis of auto safety is an example of the general principle that people respond to incentives. Many incentives that economists study are more straightforward than those of the auto-safety laws. No one is surprised that people drive smaller cars in Europe, where gasoline taxes are high, than in the United States, where gasoline taxes are low. Yet, as the seat belt example shows, policies can have effects that are not obvious in advance. When analyzing any policy, we must consider not only the direct effects but also the indirect effects that work through incentives. If the policy changes incentives, it will cause people to alter their behavior.

QuickQuiz List and briefly explain the four principles of individual decisionmaking.

HOW PEOPLE INTERACT

The first four principles discussed how individuals make decisions. As we go about our lives, many of our decisions affect not only ourselves but other people as well. The next three principles concern how people interact with one another.

Principle #5: Trade Can Make Everyone Better Off

You have probably heard on the news that the Japanese are our competitors in the world economy. In some ways this is true, for American and Japanese firms do produce many of the same goods. Ford and Toyota compete for the same customers in the market for automobiles. Compaq and Toshiba compete for the same customers in the market for personal computers.

Yet it is easy to be misled when thinking about competition among countries. Trade between the United States and Japan is not like a sports contest, where one side wins and the other side loses. In fact, the opposite is true: Trade between two countries can make each country better off.

To see why, consider how trade affects your family. When a member of your family looks for a job, he or she competes against members of other families who are looking for jobs. Families also compete against one another when they go shopping, because each family wants to buy the best goods at the lowest prices. So, in a sense, each family in the economy is competing with all other families.

Despite this competition, your family would not be better off isolating itself from all other families. If it did, your family would need to grow its own food, make its own clothes, and build its own home. Clearly, your family gains much from its ability to trade with others. Trade allows each person to specialize in the activities he or she does best, whether it is farming, sewing, or home building. By trading with others, people can buy a greater variety of goods and services at lower cost.

Countries as well as families benefit from the ability to trade with one another. Trade allows countries to specialize in what they do best and to enjoy a greater

"For $5 a week you can watch baseball without being nagged to cut the grass!"

variety of goods and services. The Japanese, as well as the French and the Egyptians and the Brazilians, are as much our partners in the world economy as they are our competitors.

Principle #6: Markets Are Usually a Good Way to Organize Economic Activity

The collapse of communism in the Soviet Union and Eastern Europe in the 1980s may be the most important change in the world during the past half century. Communist countries worked on the premise that central planners in the government were in the best position to guide economic activity. These planners decided what goods and services were produced, how much was produced, and who produced and consumed these goods and services. The theory behind central planning was that only the government could organize economic activity in a way that promoted economic well-being for the country as a whole.

Today, most countries that once had centrally planned economies have abandoned this system and are trying to develop market economies. In a **market economy,** the decisions of a central planner are replaced by the decisions of millions of firms and households. Firms decide whom to hire and what to make. Households decide which firms to work for and what to buy with their incomes. These firms and households interact in the marketplace, where prices and self-interest guide their decisions.

market economy
an economy that allocates resources through the decentralized decisions of many firms and households as they interact in markets for goods and services

At first glance, the success of market economies is puzzling. After all, in a market economy, no one is looking out for the economic well-being of society as a whole. Free markets contain many buyers and sellers of numerous goods and services, and all of them are interested primarily in their own well-being. Yet, despite decentralized decisionmaking and self-interested decisionmakers, market economies have proven remarkably successful in organizing economic activity in a way that promotes overall economic well-being.

In his 1776 book *An Inquiry into the Nature and Causes of the Wealth of Nations,* economist Adam Smith made the most famous observation in all of economics: Households and firms interacting in markets act as if they are guided by an "invisible hand" that leads them to desirable market outcomes. One of our goals in this book is to understand how this invisible hand works its magic. As you study economics, you will learn that prices are the instrument with which the invisible hand directs economic activity. Prices reflect both the value of a good to society and the cost to society of making the good. Because households and firms look at prices when deciding what to buy and sell, they unknowingly take into account the social benefits and costs of their actions. As a result, prices guide these individual decisionmakers to reach outcomes that, in many cases, maximize the welfare of society as a whole.

There is an important corollary to the skill of the invisible hand in guiding economic activity: When the government prevents prices from adjusting naturally to supply and demand, it impedes the invisible hand's ability to coordinate the millions of households and firms that make up the economy. This corollary explains why taxes adversely affect the allocation of resources: Taxes distort prices and thus the decisions of households and firms. It also explains the even greater harm caused by policies that directly control prices, such as rent control. And it explains the failure of communism. In communist countries, prices were not determined in the marketplace but were dictated by central planners. These planners lacked the information that gets reflected in prices when prices are free to respond to market forces. Central planners failed because they tried to run the economy with one hand tied behind their backs—the invisible hand of the marketplace.

Principle #7: Governments Can Sometimes Improve Market Outcomes

If the invisible hand of the market is so great, why do we need government? One answer is that the invisible hand needs government to protect it. Markets work only if property rights are enforced. A farmer won't grow food if he expects his crop to be stolen, and a restaurant won't serve meals unless it is assured that customers will pay before they leave. We all rely on government-provided police and courts to enforce our rights over the things we produce.

Yet there is another answer to why we need government: Although markets are usually a good way to organize economic activity, this rule has some important exceptions. There are two broad reasons for a government to intervene in the

FYI

ADAM SMITH AND THE INVISIBLE HAND

It may be only a coincidence that Adam Smith's great book *The Wealth of Nations* was published in 1776, the exact year American revolutionaries signed the Declaration of Independence. But the two documents do share a point of view that was prevalent at the time—that individuals are usually best left to their own devices, without the heavy hand of government guiding their actions. This political philosophy provides the intellectual basis for the market economy, and for free society more generally.

Why do decentralized market economies work so well? Is it because people can be counted on to treat one another with love and kindness? Not at all. Here is Adam Smith's description of how people interact in a market economy:

Adam Smith

Man has almost constant occasion for the help of his brethren, and it is vain for him to expect it from their benevolence only. He will be more likely to prevail if he can interest their self-love in his favor, and show them that it is for their own advantage to do for him what he requires of them. . . . It is not from the benevolence of the butcher, the brewer, or the baker that we expect our dinner, but from their regard to their own interest. . . .

Every individual . . . neither intends to promote the public interest, nor knows how much he is promoting it. . . . He intends only his own gain, and he is in this, as in many other cases, led by an invisible hand to promote an end which was no part of his intention. Nor is it always the worse for the society that it was no part of it. By pursuing his own interest he frequently promotes that of the society more effectually than when he really intends to promote it.

Smith is saying that participants in the economy are motivated by self-interest and that the "invisible hand" of the marketplace guides this self-interest into promoting general economic well-being.

Many of Smith's insights remain at the center of modern economics. Our analysis in the coming chapters will allow us to express Smith's conclusions more precisely and to analyze fully the strengths and weaknesses of the market's invisible hand.

economy—to promote efficiency and to promote equity. That is, most policies aim either to enlarge the economic pie or to change how the pie is divided.

Although the invisible hand usually leads markets to allocate resources efficiently, that is not always the case. Economists use the term **market failure** to refer to a situation in which the market on its own fails to produce an efficient allocation of resources. One possible cause of market failure is an **externality,** which is the impact of one person's actions on the well-being of a bystander. For instance, the classic example of an external cost is pollution. Another possible cause of market failure is **market power,** which refers to the ability of a single person (or small group) to unduly influence market prices. For example, if everyone in town needs water but there is only one well, the owner of the well is not subject to the rigorous competition with which the invisible hand normally keeps self-interest in check. In the presence of externalities or market power, well-designed public policy can enhance economic efficiency.

The invisible hand may also fail to ensure that economic prosperity is distributed equitably. A market economy rewards people according to their ability to produce things that other people are willing to pay for. The world's best basketball player earns more than the world's best chess player simply because people are willing to pay more to watch basketball than chess. The invisible hand does not ensure that everyone has sufficient food, decent clothing, and adequate health care. Many public policies, such as the income tax and the welfare system, aim to achieve a more equitable distribution of economic well-being.

To say that the government *can* improve on market outcomes at times does not mean that it always *will*. Public policy is made not by angels but by a political process that is far from perfect. Sometimes policies are designed simply to reward the politically powerful. Sometimes they are made by well-intentioned leaders who are not fully informed. One goal of the study of economics is to help you judge when a government policy is justifiable to promote efficiency or equity, and when it is not.

> **market failure**
> a situation in which a market left on its own fails to allocate resources efficiently
>
> **externality**
> the impact of one person's actions on the well-being of a bystander
>
> **market power**
> the ability of a single economic actor (or small group of actors) to have a substantial influence on market prices

QuickQuiz List and briefly explain the three principles concerning economic interactions.

HOW THE ECONOMY AS A WHOLE WORKS

We started by discussing how individuals make decisions and then looked at how people interact with one another. All these decisions and interactions together make up "the economy." The last three principles concern the workings of the economy as a whole.

Principle #8: A Country's Standard of Living Depends on Its Ability to Produce Goods and Services

The differences in living standards around the world are staggering. In 2000 the average American had an income of about $34,100. In the same year, the average Mexican earned $8,790, and the average Nigerian earned $800. Not surprisingly, this large variation in average income is reflected in various measures of the quality of life. Citizens of high-income countries have more TV sets, more cars, better nutrition, better health care, and longer life expectancy than citizens of low-income countries.

Changes in living standards over time are also large. In the United States, incomes have historically grown about 2 percent per year (after adjusting for changes in the cost of living). At this rate, average income doubles every 35 years. Over the past century, average income has risen about eightfold.

productivity
the quantity of goods and services produced from each hour of a worker's time

What explains these large differences in living standards among countries and over time? The answer is surprisingly simple. Almost all variation in living standards is attributable to differences in countries' **productivity**—that is, the amount of goods and services produced from each hour of a worker's time. In nations where workers can produce a large quantity of goods and services per unit of time, most people enjoy a high standard of living; in nations where workers are less productive, most people must endure a more meager existence. Similarly, the growth rate of a nation's productivity determines the growth rate of its average income.

The fundamental relationship between productivity and living standards is simple, but its implications are far-reaching. If productivity is the primary determinant of living standards, other explanations must be of secondary importance. For example, it might be tempting to credit labor unions or minimum-wage laws for the rise in living standards of American workers over the past century. Yet the real hero of American workers is their rising productivity. As another example, some commentators have claimed that increased competition from Japan and other countries explained the slow growth in U.S. incomes during the 1970s and 1980s. Yet the real villain was not competition from abroad but flagging productivity growth in the United States.

The relationship between productivity and living standards also has profound implications for public policy. When thinking about how any policy will affect living standards, the key question is how it will affect our ability to produce goods and services. To boost living standards, policymakers need to raise productivity by ensuring that workers are well educated, have the tools needed to produce goods and services, and have access to the best available technology.

Principle #9: Prices Rise When the Government Prints Too Much Money

In Germany in January 1921, a daily newspaper cost 0.30 marks. Less than two years later, in November 1922, the same newspaper cost 70,000,000 marks. All other prices in the economy rose by similar amounts. This episode is one of history's most spectacular examples of **inflation,** an increase in the overall level of prices in the economy.

inflation
an increase in the overall level of prices in the economy

Although the United States has never experienced inflation even close to that in Germany in the 1920s, inflation has at times been an economic problem. During the 1970s, for instance, the overall level of prices more than doubled, and President Gerald Ford called inflation "public enemy number one." By contrast, inflation in the 1990s was about 3 percent per year; at this rate it would take more than 20 years for prices to double. Because high inflation imposes various costs on society, keeping inflation at a low level is a goal of economic policymakers around the world.

What causes inflation? In almost all cases of large or persistent inflation, the culprit turns out to be the same—growth in the quantity of money. When a

"Well it may have been 68 cents when you got in line, but it's 74 cents now!"

government creates large quantities of the nation's money, the value of the money falls. In Germany in the early 1920s, when prices were on average tripling every month, the quantity of money was also tripling every month. Although less dramatic, the economic history of the United States points to a similar conclusion: The high inflation of the 1970s was associated with rapid growth in the quantity of money, and the low inflation of the 1990s was associated with slow growth in the quantity of money.

Principle #10: Society Faces a Short-Run Tradeoff between Inflation and Unemployment

When the government increases the amount of money in the economy, one result is inflation. Another result, at least in the short run, is a lower level of unemployment. The curve that illustrates this short-run tradeoff between inflation and unemployment is called the **Phillips curve,** after the economist who first examined this relationship.

The Phillips curve remains a controversial topic among economists, but most economists today accept the idea that society faces a short-run tradeoff between inflation and unemployment. This simply means that, over a period of a year or two, many economic policies push inflation and unemployment in opposite directions. Policymakers face this tradeoff regardless of whether inflation and unemployment both start out at high levels (as they were in the early 1980s), at low levels (as they were in the late 1990s), or someplace in between.

The tradeoff between inflation and unemployment is only temporary, but it can last for several years. The Phillips curve is, therefore, crucial for understanding

Phillips curve
a curve that shows the short-run tradeoff between inflation and unemployment

business cycle
fluctuations in economic activity,
such as employment and production

many developments in the economy. In particular, it is important for understanding the **business cycle**—the irregular and largely unpredictable fluctuations in economic activity, as measured by the number of people employed or the production of goods and services.

Policymakers can exploit the short-run tradeoff between inflation and unemployment using various policy instruments. By changing the amount that the government spends, the amount it taxes, and the amount of money it prints, policymakers can influence the combination of inflation and unemployment that the economy experiences. Because these instruments of monetary and fiscal policy are potentially so powerful, how policymakers should use these instruments to control the economy, if at all, is a subject of continuing debate.

QuickQuiz List and briefly explain the three principles that describe how the economy as a whole works.

FYI

HOW TO READ THIS BOOK

Economics is fun, but it can also be hard to learn. My aim in writing this text is to make it as fun and easy as possible. But you, the student, also have a role to play. Experience shows that if you are actively involved as you study this book, you will enjoy a better outcome, both on your exams and in the years that follow. Here are a few tips about how best to read this book.

1. *Summarize, don't highlight.* Running a yellow marker over the text is too passive an activity to keep your mind engaged. Instead, when you come to the end of a section, take a minute and summarize what you just learned in your own words, writing your summary in the wide margins we've provided. When you've finished the chapter, compare your summary with the one at the end of the chapter. Did you pick up the main points?

2. *Test yourself.* Throughout the book, Quick Quizzes offer instant feedback to find out if you've learned what you are supposed to. Take the opportunity. Write your answer in the book's margin. The quizzes are meant to test your basic comprehension. If you aren't sure your answer is right, you probably need to review the section.

3. *Practice, practice, practice.* At the end of each chapter, Questions for Review test your understanding, and Problems and Applications ask you to apply and extend the material. Perhaps your instructor will assign some of these exercises as homework. If so, do them. If not, do them anyway. The more you use your new knowledge, the more solid it becomes.

4. *Study in groups.* After you've read the book and worked the problems on your own, get together with classmates to discuss the material. You will learn from each other—an example of the gains from trade.

5. *Don't forget the real world.* In the midst of all the numbers, graphs, and strange new words, it is easy to lose sight of what economics is all about. The Case Studies and In the News boxes sprinkled throughout this book should help remind you. Don't skip them. They show how the theory is tied to events happening in all of our lives. If your study is successful, you won't be able to read a newspaper again without thinking about supply, demand, and the wonderful world of economics.

TABLE 1		
Ten Principles of Economics	**How People Make Decisions**	#1: People Face Tradeoffs
		#2: The Cost of Something Is What You Give Up to Get It
		#3: Rational People Think at the Margin
		#4: People Respond to Incentives
	How People Interact	#5: Trade Can Make Everyone Better Off
		#6: Markets Are Usually a Good Way to Organize Economic Activity
		#7: Governments Can Sometimes Improve Market Outcomes
	How the Economy as a Whole Works	#8: A Country's Standard of Living Depends on Its Ability to Produce Goods and Services
		#9: Prices Rise When the Government Prints Too Much Money
		#10: Society Faces a Short-Run Tradeoff between Inflation and Unemployment

CONCLUSION

You now have a taste of what economics is all about. In the coming chapters we will develop many specific insights about people, markets, and economies. Mastering these insights will take some effort, but it is not an overwhelming task. The field of economics is based on a few basic ideas that can be applied in many different situations.

Throughout this book we will refer back to the *Ten Principles of Economics* highlighted in this chapter and summarized in Table 1. Whenever we do so, an icon will be displayed in the margin, as it is now. But even when that icon is absent, you should keep these building blocks in mind. Even the most sophisticated economic analysis is built using the ten principles introduced here.

SUMMARY

- The fundamental lessons about individual decisionmaking are that people face tradeoffs among alternative goals, that the cost of any action is measured in terms of forgone opportunities, that rational people make decisions by comparing marginal costs and marginal benefits, and that people change their behavior in response to the incentives they face.

- The fundamental lessons about interactions among people are that trade can be mutually beneficial, that markets are usually a good way of coordinating trade among people, and that the government can potentially improve market outcomes if there is some market failure or if the market outcome is inequitable.

- The fundamental lessons about the economy as a whole are that productivity is the ultimate source of living standards, that money growth is the ultimate source of inflation, and that society faces a short-run tradeoff between inflation and unemployment.

KEY CONCEPTS

scarcity, p. 4
economics, p. 4
efficiency, p. 5
equity, p. 5
opportunity cost, p. 6

marginal changes, p. 6
market economy, p. 9
market failure, p. 11
externality, p. 11
market power, p. 11

productivity, p. 12
inflation, p. 12
Phillips curve, p. 13
business cycle, p. 14

QUESTIONS FOR REVIEW

1. Give three examples of important tradeoffs that you face in your life.

2. What is the opportunity cost of seeing a movie?

3. Water is necessary for life. Is the marginal benefit of a glass of water large or small?

4. Why should policymakers think about incentives?

5. Why isn't trade among countries like a game, with some winners and some losers?

6. What does the "invisible hand" of the marketplace do?

7. Explain the two main causes of market failure and give an example of each.

8. Why is productivity important?

9. What is inflation, and what causes it?

10. How are inflation and unemployment related in the short run?

PROBLEMS AND APPLICATIONS

1. Describe some of the tradeoffs faced by each of the following.
   a. a family deciding whether to buy a new car
   b. a member of Congress deciding how much to spend on national parks
   c. a company president deciding whether to open a new factory
   d. a professor deciding how much to prepare for class

2. You are trying to decide whether to take a vacation. Most of the costs of the vacation (airfare, hotel, forgone wages) are measured in dollars, but the benefits of the vacation are psychological. How can you compare the benefits to the costs?

3. You were planning to spend Saturday working at your part-time job, but a friend asks you to go skiing. What is the true cost of going skiing? Now suppose that you had been planning to spend the day studying at the library. What is the cost of going skiing in this case? Explain.

4. You win $100 in a basketball pool. You have a choice between spending the money now or putting it away for a year in a bank account that pays 5 percent interest. What is the opportunity cost of spending the $100 now?

5. The company that you manage has invested $5 million in developing a new product, but the development is not quite finished. At a recent meeting, your salespeople report that the introduction of competing products has reduced the expected sales of your new product to $3 million. If it would cost $1 million to finish development and make the product, should you go ahead and do so? What is the most that you should pay to complete development?

6. Three managers of the Magic Potion Company are discussing a possible increase in production. Each suggests a way to make this decision.

HARRY: We should examine whether our company's productivity— gallons of potion per worker— would rise or fall.

RON: We should examine whether our average cost—cost per worker— would rise or fall.

HERMIONE: We should examine whether the extra revenue from selling the additional potion would be greater or smaller than the extra costs.

Who do you think is right? Why?

7. The Social Security system provides income for people over age 65. If a recipient of Social Security decides to work and earn some income, the amount he or she receives in Social Security benefits is typically reduced.
   a. How does the provision of Social Security affect people's incentive to save while working?
   b. How does the reduction in benefits associated with higher earnings affect people's incentive to work past age 65?

8. A recent bill reforming the government's antipoverty programs limited many welfare recipients to only two years of benefits.
   a. How does this change affect the incentives for working?
   b. How might this change represent a tradeoff between equity and efficiency?

9. Your roommate is a better cook than you are, but you can clean more quickly than your roommate can. If your roommate did all of the cooking and you did all of the cleaning, would your chores take you more or less time than if you divided each task evenly? Give a similar example of how specialization and trade can make two countries both better off.

10. Suppose the United States adopted central planning for its economy, and you became the chief planner. Among the millions of decisions that you need to make for next year are how many compact discs to produce, what artists to record, and who should receive the discs.
    a. To make these decisions intelligently, what information would you need about the compact disc industry? What information would you need about each of the people in the United States?
    b. How would your decisions about CDs affect some of your other decisions, such as how many CD players to make or cassette tapes to produce? How might some of your other decisions about the economy change your views about CDs?

11. Explain whether each of the following government activities is motivated by a concern about equity or a concern about efficiency. In the case of efficiency, discuss the type of market failure involved.
    a. regulating cable TV prices
    b. providing some poor people with vouchers that can be used to buy food
    c. prohibiting smoking in public places
    d. breaking up Standard Oil (which once owned 90 percent of all oil refineries) into several smaller companies
    e. imposing higher personal income tax rates on people with higher incomes
    f. instituting laws against driving while intoxicated

12. Discuss each of the following statements from the standpoints of equity and efficiency.
    a. "Everyone in society should be guaranteed the best health care possible."
    b. "When workers are laid off, they should be able to collect unemployment benefits until they find a new job."

13. In what ways is your standard of living different from that of your parents or grandparents when they were your age? Why have these changes occurred?

14. Suppose Americans decide to save more of their incomes. If banks lend this extra saving to businesses, which use the funds to build new factories, how might this lead to faster growth in productivity? Who do you suppose benefits from the higher productivity? Is society getting a free lunch?

15. Imagine that you are a policymaker trying to decide whether to reduce the rate of inflation. To make an intelligent decision, what would you need to know about inflation, unemployment, and the tradeoff between them?

16. Look at a newspaper or at the Web site http://www.economist.com to find three stories about the economy that have been in the news lately. For each story, identify one (or more) of the *Ten Principles of Economics* discussed in this chapter that is relevant, and explain how it is relevant. Also, for each story, look through this book's table of contents and try to find a chapter that might shed light on the news event.

For more study tools, please visit http://mankiwXtra.swlearning.com.

THINKING LIKE AN ECONOMIST

Every field of study has its own language and its own way of thinking. Mathematicians talk about axioms, integrals, and vector spaces. Psychologists talk about ego, id, and cognitive dissonance. Lawyers talk about venue, torts, and promissory estoppel.

Economics is no different. Supply, demand, elasticity, comparative advantage, consumer surplus, deadweight loss—these terms are part of the economist's language. In the coming chapters, you will encounter many new terms and some familiar words that economists use in specialized ways. At first, this new language may seem needlessly arcane. But, as you will see, its value lies in its ability to provide you a new and useful way of thinking about the world in which you live.

The single most important purpose of this book is to help you learn the economist's way of thinking. Of course, just as you cannot become a mathematician, psychologist, or lawyer overnight, learning to think like an economist will take some time. Yet with a combination of theory, case studies, and examples of economics in the news, this book will give you ample opportunity to develop and practice this skill.

Before delving into the substance and details of economics, it is helpful to have an overview of how economists approach the world. This chapter, therefore, discusses the field's methodology. What is distinctive about how economists confront a question? What does it mean to think like an economist?

THE ECONOMIST AS SCIENTIST

Economists try to address their subject with a scientist's objectivity. They approach the study of the economy in much the same way as a physicist approaches the study of matter and a biologist approaches the study of life: They devise theories, collect data, and then analyze these data in an attempt to verify or refute their theories.

To beginners, it can seem odd to claim that economics is a science. After all, economists do not work with test tubes or telescopes. The essence of science, however, is the *scientific method*—the dispassionate development and testing of theories about how the world works. This method of inquiry is as applicable to studying a nation's economy as it is to studying the earth's gravity or a species' evolution. As Albert Einstein once put it, "The whole of science is nothing more than the refinement of everyday thinking."

Although Einstein's comment is as true for social sciences such as economics as it is for natural sciences such as physics, most people are not accustomed to looking at society through the eyes of a scientist. Let's therefore discuss some of the ways in which economists apply the logic of science to examine how an economy works.

"I'm a social scientist, Michael. That means I can't explain electricity or anything like that, but if you ever want to know about people, I'm your man."

The Scientific Method: Observation, Theory, and More Observation

Isaac Newton, the famous seventeenth-century scientist and mathematician, allegedly became intrigued one day when he saw an apple fall from an apple tree. This observation motivated Newton to develop a theory of gravity that applies not only to an apple falling to the earth but to any two objects in the universe. Subsequent testing of Newton's theory has shown that it works well in many circumstances (although, as Einstein would later emphasize, not in all circumstances). Because Newton's theory has been so successful at explaining observation, it is still taught today in undergraduate physics courses around the world.

This interplay between theory and observation also occurs in the field of economics. An economist might live in a country experiencing rapid increases in prices and be moved by this observation to develop a theory of inflation. The theory might assert that high inflation arises when the government prints too much money. (As you may recall, this was one of the *Ten Principles of Economics* in Chapter 1.) To test this theory, the economist could collect and analyze data on prices and money from many different countries. If growth in the quantity of money were not at all related to the rate at which prices are rising, the economist would start to doubt the validity of his theory of inflation. If money growth and inflation were strongly correlated in international data, as in fact they are, the economist would become more confident in his theory.

Although economists use theory and observation like other scientists, they do face an obstacle that makes their task especially challenging: Experiments are often difficult in economics. Physicists studying gravity can drop many objects in their laboratories to generate data to test their theories. By contrast, economists studying inflation are not allowed to manipulate a nation's monetary policy simply to generate useful data. Economists, like astronomers and evolutionary biologists, usually have to make do with whatever data the world happens to give them.

To find a substitute for laboratory experiments, economists pay close attention to the natural experiments offered by history. When a war in the Middle East interrupts the flow of crude oil, for instance, oil prices skyrocket around the world. For consumers of oil and oil products, such an event depresses living standards. For economic policymakers, it poses a difficult choice about how best to respond. But for economic scientists, it provides an opportunity to study the effects of a key natural resource on the world's economies, and this opportunity persists long after the wartime increase in oil prices is over. Throughout this book, therefore, we consider many historical episodes. These episodes are valuable to study because they give us insight into the economy of the past and, more important, because they allow us to illustrate and evaluate economic theories of the present.

The Role of Assumptions

If you ask a physicist how long it would take for a marble to fall from the top of a ten-story building, she will answer the question by assuming that the marble falls in a vacuum. Of course, this assumption is false. In fact, the building is surrounded by air, which exerts friction on the falling marble and slows it down. Yet the physicist will correctly point out that friction on the marble is so small that its effect is negligible. Assuming the marble falls in a vacuum greatly simplifies the problem without substantially affecting the answer.

Economists make assumptions for the same reason: Assumptions can simplify the complex world and make it easier to understand. To study the effects of international trade, for example, we may assume that the world consists of only two countries and that each country produces only two goods. Of course, the real world consists of dozens of countries, each of which produces thousands of different types of goods. But by assuming two countries and two goods, we can focus our thinking. Once we understand international trade in an imaginary world with two countries and two goods, we are in a better position to understand international trade in the more complex world in which we live.

The art in scientific thinking—whether in physics, biology, or economics—is deciding which assumptions to make. Suppose, for instance, that we were dropping a beach ball rather than a marble from the top of the building. Our physicist would realize that the assumption of no friction is far less accurate in this case: Friction exerts a greater force on a beach ball than on a marble because a beach ball is much larger. The assumption that gravity works in a vacuum is reasonable for studying a falling marble but not for studying a falling beach ball.

Similarly, economists use different assumptions to answer different questions. Suppose that we want to study what happens to the economy when the government changes the number of dollars in circulation. An important piece of this analysis, it turns out, is how prices respond. Many prices in the economy change infrequently; the newsstand prices of magazines, for instance, are changed only every few years. Knowing this fact may lead us to make different assumptions when studying the effects of the policy change over different time horizons. For studying the short-run effects of the policy, we may assume that prices do not change much. We may even make the extreme and artificial assumption that all prices are completely fixed. For studying the long-run effects of the policy, however, we may assume that all prices are completely flexible. Just as a physicist uses different assumptions when studying falling marbles and falling beach balls, economists use different assumptions when studying the short-run and long-run effects of a change in the quantity of money.

Economic Models

High school biology teachers teach basic anatomy with plastic replicas of the human body. These models have all the major organs—the heart, the liver, the kidneys, and so on. The models allow teachers to show their students in a simple way how the important parts of the body fit together. Of course, these plastic models are not actual human bodies, and no one would mistake the model for a real person. These models are stylized, and they omit many details. Yet despite this lack of realism—indeed, because of this lack of realism—studying these models is useful for learning how the human body works.

Economists also use models to learn about the world, but instead of being made of plastic, they are most often composed of diagrams and equations. Like a biology teacher's plastic model, economic models omit many details to allow us to see what is truly important. Just as the biology teacher's model does not include all of the body's muscles and capillaries, an economist's model does not include every feature of the economy.

As we use models to examine various economic issues throughout this book, you will see that all the models are built with assumptions. Just as a physicist begins the analysis of a falling marble by assuming away the existence of friction, economists assume away many of the details of the economy that are irrelevant for studying the question at hand. All models—in physics, biology, or economics—simplify reality in order to improve our understanding of it.

Our First Model: The Circular-Flow Diagram

The economy consists of millions of people engaged in many activities—buying, selling, working, hiring, manufacturing, and so on. To understand how the economy works, we must find some way to simplify our thinking about all these activities. In other words, we need a model that explains, in general terms, how the economy is organized and how participants in the economy interact with one another.

Figure 1 presents a visual model of the economy, called a **circular-flow diagram.** In this model, the economy is simplified to include only two types of decision-makers—households and firms. Firms produce goods and services using inputs, such as labor, land, and capital (buildings and machines). These inputs are called the *factors of production.* Households own the factors of production and consume all the goods and services that the firms produce.

circular-flow diagram
a visual model of the economy that shows how dollars flow through markets among households and firms

FIGURE 1

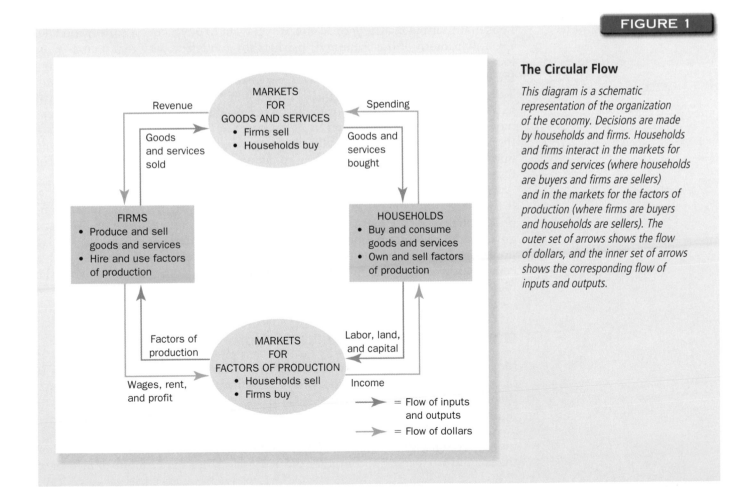

The Circular Flow

This diagram is a schematic representation of the organization of the economy. Decisions are made by households and firms. Households and firms interact in the markets for goods and services (where households are buyers and firms are sellers) and in the markets for the factors of production (where firms are buyers and households are sellers). The outer set of arrows shows the flow of dollars, and the inner set of arrows shows the corresponding flow of inputs and outputs.

Households and firms interact in two types of markets. In the *markets for goods and services,* households are buyers, and firms are sellers. In particular, households buy the output of goods and services that firms produce. In the *markets for the factors of production,* households are sellers, and firms are buyers. In these markets, households provide the inputs that the firms use to produce goods and services. The circular-flow diagram offers a simple way of organizing all the economic transactions that occur between households and firms in the economy.

The inner loop of the circular-flow diagram represents the flows of inputs and outputs. The households sell the use of their labor, land, and capital to the firms in the markets for the factors of production. The firms then use these factors to produce goods and services, which in turn are sold to households in the markets for goods and services. Hence, the factors of production flow from households to firms, and goods and services flow from firms to households.

The outer loop of the circular-flow diagram represents the corresponding flow of dollars. The households spend money to buy goods and services from the firms. The firms use some of the revenue from these sales to pay for the factors of production, such as the wages of their workers. What's left is the profit of the firm owners, who themselves are members of households. Hence, spending on goods and services flows from households to firms, and income in the form of wages, rent, and profit flows from firms to households.

Let's take a tour of the circular flow by following a dollar bill as it makes its way from person to person through the economy. Imagine that the dollar begins at a household, sitting in, say, your wallet. If you want to buy a cup of coffee, you take the dollar to one of the economy's markets for goods and services, such as your local Starbucks coffee shop. There you spend it on your favorite drink. When the dollar moves into the Starbucks cash register, it becomes revenue for the firm. The dollar doesn't stay at Starbucks for long, however, because the firm uses it to buy inputs in the markets for the factors of production. For instance, Starbucks might use the dollar to pay rent to its landlord for the space it occupies or to pay the wages of its workers. In either case, the dollar enters the income of some household and, once again, is back in someone's wallet. At that point, the story of the economy's circular flow starts once again.

The circular-flow diagram in Figure 1 is one simple model of the economy. It dispenses with details that, for some purposes, are significant. A more complex and realistic circular-flow model would include, for instance, the roles of government and international trade. Yet these details are not crucial for a basic understanding of how the economy is organized. Because of its simplicity, this circular-flow diagram is useful to keep in mind when thinking about how the pieces of the economy fit together.

Our Second Model: The Production Possibilities Frontier

Most economic models, unlike the circular-flow diagram, are built using the tools of mathematics. Here we consider one of the simplest such models, called the production possibilities frontier, and see how this model illustrates some basic economic ideas.

Although real economies produce thousands of goods and services, let's imagine an economy that produces only two goods—cars and computers. Together the car industry and the computer industry use all of the economy's factors of production. The **production possibilities frontier** is a graph that shows the various combinations of output—in this case, cars and computers—that the economy can possibly produce given the available factors of production and the available production technology that firms can use to turn these factors into output.

Figure 2 is an example of a production possibilities frontier. In this economy, if all resources were used in the car industry, the economy would produce 1,000 cars and no computers. If all resources were used in the computer industry, the economy would produce 3,000 computers and no cars. The two end points of the production possibilities frontier represent these extreme possibilities. If the economy were to divide its resources between the two industries, it could produce 700 cars and 2,000 computers, shown in the figure by point A. By contrast, the outcome at point D is not possible because resources are scarce: The economy does not have enough of the factors of production to support that level of output. In other words, the economy can produce at any point on or inside the production possibilities frontier, but it cannot produce at points outside the frontier.

An outcome is said to be *efficient* if the economy is getting all it can from the scarce resources it has available. Points on (rather than inside) the production possibilities frontier represent efficient levels of production. When the economy is producing at such a point, say point A, there is no way to produce more of one good without producing less of the other. Point B represents an *inefficient* outcome. For some reason, perhaps widespread unemployment, the economy is producing less than it could from the resources it has available: It is producing only 300 cars and 1,000 computers. If the source of the inefficiency were eliminated, the economy could move from point B to point A, increasing production of both cars (to 700) and computers (to 2,000).

production possibilities frontier
a graph that shows the combinations of output that the economy can possibly produce given the available factors of production and the available production technology

FIGURE 2

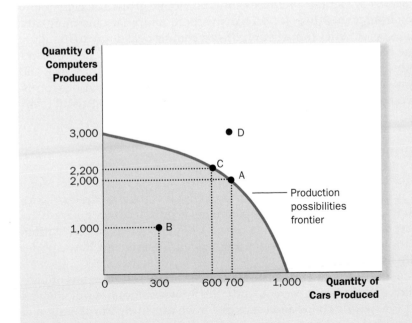

The Production Possibilities Frontier

The production possibilities frontier shows the combinations of output—in this case, cars and computers—that the economy can possibly produce. The economy can produce any combination on or inside the frontier. Points outside the frontier are not feasible given the economy's resources.

One of the *Ten Principles of Economics* discussed in Chapter 1 is that people face tradeoffs. The production possibilities frontier shows one tradeoff that society faces. Once we have reached the efficient points on the frontier, the only way of getting more of one good is to get less of the other. When the economy moves from point A to point C, for instance, society produces more computers but at the expense of producing fewer cars.

Another of the *Ten Principles of Economics* is that the cost of something is what you give up to get it. This is called the *opportunity cost*. The production possibilities frontier shows the opportunity cost of one good as measured in terms of the other good. When society reallocates some of the factors of production from the car industry to the computer industry, moving the economy from point A to point C, it gives up 100 cars to get 200 additional computers. In other words, when the economy is at point A, the opportunity cost of 200 computers is 100 cars.

Notice that the production possibilities frontier in Figure 2 is bowed outward. This means that the opportunity cost of cars in terms of computers depends on how much of each good the economy is producing. When the economy is using most of its resources to make cars, the production possibilities frontier is quite steep. Because even workers and machines best suited to making computers are being used to make cars, the economy gets a substantial increase in the number of computers for each car it gives up. By contrast, when the economy is using most of its resources to make computers, the production possibilities frontier is quite flat. In this case, the resources best suited to making computers are already in the computer industry, and each car the economy gives up yields only a small increase in the number of computers.

The production possibilities frontier shows the tradeoff between the production of different goods at a given time, but the tradeoff can change over time. For example, if a technological advance in the computer industry raises the number of computers that a worker can produce per week, the economy can make more computers for any given number of cars. As a result, the production possibilities frontier shifts outward, as in Figure 3. Because of this economic growth, society might move production from point A to point E, enjoying more computers and more cars.

The production possibilities frontier simplifies a complex economy to highlight and clarify some basic ideas. We have used it to illustrate some of the concepts mentioned briefly in Chapter 1: scarcity, efficiency, tradeoffs, opportunity cost, and economic growth. As you study economics, these ideas will recur in various forms. The production possibilities frontier offers one simple way of thinking about them.

Microeconomics and Macroeconomics

Many subjects are studied on various levels. Consider biology, for example. Molecular biologists study the chemical compounds that make up living things. Cellular biologists study cells, which are made up of many chemical compounds and, at the same time, are themselves the building blocks of living organisms. Evolutionary biologists study the many varieties of animals and plants and how species change gradually over the centuries.

Economics is also studied on various levels. We can study the decisions of individual households and firms. Or we can study the interaction of households and firms in markets for specific goods and services. Or we can study the operation of the economy as a whole, which is just the sum of the activities of all these decisionmakers in all these markets.

FIGURE 3

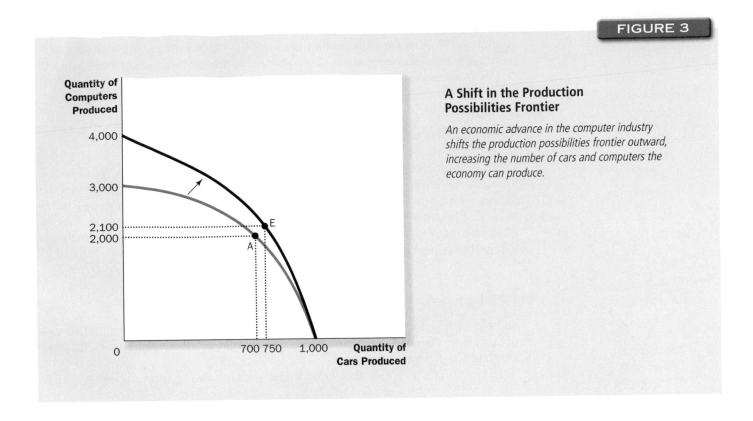

A Shift in the Production Possibilities Frontier

An economic advance in the computer industry shifts the production possibilities frontier outward, increasing the number of cars and computers the economy can produce.

The field of economics is traditionally divided into two broad subfields. **Microeconomics** is the study of how households and firms make decisions and how they interact in specific markets. **Macroeconomics** is the study of economy-wide phenomena. A microeconomist might study the effects of rent control on housing in New York City, the impact of foreign competition on the U.S. auto industry, or the effects of compulsory school attendance on workers' earnings. A macroeconomist might study the effects of borrowing by the federal government, the changes over time in the economy's rate of unemployment, or alternative policies to raise growth in national living standards.

Microeconomics and macroeconomics are closely intertwined. Because changes in the overall economy arise from the decisions of millions of individuals, it is impossible to understand macroeconomic developments without considering the associated microeconomic decisions. For example, a macroeconomist might study the effect of a cut in the federal income tax on the overall production of goods and services. To analyze this issue, he or she must consider how the tax cut affects the decisions of households about how much to spend on goods and services.

Despite the inherent link between microeconomics and macroeconomics, the two fields are distinct. In economics, as in biology, it may seem natural to begin with the smallest unit and build up. Yet doing so is neither necessary nor always the best way to proceed. Evolutionary biology is, in a sense, built upon molecular biology, since species are made up of molecules. Yet molecular biology and evolutionary biology are separate fields, each with its own questions and its own methods. Similarly, because microeconomics and macroeconomics address different questions, they sometimes take quite different approaches and are often taught in separate courses.

microeconomics
the study of how households and firms make decisions and how they interact in markets

macroeconomics
the study of economy-wide phenomena, including inflation, unemployment, and economic growth

QuickQuiz   In what sense is economics like a science?   •   Draw a production possibilities frontier for a society that produces food and clothing. Show an efficient point, an inefficient point, and an infeasible point. Show the effects of a drought.   • Define *microeconomics* and *macroeconomics*.

THE ECONOMIST AS POLICY ADVISER

Often economists are asked to explain the causes of economic events. Why, for example, is unemployment higher for teenagers than for older workers? Sometimes economists are asked to recommend policies to improve economic outcomes. What, for instance, should the government do to improve the economic well-being of teenagers? When economists are trying to explain the world, they are scientists. When they are trying to help improve it, they are policy advisers.

Positive versus Normative Analysis

To help clarify the two roles that economists play, we begin by examining the use of language. Because scientists and policy advisers have different goals, they use language in different ways.

For example, suppose that two people are discussing minimum-wage laws. Here are two statements you might hear:

POLLY: Minimum-wage laws cause unemployment.
NORMA: The government should raise the minimum wage.

Ignoring for now whether you agree with these statements, notice that Polly and Norma differ in what they are trying to do. Polly is speaking like a scientist: She is making a claim about how the world works. Norma is speaking like a policy adviser: She is making a claim about how she would like to change the world.

In general, statements about the world are of two types. One type, such as Polly's, is positive. **Positive statements** are descriptive. They make a claim about how the world *is*. A second type of statement, such as Norma's, is normative. **Normative statements** are prescriptive. They make a claim about how the world *ought to be.*

A key difference between positive and normative statements is how we judge their validity. We can, in principle, confirm or refute positive statements by examining evidence. An economist might evaluate Polly's statement by analyzing data on changes in minimum wages and changes in unemployment over time. By contrast, evaluating normative statements involves values as well as facts. Norma's statement cannot be judged using data alone. Deciding what is good or bad policy is not merely a matter of science. It also involves our views on ethics, religion, and political philosophy.

Of course, positive and normative statements may be related. Our positive views about how the world works affect our normative views about what policies are desirable. Polly's claim that the minimum wage causes unemployment, if true, might lead us to reject Norma's conclusion that the government should raise the minimum wage. Yet our normative conclusions cannot come from positive analysis alone; they involve value judgments as well.

positive statements
claims that attempt to describe the world as it is

normative statements
claims that attempt to prescribe how the world should be

As you study economics, keep in mind the distinction between positive and normative statements. Much of economics just tries to explain how the economy works. Yet often the goal of economics is to improve how the economy works. When you hear economists making normative statements, you know they have crossed the line from scientist to policy adviser.

Economists in Washington

President Harry Truman once said that he wanted to find a one-armed economist. When he asked his economists for advice, they always answered, "On the one hand, . . . On the other hand, ..."

Truman was right in realizing that economists' advice is not always straightforward. This tendency is rooted in one of the *Ten Principles of Economics* in Chapter 1: People face tradeoffs. Economists are aware that tradeoffs are involved in most policy decisions. A policy might increase efficiency at the cost of equity. It might help future generations but hurt current generations. An economist who says that all policy decisions are easy is an economist not to be trusted.

Truman was also not alone among presidents in relying on the advice of economists. Since 1946, the president of the United States has received guidance from the Council of Economic Advisers, which consists of three members and a staff of several dozen economists. The council, whose offices are just a few steps from the White House, has no duty other than to advise the president and to write the annual *Economic Report of the President*.

The president also receives input from economists in many administrative departments. Economists at the Department of Treasury help design tax policy. Economists at the Department of Labor analyze data on workers and those looking for work in order to help formulate labor-market policies. Economists at the Department of Justice help enforce the nation's antitrust laws.

Economists are also found outside the administrative branch of government. To obtain independent evaluations of policy proposals, Congress relies on the advice of the Congressional Budget Office, which is staffed by economists. The Federal Reserve, the institution that sets the nation's monetary policy, employs hundreds of economists to analyze economic developments in the United States and throughout the world. Table 1 lists the Web sites of some of these agencies.

The influence of economists on policy goes beyond their role as advisers: Their research and writings often affect policy indirectly. Economist John Maynard Keynes offered this observation:

"Let's switch. I'll make the policy, you implement it, and he'll explain it."

TABLE 1

Web Sites

Here are the Web sites for a few of the government agencies that are responsible for collecting economic data and making economic policy.

Department of Commerce	http://www.commerce.gov
Bureau of Labor Statistics	http://www.bls.gov
Congressional Budget Office	http://www.cbo.gov
Federal Reserve Board	http://www.federalreserve.gov

The ideas of economists and political philosophers, both when they are right and when they are wrong, are more powerful than is commonly understood. Indeed, the world is ruled by little else. Practical men, who believe themselves to be quite exempt from intellectual influences, are usually the slaves of some defunct economist. Madmen in authority, who hear voices in the air, are distilling their frenzy from some academic scribbler of a few years back.

Although these words were written in 1935, they remain true today. Indeed, the "academic scribbler" now influencing public policy is often Keynes himself.

QuickQuiz Give an example of a positive statement and an example of a normative statement. • Name three parts of government that regularly rely on advice from economists.

WHY ECONOMISTS DISAGREE

"If all economists were laid end to end, they would not reach a conclusion." This quip from George Bernard Shaw is revealing. Economists as a group are often criticized for giving conflicting advice to policymakers. President Ronald Reagan once joked that if the game Trivial Pursuit were designed for economists, it would have 100 questions and 3,000 answers.

Why do economists so often appear to give conflicting advice to policymakers? There are two basic reasons:

- Economists may disagree about the validity of alternative positive theories about how the world works.
- Economists may have different values and, therefore, different normative views about what policy should try to accomplish.

Let's discuss each of these reasons.

Differences in Scientific Judgments

Several centuries ago, astronomers debated whether the earth or the sun was at the center of the solar system. More recently, meteorologists have debated whether the earth is experiencing global warming and, if so, why. Science is a search for understanding about the world around us. It is not surprising that as the search continues, scientists can disagree about the direction in which truth lies.

Economists often disagree for the same reason. Economics is a young science, and there is still much to be learned. Economists sometimes disagree because they have different hunches about the validity of alternative theories or about the size of important parameters.

For example, economists disagree about whether the government should levy taxes based on a household's income or its consumption (spending). Advocates of a switch from the current income tax to a consumption tax believe that the change would encourage households to save more, because income that is saved would not be taxed. Higher saving, in turn, would lead to more rapid growth in productivity and living standards. Advocates of the current income tax system believe that household saving would not respond much to a change in the tax laws. These two groups of economists hold different normative views about the tax system because they have different positive views about the responsiveness of saving to tax incentives.

Differences in Values

Suppose that Peter and Paul both take the same amount of water from the town well. To pay for maintaining the well, the town taxes its residents. Peter has income of $50,000 and is taxed $5,000, or 10 percent of his income. Paul has income of $10,000 and is taxed $2,000, or 20 percent of his income.

Is this policy fair? If not, who pays too much and who pays too little? Does it matter whether Paul's low income is due to a medical disability or to his decision to pursue a career in acting? Does it matter whether Peter's high income is due to a large inheritance or to his willingness to work long hours at a dreary job?

These are difficult questions on which people are likely to disagree. If the town hired two experts to study how the town should tax its residents to pay for the well, we would not be surprised if they offered conflicting advice.

This simple example shows why economists sometimes disagree about public policy. As we learned earlier in our discussion of normative and positive analysis, policies cannot be judged on scientific grounds alone. Economists give conflicting advice sometimes because they have different values. Perfecting the science of economics will not tell us whether it is Peter or Paul who pays too much.

Perception versus Reality

Because of differences in scientific judgments and differences in values, some disagreement among economists is inevitable. Yet one should not overstate the amount of disagreement. In many cases, economists do offer a united view.

Table 2 (p. 32) contains ten propositions about economic policy. In a survey of economists in business, government, and academia, these propositions were endorsed by an overwhelming majority of respondents. Most of these propositions would fail to command a similar consensus among the general public.

The first proposition in the table is about rent control. For reasons we will discuss later, almost all economists believe that rent control adversely affects the availability and quality of housing and is a very costly way of helping the most needy members of society. Nonetheless, many city governments choose to ignore the advice of economists and place ceilings on the rents that landlords may charge their tenants.

The second proposition in the table concerns tariffs and import quotas, two policies that restrict trade among nations. For reasons we will discuss more fully in later chapters, almost all economists oppose such barriers to free trade. Nonetheless, over the years, the president and Congress have chosen to restrict the import of certain goods. In 2002, for example, the Bush administration imposed large tariffs on steel to protect domestic steel producers from foreign competition. In this case, economists did offer united advice, but policymakers chose to ignore it.

TABLE 2

Ten Propositions about Which Most Economists Agree

Source: Richard M. Alston, J. R. Kearl, and Michael B. Vaughn, "Is There Consensus among Economists in the 1990s?" *American Economic Review* (May 1992): 203–209. Reprinted by permission.

Proposition (and percentage of economists who agree)

1. A ceiling on rents reduces the quantity and quality of housing available. (93%)
2. Tariffs and import quotas usually reduce general economic welfare. (93%)
3. Flexible and floating exchange rates offer an effective international monetary arrangement. (90%)
4. Fiscal policy (e.g., tax cut and/or government expenditure increase) has a significant stimulative impact on a less than fully employed economy. (90%)
5. If the federal budget is to be balanced, it should be done over the business cycle rather than yearly. (85%)
6. Cash payments increase the welfare of recipients to a greater degree than do transfers-in-kind of equal cash value. (84%)
7. A large federal budget deficit has an adverse effect on the economy. (83%)
8. A minimum wage increases unemployment among young and unskilled workers. (79%)
9. The government should restructure the welfare system along the lines of a "negative income tax." (79%)
10. Effluent taxes and marketable pollution permits represent a better approach to pollution control than imposition of pollution ceilings. (78%)

Why do policies such as rent control and trade barriers persist if the experts are united in their opposition? The reason may be that economists have not yet convinced the general public that these policies are undesirable. One purpose of this book is to make you understand the economist's view of these and other subjects and, perhaps, to persuade you that it is the right one.

QuickQuiz Why might economic advisers to the president disagree about a question of policy?

LET'S GET GOING

The first two chapters of this book have introduced you to the ideas and methods of economics. We are now ready to get to work. In the next chapter we start learning in more detail the principles of economic behavior and economic policy.

As you proceed through this book, you will be asked to draw on many of your intellectual skills. You might find it helpful to keep in mind some advice from the great economist John Maynard Keynes:

The study of economics does not seem to require any specialized gifts of an unusually high order. Is it not . . . a very easy subject compared with the higher branches of philosophy or pure science? An easy subject, at which very few excel! The paradox finds its explanation, perhaps, in that the master-economist must possess a rare *combination* of gifts. He must be mathematician, historian, statesman, philosopher—in some degree. He must understand symbols and speak in words. He must contemplate the particular in terms of the general, and touch abstract and concrete in the same flight of thought. He must study the present in the light of the past for the purposes of the future. No part of man's nature or his institutions must lie entirely outside his regard. He must be purposeful and disinterested in a simultaneous mood; as aloof and incorruptible as an artist, yet sometimes as near the earth as a politician.

It is a tall order. But with practice, you will become more and more accustomed to thinking like an economist.

SUMMARY

- Economists try to address their subject with a scientist's objectivity. Like all scientists, they make appropriate assumptions and build simplified models in order to understand the world around them. Two simple economic models are the circular-flow diagram and the production possibilities frontier.

- The field of economics is divided into two subfields: microeconomics and macroeconomics. Microeconomists study decisionmaking by households and firms and the interaction among households and firms in the marketplace. Macroeconomists study the forces and trends that affect the economy as a whole.

- A positive statement is an assertion about how the world *is*. A normative statement is an assertion about how the world *ought to be*. When economists make normative statements, they are acting more as policy advisers than scientists.

- Economists who advise policymakers offer conflicting advice either because of differences in scientific judgments or because of differences in values. At other times, economists are united in the advice they offer, but policymakers may choose to ignore it.

KEY CONCEPTS

circular-flow diagram, p. 23
production possibilities frontier, p. 25

microeconomics, p. 27
macroeconomics, p. 27
positive statements, p. 28

normative statements, p. 28

QUESTIONS FOR REVIEW

1. How is economics like a science?

2. Why do economists make assumptions?

3. Should an economic model describe reality exactly?

4. Draw and explain a production possibilities frontier for an economy that produces milk and cookies. What happens to this frontier if disease kills half of the economy's cow population?

5. Use a production possibilities frontier to describe the idea of "efficiency."

6. What are the two subfields into which economics is divided? Explain what each subfield studies.

7. What is the difference between a positive and a normative statement? Give an example of each.

8. What is the Council of Economic Advisers?

9. Why do economists sometimes offer conflicting advice to policymakers?

PROBLEMS AND APPLICATIONS

1. Describe some unusual language used in one of the other fields that you are studying. Why are these special terms useful?

2. One common assumption in economics is that the products of different firms in the same industry are indistinguishable. For each of the following industries, discuss whether this is a reasonable assumption.
   a. steel
   b. novels
   c. wheat
   d. fast food

3. Draw a circular-flow diagram. Identify the parts of the model that correspond to the flow of goods and services and the flow of dollars for each of the following activities.
   a. Sam pays a storekeeper $1 for a quart of milk.
   b. Sally earns $4.50 per hour working at a fast food restaurant.
   c. Serena spends $7 to see a movie.
   d. Stuart earns $10,000 from his 10 percent ownership of Acme Industrial.

4. Imagine a society that produces military goods and consumer goods, which we'll call "guns" and "butter."
   a. Draw a production possibilities frontier for guns and butter. Explain why it most likely has a bowed-out shape.
   b. Show a point that is impossible for the economy to achieve. Show a point that is feasible but inefficient.
   c. Imagine that the society has two political parties, called the Hawks (who want a strong military) and the Doves (who want a smaller military). Show a point on your production possibilities frontier that the Hawks might choose and a point the Doves might choose.
   d. Imagine that an aggressive neighboring country reduces the size of its military. As a result, both the Hawks and the Doves reduce their desired production of guns by the same amount. Which party would get the bigger "peace dividend," measured by the increase in butter production? Explain.

5. The first principle of economics discussed in Chapter 1 is that people face tradeoffs. Use a production possibilities frontier to illustrate society's tradeoff between a clean environment and the quantity of industrial output. What do you suppose determines the shape and position of the frontier? Show what happens to the frontier if engineers develop an automobile engine with almost no emissions.

6. Classify the following topics as relating to microeconomics or macroeconomics.
   a. a family's decision about how much income to save
   b. the effect of government regulations on auto emissions
   c. the impact of higher national saving on economic growth
   d. a firm's decision about how many workers to hire
   e. the relationship between the inflation rate and changes in the quantity of money

7. Classify each of the following statements as positive or normative. Explain.
   a. Society faces a short-run tradeoff between inflation and unemployment.
   b. A reduction in the rate of growth of money will reduce the rate of inflation.
   c. The Federal Reserve should reduce the rate of growth of money.
   d. Society ought to require welfare recipients to look for jobs.
   e. Lower tax rates encourage more work and more saving.

8. Classify each of the statements in Table 2 as positive, normative, or ambiguous. Explain.

9. If you were president, would you be more interested in your economic advisers' positive views or their normative views? Why?

10. The *Economic Report of the President* contains statistical information about the economy as well as the Council of Economic Advisers' analysis of current policy issues. Find a recent copy of this annual report at your library and read a chapter about an issue that interests you. Summarize the economic problem at hand and describe the council's recommended policy.

11. Who is the current chairman of the Federal Reserve? Who is the current chair of the Council

of Economic Advisers? Who is the current secretary of the treasury?

12. Would you expect economists to disagree less about public policy as time goes on? Why or why not? Can their differences be completely eliminated? Why or why not?

13. Look up one of the Web sites listed in Table 1. What recent economic trends or issues are addressed there?

http://   For more study tools, please visit http://mankiwXtra.swlearning.com.

APPENDIX
Graphing: A Brief Review

Many of the concepts that economists study can be expressed with numbers—the price of bananas, the quantity of bananas sold, the cost of growing bananas, and so on. Often these economic variables are related to one another. When the price of bananas rises, people buy fewer bananas. One way of expressing the relationships among variables is with graphs.

Graphs serve two purposes. First, when developing economic theories, graphs offer a way to visually express ideas that might be less clear if described with equations or words. Second, when analyzing economic data, graphs provide a way of finding how variables are in fact related in the world. Whether we are working with theory or with data, graphs provide a lens through which a recognizable forest emerges from a multitude of trees.

Numerical information can be expressed graphically in many ways, just as a thought can be expressed in words in many ways. A good writer chooses words that will make an argument clear, a description pleasing, or a scene dramatic. An effective economist chooses the type of graph that best suits the purpose at hand.

In this appendix we discuss how economists use graphs to study the mathematical relationships among variables. We also discuss some of the pitfalls that can arise in the use of graphical methods.

Graphs of a Single Variable

Three common graphs are shown in Figure A-1. The *pie chart* in panel (a) shows how total income in the United States is divided among the sources of income, including compensation of employees, corporate profits, and so on. A slice of the pie represents each source's share of the total. The *bar graph* in panel (b) compares income for four countries. The height of each bar represents the average income in each country. The *time-series graph* in panel (c) traces the rising productivity in the U.S. business sector over time. The height of the line shows output per hour in each year. You have probably seen similar graphs presented in newspapers and magazines.

Graphs of Two Variables: The Coordinate System

Although the three graphs in Figure A-1 are useful in showing how a variable changes over time or across individuals, such graphs are limited in how much they can tell us. These graphs display information only on a single variable. Economists are often concerned with the relationships between variables. Thus, they need to be able to display two variables on a single graph. The *coordinate system* makes this possible.

Suppose you want to examine the relationship between study time and grade point average. For each student in your class, you could record a pair of numbers: hours per week spent studying and grade point average. These numbers could then be placed in parentheses as an *ordered pair* and appear as a single point on the

Types of Graphs

The pie chart in panel (a) shows how U.S. national income is derived from various sources. The bar graph in panel (b) compares the average income in four countries. The time-series graph in panel (c) shows the productivity of labor in U.S. businesses from 1950 to 2000.

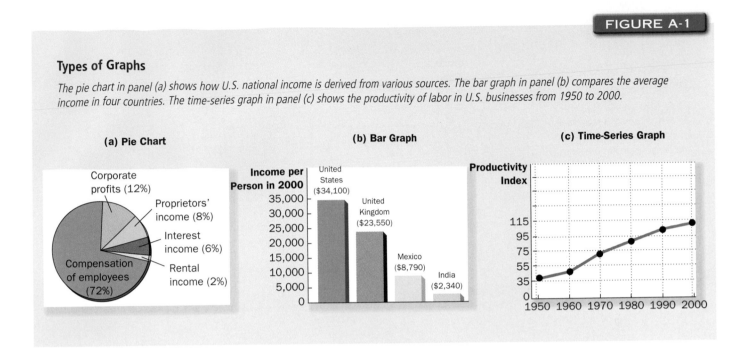

(a) Pie Chart

Corporate profits (12%)

Proprietors' income (8%)

Interest income (6%)

Rental income (2%)

Compensation of employees (72%)

(b) Bar Graph

Income per Person in 2000

United States ($34,100)

United Kingdom ($23,550)

Mexico ($8,790)

India ($2,340)

35,000
30,000
25,000
20,000
15,000
10,000
5,000
0

(c) Time-Series Graph

Productivity Index

115
95
75
55
35
0

1950 1960 1970 1980 1990 2000

graph. Albert E., for instance, is represented by the ordered pair (25 hours/week, 3.5 GPA), while his "what-me-worry?" classmate Alfred E. is represented by the ordered pair (5 hours/week, 2.0 GPA).

We can graph these ordered pairs on a two-dimensional grid. The first number in each ordered pair, called the *x-coordinate*, tells us the horizontal location of the point. The second number, called the *y-coordinate*, tells us the vertical location of the point. The point with both an x-coordinate and a y-coordinate of zero is known as the *origin*. The two coordinates in the ordered pair tell us where the point is located in relation to the origin: x units to the right of the origin and y units above it.

Figure A-2 (p. 38) graphs grade point average against study time for Albert E., Alfred E., and their classmates. This type of graph is called a *scatterplot* because it plots scattered points. Looking at this graph, we immediately notice that points farther to the right (indicating more study time) also tend to be higher (indicating a better grade point average). Because study time and grade point average typically move in the same direction, we say that these two variables have a *positive correlation*. By contrast, if we were to graph party time and grades, we would likely find that higher party time is associated with lower grades; because these variables typically move in opposite directions, we would call this a *negative correlation*. In either case, the coordinate system makes the correlation between the two variables easy to see.

Curves in the Coordinate System

Students who study more do tend to get higher grades, but other factors also influence a student's grade. Previous preparation is an important factor, for instance,

FIGURE A-2

Using the Coordinate System

Grade point average is measured on the vertical axis and study time on the horizontal axis. Albert E., Alfred E., and their classmates are represented by various points. We can see from the graph that students who study more tend to get higher grades.

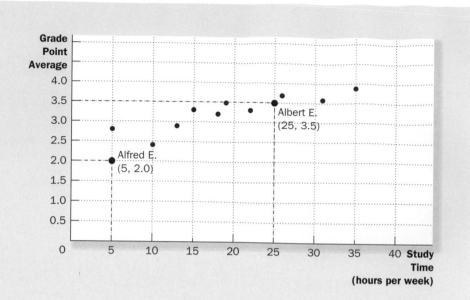

as are talent, attention from teachers, even eating a good breakfast. A scatterplot like Figure A-2 does not attempt to isolate the effect that study has on grades from the effects of other variables. Often, however, economists prefer looking at how one variable affects another holding everything else constant.

To see how this is done, let's consider one of the most important graphs in economics—the *demand curve*. The demand curve traces out the effect of a good's price on the quantity of the good consumers want to buy. Before showing a demand curve, however, consider Table A-1, which shows how the number of novels that Emma buys depends on her income and on the price of novels. When novels are cheap, Emma buys them in large quantities. As they become more expensive, she borrows books from the library instead of buying them or chooses to go to the movies instead of reading. Similarly, at any given price, Emma buys more novels when she has a higher income. That is, when her income increases, she spends part of the additional income on novels and part on other goods.

We now have three variables—the price of novels, income, and the number of novels purchased—which is more than we can represent in two dimensions. To put the information from Table A-1 in graphical form, we need to hold one of the three variables constant and trace out the relationship between the other two. Because the demand curve represents the relationship between price and quantity demanded, we hold Emma's income constant and show how the number of novels she buys varies with the price of novels.

Suppose that Emma's income is $30,000 per year. If we place the number of novels Emma purchases on the *x*-axis and the price of novels on the *y*-axis, we can graphically represent the middle column of Table A-1. When the points that represent these entries from the table—(5 novels, $10), (9 novels, $9), and so on—are connected, they form a line. This line, pictured in Figure A-3, is known as Emma's demand curve for novels; it tells us how many novels Emma purchases at any

	Income			
Price	$20,000	$30,000	$40,000	
$10	2 novels	5 novels	8 novels	
9	6	9	12	
8	10	13	16	
7	14	17	20	
6	18	21	24	
5	22	25	28	
	Demand curve, D_3	Demand curve, D_1	Demand curve, D_2	

Novels Purchased by Emma

This table shows the number of novels Emma buys at various incomes and prices. For any given level of income, the data on price and quantity demanded can be graphed to produce Emma's demand curve for novels, as shown in Figures A-3 and A-4.

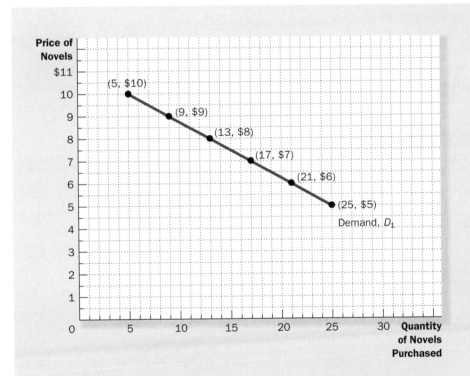

Demand Curve

The line D_1 shows how Emma's purchases of novels depend on the price of novels when her income is held constant. Because the price and the quantity demanded are negatively related, the demand curve slopes downward.

given price. The demand curve is downward sloping, indicating that a higher price reduces the quantity of novels demanded. Because the quantity of novels demanded and the price move in opposite directions, we say that the two variables are *negatively related*. (Conversely, when two variables move in the same direction, the curve relating them is upward sloping, and we say the variables are *positively related*.)

Now suppose that Emma's income rises to $40,000 per year. At any given price, Emma will purchase more novels than she did at her previous level of income. Just as earlier we drew Emma's demand curve for novels using the entries from the middle column of Table A-1, we now draw a new demand curve using the entries from the right-hand column of the table. This new demand curve (curve D_2) is pictured alongside the old one (curve D_1) in Figure A-4; the new curve is a similar line drawn farther to the right. We therefore say that Emma's demand curve for novels *shifts* to the right when her income increases. Likewise, if Emma's income were to fall to $20,000 per year, she would buy fewer novels at any given price and her demand curve would shift to the left (to curve D_3).

In economics, it is important to distinguish between *movements along a curve* and *shifts of a curve.* As we can see from Figure A-3, if Emma earns $30,000 per year and novels cost $8 apiece, she will purchase 13 novels per year. If the price of novels falls to $7, Emma will increase her purchases of novels to 17 per year. The demand curve, however, stays fixed in the same place. Emma still buys the same number of novels *at each price,* but as the price falls she moves along her demand curve from left to right. By contrast, if the price of novels remains fixed at $8 but her income rises to $40,000, Emma increases her purchases of novels from 13 to 16 per year. Because Emma buys more novels *at each price,* her demand curve shifts out, as shown in Figure A-4.

There is a simple way to tell when it is necessary to shift a curve. When a variable that is not named on either axis changes, the curve shifts. Income is on neither the *x*-axis nor the *y*-axis of the graph, so when Emma's income changes, her de-

FIGURE A-4

Shifting Demand Curves

The location of Emma's demand curve for novels depends on how much income she earns. The more she earns, the more novels she will purchase at any given price, and the farther to the right her demand curve will lie. Curve D_1 represents Emma's original demand curve when her income is $30,000 per year. If her income rises to $40,000 per year, her demand curve shifts to D_2. If her income falls to $20,000 per year, her demand curve shifts to D_3.

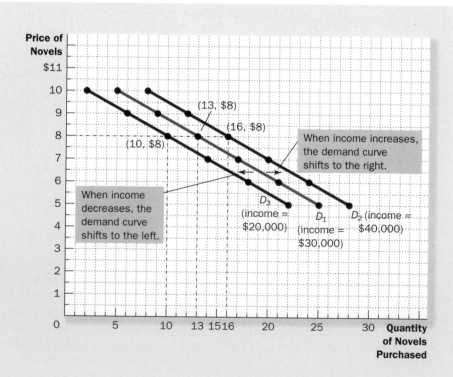

mand curve must shift. Any change that affects Emma's purchasing habits besides a change in the price of novels will result in a shift in her demand curve. If, for instance, the public library closes and Emma must buy all the books she wants to read, she will demand more novels at each price, and her demand curve will shift to the right. Or, if the price of movies falls and Emma spends more time at the movies and less time reading, she will demand fewer novels at each price, and her demand curve will shift to the left. By contrast, when a variable on an axis of the graph changes, the curve does not shift. We read the change as a movement along the curve.

Slope

One question we might want to ask about Emma is how much her purchasing habits respond to price. Look at the demand curve pictured in Figure A-5. If this curve is very steep, Emma purchases nearly the same number of novels regardless of whether they are cheap or expensive. If this curve is much flatter, Emma purchases many fewer novels when the price rises. To answer questions about how much one variable responds to changes in another variable, we can use the concept of *slope*.

The slope of a line is the ratio of the vertical distance covered to the horizontal distance covered as we move along the line. This definition is usually written out in mathematical symbols as follows:

$$\text{slope} = \frac{\Delta y}{\Delta x},$$

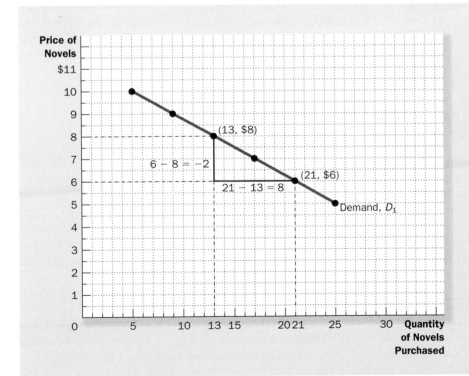

Calculating the Slope of a Line

To calculate the slope of the demand curve, we can look at the changes in the x- and y-coordinates as we move from the point (21 novels, $6) to the point (13 novels, $8). The slope of the line is the ratio of the change in the y-coordinate (-2) to the change in the x-coordinate ($+8$), which equals $-1/4$.

where the Greek letter Δ (delta) stands for the change in a variable. In other words, the slope of a line is equal to the "rise" (change in y) divided by the "run" (change in x). The slope will be a small positive number for a fairly flat upward-sloping line, a large positive number for a steep upward-sloping line, and a negative number for a downward-sloping line. A horizontal line has a slope of zero because in this case the y-variable never changes; a vertical line is said to have an infinite slope because the y-variable can take any value without the x-variable changing at all.

What is the slope of Emma's demand curve for novels? First of all, because the curve slopes down, we know the slope will be negative. To calculate a numerical value for the slope, we must choose two points on the line. With Emma's income at $30,000, she will purchase 21 novels at a price of $6 or 13 novels at a price of $8. When we apply the slope formula, we are concerned with the change between these two points; in other words, we are concerned with the difference between them, which lets us know that we will have to subtract one set of values from the other, as follows:

$$\text{slope} = \frac{\Delta y}{\Delta x} = \frac{\text{first } y\text{-coordinate} - \text{second } y\text{-coordinate}}{\text{first } x\text{-coordinate} - \text{second } x\text{-coordinate}} = \frac{6-8}{21-13} = \frac{-2}{8} = \frac{-1}{4}$$

Figure A-5 shows graphically how this calculation works. Try computing the slope of Emma's demand curve using two different points. You should get exactly the same result, $-1/4$. One of the properties of a straight line is that it has the same slope everywhere. This is not true of other types of curves, which are steeper in some places than in others.

The slope of Emma's demand curve tells us something about how responsive her purchases are to changes in the price. A small slope (a number close to zero) means that Emma's demand curve is relatively flat; in this case, she adjusts the number of novels she buys substantially in response to a price change. A larger slope (a number farther from zero) means that Emma's demand curve is relatively steep; in this case, she adjusts the number of novels she buys only slightly in response to a price change.

Cause and Effect

Economists often use graphs to advance an argument about how the economy works. In other words, they use graphs to argue about how one set of events *causes* another set of events. With a graph like the demand curve, there is no doubt about cause and effect. Because we are varying price and holding all other variables constant, we know that changes in the price of novels cause changes in the quantity Emma demands. Remember, however, that our demand curve came from a hypothetical example. When graphing data from the real world, it is often more difficult to establish how one variable affects another.

The first problem is that it is difficult to hold everything else constant when measuring how one variable affects another. If we are not able to hold variables constant, we might decide that one variable on our graph is causing changes in the other variable when actually those changes are caused by a third *omitted variable* not pictured on the graph. Even if we have identified the correct two variables to look at, we might run into a second problem—*reverse causality*. In other words, we might decide that A causes B when in fact B causes A. The omitted-variable and reverse-causality traps require us to proceed with caution when using graphs to draw conclusions about causes and effects.

Omitted Variables   To see how omitting a variable can lead to a deceptive graph, let's consider an example. Imagine that the government, spurred by public concern about the large number of deaths from cancer, commissions an exhaustive study from Big Brother Statistical Services, Inc. Big Brother examines many of the items found in people's homes to see which of them are associated with the risk of cancer. Big Brother reports a strong relationship between two variables: the number of cigarette lighters that a household owns and the probability that someone in the household will develop cancer. Figure A-6 shows this relationship.

What should we make of this result? Big Brother advises a quick policy response. It recommends that the government discourage the ownership of cigarette lighters by taxing their sale. It also recommends that the government require warning labels: "Big Brother has determined that this lighter is dangerous to your health."

In judging the validity of Big Brother's analysis, one question is paramount: Has Big Brother held constant every relevant variable except the one under consideration? If the answer is no, the results are suspect. An easy explanation for Figure A-6 is that people who own more cigarette lighters are more likely to smoke cigarettes and that cigarettes, not lighters, cause cancer. If Figure A-6 does not hold constant the amount of smoking, it does not tell us the true effect of owning a cigarette lighter.

This story illustrates an important principle: When you see a graph being used to support an argument about cause and effect, it is important to ask whether the movements of an omitted variable could explain the results you see.

Reverse Causality   Economists can also make mistakes about causality by misreading its direction. To see how this is possible, suppose the Association of American Anarchists commissions a study of crime in America and arrives at Figure A-7 (p. 44), which plots the number of violent crimes per thousand people in major cities against the number of police officers per thousand people. The anarchists

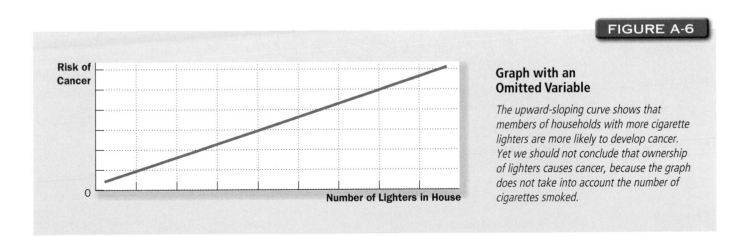

FIGURE A-6

Graph with an Omitted Variable

The upward-sloping curve shows that members of households with more cigarette lighters are more likely to develop cancer. Yet we should not conclude that ownership of lighters causes cancer, because the graph does not take into account the number of cigarettes smoked.

Risk of Cancer

0

Number of Lighters in House

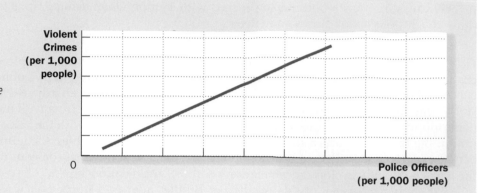

FIGURE A-7

Graph Suggesting Reverse Causality

The upward-sloping curve shows that cities with a higher concentration of police are more dangerous. Yet the graph does not tell us whether police cause crime or crime-plagued cities hire more police.

Violent Crimes (per 1,000 people)

Police Officers (per 1,000 people)

note the curve's upward slope and argue that because police increase rather than decrease the amount of urban violence, law enforcement should be abolished.

If we could run a controlled experiment, we would avoid the danger of reverse causality. To run an experiment, we would set the number of police officers in different cities randomly and then examine the correlation between police and crime. Figure A-7, however, is not based on such an experiment. We simply observe that more dangerous cities have more police officers. The explanation for this may be that more dangerous cities hire more police. In other words, rather than police causing crime, crime may cause police. Nothing in the graph itself allows us to establish the direction of causality.

It might seem that an easy way to determine the direction of causality is to examine which variable moves first. If we see crime increase and then the police force expand, we reach one conclusion. If we see the police force expand and then crime increase, we reach the other. Yet there is also a flaw with this approach: Often people change their behavior not in response to a change in their present conditions but in response to a change in their *expectations* of future conditions. A city that expects a major crime wave in the future, for instance, might well hire more police now. This problem is even easier to see in the case of babies and minivans. Couples often buy a minivan in anticipation of the birth of a child. The minivan comes before the baby, but we wouldn't want to conclude that the sale of minivans causes the population to grow!

There is no complete set of rules that says when it is appropriate to draw causal conclusions from graphs. Yet just keeping in mind that cigarette lighters don't cause cancer (omitted variable) and minivans don't cause larger families (reverse causality) will keep you from falling for many faulty economic arguments.

INTERDEPENDENCE AND
THE GAINS FROM TRADE

Consider your typical day. You wake up in the morning, and you pour yourself juice from oranges grown in Florida and coffee from beans grown in Brazil. Over breakfast, you watch a news program broadcast from New York on your television made in Japan. You get dressed in clothes made of cotton grown in Georgia and sewn in factories in Thailand. You drive to class in a car made of parts manufactured in more than a dozen countries around the world. Then you open up your economics textbook written by an author living in Massachusetts, published by a company located in Ohio, and printed on paper made from trees grown in Oregon.

Every day you rely on many people from around the world, most of whom you do not know, to provide you with the goods and services that you enjoy. Such interdependence is possible because people trade with one another. Those people who provide you with goods and services are not acting out of generosity or concern for your welfare. Nor is some government agency directing them to make what you want and to give it to you. Instead, people provide you and other consumers with the goods and services they produce because they get something in return.

In subsequent chapters we will examine how our economy coordinates the activities of millions of people with varying tastes and abilities. As a starting point for this analysis, here we consider the reasons for economic interdependence. One of the *Ten Principles of Economics* highlighted in Chapter 1 is that trade can make everyone better off. This principle explains why people trade with their neighbors and why nations trade with other nations. In this chapter we examine this principle more closely. What exactly do people gain when they trade with one another? Why do people choose to become interdependent?

A PARABLE FOR THE MODERN ECONOMY

To understand why people choose to depend on others for goods and services and how this choice improves their lives, let's look at a simple economy. Imagine that there are two goods in the world—meat and potatoes. And there are two people in the world—a cattle rancher and a potato farmer—each of whom would like to eat both meat and potatoes.

The gains from trade are most obvious if the rancher can produce only meat and the farmer can produce only potatoes. In one scenario, the rancher and the farmer could choose to have nothing to do with each other. But after several months of eating beef roasted, boiled, broiled, and grilled, the rancher might decide that self-sufficiency is not all it's cracked up to be. The farmer, who has been eating potatoes mashed, fried, baked, and scalloped, would likely agree. It is easy to see that trade would allow them to enjoy greater variety: Each could then have a steak with baked potato.

Although this scene illustrates most simply how everyone can benefit from trade, the gains would be similar if the rancher and the farmer were each capable of producing the other good, but only at great cost. Suppose, for example, that the potato farmer is able to raise cattle and produce meat, but that he is not very good at it. Similarly, suppose that the cattle rancher is able to grow potatoes, but that her land is not very well suited for it. In this case, it is easy to see that the farmer and the rancher can each benefit by specializing in what he or she does best and then trading with the other.

The gains from trade are less obvious, however, when one person is better at producing *every* good. For example, suppose that the rancher is better at raising cattle *and* better at growing potatoes than the farmer. In this case, should the rancher or farmer choose to remain self-sufficient? Or is there still reason for them to trade with each other? To answer this question, we need to look more closely at the factors that affect such a decision.

Production Possibilities

Suppose that the farmer and the rancher each work 8 hours a day and can devote this time to growing potatoes, raising cattle, or a combination of the two. Table 1 shows the amount of time each person requires to produce 1 ounce of each good. The farmer can produce an ounce of potatoes in 15 minutes and an ounce of meat in 60 minutes. The rancher, who is more productive in both activities, can produce an ounce of potatoes in 10 minutes and an ounce of meat in 20 minutes. The last columns in Table 1 show the amounts of meat or potatoes the farmer and rancher can produce if they work an 8-hour day, producing only that good.

Panel (a) of Figure 1 illustrates the amounts of meat and potatoes that the farmer can produce. If the farmer devotes all 8 hours of his time to potatoes, he produces

TABLE 1

	Minutes Needed to Make 1 Ounce of:		Amount of Meat or Potatoes Produced in 8 Hours	
	Meat	Potatoes	Meat	Potatoes
Farmer	60 min/oz	15 min/oz	8 oz	32 oz
Rancher	20 min/oz	10 min/oz	24 oz	48 oz

The Production Opportunities of the Farmer and the Rancher

FIGURE 1

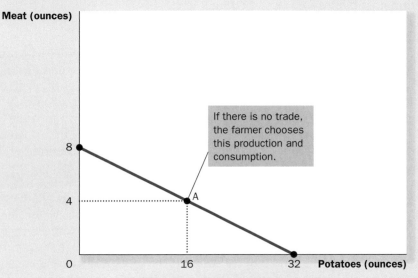

(a) The Farmer's Production Possibilities Frontier

The Production Possibilities Frontier

Panel (a) shows the combinations of meat and potatoes that the farmer can produce. Panel (b) shows the combinations of meat and potatoes that the rancher can produce. Both production possibilities frontiers are derived from Table 1 and the assumption that the farmer and rancher each work 8 hours a day.

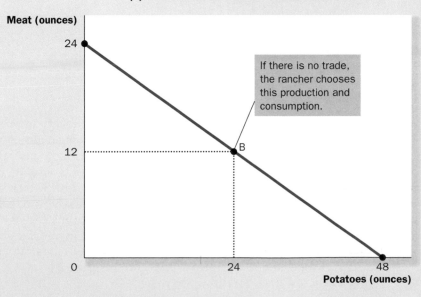

(b) The Rancher's Production Possibilities Frontier

32 ounces of potatoes (measured on the horizontal axis) and no meat. If he devotes all his time to meat, he produces 8 ounces of meat (measured on the vertical axis) and no potatoes. If the farmer divides his time equally between the two activities, spending 4 hours on each, he produces 16 ounces of potatoes and 4 ounces of meat. The figure shows these three possible outcomes and all others in between.

This graph is the farmer's production possibilities frontier. As we discussed in Chapter 2, a production possibilities frontier shows the various mixes of output that an economy can produce. It illustrates one of the *Ten Principles of Economics* in Chapter 1: People face tradeoffs. Here the farmer faces a tradeoff between producing meat and producing potatoes. You may recall that the production possibilities frontier in Chapter 2 was drawn bowed out; in that case, the tradeoff between the two goods depended on the amounts being produced. Here, however, the farmer's technology for producing meat and potatoes (as summarized in Table 1) allows him to switch between one good and the other at a constant rate. In this case, the production possibilities frontier is a straight line.

Panel (b) of Figure 1 shows the production possibilities frontier for the rancher. If the rancher devotes all 8 hours of her time to potatoes, she produces 48 ounces of potatoes and no meat. If she devotes all her time to meat, she produces 24 ounces of meat and no potatoes. If the rancher divides her time equally, spending 4 hours on each activity, she produces 24 ounces of potatoes and 12 ounces of meat. Once again, the production possibilities frontier shows all the possible outcomes.

If the farmer and rancher choose to be self-sufficient, rather than trade with each other, then each consumes exactly what he or she produces. In this case, the production possibilities frontier is also the consumption possibilities frontier. That is, without trade, Figure 1 shows the possible combinations of meat and potatoes that the farmer and rancher can each consume.

Although these production possibilities frontiers are useful in showing the tradeoffs that the farmer and rancher face, they do not tell us what the farmer and rancher will actually choose to do. To determine their choices, we need to know the tastes of the farmer and the rancher. Let's suppose they choose the combinations identified by points A and B in Figure 1: The farmer produces and consumes 16 ounces of potatoes and 4 ounces of meat, while the rancher produces and consumes 24 ounces of potatoes and 12 ounces of meat.

Specialization and Trade

After several years of eating combination B, the rancher gets an idea and goes to talk to the farmer:

RANCHER: Farmer, my friend, have I got a deal for you! I know how to improve life for both of us. I think you should stop producing meat altogether and devote all your time to growing potatoes. According to my calculations, if you work 8 hours a day growing potatoes, you'll produce 32 ounces of potatoes. If you give me 15 of those 32 ounces, I'll give you 5 ounces of meat in return. In the end, you'll get to eat 17 ounces of potatoes and 5 ounces of meat every day, instead of the 16 ounces of potatoes and 4 ounces of meat you now get. If you go along with my plan, you'll have more of *both* foods. [To illustrate her point, the rancher shows the farmer panel (a) of Figure 2.]

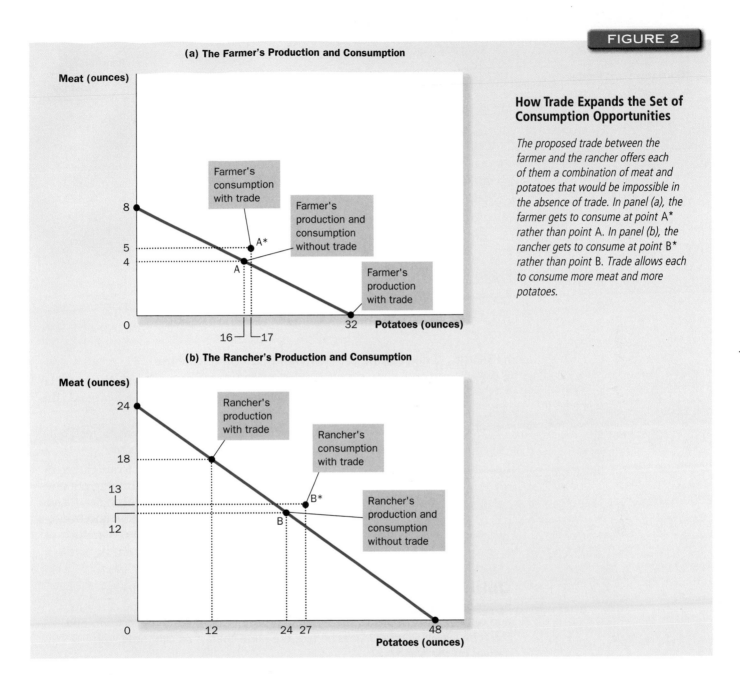

FIGURE 2

How Trade Expands the Set of Consumption Opportunities

The proposed trade between the farmer and the rancher offers each of them a combination of meat and potatoes that would be impossible in the absence of trade. In panel (a), the farmer gets to consume at point A* rather than point A. In panel (b), the rancher gets to consume at point B* rather than point B. Trade allows each to consume more meat and more potatoes.

FARMER: *(sounding skeptical)* That seems like a good deal for me. But I don't understand why you are offering it. If the deal is so good for me, it can't be good for you too.

RANCHER: Oh, but it is! Suppose I spend 6 hours a day raising cattle and 2 hours growing potatoes. Then I can produce 18 ounces of meat and 12 ounces of potatoes. After I give you 5 ounces of my meat in exchange for 15 ounces of your potatoes, I'll end up with 13 ounces of meat and 27 ounces of potatoes. So I will also consume more of both foods than I do now. [She points out panel (b) of Figure 2.]

TABLE 2

The Gains from Trade:
A Summary

	Farmer		Rancher	
	Meat	Potatoes	Meat	Potatoes
Without Trade:				
Production and Consumption	4 oz	16 oz	12 oz	24 oz
With Trade:				
Production	0 oz	32 oz	18 oz	12 oz
Trade	Gets 5 oz	Gives 15 oz	Gives 5 oz	Gets 15 oz
Consumption	5 oz	17 oz	13 oz	27 oz
Gains from Trade:				
Increase in Consumption	+1 oz	+1 oz	+1 oz	+3 oz

FARMER: I don't know. . . . This sounds too good to be true.

RANCHER: It's really not as complicated as it seems at first. Here—I've summarized my proposal for you in a simple table. [The rancher hands the farmer a copy of Table 2.]

FARMER: *(after pausing to study the table)* These calculations seem correct, but I am puzzled. How can this deal make us both better off?

RANCHER: We can both benefit because trade allows each of us to specialize in doing what we do best. You will spend more time growing potatoes and less time raising cattle. I will spend more time raising cattle and less time growing potatoes. As a result of specialization and trade, each of us can consume more meat and more potatoes without working any more hours.

QuickQuiz Draw an example of a production possibilities frontier for Robinson Crusoe, a shipwrecked sailor who spends his time gathering coconuts and catching fish. Does this frontier limit Crusoe's consumption of coconuts and fish if he lives by himself? Does he face the same limits if he can trade with natives on the island?

THE PRINCIPLE OF COMPARATIVE ADVANTAGE

The rancher's explanation of the gains from trade, though correct, poses a puzzle: If the rancher is better at both raising cattle and growing potatoes, how can the farmer ever specialize in doing what he does best? The farmer doesn't seem to do anything best. To solve this puzzle, we need to look at the principle of *comparative advantage*.

As a first step in developing this principle, consider the following question: In our example, who can produce potatoes at lower cost—the farmer or the rancher? There are two possible answers, and in these two answers lie the solution to our puzzle and the key to understanding the gains from trade.

Absolute Advantage

One way to answer the question about the cost of producing potatoes is to compare the inputs required by the two producers. Economists use the term **absolute advantage** when comparing the productivity of one person, firm, or nation to that of another. The producer that requires a smaller quantity of inputs to produce a good is said to have an absolute advantage in producing that good.

absolute advantage
the comparison among producers of a good according to their productivity

In our example, the rancher has an absolute advantage both in producing meat and in producing potatoes, because she requires less time than the farmer to produce a unit of either good. The rancher needs to input only 20 minutes to produce an ounce of meat, whereas the farmer needs 60 minutes. Similarly, the rancher needs only 10 minutes to produce an ounce of potatoes, whereas the farmer needs 15 minutes. Based on this information, we can conclude that the rancher has the lower cost of producing potatoes, if we measure cost in terms of the quantity of inputs.

Opportunity Cost and Comparative Advantage

There is another way to look at the cost of producing potatoes. Rather than comparing inputs required, we can compare the opportunity costs. Recall from Chapter 1 that the **opportunity cost** of some item is what we give up to get that item. In our example, we assumed that the farmer and the rancher each spend 8 hours a day working. Time spent producing potatoes, therefore, takes away from time available for producing meat. As the rancher and farmer reallocate time between producing the two goods, they move along their production possibility frontiers; they give up units of one good to produce units of the other. The opportunity cost measures the tradeoff between the two goods that each producer faces.

opportunity cost
whatever must be given up to obtain some item

Let's first consider the rancher's opportunity cost. According to Table 1, producing 1 ounce of potatoes takes her 10 minutes of work. When the rancher spends that 10 minutes producing potatoes, she spends 10 minutes less producing meat. Because the rancher needs 20 minutes to produce 1 ounce of meat, 10 minutes of work would yield ½ ounce of meat. Hence, the rancher's opportunity cost of producing 1 ounce of potatoes is ½ ounce of meat.

Now consider the farmer's opportunity cost. Producing 1 ounce of potatoes takes him 15 minutes. Because he needs 60 minutes to produce 1 ounce of meat, 15 minutes of work would yield ¼ ounce of meat. Hence, the farmer's opportunity cost of 1 ounce of potatoes is ¼ ounce of meat.

Table 3 (p. 52) shows the opportunity costs of meat and potatoes for the two producers. Notice that the opportunity cost of meat is the inverse of the opportunity cost of potatoes. Because 1 ounce of potatoes costs the rancher ½ ounce of meat, 1 ounce of meat costs the rancher 2 ounces of potatoes. Similarly, because 1 ounce of potatoes costs the farmer ¼ ounce of meat, 1 ounce of meat costs the farmer 4 ounces of potatoes.

TABLE 3		Opportunity Cost of:	
The Opportunity Cost of Meat and Potatoes		**1 Ounce of Meat**	**1 Ounce of Potatoes**
	Farmer	4 oz potatoes	¼ oz meat
	Rancher	2 oz potatoes	½ oz meat

comparative advantage
the comparison among producers of a good according to their opportunity cost

Economists use the term **comparative advantage** when describing the opportunity cost of two producers. The producer who gives up less of other goods to produce good X has the smaller opportunity cost of producing good X and is said to have a comparative advantage in producing it. In our example, the farmer has a lower opportunity cost of producing potatoes than does the rancher: An ounce of potatoes costs the farmer only ¼ ounce of meat, while it costs the rancher ½ ounce of meat. Conversely, the rancher has a lower opportunity cost of producing meat than does the farmer: An ounce of meat costs the rancher 2 ounces of potatoes, while it costs the farmer 4 ounces of potatoes. Thus, the farmer has a comparative advantage in growing potatoes, and the rancher has a comparative advantage in producing meat.

Although it is possible for one person to have an absolute advantage in both goods (as the rancher does in our example), it is impossible for one person to have a comparative advantage in both goods. Because the opportunity cost of one good is the inverse of the opportunity cost of the other, if a person's opportunity cost of one good is relatively high, his opportunity cost of the other good must be relatively low. Comparative advantage reflects the relative opportunity cost. Unless two people have exactly the same opportunity cost, one person will have a comparative advantage in one good, and the other person will have a comparative advantage in the other good.

Comparative Advantage and Trade

Differences in opportunity cost and comparative advantage create the gains from trade. When each person specializes in producing the good for which he or she has a comparative advantage, total production in the economy rises, and this increase in the size of the economic pie can be used to make everyone better off. In other words, as long as two people have different opportunity costs, each can benefit from trade by obtaining a good at a price that is lower than his or her opportunity cost of that good.

Consider the proposed deal from the viewpoint of the farmer. The farmer gets 5 ounces of meat in exchange for 15 ounces of potatoes. In other words, the farmer buys each ounce of meat for a price of 3 ounces of potatoes. This price of meat is lower than his opportunity cost for 1 ounce of meat, which is 4 ounces of potatoes. Thus, the farmer benefits from the deal because he gets to buy meat at a good price.

Now consider the deal from the rancher's viewpoint. The rancher buys 15 ounces of potatoes for a price of 5 ounces of meat. That is, the price of potatoes is

FYI

THE LEGACY OF ADAM SMITH AND DAVID RICARDO

Economists have long understood the principle of comparative advantage. Here is how the great economist Adam Smith put the argument:

It is a maxim of every prudent master of a family, never to attempt to make at home what it will cost him more to make than to buy. The tailor does not attempt to make his own shoes, but buys them of the shoemaker. The shoemaker does not attempt to make his own clothes but employs a tailor. The farmer attempts to make neither the one nor the other, but employs those different artificers. All of them find it for their interest to employ their whole industry in a way in which they have some advantage over their neighbors,

and to purchase with a part of its produce, or what is the same thing, with the price of part of it, whatever else they have occasion for.

This quotation is from Smith's 1776 book *An Inquiry into the Nature and Causes of the Wealth of Nations,* which was a landmark in the analysis of trade and economic interdependence.

Smith's book inspired David Ricardo, a millionaire stockbroker, to become an economist. In his 1817 book *Principles of Political Economy and Taxation,* Ricardo developed the principle of comparative advantage as we know it today. His defense of free trade was not a mere academic exercise. Ricardo put his economic beliefs to work as a member of the British Parliament, where he opposed the Corn Laws, which restricted the import of grain.

The conclusions of Adam Smith and David Ricardo on the gains from trade have held up well over time. Although economists often disagree on questions of policy, they are united in their support of free trade. Moreover, the central argument for free trade has not changed much in the past two centuries. Even though the field of economics has broadened its scope and refined its theories since the time of Smith and Ricardo, economists' opposition to trade restrictions is still based largely on the principle of comparative advantage.

David Ricardo

⅓ ounce of meat. This price of potatoes is lower than her opportunity cost of 1 ounce of potatoes, which is ½ ounce of meat. The rancher benefits because she gets to buy potatoes at a good price.

These benefits arise because each person concentrates on the activity for which he or she has the lower opportunity cost: The farmer spends more time growing potatoes, and the rancher spends more time producing meat. As a result, the total production of potatoes and the total production of meat both rise. In our example, potato production rises from 40 to 44 ounces, and meat production rises from 16 to 18 ounces. The farmer and rancher share the benefits of this increased production. The moral of the story of the farmer and the rancher should now be clear: *Trade can benefit everyone in society because it allows people to specialize in activities in which they have a comparative advantage.*

QuickQuiz Robinson Crusoe can gather 10 coconuts or catch 1 fish per hour. His friend Friday can gather 30 coconuts or catch 2 fish per hour. What is Crusoe's opportunity cost of catching one fish? What is Friday's? Who has an absolute advantage in catching fish? Who has a comparative advantage in catching fish?

APPLICATIONS OF COMPARATIVE ADVANTAGE

The principle of comparative advantage explains interdependence and the gains from trade. Because interdependence is so prevalent in the modern world, the principle of comparative advantage has many applications. Here are two examples, one fanciful and one of great practical importance.

Should Tiger Woods Mow His Own Lawn?

Tiger Woods spends a lot of time walking around on grass. One of the most talented golfers of all time, he can hit a drive and sink a putt in a way that most casual golfers only dream of doing. Most likely, he is talented at other activities too.

IN THE NEWS

WHO HAS A COMPARATIVE ADVANTAGE IN PRODUCING LAMB?

A common barrier to free trade among countries is tariffs, which are taxes on the import of goods from abroad. In the following opinion column, economist Douglas Irwin discusses a recent example of their use.

Lamb Tariffs Fleece U.S. Consumers

By Douglas A. Irwin

President Clinton dealt a serious blow to free trade last Wednesday, when he announced that the U.S. would impose stiff import tariffs on lamb from Australia and New Zealand. His decision undercuts American leadership and makes a mockery of the administration's claims that it favors free and fair trade.

U.S. sheep producers have long been dependent on government. For more than half a century, until Congress enacted farm-policy reforms in 1995, they received subsidies for wool. Having lost that handout, saddled with high costs and inefficiencies, and facing domestic competition from chicken, beef, and pork, sheep producers sought to stop foreign competition by filing for import relief.

Almost all U.S. lamb imports come from Australia and New Zealand, major agricultural producers with a crushing comparative advantage. New Zealand has fewer than four million people but as many as 60 million sheep (compared with about seven million sheep in the U.S.). New Zealand's farmers have invested substantial resources in new technology and effective marketing, making them among the most efficient producers in the world. New Zealand also eliminated domestic agricultural subsidies in the free-market reforms of the 1950s, and is a free-trading country, on track to eliminate all import tariffs by 2006.

Rather than emulate this example, the American Sheep Industry Association, among others, filed an "escape clause" petition under the Trade Act of 1974, which allows temporary "breathing space" protection to import-competing industries. Under the escape-clause provision, a petitioning industry is required to present an adjustment plan to ensure that it undertakes steps to become competitive in the future. The tariff protection is usually limited and scheduled to be phased out.

For example, let's imagine that Woods can mow his lawn faster than anyone else. But just because he *can* mow his lawn fast, does this mean he *should?*

To answer this question, we can use the concepts of opportunity cost and comparative advantage. Let's say that Woods can mow his lawn in 2 hours. In that same 2 hours, he could film a television commercial for Nike and earn $10,000. By contrast, Forrest Gump, the boy next door, can mow Woods's lawn in 4 hours. In that same 4 hours, he could work at McDonald's and earn $20.

In this example, Woods's opportunity cost of mowing the lawn is $10,000 and Forrest's opportunity cost is $20. Woods has an absolute advantage in mowing lawns because he can do the work in less time. Yet Forrest has a comparative advantage in mowing lawns because he has the lower opportunity cost.

The gains from trade in this example are tremendous. Rather than mowing his own lawn, Woods should make the commercial and hire Forrest to mow the lawn.

The U.S. International Trade Commission determines whether imports are a cause of "serious injury" to the domestic industry and, if so, proposes a remedy, which the president has full discretion to adopt, change or reject. In February, the ITC did not find that the domestic industry had suffered "serious injury," but rather adopted the weaker ruling that imports were "a substantial cause of threat of serious injury." The ITC did not propose to roll back imports, only to impose a 20% tariff (declining over four years) on imports above last year's levels.

The administration at first appeared to be considering less restrictive measures. Australia and New Zealand even offered financial assistance to the U.S. producers, and the administration delayed any announcement and appeared to be working toward a compromise. But these hopes were completely dashed with the shocking final decision, in which the administration capitulated to the demands of the sheep industry and its advocates in Congress.

The congressional charge was led by Sen. Max Baucus (D., Mont.), a member of the Agriculture Committee whose sister, a sheep producer, had appeared before the ITC to press for higher tariffs. The administration opted for . . . [the following:] On top of existing tariffs, the president imposed a 9% tariff on *all* imports in the first year (declining to 6% and then 3% in years two and three), and a whopping 40% tariff on imports above last year's levels (dropping to 32% and 24%). . . .

The American Sheep Industry Association's president happily announced that the move will "bring some stability to the market." Whenever producers speak of bringing stability to the market, you know that consumers are getting fleeced.

The lamb decision, while little noticed at home, has been closely followed abroad. The decision undercuts the administration's free-trade rhetoric and harms its efforts to get other countries to open up their markets. Some import relief had been expected, but not so clearly protectionist as what finally materialized. The extreme decision has outraged farmers in Australia and New Zealand, and officials there have vowed to take the U.S. to a WTO dispute settlement panel.

The administration's timing could not have been worse. The decision came right after an Asia Pacific Economic Co-operation summit reaffirmed its commitment to reduce trade barriers, and a few months before the World Trade Organization's November meeting in Seattle, where the WTO is to launch a new round of multilateral trade negotiations. A principal U.S. objective at the summit is the reduction of agricultural protection in Europe and elsewhere.

In 1947, facing an election the next year, President Truman courageously resisted special interest pressure and vetoed a bill to impose import quotas on wool, which would have jeopardized the first postwar multilateral trade negotiations due to start later that year. In contrast, Mr. Clinton, though a lame duck, caved in to political pressure. If the U.S., whose booming economy is the envy of the world, cannot resist protectionism, how can it expect other countries to do so?

Source: *The Wall Street Journal,* July 12, 1999, p. A28. © 1999 by Dow Jones & Co. Inc. Reproduced with permission of DOW JONES & CO INC in the format Textbook via Copyright Clearance Center.

As long as Woods pays Forrest more than $20 and less than $10,000, both of them are better off.

Should the United States Trade with Other Countries?

Just as individuals can benefit from specialization and trade with one another, as the farmer and rancher did, so can populations of people in different countries. Many of the goods that Americans enjoy are produced abroad, and many of the goods produced in the United States are sold abroad. Goods produced abroad and sold domestically are called **imports**. Goods produced domestically and sold abroad are called **exports**.

To see how countries can benefit from trade, suppose there are two countries, the United States and Japan, and two goods, food and cars. Imagine that the two countries produce cars equally well: An American worker and a Japanese worker can each produce 1 car per month. By contrast, because the United States has more and better land, it is better at producing food: A U.S. worker can produce 2 tons of food per month, whereas a Japanese worker can produce only 1 ton of food per month.

The principle of comparative advantage states that each good should be produced by the country that has the smaller opportunity cost of producing that good. Because the opportunity cost of a car is 2 tons of food in the United States but only 1 ton of food in Japan, Japan has a comparative advantage in producing cars. Japan should produce more cars than it wants for its own use and export some of them to the United States. Similarly, because the opportunity cost of a ton of food is 1 car in Japan but only ½ car in the United States, the United States has a comparative advantage in producing food. The United States should produce more food than it wants to consume and export some of it to Japan. Through specialization and trade, both countries can have more food and more cars.

In reality, of course, the issues involved in trade among nations are more complex than this example suggests, as we will see in Chapter 9. Most important among these issues is that each country has many citizens with different interests. International trade can make some individuals worse off, even as it makes the country as a whole better off. When the United States exports food and imports cars, the impact on an American farmer is not the same as the impact on an American autoworker. Yet, contrary to the opinions sometimes voiced by politicians and political commentators, international trade is not like war, in which some countries win and others lose. Trade allows all countries to achieve greater prosperity.

QuickQuiz Suppose that the world's fastest typist happens to be trained in brain surgery. Should he do his own typing or hire a secretary? Explain.

CONCLUSION

The principle of comparative advantage shows that trade can make everyone better off. You should now understand more fully the benefits of living in an interdependent economy. But having seen why interdependence is desirable, you might

---

imports
goods produced abroad and sold domestically

exports
goods produced domestically and sold abroad

naturally ask how it is possible. How do free societies coordinate the diverse activities of all the people involved in their economies? What ensures that goods and services will get from those who should be producing them to those who should be consuming them?

In a world with only two people, such as the rancher and the farmer, the answer is simple: These two people can directly bargain and allocate resources between themselves. In the real world with billions of people, the answer is less obvious. We take up this issue in the next chapter, where we see that free societies allocate resources through the market forces of supply and demand.

SUMMARY

- Each person consumes goods and services produced by many other people both in our country and around the world. Interdependence and trade are desirable because they allow everyone to enjoy a greater quantity and variety of goods and services.

- There are two ways to compare the ability of two people in producing a good. The person who can produce the good with the smaller quantity of inputs is said to have an *absolute advantage* in producing the good. The person who has the smaller opportunity cost of producing the good is said to have a *comparative advantage*. The gains from trade are based on comparative advantage, not absolute advantage.

- Trade makes everyone better off because it allows people to specialize in those activities in which they have a comparative advantage.

- The principle of comparative advantage applies to countries as well as to people. Economists use the principle of comparative advantage to advocate free trade among countries.

KEY CONCEPTS

absolute advantage, p. 51
opportunity cost, p. 51

comparative advantage, p. 52
imports, p. 56

exports, p. 56

QUESTIONS FOR REVIEW

1. Explain how absolute advantage and comparative advantage differ.

2. Give an example in which one person has an absolute advantage in doing something but another person has a comparative advantage.

3. Is absolute advantage or comparative advantage more important for trade? Explain your

reasoning using the example in your answer to Question 2.

4. Will a nation tend to export or import goods for which it has a comparative advantage? Explain.

5. Why do economists oppose policies that restrict trade among nations?

PROBLEMS AND APPLICATIONS

1. Consider the farmer and the rancher from our example in this chapter. Explain why the farmer's opportunity cost of producing 1 ounce of meat is 4 ounces of potatoes. Explain why the rancher's opportunity cost

of producing 1 ounce of meat is 2 ounces of potatoes.

2. Maria can read 20 pages of economics in an hour. She can also read 50 pages of sociology in an hour. She spends 5 hours per day studying.

a. Draw Maria's production possibilities frontier for reading economics and sociology.

b. What is Maria's opportunity cost of reading 100 pages of sociology?

3. American and Japanese workers can each produce 4 cars a year. An American worker can produce 10 tons of grain a year, whereas a Japanese worker can produce 5 tons of grain a year. To keep things simple, assume that each country has 100 million workers.

a. For this situation, construct a table analogous to Table 1.

b. Graph the production possibilities frontier of the American and Japanese economies.

c. For the United States, what is the opportunity cost of a car? Of grain? For Japan, what is the opportunity cost of a car? Of grain? Put this information in a table analogous to Table 3.

d. Which country has an absolute advantage in producing cars? In producing grain?

e. Which country has a comparative advantage in producing cars? In producing grain?

f. Without trade, half of each country's workers produce cars and half produce grain. What quantities of cars and grain does each country produce?

g. Starting from a position without trade, give an example in which trade makes each country better off.

4. Pat and Kris are roommates. They spend most of their time studying (of course), but they leave some time for their favorite activities: making pizza and brewing root beer. Pat takes 4 hours to brew a gallon of root beer and 2 hours to make a pizza. Kris takes 6 hours to brew a gallon of root beer and 4 hours to make a pizza.

a. What is each roommate's opportunity cost of making a pizza? Who has the absolute advantage in making pizza? Who has the comparative advantage in making pizza?

b. If Pat and Kris trade foods with each other, who will trade away pizza in exchange for root beer?

c. The price of pizza can be expressed in terms of gallons of root beer. What is the highest price at which pizza can be traded that would make both roommates better off? What is the lowest price? Explain.

5. Suppose that there are 10 million workers in Canada, and that each of these workers can produce either 2 cars or 30 bushels of wheat in a year.

a. What is the opportunity cost of producing a car in Canada? What is the opportunity cost of producing a bushel of wheat in Canada? Explain the relationship between the opportunity costs of the two goods.

b. Draw Canada's production possibilities frontier. If Canada chooses to consume 10 million cars, how much wheat can it consume without trade? Label this point on the production possibilities frontier.

c. Now suppose that the United States offers to buy 10 million cars from Canada in exchange for 20 bushels of wheat per car. If Canada continues to consume 10 million cars, how much wheat does this deal allow Canada to consume? Label this point on your diagram. Should Canada accept the deal?

6. Consider a professor who is writing a book. The professor can both write the chapters and gather the needed data faster than anyone else at his university. Still, he pays a student to collect data at the library. Is this sensible? Explain.

7. England and Scotland both produce scones and sweaters. Suppose that an English worker can produce 50 scones per hour or 1 sweater per hour. Suppose that a Scottish worker can produce 40 scones per hour or 2 sweaters per hour.

a. Which country has the absolute advantage in the production of each good? Which country has the comparative advantage?

b. If England and Scotland decide to trade, which commodity will Scotland trade to England? Explain.

c. If a Scottish worker could produce only 1 sweater per hour, would Scotland still gain from trade? Would England still gain from trade? Explain.

8. The following table describes the production possibilities of two cities in the country of Baseballia:

	Pairs of Red Socks per Worker per Hour	Pairs of White Socks per Worker per Hour
Boston	3	3
Chicago	2	1

a. Without trade, what is the price of white socks (in terms of red socks) in Boston? What is the price in Chicago?

b. Which city has an absolute advantage in the production of each color sock? Which city has a comparative advantage in the production of each color sock?

c. If the cities trade with each other, which color sock will each export?

d. What is the range of prices at which trade can occur?

9. Suppose that all goods can be produced with fewer worker hours in Germany than in France.

a. In what sense is the cost of all goods lower in Germany than in France?

b. In what sense is the cost of some goods lower in France?

c. If Germany and France traded with each other, would both countries be better off as a result? Explain in the context of your answers to parts (a) and (b).

10. Are the following statements true or false? Explain in each case.

a. "Two countries can achieve gains from trade even if one of the countries has an absolute advantage in the production of all goods."

b. "Certain very talented people have a comparative advantage in everything they do."

c. "If a certain trade is good for one person, it can't be good for the other one."

http://   For more study tools, please visit http://mankiwXtra.swlearning.com.

2

SUPPLY AND DEMAND I: HOW MARKETS WORK

THE MARKET FORCES
OF SUPPLY AND DEMAND

When a cold snap hits Florida, the price of orange juice rises in supermarkets throughout the country. When the weather turns warm in New England every summer, the price of hotel rooms in the Caribbean plummets. When a war breaks out in the Middle East, the price of gasoline in the United States rises, and the price of a used Cadillac falls. What do these events have in common? They all show the workings of supply and demand.

Supply and *demand* are the two words that economists use most often—and for good reason. Supply and demand are the forces that make market economies work. They determine the quantity of each good produced and the price at which it is sold. If you want to know how any event or policy will affect the economy, you must think first about how it will affect supply and demand.

This chapter introduces the theory of supply and demand. It considers how buyers and sellers behave and how they interact with one another. It shows how supply and demand determine prices in a market economy and how prices, in turn, allocate the economy's scarce resources.

MARKETS AND COMPETITION

market
a group of buyers and sellers
of a particular good or service

The terms *supply* and *demand* refer to the behavior of people as they interact with one another in markets. A **market** is a group of buyers and sellers of a particular good or service. The buyers as a group determine the demand for the product, and the sellers as a group determine the supply of the product. Before discussing how buyers and sellers behave, let's first consider more fully what we mean by a "market" and the various types of markets we observe in the economy.

Competitive Markets

Markets take many forms. Sometimes markets are highly organized, such as the markets for many agricultural commodities. In these markets, buyers and sellers meet at a specific time and place, where an auctioneer helps set prices and arrange sales.

More often, markets are less organized. For example, consider the market for ice cream in a particular town. Buyers of ice cream do not meet together at any one time. The sellers of ice cream are in different locations and offer somewhat different products. There is no auctioneer calling out the price of ice cream. Each seller posts a price for an ice-cream cone, and each buyer decides how much ice cream to buy at each store.

Even though it is not organized, the group of ice-cream buyers and ice-cream sellers forms a market. Each buyer knows that there are several sellers from which to choose, and each seller is aware that his product is similar to that offered by other sellers. The price of ice cream and the quantity of ice cream sold are not determined by any single buyer or seller. Rather, price and quantity are determined by all buyers and sellers as they interact in the marketplace.

competitive market
a market in which there are many
buyers and many sellers so that
each has a negligible impact on
the market price

The market for ice cream, like most markets in the economy, is highly competitive. A **competitive market** is a market in which there are many buyers and many sellers so that each has a negligible impact on the market price. Each seller of ice cream has limited control over the price because other sellers are offering similar products. A seller has little reason to charge less than the going price, and if he or she charges more, buyers will make their purchases elsewhere. Similarly, no single buyer of ice cream can influence the price of ice cream because each buyer purchases only a small amount.

In this chapter we examine how buyers and sellers interact in competitive markets. We see how the forces of supply and demand determine both the quantity of the good sold and its price.

Competition: Perfect and Otherwise

We assume in this chapter that markets are *perfectly competitive*. Perfectly competitive markets are defined by two primary characteristics: (1) the goods being offered for sale are all the same, and (2) the buyers and sellers are so numerous that no single buyer or seller can influence the market price. Because buyers and sellers in perfectly competitive markets must accept the price the market determines, they are said to be *price takers*.

There are some markets in which the assumption of perfect competition applies perfectly. In the wheat market, for example, there are thousands of farmers who sell wheat and millions of consumers who use wheat and wheat products. Because no single buyer or seller can influence the price of wheat, each takes the price as given.

Not all goods and services, however, are sold in perfectly competitive markets. Some markets have only one seller, and this seller sets the price. Such a seller is called a *monopoly*. Your local cable television company, for instance, may be a monopoly. Residents of your town probably have only one cable company from which to buy this service.

Some markets fall between the extremes of perfect competition and monopoly. One such market, called an *oligopoly*, has a few sellers that do not always compete aggressively. Airline routes are an example. If a route between two cities is serviced by only two or three carriers, the carriers may avoid rigorous competition so they can keep prices high. Another type of market is *monopolistically competitive*; it contains many sellers but each offers a slightly different product. Because the products are not exactly the same, each seller has some ability to set the price for its own product. An example is the market for magazines. Magazines compete with one another for readers and anyone can enter the market by starting a new one, but each magazine offers different articles and can set its own price.

Despite the diversity of market types we find in the world, we begin by studying perfect competition. Perfectly competitive markets are the easiest to analyze. Moreover, because some degree of competition is present in most markets, many of the lessons that we learn by studying supply and demand under perfect competition apply in more complicated markets as well.

QuickQuiz What is a market? • What are the characteristics of a competitive market?

DEMAND

We begin our study of markets by examining the behavior of buyers. To focus our thinking, let's keep in mind a particular good—ice cream.

The Demand Curve: The Relationship between Price and Quantity Demanded

The **quantity demanded** of any good is the amount of the good that buyers are willing and able to purchase. As we will see, many things determine the quantity demanded of any good, but when analyzing how markets work, one determinant plays a central role—the price of the good. If the price of ice cream rose to $20 per scoop, you would buy less ice cream. You might buy frozen yogurt instead. If the price of ice cream fell to $0.20 per scoop, you would buy more. Because the quantity demanded falls as the price rises and rises as the price falls, we say that the quantity demanded is *negatively related* to the price. This relationship between price and quantity demanded is true for most goods in the economy and, in fact, is

quantity demanded
the amount of a good that buyers are willing and able to purchase

FIGURE 1

FIGURE 1

Catherine's Demand Schedule and Demand Curve

The demand schedule shows the quantity demanded at each price. The demand curve, which graphs the demand schedule, shows how the quantity demanded of the good changes as its price varies. Because a lower price increases the quantity demanded, the demand curve slopes downward.

Price of Ice-Cream Cone	Quantity of Cones Demanded
$0.00	12
0.50	10
1.00	8
1.50	6
2.00	4
2.50	2
3.00	0

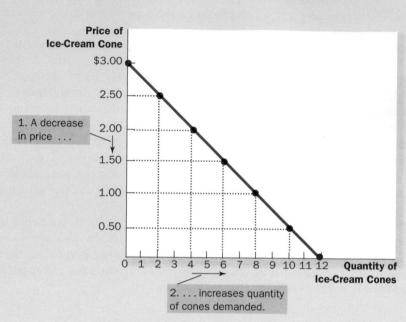

1. A decrease in price . . .

2. . . . increases quantity of cones demanded.

law of demand
the claim that, other things equal, the quantity demanded of a good falls when the price of the good rises

demand schedule
a table that shows the relationship between the price of a good and the quantity demanded

demand curve
a graph of the relationship between the price of a good and the quantity demanded

so pervasive that economists call it the **law of demand:** Other things equal, when the price of a good rises, the quantity demanded of the good falls, and when the price falls, the quantity demanded rises.

The table in Figure 1 shows how many ice-cream cones Catherine buys each month at different prices of ice cream. If ice cream is free, Catherine eats 12 cones. At $0.50 per cone, Catherine buys 10 cones. As the price rises further, she buys fewer and fewer cones. When the price reaches $3.00, Catherine doesn't buy any ice cream at all. This table is a **demand schedule,** a table that shows the relationship between the price of a good and the quantity demanded, holding constant everything else that influences how much consumers of the good want to buy.

The graph in Figure 1 uses the numbers from the table to illustrate the law of demand. By convention, the price of ice cream is on the vertical axis, and the quantity of ice cream demanded is on the horizontal axis. The downward-sloping line relating price and quantity demanded is called the **demand curve.**

Market Demand versus Individual Demand

The demand curve in Figure 1 shows an individual's demand for a product. To analyze how markets work, we need to determine the *market demand*, which is the sum of all the individual demands for a particular good or service.

FIGURE 2

Market Demand as the Sum of Individual Demands

The quantity demanded in a market is the sum of the quantities demanded by all the buyers at each price. Thus, the market demand curve is found by adding horizontally the individual demand curves. At a price of $2, Catherine demands 4 ice-cream cones, and Nicholas demands 3 ice-cream cones. The quantity demanded in the market at this price is 7 cones.

Price of Ice-Cream Cone	Catherine		Nicholas		Market
$0.00	12	+	7	=	19
0.50	10		6		16
1.00	8		5		13
1.50	6		4		10
2.00	4		3		7
2.50	2		2		4
3.00	0		1		1

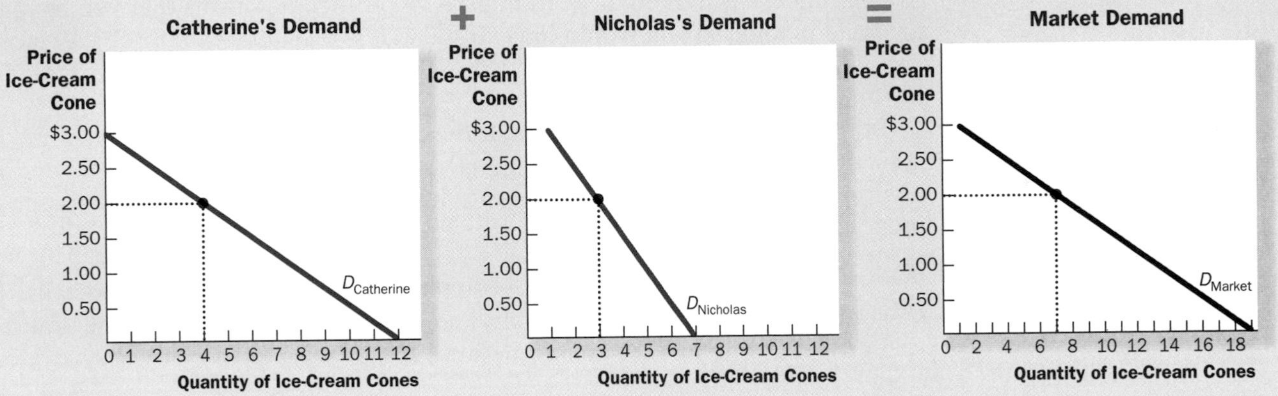

The table in Figure 2 shows the demand schedules for ice cream of two individuals—Catherine and Nicholas. At any price, Catherine's demand schedule tells us how much ice cream she buys, and Nicholas's demand schedule tells us how much ice cream he buys. The market demand at each price is the sum of the two individual demands.

The graph in Figure 2 shows the demand curves that correspond to these demand schedules. Notice that we sum the individual demand curves *horizontally* to obtain the market demand curve. That is, to find the total quantity demanded at any price, we add the individual quantities found on the horizontal axis of the individual demand curves. Because we are interested in analyzing how markets work, we will work most often with the market demand curve. The market demand curve shows how the total quantity demanded of a good varies as the price of the good varies, while all the other factors that affect how much consumers want to buy are held constant.

Shifts in the Demand Curve

The demand curve for ice cream shows how much ice cream people buy at any given price, holding constant the many other factors beyond price that influence consumers' buying decisions. As a result, this demand curve need not be stable over time. If something happens to alter the quantity demanded at any given price, the demand curve shifts. For example, suppose the American Medical Association discovered that people who regularly eat ice cream live longer, healthier lives. The discovery would raise the demand for ice cream. At any given price, buyers would now want to purchase a larger quantity of ice cream, and the demand curve for ice cream would shift.

Figure 3 illustrates shifts in demand. Any change that increases the quantity demanded at every price, such as our imaginary discovery by the American Medical Association, shifts the demand curve to the right and is called *an increase in demand*. Any change that reduces the quantity demanded at every price shifts the demand curve to the left and is called *a decrease in demand*.

There are many variables that can shift the demand curve. Here are the most important:

Income   What would happen to your demand for ice cream if you lost your job one summer? Most likely, it would fall. A lower income means that you have less to spend in total, so you would have to spend less on some—and probably most—goods. If the demand for a good falls when income falls, the good is called a **normal good.**

Not all goods are normal goods. If the demand for a good rises when income falls, the good is called an **inferior good.** An example of an inferior good might be bus rides. As your income falls, you are less likely to buy a car or take a cab, and more likely to ride the bus.

Prices of Related Goods   Suppose that the price of frozen yogurt falls. The law of demand says that you will buy more frozen yogurt. At the same time, you will probably buy less ice cream. Because ice cream and frozen yogurt are both

normal good
a good for which, other things equal, an increase in income leads to an increase in demand

inferior good
a good for which, other things equal, an increase in income leads to a decrease in demand

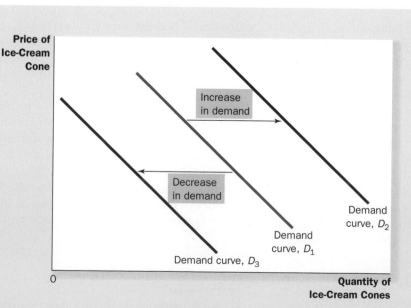

FIGURE 3

Shifts in the Demand Curve

Any change that raises the quantity that buyers wish to purchase at a given price shifts the demand curve to the right. Any change that lowers the quantity that buyers wish to purchase at a given price shifts the demand curve to the left.

cold, sweet, creamy desserts, they satisfy similar desires. When a fall in the price of one good reduces the demand for another good, the two goods are called **substitutes.** Substitutes are often pairs of goods that are used in place of each other, such as hot dogs and hamburgers, sweaters and sweatshirts, and movie tickets and video rentals.

substitutes
two goods for which an increase in the price of one leads to an increase in the demand for the other

Now suppose that the price of hot fudge falls. According to the law of demand, you will buy more hot fudge. Yet, in this case, you will buy more ice cream as well, because ice cream and hot fudge are often used together. When a fall in the price of one good raises the demand for another good, the two goods are called **complements.** Complements are often pairs of goods that are used together, such as gasoline and automobiles, computers and software, and peanut butter and jelly.

complements
two goods for which an increase in the price of one leads to a decrease in the demand for the other

Tastes The most obvious determinant of your demand is your tastes. If you like ice cream, you buy more of it. Economists normally do not try to explain people's tastes because tastes are based on historical and psychological forces that are beyond the realm of economics. Economists do, however, examine what happens when tastes change.

Expectations Your expectations about the future may affect your demand for a good or service today. For example, if you expect to earn a higher income next month, you may be more willing to spend some of your current savings buying ice cream. As another example, if you expect the price of ice cream to fall tomorrow, you may be less willing to buy an ice-cream cone at today's price.

Number of Buyers Because market demand is derived from individual demands, it depends on all those factors that determine the demand of individual buyers, including buyers' incomes, tastes, expectations, and the prices of related goods. In addition, it depends on the number of buyers. If Peter, another consumer of ice cream, were to join Catherine and Nicholas, the quantity demanded in the market would be higher at every price and the demand curve would shift to the right.

Summary The demand curve shows what happens to the quantity demanded of a good when its price varies, holding constant all the other variables that influence buyers. When one of these other variables changes, the demand curve shifts. Table 1 lists all the variables that influence how much consumers choose to buy of a good.

TABLE 1

Variables That Influence Buyers

This table lists the variables that affect how much consumers choose to buy of any good. Notice the special role that the price of the good plays: A change in the good's price represents a movement along the demand curve, whereas a change in one of the other variables shifts the demand curve.

Variable	A Change in This Variable . . .
Price	Represents a movement along the demand curve
Income	Shifts the demand curve
Prices of related goods	Shifts the demand curve
Tastes	Shifts the demand curve
Expectations	Shifts the demand curve
Number of buyers	Shifts the demand curve

Case Study

TWO WAYS TO REDUCE THE QUANTITY OF SMOKING DEMANDED

Public policymakers often want to reduce the amount that people smoke. There are two ways that policy can attempt to achieve this goal.

One way to reduce smoking is to shift the demand curve for cigarettes and other tobacco products. Public service announcements, mandatory health warnings on cigarette packages, and the prohibition of cigarette advertising on television are all policies aimed at reducing the quantity of cigarettes demanded at any given price. If successful, these policies shift the demand curve for cigarettes to the left, as in panel (a) of Figure 4.

Alternatively, policymakers can try to raise the price of cigarettes. If the government taxes the manufacture of cigarettes, for example, cigarette companies pass much of this tax on to consumers in the form of higher prices. A higher price encourages smokers to reduce the numbers of cigarettes they smoke. In this case,

---

FIGURE 4

Shifts in the Demand Curve versus Movements along the Demand Curve

If warnings on cigarette packages convince smokers to smoke less, the demand curve for cigarettes shifts to the left. In panel (a), the demand curve shifts from D_1 to D_2. At a price of $2 per pack, the quantity demanded falls from 20 to 10 cigarettes per day, as reflected by the shift from point A to point B. By contrast, if a tax raises the price of cigarettes, the demand curve does not shift. Instead, we observe a movement to a different point on the demand curve. In panel (b), when the price rises from $2 to $4, the quantity demanded falls from 20 to 12 cigarettes per day, as reflected by the movement from point A to point C.

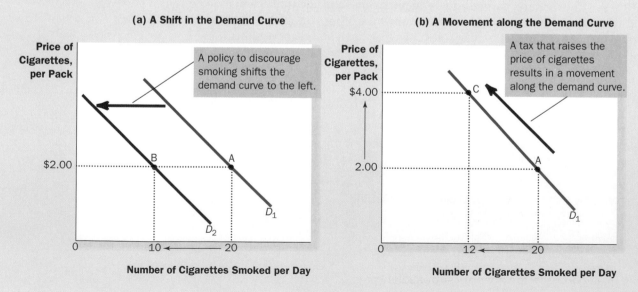

(a) A Shift in the Demand Curve

(b) A Movement along the Demand Curve

the reduced amount of smoking does not represent a shift in the demand curve. Instead, it represents a movement along the same demand curve to a point with a higher price and lower quantity, as in panel (b) of Figure 4.

How much does the amount of smoking respond to changes in the price of cigarettes? Economists have attempted to answer this question by studying what happens when the tax on cigarettes changes. They have found that a 10 percent increase in the price causes a 4 percent reduction in the quantity demanded. Teenagers are found to be especially sensitive to the price of cigarettes: A 10 percent increase in the price causes a 12 percent drop in teenage smoking.

A related question is how the price of cigarettes affects the demand for illicit drugs, such as marijuana. Opponents of cigarette taxes often argue that tobacco and marijuana are substitutes, so that high cigarette prices encourage marijuana use. By contrast, many experts on substance abuse view tobacco as a "gateway drug" leading the young to experiment with other harmful substances. Most studies of the data are consistent with this view: They find that lower cigarette prices are associated with greater use of marijuana. In other words, tobacco and marijuana appear to be complements rather than substitutes. ●

QuickQuiz Make up an example of a demand schedule for pizza, and graph the implied demand curve. • Give an example of something that would shift this demand curve. • Would a change in the price of pizza shift this demand curve?

What is the best way to stop this?

SUPPLY

We now turn to the other side of the market and examine the behavior of sellers. Once again, to focus our thinking, let's consider the market for ice cream.

The Supply Curve: The Relationship between Price and Quantity Supplied

The **quantity supplied** of any good or service is the amount that sellers are willing and able to sell. There are many determinants of quantity supplied, but once again price plays a special role in our analysis. When the price of ice cream is high, selling ice cream is profitable, and so the quantity supplied is large. Sellers of ice cream work long hours, buy many ice-cream machines, and hire many workers. By contrast, when the price of ice cream is low, the business is less profitable, and so sellers produce less ice cream. At a low price, some sellers may even choose to shut down, and their quantity supplied falls to zero. Because the quantity supplied rises as the price rises and falls as the price falls, we say that the quantity supplied is *positively related* to the price of the good. This relationship between price and quantity supplied is called the **law of supply:** Other things equal, when the price of a good rises, the quantity supplied of the good also rises, and when the price falls, the quantity supplied falls as well.

quantity supplied
the amount of a good that sellers are willing and able to sell

law of supply
the claim that, other things equal, the quantity supplied of a good rises when the price of the good rises

FIGURE 5

Ben's Supply Schedule and Supply Curve

The supply schedule shows the quantity supplied at each price. This supply curve, which graphs the supply schedule, shows how the quantity supplied of the good changes as its price varies. Because a higher price increases the quantity supplied, the supply curve slopes upward.

Price of Ice-Cream Cone	Quantity of Cones Demanded
$0.00	0
0.50	0
1.00	1
1.50	2
2.00	3
2.50	4
3.00	5

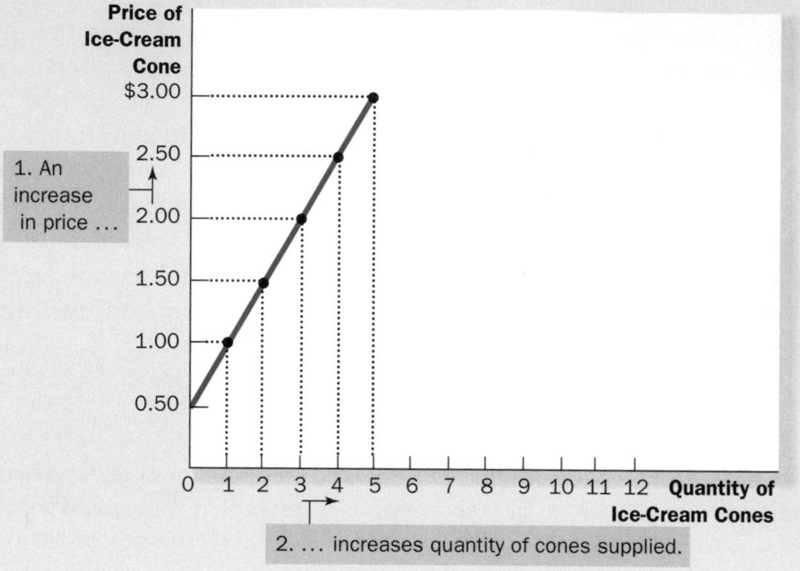

1. An increase in price ...

2. ... increases quantity of cones supplied.

The table in Figure 5 shows the quantity supplied by Ben, an ice-cream seller, at various prices of ice cream. At a price below $1.00, Ben does not supply any ice cream at all. As the price rises, he supplies a greater and greater quantity. This is the **supply schedule,** a table that shows the relationship between the price of a good and the quantity supplied, holding constant everything else that influences how much producers of the good want to sell.

The graph in Figure 5 uses the numbers from the table to illustrate the law of supply. The curve relating price and quantity supplied is called the **supply curve.** The supply curve slopes upward because, other things equal, a higher price means a greater quantity supplied.

supply schedule
a table that shows the relationship between the price of a good and the quantity supplied

supply curve
a graph of the relationship between the price of a good and the quantity supplied

Market Supply versus Individual Supply

Just as market demand is the sum of the demands of all buyers, market supply is the sum of the supplies of all sellers. The table in Figure 6 shows the supply schedules for two ice-cream producers—Ben and Jerry. At any price, Ben's supply schedule tells us the quantity of ice cream Ben supplies, and Jerry's supply schedule tells us the quantity of ice cream Jerry supplies. The market supply is the sum of the two individual supplies.

FIGURE 6

Market Supply as the Sum of Individual Supplies

The quantity supplied in a market is the sum of the quantities supplied by all the sellers at each price. Thus, the market supply curve is found by adding horizontally the individual supply curves. At a price of $2, Ben supplies 3 ice-cream cones, and Jerry supplies 4 ice-cream cones. The quantity supplied in the market at this price is 7 cones.

Price of Ice-Cream Cone	Ben		Jerry		Market
$0.00	0	+	0	=	0
0.50	0		0		0
1.00	1		0		1
1.50	2		2		4
2.00	3		4		7
2.50	4		6		10
3.00	5		8		13

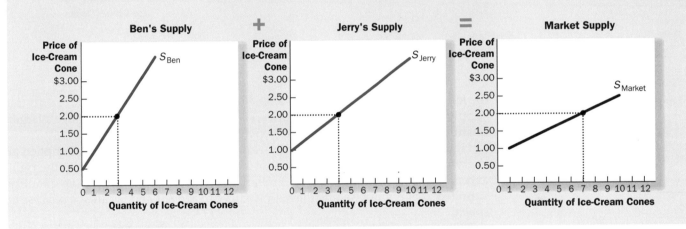

The graph in Figure 6 shows the supply curves that correspond to the supply schedules. As with demand curves, we sum the individual supply curves *horizontally* to obtain the market supply curve. That is, to find the total quantity supplied at any price, we add the individual quantities found on the horizontal axis of the individual supply curves. The market supply curve shows how the total quantity supplied varies as the price of the good varies.

Shifts in the Supply Curve

The supply curve for ice cream shows how much ice cream producers offer for sale at any given price, holding constant all the other factors beyond price that influence producers' decisions about how much to sell. This relationship can change over time, which is represented by a shift in the supply curve. For example, suppose the price of sugar falls. Because sugar is an input into producing ice cream,

FIGURE 7

Shifts in the Supply Curve

Any change that raises the quantity that sellers wish to produce at a given price shifts the supply curve to the right. Any change that lowers the quantity that sellers wish to produce at a given price shifts the supply curve to the left.

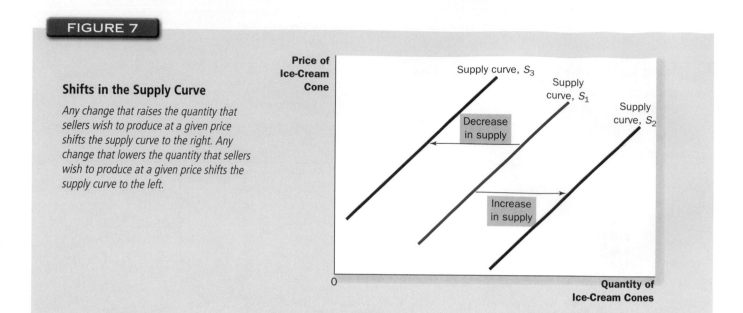

the fall in the price of sugar makes selling ice cream more profitable. This raises the supply of ice cream: At any given price, sellers are now willing to produce a larger quantity. Thus, the supply curve for ice cream shifts to the right.

Figure 7 illustrates shifts in supply. Any change that raises quantity supplied at every price, such as a fall in the price of sugar, shifts the supply curve to the right and is called *an increase in supply*. Similarly, any change that reduces the quantity supplied at every price shifts the supply curve to the left and is called *a decrease in supply*.

There are many variables that can shift the supply curve. Here are some of the most important:

Input Prices   To produce its output of ice cream, sellers use various inputs: cream, sugar, flavoring, ice-cream machines, the buildings in which the ice cream is made, and the labor of workers to mix the ingredients and operate the machines. When the price of one or more of these inputs rises, producing ice cream is less profitable, and firms supply less ice cream. If input prices rise substantially, a firm might shut down and supply no ice cream at all. Thus, the supply of a good is negatively related to the price of the inputs used to make the good.

Technology   The technology for turning the inputs into ice cream is yet another determinant of supply. The invention of the mechanized ice-cream machine, for example, reduced the amount of labor necessary to make ice cream. By reducing firms' costs, the advance in technology raised the supply of ice cream.

Expectations   The amount of ice cream a firm supplies today may depend on its expectations of the future. For example, if it expects the price of ice cream to rise

---

TABLE 2

Variables That Influence Sellers

This table lists the variables that affect how much producers choose to sell of any good. Notice the special role that the price of the good plays: A change in the good's price represents a movement along the supply curve, whereas a change in one of the other variables shifts the supply curve.

Variable	A Change in This Variable . . .
Price	Represents a movement along the supply curve
Input prices	Shifts the supply curve
Technology	Shifts the supply curve
Expectations	Shifts the supply curve
Number of sellers	Shifts the supply curve

---

in the future, it will put some of its current production into storage and supply less to the market today.

Number of Sellers Market supply depends on all those factors that influence the supply of individual sellers, such as the prices of inputs used to produce the good, the available technology, and expectations. In addition, the supply in a market depends on the number of sellers. If Ben or Jerry were to retire from the ice-cream business, the supply in the market would fall.

Summary The supply curve shows what happens to the quantity supplied of a good when its price varies, holding constant all the other variables that influence sellers. When one of these other variables changes, the supply curve shifts. Table 2 lists all the variables that influence how much producers choose to sell of a good.

QuickQuiz Make up an example of a supply schedule for pizza, and graph the implied supply curve. • Give an example of something that would shift this supply curve. • Would a change in the price of pizza shift this supply curve?

SUPPLY AND DEMAND TOGETHER

Having analyzed supply and demand separately, we now combine them to see how they determine the quantity of a good sold in a market and its price.

Equilibrium

Figure 8 (p. 76) shows the market supply curve and market demand curve together. Notice that there is one point at which the supply and demand curves intersect. This point is called the market's **equilibrium.** The price at this intersection is called the **equilibrium price,** and the quantity is called the **equilibrium quantity.** Here

equilibrium
a situation in which the price has reached the level where quantity supplied equals quantity demanded

equilibrium price
the price that balances quantity supplied and quantity demanded

equilibrium quantity
the quantity supplied and the quantity demanded at the equilibrium price

FIGURE 8

**The Equilibrium
of Supply and Demand**

*The equilibrium is found where
the supply and demand curves
intersect. At the equilibrium price, the
quantity supplied equals the quantity
demanded. Here the equilibrium price
is $2: At this price, 7 ice-cream cones
are supplied, and 7 ice-cream cones
are demanded.*

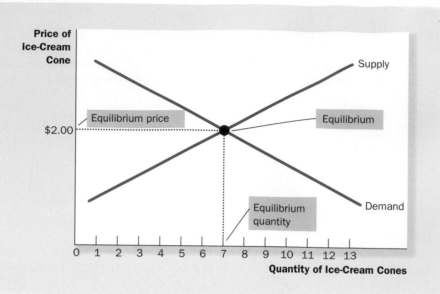

the equilibrium price is $2.00 per cone, and the equilibrium quantity is 7 ice-cream cones.

The dictionary defines the word *equilibrium* as a situation in which various forces are in balance—and this also describes a market's equilibrium. *At the equilibrium price, the quantity of the good that buyers are willing and able to buy exactly balances the quantity that sellers are willing and able to sell.* The equilibrium price is sometimes called the *market-clearing price* because, at this price, everyone in the market has been satisfied: Buyers have bought all they want to buy, and sellers have sold all they want to sell.

The actions of buyers and sellers naturally move markets toward the equilibrium of supply and demand. To see why, consider what happens when the market price is not equal to the equilibrium price.

Suppose first that the market price is above the equilibrium price, as in panel (a) of Figure 9. At a price of $2.50 per cone, the quantity of the good supplied (10 cones) exceeds the quantity demanded (4 cones). There is a **surplus** of the good: Suppliers are unable to sell all they want at the going price. A surplus is sometimes called a situation of *excess supply*. When there is a surplus in the ice-cream market, sellers of ice cream find their freezers increasingly full of ice cream they would like to sell but cannot. They respond to the surplus by cutting their prices. Falling prices, in turn, increase the quantity demanded and decrease the quantity supplied. Prices continue to fall until the market reaches the equilibrium.

Suppose now that the market price is below the equilibrium price, as in panel (b) of Figure 9. In this case, the price is $1.50 per cone, and the quantity of the good demanded exceeds the quantity supplied. There is a **shortage** of the good: Demanders are unable to buy all they want at the going price. A shortage is sometimes called a situation of *excess demand*. When a shortage occurs in the ice-cream market, buyers have to wait in long lines for a chance to buy one of the few cones

surplus
a situation in which quantity supplied is greater than quantity demanded

shortage
a situation in which quantity demanded is greater than quantity supplied

FIGURE 9

Markets Not in Equilibrium

In panel (a), there is a surplus. Because the market price of $2.50 is above the equilibrium price, the quantity supplied (10 cones) exceeds the quantity demanded (4 cones). Suppliers try to increase sales by cutting the price of a cone, and this moves the price toward its equilibrium level. In panel (b), there is a shortage. Because the market price of $1.50 is below the equilibrium price, the quantity demanded (10 cones) exceeds the quantity supplied (4 cones). With too many buyers chasing too few goods, suppliers can take advantage of the shortage by raising the price. Hence, in both cases, the price adjustment moves the market toward the equilibrium of supply and demand.

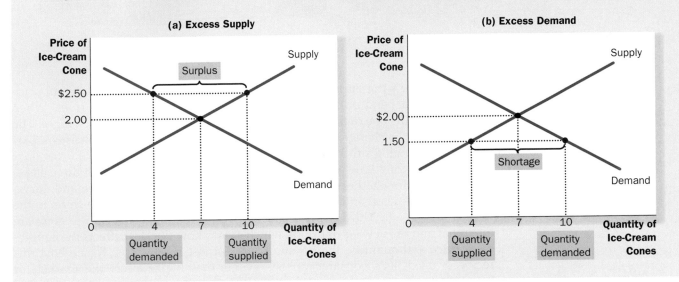

that are available. With too many buyers chasing too few goods, sellers can respond to the shortage by raising their prices without losing sales. As the price rises, quantity demanded falls, quantity supplied rises, and the market once again moves toward the equilibrium.

Thus, the activities of the many buyers and sellers automatically push the market price toward the equilibrium price. Once the market reaches its equilibrium, all buyers and sellers are satisfied, and there is no upward or downward pressure on the price. How quickly equilibrium is reached varies from market to market, depending on how quickly prices adjust. In most free markets, surpluses and shortages are only temporary because prices eventually move toward their equilibrium levels. Indeed, this phenomenon is so pervasive that it is called the **law of supply and demand**: The price of any good adjusts to bring the quantity supplied and quantity demanded for that good into balance.

law of supply and demand
the claim that the price of any good adjusts to bring the quantity supplied and the quantity demanded for that good into balance

Three Steps to Analyzing Changes in Equilibrium

So far we have seen how supply and demand together determine a market's equilibrium, which in turn determines the price of the good and the amount of the

good that buyers purchase and sellers produce. Of course, the equilibrium price and quantity depend on the position of the supply and demand curves. When some event shifts one of these curves, the equilibrium in the market changes. The analysis of such a change is called *comparative statics* because it involves comparing two unchanging situations—an initial and a new equilibrium.

When analyzing how some event affects a market, we proceed in three steps. First, we decide whether the event shifts the supply curve, the demand curve, or in some cases both curves. Second, we decide whether the curve shifts to the right or to the left. Third, we use the supply-and-demand diagram to compare the initial and the new equilibrium, which shows how the shift affects the equilibrium price and quantity. Table 3 summarizes these three steps. To see how this recipe is used, let's consider various events that might affect the market for ice cream.

Example: A Change in Demand   Suppose that one summer the weather is very hot. How does this event affect the market for ice cream? To answer this question, let's follow our three steps.

1. The hot weather affects the demand curve by changing people's taste for ice cream. That is, the weather changes the amount of ice cream that people want to buy at any given price. The supply curve is unchanged because the weather does not directly affect the firms that sell ice cream.

TABLE 3

A Three-Step Program for Analyzing Changes in Equilibrium

1. Decide whether the event shifts the supply or demand curve (or perhaps both).
2. Decide in which direction the curve shifts.
3. Use the supply-and-demand diagram to see how the shift changes the equilibrium price and quantity.

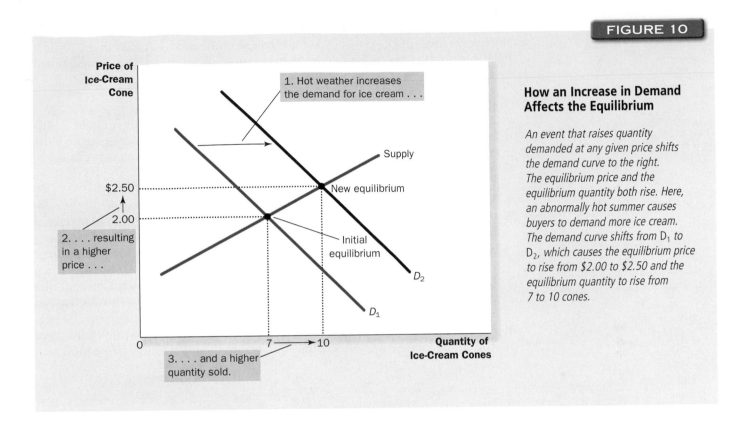

FIGURE 10

How an Increase in Demand Affects the Equilibrium

An event that raises quantity demanded at any given price shifts the demand curve to the right. The equilibrium price and the equilibrium quantity both rise. Here, an abnormally hot summer causes buyers to demand more ice cream. The demand curve shifts from D_1 to D_2, which causes the equilibrium price to rise from $2.00 to $2.50 and the equilibrium quantity to rise from 7 to 10 cones.

2. Because hot weather makes people want to eat more ice cream, the demand curve shifts to the right. Figure 10 shows this increase in demand as the shift in the demand curve from D_1 to D_2. This shift indicates that the quantity of ice cream demanded is higher at every price.
3. As Figure 10 shows, the increase in demand raises the equilibrium price from $2.00 to $2.50 and the equilibrium quantity from 7 to 10 cones. In other words, the hot weather increases the price of ice cream and the quantity of ice cream sold.

Shifts in Curves versus Movements along Curves   Notice that when hot weather drives up the price of ice cream, the quantity of ice cream that firms supply rises, even though the supply curve remains the same. In this case, economists say there has been an increase in "quantity supplied" but no change in "supply."

"Supply" refers to the position of the supply curve, whereas the "quantity supplied" refers to the amount suppliers wish to sell. In this example, supply does not change because the weather does not alter firms' desire to sell at any given price. Instead, the hot weather alters consumers' desire to buy at any given price and thereby shifts the demand curve. The increase in demand causes the equilibrium price to rise. When the price rises, the quantity supplied rises. This increase in quantity supplied is represented by the movement along the supply curve.

To summarize, a shift *in* the supply curve is called a "change in supply," and a shift *in* the demand curve is called a "change in demand." A movement *along* a fixed supply curve is called a "change in the quantity supplied," and a movement *along* a fixed demand curve is called a "change in the quantity demanded."

Example: A Change in Supply Suppose that, during another summer, a hurricane destroys part of the sugar cane crop and drives up the price of sugar. How does this event affect the market for ice cream? Once again, to answer this question, we follow our three steps.

1. The change in the price of sugar, an input into making ice cream, affects the supply curve. By raising the costs of production, it reduces the amount of ice cream that firms produce and sell at any given price. The demand curve does not change because the higher cost of inputs does not directly affect the amount of ice cream households wish to buy.
2. The supply curve shifts to the left because, at every price, the total amount that firms are willing and able to sell is reduced. Figure 11 illustrates this decrease in supply as a shift in the supply curve from S_1 to S_2.
3. As Figure 11 shows, the shift in the supply curve raises the equilibrium price from $2.00 to $2.50 and lowers the equilibrium quantity from 7 to 4 cones. As a

FIGURE 11

How a Decrease in Supply Affects the Equilibrium

An event that reduces quantity supplied at any given price shifts the supply curve to the left. The equilibrium price rises, and the equilibrium quantity falls. Here, an increase in the price of sugar (an input) causes sellers to supply less ice cream. The supply curve shifts from S_1 to S_2, which causes the equilibrium price of ice cream to rise from $2.00 to $2.50 and the equilibrium quantity to fall from 7 to 4 cones.

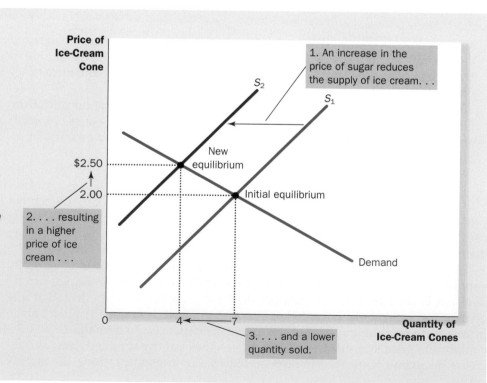

Price of Ice-Cream Cone

1. An increase in the price of sugar reduces the supply of ice cream. . .

S_2

S_1

New equilibrium

$2.50

2.00 .... Initial equilibrium

2. . . . resulting in a higher price of ice cream . . .

Demand

0   4◄—7

Quantity of Ice-Cream Cones

3. . . . and a lower quantity sold.

IN THE NEWS

MOTHER NATURE SHIFTS THE SUPPLY CURVE

According to our analysis, a natural disaster that reduces supply reduces the quantity sold and raises the price. Here's a recent example.

4-Day Cold Spell Slams California: Crops Devastated; Price of Citrus to Rise

By Todd S. Purdum

A brutal four-day freeze has destroyed more than a third of California's annual citrus crop, inflicting upwards of a half-billion dollars in damage and raising the prospect of tripled orange prices in supermarkets by next week.

Throughout the Golden State, cold, dry air from the Gulf of Alaska sent temperatures below freezing beginning Monday, with readings in the high teens and low 20's in agriculturally rich Central Valley early today—the worst cold spell since a 10-day freeze in 1990. Farmers frantically ran wind and irrigation machines overnight to keep trees warm, but officials pronounced a near total loss in the valley, and said perhaps half of the state's orange crop was lost as well....

California grows about 80 percent of the nation's oranges eaten as fruit, and 90 percent of lemons, and wholesalers said the retail prices of oranges could triple in the next few days. The price of lemons was certain to rise as well, but the price of orange juice should be less affected because most juice oranges are grown in Florida.

In some California markets, wholesalers reported that the price of navel or-

anges had increased to 90 cents a pound on Wednesday from 35 cents on Tuesday.

Source: *The New York Times,* December 25, 1998, p. A1. Copyright © 1998 by The New York Times Co. Reprinted by permission.

result of the sugar price increase, the price of ice cream rises, and the quantity of ice cream sold falls.

Example: A Change in Both Supply and Demand   Now suppose that the heat wave and the hurricane occur during the same summer. To analyze this combination of events, we again follow our three steps.

1. We determine that both curves must shift. The hot weather affects the demand curve because it alters the amount of ice cream that households want to buy at any given price. At the same time, when the hurricane drives up sugar prices, it alters the supply curve for ice cream because it changes the amount of ice cream that firms want to sell at any given price.

FIGURE 12

A Shift in Both Supply and Demand

Here we observe a simultaneous increase in demand and decrease in supply. Two outcomes are possible. In panel (a), the equilibrium price rises from P_1 to P_2, and the equilibrium quantity rises from Q_1 to Q_2. In panel (b), the equilibrium price again rises from P_1 to P_2, but the equilibrium quantity falls from Q_1 to Q_2.

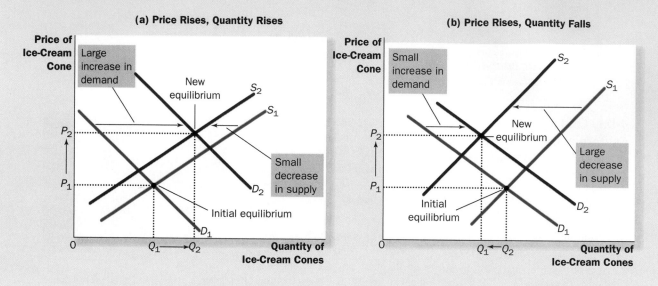

2. The curves shift in the same directions as they did in our previous analysis: The demand curve shifts to the right, and the supply curve shifts to the left. Figure 12 illustrates these shifts.

3. As Figure 12 shows, there are two possible outcomes that might result, depending on the relative size of the demand and supply shifts. In both cases, the equilibrium price rises. In panel (a), where demand increases substantially while supply falls just a little, the equilibrium quantity also rises. By contrast, in panel (b), where supply falls substantially while demand rises just a little, the equilibrium quantity falls. Thus, these events certainly raise the price of ice cream, but their impact on the amount of ice cream sold is ambiguous (that is, it could go either way).

Summary   We have just seen three examples of how to use supply and demand curves to analyze a change in equilibrium. Whenever an event shifts the supply curve, the demand curve, or perhaps both curves, you can use these tools to predict how the event will alter the amount sold in equilibrium and the price at which the good is sold. Table 4 shows the predicted outcome for any combination of shifts in the two curves. To make sure you understand how to use the tools of supply and demand, pick a few entries in this table and make sure you can explain to yourself why the table contains the prediction it does.

TABLE 4

What Happens to Price and Quantity When Supply or Demand Shifts?

As a quick quiz, make sure you can explain each of the entries in this table using a supply-and-demand diagram.

	No Change in Supply	An Increase in Supply	A Decrease in Supply
No Change in Demand	P same Q same	P down Q up	P up Q down
An Increase in Demand	P up Q up	P ambiguous Q up	P up Q ambiguous
A Decrease in Demand	P down Q down	P down Q ambiguous	P ambiguous Q down

QuickQuiz Analyze what happens to the market for pizza if the price of tomatoes rises. • Analyze what happens to the market for pizza if the price of hamburgers falls.

CONCLUSION: HOW PRICES ALLOCATE RESOURCES

This chapter has analyzed supply and demand in a single market. Although our discussion has centered around the market for ice cream, the lessons learned here apply in most other markets as well. Whenever you go to a store to buy something, you are contributing to the demand for that item. Whenever you look for a job, you are contributing to the supply of labor services. Because supply and demand

"Two dollars."

"—and seventy-five cents."

are such pervasive economic phenomena, the model of supply and demand is a powerful tool for analysis. We will be using this model repeatedly in the following chapters.

One of the *Ten Principles of Economics* discussed in Chapter 1 is that markets are usually a good way to organize economic activity. Although it is still too early to judge whether market outcomes are good or bad, in this chapter we have begun to see how markets work. In any economic system, scarce resources have to be allocated among competing uses. Market economies harness the forces of supply and demand to serve that end. Supply and demand together determine the prices of the economy's many different goods and services; prices in turn are the signals that guide the allocation of resources.

For example, consider the allocation of beachfront land. Because the amount of this land is limited, not everyone can enjoy the luxury of living by the beach. Who gets this resource? The answer is: whoever is willing and able to pay the price. The price of beachfront land adjusts until the quantity of land demanded exactly balances the quantity supplied. Thus, in market economies, prices are the mechanism for rationing scarce resources.

Similarly, prices determine who produces each good and how much is produced. For instance, consider farming. Because we need food to survive, it is crucial that some people work on farms. What determines who is a farmer and who is not? In a free society, there is no government planning agency making this decision and ensuring an adequate supply of food. Instead, the allocation of workers to farms is based on the job decisions of millions of workers. This decentralized system works well because these decisions depend on prices. The prices of food and the wages of farmworkers (the price of their labor) adjust to ensure that enough people choose to be farmers.

If a person had never seen a market economy in action, the whole idea might seem preposterous. Economies are large groups of people engaged in many interdependent activities. What prevents decentralized decisionmaking from degenerating into chaos? What coordinates the actions of the millions of people with their varying abilities and desires? What ensures that what needs to get done does in fact get done? The answer, in a word, is *prices*. If market economies are guided by an invisible hand, as Adam Smith famously suggested, then the price system is the baton that the invisible hand uses to conduct the economic orchestra.

SUMMARY

- Economists use the model of supply and demand to analyze competitive markets. In a competitive market, there are many buyers and sellers, each of whom has little or no influence on the market price.

- The demand curve shows how the quantity of a good demanded depends on the price. According to the law of demand, as the price of a good falls, the quantity demanded rises. Therefore, the demand curve slopes downward.

- In addition to price, other determinants of how much consumers want to buy include income, the prices of substitutes and complements, tastes, expectations, and the number of buyers. If one of these factors changes, the demand curve shifts.

- The supply curve shows how the quantity of a good supplied depends on the price. According to the law of supply, as the price of a good rises, the quantity supplied rises. Therefore, the supply curve slopes upward.

- In addition to price, other determinants of how much producers want to sell include input prices, technology, expectations, and the number of sellers. If one of these factors changes, the supply curve shifts.

- The intersection of the supply and demand curves determines the market equilibrium. At the equilibrium price, the quantity demanded equals the quantity supplied.

- The behavior of buyers and sellers naturally drives markets toward their equilibrium. When the market price is above the equilibrium price, there is a surplus of the good, which causes the market price to fall. When the market price is below the equilibrium price, there is a shortage, which causes the market price to rise.

- To analyze how any event influences a market, we use the supply-and-demand diagram to examine how the event affects the equilibrium price and quantity. To do this we follow three steps. First, we decide whether the event shifts the supply curve or the demand curve (or both). Second, we decide which direction the curve shifts. Third, we compare the new equilibrium with the initial equilibrium.

- In market economies, prices are the signals that guide economic decisions and thereby allocate scarce resources. For every good in the economy, the price ensures that supply and demand are in balance. The equilibrium price then determines how much of the good buyers choose to purchase and how much sellers choose to produce.

KEY CONCEPTS

market, p. 64
competitive market, p. 64
quantity demanded, p. 65
law of demand, p. 66
demand schedule, p. 66
demand curve, p. 66
normal good, p. 68

inferior good, p. 68
substitutes, p. 69
complements, p. 69
quantity supplied, p. 71
law of supply, p. 71
supply schedule, p. 72
supply curve, p. 72

equilibrium, p. 75
equilibrium price, p. 75
equilibrium quantity, p. 75
surplus, p. 76
shortage, p. 76
law of supply and demand, p. 77

QUESTIONS FOR REVIEW

1. What is a competitive market? Briefly describe the types of markets other than perfectly competitive markets.

2. What determines the quantity of a good that buyers demand?

3. What are the demand schedule and the demand curve, and how are they related? Why does the demand curve slope downward?

4. Does a change in consumers' tastes lead to a movement along the demand curve or a shift in the demand curve? Does a change in price lead to a movement along the demand curve or a shift in the demand curve?

5. Popeye's income declines and, as a result, he buys more spinach. Is spinach an inferior or a normal good? What happens to Popeye's demand curve for spinach?

6. What determines the quantity of a good that sellers supply?

7. What are the supply schedule and the supply curve, and how are they related? Why does the supply curve slope upward?

8. Does a change in producers' technology lead to a movement along the supply curve or a shift in the supply curve? Does a change in price lead to a movement along the supply curve or a shift in the supply curve?

9. Define the equilibrium of a market. Describe the forces that move a market toward its equilibrium.

10. Beer and pizza are complements because they are often enjoyed together. When the price of beer rises, what happens to the supply, demand, quantity supplied, quantity demanded, and the price in the market for pizza?

11. Describe the role of prices in market economies.

PROBLEMS AND APPLICATIONS

1. Explain each of the following statements using supply-and-demand diagrams.
   a. When a cold snap hits Florida, the price of orange juice rises in supermarkets throughout the country.
   b. When the weather turns warm in New England every summer, the prices of hotel rooms in Caribbean resorts plummet.
   c. When a war breaks out in the Middle East, the price of gasoline rises, while the price of a used Cadillac falls.

2. "An increase in the demand for notebooks raises the quantity of notebooks demanded, but not the quantity supplied." Is this statement true or false? Explain.

3. Consider the market for minivans. For each of the events listed here, identify which of the determinants of demand or supply are affected. Also indicate whether demand or supply is increased or decreased. Then show the effect on the price and quantity of minivans.
   a. People decide to have more children.
   b. A strike by steelworkers raises steel prices.
   c. Engineers develop new automated machinery for the production of minivans.
   d. The price of sports utility vehicles rises.
   e. A stock-market crash lowers people's wealth.

4. During the 1990s, technological advances reduced the cost of computer chips. How do you think this affected the market for computers? For computer software? For typewriters?

5. Using supply-and-demand diagrams, show the effect of the following events on the market for sweatshirts.
   a. A hurricane in South Carolina damages the cotton crop.
   b. The price of leather jackets falls.
   c. All colleges require morning calisthenics in appropriate attire.
   d. New knitting machines are invented.

6. Suppose that in the year 2005 the number of births is temporarily high. How does this baby boom affect the price of baby-sitting services in 2010 and 2020? (Hint: 5-year-olds need baby-sitters, whereas 15-year-olds can be baby-sitters.)

7. Ketchup is a complement (as well as a condiment) for hot dogs. If the price of hot dogs rises, what happens to the market for ketchup? For tomatoes? For tomato juice? For orange juice?

8. The case study presented in the chapter discussed cigarette taxes as a way to reduce smoking. Now think about the markets for other tobacco products such as cigars and chewing tobacco.
   a. Are these goods substitutes or complements for cigarettes?
   b. Using a supply-and-demand diagram, show what happens in the markets for cigars and chewing tobacco if the tax on cigarettes is increased.
   c. If policymakers wanted to reduce total tobacco consumption, what policies could they combine with the cigarette tax?

9. The market for pizza has the following demand and supply schedules:

Price	Quantity Demanded	Quantity Supplied
$4	135	26
5	104	53
6	81	81
7	68	98
8	53	110
9	39	121

Graph the demand and supply curves. What is the equilibrium price and quantity in this market? If the actual price in this market were *above* the equilibrium price, what would drive the market toward the equilibrium? If the actual price in this market were *below* the equilibrium price, what would drive the market toward the equilibrium?

10. Because bagels and cream cheese are often eaten together, they are complements.
    a. We observe that both the equilibrium price of cream cheese and the equilibrium quantity of bagels have risen. What could be responsible for this pattern—a fall in the price of flour or a fall in the price of milk? Illustrate and explain your answer.
    b. Suppose instead that the equilibrium price of cream cheese has risen but the equilibrium quantity of bagels has fallen. What could be responsible for this pattern— a rise in the price of flour or a rise in the price of milk? Illustrate and explain your answer.

11. Suppose that the price of basketball tickets at your college is determined by market forces. Currently, the demand and supply schedules are as follows:

Price	Quantity Demanded	Quantity Supplied
$4	10,000	8,000
8	8,000	8,000
12	6,000	8,000
16	4,000	8,000
20	2,000	8,000

   a. Draw the demand and supply curves. What is unusual about this supply curve? Why might this be true?
   b. What are the equilibrium price and quantity of tickets?

c. Your college plans to increase total enrollment next year by 5,000 students. The additional students will have the following demand schedule:

Price	Quantity Demanded
$4	4,000
8	3,000
12	2,000
16	1,000
20	0

Now add the old demand schedule and the demand schedule for the new students to calculate the new demand schedule for the entire college. What will be the new equilibrium price and quantity?

12. An article in *The New York Times* described a successful marketing campaign by the French champagne industry. The article noted that "many executives felt giddy about the stratospheric champagne prices. But they also feared that such sharp price increases would cause demand to decline, which would then cause prices to plunge." What mistake are the executives making in their analysis of the situation? Illustrate your answer with a graph.

13. Market research has revealed the following information about the market for chocolate bars: The demand schedule can be represented by the equation $Q^D = 1,600 - 300P$, where Q^D is the quantity demanded and P is the price. The supply schedule can be represented by the equation $Q^S = 1,400 + 700P$, where Q^S is the quantity supplied. Calculate the equilibrium price and quantity in the market for chocolate bars.

14. What do we mean by a perfectly competitive market? Do you think that the example of ice cream used in this chapter fits this description? Is there another type of market that better characterizes the market for ice cream?

http://

For more study tools, please visit http://mankiwXtra.swlearning.com.

ELASTICITY AND ITS APPLICATION

Imagine yourself as a Kansas wheat farmer. Because you earn all your income from selling wheat, you devote much effort to making your land as productive as it can be. You monitor weather and soil conditions, check your fields for pests and disease, and study the latest advances in farm technology. You know that the more wheat you grow, the more you will have to sell after the harvest, and the higher will be your income and your standard of living.

One day Kansas State University announces a major discovery. Researchers in its agronomy department have devised a new hybrid of wheat that raises the amount farmers can produce from each acre of land by 20 percent. How should you react to this news? Should you use the new hybrid? Does this discovery make you better off or worse off than you were before? In this chapter we will see that these questions can have surprising answers. The surprise will come from applying the most basic tools of economics—supply and demand—to the market for wheat.

The previous chapter introduced supply and demand. In any competitive market, such as the market for wheat, the upward-sloping supply curve represents the behavior of sellers, and the downward-sloping demand curve represents the behavior of buyers. The price of the good adjusts to bring the quantity supplied and quantity demanded of the good into balance. To apply this basic analysis to understand the impact of the agronomists' discovery, we must first develop one more tool: the concept of *elasticity*. Elasticity, a measure of how much buyers and sellers respond to changes in market conditions, allows us to analyze supply and demand with greater precision. When studying how some event or policy affects a market, we can discuss not only the direction of the effects but their magnitude as well.

THE ELASTICITY OF DEMAND

When we introduced demand in Chapter 4, we noted that consumers usually buy more of a good when its price is lower, when their incomes are higher, when the prices of substitutes for the good are higher, or when the prices of complements of the good are lower. Our discussion of demand was qualitative, not quantitative. That is, we discussed the direction in which quantity demanded moves, but not the size of the change. To measure how much consumers respond to changes in these variables, economists use the concept of **elasticity.**

elasticity
a measure of the responsiveness of quantity demanded or quantity supplied to one of its determinants

The Price Elasticity of Demand and Its Determinants

price elasticity of demand
a measure of how much the quantity demanded of a good responds to a change in the price of that good, computed as the percentage change in quantity demanded divided by the percentage change in price

The law of demand states that a fall in the price of a good raises the quantity demanded. The **price elasticity of demand** measures how much the quantity demanded responds to a change in price. Demand for a good is said to be *elastic* if the quantity demanded responds substantially to changes in the price. Demand is said to be *inelastic* if the quantity demanded responds only slightly to changes in the price.

The price elasticity of demand for any good measures how willing consumers are to move away from the good as its price rises. Thus, the elasticity reflects the many economic, social, and psychological forces that shape consumer tastes. Based on experience, however, we can state some general rules about what determines the price elasticity of demand.

Availability of Close Substitutes   Goods with close substitutes tend to have more elastic demand because it is easier for consumers to switch from that good to others. For example, butter and margarine are easily substitutable. A small increase in the price of butter, assuming the price of margarine is held fixed, causes the quantity of butter sold to fall by a large amount. By contrast, because eggs are a food without a close substitute, the demand for eggs is less elastic than the demand for butter.

Necessities versus Luxuries   Necessities tend to have inelastic demands, whereas luxuries have elastic demands. When the price of a visit to the doctor rises, people will not dramatically alter the number of times they go to the doctor, although they might go somewhat less often. By contrast, when the price of sailboats rises, the quantity of sailboats demanded falls substantially. The reason is that most people view doctor visits as a necessity and sailboats as a luxury. Of course, whether a good is a necessity or a luxury depends not on the intrinsic properties of the good but on the preferences of the buyer. For an avid sailor with little concern over his health, sailboats might be a necessity with inelastic demand and doctor visits a luxury with elastic demand.

Definition of the Market   The elasticity of demand in any market depends on how we draw the boundaries of the market. Narrowly defined markets tend to have more elastic demand than broadly defined markets, because it is easier to find close substitutes for narrowly defined goods. For example, food, a broad category, has a fairly inelastic demand because there are no good substitutes for food. Ice cream, a more narrow category, has a more elastic demand because it is easy to substitute other desserts for ice cream. Vanilla ice cream, a very narrow category, has a very elastic demand because other flavors of ice cream are almost perfect substitutes for vanilla.

Time Horizon   Goods tend to have more elastic demand over longer time horizons. When the price of gasoline rises, the quantity of gasoline demanded falls only slightly in the first few months. Over time, however, people buy more fuel-efficient cars, switch to public transportation, and move closer to where they work. Within several years, the quantity of gasoline demanded falls substantially.

Computing the Price Elasticity of Demand

Now that we have discussed the price elasticity of demand in general terms, let's be more precise about how it is measured. Economists compute the price elasticity of demand as the percentage change in the quantity demanded divided by the percentage change in the price. That is,

$$\text{Price elasticity of demand} = \frac{\text{Percentage change in quantity demanded}}{\text{Percentage change in price}}.$$

For example, suppose that a 10 percent increase in the price of an ice-cream cone causes the amount of ice cream you buy to fall by 20 percent. We calculate your elasticity of demand as

$$\text{Price elasticity of demand} = \frac{20 \text{ percent}}{10 \text{ percent}} = 2.$$

In this example, the elasticity is 2, reflecting that the change in the quantity demanded is proportionately twice as large as the change in the price.

Because the quantity demanded of a good is negatively related to its price, the percentage change in quantity will always have the opposite sign as the percentage change in price. In this example, the percentage change in price is a *positive* 10 percent (reflecting an increase), and the percentage change in quantity demanded is a *negative* 20 percent (reflecting a decrease). For this reason, price elasticities of demand are sometimes reported as negative numbers. In this book we follow the common practice of dropping the minus sign and reporting all price elasticities as positive numbers. (Mathematicians call this the *absolute value*.) With this convention, a larger price elasticity implies a greater responsiveness of quantity demanded to price.

The Midpoint Method: A Better Way to Calculate Percentage Changes and Elasticities

If you try calculating the price elasticity of demand between two points on a demand curve, you will quickly notice an annoying problem: The elasticity from point A to point B seems different from the elasticity from point B to point A. For example, consider these numbers:

Point A: Price = $4   Quantity = 120

Point B: Price = $6   Quantity = 80

Going from point A to point B, the price rises by 50 percent, and the quantity falls by 33 percent, indicating that the price elasticity of demand is 33/50, or 0.66. By contrast, going from point B to point A, the price falls by 33 percent, and the quantity rises by 50 percent, indicating that the price elasticity of demand is 50/33, or 1.5.

One way to avoid this problem is to use the *midpoint method* for calculating elasticities. The standard way to compute a percentage change is to divide the change by the initial level. By contrast, the midpoint method computes a percentage change by dividing the change by the midpoint (or average) of the initial and final levels. For instance, $5 is the midpoint of $4 and $6. Therefore, according to the midpoint method, a change from $4 to $6 is considered a 40 percent rise, because $(6 - 4)/5 \times 100 = 40$. Similarly, a change from $6 to $4 is considered a 40 percent fall.

Because the midpoint method gives the same answer regardless of the direction of change, it is often used when calculating the price elasticity of demand between two points. In our example, the midpoint between point A and point B is:

Midpoint: Price = $5   Quantity = 100

According to the midpoint method, when going from point A to point B, the price rises by 40 percent, and the quantity falls by 40 percent. Similarly, when going from point B to point A, the price falls by 40 percent, and the quantity rises by 40 percent. In both directions, the price elasticity of demand equals 1.

We can express the midpoint method with the following formula for the price elasticity of demand between two points, denoted (Q_1, P_1) and (Q_2, P_2):

$$\text{Price elasticity of demand} = \frac{(Q_2 - Q_1)/[(Q_2 + Q_1)/2]}{(P_2 - P_1)/[(P_2 + P_1)/2]}.$$

The numerator is the percentage change in quantity computed using the midpoint method, and the denominator is the percentage change in price computed using

FIGURE 1

The Price Elasticity of Demand

The price elasticity of demand determines whether the demand curve is steep or flat. Note that all percentage changes are calculated using the midpoint method.

(a) Perfectly Inelastic Demand: Elasticity Equals 0

Price

Demand

$5
4

1. An increase in price . . .

0   100   Quantity

2. . . . leaves the quantity demanded unchanged.

(b) Inelastic Demand: Elasticity Is Less Than 1

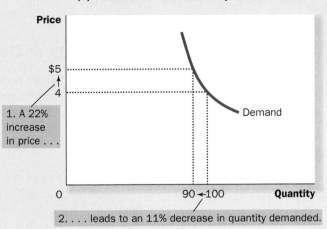

Price

$5
4

1. A 22% increase in price . . .

Demand

0   90 ← 100   Quantity

2. . . . leads to an 11% decrease in quantity demanded.

(c) Unit Elastic Demand: Elasticity Equals 1

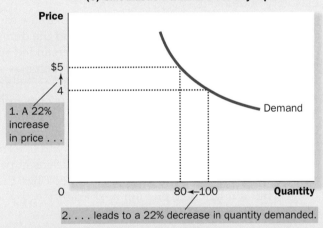

Price

$5
4

1. A 22% increase in price . . .

Demand

0   80 ← 100   Quantity

2. . . . leads to a 22% decrease in quantity demanded.

(d) Elastic Demand: Elasticity Is Greater Than 1

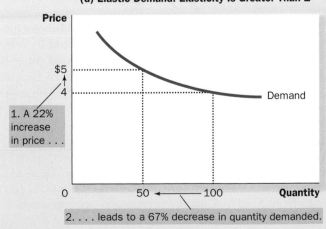

Price

$5
4

1. A 22% increase in price . . .

Demand

0   50 ← 100   Quantity

2. . . . leads to a 67% decrease in quantity demanded.

(e) Perfectly Elastic Demand: Elasticity Equals Infinity

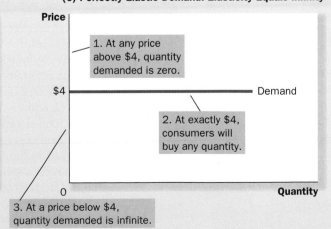

Price

1. At any price above $4, quantity demanded is zero.

$4   Demand

2. At exactly $4, consumers will buy any quantity.

0   Quantity

3. At a price below $4, quantity demanded is infinite.

the midpoint method. If you ever need to calculate elasticities, you should use this formula.

In this book, however, we rarely perform such calculations. For most of our purposes, what elasticity represents—the responsiveness of quantity demanded to price—is more important than how it is calculated.

The Variety of Demand Curves

Economists classify demand curves according to their elasticity. Demand is *elastic* when the elasticity is greater than 1, so that quantity moves proportionately more than the price. Demand is *inelastic* when the elasticity is less than 1, so that quantity moves proportionately less than the price. If the elasticity is exactly 1, so that quantity moves the same amount proportionately as price, demand is said to have *unit elasticity.*

Because the price elasticity of demand measures how much quantity demanded responds to changes in the price, it is closely related to the slope of the demand curve. The following rule of thumb is a useful guide: The flatter the demand curve that passes through a given point, the greater the price elasticity of demand. The steeper the demand curve that passes through a given point, the smaller the price elasticity of demand.

Figure 1 (p. 93) shows five cases. In the extreme case of a zero elasticity shown in panel (a), demand is *perfectly inelastic,* and the demand curve is vertical. In this case, regardless of the price, the quantity demanded stays the same. As the elasticity rises, the demand curve gets flatter and flatter, as shown in panels (b), (c), and (d). At the opposite extreme shown in panel (e), demand is *perfectly elastic.* This occurs as the price elasticity of demand approaches infinity and the demand curve becomes horizontal, reflecting the fact that very small changes in the price lead to huge changes in the quantity demanded.

Finally, if you have trouble keeping straight the terms *elastic* and *inelastic,* here's a memory trick for you: <u>I</u>nelastic curves, such as in panel (a) of Figure 1, look like the letter *I.* <u>E</u>lastic curves, as in panel (e), look like the letter *E.* This is not a deep insight, but it might help on your next exam.

Total Revenue and the Price Elasticity of Demand

total revenue
the amount paid by buyers and received by sellers of a good, computed as the price of the good times the quantity sold

When studying changes in supply or demand in a market, one variable we often want to study is **total revenue,** the amount paid by buyers and received by sellers of the good. In any market, total revenue is $P \times Q$, the price of the good times the quantity of the good sold. We can show total revenue graphically, as in Figure 2. The height of the box under the demand curve is P, and the width is Q. The area of this box, $P \times Q$, equals the total revenue in this market. In Figure 2, where $P = \$4$ and $Q = 100$, total revenue is $\$4 \times 100$, or $\$400$.

How does total revenue change as one moves along the demand curve? The answer depends on the price elasticity of demand. If demand is inelastic, as in Figure 3, then an increase in the price causes an increase in total revenue. Here an increase in price from $\$1$ to $\$3$ causes the quantity demanded to fall only from 100 to 80, and so total revenue rises from $\$100$ to $\$240$. An increase in price raises $P \times Q$ because the fall in Q is proportionately smaller than the rise in P.

FIGURE 2

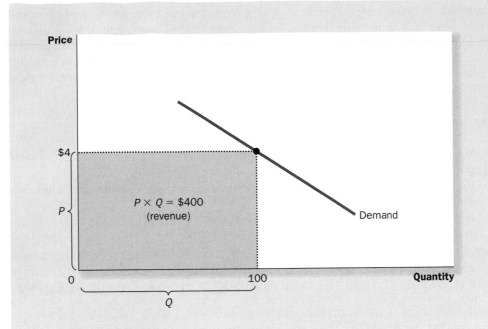

Total Revenue

The total amount paid by buyers, and received as revenue by sellers, equals the area of the box under the demand curve, P × Q. Here, at a price of $4, the quantity demanded is 100, and total revenue is $400.

FIGURE 3

How Total Revenue Changes When Price Changes: Inelastic Demand

With an inelastic demand curve, an increase in the price leads to a decrease in quantity demanded that is proportionately smaller. Therefore, total revenue (the product of price and quantity) increases. Here, an increase in the price from $1 to $3 causes the quantity demanded to fall from 100 to 80, and total revenue rises from $100 to $240.

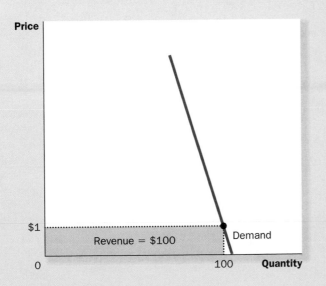

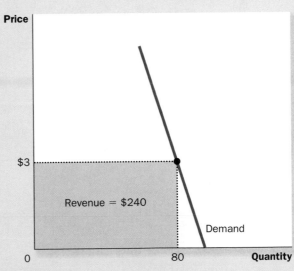

We obtain the opposite result if demand is elastic: An increase in the price causes a decrease in total revenue. In Figure 4, for instance, when the price rises from $4 to $5, the quantity demanded falls from 50 to 20, and so total revenue falls from $200 to $100. Because demand is elastic, the reduction in the quantity demanded is so great that it more than offsets the increase in the price. That is, an increase in price reduces $P \times Q$ because the fall in Q is proportionately greater than the rise in P.

Although the examples in these two figures are extreme, they illustrate a general rule:

- When demand is inelastic (a price elasticity less than 1), price and total revenue move in the same direction.
- When demand is elastic (a price elasticity greater than 1), price and total revenue move in opposite directions.
- If demand is unit elastic (a price elasticity exactly equal to 1), total revenue remains constant when the price changes.

Elasticity and Total Revenue along a Linear Demand Curve

Although some demand curves have an elasticity that is the same along the entire curve, that is not always the case. An example of a demand curve along which elasticity changes is a straight line, as shown in Figure 5. A linear demand curve

---

FIGURE 4

How Total Revenue Changes When Price Changes: Elastic Demand

With an elastic demand curve, an increase in the price leads to a decrease in quantity demanded that is proportionately larger. Therefore, total revenue (the product of price and quantity) decreases. Here, an increase in the price from $4 to $5 causes the quantity demanded to fall from 50 to 20, so total revenue falls from $200 to $100.

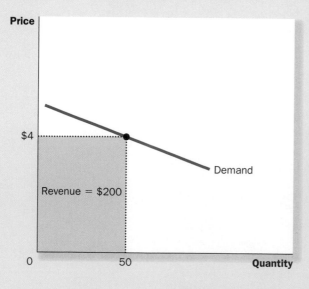
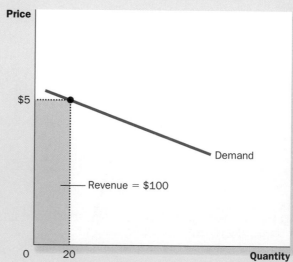

FIGURE 5

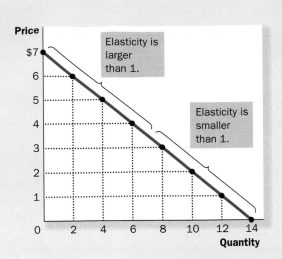

Elasticity of a Linear Demand Curve

The slope of a linear demand curve is constant, but its elasticity is not. The demand schedule in the table was used to calculate the price elasticity of demand by the midpoint method. At points with a low price and high quantity, the demand curve is inelastic. At points with a high price and low quantity, the demand curve is elastic.

Price	Quantity	Total Revenue (Price × Quantity)	Percent Change in Price	Percent Change in Quantity	Elasticity	Description
$7	0	$ 0				
			15	200	13.0	Elastic
6	2	12				
			18	67	3.7	Elastic
5	4	20				
			22	40	1.8	Elastic
4	6	24				
			29	29	1.0	Unit elastic
3	8	24				
			40	22	0.6	Inelastic
2	10	20				
			67	18	0.3	Inelastic
1	12	12				
			200	15	0.1	Inelastic
0	14	0				

has a constant slope. Recall that slope is defined as "rise over run," which here is the ratio of the change in price ("rise") to the change in quantity ("run"). This particular demand curve's slope is constant because each $1 increase in price causes the same 2-unit decrease in the quantity demanded.

Even though the slope of a linear demand curve is constant, the elasticity is not. The reason is that the slope is the ratio of *changes* in the two variables, whereas the elasticity is the ratio of *percentage changes* in the two variables. You can see this by looking at the table in Figure 5, which shows the demand schedule for the linear demand curve in the graph. The table uses the midpoint method to calculate the price elasticity of demand. At points with a low price and high quantity, the demand curve is inelastic. At points with a high price and low quantity, the demand curve is elastic.

The table also presents total revenue at each point on the demand curve. These numbers illustrate the relationship between total revenue and elasticity. When the price is $1, for instance, demand is inelastic, and a price increase to $2 raises total revenue. When the price is $5, demand is elastic, and a price increase to $6 reduces total revenue. Between $3 and $4, demand is exactly unit elastic, and total revenue is the same at these two prices.

IN THE NEWS

ON THE ROAD WITH ELASTICITY

How should a firm that operates a private toll road set a price for its service? As the following article makes clear, answering this question requires an understanding of the demand curve and its elasticity.

For Whom the Booth Tolls, Price Really Does Matter

By Steven Pearlstein

All businesses face a similar question: What price for their product will generate the maximum profit?

The answer is not always obvious: Raising the price of something often has the effect of reducing sales as price-sensitive consumers seek alternatives or simply do without. For every product, the extent of that sensitivity is different. The trick is to find the point for each where the ideal tradeoff between profit margin and sales volume is achieved.

Right now, the developers of a new private toll road between Leesburg and Washington-Dulles International Airport are trying to discern the magic point. The group originally projected that it could charge nearly $2 for the 14-mile one-way trip, while attracting 34,000 trips on an average day from overcrowded public roads such as nearby Route 7. But after spending $350 million to build their much heralded "Greenway," they

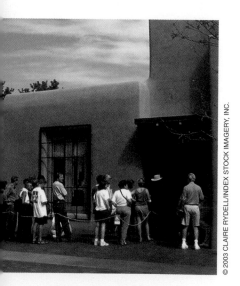

If the price of admission were higher, how much smaller would this crowd be?

© 2003 CLAIRE RYDELL/INDEX STOCK IMAGERY, INC.

Case Study

PRICING ADMISSION TO A MUSEUM

You are curator of a major art museum. Your director of finance tells you that the museum is running short of funds and suggests that you consider changing the price of admission to increase total revenue. What do you do? Do you raise the price of admission, or do you lower it?

The answer depends on the elasticity of demand. If the demand for visits to the museum is inelastic, then an increase in the price of admission would increase total revenue. But if the demand is elastic, then an increase in price would cause the number of visitors to fall by so much that total revenue would decrease. In this case, you should cut the price. The number of visitors would rise by so much that total revenue would increase.

To estimate the price elasticity of demand, you would need to turn to your statisticians. They might use historical data to study how museum attendance varied from year to year as the admission price changed. Or they might use data on attendance at the various museums around the country to see how the admission price affects attendance. In studying either of these sets of data, the statisticians would need to take account of other factors that affect attendance—weather, discovered to their dismay that only about a third that number of commuters were willing to pay that much to shave 20 minutes off their daily commute. . . .

It was only when the company, in desperation, lowered the toll to $1 that it came even close to attracting the expected traffic flows.

Although the Greenway still is losing money, it is clearly better off at this new point on the demand curve than it was when it first opened. Average daily revenue today is $22,000, compared with $14,875 when the "special introductory" price was $1.75. And with traffic still light even at rush hour, it is possible that the owners may lower tolls even further in search of higher revenue.

After all, when the price was lowered by 45 percent last spring, it generated a 200 percent increase in volume three months later. If the same ratio applies

again, lowering the toll another 25 percent would drive the daily volume up to 38,000 trips, and daily revenue up to nearly $29,000.

The problem, of course, is that the same ratio usually does not apply at every price point, which is why this pricing business is so tricky. . . .

Clifford Winston of the Brookings Institution and John Calfee of the American Enterprise Institute have considered the toll road's dilemma. . . .

Last year, the economists conducted an elaborate market test with 1,170 people across the country who were each presented with a series of options in which they were, in effect, asked to make a personal tradeoff between less commuting time and higher tolls.

In the end, they concluded that the people who placed the highest value on reducing their commuting time already

had done so by finding public transportation, living closer to their work, or selecting jobs that allowed them to commute at off-peak hours.

Conversely, those who commuted significant distances had a higher tolerance for traffic congestion and were willing to pay only 20 percent of their hourly pay to save an hour of their time.

Overall, the Winston/Calfee findings help explain why the Greenway's original toll and volume projections were too high: By their reckoning, only commuters who earned at least $30 an hour (about $60,000 a year) would be willing to pay $2 to save 20 minutes.

Source: *The Washington Post,* October 24, 1996, p. E1. Copyright © 1996, *The Washington Post.* Reprinted by permission.

population, size of collection, and so forth—to isolate the effect of price. In the end, such data analysis would provide an estimate of the price elasticity of demand, which you could use in deciding how to respond to your financial problem. ●

Other Demand Elasticities

In addition to the price elasticity of demand, economists also use other elasticities to describe the behavior of buyers in a market.

The Income Elasticity of Demand

The **income elasticity of demand** measures how the quantity demanded changes as consumer income changes. It is calculated as the percentage change in quantity demanded divided by the percentage change in income. That is,

$$\text{Income elasticity of demand} = \frac{\text{Percentage change in quantity demanded}}{\text{Percentage change in income}}.$$

income elasticity of demand
a measure of how much the quantity demanded of a good responds to a change in consumers' income, computed as the percentage change in quantity demanded divided by the percentage change in income

As we discussed in Chapter 4, most goods are *normal goods:* Higher income raises quantity demanded. Because quantity demanded and income move in the same direction, normal goods have positive income elasticities. A few goods, such as bus rides, are *inferior goods:* Higher income lowers the quantity demanded. Because quantity demanded and income move in opposite directions, inferior goods have negative income elasticities.

Even among normal goods, income elasticities vary substantially in size. Necessities, such as food and clothing, tend to have small income elasticities because consumers, regardless of how low their incomes, choose to buy some of these goods. Luxuries, such as caviar and diamonds, tend to have large income elasticities because consumers feel that they can do without these goods altogether if their income is too low.

cross-price elasticity of demand
a measure of how much the quantity demanded of one good responds to a change in the price of another good, computed as the percentage change in quantity demanded of the first good divided by the percentage change in the price of the second good

The Cross-Price Elasticity of Demand   The **cross-price elasticity of demand** measures how the quantity demanded of one good changes as the price of another good changes. It is calculated as the percentage change in quantity demanded of good 1 divided by the percentage change in the price of good 2. That is,

$$\text{Cross-price elasticity of demand} = \frac{\text{Percentage change in quantity demanded of good 1}}{\text{Percentage change in the price of good 2}}.$$

Whether the cross-price elasticity is a positive or negative number depends on whether the two goods are substitutes or complements. As we discussed in Chapter 4, substitutes are goods that are typically used in place of one another, such as hamburgers and hot dogs. An increase in hot dog prices induces people to grill hamburgers instead. Because the price of hot dogs and the quantity of hamburgers demanded move in the same direction, the cross-price elasticity is positive. Conversely, complements are goods that are typically used together, such as computers and software. In this case, the cross-price elasticity is negative, indicating that an increase in the price of computers reduces the quantity of software demanded.

QuickQuiz Define the price elasticity of demand. • Explain the relationship between total revenue and the price elasticity of demand.

THE ELASTICITY OF SUPPLY

When we introduced supply in Chapter 4, we noted that producers of a good offer to sell more of it when the price of the good rises, when their input prices fall, or when their technology improves. To turn from qualitative to quantitative statements about quantity supplied, we once again use the concept of elasticity.

The Price Elasticity of Supply and Its Determinants

price elasticity of supply
a measure of how much the quantity supplied of a good responds to a change in the price of that good, computed as the percentage change in quantity supplied divided by the percentage change in price

The law of supply states that higher prices raise the quantity supplied. The **price elasticity of supply** measures how much the quantity supplied responds to changes in the price. Supply of a good is said to be *elastic* if the quantity supplied responds substantially to changes in the price. Supply is said to be *inelastic* if the quantity supplied responds only slightly to changes in the price.

The price elasticity of supply depends on the flexibility of sellers to change the amount of the good they produce. For example, beachfront land has an inelastic supply because it is almost impossible to produce more of it. By contrast, manufactured goods, such as books, cars, and televisions, have elastic supplies because the firms that produce them can run their factories longer in response to a higher price.

In most markets, a key determinant of the price elasticity of supply is the time period being considered. Supply is usually more elastic in the long run than in the short run. Over short periods of time, firms cannot easily change the size of their factories to make more or less of a good. Thus, in the short run, the quantity supplied is not very responsive to the price. By contrast, over longer periods, firms can build new factories or close old ones. In addition, new firms can enter a market, and old firms can shut down. Thus, in the long run, the quantity supplied can respond substantially to price changes.

Computing the Price Elasticity of Supply

Now that we have some idea about what the price elasticity of supply is, let's be more precise. Economists compute the price elasticity of supply as the percentage change in the quantity supplied divided by the percentage change in the price. That is,

$$\text{Price elasticity of supply} = \frac{\text{Percentage change in quantity supplied}}{\text{Percentage change in price}}.$$

For example, suppose that an increase in the price of milk from \$2.85 to \$3.15 a gallon raises the amount that dairy farmers produce from 9,000 to 11,000 gallons per month. Using the midpoint method, we calculate the percentage change in price as

$$\text{Percentage change in price} = (3.15 - 2.85)/3.00 \times 100 = 10 \text{ percent.}$$

Similarly, we calculate the percentage change in quantity supplied as

$$\text{Percentage change in quantity supplied} = (11{,}000 - 9{,}000)/10{,}000 \times 100 = 20 \text{ percent.}$$

In this case, the price elasticity of supply is

$$\text{Price elasticity of supply} = \frac{20 \text{ percent}}{10 \text{ percent}} = 2.0.$$

In this example, the elasticity of 2 reflects the fact that the quantity supplied moves proportionately twice as much as the price.

The Variety of Supply Curves

Because the price elasticity of supply measures the responsiveness of quantity supplied to the price, it is reflected in the appearance of the supply curve. Figure 6 (p. 102) shows five cases. In the extreme case of a zero elasticity, as shown in

FIGURE 6

The Price Elasticity of Supply

The price elasticity of supply determines whether the supply curve is steep or flat. Note that all percentage changes are calculated using the midpoint method.

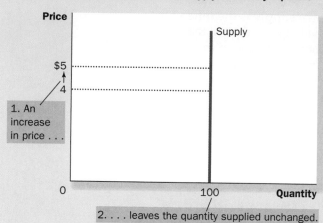

(a) Perfectly Inelastic Supply: Elasticity Equals 0

Price

$5
4

1. An increase in price . . .

0   100   Quantity

2. . . . leaves the quantity supplied unchanged.

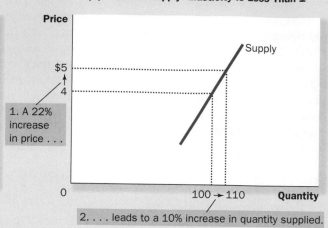

(b) Inelastic Supply: Elasticity Is Less Than 1

Price

Supply

$5
4

1. A 22% increase in price . . .

0   100 → 110   Quantity

2. . . . leads to a 10% increase in quantity supplied.

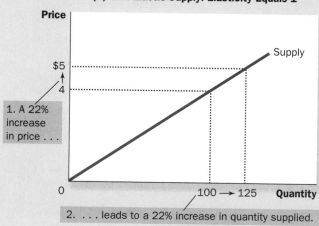

(c) Unit Elastic Supply: Elasticity Equals 1

Price

Supply

$5
4

1. A 22% increase in price . . .

0   100 → 125   Quantity

2. . . . leads to a 22% increase in quantity supplied.

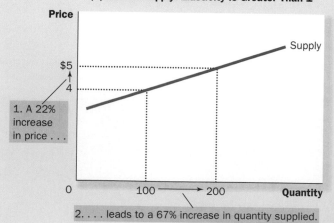

(d) Elastic Supply: Elasticity Is Greater Than 1

Price

Supply

$5
4

1. A 22% increase in price . . .

0   100 → 200   Quantity

2. . . . leads to a 67% increase in quantity supplied.

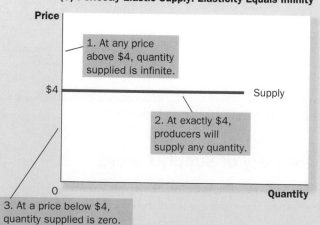

(e) Perfectly Elastic Supply: Elasticity Equals Infinity

Price

1. At any price above $4, quantity supplied is infinite.

$4   Supply

2. At exactly $4, producers will supply any quantity.

0   Quantity

3. At a price below $4, quantity supplied is zero.

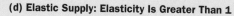

panel (a), supply is *perfectly inelastic* and the supply curve is vertical. In this case, the quantity supplied is the same regardless of the price. As the elasticity rises, the supply curve gets flatter, which shows that the quantity supplied responds more to changes in the price. At the opposite extreme shown in panel (e), supply is *perfectly elastic*. This occurs as the price elasticity of supply approaches infinity and the supply curve becomes horizontal, meaning that very small changes in the price lead to very large changes in the quantity supplied.

In some markets, the elasticity of supply is not constant but varies over the supply curve. Figure 7 shows a typical case for an industry in which firms have factories with a limited capacity for production. For low levels of quantity supplied, the elasticity of supply is high, indicating that firms respond substantially to changes in the price. In this region, firms have capacity for production that is not being used, such as plants and equipment sitting idle for all or part of the day. Small increases in price make it profitable for firms to begin using this idle capacity. As the quantity supplied rises, firms begin to reach capacity. Once capacity is fully used, increasing production further requires the construction of new plants. To induce firms to incur this extra expense, the price must rise substantially, so supply becomes less elastic.

Figure 7 presents a numerical example of this phenomenon. When the price rises from $3 to $4 (a 29 percent increase, according to the midpoint method), the quantity supplied rises from 100 to 200 (a 67 percent increase). Because quantity supplied moves proportionately more than the price, the supply curve has elasticity greater than 1. By contrast, when the price rises from $12 to $15 (a 22 percent increase), the quantity supplied rises from 500 to 525 (a 5 percent increase). In this case, quantity supplied moves proportionately less than the price, so the elasticity is less than 1.

FIGURE 7

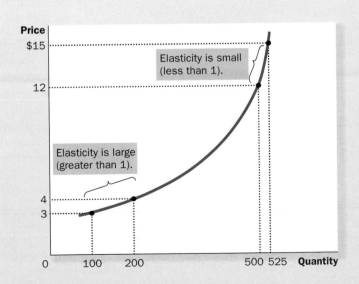

How the Price Elasticity of Supply Can Vary

Because firms often have a maximum capacity for production, the elasticity of supply may be very high at low levels of quantity supplied and very low at high levels of quantity supplied. Here, an increase in price from $3 to $4 increases the quantity supplied from 100 to 200. Because the increase in quantity supplied of 67 percent (computed using the midpoint method) is larger than the increase in price of 29 percent, the supply curve is elastic in this range. By contrast, when the price rises from $12 to $15, the quantity supplied rises only from 500 to 525. Because the increase in quantity supplied of 5 percent is smaller than the increase in price of 22 percent, the supply curve is inelastic in this range.

QuickQuiz Define the price elasticity of supply. • Explain why the price elasticity of supply might be different in the long run than in the short run.

THREE APPLICATIONS OF SUPPLY, DEMAND, AND ELASTICITY

Can good news for farming be bad news for farmers? Why did OPEC fail to keep the price of oil high? Does drug interdiction increase or decrease drug-related crime? At first, these questions might seem to have little in common. Yet all three questions are about markets, and all markets are subject to the forces of supply and demand. Here we apply the versatile tools of supply, demand, and elasticity to answer these seemingly complex questions.

Can Good News for Farming Be Bad News for Farmers?

Let's now return to the question posed at the beginning of this chapter: What happens to wheat farmers and the market for wheat when university agronomists discover a new wheat hybrid that is more productive than existing varieties? Recall from Chapter 4 that we answer such questions in three steps. First, we examine whether the supply or demand curve shifts. Second, we consider which direction the curve shifts. Third, we use the supply-and-demand diagram to see how the market equilibrium changes.

In this case, the discovery of the new hybrid affects the supply curve. Because the hybrid increases the amount of wheat that can be produced on each acre of land, farmers are now willing to supply more wheat at any given price. In other words, the supply curve shifts to the right. The demand curve remains the same because consumers' desire to buy wheat products at any given price is not affected by the introduction of a new hybrid. Figure 8 shows an example of such a change. When the supply curve shifts from S_1 to S_2, the quantity of wheat sold increases from 100 to 110, and the price of wheat falls from $3 to $2.

But does this discovery make farmers better off? As a first cut to answering this question, consider what happens to the total revenue received by farmers. Farmers' total revenue is $P \times Q$, the price of the wheat times the quantity sold. The discovery affects farmers in two conflicting ways. The hybrid allows farmers to produce more wheat (Q rises), but now each bushel of wheat sells for less (P falls).

Whether total revenue rises or falls depends on the elasticity of demand. In practice, the demand for basic foodstuffs such as wheat is usually inelastic, for these items are relatively inexpensive and have few good substitutes. When the demand curve is inelastic, as it is in Figure 8, a decrease in price causes total revenue to fall. You can see this in the figure: The price of wheat falls substantially, whereas the quantity of wheat sold rises only slightly. Total revenue falls from $300 to $220. Thus, the discovery of the new hybrid lowers the total revenue that farmers receive for the sale of their crops.

If farmers are made worse off by the discovery of this new hybrid, why do they adopt it? The answer to this question goes to the heart of how competitive markets work. Because each farmer is a small part of the market for wheat, he or she takes the price of wheat as given. For any given price of wheat, it is better to use the new

FIGURE 8

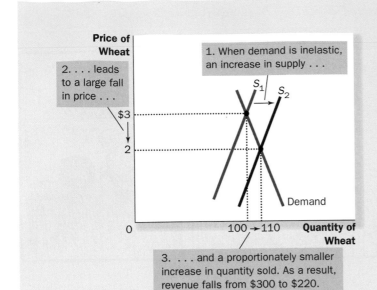

Price of Wheat

2. . . . leads to a large fall in price . . .

1. When demand is inelastic, an increase in supply . . .

S_1 S_2

$3

2

Demand

0   100 → 110   Quantity of Wheat

3. . . . and a proportionately smaller increase in quantity sold. As a result, revenue falls from $300 to $220.

An Increase in Supply in the Market for Wheat

When an advance in farm technology increases the supply of wheat from S_1 to S_2, the price of wheat falls. Because the demand for wheat is inelastic, the increase in the quantity sold from 100 to 110 is proportionately smaller than the decrease in the price from $3 to $2. As a result, farmers' total revenue falls from $300 ($3 × 100) to $220 ($2 × 110).

hybrid in order to produce and sell more wheat. Yet when all farmers do this, the supply of wheat rises, the price falls, and farmers are worse off.

Although this example may at first seem only hypothetical, in fact it helps to explain a major change in the U.S. economy over the past century. Two hundred years ago, most Americans lived on farms. Knowledge about farm methods was sufficiently primitive that most of us had to be farmers to produce enough food. Yet, over time, advances in farm technology increased the amount of food that each farmer could produce. This increase in food supply, together with inelastic food demand, caused farm revenues to fall, which in turn encouraged people to leave farming.

A few numbers show the magnitude of this historic change. As recently as 1950, there were 10 million people working on farms in the United States, representing 17 percent of the labor force. In 2000, fewer than 3 million people worked on farms, or 2 percent of the labor force. This change coincided with tremendous advances in farm productivity: Despite the 70 percent drop in the number of farmers, U.S. farms produced more than twice the output of crops and livestock in 2000 as they did in 1950.

This analysis of the market for farm products also helps to explain a seeming paradox of public policy: Certain farm programs try to help farmers by inducing them not to plant crops on all of their land. Why do these programs do this? Their purpose is to reduce the supply of farm products and thereby raise prices. With inelastic demand for their products, farmers as a group receive greater total revenue if they supply a smaller crop to the market. No single farmer would choose to leave his land fallow on his own because each takes the market price as given. But if all farmers do so together, each of them can be better off.

When analyzing the effects of farm technology or farm policy, it is important to keep in mind that what is good for farmers is not necessarily good for society as a whole. Improvement in farm technology can be bad for farmers who become increasingly unnecessary, but it is surely good for consumers who pay less for food. Similarly, a policy aimed at reducing the supply of farm products may raise the incomes of farmers, but it does so at the expense of consumers.

Why Did OPEC Fail to Keep the Price of Oil High?

Many of the most disruptive events for the world's economies over the past several decades have originated in the world market for oil. In the 1970s members of the Organization of Petroleum Exporting Countries (OPEC) decided to raise the world price of oil in order to increase their incomes. These countries accomplished this goal by jointly reducing the amount of oil they supplied. From 1973 to 1974, the price of oil (adjusted for overall inflation) rose more than 50 percent. Then, a few years later, OPEC did the same thing again. The price of oil rose 14 percent in 1979, followed by 34 percent in 1980, and another 34 percent in 1981.

Yet OPEC found it difficult to maintain a high price. From 1982 to 1985, the price of oil steadily declined at about 10 percent per year. Dissatisfaction and disarray soon prevailed among the OPEC countries. In 1986 cooperation among OPEC members completely broke down, and the price of oil plunged 45 percent. In 1990 the price of oil (adjusted for overall inflation) was back to where it began in 1970, and it stayed at that low level throughout most of the 1990s.

This episode shows how supply and demand can behave differently in the short run and in the long run. In the short run, both the supply and demand for oil are relatively inelastic. Supply is inelastic because the quantity of known oil reserves and the capacity for oil extraction cannot be changed quickly. Demand is inelastic because buying habits do not respond immediately to changes in price. Many drivers with old gas-guzzling cars, for instance, will just pay the higher price. Thus,

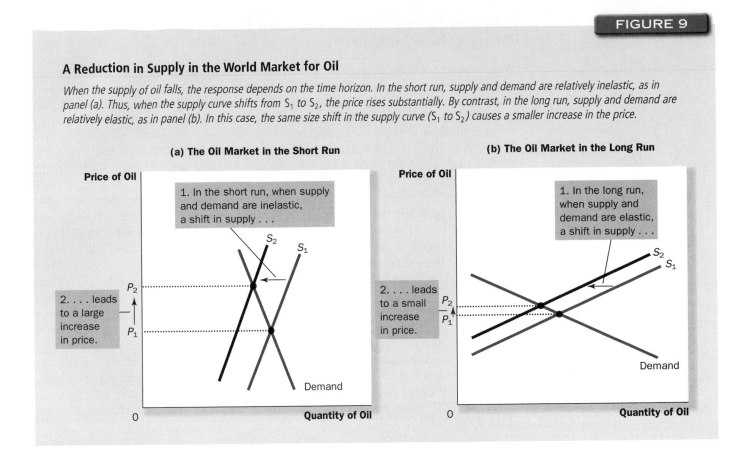

FIGURE 9

A Reduction in Supply in the World Market for Oil

When the supply of oil falls, the response depends on the time horizon. In the short run, supply and demand are relatively inelastic, as in panel (a). Thus, when the supply curve shifts from S_1 to S_2, the price rises substantially. By contrast, in the long run, supply and demand are relatively elastic, as in panel (b). In this case, the same size shift in the supply curve (S_1 to S_2) causes a smaller increase in the price.

as panel (a) of Figure 9 shows, the short-run supply and demand curves are steep. When the supply of oil shifts from S_1 to S_2, the price increase from P_1 to P_2 is large.

The situation is very different in the long run. Over long periods of time, producers of oil outside of OPEC respond to high prices by increasing oil exploration and by building new extraction capacity. Consumers respond with greater conservation, for instance by replacing old inefficient cars with newer efficient ones. Thus, as panel (b) of Figure 9 shows, the long-run supply and demand curves are more elastic. In the long run, the shift in the supply curve from S_1 to S_2 causes a much smaller increase in the price.

This analysis shows why OPEC succeeded in maintaining a high price of oil only in the short run. When OPEC countries agreed to reduce their production of oil, they shifted the supply curve to the left. Even though each OPEC member sold less oil, the price rose by so much in the short run that OPEC incomes rose. By contrast, in the long run when supply and demand are more elastic, the same reduction in supply, measured by the horizontal shift in the supply curve, caused a smaller increase in the price. Thus, OPEC's coordinated reduction in supply proved less profitable in the long run.

OPEC still exists today, and it has from time to time succeeded at reducing supply and raising prices. But the price of oil (adjusted for overall inflation) has never returned to the peak reached in 1981. The cartel now seems to understand that raising prices is easier in the short run than in the long run.

Does Drug Interdiction Increase or Decrease Drug-Related Crime?

A persistent problem facing our society is the use of illegal drugs, such as heroin, cocaine, ecstasy, and crack. Drug use has several adverse effects. One is that drug dependency can ruin the lives of drug users and their families. Another is that drug addicts often turn to robbery and other violent crimes to obtain the money needed to support their habit. To discourage the use of illegal drugs, the U.S. government devotes billions of dollars each year to reduce the flow of drugs into the country. Let's use the tools of supply and demand to examine this policy of drug interdiction.

Suppose the government increases the number of federal agents devoted to the war on drugs. What happens in the market for illegal drugs? As is usual, we answer this question in three steps. First, we consider whether the supply or demand curve shifts. Second, we consider the direction of the shift. Third, we see how the shift affects the equilibrium price and quantity.

Although the purpose of drug interdiction is to reduce drug use, its direct impact is on the sellers of drugs rather than the buyers. When the government stops some drugs from entering the country and arrests more smugglers, it raises the cost of selling drugs and, therefore, reduces the quantity of drugs supplied at any given price. The demand for drugs—the amount buyers want at any given price—is not changed. As panel (a) of Figure 10 shows, interdiction shifts the supply curve to the left from S_1 to S_2 and leaves the demand curve the same. The equilibrium price of drugs rises from P_1 to P_2, and the equilibrium quantity falls from Q_1 to Q_2. The fall in the equilibrium quantity shows that drug interdiction does reduce drug use.

But what about the amount of drug-related crime? To answer this question, consider the total amount that drug users pay for the drugs they buy. Because few drug addicts are likely to break their destructive habits in response to a higher price, it is likely that the demand for drugs is inelastic, as it is drawn in the figure. If demand is inelastic, then an increase in price raises total revenue in the drug market. That is, because drug interdiction raises the price of drugs proportionately more than it reduces drug use, it raises the total amount of money that drug users pay for drugs. Addicts who already had to steal to support their habits would have an even greater need for quick cash. Thus, drug interdiction could increase drug-related crime.

Because of this adverse effect of drug interdiction, some analysts argue for alternative approaches to the drug problem. Rather than trying to reduce the supply of drugs, policymakers might try to reduce the demand by pursuing a policy of drug education. Successful drug education has the effects shown in panel (b) of Figure 10. The demand curve shifts to the left from D_1 to D_2. As a result, the equilibrium quantity falls from Q_1 to Q_2, and the equilibrium price falls from P_1 to P_2. Total revenue, which is price times quantity, also falls. Thus, in contrast to drug interdiction, drug education can reduce both drug use and drug-related crime.

Advocates of drug interdiction might argue that the effects of this policy are different in the long run than in the short run, because the elasticity of demand may depend on the time horizon. The demand for drugs is probably inelastic over short periods of time because higher prices do not substantially affect drug use by established addicts. But demand may be more elastic over longer periods of time

FIGURE 10

Policies to Reduce the Use of Illegal Drugs

Drug interdiction reduces the supply of drugs from S_1 to S_2, as in panel (a). If the demand for drugs is inelastic, then the total amount paid by drug users rises, even as the amount of drug use falls. By contrast, drug education reduces the demand for drugs from D_1 to D_2, as in panel (b). Because both price and quantity fall, the amount paid by drug users falls.

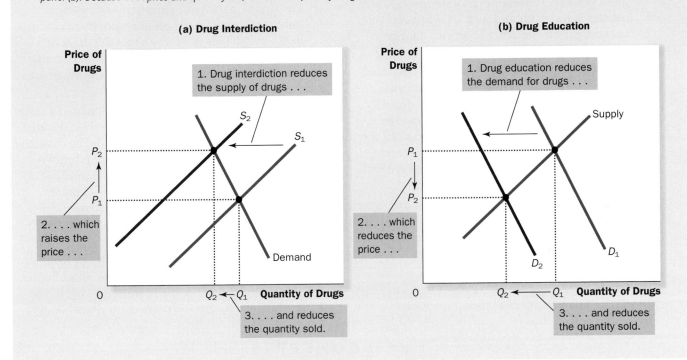

because higher prices would discourage experimentation with drugs among the young and, over time, lead to fewer drug addicts. In this case, drug interdiction would increase drug-related crime in the short run while decreasing it in the long run.

QuickQuiz How might a drought that destroys half of all farm crops be good for farmers? If such a drought is good for farmers, why don't farmers destroy their own crops in the absence of a drought?

Conclusion

According to an old quip, even a parrot can become an economist simply by learning to say "supply and demand." These last two chapters should have convinced you that there is much truth in this statement. The tools of supply and demand allow you to analyze many of the most important events and policies that shape the economy. You are now well on your way to becoming an economist (or, at least, a well-educated parrot).

SUMMARY

- The price elasticity of demand measures how much the quantity demanded responds to changes in the price. Demand tends to be more elastic if close substitutes are available, if the good is a luxury rather than a necessity, if the market is narrowly defined, or if buyers have substantial time to react to a price change.

- The price elasticity of demand is calculated as the percentage change in quantity demanded divided by the percentage change in price. If the elasticity is less than 1, so that quantity demanded moves proportionately less than the price, demand is said to be inelastic. If the elasticity is greater than 1, so that quantity demanded moves proportionately more than the price, demand is said to be elastic.

- Total revenue, the total amount paid for a good, equals the price of the good times the quantity sold. For inelastic demand curves, total revenue rises as price rises. For elastic demand curves, total revenue falls as price rises.

- The income elasticity of demand measures how much the quantity demanded responds to changes in consumers' income. The cross-price elasticity of demand measures how much the quantity demanded of one good responds to changes in the price of another good.

- The price elasticity of supply measures how much the quantity supplied responds to changes in the price. This elasticity often depends on the time horizon under consideration. In most markets, supply is more elastic in the long run than in the short run.

- The price elasticity of supply is calculated as the percentage change in quantity supplied divided by the percentage change in price. If the elasticity is less than 1, so that quantity supplied moves proportionately less than the price, supply is said to be inelastic. If the elasticity is greater than 1, so that quantity supplied moves proportionately more than the price, supply is said to be elastic.

- The tools of supply and demand can be applied in many different kinds of markets. This chapter uses them to analyze the market for wheat, the market for oil, and the market for illegal drugs.

KEY CONCEPTS

elasticity, p. 90
price elasticity of
   demand, p. 90
total revenue, p. 94

income elasticity of
   demand, p. 99
cross-price elasticity of
   demand, p. 100

price elasticity of supply, p. 100

QUESTIONS FOR REVIEW

1. Define the price elasticity of demand and the income elasticity of demand.

2. List and explain some of the determinants of the price elasticity of demand.

3. If the elasticity is greater than 1, is demand elastic or inelastic? If the elasticity equals 0, is demand perfectly elastic or perfectly inelastic?

4. On a supply-and-demand diagram, show equilibrium price, equilibrium quantity, and the total revenue received by producers.

5. If demand is elastic, how will an increase in price change total revenue? Explain.

6. What do we call a good whose income elasticity is less than 0?

7. How is the price elasticity of supply calculated? Explain what this measures.

8. What is the price elasticity of supply of Picasso paintings?

9. Is the price elasticity of supply usually larger in the short run or in the long run? Why?

10. In the 1970s, OPEC caused a dramatic increase in the price of oil. What prevented it from maintaining this high price through the 1980s?

PROBLEMS AND APPLICATIONS

1. For each of the following pairs of goods, which good would you expect to have more elastic demand and why?
   a. required textbooks or mystery novels
   b. Beethoven recordings or classical music recordings in general
   c. heating oil during the next six months or heating oil during the next five years
   d. root beer or water

2. Suppose that business travelers and vacationers have the following demand for airline tickets from New York to Boston:

Price	Quantity Demanded (business travelers)	Quantity Demanded (vacationers)
$150	2,100	1,000
200	2,000	800
250	1,900	600
300	1,800	400

   a. As the price of tickets rises from $200 to $250, what is the price elasticity of demand for (i) business travelers and (ii) vacationers? (Use the midpoint method in your calculations.)
   b. Why might vacationers have a different elasticity than business travelers?

3. Suppose that your demand schedule for compact discs is as follows:

Price	Quantity Demanded (income = $10,000)	Quantity Demanded (income = $12,000)
$ 8	40	50
10	32	45
12	24	30
14	16	20
16	8	12

   a. Use the midpoint method to calculate your price elasticity of demand as the price of compact discs increases from $8 to $10 if (i) your income is $10,000, and (ii) your income is $12,000.
   b. Calculate your income elasticity of demand as your income increases from $10,000 to $12,000 if (i) the price is $12, and (ii) the price is $16.

4. Emily has decided always to spend one-third of her income on clothing.
   a. What is her income elasticity of clothing demand?
   b. What is her price elasticity of clothing demand?
   c. If Emily's tastes change and she decides to spend only one-fourth of her income on clothing, how does her demand curve change? What are her income elasticity and price elasticity now?

5. *The New York Times* reported (Feb. 17, 1996, p. 25) that subway ridership declined after a fare increase: "There were nearly four million fewer riders in December 1995, the first full month after the price of a token increased 25 cents to $1.50, than in the previous December, a 4.3 percent decline."
   a. Use these data to estimate the price elasticity of demand for subway rides.
   b. According to your estimate, what happens to the Transit Authority's revenue when the fare rises?
   c. Why might your estimate of the elasticity be unreliable?

6. Two drivers—Tom and Jerry—each drive up to a gas station. Before looking at the price, each places an order. Tom says, "I'd like 10 gallons of gas." Jerry says, "I'd like $10 of gas." What is each driver's price elasticity of demand?

7. Economists have observed that spending on restaurant meals declines more during economic downturns than does spending on food to be eaten at home. How might the concept of elasticity help to explain this phenomenon?

8. Consider public policy aimed at smoking.
   a. Studies indicate that the price elasticity of demand for cigarettes is about 0.4. If a pack of cigarettes currently costs $2 and the government wants to reduce smoking by 20 percent, by how much should it increase the price?
   b. If the government permanently increases the price of cigarettes, will the policy have a larger effect on smoking one year from now or five years from now?
   c. Studies also find that teenagers have a higher price elasticity than do adults. Why might this be true?

9. Would you expect the price elasticity of *demand* to be larger in the market for all ice cream or the market for vanilla ice cream? Would you expect the price elasticity of *supply* to be larger in the market for all ice cream or the market for vanilla ice cream? Be sure to explain your answers.

10. Pharmaceutical drugs have an inelastic demand, and computers have an elastic demand. Suppose that technological advance doubles the supply of both products (that is, the quantity supplied at each price is twice what it was).
    a. What happens to the equilibrium price and quantity in each market?
    b. Which product experiences a larger change in price?
    c. Which product experiences a larger change in quantity?
    d. What happens to total consumer spending on each product?

11. Beachfront resorts have an inelastic supply, and automobiles have an elastic supply. Suppose that a rise in population doubles the demand for both products (that is, the quantity demanded at each price is twice what it was).
    a. What happens to the equilibrium price and quantity in each market?
    b. Which product experiences a larger change in price?
    c. Which product experiences a larger change in quantity?
    d. What happens to total consumer spending on each product?

12. Several years ago, flooding along the Missouri and Mississippi rivers destroyed thousands of acres of wheat.
    a. Farmers whose crops were destroyed by the floods were much worse off, but farmers whose crops were not destroyed benefited from the floods. Why?
    b. What information would you need about the market for wheat to assess whether farmers as a group were hurt or helped by the floods?

13. Explain why the following might be true: A drought around the world raises the total revenue that farmers receive from the sale of grain, but a drought only in Kansas reduces the total revenue that Kansas farmers receive.

14. Because better weather makes farmland more productive, farmland in regions with good weather conditions is more expensive than farmland in regions with bad weather conditions. Over time, however, as advances in technology have made all farmland more productive, the price of farmland (adjusted for overall inflation) has fallen. Use the concept of elasticity to explain why productivity and farmland prices are positively related across space but negatively related over time.

http://   For more study tools, please visit http://mankiwXtra.swlearning.com.

SUPPLY, DEMAND,
AND GOVERNMENT POLICIES

Economists have two roles. As scientists, they develop and test theories to explain the world around them. As policy advisers, they use their theories to help change the world for the better. The focus of the preceding two chapters has been scientific. We have seen how supply and demand determine the price of a good and the quantity of the good sold. We have also seen how various events shift supply and demand and thereby change the equilibrium price and quantity.

This chapter offers our first look at policy. Here we analyze various types of government policy using only the tools of supply and demand. As you will see, the analysis yields some surprising insights. Policies often have effects that their architects did not intend or anticipate.

We begin by considering policies that directly control prices. For example, rent-control laws dictate a maximum rent that landlords may charge tenants. Minimum-wage laws dictate the lowest wage that firms may pay workers. Price controls are usually enacted when policymakers believe that the market price of a good or service is unfair to buyers or sellers. Yet, as we will see, these policies can generate inequities of their own.

After our discussion of price controls, we next consider the impact of taxes. Policymakers use taxes both to influence market outcomes and to raise revenue for public purposes. Although the prevalence of taxes in our economy is obvious, their effects are not. For example, when the government levies a tax on the amount that firms pay their workers, do the firms or the workers bear the burden of the tax? The answer is not at all clear—until we apply the powerful tools of supply and demand.

CONTROLS ON PRICES

To see how price controls affect market outcomes, let's look once again at the market for ice cream. As we saw in Chapter 4, if ice cream is sold in a competitive market free of government regulation, the price of ice cream adjusts to balance supply and demand: At the equilibrium price, the quantity of ice cream that buyers want to buy exactly equals the quantity that sellers want to sell. To be concrete, suppose the equilibrium price is $3 per cone.

Not everyone may be happy with the outcome of this free-market process. Let's say the American Association of Ice-Cream Eaters complains that the $3 price is too high for everyone to enjoy a cone a day (their recommended diet). Meanwhile, the National Organization of Ice-Cream Makers complains that the $3 price—the result of "cutthroat competition"—is too low and is depressing the incomes of its members. Each of these groups lobbies the government to pass laws that alter the market outcome by directly controlling the price of an ice-cream cone.

Of course, because buyers of any good always want a lower price while sellers want a higher price, the interests of the two groups conflict. If the Ice-Cream Eaters are successful in their lobbying, the government imposes a legal maximum on the price at which ice cream can be sold. Because the price is not allowed to rise above this level, the legislated maximum is called a **price ceiling.** By contrast, if the Ice-Cream Makers are successful, the government imposes a legal minimum on the price. Because the price cannot fall below this level, the legislated minimum is called a **price floor.** Let us consider the effects of these policies in turn.

price ceiling
a legal maximum on the price at which a good can be sold

price floor
a legal minimum on the price at which a good can be sold

How Price Ceilings Affect Market Outcomes

When the government, moved by the complaints and campaign contributions of the Ice-Cream Eaters, imposes a price ceiling on the market for ice cream, two outcomes are possible. In panel (a) of Figure 1, the government imposes a price ceiling of $4 per cone. In this case, because the price that balances supply and demand ($3) is below the ceiling, the price ceiling is *not binding*. Market forces naturally move the economy to the equilibrium, and the price ceiling has no effect on the price or the quantity sold.

Panel (b) of Figure 1 shows the other, more interesting, possibility. In this case, the government imposes a price ceiling of $2 per cone. Because the equilibrium price of $3 is above the price ceiling, the ceiling is a *binding constraint* on the market. The forces of supply and demand tend to move the price toward the equilibrium price, but when the market price hits the ceiling, it can rise no further. Thus, the market price equals the price ceiling. At this price, the quantity of ice cream demanded (125 cones in the figure) exceeds the quantity supplied (75 cones). There

FIGURE 1

A Market with a Price Ceiling

In panel (a), the government imposes a price ceiling of $4. Because the price ceiling is above the equilibrium price of $3, the price ceiling has no effect, and the market can reach the equilibrium of supply and demand. In this equilibrium, quantity supplied and quantity demanded both equal 100 cones. In panel (b), the government imposes a price ceiling of $2. Because the price ceiling is below the equilibrium price of $3, the market price equals $2. At this price, 125 cones are demanded and only 75 are supplied, so there is a shortage of 50 cones.

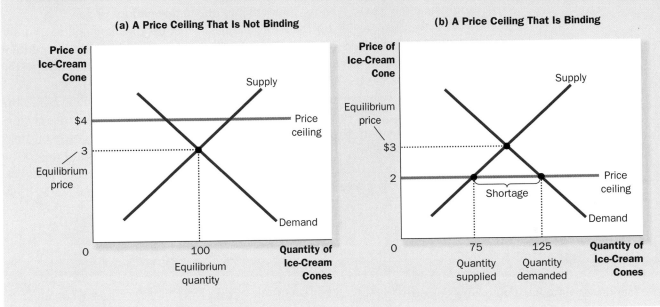

is a shortage of ice cream, so some people who want to buy ice cream at the going price are unable to.

When a shortage of ice cream develops because of this price ceiling, some mechanism for rationing ice cream will naturally develop. The mechanism could be long lines: Buyers who are willing to arrive early and wait in line get a cone, while those unwilling to wait do not. Alternatively, sellers could ration ice cream according to their own personal biases, selling it only to friends, relatives, or members of their own racial or ethnic group. Notice that even though the price ceiling was motivated by a desire to help buyers of ice cream, not all buyers benefit from the policy. Some buyers do get to pay a lower price, although they may have to wait in line to do so, but other buyers cannot get any ice cream at all.

This example in the market for ice cream shows a general result: *When the government imposes a binding price ceiling on a competitive market, a shortage of the good arises, and sellers must ration the scarce goods among the large number of potential buyers.* The rationing mechanisms that develop under price ceilings are rarely desirable. Long lines are inefficient, because they waste buyers' time. Discrimination according to seller bias is both inefficient (because the good does not necessarily go to the buyer who values it most highly) and potentially unfair. By contrast, the rationing mechanism in a free, competitive market is both efficient and impersonal. When the market for ice cream reaches its equilibrium, anyone who wants to pay the market price can get a cone. Free markets ration goods with prices.

Case Study

LINES AT THE GAS PUMP

As we discussed in the preceding chapter, in 1973 the Organization of Petroleum Exporting Countries (OPEC) raised the price of crude oil in world oil markets. Because crude oil is the major input used to make gasoline, the higher oil prices reduced the supply of gasoline. Long lines at gas stations became commonplace, and motorists often had to wait for hours to buy only a few gallons of gas.

What was responsible for the long gas lines? Most people blame OPEC. Surely, if OPEC had not raised the price of crude oil, the shortage of gasoline would not have occurred. Yet economists blame U.S. government regulations that limited the price oil companies could charge for gasoline.

Figure 2 shows what happened. As shown in panel (a), before OPEC raised the price of crude oil, the equilibrium price of gasoline P_1 was below the price ceiling. The price regulation, therefore, had no effect. When the price of crude oil rose, however, the situation changed. The increase in the price of crude oil raised the cost of producing gasoline, and this reduced the supply of gasoline. As panel (b) shows, the supply curve shifted to the left from S_1 to S_2. In an unregulated market,

FIGURE 2

The Market for Gasoline with a Price Ceiling

Panel (a) shows the gasoline market when the price ceiling is not binding because the equilibrium price, P_1, is below the ceiling. Panel (b) shows the gasoline market after an increase in the price of crude oil (an input into making gasoline) shifts the supply curve to the left from S_1 to S_2. In an unregulated market, the price would have risen from P_1 to P_2. The price ceiling, however, prevents this from happening. At the binding price ceiling, consumers are willing to buy Q_D, but producers of gasoline are willing to sell only Q_S. The difference between quantity demanded and quantity supplied, $Q_D - Q_S$, measures the gasoline shortage.

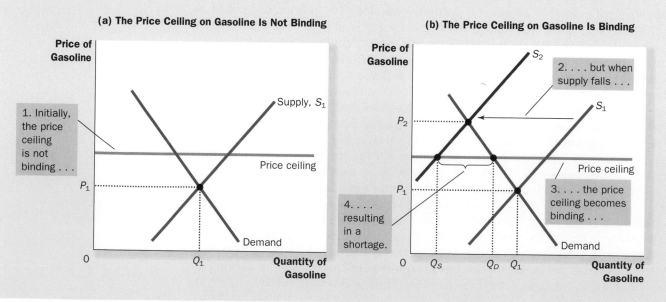

this shift in supply would have raised the equilibrium price of gasoline from P_1 to P_2, and no shortage would have resulted. Instead, the price ceiling prevented the price from rising to the equilibrium level. At the price ceiling, producers were willing to sell Q_S, and consumers were willing to buy Q_D. Thus, the shift in supply caused a severe shortage at the regulated price.

Eventually, the laws regulating the price of gasoline were repealed. Lawmakers came to understand that they were partly responsible for the many hours Americans lost waiting in line to buy gasoline. Today, when the price of crude oil changes, the price of gasoline can adjust to bring supply and demand into equilibrium. ●

Case Study
RENT CONTROL IN THE SHORT RUN AND LONG RUN

One common example of a price ceiling is rent control. In many cities, the local government places a ceiling on rents that landlords may charge their tenants. The goal of this policy is to help the poor by making housing more affordable. Economists often criticize rent control, arguing that it is a highly inefficient way to help the poor raise their standard of living. One economist called rent control "the best way to destroy a city, other than bombing."

The adverse effects of rent control are less apparent to the general population because these effects occur over many years. In the short run, landlords have a fixed number of apartments to rent, and they cannot adjust this number quickly as market conditions change. Moreover, the number of people searching for housing in a city may not be highly responsive to rents in the short run because people take time to adjust their housing arrangements. Therefore, the short-run supply and demand for housing are relatively inelastic.

Panel (a) of Figure 3 (p. 118) shows the short-run effects of rent control on the housing market. As with any binding price ceiling, rent control causes a shortage. Yet because supply and demand are inelastic in the short run, the initial shortage caused by rent control is small. The primary effect in the short run is to reduce rents.

The long-run story is very different because the buyers and sellers of rental housing respond more to market conditions as time passes. On the supply side, landlords respond to low rents by not building new apartments and by failing to maintain existing ones. On the demand side, low rents encourage people to find their own apartments (rather than living with their parents or sharing apartments with roommates) and induce more people to move into a city. Therefore, both supply and demand are more elastic in the long run.

Panel (b) of Figure 3 illustrates the housing market in the long run. When rent control depresses rents below the equilibrium level, the quantity of apartments supplied falls substantially, and the quantity of apartments demanded rises substantially. The result is a large shortage of housing.

In cities with rent control, landlords use various mechanisms to ration housing. Some landlords keep long waiting lists. Others give a preference to tenants without children. Still others discriminate on the basis of race. Sometimes, apartments

FIGURE 3

Rent Control in the Short Run and in the Long Run

Panel (a) shows the short-run effects of rent control: Because the supply and demand for apartments are relatively inelastic, the price ceiling imposed by a rent-control law causes only a small shortage of housing. Panel (b) shows the long-run effects of rent control: Because the supply and demand for apartments are more elastic, rent control causes a large shortage.

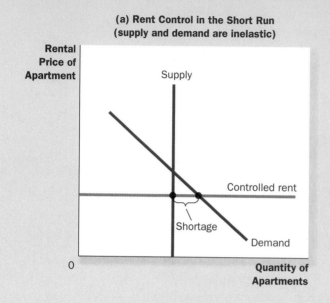

**(a) Rent Control in the Short Run
(supply and demand are inelastic)**

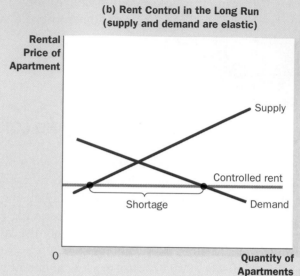

**(b) Rent Control in the Long Run
(supply and demand are elastic)**

are allocated to those willing to offer under-the-table payments to building super-intendents. In essence, these bribes bring the total price of an apartment (including the bribe) closer to the equilibrium price.

To understand fully the effects of rent control, we have to remember one of the *Ten Principles of Economics* from Chapter 1: People respond to incentives. In free markets, landlords try to keep their buildings clean and safe because desirable apartments command higher prices. By contrast, when rent control creates short-ages and waiting lists, landlords lose their incentive to respond to tenants' con-cerns. Why should a landlord spend his money to maintain and improve his property when people are waiting to get in as it is? In the end, tenants get lower rents, but they also get lower-quality housing.

Policymakers often react to the effects of rent control by imposing additional regulations. For example, there are laws that make racial discrimination in hous-ing illegal and require landlords to provide minimally adequate living conditions. These laws, however, are difficult and costly to enforce. By contrast, when rent control is eliminated and a market for housing is regulated by the forces of com-petition, such laws are less necessary. In a free market, the price of housing adjusts to eliminate the shortages that give rise to undesirable landlord behavior. ●

IN THE NEWS

DOES A DROUGHT NEED TO CAUSE A WATER SHORTAGE?

During the summer of 1999, the east coast of the United States experienced unusually little rain and a shortage of water. The following article suggests a way that the shortage could have been averted.

Trickle-Down Economics

By Terry L. Anderson and Clay J. Landry

Water shortages are being blamed on the drought in the East, but that's giving Mother Nature a bum rap. Certainly the drought is the immediate cause, but the real culprit is regulations that don't allow markets and prices to equalize demand and supply.

The similarity between water and gasoline is instructive. The energy crisis of the 1970s, too, was blamed on nature's stingy supply of oil, but in fact it was the actions of the Organization of Petroleum Exporting Countries, combined with price controls, that was the main cause of the shortages. . . .

Once again, regulators are responding to shortages—in this case of water—with controls and regulations rather than allowing the market to work. Cities are restricting water usage; some have even gone so far as to prohibit restaurants from serving water except if the customer asks for a glass. But although cities initially saw declines in water use, some are starting to report increases in consumption. This has prompted some police departments to collect lists of residents suspected of wasting water.

There's a better answer than sending out the cops. Market forces could ensure plentiful water availability even in drought years. Contrary to popular belief, the supply of water is no more fixed than the supply of oil. Like all resources, water supplies change in response to economic growth and to the price. In developing countries, despite population growth, the percentage of people with access to safe drinking water has increased to 74 percent in 1994 from 44 percent in 1980. Rising incomes have given those countries the wherewithal to supply potable water.

Supplies also increase when current users have an incentive to conserve their surplus in the marketplace. California's drought-emergency water bank illustrates this. The bank allows farmers to lease water from other users during dry spells. In 1991, the first year the bank was tried, when the price was $125 per acre-foot (326,000 gallons), supply exceeded demand by two to one. That is, many more people wanted to sell their water than wanted to buy.

Data from every corner of the world show that when cities raise the price of water by 10 percent, water use goes down by as much as 12 percent. When the price of agricultural water goes up 10 percent, usage goes down by 20 percent. . . .

Unfortunately, Eastern water users do not pay realistic prices for water. According to the American Water Works Association, only 2 percent of municipal water suppliers adjust prices seasonally. . . .

Even more egregious, Eastern water laws bar people from buying and selling water. Just as tradable pollution permits established under the Clean Air Act have encouraged polluters to find efficient ways to reduce emissions, tradable water rights can encourage conservation and increase supplies. It is mainly a matter of following the lead of Western water courts that have quantified water rights and Western legislatures that have allowed trades.

By making water a commodity and unleashing market forces, policymakers can ensure plentiful water supplies for all. New policies won't make droughts disappear, but they will ease the pain they impose by priming the invisible pump of water markets.

How Price Floors Affect Market Outcomes

To examine the effects of another kind of government price control, let's return to the market for ice cream. Imagine now that the government is persuaded by the pleas of the National Organization of Ice-Cream Makers. In this case, the government might institute a price floor. Price floors, like price ceilings, are an attempt by the government to maintain prices at other than equilibrium levels. Whereas a price ceiling places a legal maximum on prices, a price floor places a legal minimum.

When the government imposes a price floor on the ice-cream market, two outcomes are possible. If the government imposes a price floor of $2 per cone when the equilibrium price is $3, we obtain the outcome in panel (a) of Figure 4. In this case, because the equilibrium price is above the floor, the price floor is not binding. Market forces naturally move the economy to the equilibrium, and the price floor has no effect.

Panel (b) of Figure 4 shows what happens when the government imposes a price floor of $4 per cone. In this case, because the equilibrium price of $3 is below the floor, the price floor is a binding constraint on the market. The forces of supply and demand tend to move the price toward the equilibrium price, but when the market price hits the floor, it can fall no further. The market price equals the price floor. At this floor, the quantity of ice cream supplied (120 cones) exceeds the quantity demanded (80 cones). Some people who want to sell ice cream at the going price are unable to. *Thus, a binding price floor causes a surplus.*

FIGURE 4

A Market with a Price Floor

In panel (a), the government imposes a price floor of $2. Because this is below the equilibrium price of $3, the price floor has no effect. The market price adjusts to balance supply and demand. At the equilibrium, quantity supplied and quantity demanded both equal 100 cones. In panel (b), the government imposes a price floor of $4, which is above the equilibrium price of $3. Therefore, the market price equals $4. Because 120 cones are supplied at this price and only 80 are demanded, there is a surplus of 40 cones.

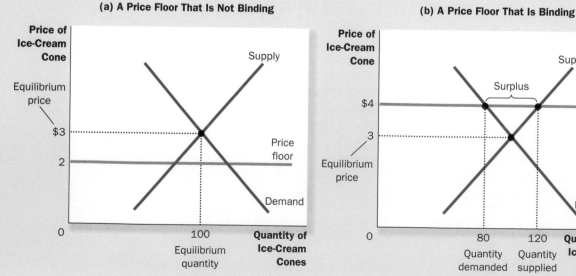
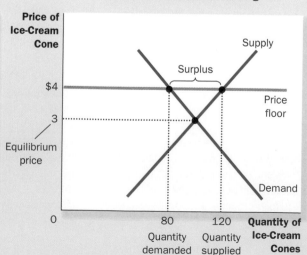

Just as price ceilings and shortages can lead to undesirable rationing mechanisms, so can price floors and surpluses. In the case of a price floor, some sellers are unable to sell all they want at the market price. The sellers who appeal to the personal biases of the buyers, perhaps due to racial or familial ties, are better able to sell their goods than those who do not. By contrast, in a free market, the price serves as the rationing mechanism, and sellers can sell all they want at the equilibrium price.

Case Study
THE MINIMUM WAGE

An important example of a price floor is the minimum wage. Minimum-wage laws dictate the lowest price for labor that any employer may pay. The U.S. Congress first instituted a minimum wage with the Fair Labor Standards Act of 1938 to ensure workers a minimally adequate standard of living. In 2002 the minimum wage according to federal law was $5.15 per hour, and some state laws imposed higher minimum wages.

To examine the effects of a minimum wage, we must consider the market for labor. Panel (a) of Figure 5 shows the labor market which, like all markets, is subject to the forces of supply and demand. Workers determine the supply of labor, and firms determine the demand. If the government doesn't intervene, the wage normally adjusts to balance labor supply and labor demand.

FIGURE 5

How the Minimum Wage Affects the Labor Market

Panel (a) shows a labor market in which the wage adjusts to balance labor supply and labor demand. Panel (b) shows the impact of a binding minimum wage. Because the minimum wage is a price floor, it causes a surplus: The quantity of labor supplied exceeds the quantity demanded. The result is unemployment.

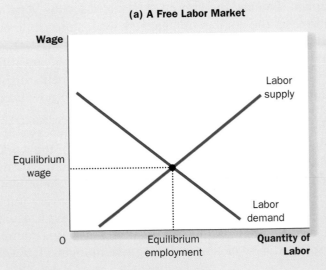
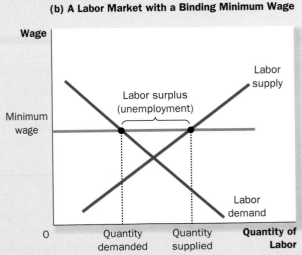

Panel (b) of Figure 5 shows the labor market with a minimum wage. If the minimum wage is above the equilibrium level, as it is here, the quantity of labor supplied exceeds the quantity demanded. The result is unemployment. Thus, the minimum wage raises the incomes of those workers who have jobs, but it lowers the incomes of those workers who cannot find jobs.

To fully understand the minimum wage, keep in mind that the economy contains not a single labor market, but many labor markets for different types of workers. The impact of the minimum wage depends on the skill and experience of the worker. Workers with high skills and much experience are not affected, because their equilibrium wages are well above the minimum. For these workers, the minimum wage is not binding.

The minimum wage has its greatest impact on the market for teenage labor. The equilibrium wages of teenagers are low because teenagers are among the least skilled and least experienced members of the labor force. In addition, teenagers are often willing to accept a lower wage in exchange for on-the-job training. (Some teenagers are willing to work as "interns" for no pay at all. Because internships pay nothing, however, the minimum wage does not apply to them. If it did, these jobs might not exist.) As a result, the minimum wage is more often binding for teenagers than for other members of the labor force.

Many economists have studied how minimum-wage laws affect the teenage labor market. These researchers compare the changes in the minimum wage over time with the changes in teenage employment. Although there is some debate about how much the minimum wage affects employment, the typical study finds that a 10 percent increase in the minimum wage depresses teenage employment between 1 and 3 percent. In interpreting this estimate, note that a 10 percent increase in the minimum wage does not raise the average wage of teenagers by 10 percent. A change in the law does not directly affect those teenagers who are already paid well above the minimum, and enforcement of minimum-wage laws is not perfect. Thus, the estimated drop in employment of 1 to 3 percent is significant.

In addition to altering the quantity of labor demanded, the minimum wage also alters the quantity supplied. Because the minimum wage raises the wage that teenagers can earn, it increases the number of teenagers who choose to look for jobs. Studies have found that a higher minimum wage influences which teenagers are employed. When the minimum wage rises, some teenagers who are still attending school choose to drop out and take jobs. These new dropouts displace other teenagers who had already dropped out of school and who now become unemployed.

The minimum wage is a frequent topic of political debate. Advocates of the minimum wage view the policy as one way to raise the income of the working poor. They correctly point out that workers who earn the minimum wage can afford only a meager standard of living. In 2002, for instance, when the minimum wage was $5.15 per hour, two adults working 40 hours a week for every week of the year at minimum-wage jobs had a total annual income of only $21,424, which was less than half of the median family income. Many advocates of the minimum wage admit that it has some adverse effects, including unemployment, but they believe that these effects are small and that, all things considered, a higher minimum wage makes the poor better off.

Opponents of the minimum wage contend that it is not the best way to combat poverty. They note that a high minimum wage causes unemployment, encourages teenagers to drop out of school, and prevents some unskilled workers from getting the on-the-job training they need. Moreover, opponents of the minimum wage point out that the minimum wage is a poorly targeted policy. Not all minimum-wage workers are heads of households trying to help their families escape poverty. In fact, fewer than a third of minimum-wage earners are in families with incomes below the poverty line. Many are teenagers from middle-class homes working at part-time jobs for extra spending money. ●

Evaluating Price Controls

One of the *Ten Principles of Economics* discussed in Chapter 1 is that markets are usually a good way to organize economic activity. This principle explains why economists usually oppose price ceilings and price floors. To economists, prices are not the outcome of some haphazard process. Prices, they contend, are the result of the millions of business and consumer decisions that lie behind the supply and demand curves. Prices have the crucial job of balancing supply and demand and, thereby, coordinating economic activity. When policymakers set prices by legal decree, they obscure the signals that normally guide the allocation of society's resources.

Another one of the *Ten Principles of Economics* is that governments can sometimes improve market outcomes. Indeed, policymakers are led to control prices because they view the market's outcome as unfair. Price controls are often aimed at helping the poor. For instance, rent-control laws try to make housing affordable for everyone, and minimum-wage laws try to help people escape poverty.

Yet price controls often hurt those they are trying to help. Rent control may keep rents low, but it also discourages landlords from maintaining their buildings and makes housing hard to find. Minimum-wage laws may raise the incomes of some workers, but they also cause other workers to be unemployed.

Helping those in need can be accomplished in ways other than controlling prices. For instance, the government can make housing more affordable by paying a fraction of the rent for poor families. Unlike rent control, such rent subsidies do not reduce the quantity of housing supplied and, therefore, do not lead to housing shortages. Similarly, wage subsidies raise the living standards of the working poor without discouraging firms from hiring them. An example of a wage subsidy is the *earned income tax credit,* a government program that supplements the incomes of low-wage workers.

Although these alternative policies are often better than price controls, they are not perfect. Rent and wage subsidies cost the government money and, therefore, require higher taxes. As we see in the next section, taxation has costs of its own.

QuickQuiz Define *price ceiling* and *price floor,* and give an example of each. Which leads to a shortage? Which leads to a surplus? Why?

TAXES

All governments—from the federal government in Washington, D.C., to the local governments in small towns—use taxes to raise revenue for public projects, such as roads, schools, and national defense. Because taxes are such an important policy instrument, and because they affect our lives in many ways, the study of taxes is a topic to which we return several times throughout this book. In this section we begin our study of how taxes affect the economy.

To set the stage for our analysis, imagine that a local government decides to hold an annual ice-cream celebration—with a parade, fireworks, and speeches by town officials. To raise revenue to pay for the event, it decides to place a $0.50 tax on the sale of ice-cream cones. When the plan is announced, our two lobbying groups swing into action. The National Organization of Ice-Cream Makers claims that its members are struggling to survive in a competitive market, and it argues that *buyers* of ice cream should have to pay the tax. The American Association of Ice-Cream Eaters claims that consumers of ice cream are having trouble making ends meet, and it argues that *sellers* of ice cream should pay the tax. The town mayor, hoping to reach a compromise, suggests that half the tax be paid by the buyers and half be paid by the sellers.

To analyze these proposals, we need to address a simple but subtle question: When the government levies a tax on a good, who bears the burden of the tax? The people buying the good? The people selling the good? Or, if buyers and sellers share the tax burden, what determines how the burden is divided? Can the government simply legislate the division of the burden, as the mayor is suggesting, or is the division determined by more fundamental forces in the economy? Economists use the term **tax incidence** to refer to the distribution of a tax burden. As we will see, some surprising lessons about tax incidence arise just by applying the tools of supply and demand.

tax incidence
the manner in which the burden of a tax is shared among participants in a market

How Taxes on Buyers Affect Market Outcomes

We first consider a tax levied on buyers of a good. Suppose, for instance, that our local government passes a law requiring buyers of ice-cream cones to send $0.50 to the government for each ice-cream cone they buy. How does this law affect the buyers and sellers of ice cream? To answer this question, we can follow the three steps in Chapter 4 for analyzing supply and demand: (1) We decide whether the law affects the supply curve or demand curve. (2) We decide which way the curve shifts. (3) We examine how the shift affects the equilibrium.

Step One   The initial impact of the tax is on the demand for ice cream. The supply curve is not affected because, for any given price of ice cream, sellers have the same incentive to provide ice cream to the market. By contrast, buyers now have to pay a tax to the government (as well as the price to the sellers) whenever they buy ice cream. Thus, the tax shifts the demand curve for ice cream.

Step Two   The direction of the shift is easy to determine. Because the tax on buyers makes buying ice cream less attractive, buyers demand a smaller quantity of ice cream at every price. As a result, the demand curve shifts to the left (or, equivalently, downward), as shown in Figure 6.

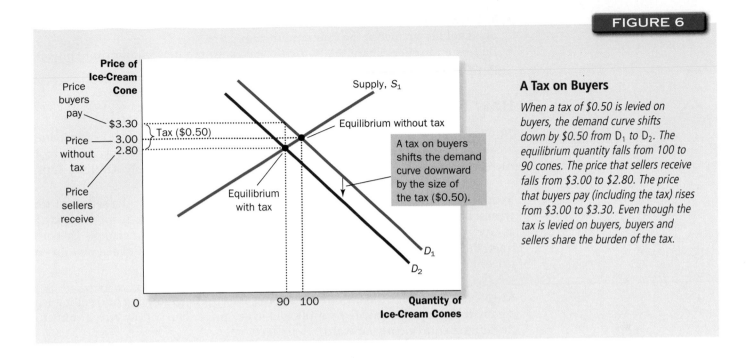

FIGURE 6

A Tax on Buyers

When a tax of $0.50 is levied on buyers, the demand curve shifts down by $0.50 from D₁ to D₂. The equilibrium quantity falls from 100 to 90 cones. The price that sellers receive falls from $3.00 to $2.80. The price that buyers pay (including the tax) rises from $3.00 to $3.30. Even though the tax is levied on buyers, buyers and sellers share the burden of the tax.

We can, in this case, be precise about how much the curve shifts. Because of the $0.50 tax levied on buyers, the effective price to buyers is now $0.50 higher than the market price (whatever the market price happens to be). For example, if the market price of a cone happened to be $2.00, the effective price to buyers would be $2.50. Because buyers look at their total cost including the tax, they demand a quantity of ice cream as if the market price were $0.50 higher than it actually is. In other words, to induce buyers to demand any given quantity, the market price must now be $0.50 lower to make up for the effect of the tax. Thus, the tax shifts the demand curve *downward* from D_1 to D_2 by exactly the size of the tax ($0.50).

Step Three Having determined how the demand curve shifts, we can now see the effect of the tax by comparing the initial equilibrium and the new equilibrium. You can see in the figure that the equilibrium price of ice cream falls from $3.00 to $2.80 and the equilibrium quantity falls from 100 to 90 cones. Because sellers sell less and buyers buy less in the new equilibrium, the tax on ice cream reduces the size of the ice-cream market.

Implications We can now return to the question of tax incidence: Who pays the tax? Although buyers send the entire tax to the government, buyers and sellers share the burden. Because the market price falls from $3.00 to $2.80 when the tax is introduced, sellers receive $0.20 less for each ice-cream cone than they did without the tax. Thus, the tax makes sellers worse off. Buyers pay sellers a lower price ($2.80), but the effective price including the tax rises from $3.00 before the tax to $3.30 with the tax ($2.80 + $0.50 = $3.30). Thus, the tax also makes buyers worse off.

To sum up, the analysis yields two lessons:

- Taxes discourage market activity. When a good is taxed, the quantity of the good sold is smaller in the new equilibrium.
- Buyers and sellers share the burden of taxes. In the new equilibrium, buyers pay more for the good, and sellers receive less.

How Taxes on Sellers Affect Market Outcomes

Now consider a tax levied on sellers of a good. Suppose the local government passes a law requiring sellers of ice-cream cones to send $0.50 to the government for each cone they sell. What are the effects of this law? Again, we apply our three steps.

Step One   In this case, the immediate impact of the tax is on the sellers of ice cream. Because the tax is not levied on buyers, the quantity of ice cream demanded at any given price is the same; thus, the demand curve does not change. By contrast, the tax on sellers makes the ice-cream business less profitable at any given price, so it shifts the supply curve.

Step Two   Because the tax on sellers raises the cost of producing and selling ice cream, it reduces the quantity supplied at every price. The supply curve shifts to the left (or, equivalently, upward).

Once again, we can be precise about the magnitude of the shift. For any market price of ice cream, the effective price to sellers—the amount they get to keep after paying the tax—is $0.50 lower. For example, if the market price of a cone happened to be $2.00, the effective price received by sellers would be $1.50. Whatever the market price, sellers will supply a quantity of ice cream as if the price were $0.50 lower than it is. Put differently, to induce sellers to supply any given quantity, the market price must now be $0.50 higher to compensate for the effect of the tax. Thus, as shown in Figure 7, the supply curve shifts *upward* from S_1 to S_2 by exactly the size of the tax ($0.50).

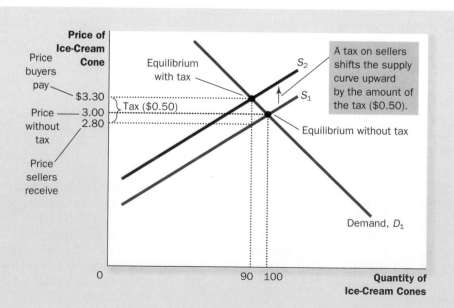

FIGURE 7

A Tax on Sellers

When a tax of $0.50 is levied on sellers, the supply curve shifts up by $0.50 from S_1 to S_2. The equilibrium quantity falls from 100 to 90 cones. The price that buyers pay rises from $3.00 to $3.30. The price that sellers receive (after paying the tax) falls from $3.00 to $2.80. Even though the tax is levied on sellers, buyers and sellers share the burden of the tax.

Step Three Having determined how the supply curve shifts, we can now compare the initial and the new equilibrium. The figure shows that the equilibrium price of ice cream rises from $3.00 to $3.30, and the equilibrium quantity falls from 100 to 90 cones. Once again, the tax reduces the size of the ice-cream market. And once again, buyers and sellers share the burden of the tax. Because the market price rises, buyers pay $0.30 more for each cone than they did before the tax was enacted. Sellers receive a higher price than they did without the tax, but the effective price (after paying the tax) falls from $3.00 to $2.80.

Implications If you compare Figures 6 and 7, you will notice a surprising conclusion: *Taxes on buyers and taxes on sellers are equivalent.* In both cases, the tax places a wedge between the price that buyers pay and the price that sellers receive. The wedge between the buyers' price and the sellers' price is the same, regardless of whether the tax is levied on buyers or sellers. In either case, the wedge shifts the relative position of the supply and demand curves. In the new equilibrium, buyers and sellers share the burden of the tax. The only difference between taxes on buyers and taxes on sellers is who sends the money to the government.

The equivalence of these two taxes is easy to understand if we imagine that the government collects the $0.50 ice-cream tax in a bowl on the counter of each ice-cream store. When the government levies the tax on buyers, the buyer is required to place $0.50 in the bowl every time a cone is bought. When the government levies the tax on sellers, the seller is required to place $0.50 in the bowl after the sale of each cone. Whether the $0.50 goes directly from the buyer's pocket into the bowl, or indirectly from the buyer's pocket into the seller's hand and then into the bowl, does not matter. Once the market reaches its new equilibrium, buyers and sellers share the burden, regardless of how the tax is levied.

Case Study
CAN CONGRESS DISTRIBUTE THE BURDEN OF A PAYROLL TAX?

If you have ever received a paycheck, you probably noticed that taxes were deducted from the amount you earned. One of these taxes is called FICA, an acronym for the Federal Insurance Contribution Act. The federal government uses the revenue from the FICA tax to pay for Social Security and Medicare, the income support and health care programs for the elderly. FICA is an example of a *payroll tax*, which is a tax on the wages that firms pay their workers. In 2002, the total FICA tax for the typical worker was 15.3 percent of earnings.

Who do you think bears the burden of this payroll tax—firms or workers? When Congress passed this legislation, it tried to mandate a division of the tax burden. According to the law, half of the tax is paid by firms, and half is paid by workers. That is, half of the tax is paid out of firm revenue, and half is deducted from workers' paychecks. The amount that shows up as a deduction on your pay stub is the worker contribution.

Our analysis of tax incidence, however, shows that lawmakers cannot so easily dictate the distribution of a tax burden. To illustrate, we can analyze a payroll tax as merely a tax on a good, where the good is labor and the price is the wage. The

FIGURE 8

A Payroll Tax

A payroll tax places a wedge between the wage that workers receive and the wage that firms pay. Comparing wages with and without the tax, you can see that workers and firms share the tax burden. This division of the tax burden between workers and firms does not depend on whether the government levies the tax on workers, levies the tax on firms, or divides the tax equally between the two groups.

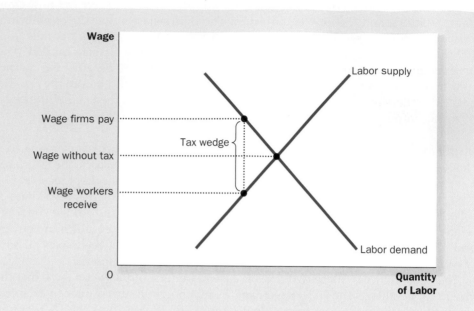

key feature of the payroll tax is that it places a wedge between the wage that firms pay and the wage that workers receive. Figure 8 shows the outcome. When a payroll tax is enacted, the wage received by workers falls, and the wage paid by firms rises. In the end, workers and firms share the burden of the tax, much as the legislation requires. Yet this division of the tax burden between workers and firms has nothing to do with the legislated division: The division of the burden in Figure 8 is not necessarily fifty-fifty, and the same outcome would prevail if the law levied the entire tax on workers or if it levied the entire tax on firms.

This example shows that the most basic lesson of tax incidence is often overlooked in public debate. Lawmakers can decide whether a tax comes from the buyer's pocket or from the seller's, but they cannot legislate the true burden of a tax. Rather, tax incidence depends on the forces of supply and demand. ●

Elasticity and Tax Incidence

When a good is taxed, buyers and sellers of the good share the burden of the tax. But how exactly is the tax burden divided? Only rarely will it be shared equally. To see how the burden is divided, consider the impact of taxation in the two markets in Figure 9. In both cases, the figure shows the initial demand curve, the initial supply curve, and a tax that drives a wedge between the amount paid by buyers and the amount received by sellers. (Not drawn in either panel of the figure is the new supply or demand curve. Which curve shifts depends on whether the tax is levied on buyers or sellers. As we have seen, this is irrelevant for the incidence of the tax.) The difference in the two panels is the relative elasticity of supply and demand.

Panel (a) of Figure 9 shows a tax in a market with very elastic supply and relatively inelastic demand. That is, sellers are very responsive to changes in the price

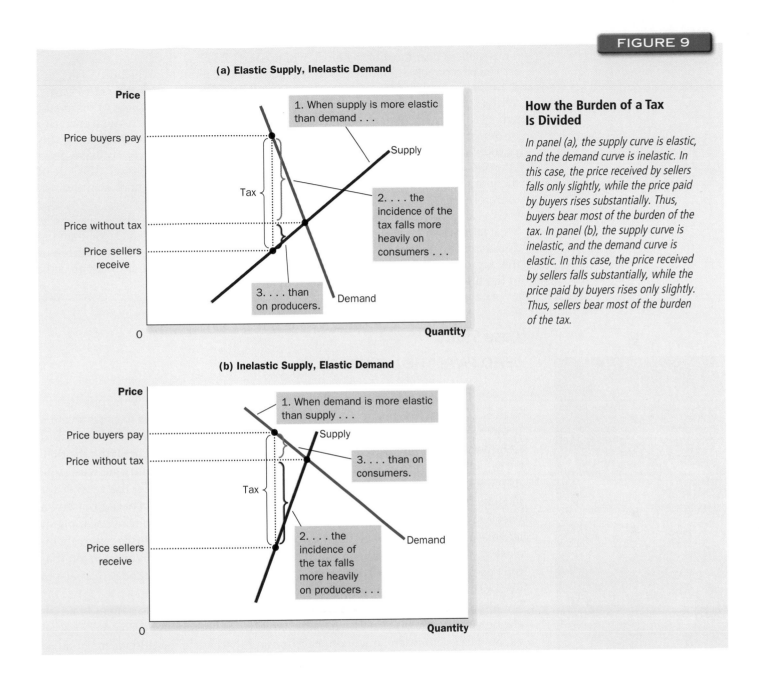

FIGURE 9

(a) Elastic Supply, Inelastic Demand

Price

1. When supply is more elastic than demand . . .

Price buyers pay

Supply

Tax

2. . . . the incidence of the tax falls more heavily on consumers . . .

Price without tax

Price sellers receive

3. . . . than on producers.

Demand

0

Quantity

(b) Inelastic Supply, Elastic Demand

Price

1. When demand is more elastic than supply . . .

Price buyers pay

Supply

Price without tax

3. . . . than on consumers.

Tax

Price sellers receive

2. . . . the incidence of the tax falls more heavily on producers . . .

Demand

0

Quantity

How the Burden of a Tax Is Divided

In panel (a), the supply curve is elastic, and the demand curve is inelastic. In this case, the price received by sellers falls only slightly, while the price paid by buyers rises substantially. Thus, buyers bear most of the burden of the tax. In panel (b), the supply curve is inelastic, and the demand curve is elastic. In this case, the price received by sellers falls substantially, while the price paid by buyers rises only slightly. Thus, sellers bear most of the burden of the tax.

of the good (so the supply curve is relatively flat), whereas buyers are not very responsive (so the demand curve is relatively steep). When a tax is imposed on a market with these elasticities, the price received by sellers does not fall much, so sellers bear only a small burden. By contrast, the price paid by buyers rises substantially, indicating that buyers bear most of the burden of the tax.

Panel (b) of Figure 9 shows a tax in a market with relatively inelastic supply and very elastic demand. In this case, sellers are not very responsive to changes in the price (so the supply curve is steeper), while buyers are very responsive (so the demand curve is flatter). The figure shows that when a tax is imposed, the price paid by buyers does not rise much, while the price received by sellers falls substantially. Thus, sellers bear most of the burden of the tax.

The two panels of Figure 9 show a general lesson about how the burden of a tax is divided: *A tax burden falls more heavily on the side of the market that is less elastic.* Why is this true? In essence, the elasticity measures the willingness of buyers or sellers to leave the market when conditions become unfavorable. A small elasticity of demand means that buyers do not have good alternatives to consuming this particular good. A small elasticity of supply means that sellers do not have good alternatives to producing this particular good. When the good is taxed, the side of the market with fewer good alternatives cannot easily leave the market and must, therefore, bear more of the burden of the tax.

We can apply this logic to the payroll tax discussed in the previous case study. Most labor economists believe that the supply of labor is much less elastic than the demand. This means that workers, rather than firms, bear most of the burden of the payroll tax. In other words, the distribution of the tax burden is not at all close to the fifty-fifty split that lawmakers intended.

Case Study

WHO PAYS THE LUXURY TAX?

In 1990, Congress adopted a new luxury tax on items such as yachts, private airplanes, furs, jewelry, and expensive cars. The goal of the tax was to raise revenue from those who could most easily afford to pay. Because only the rich could afford to buy such extravagances, taxing luxuries seemed a logical way of taxing the rich.

Yet, when the forces of supply and demand took over, the outcome was quite different from what Congress intended. Consider, for example, the market for yachts. The demand for yachts is quite elastic. A millionaire can easily not buy a yacht; she can use the money to buy a bigger house, take a European vacation, or leave a larger bequest to her heirs. By contrast, the supply of yachts is relatively inelastic, at least in the short run. Yacht factories are not easily converted to alternative uses, and workers who build yachts are not eager to change careers in response to changing market conditions.

Our analysis makes a clear prediction in this case. With elastic demand and inelastic supply, the burden of a tax falls largely on the suppliers. That is, a tax on yachts places a burden largely on the firms and workers who build yachts because they end up getting a lower price for their product. The workers, however, are not wealthy. Thus, the burden of a luxury tax falls more on the middle class than on the rich.

The mistaken assumptions about the incidence of the luxury tax quickly became apparent after the tax went into effect. Suppliers of luxuries made their congressional representatives well aware of the economic hardship they experienced, and Congress repealed most of the luxury tax in 1993. ●

© HANS GEORG ROTH/CORBIS

"If this boat were any more expensive, we'd be playing golf."

QuickQuiz In a supply-and-demand diagram, show how a tax on car buyers of $1,000 per car affects the quantity of cars sold and the price of cars. In another diagram, show how a tax on car sellers of $1,000 per car affects the quantity of cars sold and the price of cars. In both of your diagrams, show the change in the price paid by car buyers and the change in price received by car sellers.

CONCLUSION

The economy is governed by two kinds of laws: the laws of supply and demand and the laws enacted by governments. In this chapter we have begun to see how these laws interact. Price controls and taxes are common in various markets in the economy, and their effects are frequently debated in the press and among policymakers. Even a little bit of economic knowledge can go a long way toward understanding and evaluating these policies.

In subsequent chapters we will analyze many government policies in greater detail. We will examine the effects of taxation more fully, and we will consider a broader range of policies than we considered here. Yet the basic lessons of this chapter will not change: When analyzing government policies, supply and demand are the first and most useful tools of analysis.

SUMMARY

- A price ceiling is a legal maximum on the price of a good or service. An example is rent control. If the price ceiling is below the equilibrium price, the quantity demanded exceeds the quantity supplied. Because of the resulting shortage, sellers must in some way ration the good or service among buyers.

- A price floor is a legal minimum on the price of a good or service. An example is the minimum wage. If the price floor is above the equilibrium price, the quantity supplied exceeds the quantity demanded. Because of the resulting surplus, buyers' demands for the good or service must in some way be rationed among sellers.

- When the government levies a tax on a good, the equilibrium quantity of the good falls. That is, a tax on a market shrinks the size of the market.

- A tax on a good places a wedge between the price paid by buyers and the price received by sellers. When the market moves to the new equilibrium, buyers pay more for the good and sellers receive less for it. In this sense, buyers and sellers share the tax burden. The incidence of a tax (that is, the division of the tax burden) does not depend on whether the tax is levied on buyers or sellers.

- The incidence of a tax depends on the price elasticities of supply and demand. The burden tends to fall on the side of the market that is less elastic because that side of the market can respond less easily to the tax by changing the quantity bought or sold.

KEY CONCEPTS

price ceiling, p. 114   price floor, p. 114   tax incidence, p. 124

QUESTIONS FOR REVIEW

1. Give an example of a price ceiling and an example of a price floor.

2. Which causes a shortage of a good—a price ceiling or a price floor? Which causes a surplus?

3. What mechanisms allocate resources when the price of a good is not allowed to bring supply and demand into equilibrium?

4. Explain why economists usually oppose controls on prices.

5. What is the difference between a tax paid by buyers and a tax paid by sellers?

6. How does a tax on a good affect the price paid by buyers, the price received by sellers, and the quantity sold?

7. What determines how the burden of a tax is divided between buyers and sellers? Why?

PROBLEMS AND APPLICATIONS

1. Lovers of classical music persuade Congress to impose a price ceiling of $40 per ticket. Does this policy get more or fewer people to attend classical music concerts?

2. The government has decided that the free-market price of cheese is too low.
   a. Suppose the government imposes a binding price floor in the cheese market. Use a supply-and-demand diagram to show the effect of this policy on the price of cheese and the quantity of cheese sold. Is there a shortage or surplus of cheese?
   b. Farmers complain that the price floor has reduced their total revenue. Is this possible? Explain.
   c. In response to farmers' complaints, the government agrees to purchase all of the surplus cheese at the price floor. Compared to the basic price floor, who benefits from this new policy? Who loses?

3. A recent study found that the demand and supply schedules for Frisbees are as follows:

Price per Frisbee	Quantity Demanded	Quantity Supplied
$11	1 million	15 million
10	2	12
9	4	9
8	6	6
7	8	3
6	10	1

   a. What are the equilibrium price and quantity of Frisbees?
   b. Frisbee manufacturers persuade the government that Frisbee production improves scientists' understanding of aerodynamics and thus is important for national security. A concerned Congress votes to impose a price floor $2 above the equilibrium price. What is the new market price? How many Frisbees are sold?
   c. Irate college students march on Washington and demand a reduction in the price of Frisbees. An even more concerned Congress votes to repeal the price floor and impose a price ceiling $1 below the former price floor. What is the new market price? How many Frisbees are sold?

4. Suppose the federal government requires beer drinkers to pay a $2 tax on each case of beer purchased. (In fact, both the federal and state governments impose beer taxes of some sort.)
   a. Draw a supply-and-demand diagram of the market for beer without the tax. Show the price paid by consumers, the price received by producers, and the quantity of beer sold. What is the difference between the price paid by consumers and the price received by producers?
   b. Now draw a supply-and-demand diagram for the beer market with the tax. Show the price paid by consumers, the price received by producers, and the quantity of beer sold. What is the difference between the price paid by consumers and the price received by producers? Has the quantity of beer sold increased or decreased?

5. A senator wants to raise tax revenue and make workers better off. A staff member proposes raising the payroll tax paid by firms and using part of the extra revenue to reduce the payroll tax paid by workers. Would this accomplish the senator's goal?

6. If the government places a $500 tax on luxury cars, will the price paid by consumers rise by

more than $500, less than $500, or exactly $500? Explain.

7. Congress and the president decide that the United States should reduce air pollution by reducing its use of gasoline. They impose a $0.50 tax for each gallon of gasoline sold.
   a. Should they impose this tax on producers or consumers? Explain carefully, using a supply-and-demand diagram.
   b. If the demand for gasoline were more elastic, would this tax be more effective or less effective in reducing the quantity of gasoline consumed? Explain with both words and a diagram.
   c. Are consumers of gasoline helped or hurt by this tax? Why?
   d. Are workers in the oil industry helped or hurt by this tax? Why?

8. A case study in this chapter discusses the federal minimum-wage law.
   a. Suppose the minimum wage is above the equilibrium wage in the market for unskilled labor. Using a supply-and-demand diagram of the market for unskilled labor, show the market wage, the number of workers who are employed, and the number of workers who are unemployed. Also show the total wage payments to unskilled workers.
   b. Now suppose the secretary of labor proposes an increase in the minimum wage. What effect would this increase have on employment? Does the change in employment depend on the elasticity of demand, the elasticity of supply, both elasticities, or neither?
   c. What effect would this increase in the minimum wage have on unemployment? Does the change in unemployment depend on the elasticity of demand, the elasticity of supply, both elasticities, or neither?
   d. If the demand for unskilled labor were inelastic, would the proposed increase in the minimum wage raise or lower total wage

payments to unskilled workers? Would your answer change if the demand for unskilled labor were elastic?

9. Consider the following policies, each of which is aimed at reducing violent crime by reducing the use of guns. Illustrate each of these proposed policies in a supply-and-demand diagram of the gun market.
   a. a tax on gun buyers
   b. a tax on gun sellers
   c. a price floor on guns
   d. a tax on ammunition

10. The U.S. government administers two programs that affect the market for cigarettes. Media campaigns and labeling requirements are aimed at making the public aware of the dangers of cigarette smoking. At the same time, the Department of Agriculture maintains a price-support program for tobacco farmers, which raises the price of tobacco above the equilibrium price.
    a. How do these two programs affect cigarette consumption? Use a graph of the cigarette market in your answer.
    b. What is the combined effect of these two programs on the price of cigarettes?
    c. Cigarettes are also heavily taxed. What effect does this tax have on cigarette consumption?

11. A subsidy is the opposite of a tax. With a $0.50 tax on the buyers of ice-cream cones, the government collects $0.50 for each cone purchased; with a $0.50 subsidy for the buyers of ice-cream cones, the government pays buyers $0.50 for each cone purchased.
    a. Show the effect of a $0.50 per cone subsidy on the demand curve for ice-cream cones, the effective price paid by consumers, the effective price received by sellers, and the quantity of cones sold.
    b. Do consumers gain or lose from this policy? Do producers gain or lose? Does the government gain or lose?

http://

For more study tools, please visit http://mankiwXtra.swlearning.com.

3

SUPPLY AND DEMAND II:
MARKETS AND WELFARE

7

CONSUMERS, PRODUCERS, AND THE EFFICIENCY OF MARKETS

When consumers go to grocery stores to buy their turkeys for Thanksgiving dinner, they may be disappointed that the price of turkey is as high as it is. At the same time, when farmers bring to market the turkeys they have raised, they wish the price of turkey were even higher. These views are not surprising: Buyers always want to pay less, and sellers always want to get paid more. But is there a "right price" for turkey from the standpoint of society as a whole?

In previous chapters we saw how, in market economies, the forces of supply and demand determine the prices of goods and services and the quantities sold. So far, however, we have described the way markets allocate scarce resources without directly addressing the question of whether these market allocations are desirable. In other words, our analysis has been *positive* (what is) rather than *normative* (what should be). We know that the price of turkey adjusts to ensure that the quantity of turkey supplied equals the quantity of turkey demanded. But, at this equilibrium, is the quantity of turkey produced and consumed too small, too large, or just right?

welfare economics
the study of how the allocation of resources affects economic well-being

In this chapter we take up the topic of **welfare economics,** the study of how the allocation of resources affects economic well-being. We begin by examining the benefits that buyers and sellers receive from taking part in a market. We then examine how society can make these benefits as large as possible. This analysis leads to a profound conclusion: The equilibrium of supply and demand in a market maximizes the total benefits received by buyers and sellers.

As you may recall from Chapter 1, one of the *Ten Principles of Economics* is that markets are usually a good way to organize economic activity. The study of welfare economics explains this principle more fully. It also answers our question about the right price of turkey: The price that balances the supply and demand for turkey is, in a particular sense, the best one because it maximizes the total welfare of turkey consumers and turkey producers.

CONSUMER SURPLUS

We begin our study of welfare economics by looking at the benefits buyers receive from participating in a market.

Willingness to Pay

Imagine that you own a mint-condition recording of Elvis Presley's first album. Because you are not an Elvis Presley fan, you decide to sell it. One way to do so is to hold an auction.

Four Elvis fans show up for your auction: John, Paul, George, and Ringo. Each of them would like to own the album, but there is a limit to the amount that each is willing to pay for it. Table 1 shows the maximum price that each of the four possible buyers would pay. Each buyer's maximum is called his **willingness to pay,** and it measures how much that buyer values the good. Each buyer would be eager to buy the album at a price less than his willingness to pay, would refuse to buy the album at a price more than his willingness to pay, and would be indifferent about buying the album at a price exactly equal to his willingness to pay.

willingness to pay
the maximum amount that a buyer will pay for a good

To sell your album, you begin the bidding at a low price, say $10. Because all four buyers are willing to pay much more, the price rises quickly. The bidding stops when John bids $80 (or slightly more). At this point, Paul, George, and Ringo

TABLE 1

Four Possible Buyers' Willingness to Pay

Buyer	Willingness to Pay
John	$100
Paul	80
George	70
Ringo	50

have dropped out of the bidding, because they are unwilling to bid any more than $80. John pays you $80 and gets the album. Note that the album has gone to the buyer who values the album most highly.

What benefit does John receive from buying the Elvis Presley album? In a sense, John has found a real bargain: He is willing to pay $100 for the album but pays only $80 for it. We say that John receives *consumer surplus* of $20. **Consumer surplus** is the amount a buyer is willing to pay for a good minus the amount the buyer actually pays for it.

consumer surplus
a buyer's willingness to pay minus the amount the buyer actually pays

Consumer surplus measures the benefit to buyers of participating in a market. In this example, John receives a $20 benefit from participating in the auction because he pays only $80 for a good he values at $100. Paul, George, and Ringo get no consumer surplus from participating in the auction, because they left without the album and without paying anything.

Now consider a somewhat different example. Suppose that you had two identical Elvis Presley albums to sell. Again, you auction them off to the four possible buyers. To keep things simple, we assume that both albums are to be sold for the same price and that no buyer is interested in buying more than one album. Therefore, the price rises until two buyers are left.

In this case, the bidding stops when John and Paul bid $70 (or slightly higher). At this price, John and Paul are each happy to buy an album, and George and Ringo are not willing to bid any higher. John and Paul each receive consumer surplus equal to his willingness to pay minus the price. John's consumer surplus is $30, and Paul's is $10. John's consumer surplus is higher now than it was previously, because he gets the same album but pays less for it. The total consumer surplus in the market is $40.

Using the Demand Curve to Measure Consumer Surplus

Consumer surplus is closely related to the demand curve for a product. To see how they are related, let's continue our example and consider the demand curve for this rare Elvis Presley album.

We begin by using the willingness to pay of the four possible buyers to find the demand schedule for the album. The table in Figure 1 (p. 140) shows the demand schedule that corresponds to Table 1. If the price is above $100, the quantity demanded in the market is 0, because no buyer is willing to pay that much. If the price is between $80 and $100, the quantity demanded is 1, because only John is willing to pay such a high price. If the price is between $70 and $80, the quantity demanded is 2, because both John and Paul are willing to pay the price. We can continue this analysis for other prices as well. In this way, the demand schedule is derived from the willingness to pay of the four possible buyers.

The graph in Figure 1 shows the demand curve that corresponds to this demand schedule. Note the relationship between the height of the demand curve and the buyers' willingness to pay. At any quantity, the price given by the demand curve shows the willingness to pay of the *marginal buyer*, the buyer who would leave the market first if the price were any higher. At a quantity of 4 albums, for instance, the demand curve has a height of $50, the price that Ringo (the marginal buyer) is willing to pay for an album. At a quantity of 3 albums, the demand curve has a height of $70, the price that George (who is now the marginal buyer) is willing to pay.

FIGURE 1

The Demand Schedule and the Demand Curve

The table shows the demand schedule for the buyers in Table 1. The graph shows the corresponding demand curve. Note that the height of the demand curve reflects buyers' willingness to pay.

Price	Buyers	Quantity Demanded
More than $100	None	0
$80 to $100	John	1
$70 to $80	John, Paul	2
$50 to $70	John, Paul, George	3
$50 or less	John, Paul, George, Ringo	4

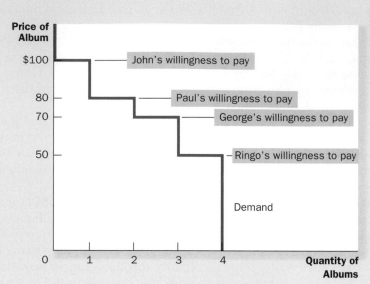

Because the demand curve reflects buyers' willingness to pay, we can also use it to measure consumer surplus. Figure 2 uses the demand curve to compute consumer surplus in our example. In panel (a), the price is $80 (or slightly above), and the quantity demanded is 1. Note that the area above the price and below the demand curve equals $20. This amount is exactly the consumer surplus we computed earlier when only 1 album is sold.

Panel (b) of Figure 2 shows consumer surplus when the price is $70 (or slightly above). In this case, the area above the price and below the demand curve equals the total area of the two rectangles: John's consumer surplus at this price is $30 and Paul's is $10. This area equals a total of $40. Once again, this amount is the consumer surplus we computed earlier.

The lesson from this example holds for all demand curves: *The area below the demand curve and above the price measures the consumer surplus in a market.* The reason is that the height of the demand curve measures the value buyers place on the good, as measured by their willingness to pay for it. The difference between this willingness to pay and the market price is each buyer's consumer surplus. Thus, the total area below the demand curve and above the price is the sum of the consumer surplus of all buyers in the market for a good or service.

How a Lower Price Raises Consumer Surplus

Because buyers always want to pay less for the goods they buy, a lower price makes buyers of a good better off. But how much does buyers' well-being rise in

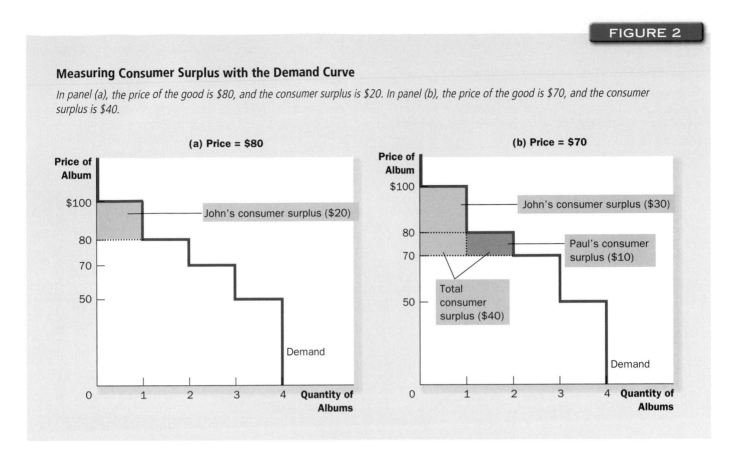

FIGURE 2

Measuring Consumer Surplus with the Demand Curve

In panel (a), the price of the good is $80, and the consumer surplus is $20. In panel (b), the price of the good is $70, and the consumer surplus is $40.

response to a lower price? We can use the concept of consumer surplus to answer this question precisely.

Figure 3 (p. 142) shows a typical downward-sloping demand curve. Although this demand curve appears somewhat different in shape from the steplike demand curves in our previous two figures, the ideas we have just developed apply nonetheless: Consumer surplus is the area above the price and below the demand curve. In panel (a), consumer surplus at a price of P_1 is the area of triangle ABC.

Now suppose that the price falls from P_1 to P_2, as shown in panel (b). The consumer surplus now equals area ADF. The increase in consumer surplus attributable to the lower price is the area BCFD.

This increase in consumer surplus is composed of two parts. First, those buyers who were already buying Q_1 of the good at the higher price P_1 are better off because they now pay less. The increase in consumer surplus of existing buyers is the reduction in the amount they pay; it equals the area of the rectangle BCED. Second, some new buyers enter the market because they are now willing to buy the good at the lower price. As a result, the quantity demanded in the market increases from Q_1 to Q_2. The consumer surplus these newcomers receive is the area of the triangle CEF.

What Does Consumer Surplus Measure?

Our goal in developing the concept of consumer surplus is to make normative judgments about the desirability of market outcomes. Now that you have seen

FIGURE 3

How the Price Affects Consumer Surplus

In panel (a), the price is P_1, the quantity demanded is Q_1, and consumer surplus equals the area of the triangle ABC. When the price falls from P_1 to P_2, as in panel (b), the quantity demanded rises from Q_1 to Q_2, and the consumer surplus rises to the area of the triangle ADF. The increase in consumer surplus (area BCFD) occurs in part because existing consumers now pay less (area BCED) and in part because new consumers enter the market at the lower price (area CEF).

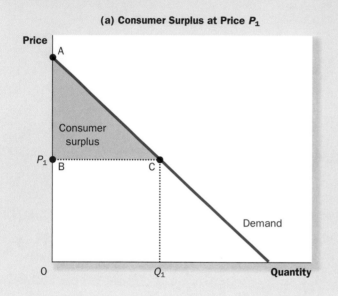

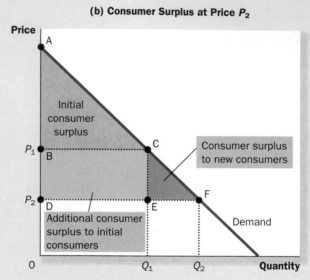

what consumer surplus is, let's consider whether it is a good measure of economic well-being.

Imagine that you are a policymaker trying to design a good economic system. Would you care about the amount of consumer surplus? Consumer surplus, the amount that buyers are willing to pay for a good minus the amount they actually pay for it, measures the benefit that buyers receive from a good *as the buyers themselves perceive it*. Thus, consumer surplus is a good measure of economic well-being if policymakers want to respect the preferences of buyers.

In some circumstances, policymakers might choose not to care about consumer surplus because they do not respect the preferences that drive buyer behavior. For example, drug addicts are willing to pay a high price for heroin. Yet we would not say that addicts get a large benefit from being able to buy heroin at a low price (even though addicts might say they do). From the standpoint of society, willingness to pay in this instance is not a good measure of the buyers' benefit, and consumer surplus is not a good measure of economic well-being, because addicts are not looking after their own best interests.

In most markets, however, consumer surplus does reflect economic well-being. Economists normally presume that buyers are rational when they make decisions and that their preferences should be respected. In this case, consumers are the best judges of how much benefit they receive from the goods they buy.

QuickQuiz Draw a demand curve for turkey. In your diagram, show a price of turkey and the consumer surplus that results from that price. Explain in words what this consumer surplus measures.

PRODUCER SURPLUS

We now turn to the other side of the market and consider the benefits sellers receive from participating in a market. As you will see, our analysis of sellers' welfare is similar to our analysis of buyers' welfare.

Cost and the Willingness to Sell

Imagine now that you are a homeowner, and you need to get your house painted. You turn to four sellers of painting services: Mary, Frida, Georgia, and Grandma. Each painter is willing to do the work for you if the price is right. You decide to take bids from the four painters and auction off the job to the painter who will do the work for the lowest price.

Each painter is willing to take the job if the price she would receive exceeds her cost of doing the work. Here the term **cost** should be interpreted as the painters' opportunity cost: It includes the painters' out-of-pocket expenses (for paint, brushes, and so on) as well as the value that the painters place on their own time. Table 2 shows each painter's cost. Because a painter's cost is the lowest price she would accept for her work, cost is a measure of her willingness to sell her services. Each painter would be eager to sell her services at a price greater than her cost, would refuse to sell her services at a price less than her cost, and would be indifferent about selling her services at a price exactly equal to her cost.

cost
the value of everything a seller must give up to produce a good

When you take bids from the painters, the price might start off high, but it quickly falls as the painters compete for the job. Once Grandma has bid $600 (or slightly less), she is the sole remaining bidder. Grandma is happy to do the job for this price, because her cost is only $500. Mary, Frida, and Georgia are unwilling to do the job for less than $600. Note that the job goes to the painter who can do the work at the lowest cost.

What benefit does Grandma receive from getting the job? Because she is willing to do the work for $500 but gets $600 for doing it, we say that she receives *producer*

TABLE 2

The Costs of Four Possible Sellers

Seller	Cost
Mary	$900
Frida	800
Georgia	600
Grandma	500

producer surplus
the amount a seller is paid for a good minus the seller's cost

surplus of $100. **Producer surplus** is the amount a seller is paid minus the cost of production. Producer surplus measures the benefit to sellers of participating in a market.

Now consider a somewhat different example. Suppose that you have two houses that need painting. Again, you auction off the jobs to the four painters. To keep things simple, let's assume that no painter is able to paint both houses and that you will pay the same amount to paint each house. Therefore, the price falls until two painters are left.

In this case, the bidding stops when Georgia and Grandma each offer to do the job for a price of $800 (or slightly less). At this price, Georgia and Grandma are willing to do the work, and Mary and Frida are not willing to bid a lower price. At a price of $800, Grandma receives producer surplus of $300, and Georgia receives producer surplus of $200. The total producer surplus in the market is $500.

Using the Supply Curve to Measure Producer Surplus

Just as consumer surplus is closely related to the demand curve, producer surplus is closely related to the supply curve. To see how, let's continue our example.

We begin by using the costs of the four painters to find the supply schedule for painting services. The table in Figure 4 shows the supply schedule that corresponds to the costs in Table 2. If the price is below $500, none of the four painters is willing to do the job, so the quantity supplied is zero. If the price is between $500 and $600, only Grandma is willing to do the job, so the quantity supplied is 1.

FIGURE 4

The Supply Schedule and the Supply Curve

The table shows the supply schedule for the sellers in Table 2. The graph shows the corresponding supply curve. Note that the height of the supply curve reflects sellers' costs.

Price	Sellers	Quantity Supplied
$900 or more	Mary, Frida, Georgia, Grandma	4
$800 to $900	Frida, Georgia, Grandma	3
$600 to $800	Georgia, Grandma	2
$500 to $600	Grandma	1
Less than $500	None	0

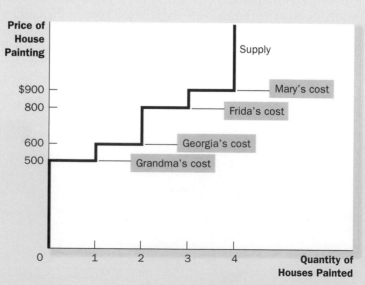

If the price is between $600 and $800, Grandma and Georgia are willing to do the job, so the quantity supplied is 2, and so on. Thus, the supply schedule is derived from the costs of the four painters.

The graph in Figure 4 shows the supply curve that corresponds to this supply schedule. Note that the height of the supply curve is related to the sellers' costs. At any quantity, the price given by the supply curve shows the cost of the *marginal seller*, the seller who would leave the market first if the price were any lower. At a quantity of 4 houses, for instance, the supply curve has a height of $900, the cost that Mary (the marginal seller) incurs to provide her painting services. At a quantity of 3 houses, the supply curve has a height of $800, the cost that Frida (who is now the marginal seller) incurs.

Because the supply curve reflects sellers' costs, we can use it to measure producer surplus. Figure 5 uses the supply curve to compute producer surplus in our example. In panel (a), we assume that the price is $600. In this case, the quantity supplied is 1. Note that the area below the price and above the supply curve equals $100. This amount is exactly the producer surplus we computed earlier for Grandma.

Panel (b) of Figure 5 shows producer surplus at a price of $800. In this case, the area below the price and above the supply curve equals the total area of the two rectangles. This area equals $500, the producer surplus we computed earlier for Georgia and Grandma when two houses needed painting.

FIGURE 5

Measuring Producer Surplus with the Supply Curve

In panel (a), the price of the good is $600, and the producer surplus is $100. In panel (b), the price of the good is $800, and the producer surplus is $500.

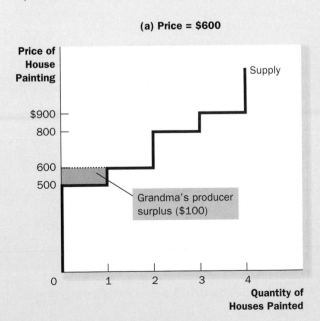

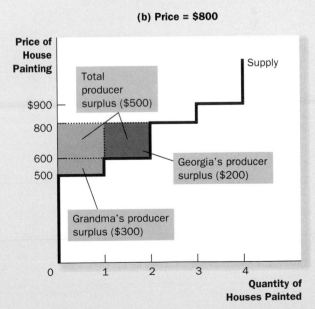

The lesson from this example applies to all supply curves: *The area below the price and above the supply curve measures the producer surplus in a market.* The logic is straightforward: The height of the supply curve measures sellers' costs, and the difference between the price and the cost of production is each seller's producer surplus. Thus, the total area is the sum of the producer surplus of all sellers.

How a Higher Price Raises Producer Surplus

You will not be surprised to hear that sellers always want to receive a higher price for the goods they sell. But how much does sellers' well-being rise in response to a higher price? The concept of producer surplus offers a precise answer to this question.

Figure 6 shows a typical upward-sloping supply curve. Even though this supply curve differs in shape from the steplike supply curves in the previous figure, we measure producer surplus in the same way: Producer surplus is the area below the price and above the supply curve. In panel (a), the price is P_1, and producer surplus is the area of triangle ABC.

FIGURE 6

How the Price Affects Producer Surplus

In panel (a), the price is P_1, the quantity demanded is Q_1, and producer surplus equals the area of the triangle ABC. When the price rises from P_1 to P_2, as in panel (b), the quantity supplied rises from Q_1 to Q_2, and the producer surplus rises to the area of the triangle ADF. The increase in producer surplus (area BCFD) occurs in part because existing producers now receive more (area BCED) and in part because new producers enter the market at the higher price (area CEF).

(a) Producer Surplus at Price P_1

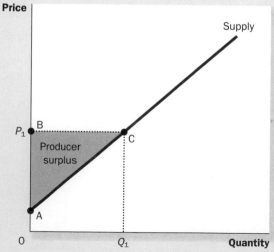

(b) Producer Surplus at Price P_2

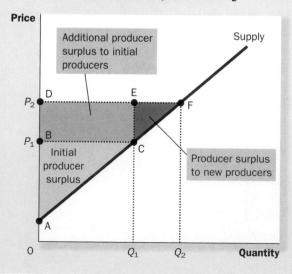

Panel (b) shows what happens when the price rises from P_1 to P_2. Producer surplus now equals area ADF. This increase in producer surplus has two parts. First, those sellers who were already selling Q_1 of the good at the lower price P_1 are better off because they now get more for what they sell. The increase in producer surplus for existing sellers equals the area of the rectangle BCED. Second, some new sellers enter the market because they are now willing to produce the good at the higher price, resulting in an increase in the quantity supplied from Q_1 to Q_2. The producer surplus of these newcomers is the area of the triangle CEF.

As this analysis shows, we use producer surplus to measure the well-being of sellers in much the same way as we use consumer surplus to measure the well-being of buyers. Because these two measures of economic welfare are so similar, it is natural to use them together. And, indeed, that is exactly what we do in the next section.

QuickQuiz Draw a supply curve for turkey. In your diagram, show a price of turkey and the producer surplus that results from that price. Explain in words what this producer surplus measures.

MARKET EFFICIENCY

Consumer surplus and producer surplus are the basic tools that economists use to study the welfare of buyers and sellers in a market. These tools can help us address a fundamental economic question: Is the allocation of resources determined by free markets in any way desirable?

The Benevolent Social Planner

To evaluate market outcomes, we introduce into our analysis a new, hypothetical character, called the benevolent social planner. The benevolent social planner is an all-knowing, all-powerful, well-intentioned dictator. The planner wants to maximize the economic well-being of everyone in society. What do you suppose this planner should do? Should he just leave buyers and sellers at the equilibrium that they reach naturally on their own? Or can he increase economic well-being by altering the market outcome in some way?

To answer this question, the planner must first decide how to measure the economic well-being of a society. One possible measure is the sum of consumer and producer surplus, which we call *total surplus*. Consumer surplus is the benefit that buyers receive from participating in a market, and producer surplus is the benefit that sellers receive. It is therefore natural to use total surplus as a measure of society's economic well-being.

To better understand this measure of economic well-being, recall how we measure consumer and producer surplus. We define consumer surplus as

Consumer surplus = Value to buyers − Amount paid by buyers.

Similarly, we define producer surplus as

Producer surplus = Amount received by sellers − Cost to sellers.

When we add consumer and producer surplus together, we obtain

Total surplus = Value to buyers − Amount paid by buyers
+ Amount received by sellers − Cost to sellers.

The amount paid by buyers equals the amount received by sellers, so the middle two terms in this expression cancel each other. As a result, we can write total surplus as

Total surplus = Value to buyers − Cost to sellers.

Total surplus in a market is the total value to buyers of the goods, as measured by their willingness to pay, minus the total cost to sellers of providing those goods.

efficiency
the property of a resource allocation of maximizing the total surplus received by all members of society

If an allocation of resources maximizes total surplus, we say that the allocation exhibits **efficiency.** If an allocation is not efficient, then some of the gains from trade among buyers and sellers are not being realized. For example, an allocation is inefficient if a good is not being produced by the sellers with lowest cost. In this case, moving production from a high-cost producer to a low-cost producer will lower the total cost to sellers and raise total surplus. Similarly, an allocation is inefficient if a good is not being consumed by the buyers who value it most highly. In this case, moving consumption of the good from a buyer with a low valuation to a buyer with a high valuation will raise total surplus.

equity
the fairness of the distribution of well-being among the members of society

In addition to efficiency, the social planner might also care about **equity**—the fairness of the distribution of well-being among the various buyers and sellers. In essence, the gains from trade in a market are like a pie to be distributed among the market participants. The question of efficiency is whether the pie is as big as possible. The question of equity is whether the pie is divided fairly. Evaluating the equity of a market outcome is more difficult than evaluating the efficiency. Whereas efficiency is an objective goal that can be judged on strictly positive grounds, equity involves normative judgments that go beyond economics and enter into the realm of political philosophy.

In this chapter we concentrate on efficiency as the social planner's goal. Keep in mind, however, that real policymakers often care about equity as well. That is, they care about both the size of the economic pie and how the pie gets sliced and distributed among members of society.

Evaluating the Market Equilibrium

Figure 7 shows consumer and producer surplus when a market reaches the equilibrium of supply and demand. Recall that consumer surplus equals the area above the price and under the demand curve and producer surplus equals the area below the price and above the supply curve. Thus, the total area between the

FIGURE 7

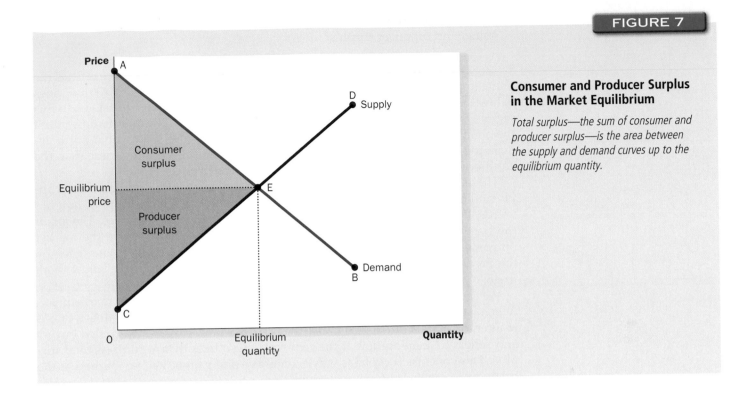

Consumer and Producer Surplus in the Market Equilibrium

Total surplus—the sum of consumer and producer surplus—is the area between the supply and demand curves up to the equilibrium quantity.

supply and demand curves up to the point of equilibrium represents the total surplus in this market.

Is this equilibrium allocation of resources efficient? Does it maximize total surplus? To answer these questions, keep in mind that when a market is in equilibrium, the price determines which buyers and sellers participate in the market. Those buyers who value the good more than the price (represented by the segment AE on the demand curve) choose to buy the good; those buyers who value it less than the price (represented by the segment EB) do not. Similarly, those sellers whose costs are less than the price (represented by the segment CE on the supply curve) choose to produce and sell the good; those sellers whose costs are greater than the price (represented by the segment ED) do not.

These observations lead to two insights about market outcomes:

1. Free markets allocate the supply of goods to the buyers who value them most highly, as measured by their willingness to pay.
2. Free markets allocate the demand for goods to the sellers who can produce them at least cost.

Thus, given the quantity produced and sold in a market equilibrium, the social planner cannot increase economic well-being by changing the allocation of consumption among buyers or the allocation of production among sellers.

But can the social planner raise total economic well-being by increasing or decreasing the quantity of the good? The answer is no, as stated in this third insight about market outcomes:

3. Free markets produce the quantity of goods that maximizes the sum of consumer and producer surplus.

To see why this is true, consider Figure 8. Recall that the demand curve reflects the value to buyers and that the supply curve reflects the cost to sellers. At quantities below the equilibrium level, the value to buyers exceeds the cost to sellers. In this region, increasing the quantity raises total surplus, and it continues to do so until the quantity reaches the equilibrium level. Beyond the equilibrium quantity, however, the value to buyers is less than the cost to sellers. Producing more than the equilibrium quantity would, therefore, lower total surplus.

These three insights about market outcomes tell us that the equilibrium of supply and demand maximizes the sum of consumer and producer surplus. In other words, the equilibrium outcome is an efficient allocation of resources. The job of the benevolent social planner is, therefore, very easy: He can leave the market outcome just as he finds it. This policy of leaving well enough alone goes by the French expression *laissez-faire*, which literally translated means "allow them to do."

We can now better appreciate Adam Smith's invisible hand of the marketplace, which we first discussed in Chapter 1. The benevolent social planner doesn't need to alter the market outcome because the invisible hand has already guided buyers and sellers to an allocation of the economy's resources that maximizes total surplus. This conclusion explains why economists often advocate free markets as the best way to organize economic activity.

FIGURE 8

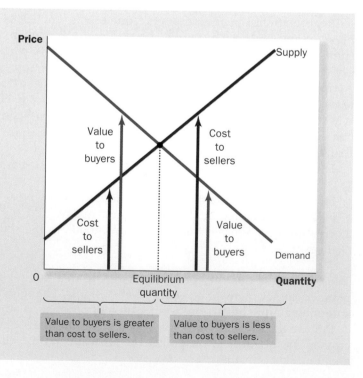

The Efficiency of the Equilibrium Quantity

At quantities less than the equilibrium quantity, the value to buyers exceeds the cost to sellers. At quantities greater than the equilibrium quantity, the cost to sellers exceeds the value to buyers. Therefore, the market equilibrium maximizes the sum of producer and consumer surplus.

IN THE NEWS

TICKET SCALPING

To allocate resources efficiently, an economy must get goods to the consumers who value them most highly. Sometimes this job falls to ticket scalpers.

Tickets? Supply Meets Demand on Sidewalk

By John Tierney

Ticket scalping has been very good to Kevin Thomas, and he makes no apologies. He sees himself as a classic American entrepreneur: a high school dropout from the Bronx who taught himself a trade, works seven nights a week, earns $40,000 a year, and at age twenty-six has $75,000 in savings, all by providing a public service outside New York's theaters and sports arenas.

He has just one complaint. "I've been busted about 30 times in the last year," he said one recent evening, just after making $280 at a Knicks game. "You learn to deal with it—I give the cops a fake name, and I pay the fines when I have to, but I don't think it's fair. I look at scalping like working as a stockbroker, buying low and selling high. If people are willing to pay me the money, what kind of problem is that?"

It is a significant problem to public officials in New York and New Jersey, who are cracking down on street scalpers like Mr. Thomas and on licensed ticket brokers. Undercover officers are enforcing new restrictions on reselling tickets at marked-up prices, and the attorneys general of the two states are pressing well-publicized cases against more than a dozen ticket brokers.

But economists tend to see scalping from Mr. Thomas's perspective. To them, the governments' crusade makes about as much sense as the old campaigns by Communist authorities against "profiteering." Economists argue that the restrictions inconvenience the public, reduce the audience for cultural and sports events, waste the police's time, deprive New York City of tens of millions of dollars of tax revenue, and actually drive up the cost of many tickets.

"It is always good politics to pose as defender of the poor by declaring high prices illegal," says William J. Baumol, the director of the C. V. Starr Center for Applied Economics at New York University. "I expect politicians to try to solve the AIDS crisis by declaring AIDS illegal as well. That would be harmless, because nothing would happen, but when you outlaw high prices you create real problems."

Dr. Baumol was one of the economists who came up with the idea of selling same-day Broadway tickets for half price at the TKTS booth in Times Square, which theater owners thought dangerously radical when the booth opened in 1973. But the owners have profited by finding a new clientele for tickets that would have gone unsold, an illustration of the free-market tenet that both buyers and sellers ultimately benefit when price is adjusted to meet demand.

Economists see another illustration of that lesson at the Museum of Modern Art, where people wait in line for up to two hours to buy tickets for the Matisse exhibit. But there is an alternative on the sidewalk: Scalpers who evade the police have been selling the $12.50 tickets to the show at prices ranging from $20 to $50.

The invisible hand at work

"You don't have to put a very high value on your time to pay $10 or $15 to avoid standing in line for two hours for a Matisse ticket," said Richard H. Thaler, an economist at Cornell University. "Some people think it's fairer to make everyone stand in line, but that forces everyone to engage in a totally unproductive activity, and it discriminates in favor of people who have the most free time. Scalping gives other people a chance, too. I can see no justification for outlawing it.". . .

Legalizing scalping, however, would not necessarily be good news for everyone. Mr. Thomas, for instance, fears that the extra competition might put him out of business. But after 16 years—he started at age ten outside of Yankee Stadium—he is thinking it might be time for a change anyway.

Source: *The New York Times,* December 26, 1992, p. A1. Copyright © 1992 by The New York Times Co. Reprinted by permission.

Case Study
SHOULD THERE BE A MARKET IN ORGANS?

On April 12, 2001, the front page of *The Boston Globe* ran the headline "How a Mother's Love Helped Save Two Lives." The newspaper told the story of Susan Stephens, a woman whose son needed a kidney transplant. When the doctor learned that the mother's kidney was not compatible, he proposed a novel solution: If Stephens donated one of her kidneys to a stranger, her son would move to the top of the kidney waiting list. The mother accepted the deal, and soon two patients had the transplant they were waiting for.

The ingenuity of the doctor's proposal and the nobility of the mother's act cannot be doubted. But the story raises many intriguing questions. If the mother could trade a kidney for a kidney, would the hospital allow her to trade a kidney for an expensive, experimental cancer treatment that she could not afford otherwise? Should she be allowed to exchange her kidney for free tuition for her son at the hospital's medical school? Should she be able to sell her kidney so she can use the cash to trade in her old Chevy for a new Lexus?

As a matter of public policy, people are not allowed to sell their organs. In essence, in the market for organs, the government has imposed a price ceiling of zero. The result, as with any binding price ceiling, is a shortage of the good. The deal in the Stephens case did not fall under this prohibition because no cash changed hands.

Many economists believe that there would be large benefits to allowing a free market in organs. People are born with two kidneys, but they usually need only one. Meanwhile, a few people suffer from illnesses that leave them without any working kidney. Despite the obvious gains from trade, the current situation is dire: The average wait for a kidney transplant is 3½ years, and about 6,000 Americans die every year because a kidney cannot be found. If those needing a kidney were allowed to buy one from those who have two, the price would rise to balance supply and demand. Sellers would be better off with the extra cash in their pockets. Buyers would be better off with the organ they need to save their lives. The shortage of kidneys would disappear.

Such a market would lead to an efficient allocation of resources, but critics of this plan worry about fairness. A market for organs, they argue, would benefit the rich at the expense of the poor, because organs would then be allocated to those most willing and able to pay. But you can also question the fairness of the current system. Now, most of us walk around with an extra organ that we don't really need, while some of our fellow citizens are dying to get one. Is that fair? ●

QuickQuiz Draw the supply and demand for turkey. In the equilibrium, show producer and consumer surplus. Explain why producing more turkey would lower total surplus.

IN THE NEWS

HOW PILGRIMS EMBRACED THE MARKET

The next time you sit down for Thanksgiving dinner, perhaps you should give thanks not only for the turkey on your plate but also for the economic system in which you live.

Thanksgiving Pays Homage to the Invisible Hand

By Caroline Baum

Most Americans think of Thanksgiving as a time to gather with friends and family and celebrate with a huge feast. If children know anything about the origins of the national holiday, declared each year by presidential proclamation, it's that the Pilgrims were grateful for a good harvest in their new land and set aside this day to give thanks.

What they don't know is that things weren't always so good for the Pilgrims, who came to the new world from England (via Holland) to escape religious persecution. Their first winters after they landed at Plymouth Rock in 1620 and established the Plymouth Bay colony were harsh. The weather was lousy and crop yields were poor. Half the Pilgrims died or returned to England.

Those who remained went hungry. Despite their deep religious convictions, the colonists took to stealing from one another. In the spring of 1623, following three grueling winters and widespread famine, Governor Bradford and the others "began to think how they might raise as much as they could, and obtain a better crop than they had done,

that they might not still thus languish in misery," Bradford relates in his history.

One of the traditions the Pilgrims brought with them from England was something called "farming in common." The colonists pooled the fruits of their labor, and the harvest was rationed among them.

The idea that "the taking away of property, and bringing them into common community was found to breed too much confusion and discontent, and retard much employment that would have been to their benefit and comfort."

Young and able men resented working hard for other men and their wives, without any compensation.

So after three winters of starvation, Bradford instituted a new policy when it came time to plant in the spring of 1623. He set aside a plot of land for each family, allowing each to "plant for his own particular, and in that regard trust to them selves."

For the colonists, the results were nothing short of miraculous. The women went willingly into the field, carrying their young children with them. Those who previously claimed to be too ill or weak to work were eager to till their own soil. . . .

Yet it was no miracle. Without knowing it, Bradford and the Pilgrims discov-

ered what Eastern Europe learned—the hard way—more than 350 years later: socialism doesn't work. Deprived of property rights and lacking economic incentives to work, produce and save, human beings behave in a predictable manner. . . .

Pretty soon, the colonists had more than enough food for their own needs and started to trade their excess corn for other commodities, such as furs.

After three winters of famine, the Pilgrims viewed their times of plenty as a stroke of good fortune when they were merely responding to market signals. Even before there was an official market, the invisible hand was at work.

Thanksgiving is a time to give thanks for our system of government, which allows the invisible hand to guide and protect us.

Source: Bloomberg News, (on-line at http://www.bloomberg.com), November 21, 2001. Reprinted with permission.

CONCLUSION: MARKET EFFICIENCY AND MARKET FAILURE

This chapter introduced the basic tools of welfare economics—consumer and producer surplus—and used them to evaluate the efficiency of free markets. We showed that the forces of supply and demand allocate resources efficiently. That is, even though each buyer and seller in a market is concerned only about his or her own welfare, they are together led by an invisible hand to an equilibrium that maximizes the total benefits to buyers and sellers.

A word of warning is in order. To conclude that markets are efficient, we made several assumptions about how markets work. When these assumptions do not hold, our conclusion that the market equilibrium is efficient may no longer be true. As we close this chapter, let's consider briefly two of the most important of these assumptions.

First, our analysis assumed that markets are perfectly competitive. In the world, however, competition is sometimes far from perfect. In some markets, a single buyer or seller (or a small group of them) may be able to control market prices. This ability to influence prices is called *market power*. Market power can cause markets to be inefficient because it keeps the price and quantity away from the equilibrium of supply and demand.

Second, our analysis assumed that the outcome in a market matters only to the buyers and sellers in that market. Yet, in the world, the decisions of buyers and sellers sometimes affect people who are not participants in the market at all. Pollution is the classic example of a market outcome that affects people not in the market. Such side effects, called *externalities*, cause welfare in a market to depend on more than just the value to the buyers and the cost to the sellers. Because buyers and sellers do not take these side effects into account when deciding how much to consume and produce, the equilibrium in a market can be inefficient from the standpoint of society as a whole.

Market power and externalities are examples of a general phenomenon called *market failure*—the inability of some unregulated markets to allocate resources efficiently. When markets fail, public policy can potentially remedy the problem and increase economic efficiency. Microeconomists devote much effort to studying when market failure is likely and what sorts of policies are best at correcting market failures. As you continue your study of economics, you will see that the tools of welfare economics developed here are readily adapted to that endeavor.

Despite the possibility of market failure, the invisible hand of the marketplace is extraordinarily important. In many markets, the assumptions we made in this chapter work well, and the conclusion of market efficiency applies directly. Moreover, our analysis of welfare economics and market efficiency can be used to shed light on the effects of various government policies. In the next two chapters we apply the tools we have just developed to study two important policy issues—the welfare effects of taxation and of international trade.

SUMMARY

- Consumer surplus equals buyers' willingness to pay for a good minus the amount they actually pay for it, and it measures the benefit buyers get from participating in a market. Consumer surplus can be computed by finding the area below the demand curve and above the price.

- Producer surplus equals the amount sellers receive for their goods minus their costs of production, and it measures the benefit sellers get from participating in a market. Producer surplus can be computed by finding the area below the price and above the supply curve.

- An allocation of resources that maximizes the sum of consumer and producer surplus is said to be efficient. Policymakers are often concerned with the efficiency, as well as the equity, of economic outcomes.

- The equilibrium of supply and demand maximizes the sum of consumer and producer surplus. That is, the invisible hand of the marketplace leads buyers and sellers to allocate resources efficiently.

- Markets do not allocate resources efficiently in the presence of market failures such as market power or externalities.

KEY CONCEPTS

welfare economics, p. 138
willingness to pay, p. 138
consumer surplus, p. 139

cost, p. 143
producer surplus, p. 144
efficiency, p. 148

equity, p. 148

QUESTIONS FOR REVIEW

1. Explain how buyers' willingness to pay, consumer surplus, and the demand curve are related.

2. Explain how sellers' costs, producer surplus, and the supply curve are related.

3. In a supply-and-demand diagram, show producer and consumer surplus in the market equilibrium.

4. What is efficiency? Is it the only goal of economic policymakers?

5. What does the invisible hand do?

6. Name two types of market failure. Explain why each may cause market outcomes to be inefficient.

PROBLEMS AND APPLICATIONS

1. An early freeze in California sours the lemon crop. What happens to consumer surplus in the market for lemons? What happens to consumer surplus in the market for lemonade? Illustrate your answers with diagrams.

2. Suppose the demand for French bread rises. What happens to producer surplus in the market for French bread? What happens to producer surplus in the market for flour? Illustrate your answer with diagrams.

3. It is a hot day, and Bert is thirsty. Here is the value he places on a bottle of water:

Value of first bottle	$7
Value of second bottle	5
Value of third bottle	3
Value of fourth bottle	1

   a. From this information, derive Bert's demand schedule. Graph his demand curve for bottled water.

   b. If the price of a bottle of water is $4, how many bottles does Bert buy? How much consumer surplus does Bert get from his purchases? Show Bert's consumer surplus in your graph.

   c. If the price falls to $2, how does quantity demanded change? How does Bert's consumer surplus change? Show these changes in your graph.

4. Ernie owns a water pump. Because pumping large amounts of water is harder than pumping small amounts, the cost of producing a bottle of water rises as he pumps more. Here is the cost he incurs to produce each bottle of water:

Cost of first bottle	$1
Cost of second bottle	3
Cost of third bottle	5
Cost of fourth bottle	7

   a. From this information, derive Ernie's supply schedule. Graph his supply curve for bottled water.

   b. If the price of a bottle of water is $4, how many bottles does Ernie produce and sell? How much producer surplus does Ernie get from these sales? Show Ernie's producer surplus in your graph.

   c. If the price rises to $6, how does quantity supplied change? How does Ernie's producer surplus change? Show these changes in your graph.

5. Consider a market in which Bert from Problem 3 is the buyer and Ernie from Problem 4 is the seller.

   a. Use Ernie's supply schedule and Bert's demand schedule to find the quantity supplied and quantity demanded at prices of $2, $4, and $6. Which of these prices brings supply and demand into equilibrium?

   b. What are consumer surplus, producer surplus, and total surplus in this equilibrium?

   c. If Ernie produced and Bert consumed one fewer bottle of water, what would happen to total surplus?

   d. If Ernie produced and Bert consumed one additional bottle of water, what would happen to total surplus?

6. The cost of producing stereo systems has fallen over the past several decades. Let's consider some implications of this fact.

   a. Use a supply-and-demand diagram to show the effect of falling production costs on the price and quantity of stereos sold.

   b. In your diagram, show what happens to consumer surplus and producer surplus.

   c. Suppose the supply of stereos is very elastic. Who benefits most from falling production costs—consumers or producers of stereos?

7. There are four consumers willing to pay the following amounts for haircuts:

Jerry: $7   Oprah: $2   Ricki: $8   Montel: $5

There are four haircutting businesses with the following costs:

Firm A: $3   Firm B: $6   Firm C: $4   Firm D: $2

Each firm has the capacity to produce only one haircut. For efficiency, how many haircuts should be given? Which businesses should cut hair, and which consumers should have their hair cut? How large is the maximum possible total surplus?

8. Suppose a technological advance reduces the cost of making computers.
   a. Use a supply-and-demand diagram to show what happens to price, quantity, consumer surplus, and producer surplus in the market for computers.
   b. Computers and adding machines are substitutes. Use a supply-and-demand diagram to show what happens to price, quantity, consumer surplus, and producer surplus in the market for adding machines. Should adding machine producers be happy or sad by the technological advance in computers?
   c. Computers and software are complements. Use a supply-and-demand diagram to show what happens to price, quantity, consumer surplus, and producer surplus in the market for software. Should software producers be happy or sad about the technological advance in computers?
   d. Does this analysis help explain why software producer Bill Gates is one of the world's richest men?

9. Consider how health insurance affects the quantity of health care services performed. Suppose that the typical medical procedure has a cost of $100, yet a person with health insurance pays only $20 out-of-pocket when she chooses to have an additional procedure performed. Her insurance company pays the remaining $80. (The insurance company will recoup the $80 through higher premiums for everybody, but the share paid by this individual is small.)

a. Draw the demand curve in the market for medical care. (In your diagram, the horizontal axis should represent the number of medical procedures.) Show the quantity of procedures demanded if each procedure has a price of $100.
   b. On your diagram, show the quantity of procedures demanded if consumers pay only $20 per procedure. If the cost of each procedure to society is truly $100, and if individuals have health insurance as just described, will the number of procedures performed maximize total surplus? Explain.
   c. Economists often blame the health insurance system for excessive use of medical care. Given your analysis, why might the use of care be viewed as "excessive"?
   d. What sort of policies might prevent this excessive use?

10. Many parts of California experienced a severe drought in the late 1980s and early 1990s.
   a. Use a diagram of the water market to show the effects of the drought on the equilibrium price and quantity of water.
   b. Many communities did not allow the price of water to change, however. What is the effect of this policy on the water market? Show on your diagram any surplus or shortage that arises.
   c. A 1991 op-ed piece in *The Wall Street Journal* stated that "all Los Angeles residents are required to cut their water usage by 10 percent as of March 1 and another 5 percent starting May 1, based on their 1986 consumption levels." The author criticized this policy on both efficiency and equity grounds, saying "not only does such a policy reward families who 'wasted' more water back in 1986, it does little to encourage consumers who could make more drastic reductions, [and] . . . punishes consumers who cannot so readily reduce their water use." In what way is the

Los Angeles system for allocating water inefficient? In what way does the system seem unfair?

d. Suppose instead that Los Angeles allowed the price of water to increase until the quantity demanded equaled the quantity supplied. Would the resulting allocation of water be more efficient? In your view, would it be more or less fair than the proportionate reductions in water use mentioned in the newspaper article? What could be done to make the market solution more fair?

http://   For more study tools, please visit http://mankiwXtra.swlearning.com.

APPLICATION: THE COSTS OF TAXATION

Taxes are often a source of heated political debate. In 1776 the anger of the American colonies over British taxes sparked the American Revolution. More than two centuries later Ronald Reagan was elected president on a platform of large cuts in personal income taxes, and during his eight years in the White House the top tax rate on income fell from 70 percent to 28 percent. In 1992 Bill Clinton was elected in part because incumbent George Bush had broken his 1988 campaign promise, "Read my lips: no new taxes." At least in this regard, the younger George Bush did not follow in his father's footsteps: As a candidate he promised a tax cut, and as president he made sure to deliver.

We began our study of taxes in Chapter 6. There we saw how a tax on a good affects its price and the quantity sold and how the forces of supply and demand divide the burden of a tax between buyers and sellers. In this chapter we extend this analysis and look at how taxes affect welfare, the economic well-being of participants in a market.

The effects of taxes on welfare might at first seem obvious. The government enacts taxes to raise revenue, and that revenue must come out of someone's pocket. As we saw in Chapter 6, both buyers and sellers are worse off when a good is

"You know, the idea of taxation with representation doesn't appeal to me very much, either."

taxed: A tax raises the price buyers pay and lowers the price sellers receive. Yet to understand fully how taxes affect economic well-being, we must compare the reduced welfare of buyers and sellers to the amount of revenue the government raises. The tools of consumer and producer surplus allow us to make this comparison. The analysis will show that the costs of taxes to buyers and sellers exceeds the revenue raised by the government.

THE DEADWEIGHT LOSS OF TAXATION

We begin by recalling one of the surprising lessons from Chapter 6: It does not matter whether a tax on a good is levied on buyers or sellers of the good. When a tax is levied on buyers, the demand curve shifts downward by the size of the tax; when it is levied on sellers, the supply curve shifts upward by that amount. In either case, when the tax is enacted, the price paid by buyers rises, and the price received by sellers falls. In the end, buyers and sellers share the burden of the tax, regardless of how it is levied.

Figure 1 shows these effects. To simplify our discussion, this figure does not show a shift in either the supply or demand curve, although one curve must shift. Which curve shifts depends on whether the tax is levied on sellers (the supply curve shifts) or buyers (the demand curve shifts). In this chapter, we can simplify the graphs by not bothering to show the shift. The key result for our purposes here is that the tax places a wedge between the price buyers pay and the price sellers receive. Because of this tax wedge, the quantity sold falls below the level that would be sold without a tax. In other words, a tax on a good causes the size of the market for the good to shrink. These results should be familiar from Chapter 6.

FIGURE 1

The Effects of a Tax

A tax on a good places a wedge between the price that buyers pay and the price that sellers receive. The quantity of the good sold falls.

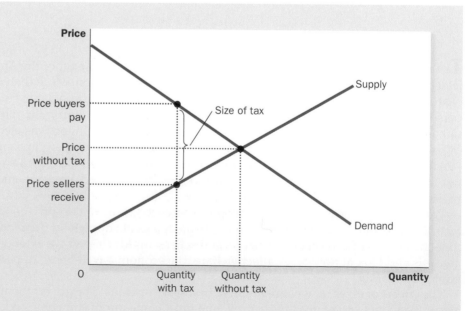

How a Tax Affects Market Participants

Now let's use the tools of welfare economics to measure the gains and losses from a tax on a good. To do this, we must take into account how the tax affects buyers, sellers, and the government. The benefit received by buyers in a market is measured by consumer surplus—the amount buyers are willing to pay for the good minus the amount they actually pay for it. The benefit received by sellers in a market is measured by producer surplus—the amount sellers receive for the good minus their costs. These are precisely the measures of economic welfare we used in Chapter 7.

What about the third interested party, the government? If T is the size of the tax and Q is the quantity of the good sold, then the government gets total tax revenue of $T \times Q$. It can use this tax revenue to provide services, such as roads, police, and public education, or to help the needy. Therefore, to analyze how taxes affect economic well-being, we use tax revenue to measure the government's benefit from the tax. Keep in mind, however, that this benefit actually accrues not to government but to those on whom the revenue is spent.

Figure 2 shows that the government's tax revenue is represented by the rectangle between the supply and demand curves. The height of this rectangle is the size of the tax, T, and the width of the rectangle is the quantity of the good sold, Q. Because a rectangle's area is its height times its width, this rectangle's area is $T \times Q$, which equals the tax revenue.

Welfare without a Tax To see how a tax affects welfare, we begin by considering welfare before the government has imposed a tax. Figure 3 (p. 162) shows the supply-and-demand diagram and marks the key areas with the letters A through F.

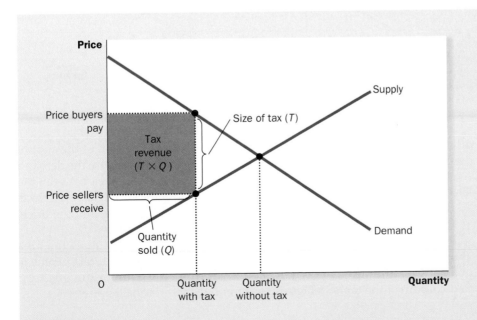

FIGURE 2

Tax Revenue

The tax revenue that the government collects equals T × Q, the size of the tax T times the quantity sold Q. Thus, tax revenue equals the area of the rectangle between the supply and demand curves.

FIGURE 3

How a Tax Affects Welfare

A tax on a good reduces consumer surplus (by the area B + C) and producer surplus (by the area D + E). Because the fall in producer and consumer surplus exceeds tax revenue (area B + D), the tax is said to impose a deadweight loss (area C + E).

	Without Tax	With Tax	Change
Consumer Surplus	A + B + C	A	−(B + C)
Producer Surplus	D + E + F	F	−(D + E)
Tax Revenue	None	B + D	+(B + D)
Total Surplus	A + B + C + D + E + F	A + B + D + F	−(C + E)

The area C + E shows the fall in total surplus and is the deadweight loss of the tax.

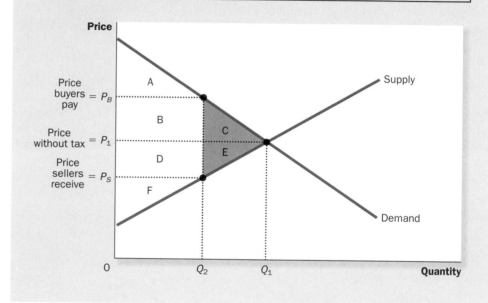

Without a tax, the price and quantity are found at the intersection of the supply and demand curves. The price is P_1, and the quantity sold is Q_1. Because the demand curve reflects buyers' willingness to pay, consumer surplus is the area between the demand curve and the price, A + B + C. Similarly, because the supply curve reflects sellers' costs, producer surplus is the area between the supply curve and the price, D + E + F. In this case, because there is no tax, tax revenue equals zero.

Total surplus—the sum of consumer and producer surplus—equals the area A + B + C + D + E + F. In other words, as we saw in Chapter 7, total surplus is the area between the supply and demand curves up to the equilibrium quantity. The first column of the table in Figure 3 summarizes these conclusions.

Welfare with a Tax Now consider welfare after the tax is enacted. The price paid by buyers rises from P_1 to P_B, so consumer surplus now equals only area A (the area below the demand curve and above the buyer's price). The price received by sellers falls from P_1 to P_S, so producer surplus now equals only area F (the area above the supply curve and below the seller's price). The quantity sold falls from Q_1 to Q_2, and the government collects tax revenue equal to the area B + D.

To compute total surplus with the tax, we add consumer surplus, producer surplus, and tax revenue. Thus, we find that total surplus is area A + B + D + F. The second column of the table provides a summary.

Changes in Welfare   We can now see the effects of the tax by comparing welfare before and after the tax is enacted. The third column in the table in Figure 3 shows the changes. The tax causes consumer surplus to fall by the area B + C and producer surplus to fall by the area D + E. Tax revenue rises by the area B + D. Not surprisingly, the tax makes buyers and sellers worse off and the government better off.

The change in total welfare includes the change in consumer surplus (which is negative), the change in producer surplus (which is also negative), and the change in tax revenue (which is positive). When we add these three pieces together, we find that total surplus in the market falls by the area C + E. *Thus, the losses to buyers and sellers from a tax exceed the revenue raised by the government.* The fall in total surplus that results when a tax (or some other policy) distorts a market outcome is called the **deadweight loss.** The area C + E measures the size of the deadweight loss.

To understand why taxes impose deadweight losses, recall one of the *Ten Principles of Economics* in Chapter 1: People respond to incentives. In Chapter 7 we saw that markets normally allocate scarce resources efficiently. That is, the equilibrium of supply and demand maximizes the total surplus of buyers and sellers in a market. When a tax raises the price to buyers and lowers the price to sellers, however, it gives buyers an incentive to consume less and sellers an incentive to produce less than they otherwise would. As buyers and sellers respond to these incentives, the size of the market shrinks below its optimum. Thus, because taxes distort incentives, they cause markets to allocate resources inefficiently.

deadweight loss
the fall in total surplus that results from a market distortion, such as a tax

Deadweight Losses and the Gains from Trade

To gain some intuition for why taxes result in deadweight losses, consider an example. Imagine that Joe cleans Jane's house each week for $100. The opportunity cost of Joe's time is $80, and the value of a clean house to Jane is $120. Thus, Joe and Jane each receive a $20 benefit from their deal. The total surplus of $40 measures the gains from trade in this particular transaction.

Now suppose that the government levies a $50 tax on the providers of cleaning services. There is now no price that Jane can pay Joe that will leave both of them better off after paying the tax. The most Jane would be willing to pay is $120, but then Joe would be left with only $70 after paying the tax, which is less than his $80 opportunity cost. Conversely, for Joe to receive his opportunity cost of $80, Jane would need to pay $130, which is above the $120 value she places on a clean house. As a result, Jane and Joe cancel their arrangement. Joe goes without the income, and Jane lives in a dirtier house.

The tax has made Joe and Jane worse off by a total of $40, because they have lost this amount of surplus. At the same time, the government collects no revenue from Joe and Jane because they decide to cancel their arrangement. The $40 is pure deadweight loss: It is a loss to buyers and sellers in a market not offset by an increase in government revenue. From this example, we can see the ultimate source of deadweight losses: *Taxes cause deadweight losses because they prevent buyers and sellers from realizing some of the gains from trade.*

The area of the triangle between the supply and demand curves (area C + E in Figure 3) measures these losses. This loss can be seen most easily in Figure 4 by recalling that the demand curve reflects the value of the good to consumers and that the supply curve reflects the costs of producers. When the tax raises the price to buyers to P_B and lowers the price to sellers to P_S, the marginal buyers and sellers leave the market, so the quantity sold falls from Q_1 to Q_2. Yet, as the figure shows, the value of the good to these buyers still exceeds the cost to these sellers. As in our example with Joe and Jane, the gains from trade—the difference between buyers' value and sellers' cost—is less than the tax. Thus, these trades do not get made once the tax is imposed. The deadweight loss is the surplus lost because the tax discourages these mutually advantageous trades.

QuickQuiz Draw the supply and demand curve for cookies. If the government imposes a tax on cookies, show what happens to the quantity sold, the price paid by buyers, and the price paid by sellers. In your diagram, show the deadweight loss from the tax. Explain the meaning of the deadweight loss.

THE DETERMINANTS OF THE DEADWEIGHT LOSS

What determines whether the deadweight loss from a tax is large or small? The answer is the price elasticities of supply and demand, which measure how much the quantity supplied and quantity demanded respond to changes in the price.

FIGURE 4

The Deadweight Loss

When the government imposes a tax on a good, the quantity sold falls from Q_1 to Q_2. As a result, some of the potential gains from trade among buyers and sellers do not get realized. These lost gains from trade create the deadweight loss.

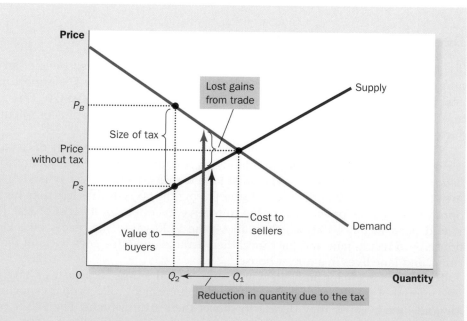

Let's consider first how the elasticity of supply affects the size of the dead-weight loss. In the top two panels of Figure 5, the demand curve and the size of the tax are the same. The only difference in these figures is the elasticity of the supply curve. In panel (a), the supply curve is relatively inelastic: Quantity supplied

FIGURE 5

Tax Distortions and Elasticities

In panels (a) and (b), the demand curve and the size of the tax are the same, but the price elasticity of supply is different. Notice that the more elastic the supply curve, the larger the deadweight loss of the tax. In panels (c) and (d), the supply curve and the size of the tax are the same, but the price elasticity of demand is different. Notice that the more elastic the demand curve, the larger the deadweight loss of the tax.

(a) Inelastic Supply

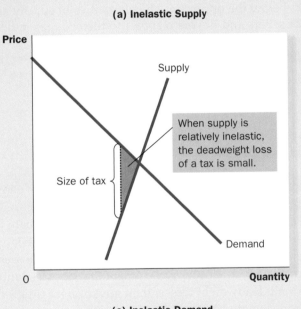

(b) Elastic Supply

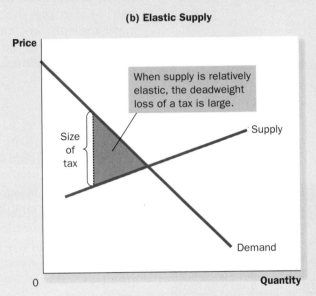

(c) Inelastic Demand

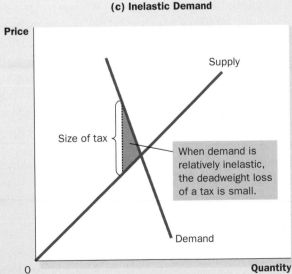

(d) Elastic Demand

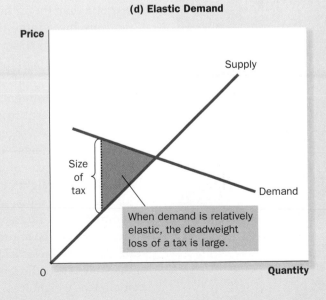

responds only slightly to changes in the price. In panel (b), the supply curve is relatively elastic: Quantity supplied responds substantially to changes in the price. Notice that the deadweight loss, the area of the triangle between the supply and demand curves, is larger when the supply curve is more elastic.

Similarly, the bottom two panels of Figure 5 show how the elasticity of demand affects the size of the deadweight loss. Here the supply curve and the size of the tax are held constant. In panel (c) the demand curve is relatively inelastic, and the deadweight loss is small. In panel (d) the demand curve is more elastic, and the deadweight loss from the tax is larger.

The lesson from this figure is easy to explain. A tax has a deadweight loss because it induces buyers and sellers to change their behavior. The tax raises the price paid by buyers, so they consume less. At the same time, the tax lowers the price received by sellers, so they produce less. Because of these changes in behavior, the size of the market shrinks below the optimum. The elasticities of supply and demand measure how much sellers and buyers respond to the changes in the price and, therefore, determine how much the tax distorts the market outcome. Hence, *the greater the elasticities of supply and demand, the greater the deadweight loss of a tax.*

Case Study

THE DEADWEIGHT LOSS DEBATE

Supply, demand, elasticity, deadweight loss—all this economic theory is enough to make your head spin. But believe it or not, these ideas go to the heart of a profound political question: How big should the government be? The debate hinges on these concepts because the larger the deadweight loss of taxation, the larger the cost of any government program. If taxation entails large deadweight losses, then these losses are a strong argument for a leaner government that does less and taxes less. But if taxes impose small deadweight losses, then government programs are less costly than they otherwise might be.

So how big are the deadweight losses of taxation? This is a question about which economists disagree. To see the nature of this disagreement, consider the most important tax in the U.S. economy—the tax on labor. The Social Security tax, the Medicare tax, and, to a large extent, the federal income tax are labor taxes. Many state governments also tax labor earnings. A labor tax places a wedge between the wage that firms pay and the wage that workers receive. If we add all forms of labor taxes together, the *marginal tax rate* on labor income—the tax on the last dollar of earnings—is almost 50 percent for many workers.

Although the size of the labor tax is easy to determine, the deadweight loss of this tax is less straightforward. Economists disagree about whether this 50 percent labor tax has a small or a large deadweight loss. This disagreement arises because economists hold different views about the elasticity of labor supply.

Economists who argue that labor taxes are not very distorting believe that labor supply is fairly inelastic. Most people, they claim, would work full-time regardless of the wage. If so, the labor supply curve is almost vertical, and a tax on labor has a small deadweight loss.

"Here's what I think about the elasticity of labor supply."

Economists who argue that labor taxes are highly distorting believe that labor supply is more elastic. They admit that some groups of workers may supply their labor inelastically but claim that many other groups respond more to incentives. Here are some examples:

- Many workers can adjust the number of hours they work—for instance, by working overtime. The higher the wage, the more hours they choose to work.
- Some families have second earners—often married women with children—with some discretion over whether to do unpaid work at home or paid work in the marketplace. When deciding whether to take a job, these second earners compare the benefits of being at home (including savings on the cost of child care) with the wages they could earn.
- Many of the elderly can choose when to retire, and their decisions are partly based on the wage. Once they are retired, the wage determines their incentive to work part-time.
- Some people consider engaging in illegal economic activity, such as the drug trade, or working at jobs that pay "under the table" to evade taxes. Economists call this the *underground economy*. In deciding whether to work in the underground economy or at a legitimate job, these potential criminals compare what they can earn by breaking the law with the wage they can earn legally.

In each of these cases, the quantity of labor supplied responds to the wage (the price of labor). Thus, the decisions of these workers are distorted when their labor earnings are taxed. Labor taxes encourage workers to work fewer hours, second earners to stay at home, the elderly to retire early, and the unscrupulous to enter the underground economy.

These two views of labor taxation persist to this day. Indeed, whenever you see two political candidates debating whether the government should provide more services or reduce the tax burden, keep in mind that part of the disagreement may rest on different views about the elasticity of labor supply and the deadweight loss of taxation. ●

QuickQuiz The demand for beer is more elastic than the demand for milk. Would a tax on beer or a tax on milk have larger deadweight loss? Why?

DEADWEIGHT LOSS AND TAX REVENUE AS TAXES VARY

Taxes rarely stay the same for long periods of time. Policymakers in local, state, and federal governments are always considering raising one tax or lowering another. Here we consider what happens to the deadweight loss and tax revenue when the size of a tax changes.

HENRY GEORGE AND THE LAND TAX

Is there an ideal tax? Henry George, the nineteenth-century American economist and social philosopher, thought so. In his 1879 book *Progress and Poverty*, George argued that the government should raise all its revenue from a tax on land. This "single tax" was, he claimed, both equitable and efficient. George's ideas won him a large political following, and in 1886 he lost a close race for mayor of New York City (although he finished well ahead of Republican candidate Theodore Roosevelt).

George's proposal to tax land was motivated largely by a concern over the distribution of economic well-being. He deplored the "shocking contrast between monstrous wealth and debasing want" and thought landowners benefited more than they should from the rapid growth in the overall economy.

George's arguments for the land tax can be understood using the tools of modern economics. Consider first supply and demand in the market for renting land. As immigration causes the population to rise and technological progress causes incomes to grow, the demand for land rises over time. Yet because the amount of land is fixed, the supply is perfectly inelastic. Rapid increases in demand together with inelastic supply lead to large increases in the equilibrium rents on land, so that economic growth makes rich landowners even richer.

Henry George

Now consider the incidence of a tax on land. As we first saw in Chapter 6, the burden of a tax falls more heavily on the side of the market that is less elastic. A tax on land takes this principle to an extreme. Because the elasticity of supply is zero, the landowners bear the entire burden of the tax.

Consider next the question of efficiency. As we just discussed, the deadweight loss of a tax depends on the elasticities of supply and demand. Again, a tax on land is an extreme case. Because supply is perfectly inelastic, a tax on land does not alter the market allocation. There is no deadweight loss, and the government's tax revenue exactly equals the loss of the landowners.

Although taxing land may look attractive in theory, it is not as straightforward in practice as it may appear. For a tax on land not to distort economic incentives, it must be a tax on raw land. Yet the value of land often comes from improvements, such as clearing trees, providing sewers, and building roads. Unlike the supply of raw land, the supply of improvements has an elasticity greater than zero. If a land tax were imposed on improvements, it would distort incentives. Landowners would respond by devoting fewer resources to improving their land.

Today, few economists support George's proposal for a single tax on land. Not only is taxing improvements a potential problem, but the tax would not raise enough revenue to pay for the much larger government we have today. Yet many of George's arguments remain valid. Here is the assessment of the eminent economist Milton Friedman a century after George's book:

"In my opinion, the least bad tax is the property tax on the unimproved value of land, the Henry George argument of many, many years ago."

Figure 6 shows the effects of a small, medium, and large tax, holding constant the market's supply and demand curves. The deadweight loss—the reduction in total surplus that results when the tax reduces the size of a market below the optimum—equals the area of the triangle between the supply and demand curves. For the small tax in panel (a), the area of the deadweight loss triangle is quite small. But as the size of a tax rises in panels (b) and (c), the deadweight loss grows larger and larger.

Indeed, the deadweight loss of a tax rises even more rapidly than the size of the tax. The reason is that the deadweight loss is an area of a triangle, and an area of a triangle depends on the *square* of its size. If we double the size of a tax, for instance, the base and height of the triangle double, so the deadweight loss rises by a factor of 4. If we triple the size of a tax, the base and height triple, so the deadweight loss rises by a factor of 9.

FIGURE 6

Deadweight Loss and Tax Revenue from Three Taxes of Different Size

The deadweight loss is the reduction in total surplus due to the tax. Tax revenue is the amount of the tax times the amount of the good sold. In panel (a), a small tax has a small deadweight loss and raises a small amount of revenue. In panel (b), a somewhat larger tax has a larger deadweight loss and raises a larger amount of revenue. In panel (c), a very large tax has a very large deadweight loss, but because it has reduced the size of the market so much, the tax raises only a small amount of revenue.

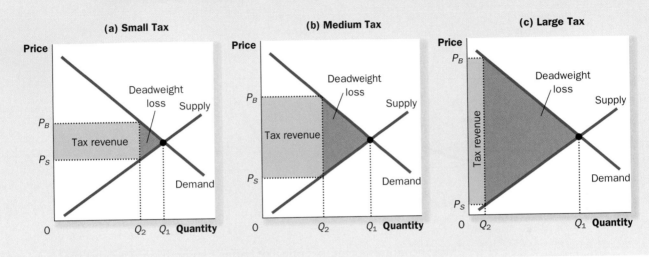

The government's tax revenue is the size of the tax times the amount of the good sold. As Figure 6 shows, tax revenue equals the area of the rectangle between the supply and demand curves. For the small tax in panel (a), tax revenue is small. As the size of a tax rises from panel (a) to panel (b), tax revenue grows. But as the size of the tax rises further from panel (b) to panel (c), tax revenue falls because the higher tax drastically reduces the size of the market. For a very large tax, no revenue would be raised, because people would stop buying and selling the good altogether.

Figure 7 (p. 170) summarizes these results. In panel (a) we see that as the size of a tax increases, its deadweight loss quickly gets larger. By contrast, panel (b) shows that tax revenue first rises with the size of the tax; but then, as the tax gets larger, the market shrinks so much that tax revenue starts to fall.

Case Study

THE LAFFER CURVE AND SUPPLY-SIDE ECONOMICS

One day in 1974, economist Arthur Laffer sat in a Washington restaurant with some prominent journalists and politicians. He took out a napkin and drew a figure on it to show how tax rates affect tax revenue. It looked much like panel (b) of our Figure 7. Laffer then suggested that the United States was on the downward-sloping side of this curve. Tax rates were so high, he argued, that reducing them would actually raise tax revenue.

FIGURE 7

How Deadweight Loss and Tax Revenue Vary with the Size of a Tax

Panel (a) shows that as the size of a tax grows larger, the deadweight loss grows larger. Panel (b) shows that tax revenue first rises, then falls. This relationship is sometimes called the Laffer curve.

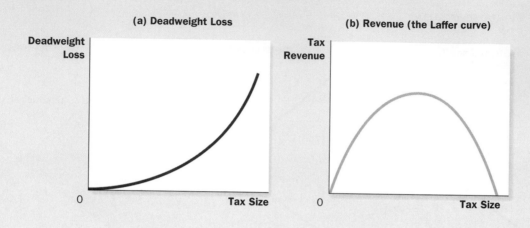

Most economists were skeptical of Laffer's suggestion. The idea that a cut in tax rates could raise tax revenue was correct as a matter of economic theory, but there was more doubt about whether it would do so in practice. There was little evidence for Laffer's view that U.S. tax rates had in fact reached such extreme levels.

Nonetheless, the *Laffer curve* (as it became known) captured the imagination of Ronald Reagan. David Stockman, budget director in the first Reagan administration, offers the following story:

> [Reagan] had once been on the Laffer curve himself. "I came into the Big Money making pictures during World War II," he would always say. At that time the wartime income surtax hit 90 percent. "You could only make four pictures and then you were in the top bracket," he would continue. "So we all quit working after four pictures and went off to the country." High tax rates caused less work. Low tax rates caused more. His experience proved it.

When Reagan ran for president in 1980, he made cutting taxes part of his platform. Reagan argued that taxes were so high that they were discouraging hard work. He argued that lower taxes would give people the proper incentive to work, which would raise economic well-being and perhaps even tax revenue. Because the cut in tax rates was intended to encourage people to increase the quantity of labor they supplied, the views of Laffer and Reagan became known as *supply-side economics.*

Subsequent history failed to confirm Laffer's conjecture that lower tax rates would raise tax revenue. When Reagan cut taxes after he was elected, the result was less tax revenue, not more. Revenue from personal income taxes (per person, adjusted for inflation) fell by 9 percent from 1980 to 1984, even though average income (per person, adjusted for inflation) grew by 4 percent over this period. The tax cut, together with policymakers' unwillingness to restrain spending, began a long period during which the government spent more than it collected in taxes. Throughout Reagan's two terms in office, and for many years thereafter, the government ran large budget deficits.

Yet Laffer's argument is not completely without merit. Although an overall cut in tax rates normally reduces revenue, some taxpayers at some times may be on the wrong side of the Laffer curve. In the 1980s, tax revenue collected from the richest Americans, who face the highest tax rates, did rise when their taxes were cut. The idea that cutting taxes can raise revenue may be correct if applied to those taxpayers facing the highest tax rates. In addition, Laffer's argument may be more plausible when applied to other countries, where tax rates are much higher than in the United States. In Sweden in the early 1980s, for instance, the typical worker faced a marginal tax rate of about 80 percent. Such a high tax rate provides a substantial disincentive to work. Studies have suggested that Sweden would indeed have raised more tax revenue if it had lowered its tax rates.

These ideas arise frequently in political debate. When Bill Clinton moved into the White House in 1993, he increased the federal income tax rates on high-income taxpayers to about 40 percent. Some economists criticized the policy, arguing that the plan would not yield as much revenue as the Clinton administration estimated. They claimed that the administration did not fully take into account how taxes alter behavior. Conversely, when Bob Dole challenged Bill Clinton in the election of 1996, Dole proposed cutting personal income taxes. Although Dole rejected the idea that tax cuts would completely pay for themselves, he did claim that 28 percent of the tax cut would be recouped because lower tax rates would lead to more rapid economic growth. Economists debated whether Dole's 28 percent projection was reasonable, excessively optimistic, or (as Laffer might suggest) excessively pessimistic.

Policymakers disagree about these issues in part because they disagree about the size of the relevant elasticities. The more elastic that supply and demand are in any market, the more taxes in that market distort behavior, and the more likely it is that a tax cut will raise tax revenue. There is no debate, however, about the general lesson: How much revenue the government gains or loses from a tax change cannot be computed just by looking at tax rates. It also depends on how the tax change affects people's behavior. ●

QuickQuiz If the government doubles the tax on gasoline, can you be sure that revenue from the gasoline tax will rise? Can you be sure that the deadweight loss from the gasoline tax will rise? Explain.

CONCLUSION

Taxes, Oliver Wendell Holmes once said, are the price we pay for a civilized society. Indeed, our society cannot exist without some form of taxes. We all expect the government to provide us certain services, such as roads, parks, police, and national defense. These public services require tax revenue.

This chapter has shed some light on how high the price of civilized society can be. One of the *Ten Principles of Economics* discussed in Chapter 1 is that markets are usually a good way to organize economic activity. When the government imposes taxes on buyers or sellers of a good, however, society loses some of the benefits of market efficiency. Taxes are costly to market participants not only because taxes transfer resources from those participants to the government, but also because they alter incentives and distort market outcomes.

SUMMARY

- A tax on a good reduces the welfare of buyers and sellers of the good, and the reduction in consumer and producer surplus usually exceeds the revenue raised by the government. The fall in total surplus—the sum of consumer surplus, producer surplus, and tax revenue—is called the deadweight loss of the tax.

- Taxes have deadweight losses because they cause buyers to consume less and sellers to produce less, and this change in behavior shrinks the size

of the market below the level that maximizes total surplus. Because the elasticities of supply and demand measure how much market participants respond to market conditions, larger elasticities imply larger deadweight losses.

- As a tax grows larger, it distorts incentives more, and its deadweight loss grows larger. Tax revenue first rises with the size of a tax. Eventually, however, a larger tax reduces tax revenue because it reduces the size of the market.

KEY CONCEPTS

deadweight loss, p. 163

QUESTIONS FOR REVIEW

1. What happens to consumer and producer surplus when the sale of a good is taxed? How does the change in consumer and producer surplus compare to the tax revenue? Explain.

2. Draw a supply-and-demand diagram with a tax on the sale of the good. Show the deadweight loss. Show the tax revenue.

3. How do the elasticities of supply and demand affect the deadweight loss of a tax? Why do they have this effect?

4. Why do experts disagree about whether labor taxes have small or large deadweight losses?

5. What happens to the deadweight loss and tax revenue when a tax is increased?

PROBLEMS AND APPLICATIONS

1. The market for pizza is characterized by a downward-sloping demand curve and an upward-sloping supply curve.
   a. Draw the competitive market equilibrium. Label the price, quantity, consumer surplus, and producer surplus. Is there any deadweight loss? Explain.
   b. Suppose that the government forces each pizzeria to pay a $1 tax on each pizza sold. Illustrate the effect of this tax on the pizza market, being sure to label the consumer

surplus, producer surplus, government revenue, and deadweight loss. How does each area compare to the pre-tax case?

   c. If the tax were removed, pizza eaters and sellers would be better off, but the government would lose tax revenue. Suppose that consumers and producers voluntarily transferred some of their gains to the government. Could all parties (including the government) be better off than they were with a tax? Explain using the labeled areas in your graph.

2. Evaluate the following two statements. Do you agree? Why or why not?
   a. "If the government taxes land, wealthy landowners will pass the tax on to their poorer renters."
   b. "If the government taxes apartment buildings, wealthy landlords will pass the tax on to their poorer renters."

3. Evaluate the following two statements. Do you agree? Why or why not?
   a. "A tax that has no deadweight loss cannot raise any revenue for the government."
   b. "A tax that raises no revenue for the government cannot have any deadweight loss."

4. Consider the market for rubber bands.
   a. If this market has very elastic supply and very inelastic demand, how would the burden of a tax on rubber bands be shared between consumers and producers? Use the tools of consumer surplus and producer surplus in your answer.
   b. If this market has very inelastic supply and very elastic demand, how would the burden of a tax on rubber bands be shared between consumers and producers? Contrast your answer with your answer to part (a).

5. Suppose that the government imposes a tax on heating oil.
   a. Would the deadweight loss from this tax likely be greater in the first year after it is imposed or in the fifth year? Explain.
   b. Would the revenue collected from this tax likely be greater in the first year after it is imposed or in the fifth year? Explain.

6. After economics class one day, your friend suggests that taxing food would be a good way to raise revenue because the demand for food is quite inelastic. In what sense is taxing food a "good" way to raise revenue? In what sense is it not a "good" way to raise revenue?

7. Senator Daniel Patrick Moynihan once introduced a bill that would levy a 10,000 percent tax on certain hollow-tipped bullets.
   a. Do you expect that this tax would raise much revenue? Why or why not?

   b. Even if the tax would raise no revenue, what might be Senator Moynihan's reason for proposing it?

8. The government places a tax on the purchase of socks.
   a. Illustrate the effect of this tax on equilibrium price and quantity in the sock market. Identify the following areas both before and after the imposition of the tax: total spending by consumers, total revenue for producers, and government tax revenue.
   b. Does the price received by producers rise or fall? Can you tell whether total receipts for producers rise or fall? Explain.
   c. Does the price paid by consumers rise or fall? Can you tell whether total spending by consumers rises or falls? Explain carefully. (Hint: Think about elasticity.) If total consumer spending falls, does consumer surplus rise? Explain.

9. Suppose the government currently raises $100 million through a $0.01 tax on widgets, and another $100 million through a $0.10 tax on gadgets. If the government doubled the tax rate on widgets and eliminated the tax on gadgets, would it raise more money than today, less money, or the same amount of money? Explain.

10. Most states tax the purchase of new cars. Suppose that New Jersey currently requires car dealers to pay the state $100 for each car sold, and plans to increase the tax to $150 per car next year.
    a. Illustrate the effect of this tax increase on the quantity of cars sold in New Jersey, the price paid by consumers, and the price received by producers.
    b. Create a table that shows the levels of consumer surplus, producer surplus, government revenue, and total surplus both before and after the tax increase.
    c. What is the change in government revenue? Is it positive or negative?
    d. What is the change in deadweight loss? Is it positive or negative?
    e. Give one reason why the demand for cars in New Jersey might be fairly elastic. Does this make the additional tax more or less likely to increase government revenue? How might states try to reduce the elasticity of demand?

11. Several years ago the British government imposed a "poll tax" that required each person to pay a flat amount to the government independent of his or her income or wealth. What is the effect of such a tax on economic efficiency? What is the effect on economic equity? Do you think this was a popular tax?

12. This chapter analyzed the welfare effects of a tax on a good. Consider now the opposite policy. Suppose that the government *subsidizes* a good: For each unit of the good sold, the government pays $2 to the buyer. How does the subsidy affect consumer surplus, producer surplus, tax revenue, and total surplus? Does a subsidy lead to a deadweight loss? Explain.

13. (This problem uses some high school algebra and is challenging.) Suppose that a market is described by the following supply and demand equations:

$$Q^S = 2P$$

$$Q^D = 300 - P$$

a. Solve for the equilibrium price and the equilibrium quantity.

b. Suppose that a tax of T is placed on buyers, so the new demand equation is

$$Q^D = 300 - (P + T).$$

Solve for the new equilibrium. What happens to the price received by sellers, the price paid by buyers, and the quantity sold?

c. Tax revenue is $T \times Q$. Use your answer to part (b) to solve for tax revenue as a function of T. Graph this relationship for T between 0 and 300.

d. The deadweight loss of a tax is the area of the triangle between the supply and demand curves. Recalling that the area of a triangle is $1/2 \times$ base $\times$ height, solve for deadweight loss as a function of T. Graph this relationship for T between 0 and 300. (Hint: Looking sideways, the base of the deadweight loss triangle is T, and the height is the difference between the quantity sold with the tax and the quantity sold without the tax.)

e. The government now levies a tax on this good of $200 per unit. Is this a good policy? Why or why not? Can you propose a better policy?

http://   For more study tools, please visit http://mankiwXtra.swlearning.com.

APPLICATION: INTERNATIONAL TRADE

If you check the labels on the clothes you are now wearing, you will probably find that some of your clothes were made in another country. A century ago the textiles and clothing industry was a major part of the U.S. economy, but that is no longer the case. Faced with foreign competitors that could produce quality goods at low cost, many U.S. firms found it increasingly difficult to produce and sell textiles and clothing at a profit. As a result, they laid off their workers and shut down their factories. Today, much of the textiles and clothing that Americans consume is imported from abroad.

The story of the textiles industry raises important questions for economic policy: How does international trade affect economic well-being? Who gains and who loses from free trade among countries, and how do the gains compare to the losses?

Chapter 3 introduced the study of international trade by applying the principle of comparative advantage. According to this principle, all countries can benefit from trading with one another because trade allows each country to specialize in doing what it does best. But the analysis in Chapter 3 was incomplete. It did not explain how the international marketplace achieves these gains from trade or how the gains are distributed among various economic actors.

We now return to the study of international trade and take up these questions. Over the past several chapters, we have developed many tools for analyzing how markets work: supply, demand, equilibrium, consumer surplus, producer surplus, and so on. With these tools we can learn more about the effects of international trade on economic well-being.

THE DETERMINANTS OF TRADE

Consider the market for steel. The steel market is well suited to examining the gains and losses from international trade: Steel is made in many countries around the world, and there is much world trade in steel. Moreover, the steel market is one in which policymakers often consider (and sometimes implement) trade restrictions to protect domestic steel producers from foreign competitors. We examine here the steel market in the imaginary country of Isoland.

The Equilibrium without Trade

As our story begins, the Isolandian steel market is isolated from the rest of the world. By government decree, no one in Isoland is allowed to import or export steel, and the penalty for violating the decree is so large that no one dares try.

Because there is no international trade, the market for steel in Isoland consists solely of Isolandian buyers and sellers. As Figure 1 shows, the domestic price adjusts to balance the quantity supplied by domestic sellers and the quantity

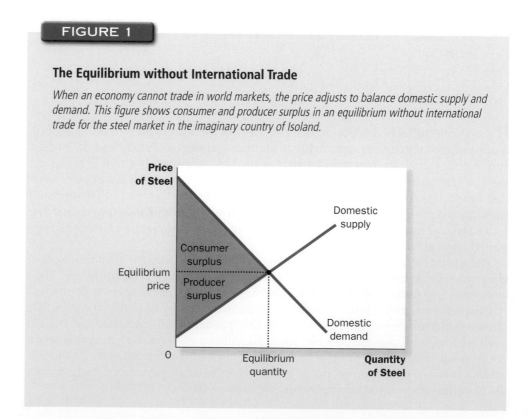

FIGURE 1

The Equilibrium without International Trade

When an economy cannot trade in world markets, the price adjusts to balance domestic supply and demand. This figure shows consumer and producer surplus in an equilibrium without international trade for the steel market in the imaginary country of Isoland.

demanded by domestic buyers. The figure shows the consumer and producer surplus in the equilibrium without trade. The sum of consumer and producer surplus measures the total benefits that buyers and sellers receive from the steel market.

Now suppose that, in an election upset, Isoland elects a new president. The president campaigned on a platform of "change" and promised the voters bold new ideas. Her first act is to assemble a team of economists to evaluate Isolandian trade policy. She asks them to report back on three questions:

- If the government allowed Isolandians to import and export steel, what would happen to the price of steel and the quantity of steel sold in the domestic steel market?
- Who would gain from free trade in steel and who would lose, and would the gains exceed the losses?
- Should a tariff (a tax on steel imports) or an import quota (a limit on steel imports) be part of the new trade policy?

After reviewing supply and demand in their favorite textbook (this one, of course), the Isolandian economics team begins its analysis.

The World Price and Comparative Advantage

The first issue our economists take up is whether Isoland is likely to become a steel importer or a steel exporter. In other words, if free trade were allowed, would Isolandians end up buying or selling steel in world markets?

To answer this question, the economists compare the current Isolandian price of steel to the price of steel in other countries. We call the price prevailing in world markets the **world price.** If the world price of steel is higher than the domestic price, then Isoland would become an exporter of steel once trade is permitted. Isolandian steel producers would be eager to receive the higher prices available abroad and would start selling their steel to buyers in other countries. Conversely, if the world price of steel is lower than the domestic price, then Isoland would become an importer of steel. Because foreign sellers offer a better price, Isolandian steel consumers would quickly start buying steel from other countries.

In essence, comparing the world price and the domestic price before trade indicates whether Isoland has a comparative advantage in producing steel. The domestic price reflects the opportunity cost of steel: It tells us how much an Isolandian must give up to get one unit of steel. If the domestic price is low, the cost of producing steel in Isoland is low, suggesting that Isoland has a comparative advantage in producing steel relative to the rest of the world. If the domestic price is high, then the cost of producing steel in Isoland is high, suggesting that foreign countries have a comparative advantage in producing steel.

As we saw in Chapter 3, trade among nations is ultimately based on comparative advantage. That is, trade is beneficial because it allows each nation to specialize in doing what it does best. By comparing the world price and the domestic price before trade, we can determine whether Isoland is better or worse at producing steel than the rest of the world.

world price
the price of a good that prevails in the world market for that good

QuickQuiz The country Autarka does not allow international trade. In Autarka, you can buy a wool suit for 3 ounces of gold. Meanwhile, in neighboring countries, you can buy the same suit for 2 ounces of gold. If Autarka were to allow free trade, would it import or export suits?

THE WINNERS AND LOSERS FROM TRADE

To analyze the welfare effects of free trade, the Isolandian economists begin with the assumption that Isoland is a small economy compared to the rest of the world so that its actions have a negligible effect on world markets. The small-economy assumption has a specific implication for analyzing the steel market: If Isoland is a small economy, then the change in Isoland's trade policy will not affect the world price of steel. The Isolandians are said to be *price takers* in the world economy. That is, they take the world price of steel as given. They can sell steel at this price and be exporters or buy steel at this price and be importers.

The small-economy assumption is not necessary to analyze the gains and losses from international trade. But the Isolandian economists know from experience that this assumption greatly simplifies the analysis. They also know that the basic lessons do not change in the more complicated case of a large economy.

The Gains and Losses of an Exporting Country

Figure 2 shows the Isolandian steel market when the domestic equilibrium price before trade is below the world price. Once free trade is allowed, the domestic price rises to equal the world price. No seller of steel would accept less than the world price, and no buyer would pay more than the world price.

With the domestic price now equal to the world price, the domestic quantity supplied differs from the domestic quantity demanded. The supply curve shows the quantity of steel supplied by Isolandian sellers. The demand curve shows the

FIGURE 2

International Trade in an Exporting Country

Once trade is allowed, the domestic price rises to equal the world price. The supply curve shows the quantity of steel produced domestically, and the demand curve shows the quantity consumed domestically. Exports from Isoland equal the difference between the domestic quantity supplied and the domestic quantity demanded at the world price.

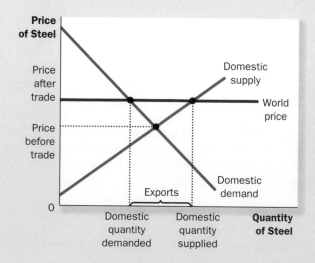

quantity of steel demanded by Isolandian buyers. Because the domestic quantity supplied is greater than the domestic quantity demanded, Isoland sells steel to other countries. Thus, Isoland becomes a steel exporter.

Although domestic quantity supplied and domestic quantity demanded differ, the steel market is still in equilibrium because there is now another participant in the market: the rest of the world. One can view the horizontal line at the world price as representing the demand for steel from the rest of the world. This demand curve is perfectly elastic because Isoland, as a small economy, can sell as much steel as it wants at the world price.

Now consider the gains and losses from opening up trade. Clearly, not everyone benefits. Trade forces the domestic price to rise to the world price. Domestic producers of steel are better off because they can now sell steel at a higher price, but domestic consumers of steel are worse off because they have to buy steel at a higher price.

To measure these gains and losses, we look at the changes in consumer and producer surplus, which are shown in the graph and table in Figure 3. Before trade is allowed, the price of steel adjusts to balance domestic supply and domestic demand. Consumer surplus, the area between the demand curve and the before-trade

FIGURE 3

How Free Trade Affects Welfare in an Exporting Country

When the domestic price rises to equal the world price, sellers are better off (producer surplus rises from C to B + C + D), and buyers are worse off (consumer surplus falls from A + B to A). Total surplus rises by an amount equal to area D, indicating that trade raises the economic well-being of the country as a whole.

	Before Trade	After Trade	Change
Consumer Surplus	A + B	A	−B
Producer Surplus	C	B + C + D	+(B + D)
Total Surplus	A + B + C	A + B + C + D	+D

The area D shows the increase in total surplus and represents the gains from trade.

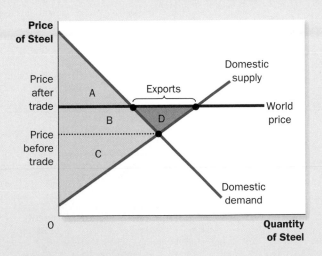

price, is area A + B. Producer surplus, the area between the supply curve and the before-trade price, is area C. Total surplus before trade, the sum of consumer and producer surplus, is area A + B + C.

After trade is allowed, the domestic price rises to the world price. Consumer surplus is area A (the area between the demand curve and the world price). Producer surplus is area B + C + D (the area between the supply curve and the world price). Thus, total surplus with trade is area A + B + C + D.

These welfare calculations show who wins and who loses from trade in an exporting country. Sellers benefit because producer surplus increases by the area B + D. Buyers are worse off because consumer surplus decreases by the area B. Because the gains of sellers exceed the losses of buyers by the area D, total surplus in Isoland increases.

This analysis of an exporting country yields two conclusions:

- When a country allows trade and becomes an exporter of a good, domestic producers of the good are better off, and domestic consumers of the good are worse off.
- Trade raises the economic well-being of a nation in the sense that the gains of the winners exceed the losses of the losers.

The Gains and Losses of an Importing Country

Now suppose that the domestic price before trade is above the world price. Once again, after free trade is allowed, the domestic price must equal the world price. As Figure 4 shows, the domestic quantity supplied is less than the domestic quantity

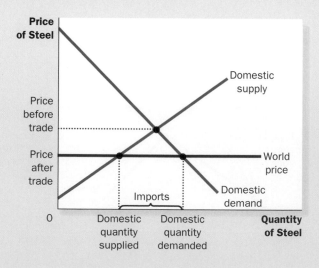

FIGURE 4

International Trade in an Importing Country

Once trade is allowed, the domestic price falls to equal the world price. The supply curve shows the amount produced domestically, and the demand curve shows the amount consumed domestically. Imports equal the difference between the domestic quantity demanded and the domestic quantity supplied at the world price.

demanded. The difference between the domestic quantity demanded and the domestic quantity supplied is bought from other countries, and Isoland becomes a steel importer.

In this case, the horizontal line at the world price represents the supply of the rest of the world. This supply curve is perfectly elastic because Isoland is a small economy and, therefore, can buy as much steel as it wants at the world price.

Now consider the gains and losses from trade. Once again, not everyone benefits. When trade forces the domestic price to fall, domestic consumers are better off (they can now buy steel at a lower price), and domestic producers are worse off (they now have to sell steel at a lower price). Changes in consumer and producer surplus measure the size of the gains and losses, as shown in the graph and table in Figure 5. Before trade, consumer surplus is area A, producer surplus is area B + C, and total surplus is area A + B + C. After trade is allowed, consumer surplus is area A + B + D, producer surplus is area C, and total surplus is area A + B + C + D.

These welfare calculations show who wins and who loses from trade in an importing country. Buyers benefit because consumer surplus increases by the

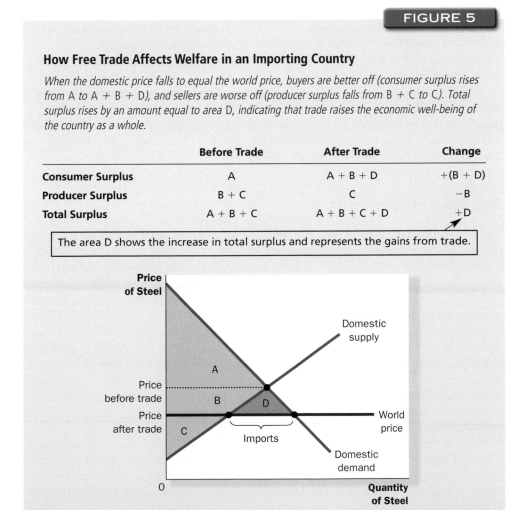

FIGURE 5

How Free Trade Affects Welfare in an Importing Country

When the domestic price falls to equal the world price, buyers are better off (consumer surplus rises from A to A + B + D), and sellers are worse off (producer surplus falls from B + C to C). Total surplus rises by an amount equal to area D, indicating that trade raises the economic well-being of the country as a whole.

	Before Trade	After Trade	Change
Consumer Surplus	A	A + B + D	+(B + D)
Producer Surplus	B + C	C	−B
Total Surplus	A + B + C	A + B + C + D	+D

The area D shows the increase in total surplus and represents the gains from trade.

area B + D. Sellers are worse off because producer surplus falls by the area B. The gains of buyers exceed the losses of sellers, and total surplus increases by the area D.

This analysis of an importing country yields two conclusions parallel to those for an exporting country:

- When a country allows trade and becomes an importer of a good, domestic consumers of the good are better off, and domestic producers of the good are worse off.
- Trade raises the economic well-being of a nation in the sense that the gains of the winners exceed the losses of the losers.

Having completed our analysis of trade, we can better understand one of the *Ten Principles of Economics* in Chapter 1: Trade can make everyone better off. If Isoland opens up its steel market to international trade, that change will create winners and losers, regardless of whether Isoland ends up exporting or importing steel. In either case, however, the gains of the winners exceed the losses of the losers, so the winners could compensate the losers and still be better off. In this sense, trade *can* make everyone better off. But *will* trade make everyone better off? Probably not. In practice, compensation for the losers from international trade is rare. Without such compensation, opening up to international trade is a policy that expands the size of the economic pie, while perhaps leaving some participants in the economy with a smaller slice.

We can now see why the debate over trade policy is so often contentious. Whenever a policy creates winners and losers, the stage is set for a political battle. Nations sometimes fail to enjoy the gains from trade simply because the losers from free trade have more political clout than the winners. The losers lobby for trade restrictions, such as tariffs and import quotas.

The Effects of a Tariff

tariff
a tax on goods produced abroad and sold domestically

The Isolandian economists next consider the effects of a **tariff**—a tax on imported goods. The economists quickly realize that a tariff on steel will have no effect if Isoland becomes a steel exporter. If no one in Isoland is interested in importing steel, a tax on steel imports is irrelevant. The tariff matters only if Isoland becomes a steel importer. Concentrating their attention on this case, the economists compare welfare with and without the tariff.

The graph in Figure 6 shows the Isolandian market for steel. Under free trade, the domestic price equals the world price. A tariff raises the price of imported steel above the world price by the amount of the tariff. Domestic suppliers of steel, who compete with suppliers of imported steel, can now sell their steel for the world price plus the amount of the tariff. Thus, the price of steel—both imported and domestic—rises by the amount of the tariff and is, therefore, closer to the price that would prevail without trade.

The change in price affects the behavior of domestic buyers and sellers. Because the tariff raises the price of steel, it reduces the domestic quantity demanded from Q_1^D to Q_2^D and raises the domestic quantity supplied from Q_1^S to Q_2^S. Thus, *the tariff reduces the quantity of imports and moves the domestic market closer to its equilibrium without trade.*

FIGURE 6

The Effects of a Tariff

A tariff reduces the quantity of imports and moves a market closer to the equilibrium that would exist without trade. Total surplus falls by an amount equal to area D + F. These two triangles represent the deadweight loss from the tariff.

	Before Tariff	After Tariff	Change
Consumer Surplus	A + B + C + D + E + F	A + B	−(C + D + E + F)
Producer Surplus	G	C + G	+C
Government Revenue	None	E	+E
Total Surplus	A + B + C + D + E + F + G	A + B + C + E + G	−(D + F)

> The area D + F shows the fall in total surplus and represents the deadweight loss of the tariff.

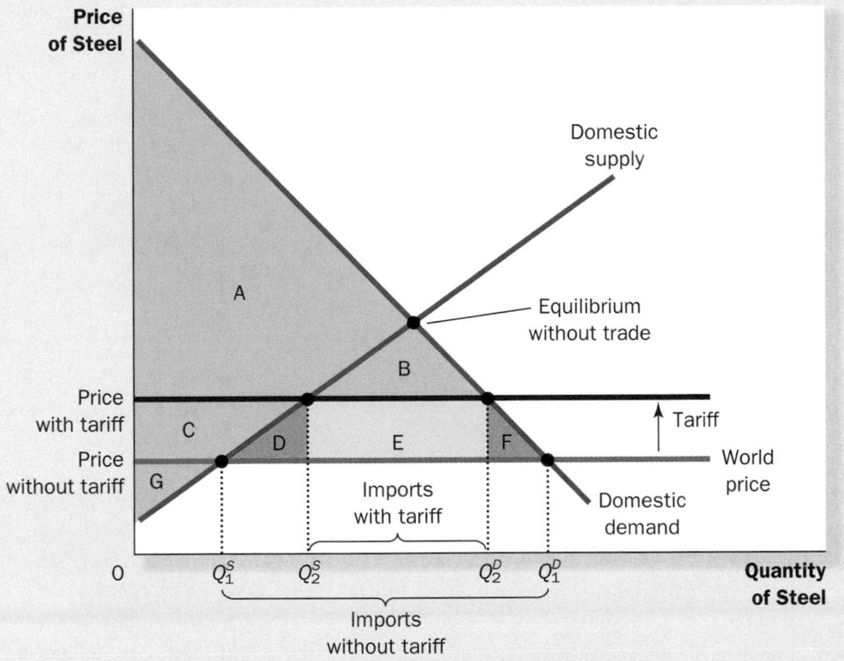

Now consider the gains and losses from the tariff. Because the tariff raises the domestic price, domestic sellers are better off, and domestic buyers are worse off. In addition, the government raises revenue. To measure these gains and losses, we look at the changes in consumer surplus, producer surplus, and government revenue. These changes are summarized in the table in Figure 6.

Before the tariff, the domestic price equals the world price. Consumer surplus, the area between the demand curve and the world price, is area A + B + C + D + E + F. Producer surplus, the area between the supply curve and the world price, is area G.

Government revenue equals zero. Total surplus—the sum of consumer surplus, producer surplus, and government revenue—is area A + B + C + D + E + F + G.

Once the government imposes a tariff, the domestic price exceeds the world price by the amount of the tariff. Consumer surplus is now area A + B. Producer surplus is area C + G. Government revenue, which is the quantity of after-tariff imports times the size of the tariff, is the area E. Thus, total surplus with the tariff is area A + B + C + E + G.

To determine the total welfare effects of the tariff, we add the change in consumer surplus (which is negative), the change in producer surplus (positive), and the change in government revenue (positive). We find that total surplus in the market decreases by the area D + F. This fall in total surplus is called the *deadweight loss* of the tariff.

A tariff causes a deadweight loss simply because a tariff is a type of tax. Like most taxes, it distorts incentives and pushes the allocation of scarce resources away from the optimum. In this case, we can identify two effects. First, the tariff on

IN THE NEWS

LIFE IN ISOLAND

Our story about the steel industry and the debate over trade policy in Isoland is just a parable. Or is it?

Bush Puts Tariffs of as Much as 30% on Steel Imports
By David E. Sanger

President Bush took some of the broadest federal action in two decades to protect a major American industry today, imposing tariffs of up to 30 percent on most types of steel imported into the United States from Europe, Asia, and South America. The tariffs will last three years, he said, to give American steel producers time to consolidate operations and stem layoffs.

Mr. Bush's action is likely to send the price of steel up sharply, perhaps as much as 10 percent, a cost American consumers will ultimately bear in higher prices for autos, appliances, and housing. The United States imports about a quarter of the steel it consumes. . . .

Within minutes of the White House announcement, America's European allies and Japan said they would almost certainly challenge the action before the World Trade Organization, setting the stage for a major trade fight with many of the same countries Mr. Bush is trying to hold together in the fractious fight against terrorism. . . .

Mr. Bush is an avowed free trader, and many members of his economic team—including Lawrence Lindsey, who runs the National Economic Council, and Glenn Hubbard, the chairman of the council of economic advisors—warned of the risks to both his free-trade credentials and the broader economy. In the past his trade representative, Robert B. Zoellick, compared raising tariffs to raising taxes, and while the White House officials sidestepped such comparisons today they admitted that the result would be greater costs to consumers.

CHAPTER 9 APPLICATION: INTERNATIONAL TRADE 185

steel raises the price of steel that domestic producers can charge above the world price and, as a result, encourages them to increase production of steel (from Q_1^S to Q_2^S). Second, the tariff raises the price that domestic steel buyers have to pay and, therefore, encourages them to reduce consumption of steel (from Q_1^D to Q_2^D). Area D represents the deadweight loss from the overproduction of steel, and area F represents the deadweight loss from the underconsumption. The total deadweight loss of the tariff is the sum of these two triangles.

The Effects of an Import Quota

The Isolandian economists next consider the effects of an **import quota**—a limit on the quantity of imports. In particular, imagine that the Isolandian government distributes a limited number of import licenses. Each license gives the license holder the right to import 1 ton of steel into Isoland from abroad. The Isolandian economists want to compare welfare under a policy of free trade and welfare with the addition of this import quota.

import quota
a limit on the quantity of a good that can be produced abroad and sold domestically

The graph and table in Figure 7 (p. 186) show how an import quota affects the Isolandian market for steel. Because the import quota prevents Isolandians from buying as much steel as they want from abroad, the supply of steel is no longer perfectly elastic at the world price. Instead, as long as the price of steel in Isoland is above the world price, the license holders import as much as they are permitted, and the total supply of steel in Isoland equals the domestic supply plus the quota amount. That is, the supply curve above the world price is shifted to the right by exactly the amount of the quota. (The supply curve below the world price does not shift because, in this case, importing is not profitable for the license holders.)

The price of steel in Isoland adjusts to balance supply (domestic plus imported) and demand. As the figure shows, the quota causes the price of steel to rise above the world price. The domestic quantity demanded falls from Q_1^D to Q_2^D, and the domestic quantity supplied rises from Q_1^S to Q_2^S. Not surprisingly, the import quota reduces steel imports.

Now consider the gains and losses from the quota. Because the quota raises the domestic price above the world price, domestic sellers are better off, and domestic buyers are worse off. In addition, the license holders are better off because they make a profit from buying at the world price and selling at the higher domestic price. To measure these gains and losses, we look at the changes in consumer surplus, producer surplus, and license-holder surplus.

Before the government imposes the quota, the domestic price equals the world price. Consumer surplus, the area between the demand curve and the world price, is area A + B + C + D + E' + E" + F. Producer surplus, the area between the supply curve and the world price, is area G. The surplus of license holders equals zero because there are no licenses. Total surplus, the sum of consumer, producer, and license-holder surplus, is area A + B + C + D + E' + E" + F + G.

After the government imposes the import quota and issues the licenses, the domestic price exceeds the world price. Domestic consumers get surplus equal to area A + B, and domestic producers get surplus equal to area C + G. The license holders make a profit on each unit imported equal to the difference between the Isolandian price of steel and the world price. Their surplus equals this price differential times the quantity of imports. Thus, it equals the area of the rectangle E' + E". Total surplus with the quota is the area A + B + C + E' + E" + G.

FIGURE 7

The Effects of an Import Quota

An import quota, like a tariff, reduces the quantity of imports and moves a market closer to the equilibrium that would exist without trade. Total surplus falls by an amount equal to area D + F. These two triangles represent the deadweight loss from the quota. In addition, the import quota transfers E' + E" to whoever holds the import licenses.

	Before Quota	After Quota	Change
Consumer Surplus	A + B + C + D + E' + E" + F	A + B	−(C + D + E' + E" + F)
Producer Surplus	G	C + G	+C
License-Holder Surplus	None	E' + E"	+(E' + E")
Total Surplus	A + B + C + D + E' + E" + F + G	A + B + C + E' + E" + G	−(D + F)

The area D + F shows the fall in total surplus and represents the deadweight loss of the quota.

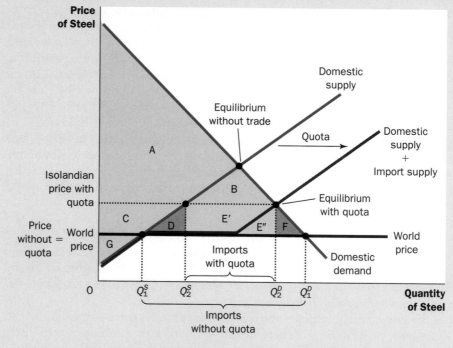

To see how total welfare changes with the imposition of the quota, we add the change in consumer surplus (which is negative), the change in producer surplus (positive), and the change in license-holder surplus (positive). We find that total surplus in the market decreases by the area D + F. This area represents the deadweight loss of the import quota.

This analysis should seem somewhat familiar. Indeed, if you compare the analysis of import quotas in Figure 7 with the analysis of tariffs in Figure 6, you will see that they are essentially identical. *Both tariffs and import quotas raise the domestic price of the good, reduce the welfare of domestic consumers, increase the welfare of domestic producers, and cause deadweight losses.* There is only one difference between these two types of trade restriction: A tariff raises revenue for the government (area E in Figure 6), whereas an import quota creates surplus for license holders (area E' + E" in Figure 7).

Tariffs and import quotas can be made to look even more similar. Suppose that the government tries to capture the license-holder surplus for itself by charging a fee for the licenses. A license to sell 1 ton of steel is worth exactly the difference between the Isolandian price of steel and the world price, and the government can set the license fee as high as this price differential. If the government does this, the license fee for imports works exactly like a tariff: Consumer surplus, producer surplus, and government revenue are exactly the same under the two policies.

In practice, however, countries that restrict trade with import quotas rarely do so by selling the import licenses. For example, the U.S. government has at times pressured Japan to "voluntarily" limit the sale of Japanese cars in the United States. In this case, the Japanese government allocates the import licenses to Japanese firms, and the surplus from these licenses (area E' + E") accrues to those firms. This kind of import quota is, from the standpoint of U.S. welfare, strictly worse than a U.S. tariff on imported cars. Both a tariff and an import quota raise prices, restrict trade, and cause deadweight losses, but at least the tariff produces revenue for the U.S. government rather than for Japanese auto companies.

Although in our analysis so far import quotas and tariffs appear to cause similar deadweight losses, a quota can potentially cause an even larger deadweight loss, depending on the mechanism used to allocate the import licenses. Suppose that when Isoland imposes a quota, everyone understands that the licenses will go to those who spend the most resources lobbying the Isolandian government. In this case, there is an implicit license fee—the cost of lobbying. The revenues from this fee, however, rather than being collected by the government, are spent on lobbying expenses. The deadweight losses from this type of quota include not only the losses from overproduction (area D) and underconsumption (area F) but also whatever part of the license-holder surplus (area E' + E") is wasted on the cost of lobbying.

The Lessons for Trade Policy

The team of Isolandian economists can now write to the new president:

Dear Madam President,

You asked us three questions about opening up trade. After much hard work, we have the answers.

Question: If the government allowed Isolandians to import and export steel, what would happen to the price of steel and the quantity of steel sold in the domestic steel market?

Answer: Once trade is allowed, the Isolandian price of steel would be driven to equal the price prevailing around the world.

If the world price is now higher than the Isolandian price, our price would rise. The higher price would reduce the amount of steel Isolandians consume and raise the amount of steel that Isolandians produce. Isoland would, therefore, become a steel exporter. This occurs because, in this case, Isoland would have a comparative advantage in producing steel.

Conversely, if the world price is now lower than the Isolandian price, our price would fall. The lower price would raise the amount of steel that

Isolandians consume and lower the amount of steel that Isolandians produce. Isoland would, therefore, become a steel importer. This occurs because, in this case, other countries would have a comparative advantage in producing steel.

Question: Who would gain from free trade in steel and who would lose, and would the gains exceed the losses?

Answer: The answer depends on whether the price rises or falls when trade is allowed. If the price rises, producers of steel gain, and consumers of steel lose. If the price falls, consumers gain, and producers lose. In both cases, the gains are larger than the losses. Thus, free trade raises the total welfare of Isolandians.

Question: Should a tariff or an import quota be part of the new trade policy?

Answer: A tariff, like most taxes, has deadweight losses: The revenue raised would be smaller than the losses to the buyers and sellers. In this case, the deadweight losses occur because the tariff would move the economy closer to our current no-trade equilibrium. An import quota works much like a tariff and would cause similar deadweight losses. The best policy, from the standpoint of economic efficiency, would be to allow trade without a tariff or an import quota.

We hope you find these answers helpful as you decide on your new policy.

Your faithful servants,
Isolandian economics team

QuickQuiz Draw the supply and demand curve for wool suits in the country of Autarka. When trade is allowed, the price of a suit falls from 3 to 2 ounces of gold. In your diagram, what is the change in consumer surplus, the change in producer surplus, and the change in total surplus? How would a tariff on suit imports alter these effects?

THE ARGUMENTS FOR RESTRICTING TRADE

The letter from the economics team persuades the new president of Isoland to consider opening up trade in steel. She notes that the domestic price is now high compared to the world price. Free trade would, therefore, cause the price of steel to fall and hurt domestic steel producers. Before implementing the new policy, she asks Isolandian steel companies to comment on the economists' advice.

Not surprisingly, the steel companies are opposed to free trade in steel. They believe that the government should protect the domestic steel industry from foreign competition. Let's consider some of the arguments they might give to support their position and how the economics team would respond.

The Jobs Argument

Opponents of free trade often argue that trade with other countries destroys domestic jobs. In our example, free trade in steel would cause the price of steel to fall, reducing the quantity of steel produced in Isoland and thus reducing employment in the Isolandian steel industry. Some Isolandian steelworkers would lose their jobs.

Yet free trade creates jobs at the same time that it destroys them. When Isolandians buy steel from other countries, those countries obtain the resources to buy

OTHER BENEFITS OF INTERNATIONAL TRADE

Our conclusions so far have been based on the standard analysis of international trade. As we have seen, there are winners and losers when a nation opens itself up to trade, but the gains to the winners exceed the losses of the losers. Yet the case for free trade can be made even stronger. There are several other economic benefits of trade beyond those emphasized in the standard analysis.

Here, in a nutshell, are some of these other benefits:

- *Increased variety of goods:* Goods produced in different countries are not exactly the same. German beer, for instance, is not the same as American beer. Free trade gives consumers in all countries greater variety from which to choose.
- *Lower costs through economies of scale:* Some goods can be produced at low cost only if they are produced in large quantities—

a phenomenon called *economies of scale.* A firm in a small country cannot take full advantage of economies of scale if it can sell only in a small domestic market. Free trade gives firms access to larger world markets and allows them to realize economies of scale more fully.

- *Increased competition:* A company shielded from foreign competitors is more likely to have market power, which in turn gives it the ability to raise prices above competitive levels. This is a type of market failure. Opening up trade fosters competition and gives the invisible hand a better chance to work its magic.
- *Enhanced flow of ideas:* The transfer of technological advances around the world is often thought to be linked to international trade in the goods that embody those advances. The best way for a poor, agricultural nation to learn about the computer revolution, for instance, is to buy some computers from abroad, rather than trying to make them domestically.

Thus, free international trade increases variety for consumers, allows firms to take advantage of economies of scale, makes markets more competitive, and facilitates the spread of technology. If the Isolandian economists thought these effects were important, their advice to their president would be even more forceful.

other goods from Isoland. Isolandian workers would move from the steel industry to those industries in which Isoland has a comparative advantage. Although the transition may impose hardship on some workers in the short run, it allows Isolandians as a whole to enjoy a higher standard of living.

Opponents of trade are often skeptical that trade creates jobs. They might respond that *everything* can be produced more cheaply abroad. Under free trade, they might argue, Isolandians could not be profitably employed in any industry. As Chapter 3 explains, however, the gains from trade are based on comparative advantage, not absolute advantage. Even if one country is better than another country at producing everything, each country can still gain from trading with the other. Workers in each country will eventually find jobs in the industry in which that country has a comparative advantage.

The National-Security Argument

When an industry is threatened with competition from other countries, opponents of free trade often argue that the industry is vital for national security. In our example, Isolandian steel companies might point out that steel is used to make guns and tanks. Free trade would allow Isoland to become dependent on foreign countries to supply steel. If a war later broke out, Isoland might be unable to produce enough steel and weapons to defend itself.

Berry's World

"You like protectionism as a 'working man.' How about as a consumer?"

Economists acknowledge that protecting key industries may be appropriate when there are legitimate concerns over national security. Yet they fear that this argument may be used too quickly by producers eager to gain at consumers' expense. The U.S. watchmaking industry, for instance, long argued that it was vital for national security, claiming that its skilled workers would be necessary in wartime. Certainly, it is tempting for those in an industry to exaggerate their role in national defense to obtain protection from foreign competition.

The Infant-Industry Argument

New industries sometimes argue for temporary trade restrictions to help them get started. After a period of protection, the argument goes, these industries will mature and be able to compete with foreign competitors. Similarly, older industries sometimes argue that they need temporary protection to help them adjust to new conditions. For example, General Motors Chairman Roger Smith once argued for temporary protection "to give U.S. automakers turnaround time to get the domestic industry back on its feet."

Economists are often skeptical about such claims. The primary reason is that the infant-industry argument is difficult to implement in practice. To apply protection successfully, the government would need to decide which industries will eventually be profitable and decide whether the benefits of establishing these industries exceed the costs to consumers of protection. Yet "picking winners" is extraordinarily difficult. It is made even more difficult by the political process, which often awards protection to those industries that are politically powerful. And once a powerful industry is protected from foreign competition, the "temporary" policy is hard to remove.

In addition, many economists are skeptical about the infant-industry argument even in principle. Suppose, for instance, that the Isolandian steel industry is young and unable to compete profitably against foreign rivals. Yet there is reason to believe that the industry can be profitable in the long run. In this case, the owners of the firms should be willing to incur temporary losses to obtain the eventual profits. Protection is not necessary for an industry to grow. Firms in various industries—such as many Internet firms today—incur temporary losses in the hope of growing and becoming profitable in the future. And many of them succeed, even without protection from foreign competition.

The Unfair-Competition Argument

A common argument is that free trade is desirable only if all countries play by the same rules. If firms in different countries are subject to different laws and regulations, then it is unfair (the argument goes) to expect the firms to compete in the international marketplace. For instance, suppose that the government of Neighborland subsidizes its steel industry by giving steel companies large tax breaks. The Isolandian steel industry might argue that it should be protected from this foreign competition because Neighborland is not competing fairly.

Would it, in fact, hurt Isoland to buy steel from another country at a subsidized price? Certainly, Isolandian steel producers would suffer, but Isolandian steel consumers would benefit from the low price. Moreover, the case for free trade is no different: The gains of the consumers from buying at the low price would exceed the losses of the producers. Neighborland's subsidy to its steel industry may be a bad policy, but it is the taxpayers of Neighborland who bear the burden. Isoland can benefit from the opportunity to buy steel at a subsidized price.

IN THE NEWS

TRADE POLICY IN INDIA

India is among the world's poorest countries. The government's trade policy is one of the reasons.

Chicken Shows Difficulty of Exporting Food to India

By Celia W. Dugger

NEW DELHI—Americans love succulent chicken breasts dressed up in every conceivable way, while Indians relish a savory tandoori drumstick brandished easily in one hand or a spicy chicken curry enriched by the marrow of the leg bone.

For Perdue Farms, America's No. 3 chicken producer, this divergence in culinary tastes seems a heaven-sent opportunity. While selling white meat at a premium to Americans, it could ship inexpensive, unwanted dark meat to India.

So as India prepared to lift its long-standing ban on chicken imports next year in a deal worked out with American trade negotiators, Perdue began developing a strategy to sell leg portions in this potentially huge new market, home

to as many as 150 million middle-class consumers.

But India does not have a reputation as one of the world's most protected economies for nothing. There is still a deep ambivalence here about foreign investment and trade, and India has taken a decidedly cautious approach to globalization. Over the last decade, it has let in ever more foreign goods and lowered barriers to trade, cutting average tariffs from 128 percent to 40 percent. Still, India has some of the world's highest tariffs.

Sure enough, as the domestic chicken industry considered the fearsome prospect of cheap imported dark meat, its lobbyists began to protest. The government hastily agreed last month to raise the tariff on chicken legs from 35 percent to 100 percent. . . .

Many Indians, from hard-line Hindu nationalists to Nehruvian socialists, believe India must shield its small producers,

Are American chickens a threat to Indian prosperity?

even at the expense of higher prices for consumers and lower-quality goods.

Source: *The New York Times,* June 14, 2000, pp. C1, C6. Copyright © 2000 by The New York Times Co. Reprinted with permission.

The Protection-as-a-Bargaining-Chip Argument

Another argument for trade restrictions concerns the strategy of bargaining. Many policymakers claim to support free trade but, at the same time, argue that trade restrictions can be useful when we bargain with our trading partners. They claim that the threat of a trade restriction can help remove a trade restriction already imposed by a foreign government. For example, Isoland might threaten to impose a tariff on steel unless Neighborland removes its tariff on wheat. If Neighborland responds to this threat by removing its tariff, the result can be freer trade.

IN THE NEWS

GLOBALIZATION

The movement toward free world trade—sometimes called globalization—has some vocal opponents, but as this article discusses, they are not always well informed.

Hearts and Heads

By Paul Krugman

There is an old European saying: anyone who is not a socialist before he is 30 has no heart, anyone who is still a socialist after he is 30 has no head. Suitably updated, this applies perfectly to the movement against globalization—the movement that made its big splash in Seattle back in 1999 and is doing its best to disrupt the Summit of the Americas in Quebec City this weekend.

The facts of globalization are not always pretty. If you buy a product made in a third-world country, it was produced by workers who are paid incredibly little by Western standards and probably work under awful conditions. Anyone who is not bothered by those facts, at least some of the time, has no heart.

But that doesn't mean the demonstrators are right. On the contrary: anyone who thinks that the answer to world poverty is simple outrage against global trade has no head—or chooses not to

use it. The anti-globalization movement already has a remarkable track record of hurting the very people and causes it claims to champion. . . .

Could anything be worse than having children work in sweatshops? Alas, yes. In 1993, child workers in Bangladesh were found to be producing clothing for Wal-Mart, and Senator Tom Harkin proposed legislation banning imports from countries employing underage workers. The direct result was that Bangladeshi textile factories stopped employing

The problem with this bargaining strategy is that the threat may not work. If it doesn't work, the country has a difficult choice. It can carry out its threat and implement the trade restriction, which would reduce its own economic welfare. Or it can back down from its threat, which would cause it to lose prestige in international affairs. Faced with this choice, the country would probably wish that it had never made the threat in the first place.

Case Study

TRADE AGREEMENTS AND THE WORLD TRADE ORGANIZATION

A country can take one of two approaches to achieving free trade. It can take a *unilateral* approach and remove its trade restrictions on its own. This is the approach that Great Britain took in the nineteenth century and that Chile and South Korea have taken in recent years. Alternatively, a country can take a *multilateral* approach and reduce its trade restrictions while other countries do the same. In other words, it can bargain with its trading partners in an attempt to reduce trade restrictions around the world.

children. But did the children go back to school? Did they return to happy homes? Not according to Oxfam, which found that the displaced child workers ended up in even worse jobs, or on the streets—and that a significant number were forced into prostitution.

The point is that third-world countries aren't poor because their export workers earn low wages; it's the other way around. Because the countries are poor, even what look to us like bad jobs at bad wages are almost always much better than the alternatives: millions of Mexicans are migrating to the north of the country to take the low-wage export jobs that outrage opponents of NAFTA. And those jobs wouldn't exist if the wages were much higher: the same factors that make poor countries poor—low productivity, bad infrastructure, general social disorganization—mean that such countries can compete on world markets only if they pay wages much lower than those paid in the West.

Of course, opponents of globalization have heard this argument, and they have answers. At a conference last week, I heard paeans to the superiority of traditional rural lifestyles over modern, urban life—a claim that not only flies in the face of the clear fact that many peasants flee to urban jobs as soon as they can, but that (it seems to me) has a disagreeable element of cultural condescension, especially given the overwhelming preponderance of white faces in the crowds of demonstrators. (Would you want to live in a pre-industrial village?) I also heard claims that rural poverty in the third world is mainly the fault of multinational corporations—which is just plain wrong, but is a convenient belief if you want to think of globalization as an unmitigated evil.

The most sophisticated answer was that the movement doesn't want to stop exports—it just wants better working conditions and higher wages.

But it's not a serious position. Third-world countries desperately need their export industries—they cannot retreat to an imaginary rural Arcadia. They can't have those export industries unless they are allowed to sell goods produced under conditions that Westerners find appalling, by workers who receive very low wages. And that's a fact the anti-globalization activists refuse to accept.

So who are the bad guys? The activists are getting the images they wanted from Quebec City: leaders sitting inside their fortified enclosure, with thousands of police protecting them from the outraged masses outside. But images can deceive. Many of the people inside that chain-link fence are sincerely trying to help the world's poor. And the people outside the fence, whatever their intentions, are doing their best to make the poor even poorer.

Source: *The New York Times,* April 22, 2001, OP-ED WK/p. 17. Copyright © 2001 by The New York Times Co. Reprinted by permission.

One important example of the multilateral approach is the North American Free Trade Agreement (NAFTA), which in 1993 lowered trade barriers among the United States, Mexico, and Canada. Another is the General Agreement on Tariffs and Trade (GATT), which is a continuing series of negotiations among many of the world's countries with the goal of promoting free trade. The United States helped to found GATT after World War II in response to the high tariffs imposed during the Great Depression of the 1930s. Many economists believe that the high tariffs contributed to the economic hardship during that period. GATT has successfully reduced the average tariff among member countries from about 40 percent after World War II to about 5 percent today.

The rules established under GATT are now enforced by an international institution called the World Trade Organization (WTO). The WTO was established in 1995 and has its headquarters in Geneva, Switzerland. As of January 2002, 144 countries have joined the organization, accounting for 97 percent of world trade. The functions of the WTO are to administer trade agreements, provide a forum for negotiations, and handle disputes that arise among member countries.

What are the pros and cons of the multilateral approach to free trade? One advantage is that the multilateral approach has the potential to result in freer trade than a unilateral approach because it can reduce trade restrictions abroad as well as at home. If international negotiations fail, however, the result could be more restricted trade than under a unilateral approach.

In addition, the multilateral approach may have a political advantage. In most markets, producers are fewer and better organized than consumers—and thus wield greater political influence. Reducing the Isolandian tariff on steel, for example, may be politically difficult if considered by itself. The steel companies would oppose free trade, and the users of steel who would benefit are so numerous that organizing their support would be difficult. Yet suppose that Neighborland promises to reduce its tariff on wheat at the same time that Isoland reduces its tariff on steel. In this case, the Isolandian wheat farmers, who are also politically powerful, would back the agreement. Thus, the multilateral approach to free trade can sometimes win political support when a unilateral reduction cannot. ●

QuickQuiz The textile industry of Autarka advocates a ban on the import of wool suits. Describe five arguments its lobbyists might make. Give a response to each of these arguments.

CONCLUSION

Economists and the general public often disagree about free trade. In May 2000, for example, the U.S. Congress debated whether to grant China "Permanent Normal Trade Relations," which would keep trade barriers low between the two countries. The public was split on the issue. In a *Wall Street Journal* poll, 48 percent agreed with the statement that, "Foreign trade is bad for the U.S. economy, as cheap imports hurt wages and cost jobs." Only 34 percent agreed that "Foreign trade is good for the U.S. economy, resulting in economic growth and jobs for Americans." By contrast, economists overwhelmingly supported the proposal. They viewed free trade as a way of allocating production efficiently and raising living standards in both countries. In the end, Congress agreed with the economists, and the bill passed the House of Representatives by a vote of 237 to 197.

Economists view the United States as an ongoing experiment that confirms the virtues of free trade. Throughout its history, the United States has allowed unrestricted trade among the states, and the country as a whole has benefited from the specialization that trade allows. Florida grows oranges, Texas pumps oil, California makes wine, and so on. Americans would not enjoy the high standard of living they do today if people could consume only those goods and services produced in their own states. The world could similarly benefit from free trade among countries.

To better understand economists' view of trade, let's continue our parable. Suppose that the country of Isoland ignores the advice of its economics team and decides not to allow free trade in steel. The country remains in the equilibrium without international trade.

Then, one day, some Isolandian inventor discovers a new way to make steel at very low cost. The process is quite mysterious, however, and the inventor insists on keeping it a secret. What is odd is that the inventor doesn't need any workers or iron ore to make steel. The only input he requires is wheat.

The inventor is hailed as a genius. Because steel is used in so many products, the invention lowers the cost of many goods and allows all Isolandians to enjoy a higher standard of living. Workers who had previously produced steel do suffer when their factories close, but eventually they find work in other industries. Some become farmers and grow the wheat that the inventor turns into steel. Others enter new industries that emerge as a result of higher Isolandian living standards. Everyone understands that the displacement of these workers is an inevitable part of progress.

After several years, a newspaper reporter decides to investigate this mysterious new steel process. She sneaks into the inventor's factory and learns that the inventor is a fraud. The inventor has not been making steel at all. Instead, he has been smuggling wheat abroad in exchange for steel from other countries. The only thing that the inventor had discovered was the gains from international trade.

When the truth is revealed, the government shuts down the inventor's operation. The price of steel rises, and workers return to jobs in steel factories. Living standards in Isoland fall back to their former levels. The inventor is jailed and held up to public ridicule. After all, he was no inventor. He was just an economist.

SUMMARY

- The effects of free trade can be determined by comparing the domestic price without trade to the world price. A low domestic price indicates that the country has a comparative advantage in producing the good and that the country will become an exporter. A high domestic price indicates that the rest of the world has a comparative advantage in producing the good and that the country will become an importer.

- When a country allows trade and becomes an exporter of a good, producers of the good are better off, and consumers of the good are worse off. When a country allows trade and becomes an importer of a good, consumers are better off, and producers are worse off. In both cases, the gains from trade exceed the losses.

- A tariff—a tax on imports—moves a market closer to the equilibrium that would exist

without trade and, therefore, reduces the gains from trade. Although domestic producers are better off and the government raises revenue, the losses to consumers exceed these gains.

- An import quota—a limit on imports—has effects that are similar to those of a tariff. Under a quota, however, the holders of the import licenses receive the revenue that the government would collect with a tariff.

- There are various arguments for restricting trade: protecting jobs, defending national security, helping infant industries, preventing unfair competition, and responding to foreign trade restrictions. Although some of these arguments have some merit in some cases, economists believe that free trade is usually the better policy.

KEY CONCEPTS

world price, p. 177   tariff, p. 182   import quota, p. 185

QUESTIONS FOR REVIEW

1. What does the domestic price that prevails without international trade tell us about a nation's comparative advantage?

2. When does a country become an exporter of a good? An importer?

3. Draw the supply-and-demand diagram for an importing country. What is consumer surplus and producer surplus before trade is allowed? What is consumer surplus and producer surplus with free trade? What is the change in total surplus?

4. Describe what a tariff is, and describe its economic effects.

5. What is an import quota? Compare its economic effects with those of a tariff.

6. List five arguments often given to support trade restrictions. How do economists respond to these arguments?

7. What is the difference between the unilateral and multilateral approaches to achieving free trade? Give an example of each.

PROBLEMS AND APPLICATIONS

1. The United States represents a small part of the world orange market.
   a. Draw a diagram depicting the equilibrium in the U.S. orange market without international trade. Identify the equilibrium price, equilibrium quantity, consumer surplus, and producer surplus.
   b. Suppose that the world orange price is below the U.S. price before trade, and that the U.S. orange market is now opened to trade. Identify the new equilibrium price, quantity consumed, quantity produced domestically, and quantity imported. Also show the change in the surplus of domestic consumers and producers. Has domestic total surplus increased or decreased?

2. The world price of wine is below the price that would prevail in the United States in the absence of trade.
   a. Assuming that American imports of wine are a small part of total world wine production, draw a graph for the U.S. market for wine under free trade. Identify consumer surplus, producer surplus, and total surplus in an appropriate table.
   b. Now suppose that an unusual shift of the Gulf Stream leads to an unseasonably cold summer in Europe, destroying much of the grape harvest there. What effect does this shock have on the world price of wine? Using your graph and table from part (a), show the effect on consumer surplus, producer

surplus, and total surplus in the United States. Who are the winners and losers? Is the United States as a whole better or worse off?

3. The world price of cotton is below the no-trade price in country A and above the no-trade price in country B. Using supply-and-demand diagrams and welfare tables such as those in the chapter, show the gains from trade in each country. Compare your results for the two countries.

4. Suppose that Congress imposes a tariff on imported autos to protect the U.S. auto industry from foreign competition. Assuming that the U.S. is a price taker in the world auto market, show on a diagram: the change in the quantity of imports, the loss to U.S. consumers, the gain to U.S. manufacturers, government revenue, and the deadweight loss associated with the tariff. The loss to consumers can be decomposed into three pieces: a transfer to domestic producers, a transfer to the government, and a deadweight loss. Use your diagram to identify these three pieces.

5. According to an article in *The New York Times* (Nov. 5, 1993), "many Midwest wheat farmers oppose the [North American] free trade agreement [NAFTA] as much as many corn farmers support it." For simplicity, assume that the United States is a small country in the markets for both corn and wheat, and that without the free trade agreement, the United States would not trade these commodities internationally. (Both of these assumptions are false, but they do not affect the qualitative responses to the following questions.)
   a. Based on this report, do you think the world wheat price is above or below the U.S. no-trade wheat price? Do you think the world corn price is above or below the U.S. no-trade corn price? Now analyze the welfare consequences of NAFTA in both markets.
   b. Considering both markets together, does NAFTA make U.S. farmers as a group better or worse off? Does it make U.S. consumers as a group better or worse off? Does it make the United States as a whole better or worse off?

6. Imagine that winemakers in the state of Washington petitioned the state government to tax wines imported from California. They argue that this tax would both raise tax revenue for the state government and raise employment in the Washington State wine industry. Do you agree with these claims? Is it a good policy?

7. Senator Ernest Hollings once wrote that "consumers *do not* benefit from lower-priced imports. Glance through some mail-order catalogs and you'll see that consumers pay exactly the same price for clothing whether it is U.S.-made or imported." Comment.

8. Write a brief essay advocating or criticizing each of the following policy positions.
   a. The government should not allow imports if foreign firms are selling below their costs of production (a phenomenon called "dumping").
   b. The government should temporarily stop the import of goods for which the domestic industry is new and struggling to survive.
   c. The government should not allow imports from countries with weaker environmental regulations than ours.

9. Suppose that a technological advance in Japan lowers the world price of televisions.

a. Assume the U.S. is an importer of televisions and there are no trade restrictions. How does the technological advance affect the welfare of U.S. consumers and U.S. producers? What happens to total surplus in the United States?

b. Now suppose the United States has a quota on television imports. How does the Japanese technological advance affect the welfare of U.S. consumers, U.S. producers, and the holders of import licenses?

10. When the government of Tradeland decides to impose an import quota on foreign cars, three proposals are suggested: (1) Sell the import licenses in an auction. (2) Distribute the licenses randomly in a lottery. (3) Let people wait in line and distribute the licenses on a first-come, first-served basis. Compare the effects of these policies. Which policy do you think has the largest deadweight losses? Which policy has the smallest deadweight losses? Why? (Hint: The government's other ways of raising tax revenue all cause deadweight losses themselves.)

11. An article about sugar beet growers in *The Wall Street Journal* (June 26, 1990) explained that "the government props up domestic sugar prices by curtailing imports of lower-cost sugar. Producers are guaranteed a 'market stabilization price' of $0.22 a pound, about $0.09 higher than the current world market price." The government maintains the higher price by imposing an import quota.

a. Illustrate the effect of this quota on the U.S. sugar market. Label the relevant prices and quantities under free trade and under the quota.

b. Analyze the effects of the sugar quota using the tools of welfare analysis.

c. The article also comments that "critics of the sugar program say that [the quota] has deprived numerous sugar-producing nations in the Caribbean, Latin America, and Far East of export earnings, harmed their economies, and caused political instability, while increasing Third World demand for U.S. foreign aid." Our usual welfare analysis includes only gains and losses to U.S. consumers and producers. What role do you think the gains or losses to people in other countries should play in our economic policymaking?

d. The article continues that "at home, the sugar program has helped make possible the spectacular rise of the high-fructose corn syrup industry." Why has the sugar program had this effect? (Hint: Are sugar and corn syrup substitutes or complements?)

12. (This question is challenging.) Consider a small country that exports steel. Suppose that a "pro-trade" government decides to subsidize the export of steel by paying a certain amount for each ton sold abroad. How does this export subsidy affect the domestic price of steel, the quantity of steel produced, the quantity of steel consumed, and the quantity of steel exported?

How does it affect consumer surplus, producer surplus, government revenue, and total surplus? (Hint: The analysis of an export subsidy is similar to the analysis of a tariff.)

13. What trade disputes or trade agreements have been in the news lately? In this case, who do you think are the winners and losers from free trade? Which group has more political clout?

Note: Places to look for this information include the Web sites of the World Trade Organization (http://www.wto.org), the U.S. International Trade Commission (http://www.usitc.gov), and the International Trade Administration in the Department of Commerce (http://www.ita.doc.gov).

http://

For more study tools, please visit http://mankiwXtra.swlearning.com.

4

THE DATA OF MACROECONOMICS

10

MEASURING A NATION'S INCOME

When you finish school and start looking for a full-time job, your experience will, to a large extent, be shaped by prevailing economic conditions. In some years, firms throughout the economy are expanding their production of goods and services, employment is rising, and jobs are easy to find. In other years, firms are cutting back on production, employment is declining, and finding a good job takes a long time. Not surprisingly, any college graduate would rather enter the labor force in a year of economic expansion than in a year of economic contraction.

Because the condition of the overall economy profoundly affects all of us, changes in economic conditions are widely reported by the media. Indeed, it is hard to pick up a newspaper without seeing some newly reported statistic about the economy. The statistic might measure the total income of everyone in the economy (GDP), the rate at which average prices are rising (inflation), the percentage of the labor force that is out of work (unemployment), total spending at stores (retail sales), or the imbalance of trade between the United States and the rest of the world (the trade deficit). All these statistics are *macroeconomic*. Rather than telling us about a particular household or firm, they tell us something about the entire economy.

microeconomics
the study of how households and firms make decisions and how they interact in markets

macroeconomics
the study of economy-wide phenomena, including inflation, unemployment, and economic growth

As you may recall from Chapter 2, economics is divided into two branches: microeconomics and macroeconomics. **Microeconomics** is the study of how individual households and firms make decisions and how they interact with one another in markets. **Macroeconomics** is the study of the economy as a whole. The goal of macroeconomics is to explain the economic changes that affect many households, firms, and markets simultaneously. Macroeconomists address diverse questions: Why is average income high in some countries while it is low in others? Why do prices rise rapidly in some periods of time while they are more stable in other periods? Why do production and employment expand in some years and contract in others? What, if anything, can the government do to promote rapid growth in incomes, low inflation, and stable employment? These questions are all macroeconomic in nature because they concern the workings of the entire economy.

Because the economy as a whole is just a collection of many households and many firms interacting in many markets, microeconomics and macroeconomics are closely linked. The basic tools of supply and demand, for instance, are as central to macroeconomic analysis as they are to microeconomic analysis. Yet studying the economy in its entirety raises some new and intriguing challenges.

In this chapter and the next one, we discuss some of the data that economists and policymakers use to monitor the performance of the overall economy. These data reflect the economic changes that macroeconomists try to explain. This chapter considers *gross domestic product,* or simply GDP, which measures the total income of a nation. GDP is the most closely watched economic statistic because it is thought to be the best single measure of a society's economic well-being.

THE ECONOMY'S INCOME AND EXPENDITURE

If you were to judge how a person is doing economically, you might first look at his or her income. A person with a high income can more easily afford life's necessities and luxuries. It is no surprise that people with higher incomes enjoy higher standards of living—better housing, better health care, fancier cars, more opulent vacations, and so on.

The same logic applies to a nation's overall economy. When judging whether the economy is doing well or poorly, it is natural to look at the total income that everyone in the economy is earning. That is the task of gross domestic product (GDP).

GDP measures two things at once: the total income of everyone in the economy and the total expenditure on the economy's output of goods and services. The reason that GDP can perform the trick of measuring both total income and total expenditure is that these two things are really the same. *For an economy as a whole, income must equal expenditure.*

Why is this true? An economy's income is the same as its expenditure because every transaction has two parties: a buyer and a seller. Every dollar of spending by some buyer is a dollar of income for some seller. Suppose, for instance, that Karen pays Doug $100 to mow her lawn. In this case, Doug is a seller of a service, and Karen is a buyer. Doug earns $100, and Karen spends $100. Thus, the transaction contributes equally to the economy's income and to its expenditure. GDP, whether measured as total income or total expenditure, rises by $100.

Another way to see the equality of income and expenditure is with the circular-flow diagram in Figure 1. (You may recall this circular-flow diagram from Chapter 2.) The diagram describes all the transactions between households and firms in

FIGURE 1

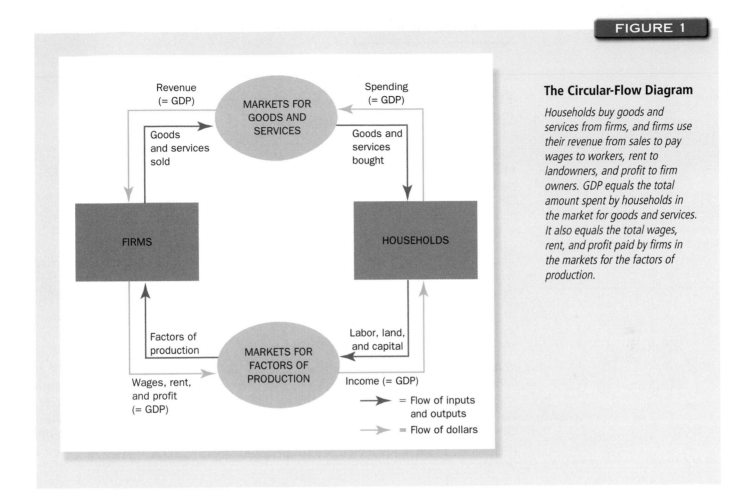

Revenue
(= GDP)

Spending
(= GDP)

MARKETS FOR
GOODS AND
SERVICES

Goods
and services
sold

Goods and
services
bought

FIRMS

HOUSEHOLDS

Factors of
production

Labor, land,
and capital

MARKETS FOR
FACTORS OF
PRODUCTION

Wages, rent,
and profit
(= GDP)

Income (= GDP)

⟶ = Flow of inputs
and outputs

⟶ = Flow of dollars

The Circular-Flow Diagram

Households buy goods and services from firms, and firms use their revenue from sales to pay wages to workers, rent to landowners, and profit to firm owners. GDP equals the total amount spent by households in the market for goods and services. It also equals the total wages, rent, and profit paid by firms in the markets for the factors of production.

a simple economy. In this economy, households buy goods and services from firms; these expenditures flow through the markets for goods and services. The firms in turn use the money they receive from sales to pay workers' wages, landowners' rent, and firm owners' profit; this income flows through the markets for the factors of production. In this economy, money flows from households to firms and then back to households.

We can compute GDP for this economy in one of two ways: by adding up the total expenditure by households or by adding up the total income (wages, rent, and profit) paid by firms. Because all expenditure in the economy ends up as someone's income, GDP is the same regardless of how we compute it.

The actual economy is, of course, more complicated than the one illustrated in Figure 1. In particular, households do not spend all of their income. They pay some of it to the government in taxes, and they save some for use in the future. In addition, households do not buy all goods and services produced in the economy. Some goods and services are bought by governments, and some are bought by firms that plan to use them in the future to produce their own output. Yet, regardless of whether a household, government, or firm buys a good or service, the transaction has a buyer and seller. Thus, for the economy as a whole, expenditure and income are always the same.

QuickQuiz What two things does gross domestic product measure? How can it measure two things at once?

THE MEASUREMENT OF GROSS DOMESTIC PRODUCT

Now that we have discussed the meaning of gross domestic product in general terms, let's be more precise about how this statistic is measured. Here is a definition of GDP:

gross domestic product (GDP)
the market value of all final goods and services produced within a country in a given period of time

- **Gross domestic product (GDP)** is the market value of all final goods and services produced within a country in a given period of time.

This definition might seem simple enough. But, in fact, many subtle issues arise when computing an economy's GDP. Let's therefore consider each phrase in this definition with some care.

"GDP Is the Market Value . . ."

You have probably heard the adage, "You can't compare apples and oranges." Yet GDP does exactly that. GDP adds together many different kinds of products into a single measure of the value of economic activity. To do this, it uses market prices. Because market prices measure the amount people are willing to pay for different goods, they reflect the value of those goods. If the price of an apple is twice the price of an orange, then an apple contributes twice as much to GDP as does an orange.

". . . Of All . . ."

GDP tries to be comprehensive. It includes all items produced in the economy and sold legally in markets. GDP measures the market value of not just apples and oranges, but also pears and grapefruit, books and movies, haircuts and health care, and on and on.

GDP also includes the market value of the housing services provided by the economy's stock of housing. For rental housing, this value is easy to calculate—the rent equals both the tenant's expenditure and the landlord's income. Yet many people own the place where they live and, therefore, do not pay rent. The government includes this owner-occupied housing in GDP by estimating its rental value. That is, GDP is based on the assumption that the owner, in effect, pays rent to himself, so the rent is included both in his expenditure and in his income.

There are some products, however, that GDP excludes because measuring them is so difficult. GDP excludes most items produced and sold illicitly, such as illegal drugs. It also excludes most items that are produced and consumed at home and, therefore, never enter the marketplace. Vegetables you buy at the grocery store are part of GDP; vegetables you grow in your garden are not.

These exclusions from GDP can at times lead to paradoxical results. For example, when Karen pays Doug to mow her lawn, that transaction is part of GDP. If Karen were to marry Doug, the situation would change. Even though Doug may continue to mow Karen's lawn, the value of the mowing is now left out of GDP because Doug's service is no longer sold in a market. Thus, when Karen and Doug marry, GDP falls.

"... Final ..."

When International Paper makes paper, which Hallmark then uses to make a greeting card, the paper is called an *intermediate good*, and the card is called a *final good*. GDP includes only the value of final goods. The reason is that the value of intermediate goods is already included in the prices of the final goods. Adding the market value of the paper to the market value of the card would be double counting. That is, it would (incorrectly) count the paper twice.

An important exception to this principle arises when an intermediate good is produced and, rather than being used, is added to a firm's inventory of goods to be used or sold at a later date. In this case, the intermediate good is taken to be "final" for the moment, and its value as inventory investment is added to GDP. When the inventory of the intermediate good is later used or sold, the firm's inventory investment is negative, and GDP for the later period is reduced accordingly.

"... Goods and Services ..."

GDP includes both tangible goods (food, clothing, cars) and intangible services (haircuts, housecleaning, doctor visits). When you buy a CD by your favorite band, you are buying a good, and the purchase price is part of GDP. When you pay to hear a concert by the same band, you are buying a service, and the ticket price is also part of GDP.

"... Produced ..."

GDP includes goods and services currently produced. It does not include transactions involving items produced in the past. When General Motors produces and sells a new car, the value of the car is included in GDP. When one person sells a used car to another person, the value of the used car is not included in GDP.

"... Within a Country ..."

GDP measures the value of production within the geographic confines of a country. When a Canadian citizen works temporarily in the United States, his production is part of U.S. GDP. When an American citizen owns a factory in Haiti, the production at his factory is not part of U.S. GDP. (It is part of Haiti's GDP.) Thus, items are included in a nation's GDP if they are produced domestically, regardless of the nationality of the producer.

"... In a Given Period of Time"

GDP measures the value of production that takes place within a specific interval of time. Usually that interval is a year or a quarter (three months). GDP measures the economy's flow of income and expenditure during that interval.

When the government reports the GDP for a quarter, it usually presents GDP "at an annual rate." This means that the figure reported for quarterly GDP is the amount of income and expenditure during the quarter multiplied by 4. The government uses this convention so that quarterly and annual figures on GDP can be compared more easily.

In addition, when the government reports quarterly GDP, it presents the data after they have been modified by a statistical procedure called *seasonal adjustment*. The unadjusted data show clearly that the economy produces more goods and services during some times of year than during others. (As you might guess, December's holiday shopping season is a high point.) When monitoring the condition of the economy, economists and policymakers often want to look beyond these regular seasonal changes. Therefore, government statisticians adjust the quarterly data to take out the seasonal cycle. The GDP data reported in the news are always seasonally adjusted.

FYI

OTHER MEASURES OF INCOME

When the U.S. Department of Commerce computes the nation's GDP every three months, it also computes various other measures of income to get a more complete picture of what's happening in the economy. These other measures differ from GDP by excluding or including certain categories of income. What follows is a brief description of five of these income measures, ordered from largest to smallest.

- *Gross national product (GNP)* is the total income earned by a nation's permanent residents (called *nationals*). It differs from GDP by including income that our citizens earn abroad and excluding income that foreigners earn here. For example, when a Canadian citizen works temporarily in the United States, his production is part of U.S. GDP, but it is not part of U.S. GNP. (It is part of Canada's GNP.) For most countries, including the United States, domestic residents are responsible for most domestic production, so GDP and GNP are quite close.
- *Net national product (NNP)* is the total income of a nation's residents (GNP) minus losses from depreciation. *Depreciation* is the wear and tear on the economy's stock of equipment and struc-

tures, such as trucks rusting and computers becoming obsolete. In the national income accounts prepared by the Department of Commerce, depreciation is called the "consumption of fixed capital."
- *National income* is the total income earned by a nation's residents in the production of goods and services. It differs from net national product by excluding indirect business taxes (such as sales taxes) and including business subsidies. NNP and national income also differ because of a "statistical discrepancy" that arises from problems in data collection.
- *Personal income* is the income that households and noncorporate businesses receive. Unlike national income, it excludes *retained earnings,* which is income that corporations have earned but have not paid out to their owners. It also subtracts corporate income taxes and contributions for social insurance (mostly Social Security taxes). In addition, personal income includes the interest income that households receive from their holdings of government debt and the income that households receive from government transfer programs, such as welfare and Social Security.
- *Disposable personal income* is the income that households and noncorporate businesses have left after satisfying all their obligations to the government. It equals personal income minus personal taxes and certain nontax payments (such as traffic tickets).

Although the various measures of income differ in detail, they almost always tell the same story about economic conditions. When GDP is growing rapidly, these other measures of income are usually growing rapidly. And when GDP is falling, these other measures are usually falling as well. For monitoring fluctuations in the overall economy, it does not matter much which measure of income we use.

Now let's repeat the definition of GDP:

- Gross domestic product (GDP) is the market value of all final goods and services produced within a country in a given period of time.

It should be apparent that GDP is a sophisticated measure of the value of economic activity. In advanced courses in macroeconomics, you will learn more about the subtleties that arise in its calculation. But even now you can see that each phrase in this definition is packed with meaning.

QuickQuiz Which contributes more to GDP—the production of a pound of hamburger or the production of a pound of caviar? Why?

THE COMPONENTS OF GDP

Spending in the economy takes many forms. At any moment, the Smith family may be having lunch at Burger King; General Motors may be building a car factory; the Navy may be procuring a submarine; and British Airways may be buying an airplane from Boeing. GDP includes all of these various forms of spending on domestically produced goods and services.

To understand how the economy is using its scarce resources, economists are often interested in studying the composition of GDP among various types of spending. To do this, GDP (which we denote as Y) is divided into four components: consumption (C), investment (I), government purchases (G), and net exports (NX):

$$Y = C + I + G + NX.$$

This equation is an *identity*—an equation that must be true by the way the variables in the equation are defined. In this case, because each dollar of expenditure included in GDP is placed into one of the four components of GDP, the total of the four components must be equal to GDP. Let's look at each of these four components more closely.

Consumption

Consumption is spending by households on goods and services. "Goods" include household spending on durable goods, such as automobiles and appliances, and nondurable goods, such as food and clothing. "Services" include such intangible items as haircuts and medical care. Household spending on education is also included in consumption of services (although one might argue that it would fit better in the next component).

consumption
spending by households on goods and services, with the exception of purchases of new housing

Investment

Investment is the purchase of goods that will be used in the future to produce more goods and services. It is the sum of purchases of capital equipment, inventories,

investment
spending on capital equipment, inventories, and structures, including household purchases of new housing

and structures. Investment in structures includes expenditure on new housing. By convention, the purchase of a new house is the one form of household spending categorized as investment rather than consumption.

As mentioned earlier in this chapter, the treatment of inventory accumulation is noteworthy. When IBM produces a computer and, instead of selling it, adds it to its inventory, IBM is assumed to have "purchased" the computer for itself. That is, the national income accountants treat the computer as part of IBM's investment spending. (If IBM later sells the computer out of inventory, IBM's inventory investment will then be negative, offsetting the positive expenditure of the buyer.) Inventories are treated this way because one aim of GDP is to measure the value of the economy's production, and goods added to inventory are part of that period's production.

Government Purchases

government purchases
spending on goods and services by local, state, and federal governments

Government purchases include spending on goods and services by local, state, and federal governments. It includes the salaries of government workers and spending on public works. Recently, the U.S. national income accounts have switched to the longer label "government consumption expenditure and gross investment," but in this book we will use the traditional and shorter term "government purchases."

The meaning of "government purchases" requires a bit of clarification. When the government pays the salary of an Army general, that salary is part of government purchases. But what happens when the government pays a Social Security benefit to one of the elderly? Such government spending is called a *transfer payment* because it is not made in exchange for a currently produced good or service. Transfer payments alter household income, but they do not reflect the economy's production. (From a macroeconomic standpoint, transfer payments are like negative taxes.) Because GDP is intended to measure income from, and expenditure on, the production of goods and services, transfer payments are not counted as part of government purchases.

Net Exports

net exports
spending on domestically produced goods by foreigners (exports) minus spending on foreign goods by domestic residents (imports)

Net exports equal the purchases of domestically produced goods by foreigners (exports) minus the domestic purchases of foreign goods (imports). A domestic firm's sale to a buyer in another country, such as the Boeing sale to British Airways, increases net exports.

The "net" in "net exports" refers to the fact that imports are subtracted from exports. This subtraction is made because imports of goods and services are included in other components of GDP. For example, suppose that a household buys a $30,000 car from Volvo, the Swedish carmaker. That transaction increases consumption by $30,000 because car purchases are part of consumer spending. It also reduces net exports by $30,000 because the car is an import. In other words, net exports include goods and services produced abroad (with a minus sign) because these goods and services are included in consumption, investment, and government purchases (with a plus sign). Thus, when a domestic household, firm, or government buys a good or service from abroad, the purchase reduces net exports—but because it also raises consumption, investment, or government purchases, it does not affect GDP.

TABLE 1

	Total (in billions of dollars)	Per Person (in dollars)	Percent of Total
Gross domestic product, Y	$10,082	$35,375	100%
Consumption, C	6,987	24,516	69
Investment, I	1,586	5,565	16
Government purchases, G	1,858	6,519	18
Net exports, NX	−349	−1,225	−3

GDP and Its Components

This table shows total GDP for the U.S. economy in 2001 and the breakdown of GDP among its four components. When reading this table, recall the identity Y = C + I + G + NX.

Source: U.S. Department of Commerce.

Case Study
THE COMPONENTS OF U.S. GDP

Table 1 shows the composition of U.S. GDP in 2001. In this year, the GDP of the United States was about $10 trillion. Dividing this number by the 2001 U.S. population of 285 million yields GDP per person (sometimes called GDP per capita). We find that in 2001 the income and expenditure of the average American was $35,375.

Consumption made up about two-thirds of GDP, or $24,516 per person. Investment was $5,565 per person. Government purchases were $6,519 per person. Net exports were −$1,225 per person. This number is negative because Americans earned less from selling to foreigners than they spent on foreign goods.

These data come from the Bureau of Economic Analysis, which is the part of the U.S. Department of Commerce that produces the national income accounts. You can find more recent data on GDP at its Web site http://www.bea.doc.gov. ●

QuickQuiz List the four components of expenditure. Which is the largest?

REAL VERSUS NOMINAL GDP

As we have seen, GDP measures the total spending on goods and services in all markets in the economy. If total spending rises from one year to the next, one of two things must be true: (1) the economy is producing a larger output of goods and services, or (2) goods and services are being sold at higher prices. When studying changes in the economy over time, economists want to separate these two effects. In particular, they want a measure of the total quantity of goods and services the economy is producing that is not affected by changes in the prices of those goods and services.

To do this, economists use a measure called *real GDP*. Real GDP answers a hypothetical question: What would be the value of the goods and services produced this year if we valued these goods and services at the prices that prevailed in some specific year in the past? By evaluating current production using prices that are fixed at past levels, real GDP shows how the economy's overall production of goods and services changes over time.

To see more precisely how real GDP is constructed, let's consider an example.

A Numerical Example

Table 2 shows some data for an economy that produces only two goods—hot dogs and hamburgers. The table shows the quantities of the two goods produced and their prices in the years 2001, 2002, and 2003.

To compute total spending in this economy, we would multiply the quantities of hot dogs and hamburgers by their prices. In the year 2001, 100 hot dogs are sold at a price of $1 per hot dog, so expenditure on hot dogs equals $100. In the same year, 50 hamburgers are sold for $2 per hamburger, so expenditure on hamburgers also equals $100. Total expenditure in the economy—the sum of expenditure on hot dogs and expenditure on hamburgers—is $200. This amount, the production of goods and services valued at current prices, is called **nominal GDP.**

The table shows the calculation of nominal GDP for these three years. Total spending rises from $200 in 2001 to $600 in 2002 and then to $1,200 in 2003. Part of this rise is attributable to the increase in the quantities of hot dogs and hamburgers, and part is attributable to the increase in the prices of hot dogs and hamburgers.

To obtain a measure of the amount produced that is not affected by changes in prices, we use **real GDP,** which is the production of goods and services valued at

nominal GDP
the production of goods and services valued at current prices

real GDP
the production of goods and services valued at constant prices

---

TABLE 2

Real and Nominal GDP

This table shows how to calculate real GDP, nominal GDP, and the GDP deflator for a hypothetical economy that produces only hot dogs and hamburgers.

		Prices and Quantities		
Year	Price of Hot Dogs	Quantity of Hot Dogs	Price of Hamburgers	Quantity of Hamburgers
2001	$1	100	$2	50
2002	2	150	3	100
2003	3	200	4	150

Year	Calculating Nominal GDP
2001	($1 per hot dog × 100 hot dogs) + ($2 per hamburger × 50 hamburgers) = $200
2002	($2 per hot dog × 150 hot dogs) + ($3 per hamburger × 100 hamburgers) = $600
2003	($3 per hot dog × 200 hot dogs) + ($4 per hamburger × 150 hamburgers) = $1,200

Year	Calculating Real GDP (base year 2001)
2001	($1 per hot dog × 100 hot dogs) + ($2 per hamburger × 50 hamburgers) = $200
2002	($1 per hot dog × 150 hot dogs) + ($2 per hamburger × 100 hamburgers) = $350
2003	($1 per hot dog × 200 hot dogs) + ($2 per hamburger × 150 hamburgers) = $500

Year	Calculating the GDP Deflator
2001	($200/$200) × 100 = 100
2002	($600/$350) × 100 = 171
2003	($1,200/$500) × 100 = 240

constant prices. We calculate real GDP by first choosing one year as a *base year*. We then use the prices of hot dogs and hamburgers in the base year to compute the value of goods and services in all of the years. In other words, the prices in the base year provide the basis for comparing quantities in different years.

Suppose that we choose 2001 to be the base year in our example. We can then use the prices of hot dogs and hamburgers in 2001 to compute the value of goods and services produced in 2001, 2002, and 2003. Table 2 shows these calculations. To compute real GDP for 2001, we use the prices of hot dogs and hamburgers in 2001 (the base year) and the quantities of hot dogs and hamburgers produced in 2001. (Thus, for the base year, real GDP always equals nominal GDP.) To compute real GDP for 2002, we use the prices of hot dogs and hamburgers in 2001 (the base year) and the quantities of hot dogs and hamburgers produced in 2002. Similarly, to compute real GDP for 2003, we use the prices in 2001 and the quantities in 2003. When we find that real GDP has risen from $200 in 2001 to $350 in 2002 and then to $500 in 2003, we know that the increase is attributable to an increase in the quantities produced, because the prices are being held fixed at base-year levels.

To sum up: *Nominal GDP uses current prices to place a value on the economy's production of goods and services. Real GDP uses constant base-year prices to place a value on the economy's production of goods and services.* Because real GDP is not affected by changes in prices, changes in real GDP reflect only changes in the amounts being produced. Thus, real GDP is a measure of the economy's production of goods and services.

Our goal in computing GDP is to gauge how well the overall economy is performing. Because real GDP measures the economy's production of goods and services, it reflects the economy's ability to satisfy people's needs and desires. Thus, real GDP is a better gauge of economic well-being than is nominal GDP. When economists talk about the economy's GDP, they usually mean real GDP rather than nominal GDP. And when they talk about growth in the economy, they measure that growth as the percentage change in real GDP from one period to another.

The GDP Deflator

As we have just seen, nominal GDP reflects both the prices of goods and services and the quantities of goods and services the economy is producing. By contrast, by holding prices constant at base-year levels, real GDP reflects only the quantities produced. From these two statistics, we can compute a third, called the GDP deflator, which reflects the prices of goods and services but not the quantities produced.

The **GDP deflator** is calculated as follows:

$$\text{GDP deflator} = \frac{\text{Nominal GDP}}{\text{Real GDP}} \times 100.$$

GDP deflator
a measure of the price level calculated as the ratio of nominal GDP to real GDP times 100

Because nominal GDP and real GDP must be the same in the base year, the GDP deflator for the base year always equals 100. The GDP deflator for subsequent years measures the change in nominal GDP from the base year that cannot be attributable to a change in real GDP.

The GDP deflator measures the current level of prices relative to the level of prices in the base year. To see why this is true, consider a couple of simple examples. First, imagine that the quantities produced in the economy rise over time but prices remain the same. In this case, both nominal and real GDP rise together, so the GDP deflator is constant. Now suppose, instead, that prices rise over time but the quantities produced stay the same. In this second case, nominal GDP rises but real GDP remains the same, so the GDP deflator rises as well. Notice that, in both cases, the GDP deflator reflects what's happening to prices, not quantities.

Let's now return to our numerical example in Table 2. The GDP deflator is computed at the bottom of the table. For year 2001, nominal GDP is $200, and real GDP is $200, so the GDP deflator is 100. For the year 2002, nominal GDP is $600, and real GDP is $350, so the GDP deflator is 171. Because the GDP deflator rose in year 2002 from 100 to 171, we can say that the price level increased by 71 percent.

The GDP deflator is one measure that economists use to monitor the average level of prices in the economy. We examine another—the consumer price index—in the next chapter, where we also describe the differences between the two measures.

Case Study
REAL GDP OVER RECENT HISTORY

Now that we know how real GDP is defined and measured, let's look at what this macroeconomic variable tells us about the recent history of the United States. Figure 2 shows quarterly data on real GDP for the U.S. economy since 1970.

The most obvious feature of these data is that real GDP grows over time. The real GDP of the U.S. economy in 2001 was more than twice its 1970 level. Put differently, the output of goods and services produced in the United States has grown on average about 3 percent per year since 1970. This continued growth in real GDP enables the typical American to enjoy greater economic prosperity than his or her parents and grandparents did.

A second feature of the GDP data is that growth is not steady. The upward climb of real GDP is occasionally interrupted by periods during which GDP declines, called *recessions*. Figure 2 marks recessions with shaded vertical bars. (There is no ironclad rule for when the official business cycle dating committee will de-

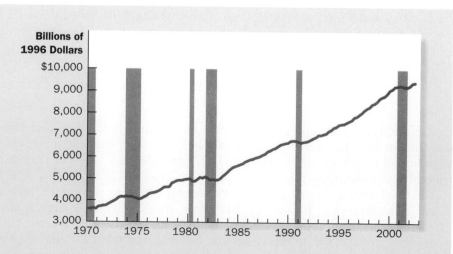

FIGURE 2

Real GDP in the United States

This figure shows quarterly data on real GDP for the U.S. economy since 1970. Recessions—periods of falling real GDP—are marked with the shaded vertical bars.

Source: U.S. Department of Commerce.

clare that a recession has occurred, but a good rule of thumb is two consecutive quarters of falling real GDP.) Recessions are associated not only with lower incomes but also with other forms of economic distress: rising unemployment, falling profits, increased bankruptcies, and so on.

IN THE NEWS

GDP LIGHTENS UP

GDP measures the value of the economy's output of goods and services. What do you think we would learn if, instead, we measured the weight of the economy's output?

From Greenspan, a (Truly) Weighty Idea

By David Wessel

Having weighed the evidence carefully, Federal Reserve Chairman Alan Greenspan wants you to know that the U.S. economy is getting lighter.

Literally.

When he refers to "downsizing" in this instance, Mr. Greenspan means that a dollar's worth of the goods and services produced in the mighty U.S. economy weighs a lot less than it used to, even after adjusting for inflation.

A modern 10-story office building, he says, weighs less than a 10-story building erected in the late 19th century. With synthetic fibers, clothes weigh less. And the electronics revolution has produced televisions so light they can be worn on the wrist.

By conventional measures, the [real] gross domestic product—the value of all goods and services produced in the nation—is five times as great as it was 50 years ago. Yet "the physical weight of our gross domestic product is evidently only modestly higher than it was 50 or

100 years ago," Mr. Greenspan told an audience in Dallas recently.

When you think about it, it's not so surprising that the economy is getting lighter. An ever-growing proportion of the U.S. GDP consists of things that don't weigh anything at all—lawyers' services, psychotherapy, e-mail, online information.

But Mr. Greenspan has a way of making the obvious sound profound. Only "a small fraction" of the nation's economic growth in the past several decades "represents growth in the tonnage of physical materials—oil, coal, ores, wood, raw chemicals," he has observed. "The remainder represents new insights into how to rearrange those physical materials to better serve human needs." . . .

The incredible shrinking GDP helps explain why American workers can produce more for each hour of work than ever before. . . . [It] also helps explain why there is so much international trade these days. "The . . . downsizing of output," Mr. Greenspan said recently, "meant that products were easier and hence less costly to move, and most especially across national borders." . . .

"The world of 1948 was vastly different," Mr. Greenspan observed a few years back. "The quintessential model of industry might in those days was the array of vast, smoke-encased integrated steel mills . . . on the shores of Lake Michigan. Output was things, big physical things."

Today, one exemplar of U.S. economic might is Microsoft Corp., with its almost weightless output. "Virtually unimaginable a half-century ago was the extent to which concepts and ideas would substitute for physical resources and human brawn in the production of goods and services," he has said.

Of course, one thing made in the U.S. is heavier than it used to be: people. The National Institutes of Health says 22.3% of Americans are obese, up from 12.8% in the early 1960s. But Mr. Greenspan doesn't talk about that.

Source: *The Wall Street Journal,* May 20, 1999, p. B1. Copyright © 1999 by Dow Jones & Co. Inc. Reproduced with permission of DOW JONES & CO INC in the format Textbook via Copyright Clearance Center.

Much of macroeconomics is aimed at explaining the long-run growth and short-run fluctuations in real GDP. As we will see in the coming chapters, we need different models for these two purposes. Because the short-run fluctuations represent deviations from the long-run trend, we first examine the behavior of key macroeconomic variables, including real GDP, in the long run. Then in later chapters we build on this analysis to explain short-run fluctuations. ●

QuickQuiz Define real and nominal GDP. Which is a better measure of economic well-being? Why?

GDP AND ECONOMIC WELL-BEING

Earlier in this chapter, GDP was called the best single measure of the economic well-being of a society. Now that we know what GDP is, we can evaluate this claim.

As we have seen, GDP measures both the economy's total income and the economy's total expenditure on goods and services. Thus, GDP per person tells us the income and expenditure of the average person in the economy. Because most people would prefer to receive higher income and enjoy higher expenditure, GDP per person seems a natural measure of the economic well-being of the average individual.

Yet some people dispute the validity of GDP as a measure of well-being. When Senator Robert Kennedy was running for president in 1968, he gave a moving critique of such economic measures:

[Gross domestic product] does not allow for the health of our children, the quality of their education, or the joy of their play. It does not include the beauty of our poetry or the strength of our marriages, the intelligence of our public debate or the integrity of our public officials. It measures neither our courage, nor our wisdom, nor our devotion to our country. It measures everything, in short, except that which makes life worthwhile, and it can tell us everything about America except why we are proud that we are Americans.

Much of what Robert Kennedy said is correct. Why then do we care about GDP?

The answer is that a large GDP does in fact help us to lead a good life. GDP does not measure the health of our children, but nations with larger GDP can afford better health care for their children. GDP does not measure the quality of their education, but nations with larger GDP can afford better educational systems. GDP does not measure the beauty of our poetry, but nations with larger GDP can afford to teach more of their citizens to read and to enjoy poetry. GDP does not take account of our intelligence, integrity, courage, wisdom, or devotion to country, but all of these laudable attributes are easier to foster when people are less concerned about being able to afford the material necessities of life. In short, GDP does not directly measure those things that make life worthwhile, but it does measure our ability to obtain the inputs into a worthwhile life.

GDP is not, however, a perfect measure of well-being. Some things that contribute to a good life are left out of GDP. One is leisure. Suppose, for instance, that everyone in the economy suddenly started working every day of the week, rather than enjoying leisure on weekends. More goods and services would be produced, and GDP would rise. Yet, despite the increase in GDP, we should not conclude that everyone would be better off. The loss from reduced leisure would offset the gain from producing and consuming a greater quantity of goods and services.

Because GDP uses market prices to value goods and services, it excludes the value of almost all activity that takes place outside of markets. In particular, GDP omits the value of goods and services produced at home. When a chef prepares a delicious meal and sells it at his restaurant, the value of that meal is part of GDP. But if the chef prepares the same meal for his spouse, the value he has added to the raw ingredients is left out of GDP. Similarly, child care provided in day care centers is part of GDP, whereas child care by parents at home is not. Volunteer work also contributes to the well-being of those in society, but GDP does not reflect these contributions.

Another thing that GDP excludes is the quality of the environment. Imagine that the government eliminated all environmental regulations. Firms could then produce goods and services without considering the pollution they create, and GDP might rise. Yet well-being would most likely fall. The deterioration in the quality of air and water would more than offset the gains from greater production.

GDP also says nothing about the distribution of income. A society in which 100 people have annual incomes of $50,000 has GDP of $5 million and, not surprisingly, GDP per person of $50,000. So does a society in which 10 people earn $500,000 and 90 suffer with nothing at all. Few people would look at those two situations and call them equivalent. GDP per person tells us what happens to the average person, but behind the average lies a large variety of personal experiences.

In the end, we can conclude that GDP is a good measure of economic well-being for most—but not all—purposes. It is important to keep in mind what GDP includes and what it leaves out.

GDP reflects the factory's production, but not the harm that it inflicts on the environment.

Case Study
INTERNATIONAL DIFFERENCES IN GDP AND THE QUALITY OF LIFE

One way to gauge the usefulness of GDP as a measure of economic well-being is to examine international data. Rich and poor countries have vastly different levels of GDP per person. If a large GDP leads to a higher standard of living, then we should observe GDP to be strongly correlated with measures of the quality of life. And, in fact, we do.

Table 3 (p. 218) shows 12 of the world's most populous countries ranked in order of GDP per person. The table also shows life expectancy (the expected life span at birth) and literacy (the percentage of the adult population who can read). These data show a clear pattern. In rich countries, such as the United States, Japan, and Germany, people can expect to live into their late seventies, and almost all of the population can read. In poor countries, such as Nigeria, Bangladesh, and Pakistan, people typically live only until their fifties or early sixties, and only about half of the population is literate.

TABLE 3

GDP, Life Expectancy, and Literacy

The table shows GDP per person and two measures of the quality of life for 12 major countries.

Source: *Human Development Report 2001*, United Nations.

Country	Real GDP per Person (1999)	Life Expectancy	Adult Literacy
United States	$31,872	77 years	99%
Japan	24,898	81	99
Germany	23,742	78	99
Mexico	8,297	72	91
Russia	7,473	66	99
Brazil	7,037	67	85
China	3,617	70	83
Indonesia	2,857	66	86
India	2,248	63	56
Pakistan	1,834	60	45
Bangladesh	1,483	59	41
Nigeria	853	52	63

Although data on other aspects of the quality of life are less complete, they tell a similar story. Countries with low GDP per person tend to have more infants with low birth weight, higher rates of infant mortality, higher rates of maternal mortality, higher rates of child malnutrition, and less common access to safe drinking water. In countries with low GDP per person, fewer school-age children are actually in school, and those who are in school must learn with fewer teachers per student. These countries also tend to have fewer televisions, fewer telephones, fewer paved roads, and fewer households with electricity. International data leave no doubt that a nation's GDP is closely associated with its citizens' standard of living. ●

Case Study
WHO WINS AT THE OLYMPICS?

Every four years, the nations of the world compete in the Olympic Games. When the games end, commentators use the number of medals a nation takes home as a measure of success. This measure seems very different from the GDP that economists use to measure success. It turns out, however, that this is not so.

Economists Andrew Bernard and Meghan Busse have examined the determinants of Olympic success. The most obvious explanation is population: Countries with more people will, other things equal, have more star athletes. But this is not the full story. China, India, Indonesia, and Bangladesh together have more than 40 percent of the world's population, but they typically win only 6 percent of the medals. The reason is that these countries are poor: Despite their large populations, they account for only 5 percent of the world's GDP. Their poverty prevents many gifted athletes from reaching their potential.

Bernard and Busse find that the best gauge of a nation's ability to produce world-class athletes is total GDP. A large total GDP means more medals, regardless of whether the total comes from high GDP per person or a large number of people. In other words, if two nations have the same total GDP, they can be expected to win the same number of medals, even if one nation (India) has many people and low GDP per person and the other nation (Netherlands) has few people and high GDP per person.

In addition to GDP, two other factors influence the number of medals won. The host country usually earns extra medals, reflecting the benefit that athletes get from competing on their home turf. In addition, the former communist countries of Eastern Europe (the Soviet Union, Romania, East Germany, and so on) earned more medals than other countries with similar GDP. These centrally planned economies devoted more of the nation's resources to training Olympic athletes than did free-market economies, where people have more control over their own lives. ●

QuickQuiz Why should policymakers care about GDP?

CONCLUSION

This chapter has discussed how economists measure the total income of a nation. Measurement is, of course, only a starting point. Much of macroeconomics is aimed at revealing the long-run and short-run determinants of a nation's gross domestic product. Why, for example, is GDP higher in the United States and Japan than in India and Nigeria? What can the governments of the poorest countries do to promote more rapid growth in GDP? Why does GDP in the United States rise rapidly in some years and fall in others? What can U.S. policymakers do to reduce the severity of these fluctuations in GDP? These are the questions we will take up shortly.

At this point, it is important to acknowledge the importance of just measuring GDP. We all get some sense of how the economy is doing as we go about our lives. But the economists who study changes in the economy and the policymakers who formulate economic policies need more than this vague sense—they need concrete data on which to base their judgments. Quantifying the behavior of the economy with statistics such as GDP is, therefore, the first step to developing a science of macroeconomics.

SUMMARY

- Because every transaction has a buyer and a seller, the total expenditure in the economy must equal the total income in the economy.

- Gross domestic product (GDP) measures an economy's total expenditure on newly produced goods and services and the total income earned from the production of these goods and services. More precisely, GDP is the market value of all

final goods and services produced within a country in a given period of time.

- GDP is divided among four components of expenditure: consumption, investment, government purchases, and net exports. Consumption includes spending on goods and services by households, with the exception of purchases of new housing. Investment includes spending on new equipment and structures, including households' purchases of new housing. Government purchases include spending on goods and services by local, state, and federal governments. Net exports equal the value of goods and services produced domestically and sold abroad (exports) minus the value of goods and services produced abroad and sold domestically (imports).

- Nominal GDP uses current prices to value the economy's production of goods and services.

Real GDP uses constant base-year prices to value the economy's production of goods and services. The GDP deflator—calculated from the ratio of nominal to real GDP—measures the level of prices in the economy.

- GDP is a good measure of economic well-being because people prefer higher to lower incomes. But it is not a perfect measure of well-being. For example, GDP excludes the value of leisure and the value of a clean environment.

KEY CONCEPTS

microeconomics, p. 204
macroeconomics, p. 204
gross domestic product
  (GDP), p. 206

consumption, p. 209
investment, p. 209
government purchases, p. 210
net exports, p. 210

nominal GDP, p. 212
real GDP, p. 212
GDP deflator, p. 213

QUESTIONS FOR REVIEW

1. Explain why an economy's income must equal its expenditure.

2. Which contributes more to GDP—the production of an economy car or the production of a luxury car? Why?

3. A farmer sells wheat to a baker for $2. The baker uses the wheat to make bread, which is sold for $3. What is the total contribution of these transactions to GDP?

4. Many years ago Peggy paid $500 to put together a record collection. Today she sold her albums at a garage sale for $100. How does this sale affect current GDP?

5. List the four components of GDP. Give an example of each.

6. Why do economists use real GDP rather than nominal GDP to gauge economic well-being?

7. In the year 2001, the economy produces 100 loaves of bread that sell for $2 each. In the year 2002, the economy produces 200 loaves of bread that sell for $3 each. Calculate nominal GDP, real GDP, and the GDP deflator for each year. (Use 2001 as the base year.) By what percentage does each of these three statistics rise from one year to the next?

8. Why is it desirable for a country to have a large GDP? Give an example of something that would raise GDP and yet be undesirable.

PROBLEMS AND APPLICATIONS

1. What components of GDP (if any) would each of the following transactions affect? Explain.
   a. A family buys a new refrigerator.
   b. Aunt Jane buys a new house.
   c. Ford sells a Thunderbird from its inventory.
   d. You buy a pizza.
   e. California repaves Highway 101.
   f. Your parents buy a bottle of French wine.
   g. Honda expands its factory in Marysville, Ohio.

2. The "government purchases" component of GDP does not include spending on transfer

payments such as Social Security. Thinking about the definition of GDP, explain why transfer payments are excluded.

3. Why do you think households' purchases of new housing are included in the investment component of GDP rather than the consumption component? Can you think of a reason why households' purchases of new cars should also be included in investment rather than in consumption? To what other consumption goods might this logic apply?

4. As the chapter states, GDP does not include the value of used goods that are resold. Why would including such transactions make GDP a less informative measure of economic well-being?

5. Below are some data from the land of milk and honey.

Year	Price of Milk	Quantity of Milk (quarts)	Price of Honey	Quantity of Honey (quarts)
2001	$1	100	$2	50
2002	1	200	2	100
2003	2	200	4	100

a. Compute nominal GDP, real GDP, and the GDP deflator for each year, using 2001 as the base year.

b. Compute the percentage change in nominal GDP, real GDP, and the GDP deflator in 2002 and 2003 from the preceding year. For each year, identify the variable that does not change. Explain in words why your answer makes sense.

c. Did economic well-being rise more in 2002 or 2003? Explain.

6. Consider the following data on U.S. GDP:

Year	Nominal GDP (in billions)	GDP Deflator (base year 1996)
2000	9,873	118
1999	9,269	113

a. What was the growth rate of nominal GDP between 1999 and 2000? (Note: The growth rate is the percentage change from one period to the next.)

b. What was the growth rate of the GDP deflator between 1999 and 2000?

c. What was real GDP in 1999 measured in 1996 prices?

d. What was real GDP in 2000 measured in 1996 prices?

e. What was the growth rate of real GDP between 1999 and 2000?

f. Was the growth rate of nominal GDP higher or lower than the growth rate of real GDP? Explain.

7. If prices rise, people's income from selling goods increases. The growth of real GDP ignores this gain, however. Why, then, do economists prefer real GDP as a measure of economic well-being?

8. Revised estimates of U.S. GDP are usually released by the government near the end of each month. Find a newspaper article that reports on the most recent release, or read the news release yourself at http://www.bea.doc.gov, the Web site of the U.S. Bureau of Economic Analysis. Discuss the recent changes in real and nominal GDP and in the components of GDP.

9. One day Barry the Barber, Inc., collects $400 for haircuts. Over this day, his equipment depreciates in value by $50. Of the remaining $350, Barry sends $30 to the government in sales taxes, takes home $220 in wages, and retains $100 in his business to add new equipment in the future. From the $220 that Barry takes home, he pays $70 in income taxes. Based on this information, compute Barry's contribution to the following measures of income.

a. gross domestic product
b. net national product
c. national income
d. personal income
e. disposable personal income

10. Goods and services that are not sold in markets, such as food produced and consumed at home, are generally not included in GDP. Can you think of how this might cause the numbers in the second column of Table 3 to be misleading in a comparison of the economic well-being of the United States and India? Explain.

11. Until the early 1990s, the U.S. government emphasized GNP rather than GDP as a measure of economic well-being. Which measure should the government prefer if it cares about the total income of Americans? Which measure should it

prefer if it cares about the total amount of economic activity occurring in the United States?

12. The participation of women in the U.S. labor force has risen dramatically since 1970.
    a. How do you think this rise affected GDP?
    b. Now imagine a measure of well-being that includes time spent working in the home and taking leisure. How would the change in this measure of well-being compare to the change in GDP?
    c. Can you think of other aspects of well-being that are associated with the rise in women's labor-force participation? Would it be practical to construct a measure of well-being that includes these aspects?

http://   For more study tools, please visit http://mankiwXtra.swlearning.com.

MEASURING THE COST OF LIVING

In 1931, as the U.S. economy was suffering through the Great Depression, famed baseball player Babe Ruth earned $80,000. At the time, this salary was extraordinary, even among the stars of baseball. According to one story, a reporter asked Ruth whether he thought it was right that he made more than President Herbert Hoover, who had a salary of only $75,000. Ruth replied, "I had a better year."

Today the average baseball player earns about 30 times Ruth's 1931 salary, and the best players can earn 200 times as much. At first, this fact might lead you to think that baseball has become much more lucrative over the past seven decades. But, as everyone knows, the prices of goods and services have also risen. In 1931, a nickel would buy an ice-cream cone, and a quarter would buy a ticket at the local movie theater. Because prices were so much lower in Babe Ruth's day than they are in ours, it is not clear whether Ruth enjoyed a higher or lower standard of living than today's players.

In the preceding chapter we looked at how economists use gross domestic product (GDP) to measure the quantity of goods and services that the economy is producing. This chapter examines how economists measure the overall cost of living. To compare Babe Ruth's salary of $80,000 to salaries from today, we need to find some way of turning dollar figures into meaningful measures of purchasing power. That is exactly the job of a statistic called the *consumer price index*. After seeing how the consumer price index is constructed, we discuss how we can use such a price index to compare dollar figures from different points in time.

The consumer price index is used to monitor changes in the cost of living over time. When the consumer price index rises, the typical family has to spend more dollars to maintain the same standard of living. Economists use the term *inflation* to describe a situation in which the economy's overall price level is rising. The *inflation rate* is the percentage change in the price level from the previous period. As we will see in the coming chapters, inflation is a closely watched aspect of macroeconomic performance and is a key variable guiding macroeconomic policy. This chapter provides the background for that analysis by showing how economists measure the inflation rate using the consumer price index.

THE CONSUMER PRICE INDEX

consumer price index (CPI)
a measure of the overall cost of the goods and services bought by a typical consumer

The **consumer price index (CPI)** is a measure of the overall cost of the goods and services bought by a typical consumer. Each month the Bureau of Labor Statistics, which is part of the Department of Labor, computes and reports the consumer price index. In this section we discuss how the consumer price index is calculated and what problems arise in its measurement. We also consider how this index compares to the GDP deflator, another measure of the overall level of prices, which we examined in the preceding chapter.

How the Consumer Price Index Is Calculated

When the Bureau of Labor Statistics calculates the consumer price index and the inflation rate, it uses data on the prices of thousands of goods and services. To see exactly how these statistics are constructed, let's consider a simple economy in which consumers buy only two goods—hot dogs and hamburgers. Table 1 shows the five steps that the Bureau of Labor Statistics follows.

1. *Fix the basket.* The first step in computing the consumer price index is to determine which prices are most important to the typical consumer. If the typical consumer buys more hot dogs than hamburgers, then the price of hot dogs is more important than the price of hamburgers and, therefore, should be given greater weight in measuring the cost of living. The Bureau of Labor Statistics sets these weights by surveying consumers and finding the basket of goods and services that the typical consumer buys. In the example in the table, the typical consumer buys a basket of 4 hot dogs and 2 hamburgers.

2. *Find the prices.* The second step in computing the consumer price index is to find the prices of each of the goods and services in the basket for each point in time. The table shows the prices of hot dogs and hamburgers for three different years.

3. *Compute the basket's cost.* The third step is to use the data on prices to calculate the cost of the basket of goods and services at different times. The table shows this calculation for each of the three years. Notice that only the prices in this calculation change. By keeping the basket of goods the same (4 hot dogs and 2

TABLE 1

Step 1: Survey Consumers to Determine a Fixed Basket of Goods

4 hot dogs, 2 hamburgers

Step 2: Find the Price of Each Good in Each Year

Year	Price of Hot Dogs	Price of Hamburgers
2001	$1	$2
2002	2	3
2003	3	4

Step 3: Compute the Cost of the Basket of Goods in Each Year

2001	($1 per hot dog × 4 hot dogs) + ($2 per hamburger × 2 hamburgers) = $8
2002	($2 per hot dog × 4 hot dogs) + ($3 per hamburger × 2 hamburgers) = $14
2003	($3 per hot dog × 4 hot dogs) + ($4 per hamburger × 2 hamburgers) = $20

Step 4: Choose One Year as a Base Year (2001) and Compute the Consumer Price Index in Each Year

2001	($8/$8) × 100 = 100
2002	($14/$8) × 100 = 175
2003	($20/$8) × 100 = 250

Step 5: Use the Consumer Price Index to Compute the Inflation Rate from Previous Year

2002	(175 − 100)/100 × 100 = 75%
2003	(250 − 175)/175 × 100 = 43%

Calculating the Consumer Price Index and the Inflation Rate: An Example

This table shows how to calculate the consumer price index and the inflation rate for a hypothetical economy in which consumers buy only hot dogs and hamburgers.

hamburgers), we are isolating the effects of price changes from the effect of any quantity changes that might be occurring at the same time.

4. *Choose a base year and compute the index.* The fourth step is to designate one year as the base year, which is the benchmark against which other years are compared. To calculate the index, the price of the basket of goods and services in each year is divided by the price of the basket in the base year, and this ratio is then multiplied by 100. The resulting number is the consumer price index.

In the example in the table, the year 2001 is the base year. In this year, the basket of hot dogs and hamburgers costs $8. Therefore, the price of the basket in all years is divided by $8 and multiplied by 100. The consumer price index is 100 in 2001. (The index is always 100 in the base year.) The consumer price index is 175 in 2002. This means that the price of the basket in 2002 is 175 percent of its price in the base year. Put differently, a basket of goods that costs $100 in the base year costs $175 in 2002. Similarly, the consumer price index is 250 in 2003, indicating that the price level in 2003 is 250 percent of the price level in the base year.

inflation rate
the percentage change in the price index from the preceding period

5. *Compute the inflation rate.* The fifth and final step is to use the consumer price index to calculate the **inflation rate,** which is the percentage change in the price index from the preceding period. That is, the inflation rate between two consecutive years is computed as follows:

$$\text{Inflation rate in year 2} = \frac{\text{CPI in year 2} - \text{CPI in year 1}}{\text{CPI in year 1}} \times 100.$$

In our example, the inflation rate is 75 percent in 2002 and 43 percent in 2003.

Although this example simplifies the real world by including only two goods, it shows how the Bureau of Labor Statistics (BLS) computes the consumer price index and the inflation rate. The BLS collects and processes data on the prices of thousands of goods and services every month and, by following the five foregoing steps, determines how quickly the cost of living for the typical consumer is rising. When the BLS makes its monthly announcement of the consumer price index, you

WHAT IS IN THE CPI'S BASKET?

When constructing the consumer price index, the Bureau of Labor Statistics tries to include all the goods and services that the typical consumer buys. Moreover, it tries to weight these goods and services according to how much consumers buy of each item.

Figure 1 shows the breakdown of consumer spending into the major categories of goods and services. By far the largest category is housing, which makes up 41 percent of the typical consumer's budget. This category includes the cost of shelter (31 percent), fuel and other utilities (5 percent), and household furnishings and operation (5 percent). The next largest category, at 17 percent, is transportation, which includes spending on cars, gasoline, buses, subways, and so on. The next category, at 16 percent, is food and beverages; this includes food at home (9 percent), food away from home (6 percent), and alcoholic beverages (1 percent). Next are medical care, recreation, and education and communication, each at about 6 percent. This last category includes, for example, college tuition and personal computers. Apparel, which includes clothing, footwear, and jewelry, makes up 4 percent of the typical consumer's budget.

Also included in the figure, at 4 percent of spending, is a category for other goods and services. This is a catchall for things consumers buy that do not naturally fit into the other categories—such as cigarettes, haircuts, and funeral expenses.

FIGURE 1

The Typical Basket of Goods and Services

This figure shows how the typical consumer divides his spending among various categories of goods and services. The Bureau of Labor Statistics calls each percentage the "relative importance" of the category.

Source: Bureau of Labor Statistics.

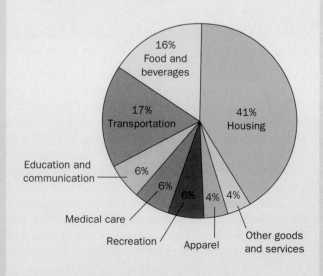

can usually hear the number on the evening television news or see it in the next day's newspaper.

In addition to the consumer price index for the overall economy, the Bureau of Labor Statistics calculates several other price indexes. It reports the index for specific regions within the country (such as Boston, New York, and Los Angeles) and for some narrow categories of goods and services (such as food, clothing, and energy). It also calculates the **producer price index,** which measures the cost of a basket of goods and services bought by firms rather than consumers. Because firms eventually pass on their costs to consumers in the form of higher consumer prices, changes in the producer price index are often thought to be useful in predicting changes in the consumer price index.

producer price index
a measure of the cost of a basket of goods and services bought by firms

Problems in Measuring the Cost of Living

The goal of the consumer price index is to measure changes in the cost of living. In other words, the consumer price index tries to gauge how much incomes must rise in order to maintain a constant standard of living. The consumer price index, however, is not a perfect measure of the cost of living. Three problems with the index are widely acknowledged but difficult to solve.

The first problem is called *substitution bias.* When prices change from one year to the next, they do not all change proportionately: Some prices rise more than others. Consumers respond to these differing price changes by buying less of the goods whose prices have risen by large amounts and by buying more of the goods whose prices have risen less or perhaps even have fallen. That is, consumers substitute toward goods that have become relatively less expensive. If a price index is computed assuming a fixed basket of goods, it ignores the possibility of consumer substitution and, therefore, overstates the increase in the cost of living from one year to the next.

Let's consider a simple example. Imagine that in the base year, apples are cheaper than pears, and so consumers buy more apples than pears. When the Bureau of Labor Statistics constructs the basket of goods, it will include more apples than pears. Suppose that next year pears are cheaper than apples. Consumers will naturally respond to the price changes by buying more pears and fewer apples. Yet, when computing the consumer price index, the Bureau of Labor Statistics uses a fixed basket, which in essence assumes that consumers continue buying the now expensive apples in the same quantities as before. For this reason, the index will measure a much larger increase in the cost of living than consumers actually experience.

The second problem with the consumer price index is the *introduction of new goods.* When a new good is introduced, consumers have more variety from which to choose. Greater variety, in turn, makes each dollar more valuable, so consumers need fewer dollars to maintain any given standard of living. Yet because the consumer price index is based on a fixed basket of goods and services, it does not reflect this change in the purchasing power of the dollar.

Again, let's consider an example. When VCRs were introduced, consumers were able to watch their favorite movies at home. Compared with going to a movie theater, the convenience was greater and the cost was less. A perfect cost-of-living index would have reflected the introduction of the VCR with a decrease in the cost of living. The consumer price index, however, did not decrease in response to the introduction of the VCR. Eventually, the Bureau of Labor Statistics did revise the

IN THE NEWS

SHOPPING FOR THE CPI

Behind every macroeconomic statistic are thousands of individual pieces of data on the economy. The following article follows some of the people who collect these data.

Is the CPI Accurate? Ask the Federal Sleuths Who Get the Numbers

By Christina Duff

TRENTON, N.J.—The hospital's finance director is relentlessly unhelpful, but she is still no match for Sabina Bloom, government gumshoe.

Mrs. Bloom wants to know the exact prices of some hospital services. "Nothing's changed," the woman says. "Well, do you have the ledger?" Mrs. Bloom asks. "We *haven't* changed any prices," the woman insists. Mrs. Bloom's fast talk finally pries the woman from behind her desk, and she gets the numbers. It turns out that a semiprivate surgery recovery room now costs $753.80 a day—or $0.04 less than a month ago.

Chalk up another small success for Mrs. Bloom, one of about 300 Bureau of Labor Statistics employees who gather the information that is fed into the monthly Consumer Price Index. . . .

Mrs. Bloom's travails sometimes read like a detective novel. Each month, she covers 900 miles in her beat-up Geo Prizm (three accidents in the past 18 months) to visit about 150 sites. Her mission: to record the prices of certain items, time and again. If prices change, she needs to find out why. Each month, some 90,000 prices are shipped to Washington, plugged into a computer, scrutinized, aggregated, adjusted for seasonal ups or downs, and then spit out as the monthly CPI report.

Choosing what to price—for example, the "regular" or "fancy" baby para-

keet—can seem arbitrary. After consulting surveys that track consumer buying habits, the labor statistics bureau selects popular stores and item categories—say, women's tops. The price-taker then asks a store employee to help zero in on an item of the price-taker's choosing. They narrow to the size of the top, its style (short-sleeve, long-sleeve, tank, or turtleneck), and so on; items that generate the most revenue in a category have the best chance of getting picked.

Shoppers know that relying on employees for anything can be chancy. At a downtown Chicago department store (the government doesn't disclose names) price-taker Mary Ann Latter squints at a sale sign above an ivory shell blouse. "Save 45%–60% when you take an additional 30% off permanently reduced

basket of goods to include VCRs, and subsequently the index reflected changes in VCR prices. But the reduction in the cost of living associated with the initial introduction of the VCR never showed up in the index.

The third problem with the consumer price index is *unmeasured quality change*. If the quality of a good deteriorates from one year to the next, the value of a dollar falls, even if the price of the good stays the same. Similarly, if the quality rises from one year to the next, the value of a dollar rises. The Bureau of Labor Statistics does its best to account for quality change. When the quality of a good in the basket changes—for example, when a car model has more horsepower or gets better gas mileage from one year to the next—the BLS adjusts the price of the good to account for the quality change. It is, in essence, trying to compute the price of a merchandise. Markdown taken at register," the sign says.

Confused, Ms. Latter asks a clerk to scan the item. There is a pause. "It's 30 percent off," she says, just before the lunch-hour rush.

"I know," Ms. Latter says, "but can you scan it just to make sure?" Under her breath, she mumbles, "So helpful."

Downstairs in the jewelry department, Ms. Latter tries to price the one 18-inch silver necklace left, but there is no tag. "Do I have to look it up now?" moans the employee behind the counter. Ms. Latter watches her wait on several customers, then asks again: "Could you find it?" The harried saleswoman throws on the counter a thick notebook with a dizzying array of jewelry sketches. Ms. Latter finally locates a silver weave that looks about right.

When the exact item can't be found, price-takers must substitute. That can be difficult. Consider a haircut: If the stylist leaves, his fill-in must have about the same experience; a newer stylist, for example, might charge less. This frigid winter afternoon, Ms. Latter needs to substitute a coat because clothing items rarely remain on the racks for more than a couple months. It must be a lightweight swing coat of less than half wool.

After digging through heavy winter wear, trying to locate tags in three departments on two floors, she gives up. It is off season anyway, so she will have to wait months to choose a substitute.

Making it harder for price detectives to grasp the true cost of living is that the master list of 207 categories they price—called the market basket—is updated only once every ten years. Cellular phones? Too new to be priced because they don't fit into any of the categories set up in the 1980s. They probably will be included when the new categories arrive in 1998.

Some changes within these categories are made every five years. So within "new cars," for example, if domestic autos overtake imports in a big way, price-takers might examine more Fords and fewer Toyotas. But that doesn't happen often enough, critics say. Ms. Latter, a city-dwelling Generation X'er, continually must price "Always Twenty-One" girdles, yet ignore the new, popular WonderBras behind her. . . .

Ms. Latter's colleague in suburban Chicago, Sheila Ward, must ignore the hoopla over Tickle Me Elmo and instead price a GI Joe Extreme doll with "painted, molded hair." Reliance on outdated goods, says Mrs. Ward, "would be one of

the criticisms of us." She recalls a music store owner who became frustrated because she kept seeking prices on a guitar he could never imagine playing—much less selling. He finally threw her out of his shop, screaming, "The damned government! Is this what I'm paying taxes for?"

Price-takers can't do much about these problems. What they can do is interrogate. At a simple restaurant, Mrs. Ward asks if food portions have changed. The owner says they haven't. But she remembers that the price of bacon has been climbing, and asks again about his BLT. Suddenly, he recalls that he has cut the number of bacon slices from three to two. And that is a very different sandwich.

Source: *The Wall Street Journal,* January 16, 1997, p. A1. © 1997 by Dow Jones & Co. Inc. Reproduced with permission of DOW JONES & CO INC in the format Textbook via Copyright Clearance Center.

basket of goods of constant quality. Despite these efforts, changes in quality remain a problem, because quality is so hard to measure.

There is still much debate among economists about how severe these measurement problems are and what should be done about them. Several studies written during the 1990s concluded that the consumer price index overstated inflation by about 1 percentage point per year. In response to this criticism, the Bureau of Labor Statistics adopted several technical changes to improve the CPI, and many economists believe the bias is now only about half as large as it once was. The issue is important because many government programs use the consumer price index to adjust for changes in the overall level of prices. Recipients of Social Security, for instance, get annual increases in benefits that are tied to the consumer price index. Some economists have suggested modifying these programs to correct for the measurement problems, such as by reducing the magnitude of the automatic benefit increases.

The GDP Deflator versus the Consumer Price Index

In the preceding chapter, we examined another measure of the overall level of prices in the economy—the GDP deflator. The GDP deflator is the ratio of nominal GDP to real GDP. Because nominal GDP is current output valued at current prices and real GDP is current output valued at base-year prices, the GDP deflator reflects the current level of prices relative to the level of prices in the base year.

Economists and policymakers monitor both the GDP deflator and the consumer price index to gauge how quickly prices are rising. Usually, these two statistics tell a similar story. Yet there are two important differences that can cause them to diverge.

The first difference is that the GDP deflator reflects the prices of all goods and services *produced domestically*, whereas the consumer price index reflects the prices of all goods and services *bought by consumers*. For example, suppose that the price of an airplane produced by Boeing and sold to the Air Force rises. Even though the plane is part of GDP, it is not part of the basket of goods and services bought by a typical consumer. Thus, the price increase shows up in the GDP deflator but not in the consumer price index.

As another example, suppose that Volvo raises the price of its cars. Because Volvos are made in Sweden, the car is not part of U.S. GDP. But U.S. consumers buy Volvos, and so the car is part of the typical consumer's basket of goods. Hence, a price increase in an imported consumption good, such as a Volvo, shows up in the consumer price index but not in the GDP deflator.

This first difference between the consumer price index and the GDP deflator is particularly important when the price of oil changes. Although the United States does produce some oil, much of the oil we use is imported from the Middle East. As a result, oil and oil products such as gasoline and heating oil comprise a much larger share of consumer spending than they do of GDP. When the price of oil rises, the consumer price index rises by much more than does the GDP deflator.

The second and more subtle difference between the GDP deflator and the consumer price index concerns how various prices are weighted to yield a single number for the overall level of prices. The consumer price index compares the price of a *fixed* basket of goods and services to the price of the basket in the base year. Only occasionally does the Bureau of Labor Statistics change the basket of goods. By contrast, the GDP deflator compares the price of *currently produced* goods and services to the price of the same goods and services in the base year. Thus, the group of goods and services used to compute the GDP deflator changes automatically over time. This difference is not important when all prices are changing proportionately. But if the prices of different goods and services are changing by varying amounts, the way we weight the various prices matters for the overall inflation rate.

Figure 2 shows the inflation rate as measured by both the GDP deflator and the consumer price index for each year since 1965. You can see that sometimes the two measures diverge. When they do diverge, it is possible to go behind these numbers and explain the divergence with the two differences we have discussed. The figure shows, however, that divergence between these two measures is the exception rather than the rule. In the late 1970s, both the GDP deflator and the consumer

THE WALL STREET JOURNAL

AUDIO - VIDEO

A. BACALL

"The price may seem a little high, but you have to remember that's in today's dollars."

FIGURE 2

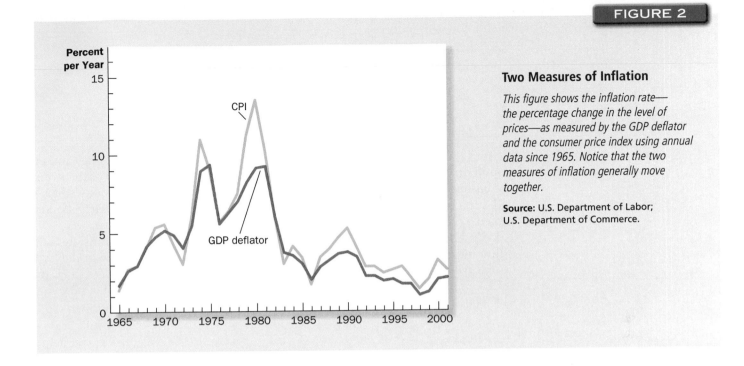

Two Measures of Inflation

This figure shows the inflation rate— the percentage change in the level of prices—as measured by the GDP deflator and the consumer price index using annual data since 1965. Notice that the two measures of inflation generally move together.

Source: U.S. Department of Labor; U.S. Department of Commerce.

price index show high rates of inflation. In the late 1980s and 1990s, both measures show low rates of inflation.

QuickQuiz Explain briefly what the consumer price index is trying to measure and how it is constructed.

CORRECTING ECONOMIC VARIABLES FOR THE EFFECTS OF INFLATION

The purpose of measuring the overall level of prices in the economy is to permit comparison between dollar figures from different points in time. Now that we know how price indexes are calculated, let's see how we might use such an index to compare a dollar figure from the past to a dollar figure in the present.

Dollar Figures from Different Times

We first return to the issue of Babe Ruth's salary. Was his salary of $80,000 in 1931 high or low compared to the salaries of today's players?

To answer this question, we need to know the level of prices in 1931 and the level of prices today. Part of the increase in baseball salaries merely compensates players for the higher level of prices today. To compare Ruth's salary to those of today's players, we need to inflate Ruth's salary to turn 1931 dollars into today's dollars. A price index determines the size of this inflation correction.

Government statistics show a consumer price index of 15.2 for 1931 and 177 for 2001. Thus, the overall level of prices has risen by a factor of 11.6 (which equals

177/15.2). We can use these numbers to measure Ruth's salary in 2001 dollars. The calculation is as follows:

$$\text{Salary in 2001 dollars} = \text{Salary in 1931 dollars} \times \frac{\text{Price level in 2001}}{\text{Price level in 1931}}$$

$$= \$80,000 \times \frac{177}{15.2}$$

$$= \$931,579.$$

We find that Babe Ruth's 1931 salary is equivalent to a salary today of just under $1 million. That is not a bad income, but it is less than half the salary of the average baseball player today, and it is far less than the amount paid to today's baseball superstars. For example, in 2001, San Francisco Giants hitter Barry Bonds signed a five-year contract that would pay him about $18 million a year.

Let's also examine President Hoover's 1931 salary of $75,000. To translate that figure into 2001 dollars, we again multiply the ratio of the price levels in the two years. We find that Hoover's salary is equivalent to $75,000 × (177/15.2), or $873,355, in 2001 dollars. This is well above President George W. Bush's salary of $400,000. It seems that President Hoover did have a pretty good year after all.

Case Study
MR. INDEX GOES TO HOLLYWOOD

What was the most popular movie of all time? The answer might surprise you.

Movie popularity is usually gauged by box office receipts. By that measure, *Titanic* is the #1 movie of all time, followed by *Star Wars, ET: The Extra-Terrestrial, Star Wars: The Phantom Menace,* and *Spiderman.* But this ranking ignores an obvious but important fact: Prices, including those of movie tickets, have been rising over time. When we correct box office receipts for the effects of inflation, the story is very different.

Table 2 shows the top ten movies of all time ranked by inflation-adjusted box office receipts. The #1 movie is *Gone with the Wind,* which was released in 1939 and is well ahead of *Titanic.* In the 1930s, before everyone had televisions in their homes, about 90 million Americans went to the cinema each week, compared to about 25 million today. But the movies from that era rarely show up in popularity rankings because ticket prices were only a quarter. Scarlett and Rhett fare a lot better once we correct for the effects of inflation. ●

"Frankly, my dear, I don't care much for the effects of inflation."

Indexation

As we have just seen, price indexes are used to correct for the effects of inflation when comparing dollar figures from different times. This type of correction shows up in many places in the economy. When some dollar amount is automatically corrected for inflation by law or contract, the amount is said to be **indexed** for inflation.

For example, many long-term contracts between firms and unions include partial or complete indexation of the wage to the consumer price index. Such a provi-

indexation
the automatic correction of a dollar amount for the effects of inflation by law or contract

TABLE 2

Film	Year of Release	Total Domestic Gross (in millions of 2001 dollars)
1. *Gone with the Wind*	1939	$1,002
2. *Star Wars*	1977	866
3. *The Sound of Music*	1965	695
4. *E.T.: The Extra-Terrestrial*	1982	687
5. *Titanic*	1997	640
6. *The Ten Commandments*	1956	639
7. *Jaws*	1975	625
8. *Doctor Zhivago*	1965	591
9. *The Jungle Book*	1967	519
10. *Snow White and the Seven Dwarfs*	1937	518

The Most Popular Movies of All Time, Inflation Adjusted

Source: The Movie Times, on-line Web site (http://www.the-movie-times.com).

sion is called a *cost-of-living allowance,* or COLA. A COLA automatically raises the wage when the consumer price index rises.

Indexation is also a feature of many laws. Social Security benefits, for example, are adjusted every year to compensate the elderly for increases in prices. The brackets of the federal income tax—the income levels at which the tax rates change—are also indexed for inflation. There are, however, many ways in which the tax system is not indexed for inflation, even when perhaps it should be. We discuss these issues more fully when we discuss the costs of inflation later in this book.

Real and Nominal Interest Rates

Correcting economic variables for the effects of inflation is particularly important, and somewhat tricky, when we look at data on interest rates. When you deposit your savings in a bank account, you will earn interest on your deposit. Conversely, when you borrow from a bank to pay your tuition, you will pay interest on your student loan. Interest represents a payment in the future for a transfer of money in the past. As a result, interest rates always involve comparing amounts of money at different points in time. To fully understand interest rates, we need to know how to correct for the effects of inflation.

Let's consider an example. Suppose that Sally Saver deposits $1,000 in a bank account that pays an annual interest rate of 10 percent. After a year passes, Sally has accumulated $100 in interest. Sally then withdraws her $1,100. Is Sally $100 richer than she was when she made the deposit a year earlier?

The answer depends on what we mean by "richer." Sally does have $100 more than she had before. In other words, the number of dollars has risen by 10 percent. But if prices have risen at the same time, each dollar now buys less than it did a year ago. Thus, her purchasing power has not risen by 10 percent. If the inflation rate was 4 percent, then the amount of goods she can buy has increased by only 6 percent. And if the inflation rate was 15 percent, then the price of goods has increased proportionately more than the number of dollars in her account. In that case, Sally's purchasing power has actually fallen by 5 percent.

The interest rate that the bank pays is called the **nominal interest rate,** and the interest rate corrected for inflation is called the **real interest rate.** We can write the

nominal interest rate
the interest rate as usually reported without a correction for the effects of inflation

real interest rate
the interest rate corrected for the effects of inflation

FIGURE 3

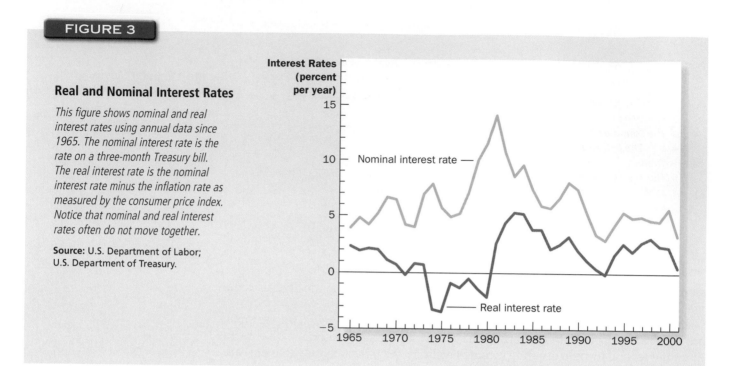

Real and Nominal Interest Rates

This figure shows nominal and real interest rates using annual data since 1965. The nominal interest rate is the rate on a three-month Treasury bill. The real interest rate is the nominal interest rate minus the inflation rate as measured by the consumer price index. Notice that nominal and real interest rates often do not move together.

Source: U.S. Department of Labor; U.S. Department of Treasury.

relationship among the nominal interest rate, the real interest rate, and inflation as follows:

$$\text{Real interest rate} = \text{Nominal interest rate} - \text{Inflation rate}$$

The real interest rate is the difference between the nominal interest rate and the rate of inflation. The nominal interest rate tells you how fast the number of dollars in your bank account rises over time. The real interest rate tells you how fast the purchasing power of your bank account rises over time.

Figure 3 shows real and nominal interest rates since 1965. The nominal interest rate is the interest rate on three-month Treasury bills. The real interest rate is computed by subtracting inflation—the percentage change in the consumer price index—from this nominal interest rate.

You can see that real and nominal interest rates do not always move together. For example, in the late 1970s, nominal interest rates were high. But because inflation was very high, real interest rates were low. Indeed, in some years, real interest rates were negative, for inflation eroded people's savings more quickly than nominal interest payments increased them. By contrast, in the 1990s, nominal interest rates were low. But because inflation was also low, real interest rates were relatively high. In the coming chapters, when we study the causes and effects of changes in interest rates, it will be important for us to keep in mind the distinction between real and nominal interest rates.

QuickQuiz   Henry Ford paid his workers $5 a day in 1914. If the consumer price index was 10 in 1914 and 177 in 2001, how much is the Ford paycheck worth in 2001 dollars?

CONCLUSION

"A nickel ain't worth a dime anymore," baseball player Yogi Berra once observed. Indeed, throughout recent history, the real values behind the nickel, the dime, and the dollar have not been stable. Persistent increases in the overall level of prices have been the norm. Such inflation reduces the purchasing power of each unit of money over time. When comparing dollar figures from different times, it is important to keep in mind that a dollar today is not the same as a dollar 20 years ago or, most likely, 20 years from now.

This chapter has discussed how economists measure the overall level of prices in the economy and how they use price indexes to correct economic variables for the effects of inflation. This analysis is only a starting point. We have not yet examined the causes and effects of inflation or how inflation interacts with other economic variables. To do that, we need to go beyond issues of measurement. Indeed, that is our next task. Having explained how economists measure macroeconomic quantities and prices in the past two chapters, we are now ready to develop the models that explain long-run and short-run movements in these variables.

SUMMARY

- The consumer price index shows the cost of a basket of goods and services relative to the cost of the same basket in the base year. The index is used to measure the overall level of prices in the economy. The percentage change in the consumer price index measures the inflation rate.

- The consumer price index is an imperfect measure of the cost of living for three reasons. First, it does not take into account consumers' ability to substitute toward goods that become relatively cheaper over time. Second, it does not take into account increases in the purchasing power of the dollar due to the introduction of new goods. Third, it is distorted by unmeasured changes in the quality of goods and services. Because of these measurement problems, the CPI overstates true inflation.

- Although the GDP deflator also measures the overall level of prices in the economy, it differs from the consumer price index because it includes goods and services produced rather than goods and services consumed. As a result, imported goods affect the consumer price index

but not the GDP deflator. In addition, while the consumer price index uses a fixed basket of goods, the GDP deflator automatically changes the group of goods and services over time as the composition of GDP changes.

- Dollar figures from different points in time do not represent a valid comparison of purchasing power. To compare a dollar figure from the past to a dollar figure today, the older figure should be inflated using a price index.

- Various laws and private contracts use price indexes to correct for the effects of inflation. The tax laws, however, are only partially indexed for inflation.

- A correction for inflation is especially important when looking at data on interest rates. The nominal interest rate is the interest rate usually reported; it is the rate at which the number of dollars in a savings account increases over time. By contrast, the real interest rate takes into account changes in the value of the dollar over time. The real interest rate equals the nominal interest rate minus the rate of inflation.

KEY CONCEPTS

consumer price index
   (CPI), p. 224
inflation rate, p. 226

producer price index, p. 227
indexation, p. 232
nominal interest rate, p. 233

real interest rate, p. 233

QUESTIONS FOR REVIEW

1. Which do you think has a greater effect on the consumer price index: a 10 percent increase in the price of chicken or a 10 percent increase in the price of caviar? Why?

2. Describe the three problems that make the consumer price index an imperfect measure of the cost of living.

3. If the price of a Navy submarine rises, is the consumer price index or the GDP deflator affected more? Why?

4. Over a long period of time, the price of a candy bar rose from $0.10 to $0.60. Over the same period, the consumer price index rose from 150 to 300. Adjusted for overall inflation, how much did the price of the candy bar change?

5. Explain the meaning of *nominal interest rate* and *real interest rate*. How are they related?

PROBLEMS AND APPLICATIONS

1. Suppose that people consume only three goods, as shown in this table:

	Tennis Balls	Tennis Racquets	Gatorade
2003 price	$2	$40	$1
2003 quantity	100	10	200
2004 price	$2	$60	$2
2004 quantity	100	10	200

   a. What is the percentage change in the price of each of the three goods? What is the percentage change in the overall price level?

   b. Do tennis racquets become more or less expensive relative to Gatorade? Does the well-being of some people change relative to the well-being of others? Explain.

2. Suppose that the residents of Vegopia spend all of their income on cauliflower, broccoli, and carrots. In 2003 they buy 100 heads of cauliflower for $200, 50 bunches of broccoli for $75, and 500 carrots for $50. In 2004 they buy 75 heads of cauliflower for $225, 80 bunches of

broccoli for $120, and 500 carrots for $100. If the base year is 2003, what is the CPI in both years? What is the inflation rate in 2004?

3. Go to the Web site of the Bureau of Labor Statistics (http://www.bls.gov) and find data on the consumer price index. By how much has the index including all items risen over the past year? For which categories of spending have prices risen the most? The least? Have any categories experienced price declines? Can you explain any of these facts?

4. Beginning in 1994, environmental regulations have required that gasoline contain a new additive to reduce air pollution. This requirement raised the cost of gasoline. The Bureau of Labor Statistics (BLS) decided that this increase in cost represented an improvement in quality.

   a. Given this decision, did the increased cost of gasoline raise the CPI?

   b. What is the argument in favor of the BLS's decision? What is the argument for a different decision?

5. Which of the problems in the construction of the CPI might be illustrated by each of the following situations? Explain.
   a. the invention of the Sony Walkman
   b. the introduction of air bags in cars
   c. increased personal computer purchases in response to a decline in their price
   d. more scoops of raisins in each package of Raisin Bran
   e. greater use of fuel-efficient cars after gasoline prices increase

6. *The New York Times* cost $0.15 in 1970 and $0.75 in 2000. The average wage in manufacturing was $3.36 per hour in 1970 and $14.26 in 1999.
   a. By what percentage did the price of a newspaper rise?
   b. By what percentage did the wage rise?
   c. In each year, how many minutes does a worker have to work to earn enough to buy a newspaper?
   d. Did workers' purchasing power in terms of newspapers rise or fall?

7. The chapter explains that Social Security benefits are increased each year in proportion to the increase in the CPI, even though most economists believe that the CPI overstates actual inflation.
   a. If the elderly consume the same market basket as other people, does Social Security provide the elderly with an improvement in their standard of living each year? Explain.
   b. In fact, the elderly consume more health care than younger people, and health care costs have risen faster than overall inflation. What would you do to determine whether the elderly are actually better off from year to year?

8. How do you think the basket of goods and services you buy differs from the basket bought by the typical U.S. household? Do you think you face a higher or lower inflation rate than is indicated by the CPI? Why?

9. Income tax brackets were not indexed until 1985. When inflation pushed up people's nominal incomes during the 1970s, what do you think happened to real tax revenue? (Hint: This phenomenon was known as "bracket creep.")

10. When deciding how much of their income to save for retirement, should workers consider the real or the nominal interest rate that their savings will earn? Explain.

11. Suppose that a borrower and a lender agree on the nominal interest rate to be paid on a loan. Then inflation turns out to be higher than they both expected.
    a. Is the real interest rate on this loan higher or lower than expected?
    b. Does the lender gain or lose from this unexpectedly high inflation? Does the borrower gain or lose?
    c. Inflation during the 1970s was much higher than most people had expected when the decade began. How did this affect homeowners who obtained fixed-rate mortgages during the 1960s? How did it affect the banks who lent the money?

http:// For more study tools, please visit http://mankiwXtra.swlearning.com.

5

THE REAL ECONOMY IN THE LONG RUN

12

PRODUCTION AND GROWTH

When you travel around the world, you see tremendous variation in the standard of living. The average person in a rich country, such as the United States, Japan, or Germany, has an income more than ten times as high as the average person in a poor country, such as India, Indonesia, or Nigeria. These large differences in income are reflected in large differences in the quality of life. Richer countries have more automobiles, more telephones, more televisions, better nutrition, safer housing, better health care, and longer life expectancy.

Even within a country, there are large changes in the standard of living over time. In the United States over the past century, average income as measured by real GDP per person has grown by about 2 percent per year. Although 2 percent might seem small, this rate of growth implies that average income doubles every 35 years. Because of this growth, average income today is about eight times as high as average income a century ago. As a result, the typical American enjoys much greater economic prosperity than did his or her parents, grandparents, and great-grandparents.

Growth rates vary substantially from country to country. In some East Asian countries, such as Singapore, South Korea, and Taiwan, average income has risen about 7 percent per year in recent decades. At this rate, average income doubles every ten years. These countries have, in the length of one generation, gone from being among the poorest in the world to being among the richest. By contrast, in some African countries, such as Chad, Ethiopia, and Nigeria, average income has been stagnant for many years.

What explains these diverse experiences? How can the rich countries be sure to maintain their high standard of living? What policies should the poor countries pursue to promote more rapid growth in order to join the developed world? These are among the most important questions in macroeconomics. As economist Robert Lucas put it, "The consequences for human welfare in questions like these are simply staggering: Once one starts to think about them, it is hard to think about anything else."

In the previous two chapters we discussed how economists measure macroeconomic quantities and prices. In this chapter we start studying the forces that determine these variables. As we have seen, an economy's gross domestic product (GDP) measures both the total income earned in the economy and the total expenditure on the economy's output of goods and services. The level of real GDP is a good gauge of economic prosperity, and the growth of real GDP is a good gauge of economic progress. Here we focus on the long-run determinants of the level and growth of real GDP. Later in this book we study the short-run fluctuations of real GDP around its long-run trend.

We proceed here in three steps. First, we examine international data on real GDP per person. These data will give you some sense of how much the level and growth of living standards vary around the world. Second, we examine the role of *productivity*—the amount of goods and services produced for each hour of a worker's time. In particular, we see that a nation's standard of living is determined by the productivity of its workers, and we consider the factors that determine a nation's productivity. Third, we consider the link between productivity and the economic policies that a nation pursues.

ECONOMIC GROWTH AROUND THE WORLD

As a starting point for our study of long-run growth, let's look at the experiences of some of the world's economies. Table 1 shows data on real GDP per person for 13 countries. For each country, the data cover about a century of history. The first and second columns of the table present the countries and time periods. (The time periods differ somewhat from country to country because of differences in data availability.) The third and fourth columns show estimates of real GDP per person about a century ago and for a recent year.

The data on real GDP per person show that living standards vary widely from country to country. Income per person in the United States, for instance, is about 9 times that in China and about 14 times that in India. The poorest countries have average levels of income that have not been seen in the developed world for many decades. The typical citizen of China in 2000 had about as much real income as the typical resident of England in 1870. The typical person in Pakistan in 2000 had about one-half the real income of a typical American a century ago.

The last column of the table shows each country's growth rate. The growth rate measures how rapidly real GDP per person grew in the typical year. In the United

TABLE 1

Country	Period	Real GDP per Person at Beginning of Period[a]	Real GDP per Person at End of Period[a]	Growth Rate (per year)
Japan	1890–2000	$1,256	$26,460	2.81%
Brazil	1900–2000	650	7,320	2.45
Mexico	1900–2000	968	8,810	2.23
Canada	1870–2000	1,984	27,330	2.04
Germany	1870–2000	1,825	25,010	2.03
China	1900–2000	598	3,940	1.90
Argentina	1900–2000	1,915	12,090	1.86
United States	1870–2000	3,347	34,260	1.81
India	1900–2000	564	2,390	1.45
Indonesia	1900–2000	743	2,840	1.35
United Kingdom	1870–2000	4,107	23,550	1.35
Pakistan	1900–2000	616	1,960	1.16
Bangladesh	1900–2000	520	1,650	1.16

[a]Real GDP is measured in 2000 dollars.

The Variety of Growth Experiences

Source: Robert J. Barro and Xavier Sala-i-Martin, *Economic Growth* (New York: McGraw-Hill, 1995), tables 10.2 and 10.3; *World Development Report 2002*, table 1; and author's calculations.

States, for example, real GDP per person was $3,347 in 1870 and $34,260 in 2000. The growth rate was 1.81 percent per year. This means that if real GDP per person, beginning at $3,347, were to increase by 1.81 percent for each of 130 years, it would end up at $34,260. Of course, real GDP per person did not actually rise exactly 1.81 percent every year: Some years it rose by more and other years by less. The growth rate of 1.81 percent per year ignores short-run fluctuations around the long-run trend and represents an average rate of growth for real GDP per person over many years.

The countries in Table 1 are ordered by their growth rate from the most to the least rapid. Japan tops the list, with a growth rate of 2.81 percent per year. A hundred years ago, Japan was not a rich country. Japan's average income was only somewhat higher than Mexico's, and it was well behind Argentina's. To put the issue another way, Japan's income in 1890 was less than India's income in 2000. But because of its spectacular growth, Japan is now an economic superpower, with average income only slightly behind that of the United States. At the bottom of the list of countries are Bangladesh and Pakistan, which have experienced growth of only 1.16 percent per year over the past century. As a result, the typical resident of these countries continues to live in abject poverty.

Because of differences in growth rates, the ranking of countries by income changes substantially over time. As we have seen, Japan is a country that has risen relative to others. One country that has fallen behind is the United Kingdom. In 1870, the United Kingdom was the richest country in the world, with average income about 20 percent higher than that of the United States and more than twice that of Canada. Today, average income in the United Kingdom is below the average income in its two former colonies.

These data show that the world's richest countries have no guarantee they will stay the richest and that the world's poorest countries are not doomed forever to remain in poverty. But what explains these changes over time? Why do some countries zoom ahead while others lag behind? These are precisely the questions that we take up next.

ARE YOU RICHER THAN THE RICHEST AMERICAN?

In October 1998 the magazine *American Heritage* published a list of the richest Americans of all time. The #1 spot went to John D. Rockefeller, the oil entrepreneur who lived from 1839 to 1937. According to the magazine's calculations, his wealth would today be the equivalent of $200 billion, more than twice that of Bill Gates, the software entrepreneur who is today's richest American.

Despite his great wealth, Rockefeller did not enjoy many of the conveniences that now we take for granted. He couldn't watch television, play video games, surf the Internet, or send an e-mail. During the heat of summer, he couldn't cool his home with

John D. Rockefeller

air-conditioning. For much of his life, he couldn't travel by car or plane, and he couldn't use a telephone to call friends or family. If he became ill, he couldn't take advantage of many medicines, such as antibiotics, that doctors today routinely use to prolong and enhance life.

Now consider: How much money would someone have to pay you to give up for the rest of your life all the modern conveniences that Rockefeller lived without? Would you do it for $200 billion? Perhaps not. And if you wouldn't, is it fair to say that you are better off than John D. Rockefeller, allegedly the richest American ever?

The preceding chapter discussed how standard price indexes, which are used to compare sums of money from different points in time, fail to fully reflect the introduction of new goods in the economy. As a result, the rate of inflation is overestimated. The flip side of this observation is that the rate of real economic growth is underestimated. Pondering Rockefeller's life shows how significant this problem might be. Because of tremendous technological advances, the average American today is arguably "richer" than the richest American a century ago, even if that fact is lost in standard economic statistics.

PHOTO: AP/WIDE WORLD PHOTOS

QuickQuiz   What is the approximate growth rate of real GDP per person in the United States? Name a country that has had faster growth and a country that has had slower growth.

PRODUCTIVITY: ITS ROLE AND DETERMINANTS

Explaining the large variation in living standards around the world is, in one sense, very easy. As we will see, the explanation can be summarized in a single word—*productivity*. But, in another sense, the international variation is deeply puzzling. To explain why incomes are so much higher in some countries than in others, we must look at the many factors that determine a nation's productivity.

Why Productivity Is So Important

Let's begin our study of productivity and economic growth by developing a simple model based loosely on Daniel Defoe's famous novel *Robinson Crusoe*. Robinson Crusoe, as you may recall, is a sailor stranded on a desert island. Because Crusoe lives alone, he catches his own fish, grows his own vegetables, and makes his own clothes. We can think of Crusoe's activities—his production and consumption of fish, vegetables, and clothing—as being a simple economy. By examining Crusoe's economy, we can learn some lessons that also apply to more complex and realistic economies.

What determines Crusoe's standard of living? The answer is obvious. If Crusoe is good at catching fish, growing vegetables, and making clothes, he lives well. If he is bad at doing these things, he lives poorly. Because Crusoe gets to consume only what he produces, his living standard is tied to his productive ability.

The term **productivity** refers to the quantity of goods and services that a worker can produce for each hour of work. In the case of Crusoe's economy, it is easy to see that productivity is the key determinant of living standards and that growth in productivity is the key determinant of growth in living standards. The more fish Crusoe can catch per hour, the more he eats at dinner. If Crusoe finds a better place to catch fish, his productivity rises. This increase in productivity makes Crusoe better off: He could eat the extra fish, or he could spend less time fishing and devote more time to making other goods he enjoys.

The key role of productivity in determining living standards is as true for nations as it is for stranded sailors. Recall that an economy's gross domestic product (GDP) measures two things at once: the total income earned by everyone in the economy and the total expenditure on the economy's output of goods and services. The reason why GDP can measure these two things simultaneously is that, for the economy as a whole, they must be equal. Put simply, an economy's income is the economy's output.

Like Crusoe, a nation can enjoy a high standard of living only if it can produce a large quantity of goods and services. Americans live better than Nigerians because American workers are more productive than Nigerian workers. The Japanese have enjoyed more rapid growth in living standards than Argentineans because Japanese workers have experienced more rapidly growing productivity. Indeed, one of the *Ten Principles of Economics* in Chapter 1 is that a country's standard of living depends on its ability to produce goods and services.

Hence, to understand the large differences in living standards we observe across countries or over time, we must focus on the production of goods and services. But seeing the link between living standards and productivity is only the first step. It leads naturally to the next question: Why are some economies so much better at producing goods and services than others?

How Productivity Is Determined

Although productivity is uniquely important in determining Robinson Crusoe's standard of living, many factors determine Crusoe's productivity. Crusoe will be better at catching fish, for instance, if he has more fishing poles, if he has been trained in the best fishing techniques, if his island has a plentiful fish supply, and if he invents a better fishing lure. Each of these determinants of Crusoe's productivity—which we can call *physical capital, human capital, natural resources,* and *technological knowledge*—has a counterpart in more complex and realistic economies. Let's consider each of these factors in turn.

Physical Capital   Workers are more productive if they have tools with which to work. The stock of equipment and structures that are used to produce goods and services is called **physical capital,** or just *capital.* For example, when woodworkers

productivity
the amount of goods and services produced from each hour of a worker's time

physical capital
the stock of equipment and structures that are used to produce goods and services

make furniture, they use saws, lathes, and drill presses. More tools allow work to be done more quickly and more accurately. That is, a worker with only basic hand tools can make less furniture each week than a worker with sophisticated and specialized woodworking equipment.

As you may recall from Chapter 2, the inputs used to produce goods and services—labor, capital, and so on—are called the *factors of production*. An important feature of capital is that it is a *produced* factor of production. That is, capital is an input into the production process that in the past was an output from the production process. The woodworker uses a lathe to make the leg of a table. Earlier the lathe itself was the output of a firm that manufactures lathes. The lathe manufacturer in turn used other equipment to make its product. Thus, capital is a factor of production used to produce all kinds of goods and services, including more capital.

human capital
the knowledge and skills that workers acquire through education, training, and experience

Human Capital   A second determinant of productivity is human capital. **Human capital** is the economist's term for the knowledge and skills that workers acquire through education, training, and experience. Human capital includes the skills accumulated in early childhood programs, grade school, high school, college, and on-the-job training for adults in the labor force.

Although education, training, and experience are less tangible than lathes, bulldozers, and buildings, human capital is like physical capital in many ways. Like physical capital, human capital raises a nation's ability to produce goods and services. Also like physical capital, human capital is a produced factor of production. Producing human capital requires inputs in the form of teachers, libraries, and student time. Indeed, students can be viewed as "workers" who have the important job of producing the human capital that will be used in future production.

natural resources
the inputs into the production of goods and services that are provided by nature, such as land, rivers, and mineral deposits

Natural Resources   A third determinant of productivity is **natural resources.** Natural resources are inputs into production that are provided by nature, such as land, rivers, and mineral deposits. Natural resources take two forms: renewable and nonrenewable. A forest is an example of a renewable resource. When one tree is cut down, a seedling can be planted in its place to be harvested in the future. Oil is an example of a nonrenewable resource. Because oil is produced by nature over many thousands of years, there is only a limited supply. Once the supply of oil is depleted, it is impossible to create more.

Differences in natural resources are responsible for some of the differences in standards of living around the world. The historical success of the United States was driven in part by the large supply of land well suited for agriculture. Today, some countries in the Middle East, such as Kuwait and Saudi Arabia, are rich simply because they happen to be on top of some of the largest pools of oil in the world.

Although natural resources can be important, they are not necessary for an economy to be highly productive in producing goods and services. Japan, for instance, is one of the richest countries in the world, despite having few natural resources. International trade makes Japan's success possible. Japan imports many of the natural resources it needs, such as oil, and exports its manufactured goods to economies rich in natural resources.

technological knowledge
society's understanding of the best ways to produce goods and services

Technological Knowledge   A fourth determinant of productivity is **technological knowledge**—the understanding of the best ways to produce goods and services. A hundred years ago, most Americans worked on farms, because farm technology required a high input of labor in order to feed the entire population.

Today, thanks to advances in the technology of farming, a small fraction of the population can produce enough food to feed the entire country. This technological change made labor available to produce other goods and services.

Technological knowledge takes many forms. Some technology is common knowledge—after it becomes used by one person, everyone becomes aware of it. For example, once Henry Ford successfully introduced production in assembly lines, other carmakers quickly followed suit. Other technology is proprietary—it is known only by the company that discovers it. Only the Coca-Cola Company, for instance, knows the secret recipe for making its famous soft drink. Still other technology is proprietary for a short time. When a pharmaceutical company discovers a new drug, the patent system gives that company a temporary right to be its exclusive manufacturer. When the patent expires, however, other companies are allowed to make the drug. All these forms of technological knowledge are important for the economy's production of goods and services.

It is worthwhile to distinguish between technological knowledge and human capital. Although they are closely related, there is an important difference. Technological knowledge refers to society's understanding about how the world works. Human capital refers to the resources expended transmitting this understanding to the labor force. To use a relevant metaphor, knowledge is the quality of society's textbooks, whereas human capital is the amount of time that the population has devoted to reading them. Workers' productivity depends on both the quality of textbooks they have available and the amount of time they have spent studying them.

FYI

THE PRODUCTION FUNCTION

Economists often use a *production function* to describe the relationship between the quantity of inputs used in production and the quantity of output from production. For example, suppose Y denotes the quantity of output, L the quantity of labor, K the quantity of physical capital, H the quantity of human capital, and N the quantity of natural resources. Then we might write

$$Y = A\, F(L, K, H, N),$$

where $F(\ )$ is a function that shows how the inputs are combined to produce output. A is a variable that reflects the available production technology. As technology improves, A rises, so the economy produces more output from any given combination of inputs.

Many production functions have a property called *constant returns to scale*. If a production function has constant returns to scale, then a doubling of all the inputs causes the amount of output to double as well. Mathematically, we write that a production function has constant returns to scale if, for any positive number x,

$$xY = A\, F(xL, xK, xH, xN).$$

A doubling of all inputs is represented in this equation by $x = 2$. The right-hand side shows the inputs doubling, and the left-hand side shows output doubling.

Production functions with constant returns to scale have an interesting implication. To see what it is, set $x = 1/L$. Then the equation above becomes

$$Y/L = A\, F(1, K/L, H/L, N/L).$$

Notice that Y/L is output per worker, which is a measure of productivity. This equation says that productivity depends on physical capital per worker (K/L), human capital per worker (H/L), and natural resources per worker (N/L). Productivity also depends on the state of technology, as reflected by the variable A. Thus, this equation provides a mathematical summary of the four determinants of productivity we have just discussed.

Case Study
ARE NATURAL RESOURCES A LIMIT TO GROWTH?

The world's population is far larger today than it was a century ago, and many people are enjoying a much higher standard of living. A perennial debate concerns whether this growth in population and living standards can continue in the future.

Many commentators have argued that natural resources provide a limit to how much the world's economies can grow. At first, this argument might seem hard to ignore. If the world has only a fixed supply of nonrenewable natural resources, how can population, production, and living standards continue to grow over time? Eventually, won't supplies of oil and minerals start to run out? When these shortages start to occur, won't they stop economic growth and, perhaps, even force living standards to fall?

Despite the apparent appeal of such arguments, most economists are less concerned about such limits to growth than one might guess. They argue that technological progress often yields ways to avoid these limits. If we compare the economy today to the economy of the past, we see various ways in which the use of natural resources has improved. Modern cars have better gas mileage. New houses have better insulation and require less energy to heat and cool them. More efficient oil rigs waste less oil in the process of extraction. Recycling allows some nonrenewable resources to be reused. The development of alternative fuels, such as ethanol instead of gasoline, allows us to substitute renewable for nonrenewable resources.

Fifty years ago, some conservationists were concerned about the excessive use of tin and copper. At the time, these were crucial commodities: Tin was used to make many food containers, and copper was used to make telephone wire. Some people advocated mandatory recycling and rationing of tin and copper so that supplies would be available for future generations. Today, however, plastic has replaced tin as a material for making many food containers, and phone calls often travel over fiber-optic cables, which are made from sand. Technological progress has made once crucial natural resources less necessary.

But are all these efforts enough to permit continued economic growth? One way to answer this question is to look at the prices of natural resources. In a market economy, scarcity is reflected in market prices. If the world were running out of natural resources, then the prices of those resources would be rising over time. But, in fact, the opposite is more nearly true. The prices of most natural resources (adjusted for overall inflation) are stable or falling. It appears that our ability to conserve these resources is growing more rapidly than their supplies are dwindling. Market prices give no reason to believe that natural resources are a limit to economic growth. ●

QuickQuiz List and describe four determinants of a country's productivity.

ECONOMIC GROWTH AND PUBLIC POLICY

So far, we have determined that a society's standard of living depends on its ability to produce goods and services and that its productivity depends on physical capital, human capital, natural resources, and technological knowledge. Let's now turn to the question faced by policymakers around the world: What can government policy do to raise productivity and living standards?

The Importance of Saving and Investment

Because capital is a produced factor of production, a society can change the amount of capital it has. If today the economy produces a large quantity of new capital goods, then tomorrow it will have a larger stock of capital and be able to produce more of all types of goods and services. Thus, one way to raise future productivity is to invest more current resources in the production of capital.

One of the *Ten Principles of Economics* presented in Chapter 1 is that people face tradeoffs. This principle is especially important when considering the accumulation of capital. Because resources are scarce, devoting more resources to producing capital requires devoting fewer resources to producing goods and services for current consumption. That is, for society to invest more in capital, it must consume less and save more of its current income. The growth that arises from capital accumulation is not a free lunch: It requires that society sacrifice consumption of goods and services in the present in order to enjoy higher consumption in the future.

The next chapter examines in more detail how the economy's financial markets coordinate saving and investment. It also examines how government policies influence the amount of saving and investment that takes place. At this point it is important to note that encouraging saving and investment is one way that a government can encourage growth and, in the long run, raise the economy's standard of living.

To see the importance of investment for economic growth, consider Figure 1 (p. 250), which displays data on 15 countries. Panel (a) shows each country's growth rate over a 31-year period. The countries are ordered by their growth rates, from most to least rapid. Panel (b) shows the percentage of GDP that each country devotes to investment. The correlation between growth and investment, although not perfect, is strong. Countries that devote a large share of GDP to investment, such as Singapore and Japan, tend to have high growth rates. Countries that devote a small share of GDP to investment, such as Rwanda and Bangladesh, tend to have low growth rates. Studies that examine a more comprehensive list of countries confirm this strong correlation between investment and growth.

There is, however, a problem in interpreting these data. As the appendix to Chapter 2 discussed, a correlation between two variables does not establish which variable is the cause and which is the effect. It is possible that high investment causes high growth, but it is also possible that high growth causes high investment. (Or, perhaps, high growth and high investment are both caused by a third variable that has been omitted from the analysis.) The data by themselves cannot tell us the direction of causation. Nonetheless, because capital accumulation affects productivity so clearly and directly, many economists interpret these data as showing that high investment leads to more rapid economic growth.

FIGURE 1

Growth and Investment

Panel (a) shows the growth rate of GDP per person for 15 countries over the period 1960–1991. Panel (b) shows the percentage of GDP that each country devoted to investment over this period. The figure shows that investment and growth are positively correlated.

Source: Robert Summers and Alan Heston, The Penn World Tables, and author's calculations.

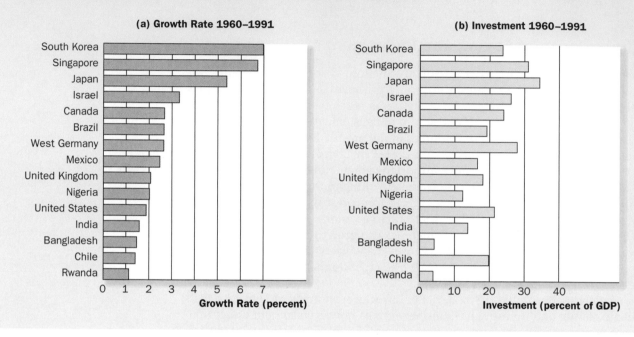

Diminishing Returns and the Catch-Up Effect

Suppose that a government, convinced by the evidence in Figure 1, pursues policies that raise the nation's saving rate—the percentage of GDP devoted to saving rather than consumption. What happens? With the nation saving more, fewer resources are needed to make consumption goods, and more resources are available to make capital goods. As a result, the capital stock increases, leading to rising productivity and more rapid growth in GDP. But how long does this higher rate of growth last? Assuming that the saving rate remains at its new higher level, does the growth rate of GDP stay high indefinitely or only for a period of time?

The traditional view of the production process is that capital is subject to **diminishing returns:** As the stock of capital rises, the extra output produced from an additional unit of capital falls. In other words, when workers already have a large quantity of capital to use in producing goods and services, giving them an additional unit of capital increases their productivity only slightly. Because of diminishing returns, an increase in the saving rate leads to higher growth only for a while. As the higher saving rate allows more capital to be accumulated, the benefits from additional capital become smaller over time, and so growth slows down. *In the long run, the higher saving rate leads to a higher level of productivity and income, but not to higher growth in these variables.* Reaching this long run, however, can take quite a while. According to studies of international data on economic growth, increasing the saving rate can lead to substantially higher growth for a period of several decades.

diminishing returns
the property whereby the benefit from an extra unit of an input declines as the quantity of the input increases

The diminishing returns to capital has another important implication: Other things equal, it is easier for a country to grow fast if it starts out relatively poor. This effect of initial conditions on subsequent growth is sometimes called the **catch-up effect.** In poor countries, workers lack even the most rudimentary tools and, as a result, have low productivity. Small amounts of capital investment would substantially raise these workers' productivity. By contrast, workers in rich countries have large amounts of capital with which to work, and this partly explains their high productivity. Yet with the amount of capital per worker already so high, additional capital investment has a relatively small effect on productivity. Studies of international data on economic growth confirm this catch-up effect: Controlling for other variables, such as the percentage of GDP devoted to investment, poor countries do tend to grow at a faster rate than rich countries.

This catch-up effect can help explain some of the puzzling results in Figure 1. Over this 31-year period, the United States and South Korea devoted a similar share of GDP to investment. Yet the United States experienced only mediocre growth of about 2 percent, while Korea experienced spectacular growth of more than 6 percent. The explanation is the catch-up effect. In 1960, Korea had GDP per person less than one-tenth the U.S. level, in part because previous investment had been so low. With a small initial capital stock, the benefits to capital accumulation were much greater in Korea, and this gave Korea a higher subsequent growth rate.

This catch-up effect shows up in other aspects of life. When a school gives an end-of-year award to the "Most Improved" student, that student is usually one who began the year with relatively poor performance. Students who began the year not studying find improvement easier than students who always worked hard. Note that it is good to be "Most Improved," given the starting point, but it is even better to be "Best Student." Similarly, economic growth over the last several decades has been much more rapid in South Korea than in the United States, but GDP per person is still higher in the United States.

catch-up effect
the property whereby countries that start off poor tend to grow more rapidly than countries that start off rich

Investment from Abroad

So far we have discussed how policies aimed at increasing a country's saving rate can increase investment and, thereby, long-term economic growth. Yet saving by domestic residents is not the only way for a country to invest in new capital. The other way is investment by foreigners.

Investment from abroad takes several forms. Ford Motor Company might build a car factory in Mexico. A capital investment that is owned and operated by a foreign entity is called *foreign direct investment*. Alternatively, an American might buy stock in a Mexican corporation (that is, buy a share in the ownership of the corporation); the Mexican corporation can use the proceeds from the stock sale to build a new factory. An investment that is financed with foreign money but operated by domestic residents is called *foreign portfolio investment*. In both cases, Americans provide the resources necessary to increase the stock of capital in Mexico. That is, American saving is being used to finance Mexican investment.

When foreigners invest in a country, they do so because they expect to earn a return on their investment. Ford's car factory increases the Mexican capital stock and, therefore, increases Mexican productivity and Mexican GDP. Yet Ford takes some of this additional income back to the United States in the form of profit. Similarly, when an American investor buys Mexican stock, the investor has a right to a portion of the profit that the Mexican corporation earns.

Investment from abroad, therefore, does not have the same effect on all measures of economic prosperity. Recall that gross domestic product (GDP) is the income earned within a country by both residents and nonresidents, whereas gross national product (GNP) is the income earned by residents of a country both at home and abroad. When Ford opens its car factory in Mexico, some of the income the factory generates accrues to people who do not live in Mexico. As a result, foreign investment in Mexico raises the income of Mexicans (measured by GNP) by less than it raises the production in Mexico (measured by GDP).

Nonetheless, investment from abroad is one way for a country to grow. Even though some of the benefits from this investment flow back to the foreign owners, this investment does increase the economy's stock of capital, leading to higher productivity and higher wages. Moreover, investment from abroad is one way for poor countries to learn the state-of-the-art technologies developed and used in richer countries. For these reasons, many economists who advise governments in less developed economies advocate policies that encourage investment from abroad. Often this means removing restrictions that governments have imposed on foreign ownership of domestic capital.

An organization that tries to encourage the flow of capital to poor countries is the World Bank. This international organization obtains funds from the world's

IN THE NEWS

PROMOTING HUMAN CAPITAL

Gary Becker won the Nobel Prize in economics in part because of his pioneering work on human capital. For many countries, he argues, it is the key to economic growth.

Bribe Third World Parents to Keep Their Kids in School

By Gary Becker

Many well-meaning Americans, including college students and religious organizations, have attacked Nike Inc. and other companies accused of using child labor in their overseas plants in poor nations. I agree that something should be done to save the children from dismal long-term economic prospects. However, effective policies must recognize that the fundamental cause of child labor is poverty, not greedy foreign and domestic employ-

ers. To combat the effects of poverty, poor mothers should be "bribed" to keep their children in school longer.

Really poor families in Brazil, Mexico, Zaire, India, and many other nations put their children to work because their meager earnings help provide basic food and medicine for themselves and younger siblings. Although parents may recognize that schooling would improve their children's marketable labor skills later in life, they cannot afford the "luxury" of taking them out of the labor market. In essence, child labor is the result of a conflict between short-term parental economic in-

terests and the long-term interests of the children.

Adequate economic growth always eliminates child labor even without laws against it. But poor nations needn't wait until they grow richer. There are short-term solutions. Many nations have compulsory schooling laws up to age 15 or so, but they are often hard to enforce, especially in rural areas and poor sections of large cities. Families who want their children to work simply do not send them to school, or the children have very high absenteeism rates. Officials are reluctant to punish parents of working children, advanced countries, such as the United States, and uses these resources to make loans to less developed countries so that they can invest in roads, sewer systems, schools, and other types of capital. It also offers the countries advice about how the funds might best be used. The World Bank, together with its sister organization, the International Monetary Fund, was set up after World War II. One lesson from the war was that economic distress often leads to political turmoil, international tensions, and military conflict. Thus, every country has an interest in promoting economic prosperity around the world. The World Bank and the International Monetary Fund are aimed at achieving that common goal.

Education

Education—investment in human capital—is at least as important as investment in physical capital for a country's long-run economic success. In the United States, each year of schooling has historically raised a person's wage on average by about 10 percent. In less developed countries, where human capital is especially scarce, the gap between the wages of educated and uneducated workers is even larger. Thus, one way in which government policy can enhance the standard of living is to provide good schools and to encourage the population to take advantage of them.

perhaps because they recognize that the problem is not selfishness but poverty.

I propose a better way: Give parents a financial incentive to keep their children in school longer. Poor mothers should be paid if schools certify that their children attend classes regularly. Parents would be strongly motivated to send their children to school—even when the children do not want to go—if these payments were not much below what the children could earn. Most poor parents would happily contribute something to improve their children's long-run chances, but they are reluctant to bear the entire burden.

I have been proposing this for some time, and the Mexican government has begun such a program, called Progresa, that covers over 2 million very poor families in Chiapas and other rural areas. Mothers whose children attend classes regularly, succeed in getting promoted, and get regular medical checkups are paid every month by the central government. These payments average about $25 per family. Most poor Mexican families earn only about $100 a month. That large a percentage increase should have a noticeable effect on their behavior.

Poor families in less developed nations whose children do go to school are likely to withdraw their daughters when they become teenagers. This tends to perpetuate economic inequalities, since the children of women who receive little schooling also tend to be badly educated. Progresa tries to combat this tendency to favor education of older sons by paying a little more to families that keep teenage daughters enrolled.

This pioneering Mexican approach appears to be highly successful. An evaluation prepared for an October economics conference in Chile shows that after only a couple of years, Progresa significantly raised the schooling of children in very poor Mexican families. It has also narrowed the education gap between girls and boys and reduced the labor force participation of boys.

Of course, governments need to find the tax revenue to finance programs like Progresa. A good start would be to recognize that Mexico and many other less developed nations typically spend disproportionately on universities and other education of their elites. Redistributing some of this spending to the poor would both reduce inequality and stimulate faster economic growth. Widespread basic education is more effective in promoting economic development than generous subsidies to the richer students who attend universities.

Child-labor critics could spend their time more fruitfully by attacking not the overseas employment policies of multinationals but the social policies of governments in poor nations that are really responsible for the prevalence of child labor there. These governments, and perhaps international organizations such as the World Bank, should follow Mexico's example and introduce programs that pay poor mothers to keep their teenage and younger sons and daughters in school and out of the labor force.

Investment in human capital, like investment in physical capital, has an opportunity cost. When students are in school, they forgo the wages they could have earned. In less developed countries, children often drop out of school at an early age, even though the benefit of additional schooling is very high, simply because their labor is needed to help support the family.

Some economists have argued that human capital is particularly important for economic growth because human capital conveys positive externalities. An *externality* is the effect of one person's actions on the well-being of a bystander. An educated person, for instance, might generate new ideas about how best to produce goods and services. If these ideas enter society's pool of knowledge, so everyone can use them, then the ideas are an external benefit of education. In this case, the return to schooling for society is even greater than the return for the individual. This argument would justify the large subsidies to human-capital investment that we observe in the form of public education.

One problem facing some poor countries is the *brain drain*—the emigration of many of the most highly educated workers to rich countries, where these workers can enjoy a higher standard of living. If human capital does have positive externalities, then this brain drain makes those people left behind poorer than they otherwise would be. This problem offers policymakers a dilemma. On the one hand, the United States and other rich countries have the best systems of higher education, and it would seem natural for poor countries to send their best students abroad to earn higher degrees. On the other hand, those students who have spent time abroad may choose not to return home, and this brain drain will reduce the poor nation's stock of human capital even further.

Property Rights and Political Stability

Another way in which policymakers can foster economic growth is by protecting property rights and promoting political stability. As we first noted when we discussed economic interdependence in Chapter 3, production in market economies arises from the interactions of millions of individuals and firms. When you buy a car, for instance, you are buying the output of a car dealer, a car manufacturer, a steel company, an iron ore mining company, and so on. This division of production among many firms allows the economy's factors of production to be used as effectively as possible. To achieve this outcome, the economy has to coordinate transactions among these firms, as well as between firms and consumers. Market economies achieve this coordination through market prices. That is, market prices are the instrument with which the invisible hand of the marketplace brings supply and demand into balance.

An important prerequisite for the price system to work is an economy-wide respect for *property rights*. Property rights refer to the ability of people to exercise authority over the resources they own. A mining company will not make the effort to mine iron ore if it expects the ore to be stolen. The company mines the ore only if it is confident that it will benefit from the ore's subsequent sale. For this reason, courts serve an important role in a market economy: They enforce property rights. Through the criminal justice system, the courts discourage direct theft. In addition, through the civil justice system, the courts ensure that buyers and sellers live up to their contracts.

Although those of us in developed countries tend to take property rights for granted, those living in less developed countries understand that lack of property rights can be a major problem. In many countries, the system of justice does not work well. Contracts are hard to enforce, and fraud often goes unpunished. In more extreme cases, the government not only fails to enforce property rights but actually infringes upon them. To do business in some countries, firms are expected to bribe powerful government officials. Such corruption impedes the coordinating power of markets. It also discourages domestic saving and investment from abroad.

One threat to property rights is political instability. When revolutions and coups are common, there is doubt about whether property rights will be respected in the future. If a revolutionary government might confiscate the capital of some businesses, as was often true after communist revolutions, domestic residents have less incentive to save, invest, and start new businesses. At the same time, foreigners have less incentive to invest in the country. Even the threat of revolution can act to depress a nation's standard of living.

Thus, economic prosperity depends in part on political prosperity. A country with an efficient court system, honest government officials, and a stable constitution will enjoy a higher economic standard of living than a country with a poor court system, corrupt officials, and frequent revolutions and coups.

Free Trade

Some of the world's poorest countries have tried to achieve more rapid economic growth by pursuing *inward-oriented policies*. These policies are aimed at raising productivity and living standards within the country by avoiding interaction with the rest of the world. This approach gets support from some domestic firms, which claim that they need protection from foreign competition in order to compete and grow. This infant-industry argument, together with a general distrust of foreigners, has at times led policymakers in less developed countries to impose tariffs and other trade restrictions.

Most economists today believe that poor countries are better off pursuing *outward-oriented policies* that integrate these countries into the world economy. When we studied international trade earlier in the book, we showed how international trade can improve the economic well-being of a country's citizens. Trade is, in some ways, a type of technology. When a country exports wheat and imports steel, the country benefits in the same way as if it had invented a technology for turning wheat into steel. A country that eliminates trade restrictions will, therefore, experience the same kind of economic growth that would occur after a major technological advance.

The adverse impact of inward orientation becomes clear when one considers the small size of many less developed economies. The total GDP of Argentina, for instance, is about that of Philadelphia. Imagine what would happen if the Philadelphia city council were to prohibit city residents from trading with people living outside the city limits. Without being able to take advantage of the gains from trade, Philadelphia would need to produce all the goods it consumes. It would also have to produce all its own capital goods, rather than importing state-of-the-art equipment from other cities. Living standards in Philadelphia would fall immediately, and the problem would likely only get worse over time. This is precisely what happened when Argentina pursued inward-oriented policies throughout much of the twentieth century. By contrast, countries pursuing outward-oriented policies, such as South Korea, Singapore, and Taiwan, have enjoyed high rates of economic growth.

The amount that a nation trades with others is determined not only by government policy but also by geography. Countries with good natural seaports find trade easier than countries without this resource. It is not a coincidence that many of the world's major cities, such as New York, San Francisco, and Hong Kong, are located next to oceans. Similarly, because landlocked countries find international trade more difficult, they tend to have lower levels of income than countries with easy access to the world's waterways.

Research and Development

The primary reason that living standards are higher today than they were a century ago is that technological knowledge has advanced. The telephone, the transistor, the computer, and the internal combustion engine are among the thousands of innovations that have improved the ability to produce goods and services.

Although most technological advance comes from private research by firms and individual inventors, there is also a public interest in promoting these efforts. To a large extent, knowledge is a *public good:* Once one person discovers an idea, the idea enters society's pool of knowledge, and other people can freely use it. Just as government has a role in providing a public good such as national defense, it also has a role in encouraging the research and development of new technologies.

The U.S. government has long played a role in the creation and dissemination of technological knowledge. A century ago, the government sponsored research about farming methods and advised farmers how best to use their land. More recently, the U.S. government has, through the Air Force and NASA, supported aerospace research; as a result, the United States is a leading maker of rockets and planes. The government continues to encourage advances in knowledge with research grants from the National Science Foundation and the National Institutes of Health and with tax breaks for firms engaging in research and development.

Yet another way in which government policy encourages research is through the patent system. When a person or firm invents a new product, such as a new drug, the inventor can apply for a patent. If the product is deemed truly original, the government awards the patent, which gives the inventor the exclusive right to make the product for a specified number of years. In essence, the patent gives the inventor a property right over his invention, turning his new idea from a public good into a private good. By allowing inventors to profit from their inventions— even if only temporarily—the patent system enhances the incentive for individuals and firms to engage in research.

Case Study
THE PRODUCTIVITY SLOWDOWN AND SPEEDUP

The rate of productivity growth is not at all steady and reliable. As measured by output per hour worked in U.S. businesses, productivity grew at an average rate of 3.2 percent per year from 1959 to 1973. Productivity then slowed down and, from 1973 to 1995, grew by only 1.5 percent per year. Productivity accelerated again in 1995, growing by 2.6 percent per year on average during the next six years.

The effects of these changes in productivity growth are easy to see. Productivity is reflected in real wages and family incomes. When productivity growth slowed, the typical worker received smaller inflation-adjusted raises, and many people experienced a general sense of economic anxiety. Accumulated over many years, even a small change in productivity growth has a large effect. If the slowdown had not occurred in 1973, the income of the average American would today be about

50 percent higher. Similarly, the acceleration in productivity growth in 1995 has already raised real incomes by about 7 percent.

The causes of these changes in productivity growth are more elusive. One fact is well established: These changes cannot be traced to the factors of production that are most easily measured. Economists can measure directly the quantity of physical capital that workers have available. They can also measure human capital in the form of years of schooling. It appears that the slowdown and speedup in productivity growth are not due primarily to changes in the growth of these inputs.

Technology is one of the few remaining culprits. That is, having ruled out other explanations, many economists attribute the slowdown and speedup in economic growth to changes in the creation of new ideas about how to produce goods and services. This explanation is difficult to confirm or refute, because the quantity of "ideas" is hard to measure, but the hypothesis is plausible. The speedup in productivity growth in 1995 coincided with the rapid growth of information technology and the Internet.

What does the future hold for technological progress and economic growth? History gives us little reason to be confident in any prediction. Neither the productivity slowdown nor the productivity speedup was foreseen by many forecasters before it arrived.

History can, however, give us a sense of what is the normal rate of technological progress. Figure 2 shows the average growth of real GDP per person in the developed world going back to 1870. The productivity slowdown is apparent:

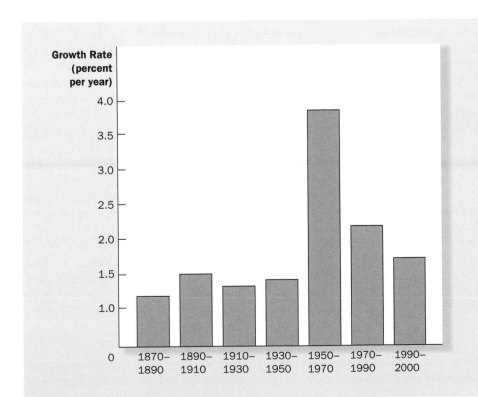

FIGURE 2

The Growth in Real GDP per Person

This figure shows the average growth rate of real GDP per person for advanced economies, including the major countries of Europe, Canada, the United States, Japan, and Australia. Notice that the growth rate rose substantially after 1950 and then fell after 1970.

Source: Robert J. Barro and Xavier Sala-i-Martin, *Economic Growth* (New York: McGraw-Hill, 1995), p. 6. Data for 1990 to 2000 from the *World Development Report, 2002.*

Around 1970, the growth rate slowed from 3.7 to 2.2 percent. (The productivity speedup is absent from these data because it is too short and primarily a U.S. phenomenon.) This figure shows an important lesson: Compared to most of history, the anomaly is the rapid growth during the 1950s and 1960s. Perhaps the decades after World War II were a period of unusually rapid technological advance, and growth slowed down in 1973 simply because technological progress was returning to a more normal rate. ●

Population Growth

Economists and other social scientists have long debated how population growth affects a society. The most direct effect is on the size of the labor force: A large population means more workers to produce goods and services. At the same time, it means more people to consume those goods and services. Beyond these obvious effects, population growth interacts with the other factors of production in ways that are less obvious and more open to debate.

Stretching Natural Resources   Thomas Robert Malthus (1766–1834), an English minister and early economic thinker, is famous for his book called *An Essay on the Principle of Population as It Affects the Future Improvement of Society.* In it, Malthus offered what may be history's most chilling forecast. Malthus argued that an ever increasing population would continually strain society's ability to provide for itself. As a result, mankind was doomed to forever live in poverty.

Malthus's logic was simple. He began by noting that "food is necessary to the existence of man" and that "the passion between the sexes is necessary and will remain nearly in its present state." He concluded that "the power of population is infinitely greater than the power in the earth to produce subsistence for man." According to Malthus, the only check on population growth was "misery and vice." Attempts by charities or governments to alleviate poverty were counterproductive, he argued, because they merely allowed the poor to have more children, placing even greater strains on society's productive capabilities.

Fortunately, Malthus's dire forecast was far off the mark. Although the world population has increased about sixfold over the past two centuries, living standards around the world are on average much higher. As a result of economic growth, chronic hunger and malnutrition are less common now than they were in Malthus's day. Famines occur from time to time, but they are more often the result of an unequal income distribution or political instability than an inadequate production of food.

Where did Malthus go wrong? As we discussed in a case study earlier in this chapter, growth in mankind's ingenuity has offset the effects of a larger population. Pesticides, fertilizers, mechanized farm equipment, new crop varieties, and other technological advances that Malthus never imagined have allowed each farmer to feed ever greater numbers of people. Even with more mouths to feed, fewer farmers are necessary because each farmer is so productive.

Diluting the Capital Stock   Whereas Mathus worried about the effects of population on the use of natural resources, some modern theories of economic growth

Thomas Robert Malthus

© BETTMANN/CORBIS

emphasize its effects on capital accumulation. According to these theories, high population growth reduces GDP per worker because rapid growth in the number of workers forces the capital stock to be spread more thinly. In other words, when population growth is rapid, each worker is equipped with less capital. A smaller quantity of capital per worker leads to lower productivity and lower GDP per worker.

This problem is most apparent in the case of human capital. Countries with high population growth have large numbers of school-age children. This places a larger burden on the educational system. It is not surprising, therefore, that educational attainment tends to be low in countries with high population growth.

The differences in population growth around the world are large. In developed countries, such as the United States and western Europe, the population has risen only about 1 percent per year in recent decades and is expected to rise even more slowly in the future. By contrast, in many poor African countries, population grows at about 3 percent per year. At this rate, the population doubles every 23 years. This rapid population growth makes it harder to provide workers with the tools and skills they need to achieve high levels of productivity.

Although rapid population growth is not the main reason that less developed countries are poor, some analysts believe that reducing the rate of population growth would help these countries raise their standards of living. In some countries, this goal is accomplished directly with laws that regulate the number of children families may have. China, for instance, allows only one child per family; couples who violate this rule are subject to substantial fines. In countries with greater freedom, the goal of reduced population growth is accomplished less directly by increasing awareness of birth control techniques.

Another way in which a country can influence population growth is to apply one of the *Ten Principles of Economics:* People respond to incentives. Bearing a child, like any decision, has an opportunity cost. When the opportunity cost rises, people will choose to have smaller families. In particular, women with the opportunity to receive good education and desirable employment tend to want fewer children than those with fewer opportunities outside the home. Hence, policies that foster equal treatment of women are one way for less developed economies to reduce the rate of population growth and, perhaps, raise their standards of living.

Promoting Technological Progress   Although rapid population growth may depress economic prosperity by reducing the amount of capital each worker has, it may also have some benefits. Some economists have suggested that world population growth has been an engine of technological progress and economic prosperity. The mechanism is simple: If there are more people, then there are more scientists, inventors, and engineers to contribute to technological advance, which benefits everyone.

Economist Michael Kremer has provided some support for this hypothesis in an article titled "Population Growth and Technological Change: One Million B.C. to 1990," which was published in the *Quarterly Journal of Economics* in 1993. Kremer begins by noting that over the broad span of human history, world growth rates have increased as world population has. For example, world growth was more rapid when the world population was 1 billion (which occurred around the year 1800) than it was when the population was only 100 million (around 500 B.C.). This fact is consistent with the hypothesis that having more people induces more technological progress.

Kremer's second piece of evidence comes from comparing regions of the world. The melting of the polar ice caps at the end of the ice age around 10,000 B.C. flooded the land bridges and separated the world into several distinct regions that could not communicate with one another for thousands of years. If technological progress is more rapid when there are more people to discover things, then larger regions should have experienced more rapid growth.

According to Kremer, that is exactly what happened. The most successful region of the world in 1500 (when Columbus reestablished technological contact) comprised the "Old World" civilizations of the large Eurasia-Africa region. Next in technological development were the Aztec and Mayan civilizations in the Americas,

IN THE NEWS

A SOLUTION TO AFRICA'S PROBLEMS

In 2000 the average income in sub-Saharan Africa was $480. Why? Here is the analysis of Jeffrey Sachs, an adviser to governments around the world and a critic of the World Bank and the International Monetary Fund (IMF), the international policy organizations that dispense advice and money to struggling countries.

Growth in Africa: It Can Be Done

By Jeffrey Sachs

In the old story, the peasant goes to the priest for advice on saving his dying chickens. The priest recommends prayer, but the chickens continue to die. The priest then recommends music for the chicken coop, but the deaths continue unabated. Pondering again, the priest recommends repainting the chicken coop in bright colors. Finally, all the chickens die. "What a shame," the priest tells the peasant. "I had so many more good ideas."

Since independence, African countries have looked to donor nations—often their former colonial rulers—and to the international finance institutions for guidance on growth. Indeed, since the onset of the African debt crises of the 1980s, the guidance has become a kind of economic receivership, with the policies of many African nations decided in a seemingly endless cycle of meetings with the IMF, the World Bank, donors, and creditors.

What a shame. So many good ideas, so few results. . . .

The IMF and World Bank would be absolved of shared responsibility for slow growth if Africa were structurally incapable of growth rates seen in other parts of the world or if the continent's low growth were an impenetrable mystery. But Africa's growth rates are not huge mysteries. . . . Studies of cross-country growth show that per capita growth is related to:

- the initial income level of the country, with poorer countries tending to grow faster than richer countries;
- the extent of overall market orientation, including openness to trade, domestic market liberalization, private rather than state ownership, protection of private property rights, and low marginal tax rates;
- the national saving rate, which in turn is strongly affected by the government's own saving rate; and
- the geographic and resource structure of the economy. . . .

These four factors can account broadly for Africa's long-term growth predicament. While it should have grown faster than other developing areas because of relatively low income per head followed by the hunter-gatherers of Australia, and then the primitive people of Tasmania, who lacked even fire-making and most stone and bone tools.

The smallest isolated region was Flinders Island, a tiny island between Tasmania and Australia. With the smallest population, Flinders Island had the fewest opportunities for technological advance and, indeed, seemed to regress. Around 3000 B.C., human society on Flinders Island died out completely. A large population, Kremer concludes, is a prequisite for technological advance.

QuickQuiz Describe three ways in which a government policymaker can try to raise the growth in living standards in a society. Are there any drawbacks to these policies?

(and hence larger opportunity for "catch-up" growth), Africa grew more slowly. This was mainly because of much higher trade barriers; excessive tax rates; lower saving rates; and adverse structural conditions, including an unusually high incidence of inaccessibility to the sea (15 of 53 countries are landlocked). . . .

If the policies are largely to blame, why, then, were they adopted? The historical origins of Africa's antimarket orientation are not hard to discern. After almost a century of colonial depredations, African nations understandably if erroneously viewed open trade and foreign capital as a threat to national sovereignty. As in Sukarno's Indonesia, Nehru's India, and Peron's Argentina, "self sufficiency" and "state leadership," including state ownership of much of industry, became the guideposts of the economy. As a result, most of Africa went into a largely self-imposed economic exile. . . .

Adam Smith in 1755 famously remarked that "little else is requisite to carry a state to the highest degrees of opulence from the lowest barbarism, but peace, easy taxes, and tolerable administration of justice." A growth agenda need not be long and complex. Take his points in turn.

Peace, of course, is not so easily guaranteed, but the conditions for peace on the continent are better than today's ghastly headlines would suggest. Several

of the large-scale conflicts that have ravaged the continent are over or nearly so. . . . The ongoing disasters, such as in Liberia, Rwanda and Somalia, would be better contained if the West were willing to provide modest support to African-based peacekeeping efforts.

"Easy taxes" are well within the ambit of the IMF and World Bank. But here, the IMF stands guilty of neglect, if not malfeasance. African nations need simple, low taxes, with modest revenue targets as a share of GDP. Easy taxes are most essential in international trade, since successful growth will depend, more than anything else, on economic integration with the rest of the world. Africa's largely self-imposed exile from world markets can end quickly by cutting import tariffs and ending export taxes on agricultural exports. Corporate tax rates should be cut. . . .

Adam Smith spoke of a "tolerable" administration of justice, not perfect justice. Market liberalization is the primary key to strengthening the rule of law. Free trade, currency convertibility and automatic incorporation of business vastly reduce the scope for official corruption and allow the government to focus on the real public goods—internal public order, the judicial system, basic public health and education, and monetary stability. . . .

All of this is possible only if the government itself has held its own spending

© TOM VAN SANT/CORBIS

to the necessary minimum. . . . Subsidies to publicly owned companies or marketing boards should be scrapped. Food and housing subsidies for urban workers cannot be financed. And, notably, interest payments on foreign debt are not budgeted for. This is because most bankrupt African states need a fresh start based on deep debt-reduction, which should be implemented in conjunction with far-reaching domestic reforms.

Source: *The Economist,* June 29, 1996, pp. 19–21. © 1996 The Economist Newspaper Ltd. All rights reserved. Reprinted with permission. Further reproduction prohibited. http://www.economist.com.

CONCLUSION: THE IMPORTANCE OF LONG-RUN GROWTH

In this chapter we have discussed what determines the standard of living in a nation and how policymakers can endeavor to raise the standard of living through policies that promote economic growth. Most of this chapter is summarized in one of the *Ten Principles of Economics:* A country's standard of living depends on its ability to produce goods and services. Policymakers who want to encourage growth in standards of living must aim to increase their nation's productive ability by encouraging rapid accumulation of the factors of production and ensuring that these factors are employed as effectively as possible.

Economists differ in their views of the role of government in promoting economic growth. At the very least, government can lend support to the invisible hand by maintaining property rights and political stability. More controversial is whether government should target and subsidize specific industries that might be especially important for technological progress. There is no doubt that these issues are among the most important in economics. The success of one generation's policymakers in learning and heeding the fundamental lessons about economic growth determines what kind of world the next generation will inherit.

SUMMARY

- Economic prosperity, as measured by GDP per person, varies substantially around the world. The average income in the world's richest countries is more than ten times that in the world's poorest countries. Because growth rates of real GDP also vary substantially, the relative positions of countries can change dramatically over time.

- The standard of living in an economy depends on the economy's ability to produce goods and services. Productivity, in turn, depends on the amounts of physical capital, human capital, natural resources, and technological knowledge available to workers.

- Government policies can try to influence the economy's growth rate in many ways: by encouraging saving and investment, encouraging

investment from abroad, fostering education, maintaining property rights and political stability, allowing free trade, promoting the research and development of new technologies, and controlling population growth.

- The accumulation of capital is subject to diminishing returns: The more capital an economy has, the less additional output the economy gets from an extra unit of capital. Because of diminishing returns, higher saving leads to higher growth for a period of time, but growth eventually slows down as the economy approaches a higher level of capital, productivity, and income. Also because of diminishing returns, the return to capital is especially high in poor countries. Other things equal, these countries can grow faster because of the catch-up effect.

KEY CONCEPTS

productivity, p. 245
physical capital, p. 245
human capital, p. 246

natural resources, p. 246
technological knowledge, p. 246
diminishing returns, p. 250

catch-up effect, p. 251

QUESTIONS FOR REVIEW

1. What does the level of a nation's GDP measure? What does the growth rate of GDP measure? Would you rather live in a nation with a high level of GDP and a low growth rate, or in a nation with a low level of GDP and a high growth rate?

2. List and describe four determinants of productivity.

3. In what way is a college degree a form of capital?

4. Explain how higher saving leads to a higher standard of living. What might deter a policymaker from trying to raise the rate of saving?

5. Does a higher rate of saving lead to higher growth temporarily or indefinitely?

6. Why would removing a trade restriction, such as a tariff, lead to more rapid economic growth?

7. How does the rate of population growth influence the level of GDP per person?

8. Describe two ways in which the U.S. government tries to encourage advances in technological knowledge.

PROBLEMS AND APPLICATIONS

1. Most countries, including the United States, import substantial amounts of goods and services from other countries. Yet the chapter says that a nation can enjoy a high standard of living only if it can produce a large quantity of goods and services itself. Can you reconcile these two facts?

2. List the capital inputs necessary to produce each of the following.
   a. cars
   b. high school educations
   c. plane travel
   d. fruits and vegetables

3. U.S. income per person today is roughly eight times what it was a century ago. Many other countries have also experienced significant growth over that period. What are some specific ways in which your standard of living differs from that of your great-grandparents?

4. The chapter discusses how employment has declined relative to output in the farm sector. Can you think of another sector of the economy where the same phenomenon has occurred more recently? Would you consider the change in employment in this sector to represent a success or a failure from the standpoint of society as a whole?

5. Suppose that society decided to reduce consumption and increase investment.
   a. How would this change affect economic growth?

   b. What groups in society would benefit from this change? What groups might be hurt?

6. Societies choose what share of their resources to devote to consumption and what share to devote to investment. Some of these decisions involve private spending; others involve government spending.
   a. Describe some forms of private spending that represent consumption, and some forms that represent investment.
   b. Describe some forms of government spending that represent consumption, and some forms that represent investment.

7. What is the opportunity cost of investing in capital? Do you think a country can "over-invest" in capital? What is the opportunity cost of investing in human capital? Do you think a country can "over-invest" in human capital? Explain.

8. Suppose that an auto company owned entirely by German citizens opens a new factory in South Carolina.
   a. What sort of foreign investment would this represent?
   b. What would be the effect of this investment on U.S. GDP? Would the effect on U.S. GNP be larger or smaller?

9. In the 1980s Japanese investors made significant direct and portfolio investments in the United States. At the time, many Americans were unhappy that this investment was occurring.

a. In what way was it better for the United States to receive this Japanese investment than not to receive it?

b. In what way would it have been better still for Americans to have done this investment?

10. In the countries of South Asia in 1992, only 56 young women were enrolled in secondary school for every 100 young men. Describe several ways in which greater educational opportunities for young women could lead to faster economic growth in these countries.

11. International data show a positive correlation between political stability and economic growth.

a. Through what mechanism could political stability lead to strong economic growth?

b. Through what mechanism could strong economic growth lead to political stability?

http://

For more study tools, please visit http://mankiwXtra.swlearning.com.

13

SAVING, INVESTMENT, AND THE FINANCIAL SYSTEM

Imagine that you have just graduated from college (with a degree in economics, of course) and you decide to start your own business—an economic forecasting firm. Before you make any money selling your forecasts, you have to incur substantial costs to set up your business. You have to buy computers with which to make your forecasts, as well as desks, chairs, and filing cabinets to furnish your new office. Each of these items is a type of capital that your firm will use to produce and sell its services.

How do you obtain the funds to invest in these capital goods? Perhaps you are able to pay for them out of your past savings. More likely, however, like most entrepreneurs, you do not have enough money of your own to finance the start of your business. As a result, you have to get the money you need from other sources.

There are various ways for you to finance these capital investments. You could borrow the money, perhaps from a bank or from a friend or relative. In this case, you would promise not only to return the money at a later date but also to pay interest for the use of the money. Alternatively, you could convince someone to provide the money you need for your business in exchange for a share of your future

financial system
the group of institutions in the economy that help to match one person's saving with another person's investment

profits, whatever they might happen to be. In either case, your investment in computers and office equipment is being financed by someone else's saving.

The **financial system** consists of those institutions in the economy that help to match one person's saving with another person's investment. As we discussed in the previous chapter, saving and investment are key ingredients to long-run economic growth: When a country saves a large portion of its GDP, more resources are available for investment in capital, and higher capital raises a country's productivity and living standard. The previous chapter, however, did not explain how the economy coordinates saving and investment. At any time, some people want to save some of their income for the future, and others want to borrow in order to finance investments in new and growing businesses. What brings these two groups of people together? What ensures that the supply of funds from those who want to save balances the demand for funds from those who want to invest?

This chapter examines how the financial system works. First, we discuss the large variety of institutions that make up the financial system in our economy. Second, we discuss the relationship between the financial system and some key macroeconomic variables—notably saving and investment. Third, we develop a model of the supply and demand for funds in financial markets. In the model, the interest rate is the price that adjusts to balance supply and demand. The model shows how various government policies affect the interest rate and, thereby, society's allocation of scarce resources.

FINANCIAL INSTITUTIONS IN THE U.S. ECONOMY

At the broadest level, the financial system moves the economy's scarce resources from savers (people who spend less than they earn) to borrowers (people who spend more than they earn). Savers save for various reasons—to put a child through college in several years or to retire comfortably in several decades. Similarly, borrowers borrow for various reasons—to buy a house in which to live or to start a business with which to make a living. Savers supply their money to the financial system with the expectation that they will get it back with interest at a later date. Borrowers demand money from the financial system with the knowledge that they will be required to pay it back with interest at a later date.

The financial system is made up of various financial institutions that help coordinate savers and borrowers. As a prelude to analyzing the economic forces that drive the financial system, let's discuss the most important of these institutions. Financial institutions can be grouped into two categories—financial markets and financial intermediaries. We consider each category in turn.

Financial Markets

financial markets
financial institutions through which savers can directly provide funds to borrowers

Financial markets are the institutions through which a person who wants to save can directly supply funds to a person who wants to borrow. The two most important financial markets in our economy are the bond market and the stock market.

The Bond Market   When Intel, the giant maker of computer chips, wants to borrow to finance construction of a new factory, it can borrow directly from the public. It does this by selling bonds. A **bond** is a certificate of indebtedness that specifies the obligations of the borrower to the holder of the bond. Put simply, a bond is an IOU. It identifies the time at which the loan will be repaid, called the *date of maturity,* and the rate of interest that will be paid periodically until the loan matures. The buyer of a bond gives his or her money to Intel in exchange for this promise of interest and eventual repayment of the amount borrowed (called the *principal*). The buyer can hold the bond until maturity or can sell the bond at an earlier date to someone else.

There are literally millions of different bonds in the U.S. economy. When large corporations, the federal government, or state and local governments need to borrow to finance the purchase of a new factory, a new jet fighter, or a new school, they usually do so by issuing bonds. If you look at *The Wall Street Journal* or the business section of your local newspaper, you will find a listing of the prices and interest rates on some of the most important bond issues. Although these bonds differ in many ways, three characteristics of bonds are most important.

The first characteristic is a bond's *term*—the length of time until the bond matures. Some bonds have short terms, such as a few months, while others have terms as long as 30 years. (The British government has even issued a bond that never matures, called a *perpetuity.* This bond pays interest forever, but the principal is never repaid.) The interest rate on a bond depends, in part, on its term. Long-term bonds are riskier than short-term bonds because holders of long-term bonds have to wait longer for repayment of principal. If a holder of a long-term bond needs his money earlier than the distant date of maturity, he has no choice but to sell the bond to someone else, perhaps at a reduced price. To compensate for this risk, long-term bonds usually pay higher interest rates than short-term bonds.

The second important characteristic of a bond is its *credit risk*—the probability that the borrower will fail to pay some of the interest or principal. Such a failure to pay is called a *default.* Borrowers can (and sometimes do) default on their loans by declaring bankruptcy. When bond buyers perceive that the probability of default is high, they demand a higher interest rate to compensate them for this risk. Because the U.S. government is considered a safe credit risk, government bonds tend to pay low interest rates. By contrast, financially shaky corporations raise money by issuing *junk bonds*, which pay very high interest rates. Buyers of bonds can judge credit risk by checking with various private agencies, such as Standard & Poor's, which rate the credit risk of different bonds.

The third important characteristic of a bond is its *tax treatment*—the way in which the tax laws treat the interest earned on the bond. The interest on most bonds is taxable income, so that the bond owner has to pay a portion of the interest in income taxes. By contrast, when state and local governments issue bonds, called *municipal bonds*, the bond owners are not required to pay federal income tax on the interest income. Because of this tax advantage, bonds issued by state and local governments pay a lower interest rate than bonds issued by corporations or the federal government.

The Stock Market Another way for Intel to raise funds to build a new semiconductor factory is to sell stock in the company. **Stock** represents ownership in a firm and is, therefore, a claim to the profits that the firm makes. For example, if Intel sells a total of 1,000,000 shares of stock, then each share represents ownership of 1/1,000,000 of the business.

bond
a certificate of indebtedness

stock
a claim to partial ownership in a firm

The sale of stock to raise money is called *equity finance*, whereas the sale of bonds is called *debt finance*. Although corporations use both equity and debt finance to raise money for new investments, stocks and bonds are very different. The owner of shares of Intel stock is a part owner of Intel; the owner of an Intel bond is a creditor of the corporation. If Intel is very profitable, the stockholders enjoy the benefits of these profits, whereas the bondholders get only the interest on their bonds. And if Intel runs into financial difficulty, the bondholders are paid what they are due before stockholders receive anything at all. Compared to bonds, stocks offer the holder both higher risk and potentially higher return.

After a corporation issues stock by selling shares to the public, these shares trade among stockholders on organized stock exchanges. In these transactions, the corporation itself receives no money when its stock changes hands. The most important stock exchanges in the U.S. economy are the New York Stock Exchange, the American Stock Exchange, and NASDAQ (National Association of Securities Dealers Automated Quotation system). Most of the world's countries have their own stock exchanges on which the shares of local companies trade.

The prices at which shares trade on stock exchanges are determined by the supply and demand for the stock in these companies. Because stock represents ownership in a corporation, the demand for a stock (and thus its price) reflects people's perception of the corporation's future profitability. When people become optimistic about a company's future, they raise their demand for its stock and thereby bid up the price of a share of stock. Conversely, when people come to expect a company to have little profit or even losses, the price of a share falls.

Various stock indexes are available to monitor the overall level of stock prices. A *stock index* is computed as an average of a group of stock prices. The most famous stock index is the Dow Jones Industrial Average, which has been computed regularly since 1896. It is now based on the prices of the stocks of 30 major U.S. companies, such as General Motors, General Electric, Microsoft, Coca-Cola, AT&T, and IBM. Another well-known stock index is the Standard & Poor's 500 Index, which is based on the prices of 500 major companies. Because stock prices reflect expected profitability, these stock indexes are watched closely as possible indicators of future economic conditions.

Financial Intermediaries

financial intermediaries
financial institutions through which savers can indirectly provide funds to borrowers

Financial intermediaries are financial institutions through which savers can indirectly provide funds to borrowers. The term *intermediary* reflects the role of these institutions in standing between savers and borrowers. Here we consider two of the most important financial intermediaries—banks and mutual funds.

Banks If the owner of a small grocery store wants to finance an expansion of his business, he probably takes a strategy quite different from Intel. Unlike Intel, a small grocer would find it difficult to raise funds in the bond and stock markets. Most buyers of stocks and bonds prefer to buy those issued by larger, more familiar companies. The small grocer, therefore, most likely finances his business expansion with a loan from a local bank.

Banks are the financial intermediaries with which people are most familiar. A primary job of banks is to take in deposits from people who want to save and use

HOW TO READ THE NEWSPAPER'S STOCK TABLES

Most daily newspapers include stock tables, which contain information about recent trading in the stocks of several thousand companies. Here is the kind of information these tables usually provide:

- *Price.* The single most important piece of information about a stock is the price of a share. The newspaper usually presents several prices. The "last" or "closing" price is the price of the last transaction that occurred before the stock exchange closed the previous day. Many newspapers also give the "high" and "low" prices over the past day of trading and, sometimes, over the past year as well.
- *Volume.* Most newspapers present the number of shares sold during the past day of trading. This figure is called the *daily volume.*
- *Dividend.* Corporations pay out some of their profits to their stockholders; this amount is called the *dividend.* (Profits not paid out are called *retained earnings* and are used by the corporation

for additional investment.) Newspapers often report the dividend paid over the previous year for each share of stock. They sometimes report the *dividend yield,* which is the dividend expressed as a percentage of the stock's price.
- *Price-earnings ratio.* A corporation's earnings, or profit, is the amount of revenue it receives for the sale of its products minus its costs of production as measured by its accountants. *Earnings per share* is the company's total earnings divided by the number of shares of stock outstanding. Companies use some of their earnings to pay dividends to stockholders; the rest is kept in the firm to make new investments. The price-earnings ratio, often called the P/E, is the price of a corporation's stock divided by the amount the corporation earned per share over the past year. Historically, the typical price-earnings ratio is about 15. A higher P/E indicates that a corporation's stock is expensive relative to its recent earnings; this might indicate either that people expect earnings to rise in the future or that the stock is overvalued. Conversely, a lower P/E indicates that a corporation's stock is cheap relative to its recent earnings; this might indicate either that people expect earnings to fall or that the stock is undervalued.

Why does the newspaper report all these data every day? Many people who invest their savings in stock follow these numbers closely when deciding which stocks to buy and sell. By contrast, other stockholders follow a buy-and-hold strategy: They buy the stock of well-run companies, hold it for long periods of time, and do not respond to the daily fluctuations reported in the paper.

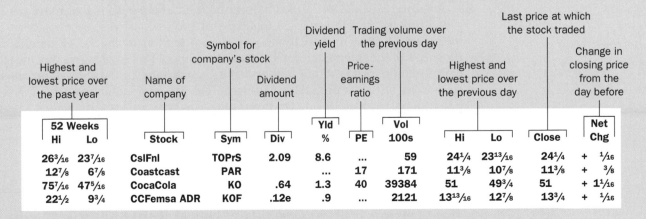

52 Weeks		Stock	Sym	Div	Yld %	PE	Vol 100s	Hi	Lo	Close	Net Chg
Hi	Lo										
$26^3/_{16}$	$23^7/_{16}$	CslFnl	TOPrS	2.09	8.6	...	59	$24^1/_4$	$23^{13}/_{16}$	$24^1/_4$	+ $^1/_{16}$
$12^7/_8$	$6^7/_8$	Coastcast	PAR		...	17	171	$11^3/_8$	$10^7/_8$	$11^3/_8$	+ $^3/_8$
$75^7/_{16}$	$47^5/_{16}$	CocaCola	KO	.64	1.3	40	39384	51	$49^3/_4$	51	+ $1^1/_{16}$
$22^1/_2$	$9^3/_4$	CCFemsa ADR	KOF	.12e	.9	...	2121	$13^{13}/_{16}$	$12^7/_8$	$13^3/_4$	+ $^1/_{16}$

these deposits to make loans to people who want to borrow. Banks pay depositors interest on their deposits and charge borrowers slightly higher interest on their loans. The difference between these rates of interest covers the banks' costs and returns some profit to the owners of the banks.

Besides being financial intermediaries, banks play a second important role in the economy: They facilitate purchases of goods and services by allowing people to write checks against their deposits. In other words, banks help create a special asset that people can use as a *medium of exchange*. A medium of exchange is an item that people can easily use to engage in transactions. A bank's role in providing a medium of exchange distinguishes it from many other financial institutions. Stocks and bonds, like bank deposits, are a possible *store of value* for the wealth that people have accumulated in past saving, but access to this wealth is not as easy, cheap, and immediate as just writing a check. For now, we ignore this second role of banks, but we will return to it when we discuss the monetary system later in the book.

Mutual Funds   A financial intermediary of increasing importance in the U.S. economy is the mutual fund. A **mutual fund** is an institution that sells shares to the public and uses the proceeds to buy a selection, or *portfolio*, of various types of stocks, bonds, or both stocks and bonds. The shareholder of the mutual fund accepts all the risk and return associated with the portfolio. If the value of the portfolio rises, the shareholder benefits; if the value of the portfolio falls, the shareholder suffers the loss.

The primary advantage of mutual funds is that they allow people with small amounts of money to diversify. Buyers of stocks and bonds are well advised to heed the adage: Don't put all your eggs in one basket. Because the value of any single stock or bond is tied to the fortunes of one company, holding a single kind of stock or bond is very risky. By contrast, people who hold a diverse portfolio of stocks and bonds face less risk because they have only a small stake in each company. Mutual funds make this diversification easy. With only a few hundred dollars, a person can buy shares in a mutual fund and, indirectly, become the part owner or creditor of hundreds of major companies. For this service, the company operating the mutual fund charges shareholders a fee, usually between 0.5 and 2.0 percent of assets each year.

A second advantage claimed by mutual fund companies is that mutual funds give ordinary people access to the skills of professional money managers. The managers of most mutual funds pay close attention to the developments and prospects of the companies in which they buy stock. These managers buy the stock of those companies that they view as having a profitable future and sell the stock of companies with less promising prospects. This professional management, it is argued, should increase the return that mutual fund depositors earn on their savings.

Financial economists, however, are often skeptical of this second argument. With thousands of money managers paying close attention to each company's

mutual fund
an institution that sells shares to the public and uses the proceeds to buy a portfolio of stocks and bonds

ARLO AND JANIS by Jimmy Johnson

IN THE NEWS

FINANCE IN CHINA

The importance of free financial markets is most apparent when a country doesn't have them.

Sharp Shift for China's Economy as Entrepreneurs Woo Investors

By Craig S. Smith

Wang Shuxian, a former farmer who now drives a Cadillac, built his successful textile company with money from friends and family. As a private businessman, he could never sell shares on the country's state-run stock market. Now he can, in a change signaling that China's economy is preparing to take a sudden turn. . . .

New rules are allowing privately owned companies access to the country's capital markets, which so far have been effectively off limits for nearly all of them. . . . With easier access to capital,

private companies have a chance at becoming the main engine of China's economy for the first time since a brief period earlier this century and otherwise since the Song Dynasty nearly 1,000 years ago.

The change also has political implications: As China's ranks of private businesses grow in number and wealth, their owners will become an increasingly powerful constituency whose demands the government will not be able to easily ignore.

"The rule of law and access to finance are the two things that will make China's private companies independent from political power," said Andy Xie, an economist for Morgan Stanley Dean Witter in Hong Kong.

Under the existing system, the government, not the market, decides which companies can sell stock to the public. That system puts the power over which concerns get investment money in the hands of local Communist Party bureaucrats, who are most concerned with helping state enterprises in their province survive. The system also encourages bribery and crams the markets with lower-quality state companies that would otherwise never be able to list their shares.

Source: *The New York Times,* December 28, 2000, p. A1. Copyright © 2000 by The New York Times Co. Reprinted by permission.

prospects, the price of a company's stock is usually a good reflection of the company's true value. As a result, it is hard to "beat the market" by buying good stocks and selling bad ones. In fact, mutual funds called *index funds,* which buy all the stocks in a given stock index, perform somewhat better on average than mutual funds that take advantage of active management by professional money managers. The explanation for the superior performance of index funds is that they keep costs low by buying and selling very rarely and by not having to pay the salaries of the professional money managers.

Summing Up

The U.S. economy contains a large variety of financial institutions. In addition to the bond market, the stock market, banks, and mutual funds, there are also pension funds, credit unions, insurance companies, and even the local loan shark.

These institutions differ in many ways. When analyzing the macroeconomic role of the financial system, however, it is more important to keep in mind the similarity of these institutions than the differences. These financial institutions all serve the same goal—directing the resources of savers into the hands of borrowers.

QuickQuiz What is stock? What is a bond? How are they different? How are they similar?

SAVING AND INVESTMENT IN THE NATIONAL INCOME ACCOUNTS

Events that occur within the financial system are central to understanding developments in the overall economy. As we have just seen, the institutions that make up this system—the bond market, the stock market, banks, and mutual funds—have the role of coordinating the economy's saving and investment. And as we saw in the previous chapter, saving and investment are important determinants of long-run growth in GDP and living standards. As a result, macroeconomists need to understand how financial markets work and how various events and policies affect them.

As a starting point for an analysis of financial markets, we discuss in this section the key macroeconomic variables that measure activity in these markets. Our emphasis here is not on behavior but on accounting. *Accounting* refers to how various numbers are defined and added up. A personal accountant might help an individual add up his income and expenses. A national income accountant does the same thing for the economy as a whole. The national income accounts include, in particular, GDP and the many related statistics.

The rules of national income accounting include several important identities. Recall that an *identity* is an equation that must be true because of the way the variables in the equation are defined. Identities are useful to keep in mind, for they clarify how different variables are related to one another. Here we consider some accounting identities that shed light on the macroeconomic role of financial markets.

Some Important Identities

Recall that gross domestic product (GDP) is both total income in an economy and the total expenditure on the economy's output of goods and services. GDP (denoted as Y) is divided into four components of expenditure: consumption (C), investment (I), government purchases (G), and net exports (NX). We write

$$Y = C + I + G + NX.$$

This equation is an identity because every dollar of expenditure that shows up on the left-hand side also shows up in one of the four components on the right-hand side. Because of the way each of the variables is defined and measured, this equation must always hold.

In this chapter, we simplify our analysis by assuming that the economy we are examining is closed. A *closed economy* is one that does not interact with other

CHAPTER 13 SAVING, INVESTMENT, AND THE FINANCIAL SYSTEM | 273

economies. In particular, a closed economy does not engage in international trade in goods and services, nor does it engage in international borrowing and lending. Of course, actual economies are *open economies*—that is, they interact with other economies around the world. Nonetheless, assuming a closed economy is a useful simplification with which we can learn some lessons that apply to all economies. Moreover, this assumption applies perfectly to the world economy (for interplanetary trade is not yet common).

Because a closed economy does not engage in international trade, imports and exports are exactly zero. Therefore, net exports (*NX*) are also zero. In this case, we can write

$$Y = C + I + G.$$

This equation states that GDP is the sum of consumption, investment, and government purchases. Each unit of output sold in a closed economy is consumed, invested, or bought by the government.

To see what this identity can tell us about financial markets, subtract *C* and *G* from both sides of this equation. We obtain

$$Y - C - G = I.$$

The left-hand side of this equation ($Y - C - G$) is the total income in the economy that remains after paying for consumption and government purchases: This amount is called **national saving,** or just **saving,** and is denoted *S*. Substituting *S* for $Y - C - G$, we can write the last equation as

$$S = I.$$

This equation states that saving equals investment.

To understand the meaning of national saving, it is helpful to manipulate the definition a bit more. Let *T* denote the amount that the government collects from households in taxes minus the amount it pays back to households in the form of transfer payments (such as Social Security and welfare). We can then write national saving in either of two ways:

$$S = Y - C - G$$

or

$$S = (Y - T - C) + (T - G).$$

These equations are the same, because the two *T*'s in the second equation cancel each other, but each reveals a different way of thinking about national saving. In particular, the second equation separates national saving into two pieces: private saving ($Y - T - C$) and public saving ($T - G$).

Consider each of these two pieces. **Private saving** is the amount of income that households have left after paying their taxes and paying for their consumption. In particular, because households receive income of *Y*, pay taxes of *T*, and spend *C* on consumption, private saving is $Y - T - C$. **Public saving** is the amount of tax revenue that the government has left after paying for its spending. The government

national saving (saving)
the total income in the economy that remains after paying for consumption and government purchases

private saving
the income that households have left after paying for taxes and consumption

public saving
the tax revenue that the government has left after paying for its spending

budget surplus
an excess of tax revenue over
government spending

budget deficit
a shortfall of tax revenue from
government spending

receives T in tax revenue and spends G on goods and services. If T exceeds G, the government runs a **budget surplus** because it receives more money than it spends. This surplus of $T - G$ represents public saving. If the government spends more than it receives in tax revenue, then G is larger than T. In this case, the government runs a **budget deficit,** and public saving $T - G$ is a negative number.

Now consider how these accounting identities are related to financial markets. The equation $S = I$ reveals an important fact: *For the economy as a whole, saving must be equal to investment.* Yet this fact raises some important questions: What mechanisms lie behind this identity? What coordinates those people who are deciding how much to save and those people who are deciding how much to invest? The answer is the financial system. The bond market, the stock market, banks, mutual funds, and other financial markets and intermediaries stand between the two sides of the $S = I$ equation. They take in the nation's saving and direct it to the nation's investment.

The Meaning of Saving and Investment

The terms *saving* and *investment* can sometimes be confusing. Most people use these terms casually and sometimes interchangeably. By contrast, the macroeconomists who put together the national income accounts use these terms carefully and distinctly.

Consider an example. Suppose that Larry earns more than he spends and deposits his unspent income in a bank or uses it to buy a bond or some stock from a corporation. Because Larry's income exceeds his consumption, he adds to the nation's saving. Larry might think of himself as "investing" his money, but a macroeconomist would call Larry's act saving rather than investment.

In the language of macroeconomics, investment refers to the purchase of new capital, such as equipment or buildings. When Moe borrows from the bank to build himself a new house, he adds to the nation's investment. Similarly, when the Curly Corporation sells some stock and uses the proceeds to build a new factory, it also adds to the nation's investment.

Although the accounting identity $S = I$ shows that saving and investment are equal for the economy as a whole, this does not have to be true for every individual household or firm. Larry's saving can be greater than his investment, and he can deposit the excess in a bank. Moe's saving can be less than his investment, and he can borrow the shortfall from a bank. Banks and other financial institutions make these individual differences between saving and investment possible by allowing one person's saving to finance another person's investment.

QuickQuiz Define *private saving, public saving, national saving,* and *investment.* How are they related?

THE MARKET FOR LOANABLE FUNDS

Having discussed some of the important financial institutions in our economy and the macroeconomic role of these institutions, we are ready to build a model of financial markets. Our purpose in building this model is to explain how financial markets coordinate the economy's saving and investment. The model also gives us a tool with which we can analyze various government policies that influence saving and investment.

To keep things simple, we assume that the economy has only one financial market, called the **market for loanable funds.** All savers go to this market to deposit their saving, and all borrowers go to this market to get their loans. Thus, the term *loanable funds* refers to all income that people have chosen to save and lend out, rather than use for their own consumption. In the market for loanable funds, there is one interest rate, which is both the return to saving and the cost of borrowing.

The assumption of a single financial market, of course, is not literally true. As we have seen, the economy has many types of financial institutions. But, as we discussed in Chapter 2, the art in building an economic model is simplifying the world in order to explain it. For our purposes here, we can ignore the diversity of financial institutions and assume that the economy has a single financial market.

market for loanable funds
the market in which those who want to save supply funds and those who want to borrow to invest demand funds

Supply and Demand for Loanable Funds

The economy's market for loanable funds, like other markets in the economy, is governed by supply and demand. To understand how the market for loanable funds operates, therefore, we first look at the sources of supply and demand in that market.

The supply of loanable funds comes from those people who have some extra income they want to save and lend out. This lending can occur directly, such as when a household buys a bond from a firm, or it can occur indirectly, such as when a household makes a deposit in a bank, which in turn uses the funds to make loans. In both cases, *saving is the source of the supply of loanable funds.*

The demand for loanable funds comes from households and firms who wish to borrow to make investments. This demand includes families taking out mortgages to buy homes. It also includes firms borrowing to buy new equipment or build factories. In both cases, *investment is the source of the demand for loanable funds.*

The interest rate is the price of a loan. It represents the amount that borrowers pay for loans and the amount that lenders receive on their saving. Because a high interest rate makes borrowing more expensive, the quantity of loanable funds demanded falls as the interest rate rises. Similarly, because a high interest rate makes saving more attractive, the quantity of loanable funds supplied rises as the interest rate rises. In other words, the demand curve for loanable funds slopes downward, and the supply curve for loanable funds slopes upward.

Figure 1 (p. 276) shows the interest rate that balances the supply and demand for loanable funds. In the equilibrium shown, the interest rate is 5 percent, and the quantity of loanable funds demanded and the quantity of loanable funds supplied both equal $1,200 billion.

The adjustment of the interest rate to the equilibrium level occurs for the usual reasons. If the interest rate were lower than the equilibrium level, the quantity of loanable funds supplied would be less than the quantity of loanable funds demanded. The resulting shortage of loanable funds would encourage lenders to raise the interest rate they charge. A higher interest rate would encourage saving (thereby increasing the quantity of loanable funds supplied) and discourage borrowing for investment (thereby decreasing the quantity of loanable funds demanded). Conversely, if the interest rate were higher than the equilibrium level,

FIGURE 1

The Market for Loanable Funds

The interest rate in the economy adjusts to balance the supply and demand for loanable funds. The supply of loanable funds comes from national saving, including both private saving and public saving. The demand for loanable funds comes from firms and households that want to borrow for purposes of investment. Here the equilibrium interest rate is 5 percent, and $1,200 billion of loanable funds are supplied and demanded.

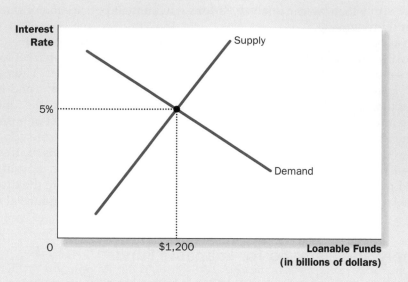

the quantity of loanable funds supplied would exceed the quantity of loanable funds demanded. As lenders competed for the scarce borrowers, interest rates would be driven down. In this way, the interest rate approaches the equilibrium level at which the supply and demand for loanable funds exactly balance.

Recall that economists distinguish between the real interest rate and the nominal interest rate. The nominal interest rate is the interest rate as usually reported—the monetary return to saving and cost of borrowing. The real interest rate is the nominal interest rate corrected for inflation; it equals the nominal interest rate minus the inflation rate. Because inflation erodes the value of money over time, the real interest rate more accurately reflects the real return to saving and cost of borrowing. Therefore, the supply and demand for loanable funds depend on the real (rather than nominal) interest rate, and the equilibrium in Figure 1 should be interpreted as determining the real interest rate in the economy. For the rest of this chapter, when you see the term *interest rate,* you should remember that we are talking about the real interest rate.

This model of the supply and demand for loanable funds shows that financial markets work much like other markets in the economy. In the market for milk, for instance, the price of milk adjusts so that the quantity of milk supplied balances the quantity of milk demanded. In this way, the invisible hand coordinates the behavior of dairy farmers and the behavior of milk drinkers. Once we realize that saving represents the supply of loanable funds and investment represents the demand, we can see how the invisible hand coordinates saving and investment. When the interest rate adjusts to balance supply and demand in the market for loanable funds, it coordinates the behavior of people who want to save (the suppliers of loanable funds) and the behavior of people who want to invest (the demanders of loanable funds).

We can now use this analysis of the market for loanable funds to examine various government policies that affect the economy's saving and investment. Because this model is just supply and demand in a particular market, we analyze any policy using the three steps discussed in Chapter 4. First, we decide whether the policy shifts the supply curve or the demand curve. Second, we determine the direction of the shift. Third, we use the supply-and-demand diagram to see how the equilibrium changes.

Policy 1: Saving Incentives

American families save a smaller fraction of their incomes than their counterparts in many other countries, such as Japan and Germany. Although the reasons for these international differences are unclear, many U.S. policymakers view the low level of U.S. saving as a major problem. One of the *Ten Principles of Economics* in Chapter 1 is that a country's standard of living depends on its ability to produce goods and services. And, as we discussed in the preceding chapter, saving is an important long-run determinant of a nation's productivity. If the United States could somehow raise its saving rate to the level that prevails in other countries, the growth rate of GDP would increase, and over time, U.S. citizens would enjoy a higher standard of living.

Another of the *Ten Principles of Economics* is that people respond to incentives. Many economists have used this principle to suggest that the low saving rate in the United States is at least partly attributable to tax laws that discourage saving. The U.S. federal government, as well as many state governments, collects revenue by taxing income, including interest and dividend income. To see the effects of this policy, consider a 25-year-old who saves $1,000 and buys a 30-year bond that pays an interest rate of 9 percent. In the absence of taxes, the $1,000 grows to $13,268 when the individual reaches age 55. Yet if that interest is taxed at a rate of, say, 33 percent, then the after-tax interest rate is only 6 percent. In this case, the $1,000 grows to only $5,743 after 30 years. The tax on interest income substantially reduces the future payoff from current saving and, as a result, reduces the incentive for people to save.

In response to this problem, many economists and lawmakers have proposed reforming the tax code to encourage greater saving. In 1995, for instance, when Congressman Bill Archer of Texas became chairman of the powerful House Ways and Means Committee, he proposed replacing the current income tax with a consumption tax. Under a consumption tax, income that is saved would not be taxed until the saving is later spent; in essence, a consumption tax is like the sales taxes that many states now use to collect revenue. A more modest proposal is to expand eligibility for special accounts, such as Individual Retirement Accounts, that allow people to shelter some of their saving from taxation. Let's consider the effect of such a saving incentive on the market for loanable funds, as illustrated in Figure 2 (p. 278).

First, which curve would this policy affect? Because the tax change would alter the incentive for households to save *at any given interest rate*, it would affect the quantity of loanable funds supplied at each interest rate. Thus, the supply of loanable funds would shift. The demand for loanable funds would remain the same, because the tax change would not directly affect the amount that borrowers want to borrow at any given interest rate.

Second, which way would the supply curve shift? Because saving would be taxed less heavily than under current law, households would increase their saving by consuming a smaller fraction of their income. Households would use this

FIGURE 2

An Increase in the Supply of Loanable Funds

A change in the tax laws to encourage Americans to save more would shift the supply of loanable funds to the right from S_1 to S_2. As a result, the equilibrium interest rate would fall, and the lower interest rate would stimulate investment. Here the equilibrium interest rate falls from 5 percent to 4 percent, and the equilibrium quantity of loanable funds saved and invested rises from $1,200 billion to $1,600 billion.

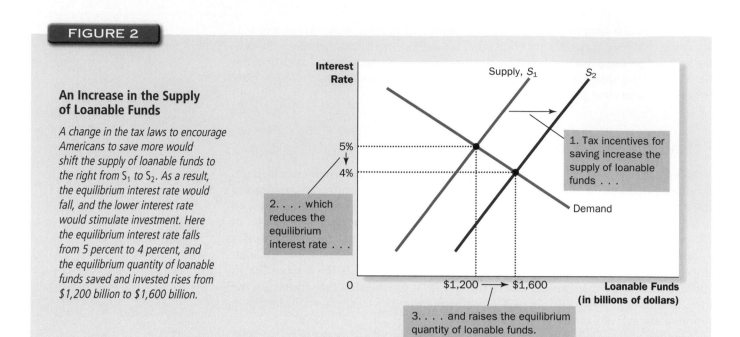

1. Tax incentives for saving increase the supply of loanable funds . . .

2. . . . which reduces the equilibrium interest rate . . .

3. . . . and raises the equilibrium quantity of loanable funds.

additional saving to increase their deposits in banks or to buy more bonds. The supply of loanable funds would increase, and the supply curve would shift to the right from S_1 to S_2, as shown in Figure 2.

Finally, we can compare the old and new equilibria. In the figure, the increased supply of loanable funds reduces the interest rate from 5 percent to 4 percent. The lower interest rate raises the quantity of loanable funds demanded from $1,200 billion to $1,600 billion. That is, the shift in the supply curve moves the market equilibrium along the demand curve. With a lower cost of borrowing, households and firms are motivated to borrow more to finance greater investment. Thus, *if a reform of the tax laws encouraged greater saving, the result would be lower interest rates and greater investment.*

Although this analysis of the effects of increased saving is widely accepted among economists, there is less consensus about what kinds of tax changes should be enacted. Many economists endorse tax reform aimed at increasing saving in order to stimulate investment and growth. Yet others are skeptical that these tax changes would have much effect on national saving. These skeptics also doubt the equity of the proposed reforms. They argue that, in many cases, the benefits of the tax changes would accrue primarily to the wealthy, who are least in need of tax relief.

Policy 2: Investment Incentives

Suppose that Congress passed a tax reform aimed at making investment more attractive. In essence, this is what Congress does when it institutes an *investment tax credit*, which it does from time to time. An investment tax credit gives a tax advantage to any firm building a new factory or buying a new piece of equipment. Let's

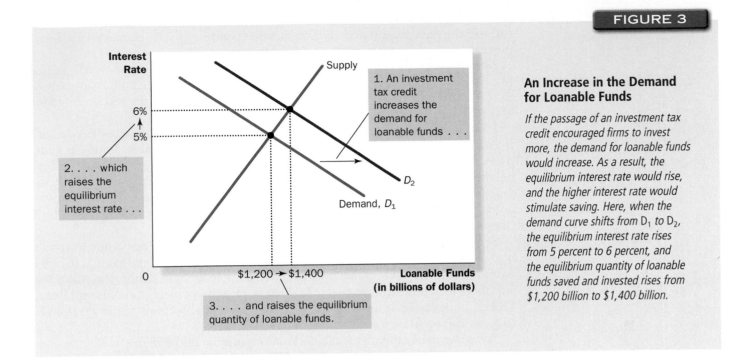

FIGURE 3

Interest Rate

Supply

6%

5%

1. An investment tax credit increases the demand for loanable funds . . .

D_2

Demand, D_1

2. . . . which raises the equilibrium interest rate . . .

0

$1,200 → $1,400

Loanable Funds (in billions of dollars)

3. . . . and raises the equilibrium quantity of loanable funds.

An Increase in the Demand for Loanable Funds

If the passage of an investment tax credit encouraged firms to invest more, the demand for loanable funds would increase. As a result, the equilibrium interest rate would rise, and the higher interest rate would stimulate saving. Here, when the demand curve shifts from D₁ to D₂, the equilibrium interest rate rises from 5 percent to 6 percent, and the equilibrium quantity of loanable funds saved and invested rises from $1,200 billion to $1,400 billion.

consider the effect of such a tax reform on the market for loanable funds, as illustrated in Figure 3.

First, would the law affect supply or demand? Because the tax credit would reward firms that borrow and invest in new capital, it would alter investment at any given interest rate and, thereby, change the demand for loanable funds. By contrast, because the tax credit would not affect the amount that households save at any given interest rate, it would not affect the supply of loanable funds.

Second, which way would the demand curve shift? Because firms would have an incentive to increase investment at any interest rate, the quantity of loanable funds demanded would be higher at any given interest rate. Thus, the demand curve for loanable funds would move to the right, as shown by the shift from D_1 to D_2 in the figure.

Third, consider how the equilibrium would change. In Figure 3, the increased demand for loanable funds raises the interest rate from 5 percent to 6 percent, and the higher interest rate in turn increases the quantity of loanable funds supplied from $1,200 billion to $1,400 billion, as households respond by increasing the amount they save. This change in household behavior is represented here as a movement along the supply curve. Thus, *if a reform of the tax laws encouraged greater investment, the result would be higher interest rates and greater saving.*

Policy 3: Government Budget Deficits and Surpluses

A perpetual topic of political debate is the status of the government budget. Recall that a *budget deficit* is an excess of government spending over tax revenue. Governments finance budget deficits by borrowing in the bond market, and the accumulation of past government borrowing is called the *government debt*. A *budget surplus,* an excess of tax revenue over government spending, can be used to repay some of the government debt. If government spending exactly equals tax revenue, the government is said to have a *balanced budget.*

Imagine that the government starts with a balanced budget and then, because of a tax cut or a spending increase, starts running a budget deficit. We can analyze the effects of the budget deficit by following our three steps in the market for loanable funds, as illustrated in Figure 4.

First, which curve shifts when the government starts running a budget deficit? Recall that national saving—the source of the supply of loanable funds—is composed of private saving and public saving. A change in the government budget balance represents a change in public saving and, thereby, in the supply of loanable funds. Because the budget deficit does not influence the amount that households and firms want to borrow to finance investment at any given interest rate, it does not alter the demand for loanable funds.

Second, which way does the supply curve shift? When the government runs a budget deficit, public saving is negative, and this reduces national saving. In other words, when the government borrows to finance its budget deficit, it reduces the supply of loanable funds available to finance investment by households and firms. Thus, a budget deficit shifts the supply curve for loanable funds to the left from S_1 to S_2, as shown in Figure 4.

Third, we can compare the old and new equilibria. In the figure, when the budget deficit reduces the supply of loanable funds, the interest rate rises from 5 percent to 6 percent. This higher interest rate then alters the behavior of the households and firms that participate in the loan market. In particular, many demanders of

---

FIGURE 4

The Effect of a Government Budget Deficit

When the government spends more than it receives in tax revenue, the resulting budget deficit lowers national saving. The supply of loanable funds decreases, and the equilibrium interest rate rises. Thus, when the government borrows to finance its budget deficit, it crowds out households and firms who otherwise would borrow to finance investment. Here, when the supply shifts from S_1 to S_2, the equilibrium interest rate rises from 5 percent to 6 percent, and the equilibrium quantity of loanable funds saved and invested falls from $1,200 billion to $800 billion.

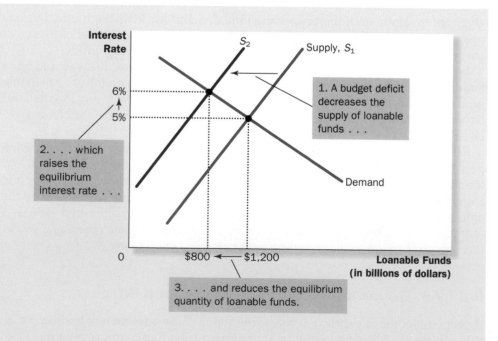

loanable funds are discouraged by the higher interest rate. Fewer families buy new homes, and fewer firms choose to build new factories. The fall in investment because of government borrowing is called **crowding out** and is represented in the figure by the movement along the demand curve from a quantity of $1,200 billion in loanable funds to a quantity of $800 billion. That is, when the government borrows to finance its budget deficit, it crowds out private borrowers who are trying to finance investment.

Thus, the most basic lesson about budget deficits follows directly from their effects on the supply and demand for loanable funds: *When the government reduces national saving by running a budget deficit, the interest rate rises, and investment falls.* Because investment is important for long-run economic growth, government budget deficits reduce the economy's growth rate.

Government budget surpluses work just the opposite as budget deficits. When government collects more in tax revenue than it spends, its saves the difference by retiring some of the outstanding government debt. This budget surplus, or public saving, contributes to national saving. Thus, *a budget surplus increases the supply of loanable funds, reduces the interest rate, and stimulates investment.* Higher investment, in turn, means greater capital accumulation and more rapid economic growth.

crowding out
a decrease in investment that results from government borrowing

Case Study
THE HISTORY OF U.S. GOVERNMENT DEBT

How indebted is the U.S. government? The answer to this question varies substantially over time. Figure 5 (p. 282) shows the debt of the U.S. federal government expressed as a percentage of U.S. GDP. It shows that the government debt has fluctuated from zero in 1836 to 107 percent of GDP in 1945. In recent years, government debt has been about 35 percent of GDP.

The behavior of the debt–GDP ratio is one gauge of what's happening with the government's finances. Because GDP is a rough measure of the government's tax base, a declining debt–GDP ratio indicates that the government indebtedness is shrinking relative to its ability to raise tax revenue. This suggests that the government is, in some sense, living within its means. By contrast, a rising debt–GDP ratio means that the government indebtedness is increasing relative to its ability to raise tax revenue. It is often interpreted as meaning that fiscal policy—government spending and taxes—cannot be sustained forever at current levels.

Throughout history, the primary cause of fluctuations in government debt is war. When wars occur, government spending on national defense rises substantially to pay for soldiers and military equipment. Taxes typically rise as well but by much less than the increase in spending. The result is a budget deficit and increasing government debt. When the war is over, government spending declines, and the debt–GDP ratio starts declining as well.

There are two reasons to believe that debt financing of war is an appropriate policy. First, it allows the government to keep tax rates smooth over time. Without debt financing, tax rates would have to rise sharply during wars, and this would cause a substantial decline in economic efficiency. Second, debt financing of wars

FIGURE 5

The U.S. Government Debt

The debt of the U.S. federal government, expressed here as a percentage of GDP, has varied substantially throughout history. It reached its highest level after the large expenditures of World War II, but then declined throughout the 1950s and 1960s. It began rising again in the early 1980s when Ronald Reagan's tax cuts were not accompanied by similar cuts in government spending. It then stabilized and even declined slightly in the late 1990s.

Source: U.S. Department of Treasury; U.S. Department of Commerce; and T. S. Berry, "Production and Population since 1789," Bostwick Paper No. 6, Richmond, 1988.

shifts part of the cost of wars to future generations, who will have to pay off the government debt. This is arguably a fair distribution of the burden, for future generations get some of the benefit when one generation fights a war to defend the nation against foreign aggressors.

One large increase in government debt that cannot be explained by war is the increase that occurred beginning around 1980. When President Ronald Reagan took office in 1981, he was committed to smaller government and lower taxes. Yet he found cutting government spending to be more difficult politically than cutting taxes. The result was the beginning of a period of large budget deficits that continued not only through Reagan's time in office but also for many years thereafter. As a result, government debt rose from 26 percent of GDP in 1980 to 50 percent of GDP in 1993.

As we discussed earlier, government budget deficits reduce national saving, investment, and long-run economic growth, and this is precisely why the rise in government debt during the 1980s troubled so many economists. Policymakers from both political parties accepted this basic argument and viewed persistent budget deficits as an important policy problem. When Bill Clinton moved into the Oval Office in 1993, deficit reduction was his first major goal. Similarly, when the Republicans took control of Congress in 1995, deficit reduction was high on their legislative agenda. Both of these efforts substantially reduced the size of the government budget deficit, and it eventually turned into a surplus. As a result, by the late 1990s, the debt–GDP ratio was declining once again.

The debt–GDP ratio stabilized during the first few years of the George W. Bush presidency, as the budget surplus turned into a small budget deficit. There were three reasons for this change. First, in 2001 President Bush signed into law the tax cut that he had promised during the campaign. Second, the war on terrorism following the September 11 attacks induced increases in government spending. Third, in 2001 the economy experienced a *recession* (a reduction in economic activity), a situation that automatically decreases tax revenue and increases government spending. Nonetheless, as of 2002 the Congressional Budget Office was projecting that, under laws in place at the time, the debt–GDP ratio would decline over the following decade and reach 15 percent in 2012. ●

QuickQuiz If more Americans adopted a "live for today" approach to life, how would this affect saving, investment, and the interest rate?

CONCLUSION

"Neither a borrower nor a lender be," Polonius advises his son in Shakespeare's *Hamlet.* If everyone followed this advice, this chapter would have been unnecessary.

Few economists would agree with Polonius. In our economy, people borrow and lend often, and usually for good reason. You may borrow one day to start your own business or to buy a home. And people may lend to you in the hope that the interest you pay will allow them to enjoy a more prosperous retirement. The financial system has the job of coordinating all this borrowing and lending activity.

In many ways, financial markets are like other markets in the economy. The price of loanable funds—the interest rate—is governed by the forces of supply and demand, just as other prices in the economy are. And we can analyze shifts in supply or demand in financial markets as we do in other markets. One of the *Ten Principles of Economics* introduced in Chapter 1 is that markets are usually a good way to organize economic activity. This principle applies to financial markets as well. When financial markets bring the supply and demand for loanable funds into balance, they help allocate the economy's scarce resources to their most efficient use.

In one way, however, financial markets are special. Financial markets, unlike most other markets, serve the important role of linking the present and the future. Those who supply loanable funds—savers—do so because they want to convert some of their current income into future purchasing power. Those who demand loanable funds—borrowers—do so because they want to invest today in order to have additional capital in the future to produce goods and services. Thus, well-functioning financial markets are important not only for current generations but also for future generations who will inherit many of the resulting benefits.

SUMMARY

- The U.S. financial system is made up of many types of financial institutions, such as the bond market, the stock market, banks, and mutual funds. All these institutions act to direct the resources of households who want to save some of their income into the hands of households and firms who want to borrow.

- National income accounting identities reveal some important relationships among macroeconomic variables. In particular, for a closed economy, national saving must equal investment. Financial institutions are the mechanism through which the economy matches one person's saving with another person's investment.

- The interest rate is determined by the supply and demand for loanable funds. The supply of loanable funds comes from households who want to save some of their income and lend it out. The demand for loanable funds comes from households and firms who want to borrow for investment. To analyze how any policy or event affects the interest rate, one must consider how it affects the supply and demand for loanable funds.

- National saving equals private saving plus public saving. A government budget deficit represents negative public saving and, therefore, reduces national saving and the supply of loanable funds available to finance investment. When a government budget deficit crowds out investment, it reduces the growth of productivity and GDP.

KEY CONCEPTS

financial system, p. 266
financial markets, p. 266
bond, p. 267
stock, p. 267
financial intermediaries, p. 268

mutual fund, p. 270
national saving (saving), p. 273
private saving, p. 273
public saving, p. 273
budget surplus, p. 274

budget deficit, p. 274
market for loanable funds, p. 275
crowding out, p. 281

QUESTIONS FOR REVIEW

1. What is the role of the financial system? Name and describe two markets that are part of the financial system in our economy. Name and describe two financial intermediaries.

2. Why is it important for people who own stocks and bonds to diversify their holdings? What type of financial institution makes diversification easier?

3. What is national saving? What is private saving? What is public saving? How are these three variables related?

4. What is investment? How is it related to national saving?

5. Describe a change in the tax code that might increase private saving. If this policy were implemented, how would it affect the market for loanable funds?

6. What is a government budget deficit? How does it affect interest rates, investment, and economic growth?

PROBLEMS AND APPLICATIONS

1. For each of the following pairs, which bond would you expect to pay a higher interest rate? Explain.
   a. a bond of the U.S. government or a bond of an East European government
   b. a bond that repays the principal in year 2005 or a bond that repays the principal in year 2025
   c. a bond from Coca-Cola or a bond from a software company you run in your garage
   d. a bond issued by the federal government or a bond issued by New York State

2. Check a newspaper or the Internet for the stock listings of two companies you know something about (perhaps as a customer). What is the price-earnings ratio for each company? Why do you think they differ? If you were to buy one of these stocks, which would you choose? Why?

3. Theodore Roosevelt once said, "There is no moral difference between gambling at cards or in lotteries or on the race track and gambling in the stock market." What social purpose do you think is served by the existence of the stock market?

4. Declines in stock prices are sometimes viewed as harbingers of future declines in real GDP. Why do you suppose that might be true?

5. When the Russian government defaulted on its debt to foreigners in 1998, interest rates rose on bonds issued by many other developing countries. Why do you suppose this happened?

6. Many workers hold large amounts of stock issued by the firms at which they work. Why do you suppose companies encourage this behavior? Why might a person *not* want to hold stock in the company where he works?

7. Explain the difference between saving and investment as defined by a macroeconomist. Which of the following situations represent investment? Saving? Explain.
   a. Your family takes out a mortgage and buys a new house.

   b. You use your $200 paycheck to buy stock in AT&T.
   c. Your roommate earns $100 and deposits it in her account at a bank.
   d. You borrow $1,000 from a bank to buy a car to use in your pizza delivery business.

8. Suppose GDP is $8 trillion, taxes are $1.5 trillion, private saving is $0.5 trillion, and public saving is $0.2 trillion. Assuming this economy is closed, calculate consumption, government purchases, national saving, and investment.

9. Suppose that Intel is considering building a new chip-making factory.
   a. Assuming that Intel needs to borrow money in the bond market, why would an increase in interest rates affect Intel's decision about whether to build the factory?
   b. If Intel has enough of its own funds to finance the new factory without borrowing, would an increase in interest rates still affect Intel's decision about whether to build the factory? Explain.

10. Suppose the government borrows $20 billion more next year than this year.
   a. Use a supply-and-demand diagram to analyze this policy. Does the interest rate rise or fall?
   b. What happens to investment? To private saving? To public saving? To national saving? Compare the size of the changes to the $20 billion of extra government borrowing.
   c. How does the elasticity of supply of loanable funds affect the size of these changes?
   d. How does the elasticity of demand for loanable funds affect the size of these changes?
   e. Suppose households believe that greater government borrowing today implies higher taxes to pay off the government debt in the future. What does this belief do to private saving and the supply of loanable funds today? Does it increase or decrease the effects you discussed in parts (a) and (b)?

11. Over the past ten years, new computer technology has enabled firms to reduce substantially the amount of inventories they hold for each dollar of sales. Illustrate the effect of this change on the market for loanable funds. (Hint: Expenditure on inventories is a type of investment.) What do you think has been the effect on investment in factories and equipment?

12. "Some economists worry that the aging populations of industrial countries are going to start running down their savings just when the investment appetite of emerging economies is growing" (*Economist,* May 6, 1995). Illustrate the effect of these phenomena on the world market for loanable funds.

13. This chapter explains that investment can be increased both by reducing taxes on private saving and by reducing the government budget deficit.
    a. Why is it difficult to implement both of these policies at the same time?
    b. What would you need to know about private saving in order to judge which of these two policies would be a more effective way to raise investment?

http://

For more study tools, please visit http://mankiwXtra.swlearning.com.

14

THE BASIC TOOLS OF FINANCE

Sometime in your life, you will have to deal with the economy's financial system. You will deposit your savings in a bank account, or you will take out a mortgage to buy a house. After you take a job, you will decide whether to invest your retirement account in stocks, bonds, or other financial instruments. You may try to put together your own stock portfolio, and then you will have to decide between betting on established companies such as General Electric or newer ones such as Cisco Systems. And whenever you watch the evening news, you will hear reports about whether the stock market is up or down, together with the often feeble attempts to explain why the market behaves as it does.

If you reflect for a moment on the many financial decisions you will make through your life, you will see two related elements in almost all of them—time and risk. As we saw in the preceding chapter, the financial system coordinates the economy's saving and investment. Thus, it concerns decisions we make today that will affect our lives in the future. But the future is unknown. When a person decides to allocate some saving, or a firm decides to undertake an investment, the decision is based on a guess about the likely future result—but the actual result could end up being very different.

finance
the field that studies how people make decisions regarding the allocation of resources over time and the handling of risk

This chapter introduces some tools that help us understand the decisions that people make as they participate in financial markets. The field of **finance** develops these tools in great detail, and you may choose to take courses that focus on this topic. But because the financial system is so important to the functioning of the economy, many of the basic insights of finance are central to understanding how the economy works. The tools of finance may also help you think through some of the decisions that you will make in your own life.

This chapter takes up three topics. First, we discuss how to compare sums of money at different points in time. Second, we discuss how to manage risk. Third, we build on our analysis of time and risk to examine what determines the value of an asset, such as a share of stock.

PRESENT VALUE: MEASURING THE TIME VALUE OF MONEY

Imagine that someone offered to give you $100 today or $100 in ten years. Which would you choose? This is an easy question. Getting $100 today is better, because you can always deposit the money in a bank, still have it in ten years, and earn interest on the $100 along the way. The lesson: Money today is more valuable than the same amount of money in the future.

Now consider a harder question: Imagine that someone offered you $100 today or $200 in ten years. Which would you choose? To answer this question, you need some way to compare sums of money from different points in time. Economists do this with a concept called *present value*. The **present value** of any future sum of money is the amount today that would be needed, at current interest rates, to produce that future sum.

present value
the amount of money today that would be needed to produce, using prevailing interest rates, a given future amount of money

To learn how to use the concept of present value, let's work through a couple of simple examples:

Question: If you put $100 in a bank account today, how much will it be worth in N years? That is, what will be the **future value** of this $100?

future value
the amount of money in the future that an amount of money today will yield, given prevailing interest rates

Answer: Let's use r to denote the interest rate expressed in decimal form (so an interest rate of 5 percent means $r = 0.05$). Suppose that interest is paid annually and that the interest paid remains in the bank account to earn more interest—a process called **compounding.** Then the $100 will become

compounding
the accumulation of a sum of money in, say, a bank account, where the interest earned remains in the account to earn additional interest in the future

$(1 + r) \times \$100$	after one year,
$(1 + r) \times (1 + r) \times \$100$	after two years,
$(1 + r) \times (1 + r) \times (1 + r) \times \$100$	after three years,...
$(1 + r)^N \times \$100$	after N years.

For example, if we are investing at an interest rate of 5 percent for 10 years, then the future value of the $100 will be $(1.05)^{10} \times \$100$, which is $163.

Question: Now suppose you are going to be paid $200 in N years. What is the *present value* of this future payment? That is, how much would you have to deposit in a bank right now to yield $200 in N years?

Answer: To answer this question, just turn the previous answer on its head. In the first question, we computed a future value from a present value by *multiplying* by the factor $(1 + r)^N$. To compute a present value from a future value, we *divide* by the factor $(1 + r)^N$. Thus, the present value of $200 in N years is $200/(1 + r)^N$. If that amount is deposited in a bank today, after N years it would become $(1 + r)^N \times [\$200/(1 + r)^N]$, which is $200. For instance, if the interest rate is 5 percent, the present value of $200 in ten years is $200/(1.05)^{10}$, which is $123.

This illustrates the general formula: *If r is the interest rate, then an amount X to be received in N years has present value of* $X/(1 + r)^N$.

Let's now return to our earlier question: Should you choose $100 today or $200 in 10 years? We can infer from our calculation of present value that if the interest rate is 5 percent, you should prefer the $200 in ten years. The future $200 has a present value of $123, which is greater than $100. You are better off waiting for the future sum.

Notice that the answer to our question depends on the interest rate. If the interest rate were 8 percent, then the $200 in ten years would have a present value of $200/(1.08)^{10}$, which is only $93. In this case, you should take the $100 today. Why

FYI

THE MAGIC OF COMPOUNDING AND THE RULE OF 70

Suppose you observe that one country has an average growth rate of 1 percent per year while another has an average growth rate of 3 percent per year. At first, this might not seem like a big deal. What difference can 2 percent make?

The answer is: a big difference. Even growth rates that seem small when written in percentage terms seem large after they are compounded for many years.

Consider an example. Suppose that two college graduates—Jerry and Elaine—both take their first jobs at the age of 22 earning $30,000 a year. Jerry lives in an economy where all incomes grow at 1 percent per year, while Elaine lives in one where incomes grow at 3 percent per year. Straightforward calculations show what happens. Forty years later, when both are 62 years old, Jerry earns $45,000 a year, while Elaine earns $98,000. Because of that difference of

2 percentage points in the growth rate, Elaine's salary is more than twice Jerry's.

An old rule of thumb, called the *rule of 70*, is helpful in understanding growth rates and the effects of compounding. According to the rule of 70, if some variable grows at a rate of x percent per year, then that variable doubles in approximately $70/x$ years. In Jerry's economy, incomes grow at 1 percent per year, so it takes about 70 years for incomes to double. In Elaine's economy, incomes grow at 3 percent per year, so it takes about 70/3, or 23, years for incomes to double.

The rule of 70 applies not only to a growing economy but also to a growing savings account. Here is an example: In 1791, Ben Franklin died and left $5,000 to be invested for a period of 200 years to benefit medical students and scientific research. If this money had earned 7 percent per year (which would, in fact, have been possible to do), the investment would have doubled in value every 10 years. Over 200 years, it would have doubled 20 times. At the end of 200 years of compounding, the investment would have been worth $2^{20} \times \$5,000$, which is about $5 billion. (In fact, Franklin's $5,000 grew to only $2 million over 200 years because some of the money was spent along the way.)

As these examples show, growth rates and interest rates compounded over many years can lead to some spectacular results. That is probably why Albert Einstein once called compounding "the greatest mathematical discovery of all time."

should the interest rate matter for your choice? The answer is that the higher the interest rate, the more you can earn by depositing your money at the bank, so the more attractive getting $100 today becomes.

The concept of present value is useful in many applications, including the decisions that companies face when evaluating investment projects. For instance, imagine that General Motors is thinking about building a new factory. Suppose that the factory will cost $100 million today and will yield the company $200 million in ten years. Should General Motors undertake the project? You can see that this decision is exactly like the one we have been studying. To make its decision, the company will compare the present value of the $200 million return to the $100 million cost.

The company's decision, therefore, will depend on the interest rate. If the interest rate is 5 percent, then the present value of the $200 million return from the factory is $123 million, and the company will choose to pay the $100 million cost. By contrast, if the interest rate is 8 percent, then the present value of the return is only $93 million, and the company will decide to forgo the project. Thus, the concept of present value helps explain why investment—and thus the quantity of loanable funds demanded—declines when the interest rate rises.

Here is another application of present value: Suppose you win a million-dollar lottery and are given a choice between $20,000 a year for 50 years (totaling $1,000,000) or an immediate payment of $400,000. Which would you choose? To make the right choice, you need to calculate the present value of the stream of payments. After performing 50 calculations similar to those above (one calculation for each payment) and adding up the results, you would learn that the present value of this million-dollar prize at a 7 percent interest rate is only $276,000. You are better off picking the immediate payment of $400,000. The million dollars may seem like more money, but the future cash flows, once discounted to the present, are worth far less.

QuickQuiz The interest rate is 7 percent. What is the present value of $150 to be received in 10 years?

MANAGING RISK

Life is full of gambles. When you go skiing, you risk breaking your leg in a fall. When you drive to work, you risk a car accident. When you put some of your savings in the stock market, you risk a fall in prices. The rational response to this risk is not necessarily to avoid it at any cost, but to take it into account in your decisionmaking. Let's consider how a person might do that.

Risk Aversion

risk averse
exhibiting a dislike of uncertainty

Most people are **risk averse.** This means more than that people dislike bad things happening to them. It means that they dislike bad things more than they like comparable good things.

For example, suppose a friend offers you the following opportunity. He will flip a coin. If it comes up heads, he will pay you $1,000. But if it comes up tails, you will have to pay him $1,000. Would you accept the bargain? You wouldn't if you

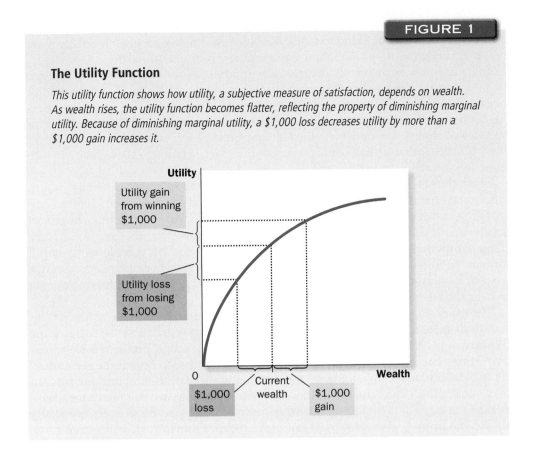

FIGURE 1

The Utility Function

This utility function shows how utility, a subjective measure of satisfaction, depends on wealth. As wealth rises, the utility function becomes flatter, reflecting the property of diminishing marginal utility. Because of diminishing marginal utility, a $1,000 loss decreases utility by more than a $1,000 gain increases it.

were risk averse. For a risk-averse person, the pain from losing the $1,000 would exceed the gain from winning $1,000.

Economists have developed models of risk aversion using the concept of *utility*, which is a person's subjective measure of well-being or satisfaction. Every level of wealth provides a certain amount of utility, as shown by the utility function in Figure 1. But the function exhibits the property of diminishing marginal utility: The more wealth a person has, the less utility he gets from an additional dollar. Thus, in the figure, the utility function gets flatter as wealth increases. Because of diminishing marginal utility, the utility lost from losing the $1,000 bet is more than the utility gained from winning it. As a result, people are risk averse.

Risk aversion provides the starting point for explaining various things we observe in the economy. Let's consider three of them: insurance, diversification, and the risk–return tradeoff.

The Markets for Insurance

One way to deal with risk is to buy insurance. The general feature of insurance contracts is that a person facing a risk pays a fee to an insurance company, which in return agrees to accept all or part of the risk. There are many types of insurance. Car insurance covers the risk of your being in an auto accident, fire insurance covers the risk that your house will burn down, health insurance covers the risk that you might need expensive medical treatment, and life insurance covers the risk that you will die and leave your family without your income. There is also insurance against the risk of living too long: For a fee paid today, an insurance company will pay you an *annuity*—a regular income every year until you die.

In a sense, every insurance contract is a gamble. It is possible that you will not be in an auto accident, that your house will not burn down, and that you will not need expensive medical treatment. In most years, you will pay the insurance company the premium and get nothing in return except peace of mind. Indeed, the insurance company is counting on the fact that most people will not make claims on their policies; otherwise, it couldn't pay out the large claims to those few who are unlucky and still stay in business.

From the standpoint of the economy as a whole, the role of insurance is not to eliminate the risks inherent in life but to spread them around more efficiently. Consider fire insurance, for instance. Owning fire insurance does not reduce the risk of losing your home in a fire. But if that unlucky event occurs, the insurance company compensates you. The risk, rather than being borne by you alone, is shared among the thousands of insurance-company shareholders. Because people are risk averse, it is easier for 10,000 people to bear 1/10,000 of the risk than for one person to bear the entire risk himself.

The markets for insurance suffer from two types of problems that impede their ability to spread risk. One problem is *adverse selection:* A high-risk person is more likely to apply for insurance than a low-risk person. A second problem is *moral hazard:* After people buy insurance, they have less incentive to be careful about their risky behavior. Insurance companies are aware of these problems, and the price of insurance reflects the actual risks that the insurance company will face after the insurance is bought. The high price of insurance is why some people, especially those who know themselves to be low-risk, decide against buying insurance and, instead, endure some of life's uncertainty on their own.

Diversification of Idiosyncratic Risk

In 2002 Enron, a large and once widely respected company, went bankrupt amid accusations of fraud and accounting irregularities. The company's top executives were called before Congress to explain their actions, and they faced the prospect of criminal prosecution. The saddest part of the story, however, involved thousands of lower-level employees. Not only did they lose their jobs, but many lost their life savings as well. The employees had about two-thirds of their retirement funds in Enron stock, which was now worthless.

If there is one piece of practical advice that finance offers to risk-averse people, it is this: "Don't put all your eggs in one basket." You may have heard this before, but finance has turned this traditional wisdom into a science. It goes by the name **diversification.**

diversification
the reduction of risk achieved by replacing a single risk with a large number of smaller unrelated risks

The market for insurance is one example of diversification. Imagine a town with 10,000 homeowners, each facing the risk of a house fire. If someone starts an insurance company and each person in town becomes both a shareholder and a policyholder of the company, they all reduce their risk through diversification. Each person now faces 1/10,000 of the risk of 10,000 possible fires, rather than the entire risk of a single fire in his own home. Unless the entire town catches fire at the same time, the downside that each person faces is much smaller.

When people use their savings to buy financial assets, they can also reduce risk through diversification. A person who buys stock in a company is placing a bet on

FIGURE 2

Diversification Reduces Risk

This figure shows how the risk of a portfolio, measured here with a statistic called standard deviation, *depends on the number of stocks in the portfolio. The investor is assumed to put an equal percentage of his portfolio in each of the stocks. Increasing the number of stocks reduces the amount of risk in a stock portfolio, but it does not eliminate it.*

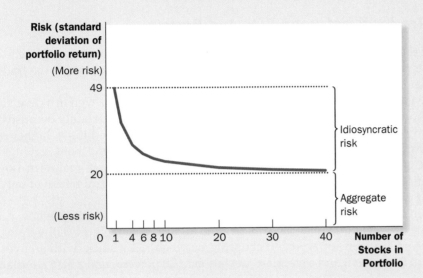

Source: Adapted from Meir Statman, "How Many Stocks Make a Diversified Portfolio?" *Journal of Financial and Quantitative Analysis* 22 (September 1987): 353–364. Reprinted by permission of School of Business Administration/University of Washington.

the future profitability of that company. That bet is often quite risky because companies' fortunes are hard to predict. Microsoft evolved from a start-up by some geeky teenagers to one of the world's most valuable companies in only a few years; Enron went from one of the world's most respected companies to an almost worthless one in only a few months. Fortunately, a shareholder need not tie his own fortune to that of any single company. Risk can be reduced by placing a large number of small bets, rather than a small number of large ones.

Figure 2 shows how the risk of a portfolio of stocks depends on the number of stocks in the portfolio. Risk is measured here with a statistic called *standard deviation*, which you may have learned about in a math or statistics class. Standard deviation measures the volatility of a variable—that is, how much the variable is likely to fluctuate. The higher the standard deviation of a portfolio's return, the riskier it is.

The figure shows that the risk of a stock portfolio falls substantially as the number of stocks increase. For a portfolio with single stock, the standard deviation is 49 percent. Going from 1 stock to 10 stocks eliminates about half the risk. Going from 10 to 20 stocks reduces the risk by another 13 percent. As the number of stocks continues to increase, risk continues to fall, although the reductions in risk after 20 or 30 stocks are small.

idiosyncratic risk
risk that affects only a single economic actor

aggregate risk
risk that affects all economic actors at once

Notice that it is impossible to eliminate all risk by increasing the number of stocks in the portfolio. Diversification can eliminate **idiosyncratic risk**—the uncertainty associated with the specific companies. But diversification cannot eliminate **aggregate risk**—the uncertainty associated with the entire economy, which affects all companies. For example, when the economy goes into a recession, most companies experience falling sales, reduced profit, and low stock returns. Diversification reduces the risk of holding stocks, but it does not eliminate it.

The Tradeoff between Risk and Return

One of the *Ten Principles of Economics* in Chapter 1 is that people face tradeoffs. The tradeoff that is most relevant for understanding financial decisions is the tradeoff between risk and return.

As we have seen, there are risks inherent in holding stocks, even in a diversified portfolio. But risk-averse people are willing to accept this uncertainty because they are compensated for doing so. Historically, stocks have offered much higher rates of return than alternative financial assets, such as bonds and bank savings accounts. Over the past two centuries, stocks offered an average real return of 8.3 percent per year, while short-term government bonds paid a real return of only 3.1 percent per year.

When deciding how to allocate their savings, people have to decide how much risk they are willing to undertake to earn the higher return. Figure 3 illustrates the risk–return tradeoff for a person choosing between risky stock, with an average return of 8.3 percent and a standard deviation of 20 percent, and a safe alternative,

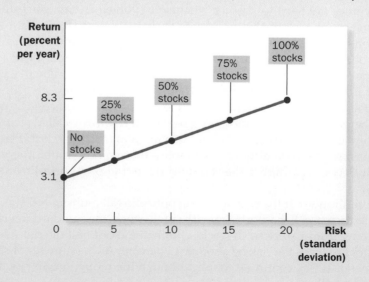

FIGURE 3

The Tradeoff Between Risk and Return

When people increase the percentage of their savings that they have invested in stocks, they increase the average return they can expect to earn, but they also increase the risks they face.

with a return of 3.1 percent and a standard deviation of zero. The safe alternative can be either a bank savings account or a government bond. Each point in this figure represents a particular allocation of a portfolio between risky stocks and the safe asset. The figure shows that the more a person puts into stock, the greater is both the risk and the return.

Acknowledging the risk–return tradeoff does not, by itself, tell us what a person should do. The choice of a particular combination of risk and return depends on a person's risk aversion, which reflects a person's own preferences. But it is important for stockholders to realize that the higher average return that they enjoy comes at the price of higher risk.

QuickQuiz Describe three ways that a risk-averse person might reduce the risk he faces.

ASSET VALUATION

Now that we have developed a basic understanding of the two building blocks of finance—time and risk—let's apply this knowledge. This section considers a simple question: What determines the price of a share of stock? Like most prices, the answer is supply and demand. But that is not the end of the story. To understand stock prices, we need to think more deeply about what determines a person's willingness to pay for a share of stock.

Fundamental Analysis

Let's imagine that you have decided to put 60 percent of your savings into stock and, to achieve diversification, you have decided to buy 20 different stocks. If you open up the newspaper, you will find thousands of stocks listed. How should you pick the 20 for your portfolio?

When you buy stock, you are buying shares in a business. When deciding which businesses you want to own, it is natural to consider two things: the value of the business and the price at which the shares are being sold. If the price is less than the value, the stock is said to be *undervalued*. If the price is more than the value, the stock is said to be *overvalued*. If the price and the value are equal, the stock is said to be *fairly valued*. When choosing 20 stocks for your portfolio, you should prefer undervalued stocks. In these cases, you are getting a bargain by paying less than the business is worth.

This is easier said than done. Learning the price is easy: You can just look it up in the newspaper. Determining the value of the business is the hard part. The term **fundamental analysis** refers to the detailed analysis of a company to determine its value. Many Wall Street firms hire stock analysts to conduct such fundamental analysis and offer advice about which stocks to buy.

The value of a stock to a stockholder is what he gets out of owning it, which includes the present value of the stream of dividend payments and the final sale price. Recall that *dividends* are the cash payments that a company makes to its shareholders. A company's ability to pay dividends, as well as the value of the stock when the stockholder sells his shares, depends on the company's ability to earn profits. Its profitability, in turn, depends on a large number of factors—the

fundamental analysis
the study of a company's accounting statements and future prospects to determine its value

demand for its product, how much competition it faces, how much capital it has in place, whether its workers are unionized, how loyal its customers are, what kinds of government regulations and taxes it faces, and so on. The job of fundamental analysts is to take all these factors into account to determine how much a share of stock in the company is worth.

If you want to rely on fundamental analysis to pick a stock portfolio, there are three ways to do it. One way is to do all the necessary research yourself, by reading through companies' annual reports and so forth. A second way is to rely on the advice of Wall Street analysts. A third way is to buy a mutual fund, which has a manager who conducts fundamental analysis and makes the decision for you.

The Efficient Markets Hypothesis

efficient markets hypothesis
the theory that asset prices reflect all publicly available information about the value of an asset

There is another way to choose 20 stocks for your portfolio: Pick them randomly by, for instance, putting the stock pages on your bulletin board and throwing darts at the page. This may sound crazy, but there is reason to believe that it won't lead you too far astray. That reason is called the **efficient markets hypothesis.**

To understand this theory, the starting point is to acknowledge that each company listed on a major stock exchange is followed closely by many money managers, such as the individuals who run mutual funds. Every day, these managers monitor news stories and conduct fundamental analysis to try to determine the stock's value. Their job is to buy a stock when its price falls below its value, and to sell it when its price rises above its value.

The second piece to the efficient markets hypothesis is that the equilibrium of supply and demand sets the market price. This means that, at the market price, the number of shares being offered for sale exactly equals the number of shares that people want to buy. In other words, at the market price, the number of people who think the stock is overvalued exactly balances the number of people who think it's undervalued. As judged by the typical person in the market, all stocks are fairly valued all the time.

informationally efficient
reflecting all available information in a rational way

According to this theory, the stock market is **informationally efficient:** It reflects all available information about the value of the asset. Stock prices change when information changes. When the good news about the company's prospects become public, the value and the stock price both rise. When the company's prospects deteriorate, the value and price both fall. But at any moment in time, the market price is the best guess of the company's value based on available information.

random walk
the path of a variable whose changes are impossible to predict

One implication of the efficient markets hypothesis is that stock prices should follow a **random walk.** This means that the changes in stock prices are impossible to predict from available information. If, based on publicly available information, a person could predict that a stock price would rise by 10 percent tomorrow, then the stock market must be failing to incorporate that information today. According to this theory, the only thing that can move stock prices is news that changes the market's perception of the company's value. But news must be unpredictable—otherwise, it wouldn't really be news. For the same reason, changes in stock prices should be unpredictable.

If the efficient markets hypothesis is correct, then there is little point in spending many hours studying the business page to decide which 20 stocks to add to your portfolio. If prices reflect all available information, no stock is a better buy than any other. The best you can do is buy a diversified portfolio.

Case Study

RANDOM WALKS AND INDEX FUNDS

The efficient markets hypothesis is a theory about how financial markets work. The theory is probably not completely true: As we discuss in the next section, there is reason to doubt that stockholders are always rational and that stock prices are informationally efficient at every moment. Nonetheless, the efficient markets hypothesis does much better as a description of the world than you might think.

There is much evidence that stock prices, even if not exactly a random walk, are very close to it. For example, you might be tempted to buy stocks that have recently risen and avoid stocks that have recently fallen (or perhaps just the opposite). But statistical studies have shown that following such trends (or bucking them) fails to outperform the market. The correlation between how well a stock does one year and how well it does the following year is almost exactly zero.

Some of the best evidence in favor of the efficient markets hypothesis comes from the performance of index funds. An index fund is a mutual fund that buys all the stocks in a given stock index. The performance of these funds can be compared with that of actively managed mutual funds, where a professional portfolio manager picks stocks based on extensive research and alleged expertise. In essence, an index fund buys all stocks, whereas active funds are supposed to buy only the best stocks.

In practice, active managers usually fail to beat index funds, and in fact, most of them do worse. For example, in the ten years ending February 2002, 82 percent of stock mutual funds failed to beat an index fund holding all 500 stocks in the Standard & Poor's 500 Index. Most active portfolio managers give a lower return than index funds because they trade more frequently, incurring more trading costs, and because they charge greater fees as compensation for their alleged expertise.

What about those 18 percent of managers who did beat the market? Perhaps they are smarter than average, or perhaps they were more lucky. If you have 5,000 people flipping coins ten times, on average about five will flip ten heads; these five might claim an exceptional coin-flipping skill, but they would have trouble replicating the feat. Similarly, studies have shown that mutual fund managers with a history of superior performance usually fail to maintain it in subsequent periods.

The efficient markets hypothesis says that it is impossible to beat the market. The accumulation of many studies in financial markets confirms that beating the market is, at best, extremely difficult. Even if the efficient markets hypothesis is not an exact description of the world, it contains a large element of truth. ●

Market Irrationality

The efficient markets hypothesis assumes that people buying and selling stock rationally process the information they have about the stock's underlying value. But is the stock market really that rational? Or do stock prices sometimes deviate from reasonable expectations of their true value?

IN THE NEWS

SOME LESSONS FROM ENRON

When many investors lost their life savings in the wake of the collapse of Enron, the rationality of stock market investors was called into question.

Investor Behavior Clouds the Wisdom of Offering Wider Choice in 401(k)'s

By Hal R. Varian

After the Enron collapse, Congress is debating whether to limit the amount of their own company's stock that employees can put into their own 401(k) retirement plans.

Those in favor of such caps, like Senators Barbara Boxer and Jon S. Corzine, see them as a way to encourage diversification and reduce risk. Those opposed, like Labor Secretary Elaine L. Chao, say such caps violate freedom of choice.

Economists generally believe that more choice is better, but even economists acknowledge that there are plenty of exceptions in real life. Offering a cigarette to someone trying to quit, a drink to a recovering alcoholic, or a candy bar to a dieter isn't doing that person a favor.

To most economists, the problems illustrated by these examples are anomalies. But to one group, behavioral economists, the examples are central.

Clearly, more choice is not better when people have problems with self-control. . . . In some investment situations, more choice can be downright dangerous. Two finance professors, Brad Barber and Terrance Odean, studied the performance of 66,465 households with discount brokerage accounts. Households

There is a long tradition suggesting that fluctuations in stock prices are partly psychological. In the 1930s, economist John Maynard Keynes suggested that asset markets are driven by the "animal spirits" of investors—irrational waves of optimism and pessimism. In the 1990s, as the stock market soared to new heights, Fed chairman Alan Greenspan questioned whether the boom reflected "irrational exuberance." Stock prices did subsequently fall, but whether the exuberance of the 1990s was irrational given the information available at the time remains debatable.

The possibility of such speculative bubbles arises in part because the value of the stock to a stockholder depends not only on the stream of dividend payments but also on the final sale price. Thus, a person might be willing to pay more than a stock is worth today if he expects another person to pay even more for it tomorrow. When you evaluate a stock, you have to estimate not only the value of the business but also what other people will think the business is worth in the future.

There is much debate among economists about whether departures from rational pricing are important or rare. Believers in market irrationality point out (correctly) that the stock market often moves in ways that are hard to explain on the basis of news that might alter a rational valuation. Believers in the efficient markets hypothesis point out (correctly) that it is impossible to know the correct, rational valuation of a company, so one should not quickly jump to the conclusion that traded infrequently received an 18 percent return on their investments, while the return for households that traded most actively was 11.3 percent.

In the words of Mr. Barber and Mr. Odean: "Trading can be hazardous to your wealth."

In later work, these two financial economists investigated who it was that traded too much. They found that one important determinant of excessive trading was gender.

Psychologists consistently find that men tend to have excessive confidence in their own abilities. . . . Mr. Barber and Mr. Odean find that on average, men trade 45 percent more than women. They also find that this excessive trading reduces men's net returns by almost a full percentage point.

Psychologists find that men tend to suffer from "self-serving attribution bias." In plain language: men tend to think their successes are the result of their own skill, rather than dumb luck, and so become overconfident.

It is not hard to see how overconfidence might lead to bubbles: Though frequent traders lose on average, sometimes they luck out. If many happen to get lucky at the same time, they will attribute this success to their superior abilities and double their bets. This pushes up the value of stocks even more, leading to more excessive confidence and an unsustainable boom in stock prices.

If we accept this evidence that investors have problems with self-control, poor decision making, and overconfidence, what can we say about the regulation of financial markets and pensions? . . . The findings from behavioral economics suggest that mandated saving plans, like conventional defined-benefit pension plans and social security, are pretty good programs. The tendency in the last several years has been to offer employees more choice of retirement options. But if individuals do not make good choices when left to their own devices, this may not be appropriate. . . .

Many employees of Enron, Global Crossing, Lucent, and Nortel have seen their pensions evaporate when the price of their company stock dropped. If these investors had held more diversified portfolios, they would be sleeping a lot more soundly today.

Source: *The New York Times,* February 14, 2002, p. C2. Copyright © 2002 by The New York Times Co. Reprinted by permission.

that any particular valuation is irrational. Moreover, if the market were irrational, a rational person should be able to take advantage of this fact; yet, as the previous case study discussed, beating the market is nearly impossible.

QuickQuiz *Fortune* magazine regularly publishes a list of the "most respected" companies. According to the efficient markets hypothesis, if you restrict your stock portfolio to these companies, would you earn a better than average return? Explain.

CONCLUSION

This chapter has developed some of the basic tools that people should (and often do) use as they make financial decisions. The concept of present value reminds us that a dollar in the future is less valuable than a dollar today, and it gives us a way to compare sums of money at different points in time. The theory of risk management reminds us that the future is uncertain and that risk-averse people can take precautions to guard against this uncertainty. The study of asset valuation tells us that the stock price of any company should reflect its expected future profitability.

Although most of the tools of finance are well established, there is more controversy about the validity of the efficient markets hypothesis and whether stock prices are, in practice, rational estimates of a company's true worth. Rational or not, the large movements in stock prices that we observe have important macroeconomic implications. Stock market fluctuations often go hand in hand with fluctuations in the economy more broadly. We will see the stock market again when we study economic fluctuations later in the book.

SUMMARY

- Because savings can earn interest, a sum of money today is more valuable than the same sum of money in the future. A person can compare sums from different times using the concept of present value. The present value of any future sum is the amount that would be needed today, given prevailing interest rates, to produce that future sum.

- Because of diminishing marginal utility, most people are risk averse. Risk-averse people can reduce risk using insurance, through diversification, and by choosing a portfolio with lower risk and lower return.

- The value of an asset, such as a share of stock, equals the present value of the cash flows the owner of the share will receive, including the stream of dividends and the final sale price. According to the efficient markets hypothesis, financial markets process available information rationally, so a stock price always equals the best estimate of the value of the underlying business. Some economists question the efficient markets hypothesis, however, and believe that irrational psychological factors also influence asset prices.

KEY CONCEPTS

finance, p. 288
present value, p. 288
future value, p. 288
compounding, p. 288
risk averse, p. 290

diversification, p. 292
idiosyncratic risk, p. 294
aggregate risk, p. 294
fundamental analysis, p. 295

efficient markets
    hypothesis, p. 296
informationally efficient, p. 296
random walk, p. 296

QUESTIONS FOR REVIEW

1. The interest rate is 7 percent. Use the concept of present value to compare $200 to be received in 10 years and $300 to be received in 20 years.

2. What benefit do people get from the market for insurance? What two problems impede the insurance company from working perfectly?

3. What is diversification? Does a stockholder get more diversification going from 1 to 10 stocks or going from 100 to 120 stocks?

4. Comparing stocks and government bonds, which has more risk? Which pays a higher average return?

5. What factors should a stock analyst think about in determining the value of a share of stock?

6. Describe the efficient markets hypothesis, and give a piece of evidence consistent with this theory.

7. Explain the view of those economists who are skeptical of the efficient markets hypothesis.

PROBLEMS AND APPLICATIONS

1. About 400 years ago, native Americans sold the island of Manhattan for $24. If they had invested this money at an interest rate of 7 percent per year, how much would they have today?

2. A company has an investment project that would cost $10 million today and yield a payoff of $15 million in four years.
   a. Should the firm undertake the project if the interest rate is 11 percent? 10 percent? 9 percent? 8 percent?
   b. Can you figure out the exact cutoff for the interest rate between profitability and nonprofitability?

3. For each of the following kinds of insurance, give an example of behavior that can be called *moral* *hazard* and another example of behavior that can be called *adverse selection.*
   a. health insurance
   b. car insurance

4. Imagine that you intend to buy a portfolio of ten stocks with some of your savings. Should the stocks be of companies in the same industry? Should the stocks be of companies located in the same country? Explain.

5. Which kind of stock would you expect to pay the higher average return: stock in an industry that is very sensitive to economic conditions (such as an automaker) or stock in an industry that is relatively insensitive to economic conditions (such as a water company). Why?

6. A company faces two kinds of risk. An idiosyncratic risk is that a competitor might enter its market and take some of its customers. An aggregate risk is that the economy might enter a recession, reducing sales. Which of these two risks would more likely cause the company's shareholders to demand a higher return? Why?

7. You have two roommates who invest in the stock market.

   a. One roommate says she buys stock only in companies that everyone believes will experience big increases in profits in the future. How do you suppose the price-earnings ratio of these companies compares to the price-earnings ratio of other companies? What might be the disadvantage of buying stock in these companies?

   b. Another roommate says she only buys stock in companies that are cheap, which she measures by a low price-earnings ratio. How do you suppose the earnings prospects of these companies compare to those of other companies? What might be the disadvantage of buying stock in these companies?

8. When company executives buy and sell stock based on private information they obtain as part of their jobs, they are engaged in *insider trading*.

   a. Give an example of inside information that might be useful for buying or selling stock.

   b. Those who trade stocks based on inside information usually earn very high rates of return. Does this fact violate the efficient market hypothesis?

   c. Insider trading is illegal. Why do you suppose that is?

9. Find some information on an index fund (such as the Vanguard 500 Index, ticker symbol VFINX). How has this fund performed compared with other stock mutual funds over the past five or ten years? (Hint: One place to look for data on mutual funds is http://www.morningstar.com.) What do you learn from this comparison?

http://   For more study tools, please visit http://mankiwXtra.swlearning.com.

15

UNEMPLOYMENT AND
ITS NATURAL RATE

Losing a job can be the most distressing economic event in a person's life. Most people rely on their labor earnings to maintain their standard of living, and many people get from their work not only income but also a sense of personal accomplishment. A job loss means a lower living standard in the present, anxiety about the future, and reduced self-esteem. It is not surprising, therefore, that politicians campaigning for office often speak about how their proposed policies will help create jobs.

In previous chapters we have seen some of the forces that determine the level and growth of a country's standard of living. A country that saves and invests a high fraction of its income, for instance, enjoys more rapid growth in its capital stock and its GDP than a similar country that saves and invests less. An even more obvious determinant of a country's standard of living is the amount of unemployment it typically experiences. People who would like to work but cannot find a job are not contributing to the economy's production of goods and services. Although some degree of unemployment is inevitable in a complex economy with thousands of firms and millions of workers, the amount of unemployment varies substantially over time and across countries. When a country keeps its workers as fully employed as possible, it achieves a higher level of GDP than it would if it left many of its workers standing idle.

This chapter begins our study of unemployment. The problem of unemployment is usefully divided into two categories—the long-run problem and the short-run problem. The economy's *natural rate of unemployment* refers to the amount of unemployment that the economy normally experiences. *Cyclical unemployment* refers to the year-to-year fluctuations in unemployment around its natural rate, and it is closely associated with the short-run ups and downs of economic activity. Cyclical unemployment has its own explanation, which we defer until we study short-run economic fluctuations later in this book. In this chapter we discuss the determinants of an economy's natural rate of unemployment. As we will see, the designation *natural* does not imply that this rate of unemployment is desirable. Nor does it imply that it is constant over time or impervious to economic policy. It merely means that this unemployment does not go away on its own even in the long run.

We begin the chapter by looking at some of the relevant facts that describe unemployment. In particular, we examine three questions: How does the government measure the economy's rate of unemployment? What problems arise in interpreting the unemployment data? How long are the unemployed typically without work?

We then turn to the reasons why economies always experience some unemployment and the ways in which policymakers can help the unemployed. We discuss four explanations for the economy's natural rate of unemployment: job search, minimum-wage laws, unions, and efficiency wages. As we will see, long-run unemployment does not arise from a single problem that has a single solution. Instead, it reflects a variety of related problems. As a result, there is no easy way for policymakers to reduce the economy's natural rate of unemployment and, at the same time, to alleviate the hardships experienced by the unemployed.

IDENTIFYING UNEMPLOYMENT

We begin this chapter by examining more precisely what the term *unemployment* means. We consider how the government measures unemployment, what problems arise in interpreting the unemployment data, how long the typical spell of unemployment lasts, and why there will always be some people unemployed.

How Is Unemployment Measured?

Measuring unemployment is the job of the Bureau of Labor Statistics (BLS), which is part of the Department of Labor. Every month the BLS produces data on unemployment and on other aspects of the labor market, such as types of employment, length of the average workweek, and the duration of unemployment. These data come from a regular survey of about 60,000 households, called the Current Population Survey.

Based on the answers to survey questions, the BLS places each adult (aged 16 and older) in each surveyed household into one of three categories:

- Employed
- Unemployed
- Not in the labor force

A person is considered employed if he or she spent some of the previous week working at a paid job. A person is unemployed if he or she is on temporary layoff or is looking for a job. A person who fits neither of the first two categories, such as a full-time student, homemaker, or retiree, is not in the labor force. Figure 1 shows this breakdown for 2001.

Once the BLS has placed all the individuals covered by the survey in a category, it computes various statistics to summarize the state of the labor market. The BLS defines the **labor force** as the sum of the employed and the unemployed:

$$\text{Labor force} = \text{Number of employed} + \text{Number of unemployed}.$$

labor force
the total number of workers, including both the employed and the unemployed

The BLS defines the **unemployment rate** as the percentage of the labor force that is unemployed:

$$\text{Unemployment rate} = \frac{\text{Number of unemployed}}{\text{Labor force}} \times 100.$$

unemployment rate
the percentage of the labor force that is unemployed

The BLS computes unemployment rates for the entire adult population and for more narrowly defined groups—blacks, whites, men, women, and so on.

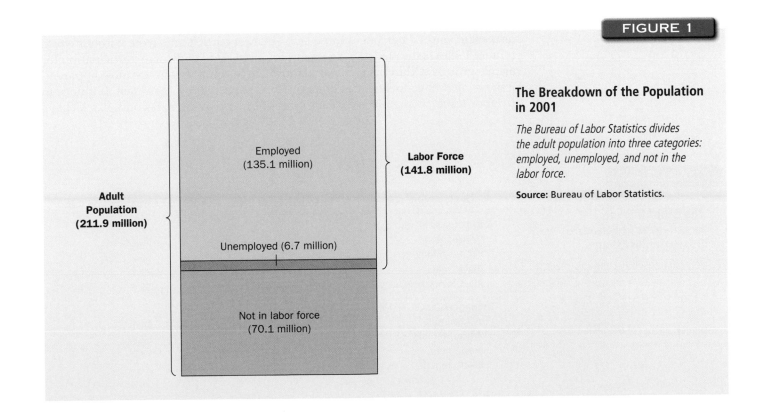

FIGURE 1

The Breakdown of the Population in 2001

The Bureau of Labor Statistics divides the adult population into three categories: employed, unemployed, and not in the labor force.

Source: Bureau of Labor Statistics.

Adult Population (211.9 million)

Employed (135.1 million)

Labor Force (141.8 million)

Unemployed (6.7 million)

Not in labor force (70.1 million)

labor-force participation rate
the percentage of the adult population that is in the labor force

The BLS uses the same survey to produce data on labor-force participation. The **labor-force participation rate** measures the percentage of the total adult population of the United States that is in the labor force:

$$\text{Labor-force participation rate} = \frac{\text{Labor force}}{\text{Adult population}} \times 100.$$

This statistic tells us the fraction of the population that has chosen to participate in the labor market. The labor-force participation rate, like the unemployment rate, is computed both for the entire adult population and for more specific groups.

To see how these data are computed, consider the figures for 2001. In that year, 135.1 million people were employed, and 6.7 million people were unemployed. The labor force was

$$\text{Labor force} = 135.1 + 6.7 = 141.8 \text{ million}.$$

The unemployment rate was

$$\text{Unemployment rate} = (6.7/141.8) \times 100 = 4.7 \text{ percent}.$$

Because the adult population was 211.9 million, the labor-force participation rate was

$$\text{Labor-force participation rate} = (141.8/211.9) \times 100 = 66.9 \text{ percent}.$$

Hence, in 2001, two-thirds of the U.S. adult population were participating in the labor market, and 4.7 percent of those labor-market participants were without work.

Table 1 shows the statistics on unemployment and labor-force participation for various groups within the U.S. population. Three comparisons are most apparent. First, women have lower rates of labor-force participation than men, but once in the labor force, women have similar rates of unemployment. Second, blacks have

TABLE 1

The Labor-Market Experiences of Various Demographic Groups

This table shows the unemployment rate and the labor-force participation rate of various groups in the population for 2001.

Source: Bureau of Labor Statistics.

Demographic Group	Unemployment Rate	Labor-Force Participation Rate
Adults (ages 20 and over)		
White, male	3.7%	76.8%
White, female	3.6	50.2
Black, male	8.0	72.1
Black, female	7.0	65.4
Teenagers (ages 16–19)		
White, male	13.8	54.1
White, female	11.4	52.8
Black, male	30.5	38.0
Black, female	27.5	37.4

FIGURE 2

Unemployment Rate since 1960

This graph uses annual data on the unemployment rate to show the fraction of the labor force without a job.

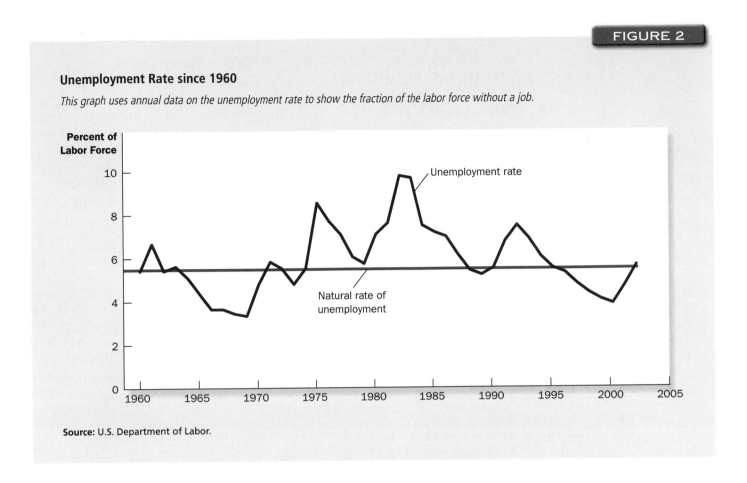

Source: U.S. Department of Labor.

similar rates of labor-force participation as whites, and they have much higher rates of unemployment. Third, teenagers have lower rates of labor-force participation and much higher rates of unemployment than the overall population. More generally, these data show that labor-market experiences vary widely among groups within the economy.

The BLS data on the labor market also allow economists and policymakers to monitor changes in the economy over time. Figure 2 shows the unemployment rate in the United States since 1960. The figure shows that the economy always has some unemployment and that the amount changes from year to year. The normal rate of unemployment around which the unemployment rate fluctuates is called the **natural rate of unemployment,** and the deviation of unemployment from its natural rate is called **cyclical unemployment.** In the figure, the natural rate is shown as a horizontal line at 5.5 percent, which is a rough estimate of the natural rate for the U.S. economy during this period. Later in this book we discuss short-run economic fluctuations, including the year-to-year fluctuations in unemployment around its natural rate. In the rest of this chapter, however, we ignore the short-run fluctuations and examine why there is always some unemployment in market economies.

natural rate of unemployment
the normal rate of unemployment around which the unemployment rate fluctuates

cyclical unemployment
the deviation of unemployment from its natural rate

Case Study

LABOR-FORCE PARTICIPATION OF MEN AND WOMEN IN THE U.S. ECONOMY

Women's role in American society has changed dramatically over the past century. Social commentators have pointed to many causes for this change. In part, it is attributable to new technologies, such as the washing machine, clothes dryer, refrigerator, freezer, and dishwasher, which have reduced the amount of time required to complete routine household tasks. In part, it is attributable to improved birth control, which has reduced the number of children born to the typical family. And, of course, this change in women's role is also partly attributable to changing political and social attitudes. Together these developments have had a profound impact on society in general and on the economy in particular.

Nowhere is that impact more obvious than in data on labor-force participation. Figure 3 shows the labor-force participation rates of men and women in the United States since 1950. Just after World War II, men and women had very different roles in society. Only 33 percent of women were working or looking for work, in contrast to 87 percent of men. Over the past several decades, the difference between the participation rates of men and women has gradually diminished, as growing numbers of women have entered the labor force and some men have left it. Data for 2001 show that 60 percent of women were in the labor force, in contrast to 74 percent of men. As measured by labor-force participation, men and women are now playing a more equal role in the economy.

FIGURE 3

Labor-Force Participation Rates for Men and Women since 1950

This figure shows the percentage of adult men and women who are members of the labor force. It shows that over the past several decades, women have entered the labor force, and men have left it.

Source: U.S. Department of Labor.

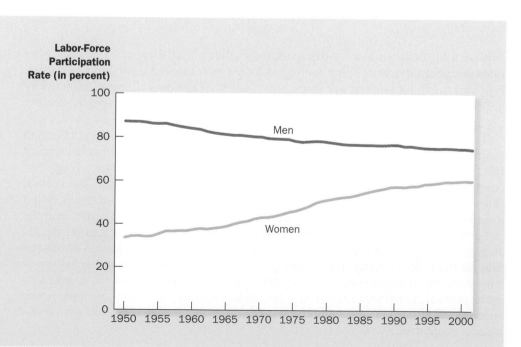

The increase in women's labor-force participation is easy to understand, but the fall in men's may seem puzzling. There are several reasons for this decline. First, young men now stay in school longer than their fathers and grandfathers did. Second, older men now retire earlier and live longer. Third, with more women employed, more fathers now stay at home to raise their children. Full-time students, retirees, and stay-at-home fathers are all counted as out of the labor force. ●

Does the Unemployment Rate Measure What We Want It To?

Measuring the amount of unemployment in the economy might seem straightforward. In fact, it is not. While it is easy to distinguish between a person with a full-time job and a person who is not working at all, it is much harder to distinguish between a person who is unemployed and a person who is not in the labor force.

Movements into and out of the labor force are, in fact, very common. More than one-third of the unemployed are recent entrants into the labor force. These entrants include young workers looking for their first jobs, such as recent college graduates. They also include, in greater numbers, older workers who had previously left the labor force but have now returned to look for work. Moreover, not all unemployment ends with the job seeker finding a job. Almost half of all spells of unemployment end when the unemployed person leaves the labor force.

Because people move into and out of the labor force so often, statistics on unemployment are difficult to interpret. On the one hand, some of those who report being unemployed may not, in fact, be trying hard to find a job. They may be calling themselves unemployed because they want to qualify for a government program that financially assists the unemployed or because they are actually working and being paid "under the table." It may be more realistic to view these individuals as out of the labor force or, in some cases, employed. On the other hand, some of those who report being out of the labor force may, in fact, want to work. These individuals may have tried to find a job but have given up after an unsuccessful search. Such individuals, called **discouraged workers,** do not show up in unemployment statistics, even though they are truly workers without jobs.

discouraged workers
individuals who would like to work but have given up looking for a job

Because of these and other problems, the BLS calculates several other measures of labor underutilization in addition to the official unemployment rate. These alternative measures are presented in Table 2 (p. 310). In the end, it is best to view the official unemployment rate as a useful but imperfect measure of joblessness.

How Long Are the Unemployed without Work?

In judging how serious the problem of unemployment is, one question to consider is whether unemployment is typically a short-term or long-term condition. If unemployment is short-term, one might conclude that it is not a big problem. Workers may require a few weeks between jobs to find the openings that best suit their tastes and skills. Yet if unemployment is long-term, one might conclude that it is a serious problem. Workers unemployed for many months are more likely to suffer economic and psychological hardship.

TABLE 2

Alternative Measures of Labor Underutilization

The table shows various measures of joblessness for the U.S. economy. The data are for August 2002.

Source: U.S. Department of Labor.

Measure and Description	Rate
U-1 Persons unemployed 15 weeks or longer, as a percent of the civilian labor force (includes only very long-term unemployed)	1.8%
U-2 Job losers and persons who have completed temporary jobs, as a percent of the civilian labor force (excludes job leavers)	3.0
U-3 Total unemployed, as a percent of the civilian labor force (official unemployment rate)	5.7
U-4 Total unemployed, plus discouraged workers, as a percent of the civilian labor force plus discouraged workers	5.9
U-5 Total unemployed plus all marginally attached workers, as a percent of the civilian labor force plus all marginally attached workers	6.6
U-6 Total unemployed, plus all marginally attached workers, plus total employed part-time for economic reasons, as a percent of the civilian labor force plus all marginally attached workers	9.5

Note: *Marginally attached workers* are persons who currently are neither working nor looking for work but indicate that they want and are available for a job and have looked for work sometime in the recent past. *Discouraged workers,* a subset of the marginally attached, have given a job-market related reason for not currently looking for a job. *Persons employed part time for economic reasons* are those who want and are available for full-time work but have had to settle for a part-time schedule.

Because the duration of unemployment can affect our view about how big a problem it is, economists have devoted much energy to studying data on the duration of unemployment spells. In this work, they have uncovered a result that is important, subtle, and seemingly contradictory: *Most spells of unemployment are short, and most unemployment observed at any given time is long-term.*

To see how this statement can be true, consider an example. Suppose that you visited the government's unemployment office every week for a year to survey the unemployed. Each week you find that there are four unemployed workers. Three of these workers are the same individuals for the whole year, while the fourth person changes every week. Based on this experience, would you say that unemployment is typically short-term or long-term?

Some simple calculations help answer this question. In this example, you meet a total of 55 unemployed people; 52 of them are unemployed for 1 week, and 3 are unemployed for the full year. This means that 52/55, or 95 percent, of unemployment spells end in 1 week. Thus, most spells of unemployment are short. Yet consider the total amount of unemployment. The 3 people unemployed for 1 year (52 weeks) make up a total of 156 weeks of unemployment. Together with the 52 people unemployed for 1 week, this makes 208 weeks of unemployment. In this example, 156/208, or 75 percent, of unemployment is attributable to those individuals who are unemployed for a full year. Thus, most unemployment observed at any given time is long-term.

This subtle conclusion implies that economists and policymakers must be careful when interpreting data on unemployment and when designing policies to help the unemployed. Most people who become unemployed will soon find jobs. Yet most of the economy's unemployment problem is attributable to the relatively few workers who are jobless for long periods of time.

Why Are There Always Some People Unemployed?

We have discussed how the government measures the amount of unemployment, the problems that arise in interpreting unemployment statistics, and the findings of labor economists on the duration of unemployment. You should now have a good idea about what unemployment is.

This discussion, however, has not explained why economies experience unemployment. In most markets in the economy, prices adjust to bring quantity supplied and quantity demanded into balance. In an ideal labor market, wages would adjust to balance the quantity of labor supplied and the quantity of labor demanded. This adjustment of wages would ensure that all workers are always fully employed.

Of course, reality does not resemble this ideal. There are always some workers without jobs, even when the overall economy is doing well. In other words, the unemployment rate never falls to zero; instead, it fluctuates around the natural rate of unemployment. To understand this natural rate, the remaining sections in the chapter examine the reasons why actual labor markets depart from the ideal of full employment.

To preview our conclusions, we will find that there are four ways to explain unemployment in the long run. The first explanation is that it takes time for workers to search for the jobs that are best suited for them. The unemployment that results from the process of matching workers and jobs is sometimes called **frictional unemployment,** and it is often thought to explain relatively short spells of unemployment.

frictional unemployment
unemployment that results because it takes time for workers to search for the jobs that best suit their tastes and skills

The next three explanations for unemployment suggest that the number of jobs available in some labor markets may be insufficient to give a job to everyone who wants one. This occurs when the quantity of labor supplied exceeds the quantity demanded. Unemployment of this sort is sometimes called **structural unemployment,** and it is often thought to explain longer spells of unemployment. As we will see, this kind of unemployment results when wages are, for some reason, set above the level that brings supply and demand into equilibrium. We will examine three possible reasons for an above-equilibrium wage: minimum-wage laws, unions, and efficiency wages.

structural unemployment
unemployment that results because the number of jobs available in some labor markets is insufficient to provide a job for everyone who wants one

QuickQuiz How is the unemployment rate measured? • How might the unemployment rate overstate the amount of joblessness? How might it understate it?

JOB SEARCH

One reason why economies always experience some unemployment is job search. **Job search** is the process of matching workers with appropriate jobs. If all workers and all jobs were the same, so that all workers were equally well suited for all jobs, job search would not be a problem. Laid-off workers would quickly find new jobs

job search
the process by which workers find appropriate jobs given their tastes and skills

that were well suited for them. But, in fact, workers differ in their tastes and skills, jobs differ in their attributes, and information about job candidates and job vacancies is disseminated slowly among the many firms and households in the economy.

Why Some Frictional Unemployment Is Inevitable

Frictional unemployment is often the result of changes in the demand for labor among different firms. When consumers decide that they prefer Compaq over Dell computers, Compaq increases employment, and Dell lays off workers. The former Dell workers must now search for new jobs, and Compaq must decide which new workers to hire for the various jobs that have opened up. The result of this transition is a period of unemployment.

Similarly, because different regions of the country produce different goods, employment can rise in one region while it falls in another. Consider, for instance, what happens when the world price of oil falls. Oil-producing firms in Texas respond to the lower price by cutting back on production and employment. At the same time, cheaper gasoline stimulates car sales, so auto-producing firms in Michigan raise production and employment. Changes in the composition of demand among industries or regions are called *sectoral shifts*. Because it takes time for workers to search for jobs in the new sectors, sectoral shifts temporarily cause unemployment.

Frictional unemployment is inevitable simply because the economy is always changing. A century ago, the four industries with the largest employment in the United States were cotton goods, woolen goods, men's clothing, and lumber. Today, the four largest industries are autos, aircraft, communications, and electrical components. As this transition took place, jobs were created in some firms and destroyed in others. The end result of this process has been higher productivity and higher living standards. But, along the way, workers in declining industries found themselves out of work and searching for new jobs.

Data show that at least 10 percent of U.S. manufacturing jobs are destroyed every year. In addition, more than 3 percent of workers leave their jobs in a typical month, sometimes because they realize that the jobs are not a good match for their tastes and skills. Many of these workers, especially younger ones, find new jobs at higher wages. This churning of the labor force is normal in a well-functioning and dynamic market economy, but the result is some amount of frictional unemployment.

Public Policy and Job Search

Even if some frictional unemployment is inevitable, the precise amount is not. The faster information spreads about job openings and worker availability, the more rapidly the economy can match workers and firms. The Internet, for instance, may help facilitate job search and reduce frictional unemployment. In addition, public policy may play a role. If policy can reduce the time it takes unemployed workers to find new jobs, it can reduce the economy's natural rate of unemployment.

Government programs try to facilitate job search in various ways. One way is through government-run employment agencies, which give out information about job vacancies. Another way is through public training programs, which aim to ease the transition of workers from declining to growing industries and to help disadvantaged groups escape poverty. Advocates of these programs believe that they make the economy operate more efficiently by keeping the labor force more fully employed, and that they reduce the inequities inherent in a constantly changing market economy.

Critics of these programs question whether the government should get involved with the process of job search. They argue that it is better to let the private market match workers and jobs. In fact, most job search in our economy takes place without intervention by the government. Newspaper ads, Internet job sites, college placement offices, headhunters, and word of mouth all help spread information about job openings and job candidates. Similarly, much worker education is done privately, either through schools or through on-the-job training. These critics contend that the government is no better—and most likely worse—at disseminating the right information to the right workers and deciding what kinds of worker training would be most valuable. They claim that these decisions are best made privately by workers and employers.

Unemployment Insurance

One government program that increases the amount of frictional unemployment, without intending to do so, is **unemployment insurance.** This program is designed to offer workers partial protection against job loss. The unemployed who quit their jobs, were fired for cause, or just entered the labor force are not eligible. Benefits are paid only to the unemployed who were laid off because their previous employers no longer needed their skills. Although the terms of the program vary over time and across states, a typical American worker covered by unemployment insurance receives 50 percent of his or her former wages for 26 weeks.

unemployment insurance
a government program that partially protects workers' incomes when they become unemployed

While unemployment insurance reduces the hardship of unemployment, it also increases the amount of unemployment. The explanation is based on one of the *Ten Principles of Economics* in Chapter 1: People respond to incentives. Because unemployment benefits stop when a worker takes a new job, the unemployed devote less effort to job search and are more likely to turn down unattractive job offers. In addition, because unemployment insurance makes unemployment less onerous, workers are less likely to seek guarantees of job security when they negotiate with employers over the terms of employment.

Many studies by labor economists have examined the incentive effects of unemployment insurance. One study examined an experiment run by the state of Illinois in 1985. When unemployed workers applied to collect unemployment insurance benefits, the state randomly selected some of them and offered each a $500 bonus if they found new jobs within 11 weeks. This group was then compared to a control group not offered the incentive. The average spell of unemployment for the group offered the bonus was 7 percent shorter than the average spell for the control group. This experiment shows that the design of the unemployment insurance system influences the effort that the unemployed devote to job search.

Several other studies examined search effort by following a group of workers over time. Unemployment insurance benefits, rather than lasting forever, usually run out after six months or a year. These studies found that when the unemployed become ineligible for benefits, the probability of their finding a new job rises markedly. Thus, receiving unemployment insurance benefits does reduce the search effort of the unemployed.

IN THE NEWS

GERMAN UNEMPLOYMENT

Many European countries have unemployment insurance that is far more generous than that offered to U.S. workers, and some economists believe that these programs explain the high European unemployment rates. The following article discusses the recent debate over unemployment insurance in Germany.

For Germany, Benefits Are Also a Burden

By Elizabeth Neuffer

BERLIN—They grumble and grouse as they wait for their benefit checks at a local unemployment office here—about the lack of jobs, about the stupidity of German politicians, about how outrageously high taxes are.

What today's unemployed Germans don't complain about is this: the size of their benefit checks.

"I get unemployment benefits, I make some money working on the black market, I make a living," says Michael Steinbach, a 30-year-old electrician who sports a well-ironed shirt, fashionable glasses, and a briefcase as he waits his turn at the Prenzlauer Berg unemployment office. "For now, it's comfortable."

Germany's social welfare system takes good care of the jobless, with initial average monthly checks of nearly $900 per month for someone married—and the prospect, for those who know how to

work the system, of remaining on benefits for life. So blatantly do people abuse this system that Chancellor Helmut Kohl once critically described his country as "Leisurepark Germany." . . .

Now—partly because . . . such generous benefits are seriously straining the nation's economy—questions are being raised about whether one way to combat unemployment is to reform the social welfare system itself. . . .

Combating unemployment, always a hot topic here, leapt back into public

Even though unemployment insurance reduces search effort and raises unemployment, we should not necessarily conclude that the policy is a bad one. The program does achieve its primary goal of reducing the income uncertainty that workers face. In addition, when workers turn down unattractive job offers, they have the opportunity to look for jobs that better suit their tastes and skills. Some economists have argued that unemployment insurance improves the ability of the economy to match each worker with the most appropriate job.

The study of unemployment insurance shows that the unemployment rate is an imperfect measure of a nation's overall level of economic well-being. Most economists agree that eliminating unemployment insurance would reduce the amount of unemployment in the economy. Yet economists disagree on whether economic well-being would be enhanced or diminished by this change in policy.

QuickQuiz How would an increase in the world price of oil affect the amount of frictional unemployment? Is this unemployment undesirable? What public policies might affect the amount of unemployment caused by this price change?

debate last week, after the German labor office released figures showing that joblessness inched up to 11.7 percent in September, the fifth consecutive postwar record. . . .

The unease here also stems from memories of when Germany last faced such levels of joblessness: 1933, when the unemployed were so desperate they begged in the streets for spare change, relied on soup kitchens for meals, and ushered the Nazis into power.

Postwar Germany's reaction was to create a massive welfare state, designed to squelch social unrest through social benevolence. "It's more important to have modestly happy people on benefits than poverty and all its side effects such as a high crime rate as in the United States," said Heiner Geissler, a leading figure in the ruling CDU party.

It is becoming increasingly clear, though, that preserving benefits has trapped Germany in something of a vicious circle.

The nation's high-cost social welfare system is one reason its labor costs are among the highest in the world: Both employees and employers must pay generously into the system, so they need higher wages and profits. More than half of a worker's paycheck goes to taxes. Employer/employee-funded taxes this year alone totaled 52.8 billion deutsche marks, or nearly $30 billion.

But high labor costs are a major reason companies are now fleeing for cheaper, neighboring Poland—meaning job losses for Germany. At the same time, unemployment benefits have become something of a velvet coffin for the unemployed, discouraging them from taking jobs. Until recently, workers who worked part-time were effectively penalized, as they would receive less unemployment benefits if they were laid off.

And generous unemployment benefits mean there is no incentive to take part-time or low-paid work—a strategy adopted to fight unemployment in other countries, including the United States. . . .

These benefits are so good that exploiting them is something of a national sport. In a recent, and not uncommon, conversation overheard in a Berlin cafe, a woman bragged about how she was using her *Sozialhilfe* to pay for a vacation in Italy. Some Germans even register in several districts, knowing it's unlikely they will be caught for receiving multiple benefits.

Not surprisingly, more than 60 percent of Germany's unemployed are long-term unemployed.

"People are used to, and heavily rely on, 'Father State,'" said Dieter Hundt, president of the Confederation of Germany Employers' Association. "We are a bit spoiled by a too tightly woven social net, which doesn't encourage the individual enough to improve his own situation."

Source: *The Boston Globe*, October 12, 1997, p. F1. Copyright © 1997 by GLOBE NEWSPAPER CO (MA). Reproduced with permission of GLOBE NEWSPAPER CO (MA) in the format Textbook via Copyright Clearance Center.

MINIMUM-WAGE LAWS

Having seen how frictional unemployment results from the process of matching workers and jobs, let's now examine how structural unemployment results when the number of jobs is insufficient for the number of workers.

To understand structural unemployment, we begin by reviewing how unemployment arises from minimum-wage laws. Although minimum wages are not the predominant reason for unemployment in our economy, they have an important effect on certain groups with particularly high unemployment rates. Moreover, the analysis of minimum wages is a natural place to start because, as we will see, it can be used to understand some of the other reasons for structural unemployment.

Figure 4 (p. 316) reviews the basic economics of a minimum wage. When a minimum-wage law forces the wage to remain above the level that balances supply and demand, it raises the quantity of labor supplied and reduces the quantity of labor demanded compared to the equilibrium level. There is a surplus of labor. Because there are more workers willing to work than there are jobs, some workers are unemployed.

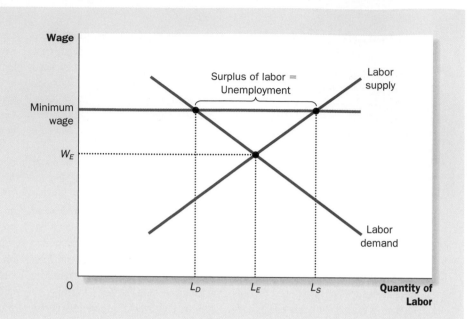

FIGURE 4

Unemployment from a Wage above the Equilibrium Level

In this labor market, the wage at which supply and demand balance is W_E. *At this equilibrium wage, the quantity of labor supplied and the quantity of labor demanded both equal* L_E. *By contrast, if the wage is forced to remain above the equilibrium level, perhaps because of a minimum-wage law, the quantity of labor supplied rises to* L_S, *and the quantity of labor demanded falls to* L_D. *The resulting surplus of labor,* L_S − L_D, *represents unemployment.*

Because we discussed minimum-wage laws extensively in Chapter 6, we will not discuss them further here. It is, however, important to note why minimum-wage laws are not a predominant reason for unemployment: Most workers in the economy have wages well above the legal minimum. Minimum-wage laws are binding most often for the least skilled and least experienced members of the labor force, such as teenagers. It is only among these workers that minimum-wage laws explain the existence of unemployment.

Although Figure 4 is drawn to show the effects of a minimum-wage law, it also illustrates a more general lesson: *If the wage is kept above the equilibrium level for any reason, the result is unemployment.* Minimum-wage laws are just one reason why wages may be "too high." In the remaining two sections of this chapter, we consider two other reasons why wages may be kept above the equilibrium level—unions and efficiency wages. The basic economics of unemployment in these cases is the same as that shown in Figure 4, but these explanations of unemployment can apply to many more of the economy's workers.

At this point, however, we should stop and notice that the structural unemployment that arises from an above-equilibrium wage is, in an important sense, different from the frictional unemployment that arises from the process of job search. The need for job search is not due to the failure of wages to balance labor supply and labor demand. When job search is the explanation for unemployment, workers are *searching* for the jobs that best suit their tastes and skills. By contrast, when the wage is above the equilibrium level, the quantity of labor supplied exceeds the quantity of labor demanded, and workers are unemployed because they are *waiting* for jobs to open up.

QuickQuiz Draw the supply curve and the demand curve for a labor market in which the wage is fixed above the equilibrium level. Show the quantity of labor supplied, the quantity demanded, and the amount of unemployment.

UNIONS AND COLLECTIVE BARGAINING

A **union** is a worker association that bargains with employers over wages and working conditions. Whereas only 16 percent of U.S. workers now belong to unions, unions played a much larger role in the U.S. labor market in the past. In the 1940s and 1950s, when unions were at their peak, about a third of the U.S. labor force was unionized. Moreover, unions continue to play a large role in many European countries. In Sweden and Denmark, for instance, more than three-fourths of workers belong to unions.

union
a worker association that bargains with employers over wages and working conditions

The Economics of Unions

A union is a type of cartel. Like any cartel, a union is a group of sellers acting together in the hope of exerting their joint market power. Most workers in the U.S. economy discuss their wages, benefits, and working conditions with their employers as individuals. By contrast, workers in a union do so as a group. The process by which unions and firms agree on the terms of employment is called **collective bargaining.**

When a union bargains with a firm, it asks for higher wages, better benefits, and better working conditions than the firm would offer in the absence of a union. If the union and the firm do not reach agreement, the union can organize a withdrawal of labor from the firm, called a **strike.** Because a strike reduces production, sales, and profit, a firm facing a strike threat is likely to agree to pay higher wages than it otherwise would. Economists who study the effects of unions typically find that union workers earn about 10 to 20 percent more than similar workers who do not belong to unions.

collective bargaining
the process by which unions and firms agree on the terms of employment

strike
the organized withdrawal of labor from a firm by a union

When a union raises the wage above the equilibrium level, it raises the quantity of labor supplied and reduces the quantity of labor demanded, resulting in unemployment. Those workers who remain employed are better off, but those who were previously employed and are now unemployed at the higher wage are worse off. Indeed, unions are often thought to cause conflict between different groups of workers—between the *insiders* who benefit from high union wages and the *outsiders* who do not get the union jobs.

The outsiders can respond to their status in one of two ways. Some of them remain unemployed and wait for the chance to become insiders and earn the high union wage. Others take jobs in firms that are not unionized. Thus, when unions raise wages in one part of the economy, the supply of labor increases in other parts of the economy. This increase in labor supply, in turn, reduces wages in industries that are not unionized. In other words, workers in unions reap the benefit of collective bargaining, while workers not in unions bear some of the cost.

The role of unions in the economy depends in part on the laws that govern union organization and collective bargaining. Normally, explicit agreements among members of a cartel are illegal. If firms that sell a common product were to agree to set a high price for that product, the agreement would be a "conspiracy in restraint of trade." The government would prosecute these firms in civil and criminal court for violating the antitrust laws. By contrast, unions are exempt from these laws. The policymakers who wrote the antitrust laws believed that workers needed greater market power as they bargained with employers. Indeed, various laws are designed to encourage the formation of unions. In particular, the Wagner Act of 1935 prevents employers from interfering when workers try to organize

"Gentlemen, nothing stands in the way of a final accord except that management wants profit maximization and the union wants more moola."

unions and requires employers to bargain with unions in good faith. The National Labor Relations Board (NLRB) is the government agency that enforces workers' right to unionize.

Legislation affecting the market power of unions is a perennial topic of political debate. State lawmakers sometimes debate *right-to-work laws*, which give workers in a unionized firm the right to choose whether to join the union. In the absence of such laws, unions can insist during collective bargaining that firms make union membership a requirement for employment. In recent years, lawmakers in Washington have debated a proposed law that would prevent firms from hiring permanent replacements for workers who are on strike. This law would make strikes more costly for firms and, thereby, would increase the market power of unions. These and similar policy decisions will help determine the future of the union movement.

Are Unions Good or Bad for the Economy?

Economists disagree about whether unions are good or bad for the economy as a whole. Let's consider both sides of the debate.

Critics of unions argue that unions are merely a type of cartel. When unions raise wages above the level that would prevail in competitive markets, they reduce the quantity of labor demanded, cause some workers to be unemployed, and reduce

IN THE NEWS

SHOULD YOU JOIN A UNION?

Someday you may face the decision about whether to vote for or against a union in your workplace. The following article discusses some issues you might consider.

On Payday, Union Jobs Stack Up Very Well

By David Cay Johnston

With the teamsters' success in their two-week strike against United Parcel Service, and with the A.F.L.-C.I.O. training thousands of union organizers in a drive to reverse a quarter-century of declining membership, millions of workers will be asked over the next few years whether they want a union to represent them.

It is a complicated question, the answer to which rests on a jumble of determinations: Do you favor collective action or individual initiative? Do you trust the union's leaders? Do you want somebody else speaking for you in dealings with your employer? Do you think you will be dismissed if you sign a union card—or that the company will send your job overseas if a union is organized?

But in one regard, the choice is simple—and it is not the choice that most workers have made during the labor movement's recent decades in the economic wilderness.

From a pocketbook perspective, workers are absolutely better off joining a union. Economists across the political spectrum agree. Turning a nonunion job into a union job very likely will have a bigger effect on lifetime finances than all the advice employees will ever read about investing their 401(k) plans, buy-ing a home or otherwise making more of what they earn.

Here is how the equation works, said Prof. Richard B. Freeman of Harvard University: "For an existing worker in a firm, if you can carry out an organizing drive, it is all to your benefit. If there are going to be losers, they are people who might have gotten a job in the future, the shareholders whose profits will go down, the managers because there will be less profit to distribute to them in pay and, maybe, consumers will pay a little more for the product. But as a worker, it is awfully hard to see why you wouldn't want a union."

Over all, union workers are paid about 20 percent more than nonunion workers, and their fringe benefits are typically worth two to four times as much, economists with a wide array of views have found. The financial advantage is even greater for workers with little formal education and training and for women, blacks, and Hispanic workers.

Moreover, 85 percent of union members have health insurance, compared with 57 percent of nonunion workers, said Barry Bluestone, a labor-friendly economics professor at the University of Massachusetts.

The conclusion draws no argument even from Prof. Leo Troy of Rutgers University, who is widely known in academic circles and among union leaders for his hostility to organized labor. "From a standpoint of wages and fringe bene-fits," Professor Troy said, "the answer is yes, you are better off in a union."

His objections to unions concern how they reduce profits for owners and distort investment decisions in ways that slow the overall growth of the economy—not how they affect workers who bargain collectively. Professor Troy points out that he belongs to a union himself—the American Association of University Professors.

Donald R. Deere, an economist at the Bush School of Government and Public Service at Texas A & M University, studied the wage differential for comparable union and nonunion workers between 1974 and 1996, a period when union membership fell to 15 percent of American workers from 22 percent.

In every educational and age category that he studied, Professor Deere found that union members increased their wage advantage over nonunion workers during those years. Last year, he estimates, unionized workers with less than a high school education earned 22 percent more than their nonunion counterparts. The differential declined as education levels rose, reaching 10 percent for college graduates.

"It makes sense to belong to a union," Professor Deere said, "so long as you don't lose your job in the long term."

Source: *The New York Times,* August 31, 1997, Money & Business Section, p. 1. Copyright © 1997 by The New York Times Co. Reprinted by permission.

the wages in the rest of the economy. The resulting allocation of labor is, critics argue, both inefficient and inequitable. It is inefficient because high union wages reduce employment in unionized firms below the efficient, competitive level. It is inequitable because some workers benefit at the expense of other workers.

Advocates of unions contend that unions are a necessary antidote to the market power of the firms that hire workers. The extreme case of this market power is the "company town," where a single firm does most of the hiring in a geographic region. In a company town, if workers do not accept the wages and working conditions that the firm offers, they have little choice but to move or stop working. In the absence of a union, therefore, the firm could use its market power to pay lower wages and offer worse working conditions than would prevail if it had to compete with other firms for the same workers. In this case, a union may balance the firm's market power and protect the workers from being at the mercy of the firm owners.

Advocates of unions also claim that unions are important for helping firms respond efficiently to workers' concerns. Whenever a worker takes a job, the worker and the firm must agree on many attributes of the job in addition to the wage: hours of work, overtime, vacations, sick leave, health benefits, promotion schedules, job security, and so on. By representing workers' views on these issues, unions allow firms to provide the right mix of job attributes. Even if unions have the adverse effect of pushing wages above the equilibrium level and causing unemployment, they have the benefit of helping firms keep a happy and productive workforce.

In the end, there is no consensus among economists about whether unions are good or bad for the economy. Like many institutions, their influence is probably beneficial in some circumstances and adverse in others.

QuickQuiz How does a union in the auto industry affect wages and employment at General Motors and Ford? How does it affect wages and employment in other industries?

THE THEORY OF EFFICIENCY WAGES

efficiency wages
above-equilibrium wages paid by firms in order to increase worker productivity

A fourth reason why economies always experience some unemployment—in addition to job search, minimum-wage laws, and unions—is suggested by the theory of **efficiency wages.** According to this theory, firms operate more efficiently if wages are above the equilibrium level. Therefore, it may be profitable for firms to keep wages high even in the presence of a surplus of labor.

In some ways, the unemployment that arises from efficiency wages is similar to the unemployment that arises from minimum-wage laws and unions. In all three cases, unemployment is the result of wages above the level that balances the quantity of labor supplied and the quantity of labor demanded. Yet there is also an important difference. Minimum-wage laws and unions prevent firms from lowering wages in the presence of a surplus of workers. Efficiency-wage theory states that such a constraint on firms is unnecessary in many cases because firms may be better off keeping wages above the equilibrium level.

Why should firms want to keep wages high? This decision may seem odd at first, for wages are a large part of firms' costs. Normally, we expect profit-maximizing firms to want to keep costs—and therefore wages—as low as possible. The novel insight of efficiency-wage theory is that paying high wages might be profitable because they might raise the efficiency of a firm's workers.

There are several types of efficiency-wage theory. Each type suggests a different explanation for why firms may want to pay high wages. Let's now consider four of these types.

Worker Health

The first and simplest type of efficiency-wage theory emphasizes the link between wages and worker health. Better paid workers eat a more nutritious diet, and workers who eat a better diet are healthier and more productive. A firm may find it more profitable to pay high wages and have healthy, productive workers than to pay lower wages and have less healthy, less productive workers.

This type of efficiency-wage theory is not relevant for firms in rich countries such as the United States. In these countries, the equilibrium wages for most workers are well above the level needed for an adequate diet. Firms are not concerned that paying equilibrium wages would place their workers' health in jeopardy.

This type of efficiency-wage theory is more relevant for firms in less developed countries where inadequate nutrition is a more common problem. Unemployment is high in the cities of many poor African countries, for example. In these countries, firms may fear that cutting wages would, in fact, adversely influence their workers' health and productivity. In other words, concern over nutrition may explain why firms do not cut wages despite a surplus of labor.

Worker Turnover

A second type of efficiency-wage theory emphasizes the link between wages and worker turnover. Workers quit jobs for many reasons—to take jobs in other firms, to move to other parts of the country, to leave the labor force, and so on. The frequency with which they quit depends on the entire set of incentives they face, including the benefits of leaving and the benefits of staying. The more a firm pays its workers, the less often its workers will choose to leave. Thus, a firm can reduce turnover among its workers by paying them a high wage.

Why do firms care about turnover? The reason is that it is costly for firms to hire and train new workers. Moreover, even after they are trained, newly hired workers are not as productive as experienced workers. Firms with higher turnover, therefore, will tend to have higher production costs. Firms may find it profitable to pay wages above the equilibrium level in order to reduce worker turnover.

Worker Effort

A third type of efficiency-wage theory emphasizes the link between wages and worker effort. In many jobs, workers have some discretion over how hard to work. As a result, firms monitor the efforts of their workers, and workers caught shirking their responsibilities are fired. But not all shirkers are caught immediately because monitoring workers is costly and imperfect. A firm can respond to this problem by paying wages above the equilibrium level. High wages make workers more eager to keep their jobs and, thereby, give workers an incentive to put forward their best effort.

This particular type of efficiency-wage theory is similar to the old Marxist idea of the "reserve army of the unemployed." Marx thought that employers benefited from unemployment because the threat of unemployment helped to discipline those workers who had jobs. In the worker-effort variant of efficiency-wage theory, unemployment fills a similar role. If the wage were at the level that balanced supply and demand, workers would have less reason to work hard because if they were fired, they could quickly find new jobs at the same wage. Therefore, firms raise wages above the equilibrium level, causing unemployment and providing an incentive for workers not to shirk their responsibilities.

Worker Quality

A fourth and final type of efficiency-wage theory emphasizes the link between wages and worker quality. When a firm hires new workers, it cannot perfectly gauge the quality of the applicants. By paying a high wage, the firm attracts a better pool of workers to apply for its jobs.

To see how this might work, consider a simple example. Waterwell Company owns one well and needs one worker to pump water from the well. Two workers, Bill and Ted, are interested in the job. Bill, a proficient worker, is willing to work for $10 per hour. Below that wage, he would rather start his own lawn-mowing business. Ted, a complete incompetent, is willing to work for anything above $2 per hour. Below that wage, he would rather sit on the beach. Economists say that Bill's *reservation wage*—the lowest wage he would accept—is $10, and Ted's reservation wage is $2.

What wage should the firm set? If the firm were interested in minimizing labor costs, it would set the wage at $2 per hour. At this wage, the quantity of workers supplied (one) would balance the quantity demanded. Ted would take the job, and Bill would not apply for it. Yet suppose Waterwell knows that only one of these two applicants is competent, but it does not know whether it is Bill or Ted. If the firm hires the incompetent worker, he may damage the well, causing the firm huge losses. In this case, the firm has a better strategy than paying the equilibrium wage of $2 and hiring Ted. It can offer $10 per hour, inducing both Bill and Ted to apply for the job. By choosing randomly between these two applicants and turning the other away, the firm has a fifty-fifty chance of hiring the competent one. By contrast, if the firm offers any lower wage, it is sure to hire the incompetent worker.

This story illustrates a general phenomenon. When a firm faces a surplus of workers, it might seem profitable to reduce the wage it is offering. But by reducing the wage, the firm induces an adverse change in the mix of workers. In this case, at a wage of $10, Waterwell has two workers applying for one job. But if Waterwell

responds to this labor surplus by reducing the wage, the competent worker (who has better alternative opportunities) will not apply. Thus, it is profitable for the firm to pay a wage above the level that balances supply and demand.

Case Study

HENRY FORD AND THE VERY GENEROUS $5-A-DAY WAGE

Henry Ford was an industrial visionary. As founder of the Ford Motor Company, he was responsible for introducing modern techniques of production. Rather than building cars with small teams of skilled craftsmen, Ford built cars on assembly lines in which unskilled workers were taught to perform the same simple tasks over and over again. The output of this assembly process was the Model T Ford, one of the most famous early automobiles.

In 1914, Ford introduced another innovation: the $5 workday. This might not seem like much today, but back then $5 was about twice the going wage. It was also far above the wage that balanced supply and demand. When the new $5-a-day wage was announced, long lines of job seekers formed outside the Ford factories. The number of workers willing to work at this wage far exceeded the number of workers Ford needed.

Ford's high-wage policy had many of the effects predicted by efficiency-wage theory. Turnover fell, absenteeism fell, and productivity rose. Workers were so much more efficient that Ford's production costs were lower even though wages were higher. Thus, paying a wage above the equilibrium level was profitable for the firm. Henry Ford himself called the $5-a-day wage "one of the finest cost-cutting moves we ever made."

Historical accounts of this episode are also consistent with efficiency-wage theory. An historian of the early Ford Motor Company wrote, "Ford and his associates freely declared on many occasions that the high-wage policy turned out to be good business. By this they meant that it had improved the discipline of the workers, given them a more loyal interest in the institution, and raised their personal efficiency."

Why did it take Henry Ford to introduce this efficiency wage? Why were other firms not already taking advantage of this seemingly profitable business strategy? According to some analysts, Ford's decision was closely linked to his use of the assembly line. Workers organized in an assembly line are highly interdependent. If one worker is absent or works slowly, other workers are less able to complete their own tasks. Thus, while assembly lines made production more efficient, they also raised the importance of low worker turnover, high worker quality, and high worker effort. As a result, paying efficiency wages may have been a better strategy for the Ford Motor Company than for other businesses at the time. ●

QuickQuiz Give four explanations for why firms might find it profitable to pay wages above the level that balances quantity of labor supplied and quantity of labor demanded.

CONCLUSION

In this chapter we discussed the measurement of unemployment and the reasons why economies always experience some degree of unemployment. We have seen how job search, minimum-wage laws, unions, and efficiency wages can all help explain why some workers do not have jobs. Which of these four explanations for the natural rate of unemployment are the most important for the U.S. economy and other economies around the world? Unfortunately, there is no easy way to tell. Economists differ in which of these explanations of unemployment they consider most important.

The analysis of this chapter yields an important lesson: Although the economy will always have some unemployment, its natural rate is not immutable. Many events and policies can change the amount of unemployment the economy typically experiences. As the information revolution changes the process of job search, as Congress adjusts the minimum wage, as workers form or quit unions, and as firms alter their reliance on efficiency wages, the natural rate of unemployment evolves. Unemployment is not a simple problem with a simple solution. But how we choose to organize our society can profoundly influence how prevalent a problem it is.

SUMMARY

- The unemployment rate is the percentage of those who would like to work who do not have jobs. The Bureau of Labor Statistics calculates this statistic monthly based on a survey of thousands of households.

- The unemployment rate is an imperfect measure of joblessness. Some people who call themselves unemployed may actually not want to work, and some people who would like to work have left the labor force after an unsuccessful search.

- In the U.S. economy, most people who become unemployed find work within a short period of time. Nonetheless, most unemployment observed at any given time is attributable to the few people who are unemployed for long periods of time.

- One reason for unemployment is the time it takes for workers to search for jobs that best suit their tastes and skills. Unemployment insurance is a government policy that, while protecting workers' incomes, increases the amount of frictional unemployment.

- A second reason why our economy always has some unemployment is minimum-wage laws. By raising the wage of unskilled and inexperienced workers above the equilibrium level, minimum-wage laws raise the quantity of labor supplied and reduce the quantity demanded. The resulting surplus of labor represents unemployment.

- A third reason for unemployment is the market power of unions. When unions push the wages in unionized industries above the equilibrium level, they create a surplus of labor.

- A fourth reason for unemployment is suggested by the theory of efficiency wages. According to this theory, firms find it profitable to pay wages above the equilibrium level. High wages can improve worker health, lower worker turnover, increase worker effort, and raise worker quality.

KEY CONCEPTS

labor force, p. 305
unemployment rate, p. 305
labor-force participation
   rate, p. 306
natural rate of
   unemployment, p. 307

cyclical unemployment, p. 307
discouraged workers, p. 309
frictional unemployment, p. 311
structural unemployment, p. 311
job search, p. 311
unemployment insurance, p. 313

union, p. 317
collective bargaining, p. 317
strike, p. 317
efficiency wages, p. 320

QUESTIONS FOR REVIEW

1. What are the three categories into which the Bureau of Labor Statistics divides everyone? How does the BLS compute the labor force, the unemployment rate, and the labor-force participation rate?

2. Is unemployment typically short-term or long-term? Explain.

3. Why is frictional unemployment inevitable? How might the government reduce the amount of frictional unemployment?

4. Are minimum-wage laws a better explanation for structural unemployment among teenagers or among college graduates? Why?

5. How do unions affect the natural rate of unemployment?

6. What claims do advocates of unions make to argue that unions are good for the economy?

7. Explain four ways in which a firm might increase its profits by raising the wages it pays.

PROBLEMS AND APPLICATIONS

1. The Bureau of Labor Statistics announced that in December 1998, of all adult Americans, 138,547,000 were employed, 6,021,000 were unemployed, and 67,723,000 were not in the labor force. How big was the labor force? What was the labor-force participation rate? What was the unemployment rate?

2. Go to the Web site of the Bureau of Labor Statistics (http://www.bls.gov). What is the national unemployment rate right now? Find the unemployment rate for the demographic group that best fits a description of you (for example, based on age, sex, and race). Is it higher or lower than the national average? Why do you think this is so?

3. As shown in Figure 3, the overall labor-force participation rate of men declined between 1970 and 1990. This overall decline reflects different patterns for different age groups, however, as shown in the following table:

	All Men	Men 16–24	Men 25–54	Men 55 and over
1970	80%	69%	96%	56%
1990	76	72	93	40

Which group experienced the largest decline? Given this information, what factor may have played an important role in the decline in overall male labor-force participation over this period?

4. The labor-force participation rate of women increased sharply between 1970 and 1990, as shown in Figure 3. As with men, however, there were different patterns for different age groups, as shown in this table:

	All Women	Women 25–54	Women 25–34	Women 35–44	Women 45–54
1970	43%	50%	45%	51%	54%
1990	58	74	74	77	71

Why do you think that younger women experienced a bigger increase in labor-force participation than older women?

5. Between 1997 and 1998, total U.S. employment increased by 2.1 million workers, but the number of unemployed workers declined by only 0.5 million. How are these numbers consistent with each other? Why might one expect a reduction in the number of people counted as unemployed to be smaller than the increase in the number of people employed?

6. Are the following workers more likely to experience short-term or long-term unemployment? Explain.
   a. a construction worker laid off because of bad weather
   b. a manufacturing worker who loses her job at a plant in an isolated area
   c. a stagecoach-industry worker laid off because of competition from railroads
   d. a short-order cook who loses his job when a new restaurant opens across the street
   e. an expert welder with little formal education who loses her job when the company installs automatic welding machinery

7. Using a diagram of the labor market, show the effect of an increase in the minimum wage on the wage paid to workers, the number of workers supplied, the number of workers demanded, and the amount of unemployment.

8. Do you think that firms in small towns or in cities have more market power in hiring? Do you think that firms generally have more market power in hiring today than 50 years ago, or less? How do you think this change over time has affected the role of unions in the economy? Explain.

9. Consider an economy with two labor markets, neither of which is unionized. Now suppose a union is established in one market.
   a. Show the effect of the union on the market in which it is formed. In what sense is the quantity of labor employed in this market an inefficient quantity?
   b. Show the effect of the union on the nonunionized market. What happens to the equilibrium wage in this market?

10. It can be shown that an industry's demand for labor will become more elastic when the demand for the industry's product becomes more elastic. Let's consider the implications of this fact for the U.S. automobile industry and the United Autoworkers Union (UAW).
   a. What happened to the elasticity of demand for American cars when the Japanese developed a strong auto industry? What happened to the elasticity of demand for American autoworkers? Explain.
   b. As the chapter explains, a union generally faces a tradeoff in deciding how much to raise wages, because a bigger increase

is better for workers who remain employed but also results in a greater reduction in employment. How did the rise in auto imports from Japan affect the wage–employment tradeoff faced by the UAW?

c. Do you think the growth of the Japanese auto industry increased or decreased the gap between the competitive wage and the wage chosen by the UAW? Explain.

11. Some workers in the economy are paid a flat salary and some are paid by commission. Which compensation scheme would require more monitoring by supervisors? In which case do firms have an incentive to pay more than the equilibrium level (as in the worker-effort variant of efficiency-wage theory)? What factors do you think determine the type of compensation firms choose?

12. (This problem is challenging.) Suppose that Congress passes a law requiring employers to provide employees some benefit (such as health care) that raises the cost of an employee by $4 per hour.

a. What effect does this employer mandate have on the demand for labor? (In answering this and the following questions, be quantitative when you can.)

b. If employees place a value on this benefit exactly equal to its cost, what effect does this employer mandate have on the supply of labor?

c. If the wage is free to balance supply and demand, how does this law affect the wage and the level of employment? Are employers better or worse off? Are employees better or worse off?

d. If a minimum-wage law prevents the wage from balancing supply and demand, how does the employer mandate affect the wage, the level of employment, and the level of unemployment? Are employers better or worse off? Are employees better or worse off?

e. Now suppose that workers do not value the mandated benefit at all. How does this alternative assumption change your answers to parts (b), (c), and (d) above?

http://   For more study tools, please visit http://mankiwXtra.swlearning.com.

6

MONEY AND PRICES IN THE LONG RUN

16

THE MONETARY SYSTEM

When you walk into a restaurant to buy a meal, you get something of value—a full stomach. To pay for this service, you might hand the restaurateur several worn-out pieces of greenish paper decorated with strange symbols, government buildings, and the portraits of famous dead Americans. Or you might hand him a single piece of paper with the name of a bank and your signature. Whether you pay by cash or check, the restaurateur is happy to work hard to satisfy your gastronomical desires in exchange for these pieces of paper which, in and of themselves, are worthless.

To anyone who has lived in a modern economy, this social custom is not at all odd. Even though paper money has no intrinsic value, the restaurateur is confident that, in the future, some third person will accept it in exchange for something that the restaurateur does value. And that third person is confident that some fourth person will accept the money, with the knowledge that yet a fifth person will accept the money . . . and so on. To the restaurateur and to other people in our society, your cash or check represents a claim to goods and services in the future.

The social custom of using money for transactions is extraordinarily useful in a large, complex society. Imagine, for a moment, that there was no item in the economy widely accepted in exchange for goods and services. People would have to rely on *barter*—the exchange of one good or service for another—to obtain the things they need. To get your restaurant meal, for instance, you would have to offer the restaurateur something of immediate value. You could offer to wash some dishes, clean his car, or give him your family's secret recipe for meat loaf. An economy that relies on barter will have trouble allocating its scarce resources efficiently. In such an economy, trade is said to require the *double coincidence of wants*—the unlikely occurrence that two people each have a good or service that the other wants.

The existence of money makes trade easier. The restaurateur does not care whether you can produce a valuable good or service for him. He is happy to accept your money, knowing that other people will do the same for him. Such a convention allows trade to be roundabout. The restaurateur accepts your money and uses it to pay his chef; the chef uses her paycheck to send her child to day care; the day care center uses this tuition to pay a teacher; and the teacher hires you to mow his lawn. As money flows from person to person in the economy, it facilitates production and trade, thereby allowing each person to specialize in what he or she does best and raising everyone's standard of living.

In this chapter we begin to examine the role of money in the economy. We discuss what money is, the various forms that money takes, how the banking system helps create money, and how the government controls the quantity of money in circulation. Because money is so important in the economy, we devote much effort in the rest of this book to learning how changes in the quantity of money affect various economic variables, including inflation, interest rates, production, and employment. Consistent with our long-run focus in the previous three chapters, in the next chapter we will examine the long-run effects of changes in the quantity of money. The short-run effects of monetary changes are a more complex topic, which we will take up later in the book. This chapter provides the background for all of this further analysis.

THE MEANING OF MONEY

What is money? This might seem like an odd question. When you read that billionaire Bill Gates has a lot of money, you know what that means: He is so rich that he can buy almost anything he wants. In this sense, the term *money* is used to mean *wealth*.

money
the set of assets in an economy that people regularly use to buy goods and services from other people

Economists, however, use the word in a more specific sense: **Money** is the set of assets in the economy that people regularly use to buy goods and services from other people. The cash in your wallet is money because you can use it to buy a meal at a restaurant or a shirt at a clothing store. By contrast, if you happened to own most of Microsoft Corporation, as Bill Gates does, you would be wealthy, but this asset is not considered a form of money. You could not buy a meal or a shirt with this wealth without first obtaining some cash. According to the economist's definition, money includes only those few types of wealth that are regularly accepted by sellers in exchange for goods and services.

The Functions of Money

Money has three functions in the economy: It is a *medium of exchange*, a *unit of account*, and a *store of value*. These three functions together distinguish money from other assets in the economy, such as stocks, bonds, real estate, art, and even baseball cards. Let's examine each of these functions of money in turn.

A **medium of exchange** is an item that buyers give to sellers when they purchase goods and services. When you buy a shirt at a clothing store, the store gives you the shirt, and you give the store your money. This transfer of money from buyer to seller allows the transaction to take place. When you walk into a store, you are confident that the store will accept your money for the items it is selling because money is the commonly accepted medium of exchange.

A **unit of account** is the yardstick people use to post prices and record debts. When you go shopping, you might observe that a shirt costs $20 and a hamburger costs $2. Even though it would be accurate to say that the price of a shirt is 10 hamburgers and the price of a hamburger is 1/10 of a shirt, prices are never quoted in this way. Similarly, if you take out a loan from a bank, the size of your future loan repayments will be measured in dollars, not in a quantity of goods and services. When we want to measure and record economic value, we use money as the unit of account.

A **store of value** is an item that people can use to transfer purchasing power from the present to the future. When a seller accepts money today in exchange for a good or service, that seller can hold the money and become a buyer of another good or service at another time. Of course, money is not the only store of value in the economy, for a person can also transfer purchasing power from the present to the future by holding other assets. The term *wealth* is used to refer to the total of all stores of value, including both money and nonmonetary assets.

Economists use the term **liquidity** to describe the ease with which an asset can be converted into the economy's medium of exchange. Because money is the economy's medium of exchange, it is the most liquid asset available. Other assets vary widely in their liquidity. Most stocks and bonds can be sold easily with small cost, so they are relatively liquid assets. By contrast, selling a house, a Rembrandt painting, or a 1948 Joe DiMaggio baseball card requires more time and effort, so these assets are less liquid.

When people decide in what form to hold their wealth, they have to balance the liquidity of each possible asset against the asset's usefulness as a store of value. Money is the most liquid asset, but it is far from perfect as a store of value. When prices rise, the value of money falls. In other words, when goods and services become more expensive, each dollar in your wallet can buy less. This link between the price level and the value of money will turn out to be important for understanding how money affects the economy.

The Kinds of Money

When money takes the form of a commodity with intrinsic value, it is called **commodity money.** The term *intrinsic value* means that the item would have value even if it were not used as money. One example of commodity money is gold. Gold has intrinsic value because it is used in industry and in the making of jewelry. Although today we no longer use gold as money, historically gold has been a common form of money because it is relatively easy to carry, measure, and verify for impurities. When an economy uses gold as money (or uses paper money that is convertible into gold on demand), it is said to be operating under a *gold standard*.

Another example of commodity money is cigarettes. In prisoner-of-war camps during World War II, prisoners traded goods and services with one another using

medium of exchange
an item that buyers give to sellers when they want to purchase goods and services

unit of account
the yardstick people use to post prices and record debts

store of value
an item that people can use to transfer purchasing power from the present to the future

liquidity
the ease with which an asset can be converted into the economy's medium of exchange

commodity money
money that takes the form of a commodity with intrinsic value

cigarettes as the store of value, unit of account, and medium of exchange. Similarly, as the Soviet Union was breaking up in the late 1980s, cigarettes started replacing the ruble as the preferred currency in Moscow. In both cases, even nonsmokers were happy to accept cigarettes in an exchange, knowing that they could use the cigarettes to buy other goods and services.

fiat money
money without intrinsic value that is used as money because of government decree

Money without intrinsic value is called **fiat money.** A *fiat* is simply an order or decree, and fiat money is established as money by government decree. For example, compare the paper dollars in your wallet (printed by the U.S. government) and the paper dollars from a game of Monopoly (printed by the Parker Brothers game company). Why can you use the first to pay your bill at a restaurant but not the second? The answer is that the U.S. government has decreed its dollars to be valid money. Each paper dollar in your wallet reads: "This note is legal tender for all debts, public and private."

Although the government is central to establishing and regulating a system of fiat money (by prosecuting counterfeiters, for example), other factors are also required for the success of such a monetary system. To a large extent, the acceptance of fiat money depends as much on expectations and social convention as on government decree. The Soviet government in the 1980s never abandoned the ruble as

IN THE NEWS

MONEY ON THE ISLAND OF YAP

The role of social custom in the monetary system is most apparent in foreign cultures with customs very different from our own. The following article describes the money on the island of Yap. As you read the article, ask yourself whether Yap is using a type of commodity money, a type of fiat money, or something in between.

Fixed Assets, or Why a Loan in Yap Is Hard to Roll Over

By Art Pine

YAP, MICRONESIA—On this tiny South Pacific island, life is easy and the currency is hard.

Elsewhere, the world's troubled monetary system creaks along; floating exchange rates wreak havoc on currency markets, and devaluations are commonplace. But on Yap the currency is as solid as a rock. In fact, it *is* rock. Limestone to be precise.

For nearly 2,000 years the Yapese have used large stone wheels to pay for major purchases, such as land, canoes and permissions to marry. Yap is a U.S. trust territory, and the dollar is used in grocery stores and gas stations. But reliance on stone money, like the island's ancient caste system and the traditional dress of loincloths and grass skirts, continues.

Buying property with stones is "much easier than buying it with U.S. dollars," says John Chodad, who recently purchased a building lot with a 30-inch stone wheel. "We don't know the value of the U.S. dollar.". . .

Stone wheels don't make good pocket money, so for small transactions, Yapese use other forms of currency, such as beer. Beer is proffered as payment for all sorts of odd jobs, including construction. The 10,000 people on Yap consume the official currency. Yet the people of Moscow preferred to accept cigarettes (or even American dollars) in exchange for goods and services, because they were more confident that these alternative monies would be accepted by others in the future.

Money in the U.S. Economy

As we will see, the quantity of money circulating in the economy, called the *money stock*, has a powerful influence on many economic variables. But before we consider why that is true, we need to ask a preliminary question: What is the quantity of money? In particular, suppose you were given the task of measuring how much money there is in the U.S. economy. What would you include in your measure?

The most obvious asset to include is **currency**—the paper bills and coins in the hands of the public. Currency is clearly the most widely accepted medium of exchange in our economy. There is no doubt that it is part of the money stock.

Yet currency is not the only asset that you can use to buy goods and services. Many stores also accept personal checks. Wealth held in your checking account is

currency
the paper bills and coins in the hands of the public

PHOTO: © ANDERS RYMAN/CORBIS

Money on the island of Yap: Not exactly pocket change.

40,000 to 50,000 cases a year, mostly of Budweiser. . . .

The people of Yap have been using stone money ever since a Yapese warrior named Anagumang first brought the huge stones from limestone caverns on neighboring Palau, some 1,500 to 2,000 years ago. Inspired by the moon, he fashioned the stone into large circles. The rest is history.

Yapese lean the stone wheels against their houses or prop up rows of them in village "banks." Most of the stones are 2 1/2 to 5 feet in diameter, but some are as much as 12 feet across. Each has a hole in the center so it can be slipped onto the trunk of a fallen betel nut tree and carried. It takes 20 men to lift some stones.

By custom, the stones are worthless when broken. You never hear people on Yap musing about wanting a piece of the rock. Rather than risk a broken stone—or back—Yapese tend to leave the larger stones where they are and make a mental accounting that the ownership has been transferred—much as gold bars used in international transactions change hands without leaving the vaults of the New York Federal Reserve Bank. . . .

There are some decided advantages to using massive stones for money. They are immune to black-market trading, for one thing, and they pose formidable obstacles to pickpockets. In addition, there aren't any sterile debates about how to stabilize the Yapese monetary system. With only 6,600 stone wheels remaining on the island, the money supply stays put. . . .

Meanwhile, Yap's stone money may be about to take on international significance. Just yesterday, Washington received notice that Tosiho Nakayama, the president of Micronesia, plans to bring a stone disk when he visits the United States next month. It will be flown by Air Force jet.

Officials say Mr. Nakayama intends the stone as Micronesia's symbolic contribution toward reducing the U.S. budget deficit.

demand deposits
balances in bank accounts that depositors can access on demand by writing a check

almost as convenient for buying things as wealth held in your wallet. To measure the money stock, therefore, you might want to include **demand deposits**—balances in bank accounts that depositors can access on demand simply by writing a check.

Once you start to consider balances in checking accounts as part of the money stock, you are led to consider the large variety of other accounts that people hold at banks and other financial institutions. Bank depositors usually cannot write checks against the balances in their savings accounts, but they can easily transfer funds from savings into checking accounts. In addition, depositors in money market mutual funds can often write checks against their balances. Thus, these other accounts should plausibly be part of the U.S. money stock.

In a complex economy such as ours, it is not easy to draw a line between assets that can be called "money" and assets that cannot. The coins in your pocket are clearly part of the money stock, and the Empire State Building clearly is not, but there are many assets in between these extremes for which the choice is less clear. Therefore, various measures of the money stock are available for the U.S. economy. Figure 1 shows the two most important, designated M1 and M2. Each of these measures uses a slightly different criterion for distinguishing monetary and nonmonetary assets.

For our purposes in this book, we need not dwell on the differences between the various measures of money. The important point is that the money stock for the U.S. economy includes not just currency but also deposits in banks and other financial institutions that can be readily accessed and used to buy goods and services.

FYI

CREDIT CARDS, DEBIT CARDS, AND MONEY

It might seem natural to include credit cards as part of the economy's stock of money. After all, people use credit cards to make many of their purchases. Aren't credit cards, therefore, a medium of exchange?

Although at first this argument may seem persuasive, credit cards are excluded from all measures of the quantity of money. The reason is that credit cards are not really a method of payment but a method of *deferring* payment. When you buy a meal with a credit card, the bank that issued the card pays the restaurant what it is due. At a later date, you will have to repay the bank (perhaps with interest). When

the time comes to pay your credit card bill, you will probably do so by writing a check against your checking account. The balance in this checking account is part of the economy's stock of money.

Notice that credit cards are very different from debit cards, which automatically withdraw funds from a bank account to pay for items bought. Rather than allowing the user to postpone payment for a purchase, a debit card allows the user immediate access to deposits in a bank account. In this sense, a debit card is more similar to a check than to a credit card. The account balances that lie behind debit cards are included in measures of the quantity of money.

Even though credit cards are not considered a form of money, they are nonetheless important for analyzing the monetary system. People who have credit cards can pay many of their bills all at once at the end of the month, rather than sporadically as they make purchases. As a result, people who have credit cards probably hold less money on average than people who do not have credit cards. Thus, the introduction and increased popularity of credit cards may reduce the amount of money that people choose to hold.

FIGURE 1

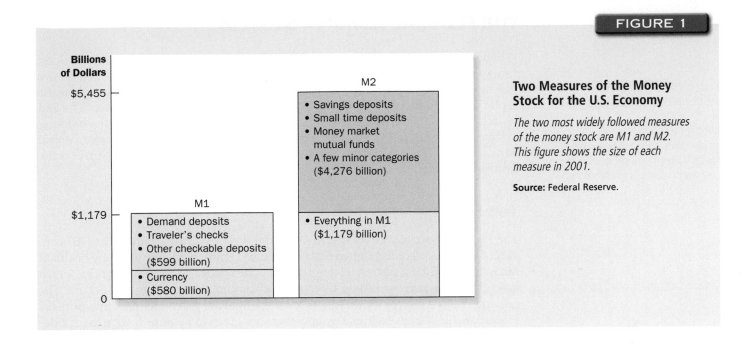

Two Measures of the Money Stock for the U.S. Economy

The two most widely followed measures of the money stock are M1 and M2. This figure shows the size of each measure in 2001.

Source: Federal Reserve.

Case Study
WHERE IS ALL THE CURRENCY?

One puzzle about the money stock of the U.S. economy concerns the amount of currency. In 2001 there was about $580 billion of currency outstanding. To put this number in perspective, we can divide it by 212 million, the number of adults (age 16 and over) in the United States. This calculation implies that the average adult holds about $2,734 of currency. Most people are surprised to learn that our economy has so much currency because they carry far less than this in their wallets.

Who is holding all this currency? No one knows for sure, but there are two plausible explanations.

The first explanation is that much of the currency is being held abroad. In foreign countries without a stable monetary system, people often prefer U.S. dollars to domestic assets. It is, in fact, not unusual to see U.S. dollars being used overseas as the medium of exchange, unit of account, and store of value.

The second explanation is that much of the currency is being held by drug dealers, tax evaders, and other criminals. For most people in the U.S. economy, currency is not a particularly good way to hold wealth. Not only can currency be lost or stolen, but it also does not earn interest, whereas a bank deposit does. Thus, most people hold only small amounts of currency. By contrast, criminals may avoid putting their wealth in banks, because a bank deposit gives police a paper trail with which to trace their illegal activities. For criminals, currency may be the best store of value available. ●

QuickQuiz List and describe the three functions of money.

THE FEDERAL RESERVE SYSTEM

Whenever an economy relies on a system of fiat money, as the U.S. economy does, some agency must be responsible for regulating the system. In the United States, that agency is the **Federal Reserve**, often simply called the **Fed.** If you look at the top of a dollar bill, you will see that it is called a "Federal Reserve Note." The Fed is an example of a **central bank**—an institution designed to oversee the banking system and regulate the quantity of money in the economy. Other major central banks around the world include the Bank of England, the Bank of Japan, and the European Central Bank.

Federal Reserve (Fed)
the central bank of the United States

central bank
an institution designed to oversee the banking system and regulate the quantity of money in the economy

The Fed's Organization

The Federal Reserve was created in 1914 after a series of bank failures in 1907 convinced Congress that the United States needed a central bank to ensure the health of the nation's banking system. Today, the Fed is run by its Board of Governors, which has seven members appointed by the president and confirmed by the Senate. The governors have 14-year terms. Just as federal judges are given lifetime appointments to insulate them from politics, Fed governors are given long terms to give them independence from short-term political pressures when they formulate monetary policy.

Among the seven members of the Board of Governors, the most important is the chairman. The chairman directs the Fed staff, presides over board meetings, and testifies regularly about Fed policy in front of congressional committees. The president appoints the chairman to a four-year term. As this book was going to press, the chairman of the Fed was Alan Greenspan, who was originally appointed in 1987 by President Reagan and was later reappointed by Presidents Bush and Clinton.

The Federal Reserve System is made up of the Federal Reserve Board in Washington, D.C., and 12 regional Federal Reserve Banks located in major cities around the country. The presidents of the regional banks are chosen by each bank's board of directors, whose members are typically drawn from the region's banking and business community.

The Fed has two related jobs. The first job is to regulate banks and ensure the health of the banking system. This task is largely the responsibility of the regional Federal Reserve Banks. In particular, the Fed monitors each bank's financial condition and facilitates bank transactions by clearing checks. It also acts as a bank's bank. That is, the Fed makes loans to banks when banks themselves want to borrow. When financially troubled banks find themselves short of cash, the Fed acts as a *lender of last resort*—a lender to those who cannot borrow anywhere else—in order to maintain stability in the overall banking system.

The Fed's second and more important job is to control the quantity of money that is made available in the economy, called the **money supply.** Decisions by policymakers concerning the money supply constitute **monetary policy.** At the Federal Reserve, monetary policy is made by the Federal Open Market Committee (FOMC). The FOMC meets about every six weeks in Washington, D.C., to discuss the condition of the economy and consider changes in monetary policy.

money supply
the quantity of money available in the economy

monetary policy
the setting of the money supply by policymakers in the central bank

The Federal Open Market Committee

The Federal Open Market Committee is made up of the seven members of the Board of Governors and five of the 12 regional bank presidents. All 12 regional presidents attend each FOMC meeting, but only five get to vote. The five with voting rights rotate among the 12 regional presidents over time. The president of the New York Fed always gets a vote, however, because New York is the traditional financial center of the U.S. economy and because all Fed purchases and sales of government bonds are conducted at the New York Fed's trading desk.

Through the decisions of the FOMC, the Fed has the power to increase or decrease the number of dollars in the economy. In simple metaphorical terms, you can imagine the Fed printing up dollar bills and dropping them around the country by helicopter. Similarly, you can imagine the Fed using a giant vacuum cleaner to suck dollar bills out of people's wallets. Although in practice the Fed's methods for changing the money supply are more complex and subtle than this, the helicopter-vacuum metaphor is a good first approximation to the meaning of monetary policy.

We discuss later in this chapter how the Fed actually changes the money supply, but it is worth noting here that the Fed's primary tool is *open-market operations*—the purchase and sale of U.S. government bonds. (Recall that a U.S. government bond is a certificate of indebtedness of the federal government.) If the FOMC decides to increase the money supply, the Fed creates dollars and uses them to buy government bonds from the public in the nation's bond markets. After the purchase, these dollars are in the hands of the public. Thus, an open-market purchase of bonds by the Fed increases the money supply. Conversely, if the FOMC decides to decrease the money supply, the Fed sells government bonds from its portfolio to the public in the nation's bond markets. After the sale, the dollars it receives for the bonds are out of the hands of the public. Thus, an open-market sale of bonds by the Fed decreases the money supply.

The Fed is an important institution because changes in the money supply can profoundly affect the economy. One of the *Ten Principles of Economics* in Chapter 1 is that prices rise when the government prints too much money. Another of the *Ten Principles of Economics* is that society faces a short-run tradeoff between inflation and unemployment. The power of the FOMC rests on these principles. For reasons we discuss more fully in the coming chapters, the FOMC's policy decisions have an important influence on the economy's rate of inflation in the long run and the economy's employment and production in the short run. Indeed, the chairman of the Federal Reserve has been called the second most powerful person in the United States.

QuickQuiz What are the primary responsibilities of the Federal Reserve? If the Fed wants to increase the supply of money, how does it usually do so?

BANKS AND THE MONEY SUPPLY

So far we have introduced the concept of "money" and discussed how the Federal Reserve controls the supply of money by buying and selling government bonds in open-market operations. Although this explanation of the money supply is correct, it is not complete. In particular, it omits the central role that banks play in the monetary system.

Recall that the amount of money you hold includes both currency (the bills in your wallet and coins in your pocket) and demand deposits (the balance in your checking account). Because demand deposits are held in banks, the behavior of banks can influence the quantity of demand deposits in the economy and,

"I've heard a lot about money, and now I'd like to try some."

therefore, the money supply. This section examines how banks affect the money supply and how they complicate the Fed's job of controlling the money supply.

The Simple Case of 100-Percent-Reserve Banking

To see how banks influence the money supply, it is useful to imagine first a world without any banks at all. In this simple world, currency is the only form of money. To be concrete, let's suppose that the total quantity of currency is $100. The supply of money is, therefore, $100.

Now suppose that someone opens a bank, appropriately called First National Bank. First National Bank is only a depository institution—that is, it accepts deposits but does not make loans. The purpose of the bank is to give depositors a safe place to keep their money. Whenever a person deposits some money, the bank keeps the money in its vault until the depositor comes to withdraw it or writes a check against his or her balance. Deposits that banks have received but have not loaned out are called **reserves.** In this imaginary economy, all deposits are held as reserves, so this system is called *100-percent-reserve banking.*

We can express the financial position of First National Bank with a *T-account,* which is a simplified accounting statement that shows changes in a bank's assets and liabilities. Here is the T-account for First National Bank if the economy's entire $100 of money is deposited in the bank:

reserves
deposits that banks have received but have not loaned out

FIRST NATIONAL BANK

Assets		Liabilities	
Reserves	$100.00	Deposits	$100.00

On the left-hand side of the T-account are the bank's assets of $100 (the reserves it holds in its vaults). On the right-hand side of the T-account are the bank's liabilities of $100 (the amount it owes to its depositors). Notice that the assets and liabilities of First National Bank exactly balance.

Now consider the money supply in this imaginary economy. Before First National Bank opens, the money supply is the $100 of currency that people are holding. After the bank opens and people deposit their currency, the money supply is the $100 of demand deposits. (There is no longer any currency outstanding, for it is all in the bank vault.) Each deposit in the bank reduces currency and raises demand deposits by exactly the same amount, leaving the money supply unchanged. Thus, *if banks hold all deposits in reserve, banks do not influence the supply of money.*

Money Creation with Fractional-Reserve Banking

Eventually, the bankers at First National Bank may start to reconsider their policy of 100-percent-reserve banking. Leaving all that money sitting idle in their vaults seems unnecessary. Why not use some of it to make loans? Families buying houses, firms building new factories, and students paying for college would all be happy to pay interest to borrow some of that money for a while. Of course, First National Bank has to keep some reserves so that currency is available if depositors want to make withdrawals. But if the flow of new deposits is roughly the same as the flow of withdrawals, First National needs to keep only a fraction of its deposits in reserve. Thus, First National adopts a system called **fractional-reserve banking.**

The fraction of total deposits that a bank holds as reserves is called the **reserve ratio.** This ratio is determined by a combination of government regulation and bank policy. As we discuss more fully later in the chapter, the Fed places a minimum on the amount of reserves that banks hold, called a *reserve requirement.* In addition, banks may hold reserves above the legal minimum, called *excess reserves,* so they can be more confident that they will not run short of cash. For our purpose here, we just take the reserve ratio as given and examine what fractional-reserve banking means for the money supply.

Let's suppose that First National has a reserve ratio of 10 percent. This means that it keeps 10 percent of its deposits in reserve and loans out the rest. Now let's look again at the bank's T-account:

fractional-reserve banking
a banking system in which banks hold only a fraction of deposits as reserves

reserve ratio
the fraction of deposits that banks hold as reserves

FIRST NATIONAL BANK

Assets		Liabilities	
Reserves	$10.00	Deposits	$100.00
Loans	90.00		

First National still has $100 in liabilities because making the loans did not alter the bank's obligation to its depositors. But now the bank has two kinds of assets: It has $10 of reserves in its vault, and it has loans of $90. (These loans are liabilities of the people taking out the loans but they are assets of the bank making the loans, because the borrowers will later repay the bank.) In total, First National's assets still equal its liabilities.

Once again consider the supply of money in the economy. Before First National makes any loans, the money supply is the $100 of deposits in the bank. Yet when First National makes these loans, the money supply increases. The depositors still have demand deposits totaling $100, but now the borrowers hold $90 in currency. The money supply (which equals currency plus demand deposits) equals $190. Thus, *when banks hold only a fraction of deposits in reserve, banks create money.*

At first, this creation of money by fractional-reserve banking may seem too good to be true because it appears that the bank has created money out of thin air. To make this creation of money seem less miraculous, note that when First National Bank loans out some of its reserves and creates money, it does not create any wealth. Loans from First National give the borrowers some currency and thus the ability to buy goods and services. Yet the borrowers are also taking on debts, so the loans do not make them any richer. In other words, as a bank creates the asset of money, it also creates a corresponding liability for its borrowers. At the end of this process of money creation, the economy is more liquid in the sense that there is more of the medium of exchange, but the economy is no wealthier than before.

The Money Multiplier

The creation of money does not stop with First National Bank. Suppose the borrower from First National uses the $90 to buy something from someone who then deposits the currency in Second National Bank. Here is the T-account for Second National Bank:

SECOND NATIONAL BANK

Assets		Liabilities	
Reserves	$ 9.00	Deposits	$90.00
Loans	81.00		

After the deposit, this bank has liabilities of $90. If Second National also has a reserve ratio of 10 percent, it keeps assets of $9 in reserve and makes $81 in loans. In this way, Second National Bank creates an additional $81 of money. If this $81 is eventually deposited in Third National Bank, which also has a reserve ratio of 10 percent, this bank keeps $8.10 in reserve and makes $72.90 in loans. Here is the T-account for Third National Bank:

THIRD NATIONAL BANK

Assets		Liabilities	
Reserves	$ 8.10	Deposits	$81.00
Loans	72.90		

The process goes on and on. Each time that money is deposited and a bank loan is made, more money is created.

How much money is eventually created in this economy? Let's add it up:

$$
\begin{aligned}
\text{Original deposit} &= \$\ 100.00 \\
\text{First National lending} &= \$\ \ \ 90.00\ [= .9 \times \$100.00] \\
\text{Second National lending} &= \$\ \ \ 81.00\ [= .9 \times \$90.00] \\
\text{Third National lending} &= \$\ \ \ 72.90\ [= .9 \times \$81.00] \\
&\quad\ \ \vdots \\
\text{Total money supply} &= \$1{,}000.00
\end{aligned}
$$

It turns out that even though this process of money creation can continue forever, it does not create an infinite amount of money. If you laboriously add the infinite sequence of numbers in the foregoing example, you find the $100 of reserves generates $1,000 of money. The amount of money the banking system generates with each dollar of reserves is called the **money multiplier.** In this imaginary economy, where the $100 of reserves generates $1,000 of money, the money multiplier is 10.

money multiplier
the amount of money the banking system generates with each dollar of reserves

What determines the size of the money multiplier? It turns out that the answer is simple: *The money multiplier is the reciprocal of the reserve ratio.* If R is the reserve ratio for all banks in the economy, then each dollar of reserves generates $1/R$ dollars of money. In our example, $R = 1/10$, so the money multiplier is 10.

This reciprocal formula for the money multiplier makes sense. If a bank holds $1,000 in deposits, then a reserve ratio of 1/10 (10 percent) means that the bank must hold $100 in reserves. The money multiplier just turns this idea around: If the banking system as a whole holds a total of $100 in reserves, it can have only $1,000 in deposits. In other words, if R is the ratio of reserves to deposits at each bank (that is, the reserve ratio), then the ratio of deposits to reserves in the banking system (that is, the money multiplier) must be $1/R$.

This formula shows how the amount of money banks create depends on the reserve ratio. If the reserve ratio were only 1/20 (5 percent), then the banking system would have 20 times as much in deposits as in reserves, implying a money multiplier of 20. Each dollar of reserves would generate $20 of money. Similarly, if the reserve ratio were 1/5 (20 percent), deposits would be 5 times reserves, the money multiplier would be 5, and each dollar of reserves would generate $5 of money. *Thus, the higher the reserve ratio, the less of each deposit banks loan out, and the smaller the money multiplier.* In the special case of 100-percent-reserve banking, the reserve ratio is 1, the money multiplier is 1, and banks do not make loans or create money.

The Fed's Tools of Monetary Control

As we have already discussed, the Federal Reserve is responsible for controlling the supply of money in the economy. Now that we understand how fractional-reserve banking works, we are in a better position to understand how the Fed carries out this job. Because banks create money in a system of fractional-reserve banking, the Fed's control of the money supply is indirect. When the Fed decides to change the money supply, it must consider how its actions will work through the banking system.

The Fed has three tools in its monetary toolbox: open-market operations, reserve requirements, and the discount rate. Let's discuss how the Fed uses each of these tools.

Open-Market Operations As we noted earlier, the Fed conducts **open-market operations** when it buys or sells government bonds. To increase the money supply, the Fed instructs its bond traders at the New York Fed to buy bonds from the public in the nation's bond markets. The dollars the Fed pays for the bonds increase the number of dollars in circulation. Some of these new dollars are held as currency, and some are deposited in banks. Each new dollar held as currency increases the money supply by exactly $1. Each new dollar deposited in a bank increases the money supply to an even greater extent because it increases reserves and, thereby, the amount of money that the banking system can create.

> **open-market operations**
> the purchase and sale of U.S. government bonds by the Fed

To reduce the money supply, the Fed does just the opposite: It sells government bonds to the public in the nation's bond markets. The public pays for these bonds with its holdings of currency and bank deposits, directly reducing the amount of money in circulation. In addition, as people make withdrawals from banks, banks find themselves with a smaller quantity of reserves. In response, banks reduce the amount of lending, and the process of money creation reverses itself.

Open-market operations are easy to conduct. In fact, the Fed's purchases and sales of government bonds in the nation's bond markets are similar to the transactions that any individual might undertake for his own portfolio. (Of course, when an individual buys or sells a bond, money changes hands, but the amount of money in circulation remains the same.) In addition, the Fed can use open-market operations to change the money supply by a small or large amount on any day without major changes in laws or bank regulations. Therefore, open-market operations are the tool of monetary policy that the Fed uses most often.

Reserve Requirements The Fed also influences the money supply with **reserve requirements,** which are regulations on the minimum amount of reserves that banks must hold against deposits. Reserve requirements influence how much money the banking system can create with each dollar of reserves. An increase in

> **reserve requirements**
> regulations on the minimum amount of reserves that banks must hold against deposits

reserve requirements means that banks must hold more reserves and, therefore, can loan out less of each dollar that is deposited; as a result, it raises the reserve ratio, lowers the money multiplier, and decreases the money supply. Conversely, a decrease in reserve requirements lowers the reserve ratio, raises the money multiplier, and increases the money supply.

The Fed uses changes in reserve requirements only rarely because frequent changes would disrupt the business of banking. When the Fed increases reserve requirements, for instance, some banks find themselves short of reserves, even though they have seen no change in deposits. As a result, they have to curtail lending until they build their level of reserves to the new required level.

discount rate
the interest rate on the loans that the Fed makes to banks

The Discount Rate The third tool in the Fed's toolbox is the **discount rate,** the interest rate on the loans that the Fed makes to banks. A bank borrows from the Fed when it has too few reserves to meet reserve requirements. This might occur because the bank made too many loans or because it has experienced recent withdrawals. When the Fed makes such a loan to a bank, the banking system has more reserves than it otherwise would, and these additional reserves allow the banking system to create more money.

The Fed can alter the money supply by changing the discount rate. A higher discount rate discourages banks from borrowing reserves from the Fed. Thus, an increase in the discount rate reduces the quantity of reserves in the banking system, which in turn reduces the money supply. Conversely, a lower discount rate encourages banks to borrow from the Fed, increases the quantity of reserves, and increases the money supply.

The Fed uses discount lending not only to control the money supply but also to help financial institutions when they are in trouble. For example, in 1984 rumors circulated that Continental Illinois National Bank had made a large number of bad loans, and these rumors induced many depositors to withdraw their deposits. As part of an effort to save the bank, the Fed acted as a lender of last resort and loaned Continental Illinois more than $5 billion. Similarly, when the stock market crashed on October 19, 1987, many Wall Street brokerage firms found themselves temporarily in need of funds to finance the high volume of stock trading. The next morning, before the stock market opened, Fed Chairman Alan Greenspan announced the Fed's "readiness to serve as a source of liquidity to support the economic and financial system." Many economists believe that Greenspan's reaction to the stock crash was an important reason why it had so few repercussions.

Problems in Controlling the Money Supply

The Fed's three tools—open-market operations, reserve requirements, and the discount rate—have powerful effects on the money supply. Yet the Fed's control of the money supply is not precise. The Fed must wrestle with two problems, each of which arises because much of the money supply is created by our system of fractional-reserve banking.

The first problem is that the Fed does not control the amount of money that households choose to hold as deposits in banks. The more money households deposit, the more reserves banks have, and the more money the banking system can create. And the less money households deposit, the less reserves banks have, and the less money the banking system can create. To see why this is a problem, suppose that one day people begin to lose confidence in the banking system and, therefore, decide to withdraw deposits and hold more currency. When this happens, the banking system loses reserves and creates less money. The money supply falls, even without any Fed action.

The second problem of monetary control is that the Fed does not control the amount that bankers choose to lend. When money is deposited in a bank, it creates more money only when the bank loans it out. Because banks can choose to hold excess reserves instead, the Fed cannot be sure how much money the banking system will create. For instance, suppose that one day bankers become more cautious about economic conditions and decide to make fewer loans and hold greater reserves. In this case, the banking system creates less money than it otherwise would. Because of the bankers' decision, the money supply falls.

Hence, in a system of fractional-reserve banking, the amount of money in the economy depends in part on the behavior of depositors and bankers. Because the Fed cannot control or perfectly predict this behavior, it cannot perfectly control the money supply. Yet, if the Fed is vigilant, these problems need not be large. The Fed collects data on deposits and reserves from banks every week, so it is quickly aware of any changes in depositor or banker behavior. It can, therefore, respond to these changes and keep the money supply close to whatever level it chooses.

Case Study

BANK RUNS AND THE MONEY SUPPLY

Although you have probably never witnessed a bank run in real life, you may have seen one depicted in movies such as *Mary Poppins* or *It's a Wonderful Life*. A bank run occurs when depositors suspect that a bank may go bankrupt and, therefore, "run" to the bank to withdraw their deposits.

Bank runs are a problem for banks under fractional-reserve banking. Because a bank holds only a fraction of its deposits in reserve, it cannot satisfy withdrawal requests from all depositors. Even if the bank is in fact *solvent* (meaning that its assets exceed its liabilities), it will not have enough cash on hand to allow all depositors immediate access to all of their money. When a run occurs, the bank is forced to close its doors until some bank loans are repaid or until some lender of last resort (such as the Fed) provides it with the currency it needs to satisfy depositors.

Bank runs complicate the control of the money supply. An important example of this problem occurred during the Great Depression in the early 1930s. After a wave of bank runs and bank closings, households and bankers became more cautious. Households withdrew their deposits from banks, preferring to hold their money in the form of currency. This decision reversed the process of money creation, as bankers responded to falling reserves by reducing bank loans. At the same time, bankers increased their reserve ratios so that they would have enough cash on hand to meet their depositors' demands in any future bank runs. The higher reserve ratio reduced the money multiplier, which also reduced the money supply. From 1929 to 1933, the money supply fell by 28 percent, even without the Federal Reserve taking any deliberate contractionary action. Many economists point to this massive fall in the money supply to explain the high unemployment and falling prices that prevailed during this period. (In future chapters we examine the mechanisms by which changes in the money supply affect unemployment and prices.)

A not-so-wonderful bank run

Today, bank runs are not a major problem for the banking system or the Fed. The federal government now guarantees the safety of deposits at most banks, primarily through the Federal Deposit Insurance Corporation (FDIC). Depositors do not run on their banks because they are confident that, even if their bank goes bankrupt, the FDIC will make good on the deposits. The policy of government deposit insurance has costs: Bankers whose deposits are guaranteed may have too little incentive to avoid bad risks when making loans. But one benefit of deposit insurance is a more stable banking system. As a result, most people see bank runs only in the movies. ●

QuickQuiz Describe how banks create money. ● If the Fed wanted to use all three of its policy tools to decrease the money supply, what would it do?

CONCLUSION

Some years ago, a book made the best-seller list with the title *Secrets of the Temple: How the Federal Reserve Runs the Country*. Although no doubt an exaggeration, this title did highlight the important role of the monetary system in our daily lives. Whenever we buy or sell anything, we are relying on the extraordinarily useful social convention called "money." Now that we know what money is and what determines its supply, we can discuss how changes in the quantity of money affect the economy. We begin to address that topic in the next chapter.

SUMMARY

- The term *money* refers to assets that people regularly use to buy goods and services.

- Money serves three functions. As a medium of exchange, it provides the item used to make transactions. As a unit of account, it provides the way in which prices and other economic values are recorded. As a store of value, it provides a way of transferring purchasing power from the present to the future.

- Commodity money, such as gold, is money that has intrinsic value: It would be valued even if it were not used as money. Fiat money, such as paper dollars, is money without intrinsic value: It would be worthless if it were not used as money.

- In the U.S. economy, money takes the form of currency and various types of bank deposits, such as checking accounts.

- The Federal Reserve, the central bank of the United States, is responsible for regulating the U.S. monetary system. The Fed chairman is appointed by the president and confirmed by Congress every four years. The chairman is the lead member of the Federal Open Market Committee, which meets about every six weeks to consider changes in monetary policy.

- The Fed controls the money supply primarily through open-market operations: The purchase of government bonds increases the money supply, and the sale of government bonds decreases the money supply. The Fed can also expand the money supply by lowering reserve requirements or decreasing the discount rate, and it can contract the money supply by raising reserve requirements or increasing the discount rate.

- When banks loan out some of their deposits, they increase the quantity of money in the economy. Because of this role of banks in determining the money supply, the Fed's control of the money supply is imperfect.

KEY CONCEPTS

money, p. 332
medium of exchange, p. 333
unit of account, p. 333
store of value, p. 333
liquidity, p. 333
commodity money, p. 333
fiat money, p. 334

currency, p. 335
demand deposits, p. 336
Federal Reserve (Fed), p. 338
central bank, p. 338
money supply, p. 338
monetary policy, p. 338
reserves, p. 340

fractional-reserve banking, p. 341
reserve ratio, p. 341
money multiplier, p. 342
open-market operations, p. 343
reserve requirements, p. 343
discount rate, p. 344

QUESTIONS FOR REVIEW

1. What distinguishes money from other assets in the economy?

2. What is commodity money? What is fiat money? Which kind do we use?

3. What are demand deposits, and why should they be included in the stock of money?

4. Who is responsible for setting monetary policy in the United States? How is this group chosen?

5. If the Fed wants to increase the money supply with open-market operations, what does it do?

6. Why don't banks hold 100 percent reserves? How is the amount of reserves banks hold related to the amount of money the banking system creates?

7. What is the discount rate? What happens to the money supply when the Fed raises the discount rate?

8. What are reserve requirements? What happens to the money supply when the Fed raises reserve requirements?

9. Why can't the Fed control the money supply perfectly?

PROBLEMS AND APPLICATIONS

1. Which of the following are money in the U.S. economy? Which are not? Explain your answers by discussing each of the three functions of money.
   a. a U.S. penny
   b. a Mexican peso
   c. a Picasso painting
   d. a plastic credit card

2. Every month *Yankee* magazine includes a "Swopper's [*sic*] Column" of offers to barter goods and services. Here is an example: "Will swop custom-designed wedding gown and up to 6 bridesmaids' gowns for 2 round-trip plane tickets and 3 nights' lodging in the countryside of England." Why would it be difficult to run our economy using a "Swopper's Column" instead of money? In light of your answer, why might the *Yankee* "Swopper's Column" exist?

3. What characteristics of an asset make it useful as a medium of exchange? As a store of value?

4. Consider how the following situations would affect the economy's monetary system.
   a. Suppose that the people on Yap discovered an easy way to make limestone wheels. How would this development affect the usefulness of stone wheels as money? Explain.
   b. Suppose that someone in the United States discovered an easy way to counterfeit $100 bills. How would this development affect the U.S. monetary system? Explain.

5. Go to the Web site of the Federal Reserve Bank of St. Louis (http://www.stls.frb.gov).
   a. Find the FRED database. Produce a graph of total currency in the U.S. economy. What happened to currency holdings at the end of 1999? Can you explain this phenomenon?
   b. Find a map of the Federal Reserve districts. If you live in the United States, find what district you live in. Where is the Federal Reserve Bank for your district located?

(Extra credit: What state has two Federal Reserve Banks?)

6. Your uncle repays a $100 loan from Tenth National Bank by writing a $100 check from his TNB checking account. Use T-accounts to show the effect of this transaction on your uncle and on TNB. Has your uncle's wealth changed? Explain.

7. Beleaguered State Bank (BSB) holds $250 million in deposits and maintains a reserve ratio of 10 percent.
   a. Show a T-account for BSB.
   b. Now suppose that BSB's largest depositor withdraws $10 million in cash from her account. If BSB decides to restore its reserve ratio by reducing the amount of loans outstanding, show its new T-account.
   c. Explain what effect BSB's action will have on other banks.
   d. Why might it be difficult for BSB to take the action described in part (b)? Discuss another way for BSB to return to its original reserve ratio.

8. You take $100 you had kept under your pillow and deposit it in your bank account. If this $100 stays in the banking system as reserves and if banks hold reserves equal to 10 percent of deposits, by how much does the total amount of deposits in the banking system increase? By how much does the money supply increase?

9. The Federal Reserve conducts a $10 million open-market purchase of government bonds. If the required reserve ratio is 10 percent, what is the largest possible increase in the money supply that could result? Explain. What is the smallest possible increase? Explain.

10. Suppose that the T-account for First National Bank is as follows:

Assets		Liabilities	
Reserves	$100,000	Deposits	$500,000
Loans	400,000		

   a. If the Fed requires banks to hold 5 percent of deposits as reserves, how much in excess reserves does First National now hold?

   b. Assume that all other banks hold only the required amount of reserves. If First National decides to reduce its reserves to only the required amount, by how much would the economy's money supply increase?

11. Suppose that the reserve requirement for checking deposits is 10 percent and that banks do not hold any excess reserves.
   a. If the Fed sells $1 million of government bonds, what is the effect on the economy's reserves and money supply?
   b. Now suppose the Fed lowers the reserve requirement to 5 percent, but banks choose to hold another 5 percent of deposits as excess reserves. Why might banks do so? What is the overall change in the money multiplier and the money supply as a result of these actions?

12. Assume that the banking system has total reserves of $100 billion. Assume also that required reserves are 10 percent of checking deposits, and that banks hold no excess reserves and households hold no currency.
   a. What is the money multiplier? What is the money supply?
   b. If the Fed now raises required reserves to 20 percent of deposits, what is the change in reserves and the change in the money supply?

13. (This problem is challenging.) The economy of Elmendyn contains 2,000 $1 bills.
   a. If people hold all money as currency, what is the quantity of money?
   b. If people hold all money as demand deposits and banks maintain 100 percent reserves, what is the quantity of money?
   c. If people hold equal amounts of currency and demand deposits and banks maintain 100 percent reserves, what is the quantity of money?
   d. If people hold all money as demand deposits and banks maintain a reserve ratio of 10 percent, what is the quantity of money?
   e. If people hold equal amounts of currency and demand deposits and banks maintain a reserve ratio of 10 percent, what is the quantity of money?

 For more study tools, please visit http://mankiwXtra.swlearning.com.

MONEY GROWTH AND INFLATION

Although today you need a dollar or two to buy yourself an ice-cream cone, life was very different 60 years ago. In one Trenton, New Jersey, candy store (run, incidentally, by this author's grandmother in the 1930s), ice-cream cones came in two sizes. A cone with a small scoop of ice cream cost three cents. Hungry customers could buy a large scoop for a nickel.

You are probably not surprised at the increase in the price of ice cream. In our economy, most prices tend to rise over time. This increase in the overall level of prices is called *inflation*. Earlier in the book we examined how economists measure the inflation rate as the percentage change in the consumer price index, the GDP deflator, or some other index of the overall price level. These price indexes show that, over the past 60 years, prices have risen on average about 5 percent per year. Accumulated over so many years, a 5 percent annual inflation rate leads to an 18-fold increase in the price level.

Inflation may seem natural and inevitable to a person who grew up in the United States during the second half of the twentieth century, but in fact it is not inevitable at all. There were long periods in the nineteenth century during which most prices fell—a phenomenon called *deflation*. The average level of prices in the

U.S. economy was 23 percent lower in 1896 than in 1880, and this deflation was a major issue in the presidential election of 1896. Farmers, who had accumulated large debts, were suffering when the fall in crop prices reduced their incomes and thus their ability to pay off their debts. They advocated government policies to reverse the deflation.

Although inflation has been the norm in more recent history, there has been substantial variation in the rate at which prices rise. During the 1990s, prices rose at an average rate of about 2 percent per year. By contrast, in the 1970s, prices rose by 7 percent per year, which meant a doubling of the price level over the decade. The public often views such high rates of inflation as a major economic problem. In fact, when President Jimmy Carter ran for reelection in 1980, challenger Ronald Reagan pointed to high inflation as one of the failures of Carter's economic policy.

International data show an even broader range of inflation experiences. Germany after World War I experienced a spectacular example of inflation. The price of a newspaper rose from 0.3 marks in January 1921 to 70,000,000 marks less than two years later. Other prices rose by similar amounts. An extraordinarily high rate of inflation such as this is called *hyperinflation*. The German hyperinflation had such an adverse effect on the German economy that it is often viewed as one contributor to the rise of Nazism and, as a result, World War II. Over the past 50 years, with this episode still in mind, German policymakers have been extraordinarily averse to inflation, and Germany has had much lower inflation than the United States.

What determines whether an economy experiences inflation and, if so, how much? This chapter answers this question by developing the *quantity theory of money*. Chapter 1 summarized this theory as one of the *Ten Principles of Economics*: Prices rise when the government prints too much money. This insight has a long and venerable tradition among economists. The quantity theory was discussed by the famous eighteenth-century philosopher David Hume and has been advocated more recently by the prominent economist Milton Friedman. This theory of inflation can explain both moderate inflations, such as those we have experienced in the United States, and hyperinflations, such as those experienced in interwar Germany and, more recently, in some Latin American countries.

After developing a theory of inflation, we turn to a related question: Why is inflation a problem? At first glance, the answer to this question may seem obvious: Inflation is a problem because people don't like it. In the 1970s, when the United States experienced a relatively high rate of inflation, opinion polls placed inflation as the most important issue facing the nation. President Ford echoed this sentiment in 1974 when he called inflation "public enemy number one." Ford wore a "WIN" button on his lapel—for Whip Inflation Now.

But what, exactly, are the costs that inflation imposes on a society? The answer may surprise you. Identifying the various costs of inflation is not as straightforward as it first appears. As a result, although all economists decry hyperinflation, some economists argue that the costs of moderate inflation are not nearly as large as the general public believes.

THE CLASSICAL THEORY OF INFLATION

We begin our study of inflation by developing the quantity theory of money. This theory is often called "classical" because it was developed by some of the earliest thinkers about economic issues. Most economists today rely on this theory to explain the long-run determinants of the price level and the inflation rate.

The Level of Prices and the Value of Money

Suppose we observe over some period of time the price of an ice-cream cone rising from a nickel to a dollar. What conclusion should we draw from the fact that people are willing to give up so much more money in exchange for a cone? It is possible that people have come to enjoy ice cream more (perhaps because some chemist has developed a miraculous new flavor). Yet that is probably not the case. It is more likely that people's enjoyment of ice cream has stayed roughly the same and that, over time, the money used to buy ice cream has become less valuable. Indeed, the first insight about inflation is that it is more about the value of money than about the value of goods.

This insight helps point the way toward a theory of inflation. When the consumer price index and other measures of the price level rise, commentators are often tempted to look at the many individual prices that make up these price indexes: "The CPI rose by 3 percent last month, led by a 20 percent rise in the price of coffee and a 30 percent rise in the price of heating oil." Although this approach does contain some interesting information about what's happening in the economy, it also misses a key point: Inflation is an economy-wide phenomenon that concerns, first and foremost, the value of the economy's medium of exchange.

The economy's overall price level can be viewed in two ways. So far, we have viewed the price level as the price of a basket of goods and services. When the price level rises, people have to pay more for the goods and services they buy. Alternatively, we can view the price level as a measure of the value of money. A rise in the price level means a lower value of money because each dollar in your wallet now buys a smaller quantity of goods and services.

It may help to express these ideas mathematically. Suppose P is the price level as measured, for instance, by the consumer price index or the GDP deflator. Then P measures the number of dollars needed to buy a basket of goods and services. Now turn this idea around: The quantity of goods and services that can be bought with \$1 equals $1/P$. In other words, if P is the price of goods and services measured in terms of money, $1/P$ is the value of money measured in terms of goods and services. Thus, when the overall price level rises, the value of money falls.

"So what's it going to be? The same size as last year or the same price as last year?"

Money Supply, Money Demand, and Monetary Equilibrium

What determines the value of money? The answer to this question, like many in economics, is supply and demand. Just as the supply and demand for bananas determines the price of bananas, the supply and demand for money determines the value of money. Thus, our next step in developing the quantity theory of money is to consider the determinants of money supply and money demand.

First consider money supply. In the preceding chapter we discussed how the Federal Reserve, together with the banking system, determines the supply of money. When the Fed sells bonds in open-market operations, it receives dollars in exchange and contracts the money supply. When the Fed buys government bonds, it pays out dollars and expands the money supply. In addition, if any of these dollars are deposited in banks which then hold them as reserves, the money multiplier swings into action, and these open-market operations can have an even greater effect on the money supply. For our purposes in this chapter, we ignore the complications introduced by the banking system and simply take the quantity of money supplied as a policy variable that the Fed controls.

Now consider money demand. Most fundamentally, the demand for money reflects how much wealth people want to hold in liquid form. Many factors influence the quantity of money demanded. The amount of currency that people hold in their wallets, for instance, depends on how much they rely on credit cards and on whether an automatic teller machine is easy to find. And, as we will emphasize in Chapter 21, the quantity of money demanded depends on the interest rate that a person could earn by using the money to buy an interest-bearing bond rather than leaving it in a wallet or low-interest checking account.

Although many variables affect the demand for money, one variable stands out in importance: the average level of prices in the economy. People hold money because it is the medium of exchange. Unlike other assets, such as bonds or stocks, people can use money to buy the goods and services on their shopping lists. How much money they choose to hold for this purpose depends on the prices of those goods and services. The higher prices are, the more money the typical transaction requires, and the more money people will choose to hold in their wallets and checking accounts. That is, a higher price level (a lower value of money) increases the quantity of money demanded.

What ensures that the quantity of money the Fed supplies balances the quantity of money people demand? The answer, it turns out, depends on the time horizon being considered. Later in this book we will examine the short-run answer, and we will see that interest rates play a key role. In the long run, however, the answer is different and much simpler. *In the long run, the overall level of prices adjusts to the level at which the demand for money equals the supply.* If the price level is above the equilibrium level, people will want to hold more money than the Fed has created, so the price level must fall to balance supply and demand. If the price level is below the equilibrium level, people will want to hold less money than the Fed has created, and the price level must rise to balance supply and demand. At the equilibrium price level, the quantity of money that people want to hold exactly balances the quantity of money supplied by the Fed.

Figure 1 illustrates these ideas. The horizontal axis of this graph shows the quantity of money. The left-hand vertical axis shows the value of money $1/P$, and the right-hand vertical axis shows the price level P. Notice that the price-level axis on the right is inverted: A low price level is shown near the top of this axis, and a high price level is shown near the bottom. This inverted axis illustrates that when the value of money is high (as shown near the top of the left axis), the price level is low (as shown near the top of the right axis).

The two curves in this figure are the supply and demand curves for money. The supply curve is vertical because the Fed has fixed the quantity of money available. The demand curve for money is downward sloping, indicating that when the value of money is low (and the price level is high), people demand a larger quantity of it to buy goods and services. At the equilibrium, shown in the figure as point A, the quantity of money demanded balances the quantity of money supplied. This equilibrium of money supply and money demand determines the value of money and the price level.

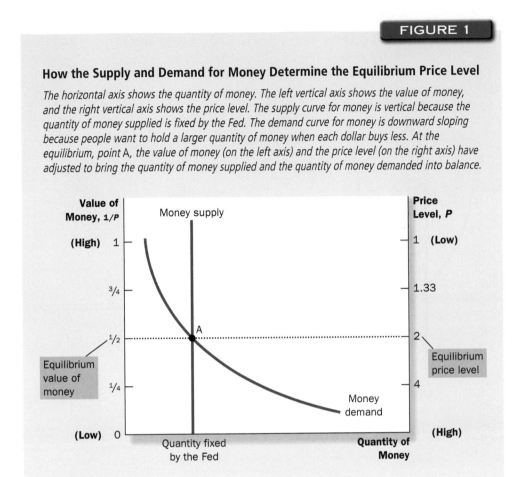

FIGURE 1

How the Supply and Demand for Money Determine the Equilibrium Price Level

The horizontal axis shows the quantity of money. The left vertical axis shows the value of money, and the right vertical axis shows the price level. The supply curve for money is vertical because the quantity of money supplied is fixed by the Fed. The demand curve for money is downward sloping because people want to hold a larger quantity of money when each dollar buys less. At the equilibrium, point A, the value of money (on the left axis) and the price level (on the right axis) have adjusted to bring the quantity of money supplied and the quantity of money demanded into balance.

The Effects of a Monetary Injection

Let's now consider the effects of a change in monetary policy. To do so, imagine that the economy is in equilibrium and then, suddenly, the Fed doubles the supply of money by printing some dollar bills and dropping them around the country from helicopters. (Or, less dramatically and more realistically, the Fed could inject money into the economy by buying some government bonds from the public in open-market operations.) What happens after such a monetary injection? How does the new equilibrium compare to the old one?

Figure 2 (p. 354) shows what happens. The monetary injection shifts the supply curve to the right from MS_1 to MS_2, and the equilibrium moves from point A to point B. As a result, the value of money (shown on the left axis) decreases from 1/2 to 1/4, and the equilibrium price level (shown on the right axis) increases from 2 to 4. In other words, when an increase in the money supply makes dollars more plentiful, the result is an increase in the price level that makes each dollar less valuable.

This explanation of how the price level is determined and why it might change over time is called the **quantity theory of money**. According to the quantity theory,

quantity theory of money
a theory asserting that the quantity of money available determines the price level and that the growth rate in the quantity of money available determines the inflation rate

FIGURE 2

An Increase in the Money Supply

When the Fed increases the supply of money, the money supply curve shifts from MS₁ to MS₂. The value of money (on the left axis) and the price level (on the right axis) adjust to bring supply and demand back into balance. The equilibrium moves from point A to point B. Thus, when an increase in the money supply makes dollars more plentiful, the price level increases, making each dollar less valuable.

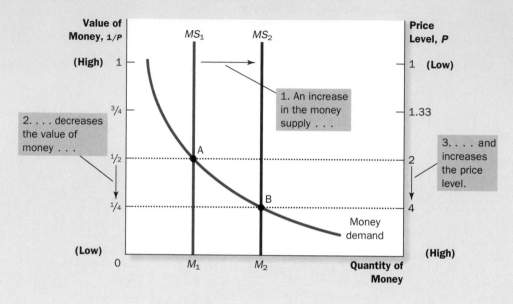

the quantity of money available in the economy determines the value of money, and growth in the quantity of money is the primary cause of inflation. As economist Milton Friedman once put it, "Inflation is always and everywhere a monetary phenomenon."

A Brief Look at the Adjustment Process

So far we have compared the old equilibrium and the new equilibrium after an injection of money. How does the economy get from the old to the new equilibrium? A complete answer to this question requires an understanding of short-run fluctuations in the economy, which we examine later in this book. Yet, even now, it is instructive to consider briefly the adjustment process that occurs after a change in money supply.

The immediate effect of a monetary injection is to create an excess supply of money. Before the injection, the economy was in equilibrium (point A in Figure 2). At the prevailing price level, people had exactly as much money as they wanted. But after the helicopters drop the new money and people pick it up off the streets, people have more dollars in their wallets than they want. At the prevailing price level, the quantity of money supplied now exceeds the quantity demanded.

People try to get rid of this excess supply of money in various ways. They might buy goods and services with their excess holdings of money. Or they might use this excess money to make loans to others by buying bonds or by depositing the money in a bank savings account. These loans allow other people to buy goods and services. In either case, the injection of money increases the demand for goods and services.

The economy's ability to supply goods and services, however, has not changed. As we saw in the chapter on production and growth, the economy's output of goods and services is determined by the available labor, physical capital, human capital, natural resources, and technological knowledge. None of these is altered by the injection of money.

Thus, the greater demand for goods and services causes the prices of goods and services to increase. The increase in the price level, in turn, increases the quantity of money demanded because people are using more dollars for every transaction. Eventually, the economy reaches a new equilibrium (point B in Figure 2) at which the quantity of money demanded again equals the quantity of money supplied. In this way, the overall price level for goods and services adjusts to bring money supply and money demand into balance.

The Classical Dichotomy and Monetary Neutrality

We have seen how changes in the money supply lead to changes in the average level of prices of goods and services. How do these monetary changes affect other important macroeconomic variables, such as production, employment, real wages, and real interest rates? This question has long intrigued economists. Indeed, the great philosopher David Hume wrote about it in the eighteenth century. The answer we give today owes much to Hume's analysis.

Hume and his contemporaries suggested that all economic variables should be divided into two groups. The first group consists of **nominal variables**—variables measured in monetary units. The second group consists of **real variables**—variables measured in physical units. For example, the income of corn farmers is a nominal variable because it is measured in dollars, whereas the quantity of corn they produce is a real variable because it is measured in bushels. Similarly, nominal GDP is a nominal variable because it measures the dollar value of the economy's output of goods and services; real GDP is a real variable because it measures the total quantity of goods and services produced and is not influenced by the current prices of those goods and services. This separation of variables into these groups is now called the **classical dichotomy.** (A *dichotomy* is a division into two groups, and *classical* refers to the earlier economic thinkers.)

Application of the classical dichotomy is somewhat tricky when we turn to prices. Prices in the economy are normally quoted in terms of money and, therefore, are nominal variables. For instance, when we say that the price of corn is $2 a bushel or that the price of wheat is $1 a bushel, both prices are nominal variables. But what about a *relative* price—the price of one thing compared to another? In our example, we could say that the price of a bushel of corn is two bushels of wheat. Notice that this relative price is no longer measured in terms of money. When comparing the prices of any two goods, the dollar signs cancel, and the resulting number is measured in physical units. The lesson is that dollar prices are nominal variables, whereas relative prices are real variables.

This lesson has several important applications. For instance, the real wage (the dollar wage adjusted for inflation) is a real variable because it measures the rate at

nominal variables
variables measured in monetary units

real variables
variables measured in physical units

classical dichotomy
the theoretical separation of nominal and real variables

which the economy exchanges goods and services for each unit of labor. Similarly, the real interest rate (the nominal interest rate adjusted for inflation) is a real variable because it measures the rate at which the economy exchanges goods and services produced today for goods and services produced in the future.

Why bother separating variables into these two groups? Hume suggested that the classical dichotomy is useful in analyzing the economy because different forces influence real and nominal variables. In particular, he argued, nominal variables are heavily influenced by developments in the economy's monetary system, whereas the monetary system is largely irrelevant for understanding the determinants of important real variables.

Notice that Hume's idea was implicit in our earlier discussions of the real economy in the long run. In previous chapters, we examined how real GDP, saving, investment, real interest rates, and unemployment are determined without any mention of the existence of money. As explained in that analysis, the economy's production of goods and services depends on productivity and factor supplies, the real interest rate adjusts to balance the supply and demand for loanable funds, the real wage adjusts to balance the supply and demand for labor, and unemployment results when the real wage is for some reason kept above its equilibrium level. These important conclusions have nothing to do with the quantity of money supplied.

Changes in the supply of money, according to Hume, affect nominal variables but not real variables. When the central bank doubles the money supply, the price level doubles, the dollar wage doubles, and all other dollar values double. Real variables, such as production, employment, real wages, and real interest rates, are unchanged. This irrelevance of monetary changes for real variables is called **monetary neutrality.**

monetary neutrality
the proposition that changes in the money supply do not affect real variables

An analogy sheds light on the meaning of monetary neutrality. Recall that, as the unit of account, money is the yardstick we use to measure economic transactions. When a central bank doubles the money supply, all prices double, and the value of the unit of account falls by half. A similar change would occur if the government were to reduce the length of the yard from 36 to 18 inches: As a result of the new unit of measurement, all *measured* distances (nominal variables) would double, but the *actual* distances (real variables) would remain the same. The dollar, like the yard, is merely a unit of measurement, so a change in its value should not have important real effects.

Is this conclusion of monetary neutrality a realistic description of the world in which we live? The answer is: not completely. A change in the length of the yard from 36 to 18 inches would not matter much in the long run, but in the short run it would certainly lead to confusion and various mistakes. Similarly, most economists today believe that over short periods of time—within the span of a year or two—there is reason to think that monetary changes do have important effects on real variables. Hume himself also doubted that monetary neutrality would apply in the short run. (We will turn to the study of short-run nonneutrality later in the book, and this topic will shed light on the reasons why the Fed changes the supply of money over time.)

Most economists today accept Hume's conclusion as a description of the economy in the long run. Over the course of a decade, for instance, monetary changes have important effects on nominal variables (such as the price level) but only negligible effects on real variables (such as real GDP). When studying long-run changes in the economy, the neutrality of money offers a good description of how the world works.

Velocity and the Quantity Equation

We can obtain another perspective on the quantity theory of money by considering the following question: How many times per year is the typical dollar bill used to pay for a newly produced good or service? The answer to this question is given by a variable called the **velocity of money.** In physics, the term *velocity* refers to the speed at which an object travels. In economics, the velocity of money refers to the speed at which the typical dollar bill travels around the economy from wallet to wallet.

velocity of money
the rate at which money changes hands

To calculate the velocity of money, we divide the nominal value of output (nominal GDP) by the quantity of money. If P is the price level (the GDP deflator), Y the quantity of output (real GDP), and M the quantity of money, then velocity is

$$V = (P \times Y)/M.$$

To see why this makes sense, imagine a simple economy that produces only pizza. Suppose that the economy produces 100 pizzas in a year, that a pizza sells for $10, and that the quantity of money in the economy is $50. Then the velocity of money is

$$V = (\$10 \times 100)/\$50$$
$$= 20.$$

In this economy, people spend a total of $1,000 per year on pizza. For this $1,000 of spending to take place with only $50 of money, each dollar bill must change hands on average 20 times per year.

With slight algebraic rearrangement, this equation can be rewritten as

$$M \times V = P \times Y.$$

This equation states that the quantity of money (M) times the velocity of money (V) equals the price of output (P) times the amount of output (Y). It is called the **quantity equation** because it relates the quantity of money (M) to the nominal value of output ($P \times Y$). The quantity equation shows that an increase in the quantity of money in an economy must be reflected in one of the other three variables: The price level must rise, the quantity of output must rise, or the velocity of money must fall.

quantity equation
the equation $M \times V = P \times Y$, which relates the quantity of money, the velocity of money, and the dollar value of the economy's output of goods and services

In many cases, it turns out that the velocity of money is relatively stable. For example, Figure 3 (p. 358) shows nominal GDP, the quantity of money (as measured by M2), and the velocity of money for the U.S. economy since 1960. Although the velocity of money is not exactly constant, it has not changed dramatically. By contrast, the money supply and nominal GDP during this period have increased more than tenfold. Thus, for some purposes, the assumption of constant velocity may be a good approximation.

We now have all the elements necessary to explain the equilibrium price level and inflation rate. Here they are:

FIGURE 3

Nominal GDP, the Quantity of Money, and the Velocity of Money

This figure shows the nominal value of output as measured by nominal GDP, the quantity of money as measured by M2, and the velocity of money as measured by their ratio. For comparability, all three series have been scaled to equal 100 in 1960. Notice that nominal GDP and the quantity of money have grown dramatically over this period, while velocity has been relatively stable.

Source: U.S. Department of Commerce; Federal Reserve Board.

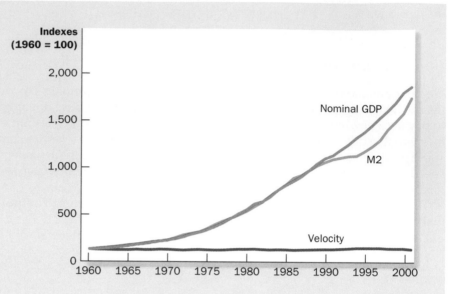

1. The velocity of money is relatively stable over time.
2. Because velocity is stable, when the central bank changes the quantity of money (M), it causes proportionate changes in the nominal value of output ($P \times Y$).
3. The economy's output of goods and services (Y) is primarily determined by factor supplies (labor, physical capital, human capital, and natural resources) and the available production technology. In particular, because money is neutral, money does not affect output.
4. With output (Y) determined by factor supplies and technology, when the central bank alters the money supply (M) and induces proportional changes in the nominal value of output ($P \times Y$), these changes are reflected in changes in the price level (P).
5. Therefore, when the central bank increases the money supply rapidly, the result is a high rate of inflation.

These five steps are the essence of the quantity theory of money.

Case Study

MONEY AND PRICES DURING FOUR HYPERINFLATIONS

Although earthquakes can wreak havoc on a society, they have the beneficial by-product of providing much useful data for seismologists. These data can shed light on alternative theories and, thereby, help society predict and deal with future

FIGURE 4

Money and Prices during Four Hyperinflations

This figure shows the quantity of money and the price level during four hyperinflations. (Note that these variables are graphed on logarithmic *scales. This means that equal vertical distances on the graph represent equal* percentage *changes in the variable.) In each case, the quantity of money and the price level move closely together. The strong association between these two variables is consistent with the quantity theory of money, which states that growth in the money supply is the primary cause of inflation.*

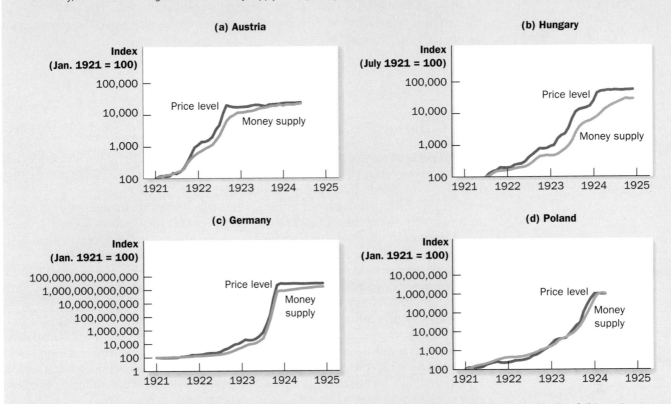

Source: Adapted from Thomas J. Sargent, "The End of Four Big Inflations," in Robert Hall, ed., *Inflation* (Chicago: University of Chicago Press, 1983), pp. 41–93. Reprinted with permission.

threats. Similarly, hyperinflations offer monetary economists a natural experiment they can use to study the effects of money on the economy.

Hyperinflations are interesting in part because the changes in the money supply and price level are so large. Indeed, hyperinflation is generally defined as inflation that exceeds 50 percent *per month*. This means that the price level increases more than 100-fold over the course of a year.

The data on hyperinflation show a clear link between the quantity of money and the price level. Figure 4 graphs data from four classic hyperinflations that occurred during the 1920s in Austria, Hungary, Germany, and Poland. Each graph shows the quantity of money in the economy and an index of the price level. The slope of the money line represents the rate at which the quantity of money was growing, and the slope of the price line represents the inflation rate. The steeper the lines, the higher the rates of money growth or inflation.

Notice that in each graph the quantity of money and the price level are almost parallel. In each instance, growth in the quantity of money is moderate at first, and so is inflation. But over time, the quantity of money in the economy starts growing faster and faster. At about the same time, inflation also takes off. Then when the quantity of money stabilizes, the price level stabilizes as well. These episodes illustrate well one of the *Ten Principles of Economics:* Prices rise when the government prints too much money. ●

The Inflation Tax

If inflation is so easy to explain, why do countries experience hyperinflation? That is, why do the central banks of these countries choose to print so much money that its value is certain to fall rapidly over time?

The answer is that the governments of these countries are using money creation as a way to pay for their spending. When the government wants to build roads, pay salaries to police officers, or give transfer payments to the poor or elderly, it first has to raise the necessary funds. Normally, the government does this by levying taxes, such as income and sales taxes, and by borrowing from the public by selling government bonds. Yet the government can also pay for spending by simply printing the money it needs.

When the government raises revenue by printing money, it is said to levy an **inflation tax.** The inflation tax is not exactly like other taxes, however, because no one receives a bill from the government for this tax. Instead, the inflation tax is more subtle. When the government prints money, the price level rises, and the dollars in your wallet are less valuable. Thus, *the inflation tax is like a tax on everyone who holds money.*

The importance of the inflation tax varies from country to country and over time. In the United States in recent years, the inflation tax has been a trivial source of revenue: It has accounted for less than 3 percent of government revenue. During the 1770s, however, the Continental Congress of the fledgling United States relied heavily on the inflation tax to pay for military spending. Because the new government had a limited ability to raise funds through regular taxes or borrowing, printing dollars was the easiest way to pay the American soldiers. As the quantity theory predicts, the result was a high rate of inflation: Prices measured in terms of the continental dollar rose more than 100-fold over a few years.

Almost all hyperinflations follow the same pattern as the hyperinflation during the American Revolution. The government has high spending, inadequate tax revenue, and limited ability to borrow. As a result, it turns to the printing press to pay for its spending. The massive increases in the quantity of money lead to massive inflation. The inflation ends when the government institutes fiscal reforms—such as cuts in government spending—that eliminate the need for the inflation tax.

inflation tax
the revenue the government raises by creating money

IN THE NEWS

RUSSIA TURNS TO THE INFLATION TAX

Whenever governments find themselves short of cash, they are tempted to solve the problem simply by printing some more. In 1998, Russian policymakers found this temptation hard to resist, and the inflation rate rose to more than 100 percent per year.

Russia's New Leaders Plan to Pay Debts by Printing Money

By Michael Wines

Moscow—Russia's new Communist-influenced Government indicated today that it plans to satisfy old debts and bail out old friends by printing new rubles, a decision that drew a swift and strong reaction from President Boris N. Yeltsin's old capitalist allies.

The deputy head of the central bank said today that the bank intends to bail out many of the nation's bankrupt financial institutions by buying back their multibillion-ruble portfolios of Government bonds and Treasury bills. The Government temporarily froze $40 billion worth of notes when the fiscal crisis erupted last month because it lacked the money to pay investors who hold them.

Asked by the Reuters news service how the near-broke Government would find the money to pay off the banks, the deputy, Andrei Kozlov, replied, "Emissions, of course, emissions." "Emissions" is a euphemism for printing money.

Hours later in Washington, Deputy Treasury Secretary Lawrence H. Summers told a House subcommittee that Russia was heading toward a return of the four-digit inflation rates that savaged consumers and almost toppled Mr. Yeltsin's Government in 1993.

Russia's new leaders cannot repeal "basic economic laws," he said.

Source: *The New York Times,* September 18, 1998, p. A3. Copyright © 1998 by The New York Times Co. Reprinted by permission.

The Fisher Effect

According to the principle of monetary neutrality, an increase in the rate of money growth raises the rate of inflation but does not affect any real variable. An important application of this principle concerns the effect of money on interest rates. Interest rates are important variables for macroeconomists to understand because they link the economy of the present and the economy of the future through their effects on saving and investment.

To understand the relationship between money, inflation, and interest rates, recall the distinction between the nominal interest rate and the real interest rate. The *nominal interest rate* is the interest rate you hear about at your bank. If you have a savings account, for instance, the nominal interest rate tells you how fast the number of dollars in your account will rise over time. The *real interest rate* corrects the nominal interest rate for the effect of inflation in order to tell you how fast the purchasing power of your savings account will rise over time. The real interest rate is the nominal interest rate minus the inflation rate:

$$\text{Real interest rate} = \text{Nominal interest rate} - \text{Inflation rate}.$$

For example, if the bank posts a nominal interest rate of 7 percent per year and the inflation rate is 3 percent per year, then the real value of the deposits grows by 4 percent per year.

We can rewrite this equation to show that the nominal interest rate is the sum of the real interest rate and the inflation rate:

$$\text{Nominal interest rate} = \text{Real interest rate} + \text{Inflation rate}.$$

This way of looking at the nominal interest rate is useful because different economic forces determine each of the two terms on the right-hand side of this equation. As we discussed earlier in the book, the supply and demand for loanable funds determine the real interest rate. And, according to the quantity theory of money, growth in the money supply determines the inflation rate.

Let's now consider how the growth in the money supply affects interest rates. In the long run over which money is neutral, a change in money growth should not affect the real interest rate. The real interest rate is, after all, a real variable. For the real interest rate not to be affected, the nominal interest rate must adjust one-for-one to changes in the inflation rate. Thus, *when the Fed increases the rate of money growth, the result is both a higher inflation rate and a higher nominal interest rate.* This adjustment of the nominal interest rate to the inflation rate is called the **Fisher effect,** after economist Irving Fisher (1867–1947), who first studied it.

Keep in mind that our analysis of the Fisher effect has maintained a long-run perspective. The Fisher effect does not hold in the short run to the extent that inflation is unanticipated. A nominal interest rate is a payment on a loan, and it is typically set when the loan is first made. If inflation catches the borrower and lender by surprise, the nominal interest rate they set will fail to reflect the rise in

Fisher effect
the one-for-one adjustment of the nominal interest rate to the inflation rate

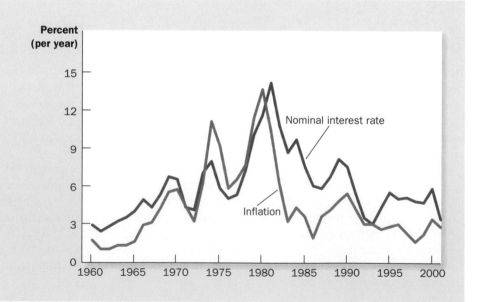

FIGURE 5

The Nominal Interest Rate and the Inflation Rate

This figure uses annual data since 1960 to show the nominal interest rate on three-month Treasury bills and the inflation rate as measured by the consumer price index. The close association between these two variables is evidence for the Fisher effect: When the inflation rate rises, so does the nominal interest rate.

Source: U.S. Department of Treasury; U.S. Department of Labor.

prices. To be precise, the Fisher effect states that the nominal interest rate adjusts to expected inflation. Expected inflation moves with actual inflation in the long run but not necessarily in the short run.

The Fisher effect is crucial for understanding changes over time in the nominal interest rate. Figure 5 shows the nominal interest rate and the inflation rate in the U.S. economy since 1960. The close association between these two variables is clear. The nominal interest rate rose from the early 1960s through the 1970s because inflation was also rising during this time. Similarly, the nominal interest rate fell from the early 1980s through the 1990s because the Fed got inflation under control.

QuickQuiz The government of a country increases the growth rate of the money supply from 5 percent per year to 50 percent per year. What happens to prices? What happens to nominal interest rates? Why might the government be doing this?

THE COSTS OF INFLATION

In the late 1970s, when the U.S. inflation rate reached about 10 percent per year, inflation dominated debates over economic policy. And even though inflation was low during the 1990s, it remained a closely watched macroeconomic variable. One recent study found that *inflation* was the economic term mentioned most often in U.S. newspapers (far ahead of second-place finisher *unemployment* and third-place finisher *productivity*).

Inflation is closely watched and widely discussed because it is thought to be a serious economic problem. But is that true? And if so, why?

A Fall in Purchasing Power? The Inflation Fallacy

If you ask the typical person why inflation is bad, he will tell you that the answer is obvious: Inflation robs him of the purchasing power of his hard-earned dollars. When prices rise, each dollar of income buys fewer goods and services. Thus, it might seem that inflation directly lowers living standards.

Yet further thought reveals a fallacy in this answer. When prices rise, buyers of goods and services pay more for what they buy. At the same time, however, sellers of goods and services get more for what they sell. Because most people earn their incomes by selling their services, such as their labor, inflation in incomes goes hand in hand with inflation in prices. Thus, *inflation does not in itself reduce people's real purchasing power.*

People believe the inflation fallacy because they do not appreciate the principle of monetary neutrality. A worker who receives an annual raise of 10 percent tends to view that raise as a reward for her own talent and effort. When an inflation rate of 6 percent reduces the real value of that raise to only 4 percent, the worker might feel that she has been cheated of what is rightfully her due. In fact, as we discussed in the chapter on production and growth, real incomes are determined by real variables, such as physical capital, human capital, natural resources, and the available production technology. Nominal incomes are determined by those factors and the overall price level. If the Fed were to lower the inflation rate from 6 percent to zero, our worker's annual raise would fall from 10 percent to 4 percent. She might feel less robbed by inflation, but her real income would not rise more quickly.

If nominal incomes tend to keep pace with rising prices, why then is inflation a problem? It turns out that there is no single answer to this question. Instead, economists have identified several costs of inflation. Each of these costs shows some way in which persistent growth in the money supply does, in fact, have some effect on real variables.

Shoeleather Costs

As we have discussed, inflation is like a tax on the holders of money. The tax itself is not a cost to society: It is only a transfer of resources from households to the government. Yet most taxes give people an incentive to alter their behavior to avoid paying the tax, and this distortion of incentives causes deadweight losses for society as a whole. Like other taxes, the inflation tax also causes deadweight losses because people waste scarce resources trying to avoid it.

How can a person avoid paying the inflation tax? Because inflation erodes the real value of the money in your wallet, you can avoid the inflation tax by holding less money. One way to do this is to go to the bank more often. For example, rather than withdrawing $200 every four weeks, you might withdraw $50 once a week. By making more frequent trips to the bank, you can keep more of your wealth in your interest-bearing savings account and less in your wallet, where inflation erodes its value.

shoeleather costs
the resources wasted when inflation encourages people to reduce their money holdings

The cost of reducing your money holdings is called the **shoeleather cost** of inflation because making more frequent trips to the bank causes your shoes to wear out more quickly. Of course, this term is not to be taken literally: The actual cost of reducing your money holdings is not the wear and tear on your shoes but the time and convenience you must sacrifice to keep less money on hand than you would if there were no inflation.

The shoeleather costs of inflation may seem trivial. And, in fact, they are in the U.S. economy, which has had only moderate inflation in recent years. But this cost is magnified in countries experiencing hyperinflation. Here is a description of one person's experience in Bolivia during its hyperinflation (as reported in the August 13, 1985, issue of *The Wall Street Journal*, p. 1):

> When Edgar Miranda gets his monthly teacher's pay of 25 million pesos, he hasn't a moment to lose. Every hour, pesos drop in value. So, while his wife rushes to market to lay in a month's supply of rice and noodles, he is off with the rest of the pesos to change them into black-market dollars.
>
> Mr. Miranda is practicing the First Rule of Survival amid the most out-of-control inflation in the world today. Bolivia is a case study of how runaway inflation undermines a society. Price increases are so huge that the figures build up almost beyond comprehension. In one six-month period, for example, prices soared at an annual rate of 38,000 percent. By official count, however, last year's inflation reached 2,000 percent, and this year's is expected to hit 8,000 percent—though other estimates range many times higher. In any event, Bolivia's rate dwarfs Israel's 370 percent and Argentina's 1,100 percent—two other cases of severe inflation.

It is easier to comprehend what happens to the thirty-eight-year-old Mr. Miranda's pay if he doesn't quickly change it into dollars. The day he was paid 25 million pesos, a dollar cost 500,000 pesos. So he received $50. Just days later, with the rate at 900,000 pesos, he would have received $27.

As this story shows, the shoeleather costs of inflation can be substantial. With the high inflation rate, Mr. Miranda does not have the luxury of holding the local money as a store of value. Instead, he is forced to convert his pesos quickly into goods or into U.S. dollars, which offer a more stable store of value. The time and effort that Mr. Miranda expends to reduce his money holdings are a waste of resources. If the monetary authority pursued a low-inflation policy, Mr. Miranda would be happy to hold pesos, and he could put his time and effort to more productive use. In fact, shortly after this article was written, the Bolivian inflation rate was reduced substantially with more restrictive monetary policy.

Menu Costs

Most firms do not change the prices of their products every day. Instead, firms often announce prices and leave them unchanged for weeks, months, or even years. One survey found that the typical U.S. firm changes its prices about once a year.

Firms change prices infrequently because there are costs of changing prices. Costs of price adjustment are called **menu costs**, a term derived from a restaurant's cost of printing a new menu. Menu costs include the cost of deciding on new prices, the cost of printing new price lists and catalogs, the cost of sending these new price lists and catalogs to dealers and customers, the cost of advertising the new prices, and even the cost of dealing with customer annoyance over price changes.

menu costs
the costs of changing prices

Inflation increases the menu costs that firms must bear. In the current U.S. economy, with its low inflation rate, annual price adjustment is an appropriate business strategy for many firms. But when high inflation makes firms' costs rise rapidly, annual price adjustment is impractical. During hyperinflations, for example, firms must change their prices daily or even more often just to keep up with all the other prices in the economy.

Relative-Price Variability and the Misallocation of Resources

Suppose that the Eatabit Eatery prints a new menu with new prices every January and then leaves its prices unchanged for the rest of the year. If there is no inflation, Eatabit's relative prices—the prices of its meals compared to other prices in the economy—would be constant over the course of the year. By contrast, if the inflation rate is 12 percent per year, Eatabit's relative prices will automatically fall by 1 percent each month. The restaurant's relative prices (that is, its prices compared with others in the economy) will be high in the early months of the year, just after it has printed a new menu, and low in the later months. And the higher the inflation rate, the greater is this automatic variability. Thus, because prices change only once in a while, inflation causes relative prices to vary more than they otherwise would.

Why does this matter? The reason is that market economies rely on relative prices to allocate scarce resources. Consumers decide what to buy by comparing the quality and prices of various goods and services. Through these decisions, they determine how the scarce factors of production are allocated among industries and firms. When inflation distorts relative prices, consumer decisions are distorted, and markets are less able to allocate resources to their best use.

Inflation-Induced Tax Distortions

Almost all taxes distort incentives, cause people to alter their behavior, and lead to a less efficient allocation of the economy's resources. Many taxes, however, become even more problematic in the presence of inflation. The reason is that lawmakers often fail to take inflation into account when writing the tax laws. Economists who have studied the tax code conclude that inflation tends to raise the tax burden on income earned from savings.

One example of how inflation discourages saving is the tax treatment of *capital gains*—the profits made by selling an asset for more than its purchase price. Suppose that in 1980 you used some of your savings to buy stock in Microsoft Corporation for $10 and that in 2000 you sold the stock for $50. According to the tax law, you have earned a capital gain of $40, which you must include in your income when computing how much income tax you owe. But suppose the overall price level doubled from 1980 to 2000. In this case, the $10 you invested in 1980 is equivalent (in terms of purchasing power) to $20 in 2000. When you sell your stock for $50, you have a real gain (an increase in purchasing power) of only $30. The tax code, however, does not take account of inflation and assesses you a tax on a gain of $40. Thus, inflation exaggerates the size of capital gains and inadvertently increases the tax burden on this type of income.

Another example is the tax treatment of interest income. The income tax treats the *nominal* interest earned on savings as income, even though part of the nominal interest rate merely compensates for inflation. To see the effects of this policy, consider the numerical example in Table 1. The table compares two economies, both of which tax interest income at a rate of 25 percent. In economy A, inflation is zero, and the nominal and real interest rates are both 4 percent. In this case, the 25 percent tax on interest income reduces the real interest rate from 4 percent to

---

TABLE 1

How Inflation Raises the Tax Burden on Saving

In the presence of zero inflation, a 25 percent tax on interest income reduces the real interest rate from 4 percent to 3 percent. In the presence of 8 percent inflation, the same tax reduces the real interest rate from 4 percent to 1 percent.

	Economy A (price stability)	Economy B (inflation)
Real interest rate	4%	4%
Inflation rate	0	8
Nominal interest rate (real interest rate + inflation rate)	4	12
Reduced interest due to 25 percent tax (.25 × nominal interest rate)	1	3
After-tax nominal interest rate (.75 × nominal interest rate)	3	9
After-tax real interest rate (after-tax nominal interest rate − inflation rate)	3	1

3 percent. In economy B, the real interest rate is again 4 percent, but the inflation rate is 8 percent. As a result of the Fisher effect, the nominal interest rate is 12 percent. Because the income tax treats this entire 12 percent interest as income, the government takes 25 percent of it, leaving an after-tax nominal interest rate of only 9 percent and an after-tax real interest rate of only 1 percent. In this case, the 25 percent tax on interest income reduces the real interest rate from 4 percent to 1 percent. Because the after-tax real interest rate provides the incentive to save, saving is much less attractive in the economy with inflation (economy B) than in the economy with stable prices (economy A).

The taxes on nominal capital gains and on nominal interest income are two examples of how the tax code interacts with inflation. There are many others. Because of these inflation-induced tax changes, higher inflation tends to discourage people from saving. Recall that the economy's saving provides the resources for investment, which in turn is a key ingredient to long-run economic growth. Thus, when inflation raises the tax burden on saving, it tends to depress the economy's long-run growth rate. There is, however, no consensus among economists about the size of this effect.

One solution to this problem, other than eliminating inflation, is to index the tax system. That is, the tax laws could be rewritten to take account of the effects of inflation. In the case of capital gains, for example, the tax code could adjust the purchase price using a price index and assess the tax only on the real gain. In the case of interest income, the government could tax only real interest income by excluding that portion of the interest income that merely compensates for inflation. To some extent, the tax laws have moved in the direction of indexation. For example, the income levels at which income tax rates change are adjusted automatically each year based on changes in the consumer price index. Yet many other aspects of the tax laws—such as the tax treatment of capital gains and interest income—are not indexed.

In an ideal world, the tax laws would be written so that inflation would not alter anyone's real tax liability. In the world in which we live, however, tax laws are far from perfect. More complete indexation would probably be desirable, but it would further complicate a tax code that many people already consider too complex.

Confusion and Inconvenience

Imagine that we took a poll and asked people the following question: "This year the yard is 36 inches. How long do you think it should be next year?" Assuming we could get people to take us seriously, they would tell us that the yard should stay the same length—36 inches. Anything else would just complicate life needlessly.

What does this finding have to do with inflation? Recall that money, as the economy's unit of account, is what we use to quote prices and record debts. In other words, money is the yardstick with which we measure economic transactions. The job of the Federal Reserve is a bit like the job of the Bureau of Standards—to ensure the reliability of a commonly used unit of measurement. When the Fed increases the money supply and creates inflation, it erodes the real value of the unit of account.

It is difficult to judge the costs of the confusion and inconvenience that arise from inflation. Earlier we discussed how the tax code incorrectly measures real incomes in the presence of inflation. Similarly, accountants incorrectly measure firms' earnings when prices are rising over time. Because inflation causes dollars at different times to have different real values, computing a firm's profit—the

IN THE NEWS

THE HYPERINFLATION IN SERBIA

Whenever governments turn to the printing press to finance substantial amounts of spending, the result is hyperinflation. As residents of Serbia learned in the early 1990s, life under such circumstances is far from easy.

Special, Today Only: 6 Million Dinars for a Snickers Bar

By Roger Thurow

BELGRADE, YUGOSLAVIA—At the Luna boutique, a Snickers bar costs 6 million dinars. Or at least it does until manager Tihomir Nikolic reads the overnight fax from his boss.

"Raise prices 99 percent," the document tersely orders. It would be an even 100 percent except that the computers at the boutique, which would be considered a dime store in other parts of the world, can't handle three-digit changes.

So for the second time in three days, Mr. Nikolic sets about raising prices. He jams a mop across the door frame to

keep customers from getting away with a bargain. The computer spits out the new prices on perforated paper. The manager and two assistants rip the paper into tags and tape them to the shelves. They used to put the prices directly on the goods, but there were so many stickers it was getting difficult to read the labels.

difference between its revenue and costs—is more complicated in an economy with inflation. Therefore, to some extent, inflation makes investors less able to sort out successful from unsuccessful firms, which in turn impedes financial markets in their role of allocating the economy's saving to alternative types of investment.

A Special Cost of Unexpected Inflation: Arbitrary Redistributions of Wealth

So far, the costs of inflation we have discussed occur even if inflation is steady and predictable. Inflation has an additional cost, however, when it comes as a surprise. Unexpected inflation redistributes wealth among the population in a way that has nothing to do with either merit or need. These redistributions occur because many loans in the economy are specified in terms of the unit of account—money.

Consider an example. Suppose that Sam Student takes out a $20,000 loan at a 7 percent interest rate from Bigbank to attend college. In ten years, the loan will come due. After his debt has compounded for ten years at 7 percent, Sam will owe Bigbank $40,000. The real value of this debt will depend on inflation over the decade. If Sam is lucky, the economy will have a hyperinflation. In this case, wages and prices will rise so high that Sam will be able to pay the $40,000 debt out of pocket change. By contrast, if the economy goes through a major deflation, then

After four hours, the mop is removed from the door. The customers wander in, rub their eyes and squint at the tags, counting the zeros. Mr. Nikolic himself squints as the computer prints another price, this one for a video recorder.

"Is that billions?" he asks himself. It is: 20,391,560,223 dinars, to be precise. He points to his T-shirt, which is emblazoned with the words "Far Out," the name of a fruit juice he once sold. He suggests it is an ideal motto for Serbia's bizarre economic situation. "It fits the craziness," he says.

How else would you describe it? Since the international community imposed economic sanctions, the inflation rate has been at least 10 percent *daily*. This translates to an annual rate in the quadrillions—so high as to be meaningless. In Serbia, one U.S. dollar will get you 10 million dinars at the Hyatt hotel, 12 million from the shady money changers on Republic Square, and 17 million from a bank run by Belgrade's underworld. Serbs complain that the dinar is as worthless as toilet paper. But for the moment, at least, there is plenty of toilet paper to go around.

The government mint, hidden in the park behind the Belgrade racetrack, is said to be churning out dinars 24 hours a day, furiously trying to keep up with the inflation that is fueled, in turn, by its own nonstop printing. The government, which believes in throwing around money to damp dissent, needs dinars to pay workers for not working at closed factories and offices. It needs them to buy the harvest from the farmers. It needs them to finance its smuggling forays and other ways to evade the sanctions, bringing in everything from oil to Mr. Nikolic's Snickers bars. It also needs them to supply brother Serbs fighting in Bosnia-Herzegovina and Croatia.

The money changers, whose fingertips detect the slightest change in paper quality, insist that the mint is even contracting out to private printers to meet demand.

"We're experts. They can't fool us," says one of the changers as he hands over 800 million worth of 5-million-dinar bills. "These," he notes confidently, "are fresh from the mint." He says he got them from a private bank, which got them from the central bank, which got them from the mint—an unholy circuit linking the black market with the Finance Ministry. "It's collective lunacy," the money changer says, laughing wickedly.

Source: *The Wall Street Journal*, August 4, 1993, p. A1. © 1993 by Dow Jones & Co. Inc. Reproduced with permission of DOW JONES & CO INC in the format Textbook via Copyright Clearance Center.

wages and prices will fall, and Sam will find the $40,000 debt a greater burden than he anticipated.

This example shows that unexpected changes in prices redistribute wealth among debtors and creditors. A hyperinflation enriches Sam at the expense of Bigbank because it diminishes the real value of the debt; Sam can repay the loan in less valuable dollars than he anticipated. Deflation enriches Bigbank at Sam's expense because it increases the real value of the debt; in this case, Sam has to repay the loan in more valuable dollars than he anticipated. If inflation were predictable, then Bigbank and Sam could take inflation into account when setting the nominal interest rate. (Recall the Fisher effect.) But if inflation is hard to predict, it imposes risk on Sam and Bigbank that both would prefer to avoid.

This cost of unexpected inflation is important to consider together with another fact: Inflation is especially volatile and uncertain when the average rate of inflation is high. This is seen most simply by examining the experience of different countries. Countries with low average inflation, such as Germany in the late twentieth century, tend to have stable inflation. Countries with high average inflation, such as many countries in Latin America, tend also to have unstable inflation. There are no known examples of economies with high, stable inflation. This relationship between the level and volatility of inflation points to another cost of inflation. If a country pursues a high-inflation monetary policy, it will have to bear not only the costs of high expected inflation but also the arbitrary redistributions of wealth associated with unexpected inflation.

Case Study

THE WIZARD OF OZ AND THE FREE-SILVER DEBATE

As a child, you probably saw the movie *The Wizard of Oz*, based on a children's book written in 1900. The movie and book tell the story of a young girl, Dorothy, who finds herself lost in a strange land far from home. You probably did not know, however, that the story is actually an allegory about U.S. monetary policy in the late nineteenth century.

From 1880 to 1896, the price level in the U.S. economy fell by 23 percent. Because this event was unanticipated, it led to a major redistribution of wealth. Most farmers in the western part of the country were debtors. Their creditors were the

IN THE NEWS

HOW TO PROTECT YOUR SAVINGS FROM INFLATION

As we have seen, unexpected changes in the price level redistribute wealth among debtors and creditors. This would no longer be true if debt contracts were written in real, rather than nominal, terms. In 1997 the U.S. Treasury started issuing bonds with a return indexed to the price level. In the following article, written a few months before the policy was implemented, two prominent economists discuss the merits of this policy.

Inflation Fighters for the Long Term

By John Y. Campbell and Robert J. Shiller

Treasury Secretary Robert Rubin announced on Thursday that the government plans to issue inflation-indexed bonds—that is, bonds whose interest and principal payments are adjusted upward for inflation, guaranteeing their real purchasing power in the future.

This is a historic moment. Economists have been advocating such bonds for many long and frustrating years. Index bonds were first called for in 1822 by the economist Joseph Lowe. In the 1870s, they were championed by the British economist William Stanley Jevons. In the early part of this century, the legendary Irving Fisher made a career of advocating them.

In recent decades, economists of every political stripe—from Milton Friedman to James Tobin, Alan Blinder to Alan Greenspan—have supported them. Yet, because there was little public clamor for such an investment, the government never issued indexed bonds.

Let's hope this lack of interest does not continue now that they will become available. The success of the indexed bonds depends on whether the public understands them—and buys them. Until now, inflation has made government bonds a risky investment. In 1966, when the inflation rate was only 3 percent, if someone had bought a 30-year government bond yielding 5 percent, he would have expected that by now his investment would be worth 180 percent of its original value. However, after years of higher-than-expected inflation, the investment is worth only 85 percent of its original value.

Because inflation has been modest in recent years, many people today are not worried about how it will affect their bankers in the east. When the price level fell, it caused the real value of these debts to rise, which enriched the banks at the expense of the farmers.

According to populist politicians of the time, the solution to the farmers' problem was the free coinage of silver. During this period, the United States was operating with a gold standard. The quantity of gold determined the money supply and, thereby, the price level. The free-silver advocates wanted silver, as well as gold, to be used as money. If adopted, this proposal would have increased the money supply, pushed up the price level, and reduced the real burden of the farmers' debts.

The debate over silver was heated, and it was central to the politics of the 1890s. A common election slogan of the populists was "We Are Mortgaged. All But Our Votes." One prominent advocate of free silver was William Jennings Bryan, the

savings. This complacency is dangerous: Even a low rate of inflation can seriously erode savings over long periods of time.

Imagine that you retire today with a pension invested in Treasury bonds that pay a fixed $10,000 each year, regardless of inflation. If there is no inflation, in 20 years the pension will have the same purchasing power that it does today. But if there is an inflation rate of only 3 percent per year, in 20 years your pension will be worth only $5,540 in today's dollars. Five percent inflation over 20 years will cut your purchasing power to $3,770, and 10 percent will reduce it to a pitiful $1,390. Which of these scenarios is likely? No one knows. Inflation ultimately depends on the people who are elected and appointed as guardians of our money supply.

At a time when Americans are living longer and planning for several decades of retirement, the insidious effects of inflation should be of serious concern. For this reason alone, the creation of inflation-indexed bonds, with their guarantee of a safe return over long periods of time, is a welcome development.

No other investment offers this kind of safety. Conventional government bonds make payments that are fixed in dollar terms; but investors should be concerned about purchasing power, not about the number of dollars they receive. Money market funds make dollar payments that increase with inflation to some degree, since short-term interest rates tend to rise with inflation. But many other factors also influence interest rates, so the real income from a money market fund is not secure.

The stock market offers a high rate of return on average, but it can fall as well as rise. Investors should remember the bear market of the 1970s as well as the bull market of the 1980s and 1990s.

Inflation-indexed government bonds have been issued in Britain for 15 years, in Canada for 5 years, and in many other countries, including Australia, New Zealand, and Sweden. In Britain, which has the world's largest indexed-bond market, the bonds have offered a yield 3 to 4 percent higher than the rate of inflation. In the United States, a safe long-term return of this sort should make indexed bonds an important part of retirement savings.

We expect that financial institutions will take advantage of the new inflation-indexed bonds and offer innovative new products. Indexed-bond funds will probably appear first, but indexed annuities and even indexed mortgages—monthly payments would be adjusted for inflation—should also become available. [*Author's note:* Since this article was written, some of these indexed products have been introduced, but their use is not yet widespread.]

Although the Clinton administration may not get much credit for it today, the decision to issue inflation-indexed bonds is an accomplishment that historians decades hence will single out for special recognition.

Source: *The New York Times,* May 18, 1996, p. 19. Copyright © 1996 by The New York Times Co. Reprinted by permission.

Democratic nominee for president in 1896. He is remembered in part for a speech at the Democratic party's nominating convention in which he said, "You shall not press down upon the brow of labor this crown of thorns. You shall not crucify mankind upon a cross of gold." Rarely since then have politicians waxed so poetic about alternative approaches to monetary policy. Nonetheless, Bryan lost the election to Republican William McKinley, and the United States remained on the gold standard.

L. Frank Baum, author of the book *The Wonderful Wizard of Oz*, was a midwestern journalist. When he sat down to write a story for children, he made the characters represent protagonists in the major political battle of his time. Although modern commentators on the story differ somewhat in the interpretation they assign to each character, there is no doubt that the story highlights the debate over monetary policy. Here is how economic historian Hugh Rockoff, writing in the August 1990 issue of the *Journal of Political Economy*, interprets the story:

DOROTHY:	Traditional American values
TOTO:	Prohibitionist party, also called the Teetotalers
SCARECROW:	Farmers
TIN WOODSMAN:	Industrial workers
COWARDLY LION:	William Jennings Bryan
MUNCHKINS:	Citizens of the east
WICKED WITCH OF THE EAST:	Grover Cleveland
WICKED WITCH OF THE WEST:	William McKinley
WIZARD:	Marcus Alonzo Hanna, chairman of the Republican party
OZ:	Abbreviation for ounce of gold
YELLOW BRICK ROAD:	Gold standard

An early debate over monetary policy

THE KOBAL COLLECTION

In the end of Baum's story, Dorothy does find her way home, but it is not by just following the yellow brick road. After a long and perilous journey, she learns that the wizard is incapable of helping her or her friends. Instead, Dorothy finally discovers the magical power of her *silver* slippers. (When the book was made into a movie in 1939, Dorothy's slippers were changed from silver to ruby. The Hollywood filmmakers were more interested in showing off the new technology of Technicolor than telling a story about nineteenth-century monetary policy.)

Although the populists lost the debate over the free coinage of silver, they did eventually get the monetary expansion and inflation that they wanted. In 1898 prospectors discovered gold near the Klondike River in the Canadian Yukon. Increased supplies of gold also arrived from the mines of South Africa. As a result, the money supply and the price level started to rise in the United States and other countries operating on the gold standard. Within 15 years, prices in the United States were back to the levels that had prevailed in the 1880s, and farmers were better able to handle their debts. ●

QuickQuiz List and describe six costs of inflation.

CONCLUSION

This chapter discussed the causes and costs of inflation. The primary cause of inflation is simply growth in the quantity of money. When the central bank creates money in large quantities, the value of money falls quickly. To maintain stable prices, the central bank must maintain strict control over the money supply.

The costs of inflation are more subtle. They include shoeleather costs, menu costs, increased variability of relative prices, unintended changes in tax liabilities, confusion and inconvenience, and arbitrary redistributions of wealth. Are these costs, in total, large or small? All economists agree that they become huge during hyperinflation. But their size for moderate inflation—when prices rise by less than 10 percent per year—is more open to debate.

Although this chapter presented many of the most important lessons about inflation, the discussion is incomplete. When the central bank reduces the rate of money growth, prices rise less rapidly, as the quantity theory suggests. Yet as the economy makes the transition to this lower inflation rate, the change in monetary policy will have disruptive effects on production and employment. That is, even though monetary policy is neutral in the long run, it has profound effects on real variables in the short run. Later in this book we will examine the reasons for short-run monetary nonneutrality in order to enhance our understanding of the causes and costs of inflation.

SUMMARY

- The overall level of prices in an economy adjusts to bring money supply and money demand into balance. When the central bank increases the supply of money, it causes the price level to rise. Persistent growth in the quantity of money supplied leads to continuing inflation.

- The principle of monetary neutrality asserts that changes in the quantity of money influence nominal variables but not real variables. Most economists believe that monetary neutrality approximately describes the behavior of the economy in the long run.

- A government can pay for some of its spending simply by printing money. When countries rely heavily on this "inflation tax," the result is hyperinflation.

- One application of the principle of monetary neutrality is the Fisher effect. According to the Fisher effect, when the inflation rate rises, the nominal interest rate rises by the same amount, so that the real interest rate remains the same.

- Many people think that inflation makes them poorer because it raises the cost of what they buy. This view is a fallacy, however, because inflation also raises nominal incomes.

- Economists have identified six costs of inflation: shoeleather costs associated with reduced money holdings, menu costs associated with more frequent adjustment of prices, increased variability of relative prices, unintended changes in tax liabilities due to nonindexation of the tax code, confusion and inconvenience resulting from a changing unit of account, and arbitrary redistributions of wealth between debtors and creditors. Many of these costs are large during hyperinflation, but the size of these costs for moderate inflation is less clear.

KEY CONCEPTS

quantity theory of money, p. 353
nominal variables, p. 355
real variables, p. 355
classical dichotomy, p. 355

monetary neutrality, p. 356
velocity of money, p. 357
quantity equation, p. 357
inflation tax, p. 360

Fisher effect, p. 362
shoeleather costs, p. 364
menu costs, p. 365

QUESTIONS FOR REVIEW

1. Explain how an increase in the price level affects the real value of money.

2. According to the quantity theory of money, what is the effect of an increase in the quantity of money?

3. Explain the difference between nominal and real variables, and give two examples of each. According to the principle of monetary neutrality, which variables are affected by changes in the quantity of money?

4. In what sense is inflation like a tax? How does thinking about inflation as a tax help explain hyperinflation?

5. According to the Fisher effect, how does an increase in the inflation rate affect the real interest rate and the nominal interest rate?

6. What are the costs of inflation? Which of these costs do you think are most important for the U.S. economy?

7. If inflation is less than expected, who benefits—debtors or creditors? Explain.

PROBLEMS AND APPLICATIONS

1. Suppose that this year's money supply is $500 billion, nominal GDP is $10 trillion, and real GDP is $5 trillion.
   a. What is the price level? What is the velocity of money?
   b. Suppose that velocity is constant and the economy's output of goods and services rises by 5 percent each year. What will happen to nominal GDP and the price level next year if the Fed keeps the money supply constant?
   c. What money supply should the Fed set next year if it wants to keep the price level stable?
   d. What money supply should the Fed set next year if it wants inflation of 10 percent?

2. Suppose that changes in bank regulations expand the availability of credit cards, so that people need to hold less cash.
   a. How does this event affect the demand for money?
   b. If the Fed does not respond to this event, what will happen to the price level?
   c. If the Fed wants to keep the price level stable, what should it do?

3. It is often suggested that the Federal Reserve try to achieve zero inflation. If we assume that velocity is constant, does this zero-inflation goal require that the rate of money growth equal zero? If yes, explain why. If no, explain what the rate of money growth should equal.

4. The economist John Maynard Keynes wrote: "Lenin is said to have declared that the best way to destroy the capitalist system was to debauch the currency. By a continuing process of inflation, governments can confiscate, secretly and unobserved, an important part of the wealth of their citizens." Justify Lenin's assertion.

5. Suppose that a country's inflation rate increases sharply. What happens to the inflation tax on the holders of money? Why is wealth that is held in savings accounts *not* subject to a change in the inflation tax? Can you think of any way in which holders of savings accounts are hurt by the increase in the inflation rate?

6. Hyperinflations are extremely rare in countries whose central banks are independent of the rest of the government. Why might this be so?

7. Let's consider the effects of inflation in an economy composed only of two people: Bob, a bean farmer, and Rita, a rice farmer. Bob and Rita both always consume equal amounts of rice and beans. In year 2000, the price of beans was $1, and the price of rice was $3.

   a. Suppose that in 2001 the price of beans was $2 and the price of rice was $6. What was inflation? Was Bob better off, worse off, or unaffected by the changes in prices? What about Rita?

   b. Now suppose that in 2001 the price of beans was $2 and the price of rice was $4. What was inflation? Was Bob better off, worse off, or unaffected by the changes in prices? What about Rita?

   c. Finally, suppose that in 2001 the price of beans was $2 and the price of rice was $1.50. What was inflation? Was Bob better off, worse off, or unaffected by the changes in prices? What about Rita?

   d. What matters more to Bob and Rita—the overall inflation rate or the relative price of rice and beans?

8. If the tax rate is 40 percent, compute the before-tax real interest rate and the after-tax real interest rate in each of the following cases.

   a. The nominal interest rate is 10 percent and the inflation rate is 5 percent.

   b. The nominal interest rate is 6 percent and the inflation rate is 2 percent.

   c. The nominal interest rate is 4 percent and the inflation rate is 1 percent.

9. What are your shoeleather costs of going to the bank? How might you measure these costs in dollars? How do you think the shoeleather costs of your college president differ from your own?

10. Recall that money serves three functions in the economy. What are those functions? How does inflation affect the ability of money to serve each of these functions?

11. Suppose that people expect inflation to equal 3 percent, but in fact prices rise by 5 percent. Describe how this unexpectedly high inflation rate would help or hurt the following:

    a. the government

    b. a homeowner with a fixed-rate mortgage

    c. a union worker in the second year of a labor contract

    d. a college that has invested some of its endowment in government bonds

12. Explain one harm associated with unexpected inflation that is *not* associated with expected inflation. Then explain one harm associated with both expected and unexpected inflation.

13. Explain whether the following statements are true, false, or uncertain.

    a. "Inflation hurts borrowers and helps lenders, because borrowers must pay a higher rate of interest."

    b. "If prices change in a way that leaves the overall price level unchanged, then no one is made better or worse off."

    c. "Inflation does not reduce the purchasing power of most workers."

http://   For more study tools, please visit http://mankiwXtra.swlearning.com.

7

THE MACROECONOMICS OF OPEN ECONOMIES

OPEN-ECONOMY MACROECONOMICS:
BASIC CONCEPTS

When you decide to buy a car, you may compare the latest models offered by Ford and Toyota. When you take your next vacation, you may consider spending it on a beach in Florida or in Mexico. When you start saving for your retirement, you may choose between a mutual fund that buys stock in U.S. companies and one that buys stock in foreign companies. In all of these cases, you are participating not just in the U.S. economy but in economies around the world.

There are clear benefits to being open to international trade: Trade allows people to produce what they produce best and to consume the great variety of goods and services produced around the world. Indeed, one of the *Ten Principles of Economics* highlighted in Chapter 1 is that trade can make everyone better off. As we saw in Chapter 3, international trade can raise living standards in all countries by allowing each country to specialize in producing those goods and services in which it has a comparative advantage.

So far our development of macroeconomics has largely ignored the economy's interaction with other economies around the world. For most questions in macroeconomics, international issues are peripheral. For instance, when we discussed the natural rate of unemployment in Chapter 15 and the causes of inflation in

closed economy
an economy that does not interact
with other economies in the world

open economy
an economy that interacts freely with
other economies around the world

Chapter 17, the effects of international trade could safely be ignored. Indeed, to keep their analysis simple, macroeconomists often assume a **closed economy**—an economy that does not interact with other economies.

Yet some new macroeconomic issues arise in an **open economy**—an economy that interacts freely with other economies around the world. This chapter and the next one, therefore, provide an introduction to open-economy macroeconomics. We begin in this chapter by discussing the key macroeconomic variables that describe an open economy's interactions in world markets. You may have noticed mention of these variables—exports, imports, the trade balance, and exchange rates—when reading the newspaper or watching the nightly news. Our first job is to understand what these data mean. In the next chapter we develop a model to explain how these variables are determined and how they are affected by various government policies.

THE INTERNATIONAL FLOWS OF GOODS AND CAPITAL

An open economy interacts with other economies in two ways: It buys and sells goods and services in world product markets, and it buys and sells capital assets such as stocks and bonds in world financial markets. Here we discuss these two activities and the close relationship between them.

The Flow of Goods: Exports, Imports, and Net Exports

exports
goods and services that are produced
domestically and sold abroad

imports
goods and services that are produced
abroad and sold domestically

net exports
the value of a nation's exports minus
the value of its imports; also called the
trade balance

trade balance
the value of a nation's exports minus
the value of its imports; also called net
exports

trade surplus
an excess of exports over imports

trade deficit
an excess of imports over exports

balanced trade
a situation in which exports equal
imports

As we first noted in Chapter 3, **exports** are domestically produced goods and services that are sold abroad, and **imports** are foreign-produced goods and services that are sold domestically. When Boeing, the U.S. aircraft manufacturer, builds a plane and sells it to Air France, the sale is an export for the United States and an import for France. When Volvo, the Swedish car manufacturer, makes a car and sells it to a U.S. resident, the sale is an import for the United States and an export for Sweden.

The **net exports** of any country are the value of its exports minus the value of its imports. The Boeing sale raises U.S. net exports, and the Volvo sale reduces U.S. net exports. Because net exports tell us whether a country is, in total, a seller or a buyer in world markets for goods and services, net exports are also called the **trade balance.** If net exports are positive, exports are greater than imports, indicating that the country sells more goods and services abroad than it buys from other countries. In this case, the country is said to run a **trade surplus.** If net exports are negative, exports are less than imports, indicating that the country sells fewer goods and services abroad than it buys from other countries. In this case, the country is said to run a **trade deficit.** If net exports are zero, its exports and imports are exactly equal, and the country is said to have **balanced trade.**

In the next chapter we develop a theory that explains an economy's trade balance, but even at this early stage it is easy to think of many factors that might influence a country's exports, imports, and net exports. Those factors include the following:

- The tastes of consumers for domestic and foreign goods
- The prices of goods at home and abroad

- The exchange rates at which people can use domestic currency to buy foreign currencies
- The incomes of consumers at home and abroad
- The cost of transporting goods from country to country
- The policies of the government toward international trade

As these variables change over time, so does the amount of international trade.

Case Study

THE INCREASING OPENNESS OF THE U.S. ECONOMY

"But we're not just talking about buying a car—we're talking about confronting this country's trade deficit with Japan."

Perhaps the most dramatic change in the U.S. economy over the past five decades has been the increasing importance of international trade and finance. This change is illustrated in Figure 1, which shows the total value of goods and services exported to other countries and imported from other countries expressed as a percentage of gross domestic product. In the 1950s exports of goods and services averaged less than 5 percent of GDP. Today they are more than twice that level. Imports of goods and services have risen by a similar amount.

This increase in international trade is partly due to improvements in transportation. In 1950 the average merchant ship carried less than 10,000 tons of cargo; today, many ships carry more than 100,000 tons. The long-distance jet was introduced in 1958, and the wide-body jet in 1967, making air transport far cheaper. Because of these developments, goods that once had to be produced locally can now be traded around the world. Cut flowers, for instance, are now grown in Israel and flown to

FIGURE 1

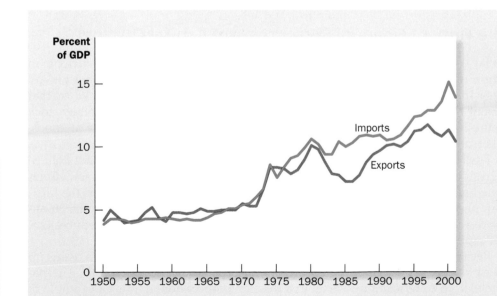

The Internationalization of the U.S. Economy

This figure shows exports and imports of the U.S. economy as a percentage of U.S. gross domestic product since 1950. The substantial increases over time show the increasing importance of international trade and finance.

Source: U.S. Department of Commerce.

the United States to be sold. Fresh fruits and vegetables that can grow only in summer can now be consumed in winter as well, because they can be shipped to the United States from countries in the southern hemisphere.

The increase in international trade has also been influenced by advances in telecommunications, which have allowed businesses to reach overseas customers more easily. For example, the first transatlantic telephone cable was not laid until 1956. As recently as 1966, the technology allowed only 138 simultaneous conversations between North America and Europe. Today, communications satellites permit more than 1 million conversations to occur at the same time.

Technological progress has also fostered international trade by changing the kinds of goods that economies produce. When bulky raw materials (such as steel) and perishable goods (such as foodstuffs) were a large part of the world's output, transporting goods was often costly and sometimes impossible. By contrast, goods produced with modern technology are often light and easy to transport. Consumer electronics, for instance, have low weight for every dollar of value, which makes them easy to produce in one country and sell in another. An even more extreme example is the film industry. Once a studio in Hollywood makes a movie, it can send copies of the film around the world at almost zero cost. And, indeed, movies are a major export of the United States.

The government's trade policies have also been a factor in increasing international trade. As we discussed earlier in this book, economists have long believed that free trade between countries is mutually beneficial. Over time, policymakers around the world have come to accept these conclusions. International agreements, such as the North American Free Trade Agreement (NAFTA) and the General Agreement on Tariffs and Trade (GATT), have gradually lowered tariffs, import quotas, and other trade barriers. The pattern of increasing trade illustrated in Figure 1 is a phenomenon that most economists and policymakers endorse and encourage. ●

The Flow of Financial Resources: Net Capital Outflow

So far we have been discussing how residents of an open economy participate in world markets for goods and services. In addition, residents of an open economy participate in world financial markets. A U.S. resident with $20,000 could use that money to buy a car from Toyota, but he could instead use that money to buy stock in the Toyota corporation. The first transaction would represent a flow of goods, whereas the second would represent a flow of capital.

net capital outflow
the purchase of foreign assets by domestic residents minus the purchase of domestic assets by foreigners

The term **net capital outflow** refers to the purchase of foreign assets by domestic residents minus the purchase of domestic assets by foreigners. (It is sometimes called *net foreign investment*.) When a U.S. resident buys stock in Telmex, the Mexican phone company, the purchase raises U.S. net capital outflow. When a Japanese resident buys a bond issued by the U.S. government, the purchase reduces U.S. net capital outflow.

Recall that the flow of capital abroad takes two forms. If McDonald's opens up a fast food outlet in Russia, that is an example of *foreign direct investment*. Alternatively, if an American buys stock in a Russian corporation, that is an example of *foreign portfolio investment*. In the first case, the American owner is actively managing the investment, whereas in the second case the American owner has a more passive role. In both cases, U.S. residents are buying assets located in another country, so both purchases increase U.S. net capital outflow.

We develop a theory to explain net capital outflow in the next chapter. Here, let's consider briefly some of the more important variables that influence net capital outflow:

- The real interest rates being paid on foreign assets
- The real interest rates being paid on domestic assets
- The perceived economic and political risks of holding assets abroad
- The government policies that affect foreign ownership of domestic assets

For example, consider U.S. investors deciding whether to buy Mexican government bonds or U.S. government bonds. (Recall that a bond is, in effect, an IOU of the issuer.) To make this decision, U.S. investors compare the real interest rates offered on the two bonds. The higher a bond's real interest rate, the more attractive it is. While making this comparison, however, U.S. investors must also take into account the risk that one of these governments might *default* on its debt (that is, not pay interest or principal when it is due), as well as any restrictions that the Mexican government has imposed, or might impose in the future, on foreign investors in Mexico.

The Equality of Net Exports and Net Capital Outflow

We have seen that an open economy interacts with the rest of the world in two ways—in world markets for goods and services and in world financial markets. Net exports and net capital outflow each measure a type of imbalance in these markets. Net exports measure an imbalance between a country's exports and its imports. Net capital outflow measures an imbalance between the amount of foreign assets bought by domestic residents and the amount of domestic assets bought by foreigners.

An important but subtle fact of accounting states that, for an economy as a whole, these two imbalances must offset each other. That is, net capital outflow (*NCO*) always equals net exports (*NX*):

$$NCO = NX.$$

This equation holds because every transaction that affects one side of this equation must also affect the other side by exactly the same amount. This equation is an *identity*—an equation that must hold because of the way the variables in the equation are defined and measured.

To see why this accounting identity is true, consider an example. Suppose that Boeing, the U.S. aircraft maker, sells some planes to a Japanese airline. In this sale, a U.S. company gives planes to a Japanese company, and a Japanese company gives yen to a U.S. company. Notice that two things have occurred simultaneously. The United States has sold to a foreigner some of its output (the planes), and this sale increases U.S. net exports. In addition, the United States has acquired some foreign assets (the yen), and this acquisition increases U.S. net capital outflow.

Although Boeing most likely will not hold on to the yen it has acquired in this sale, any subsequent transaction will preserve the equality of net exports and net capital outflow. For example, Boeing may exchange its yen for dollars with a U.S.

mutual fund that wants the yen to buy stock in Sony Corporation, the Japanese maker of consumer electronics. In this case, Boeing's net export of planes equals the mutual fund's net capital outflow in Sony stock. Hence, *NX* and *NCO* rise by an equal amount.

Alternatively, Boeing may exchange its yen for dollars with another U.S. company that wants to buy computers from Toshiba, the Japanese computer maker. In this case, U.S. imports (of computers) exactly offset U.S. exports (of planes). The sales by Boeing and Toshiba together affect neither U.S. net exports nor U.S. net capital outflow. That is, *NX* and *NCO* are the same as they were before these transactions took place.

The equality of net exports and net capital outflow follows from the fact that every international transaction is an exchange. When a seller country transfers a good or service to a buyer country, the buyer country gives up some asset to pay for this good or service. The value of that asset equals the value of the good or service sold. When we add everything up, the net value of goods and services sold by a country (*NX*) must equal the net value of assets acquired (*NCO*). The international flow of goods and services and the international flow of capital are two sides of the same coin.

IN THE NEWS

HOW THE CHINESE HELP AMERICAN HOME BUYERS

This article describes how capital is flowing from China into the United States.

China, of All Places, Sends Capital to U.S.

By Craig S. Smith

SHANGHAI, CHINA—A giant, developing nation bordered by an economic quagmire is an unlikely source of capital for the world's industrialized powers. But China, with fat trade surpluses and bulging foreign-exchange reserves, is buying U.S. government securities, especially Treasury bonds and bonds issued by Fannie Mae and Freddie Mac.

That's good for America. Such investments add liquidity to the U.S. housing market and help hold down U.S. interest rates. And China is likely to continue to buy a lot of U.S. debt for years to come.

Thanks to high domestic savings, a continuing inflow of foreign investment and tight controls on domestic spending, China is awash in capital. Last year's capital surplus . . . reached an estimated $67 billion.

China squirrels more than half of that away into foreign reserves, which are invested abroad. Chinese companies funnel much of the rest directly overseas through bank transfers—sometimes skirting Chinese capital restrictions to do so. So while the financial crisis has transformed the rest of East Asia into a capital-sucking hole, China has become a gushing fountain of capital.

This isn't the first time a developing country has sent abroad funds that could be used productively at home. Often, such money was fleeing instability, as it was in Latin America in the 1980s, Russia in the 1990s, and Africa in both decades.

Usually, however, developing countries invest their capital in their own growing economies. And some Chinese officials believe that's what China should

Saving, Investment, and Their Relationship to the International Flows

A nation's saving and investment are, as we have seen in earlier chapters, crucial to its long-run economic growth. Let's therefore consider how these variables are related to the international flows of goods and capital as measured by net exports and net capital outflow. We can do this most easily with the help of some simple mathematics.

As you may recall, the term *net exports* first appeared earlier in the book when we discussed the components of gross domestic product. The economy's gross domestic product (Y) is divided among four components: consumption (C), investment (I), government purchases (G), and net exports (NX). We write this as

$$Y = C + I + G + NX.$$

Total expenditure on the economy's output of goods and services is the sum of expenditure on consumption, investment, government purchases, and net exports. Because each dollar of expenditure is placed into one of these four components,

be doing, too. One former Chinese central bank official calls it "scandalous" that a country of poor peasants is financing investment of an industrialized power such as the United States.

Others complain that China isn't even getting good returns on its investments. It pays an average of 7 to 8 percent on its $130 billion foreign debt but earns only about 5 percent on the $140 billion of its reserves invested abroad. That's partly because yields on U.S. debt—widely considered the safest securities in the world—are relatively low.

But China has good reasons to send some of its capital overseas. Its investment in fixed assets as a percentage of its gross domestic product was an extraordinarily high 34 percent in 1996, the latest year for which figures are available. It's doubtful that China could increase that ratio without wasting money or fueling inflation. Thailand's ratio was 40 percent and Korea's 37 percent before their overspending undermined those nations' economies . . .

"They're already investing as much as they can absorb," says Andy Xie, an economist for Morgan Stanley Dean Witter & Co. in Hong Kong.

Yet while investment is constrained, savings keep growing. The percentage of working-age people in the population has climbed to 62 percent from 51 percent in the past 30 years. And those workers, often allowed only one child on which to spend, are hitting their peak saving years. With consumption low, the pileup of money pushes capital offshore.

The result: Chinese capital is spreading everywhere. The country is a big buyer of oil fields, for example, having pledged more than $8 billion for concessions in Sudan, Venezuela, Iraq and Kazakstan. Mainland capital also has poured into Hong Kong, where it helped inflate property prices before East Asia's crisis began letting out some of that air. The capital surplus has even allowed China to help its neighbors when they got into trouble: Beijing pledged $1 billion to the International Monetary Fund

bailouts in Thailand and Indonesia. Most of the money, though, goes into U.S. Treasury bonds. China won't say how much, but estimates run as high as 40 percent.

And China's central bank, like 50 others around the world, lends money to Fannie Mae and Freddie Mac, which use the funds to buy mortgage loans that banks and others extend to ordinary Americans. The flood of money keeps the market liquid and reduces the rates that U.S. home buyers pay.

Source: *The Wall Street Journal,* March 30, 1998, The Outlook, p. 1. © 1998 by Dow Jones & Co. Inc. Reproduced with permission of DOW JONES & CO INC in the format Textbook via Copyright Clearance Center.

this equation is an accounting identity: It must be true because of the way the variables are defined and measured.

Recall that national saving is the income of the nation that is left after paying for current consumption and government purchases. National saving (S) equals $Y - C - G$. If we rearrange the above equation to reflect this fact, we obtain

$$Y - C - G = I + NX$$
$$S = I + NX.$$

Because net exports (NX) also equal net capital outflow (NCO), we can write this equation as

$$S \quad = \quad I \quad + \quad NCO$$

$$\text{Saving} \quad = \quad \begin{array}{c}\text{Domestic}\\\text{investment}\end{array} \quad + \quad \begin{array}{c}\text{Net capital}\\\text{outflow.}\end{array}$$

This equation shows that a nation's saving must equal its domestic investment plus its net capital outflow. In other words, when U.S. citizens save a dollar of their income for the future, that dollar can be used to finance accumulation of domestic capital or it can be used to finance the purchase of capital abroad.

This equation should look somewhat familiar. Earlier in the book, when we analyzed the role of the financial system, we considered this identity for the special case of a closed economy. In a closed economy, net capital outflow is zero ($NCO = 0$), so saving equals investment ($S = I$). By contrast, an open economy has two uses for its saving: domestic investment and net capital outflow.

As before, we can view the financial system as standing between the two sides of this identity. For example, suppose the Smith family decides to save some of its income for retirement. This decision contributes to national saving, the left-hand side of our equation. If the Smiths deposit their saving in a mutual fund, the mutual fund may use some of the deposit to buy stock issued by General Motors, which uses the proceeds to build a factory in Ohio. In addition, the mutual fund may use some of the Smiths' deposit to buy stock issued by Toyota, which uses the proceeds to build a factory in Osaka. These transactions show up on the right-hand side of the equation. From the standpoint of U.S. accounting, the General Motors expenditure on a new factory is domestic investment, and the purchase of Toyota stock by a U.S. resident is net capital outflow. Thus, all saving in the U.S. economy shows up as investment in the U.S. economy or as U.S. net capital outflow.

Summing Up

Table 1 summarizes many of the ideas presented so far in this chapter. It describes the three possibilities for an open economy: a country with a trade deficit, a country with balanced trade, and a country with a trade surplus.

Consider first a country with a trade surplus. By definition, a trade surplus means that the value of exports exceeds the value of imports. Because net exports are exports minus imports, net exports (NX) are greater than zero. As a result, income ($Y = C + I + G + NX$) must be greater than domestic spending ($C + I + G$). But if Y is more than $C + I + G$, then $Y - C - G$ must be more than I. That is, saving ($S = Y - C - G$) must exceed investment. Because the country is saving

TABLE 1

Trade Deficit	Balanced Trade	Trade Surplus
Exports < Imports	Exports = Imports	Exports > Imports
Net exports < 0	Net exports = 0	Net exports > 0
$Y < C + I + G$	$Y = C + I + G$	$Y > C + I + G$
Saving < Investment	Saving = Investment	Saving > Investment
Net capital outflow < 0	Net capital outflow = 0	Net capital outflow > 0

International Flows of Goods and Capital: Summary

This table shows the three possible outcomes for an open economy.

more than it is investing, it must be sending some of its saving abroad. That is, the net capital outflow must be greater than zero.

The converse logic applies to a country with a trade deficit (such as the U.S. economy during the 1990s). By definition, a trade deficit means that the value of exports are less than the value of imports. Because net exports are exports minus imports, net exports (NX) are negative. Thus, income ($Y = C + I + G + NX$) must be less than domestic spending ($C + I + G$). But if Y is less than $C + I + G$, then $Y - C - G$ must be less than I. That is, saving must be less than investment. The net capital outflow must be negative.

A country with balanced trade is between these cases. Exports equal imports, so net exports are zero. Income equals domestic spending, and saving equals investment. The net capital outflow equals zero.

Case Study

IS THE U.S. TRADE DEFICIT A NATIONAL PROBLEM?

You may have heard the press call the United States "the world's largest debtor." The nation earned that description by borrowing heavily in world financial markets during the past two decades to finance large trade deficits. Why did the United States do this, and should this event give Americans reason to worry?

To answer these questions, let's see what the macroeconomic accounting identities tell us about the U.S. economy. Panel (a) of Figure 2 (p. 388) shows national saving and domestic investment as a percentage of GDP since 1960. Panel (b) shows net capital outflow (that is, the trade balance) as a percentage of GDP. Notice that, as the identities require, net capital outflow always equals national saving minus domestic investment.

The figure shows a dramatic change beginning in the early 1980s. Before 1980, national saving and domestic investment were close, and so net capital outflow was small. Yet after 1980, national saving fell below investment, and net capital outflow became a large negative number. That is, foreigners were buying more capital assets in the United States than Americans were buying abroad. The United States was going into debt.

History shows that changes in capital flows arise sometimes from changes in saving and sometimes from changes in investment. From 1980 to 1987, the flow of

FIGURE 2

National Saving, Domestic Investment, and Net Capital Outflow

Panel (a) shows national saving and domestic investment as a percentage of GDP. Panel (b) shows net capital outflow as a percentage of GDP. You can see from the figure that national saving has been lower since 1980 than it was before 1980. This fall in national saving has been reflected primarily in reduced net capital outflow rather than in reduced domestic investment.

Source: U.S. Department of Commerce.

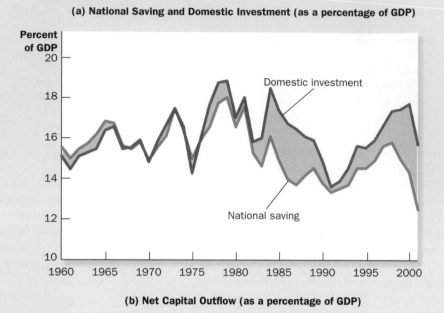

(a) National Saving and Domestic Investment (as a percentage of GDP)

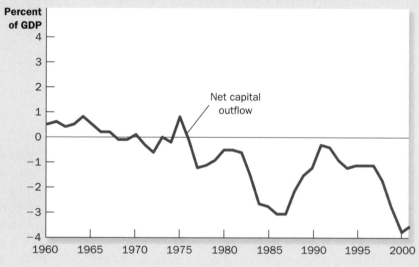

(b) Net Capital Outflow (as a percentage of GDP)

capital into the United States went from 0.5 to 3.0 percent of GDP. Of this 2.5 percentage-point change, a fall in saving accounts for 2.1 percentage points. This decline in national saving, in turn, is partly attributable to a decline in public saving—that is, an increase in the government budget deficit.

A different story explains the events of the following decade. From 1991 to 2000, the capital flow into the United States went from 0.3 to 3.7 percent of GDP. None of this 3.3 percentage-point change is attributable to a decline in saving; in fact, saving increased over this time, as the government's budget switched from deficit to surplus. But investment went from 13.4 to 17.9 percent of GDP, as the economy enjoyed a boom in information technology and many firms were eager to make these high-tech investments. (This boom ended in 2001, when a recession depressed both investment and saving; we will return to this short-run event in a later chapter.)

Are these trade deficits a problem for the U.S. economy? To answer this question, it is important to keep an eye on the nation's saving and investment.

Consider first a trade deficit induced by a fall in saving, as occurred during the 1980s. Lower saving means that the nation is putting away less of its income to provide for its future. Once national saving has fallen, however, there is no reason to deplore the resulting trade deficits. If national saving fell without inducing a trade deficit, investment in the United States would have to fall. This fall in investment, in turn, would adversely affect the growth in the capital stock, labor productivity, and real wages. In other words, given that U.S. saving has declined, it is better to have foreigners invest in the U.S. economy than no one at all.

Now consider a trade deficit induced by an investment boom, such as the trade deficits of the 1990s. In this case, the economy is borrowing from abroad to finance the purchase of new capital goods. If this additional capital provides a good return in the form of higher production of goods and services, then the economy should be able to handle the debts that are being accumulated. On the other hand, if the investment projects fail to yield the expected returns, the debts will look less desirable, at least with the benefit of hindsight.

There is no simple and correct answer to the question posed in the title to this case study. Just as an individual can go into debt in either a prudent or profligate manner, so can a nation. The trade deficit is not a problem in itself, but sometimes it can be a symptom of a problem. ●

QuickQuiz Define *net exports* and *net capital outflow*. Explain how they are related.

THE PRICES FOR INTERNATIONAL TRANSACTIONS: REAL AND NOMINAL EXCHANGE RATES

So far we have discussed measures of the flow of goods and services and the flow of capital across a nation's border. In addition to these quantity variables, macroeconomists also study variables that measure the prices at which these international transactions take place. Just as the price in any market serves the important role of coordinating buyers and sellers in that market, international prices help coordinate the decisions of consumers and producers as they interact in world markets. Here we discuss the two most important international prices—the nominal and real exchange rates.

Nominal Exchange Rates

The **nominal exchange rate** is the rate at which a person can trade the currency of one country for the currency of another. For example, if you go to a bank, you might see a posted exchange rate of 80 yen per dollar. If you give the bank one U.S.

nominal exchange rate
the rate at which a person can trade the currency of one country for the currency of another

dollar, it will give you 80 Japanese yen; and if you give the bank 80 Japanese yen, it will give you one U.S. dollar. (In actuality, the bank will post slightly different prices for buying and selling yen. The difference gives the bank some profit for offering this service. For our purposes here, we can ignore these differences.)

An exchange rate can always be expressed in two ways. If the exchange rate is 80 yen per dollar, it is also 1/80 (= 0.0125) dollar per yen. Throughout this book, we always express the nominal exchange rate as units of foreign currency per U.S. dollar, such as 80 yen per dollar.

appreciation
an increase in the value of a currency as measured by the amount of foreign currency it can buy

depreciation
a decrease in the value of a currency as measured by the amount of foreign currency it can buy

If the exchange rate changes so that a dollar buys more foreign currency, that change is called an **appreciation** of the dollar. If the exchange rate changes so that a dollar buys less foreign currency, that change is called a **depreciation** of the dollar. For example, when the exchange rate rises from 80 to 90 yen per dollar, the dollar is said to appreciate. At the same time, because a Japanese yen now buys less of the U.S. currency, the yen is said to depreciate. When the exchange rate falls from 80 to 70 yen per dollar, the dollar is said to depreciate, and the yen is said to appreciate.

At times you may have heard the media report that the dollar is either "strong" or "weak." These descriptions usually refer to recent changes in the nominal exchange rate. When a currency appreciates, it is said to *strengthen* because it can then buy more foreign currency. Similarly, when a currency depreciates, it is said to *weaken*.

For any country, there are many nominal exchange rates. The U.S. dollar can be used to buy Japanese yen, British pounds, Mexican pesos, and so on. When economists study changes in the exchange rate, they often use indexes that average these many exchange rates. Just as the consumer price index turns the many prices in the economy into a single measure of the price level, an exchange rate index turns these many exchange rates into a single measure of the international value of the currency. So when economists talk about the dollar appreciating or depreciating, they often are referring to an exchange rate index that takes into account many individual exchange rates.

Real Exchange Rates

real exchange rate
the rate at which a person can trade the goods and services of one country for the goods and services of another

The **real exchange rate** is the rate at which a person can trade the goods and services of one country for the goods and services of another. For example, suppose that you go shopping and find that a pound of Swiss cheese is twice as expensive as a pound of American cheese. We would then say that the real exchange rate is 1/2 pound of Swiss cheese per pound of American cheese. Notice that, like the nominal exchange rate, we express the real exchange rate as units of the foreign item per unit of the domestic item. But in this instance the item is a good rather than a currency.

Real and nominal exchange rates are closely related. To see how, consider an example. Suppose that a bushel of American rice sells for $100, and a bushel of Japanese rice sells for 16,000 yen. What is the real exchange rate between American and Japanese rice? To answer this question, we must first use the nominal exchange rate to convert the prices into a common currency. If the nominal exchange rate is 80 yen per dollar, then a price for American rice of $100 per bushel is equivalent to 8,000 yen per bushel. American rice is half as expensive as Japanese rice. The real exchange rate is 1/2 bushel of Japanese rice per bushel of American rice.

We can summarize this calculation for the real exchange rate with the following formula:

$$\text{Real exchange rate} = \frac{\text{Nominal exchange rate} \times \text{Domestic price}}{\text{Foreign price}}.$$

Using the numbers in our example, the formula applies as follows:

$$\text{Real exchange rate} = \frac{(80 \text{ yen per dollar}) \times (\$100 \text{ per bushel of American rice})}{16{,}000 \text{ yen per bushel of Japanese rice}}$$

$$= \frac{8{,}000 \text{ yen per bushel of American rice}}{16{,}000 \text{ yen per bushel of Japanese rice}}$$

$$= 1/2 \text{ bushel of Japanese rice per bushel of American rice}.$$

Thus, the real exchange rate depends on the nominal exchange rate and on the prices of goods in the two countries measured in the local currencies.

Why does the real exchange rate matter? As you might guess, the real exchange rate is a key determinant of how much a country exports and imports. When Uncle Ben's, Inc., is deciding whether to buy U.S. rice or Japanese rice to put into its boxes, for example, it will ask which rice is cheaper. The real exchange rate gives the answer. As another example, imagine that you are deciding whether to take a seaside vacation in Miami, Florida, or in Cancún, Mexico. You might ask your travel agent the price of a hotel room in Miami (measured in dollars), the price of a hotel room in Cancún (measured in pesos), and the exchange rate between pesos and dollars. If you decide where to vacation by comparing costs, you are basing your decision on the real exchange rate.

When studying an economy as a whole, macroeconomists focus on overall prices rather than the prices of individual items. That is, to measure the real exchange rate, they use price indexes, such as the consumer price index, which measure the price of a basket of goods and services. By using a price index for a U.S. basket (P), a price index for a foreign basket (P^*), and the nominal exchange rate between the U.S. dollar and foreign currencies (e), we can compute the overall real exchange rate between the United States and other countries as follows:

$$\text{Real exchange rate} = (e \times P)/P^*.$$

This real exchange rate measures the price of a basket of goods and services available domestically relative to a basket of goods and services available abroad.

As we examine more fully in the next chapter, a country's real exchange rate is a key determinant of its net exports of goods and services. A depreciation (fall) in the U.S. real exchange rate means that U.S. goods have become cheaper relative to foreign goods. This change encourages consumers both at home and abroad to buy more U.S. goods and fewer goods from other countries. As a result, U.S. exports rise, and U.S. imports fall, and both of these changes raise U.S. net exports. Conversely, an appreciation (rise) in the U.S. real exchange rate means that U.S. goods have become more expensive compared to foreign goods, so U.S. net exports fall.

THE EURO

You may have once heard of, or perhaps even seen, currencies such as the French franc, the German mark, or the Italian lira. These types of money no longer exist. During the 1990s, many European nations decided to give up their national currencies and use a common currency called the *euro*. The euro started circulating on January 1, 2002. Monetary policy for the euro area is now set by the European Central Bank (ECB), with representatives from all of the participating countries. The ECB issues the euro and controls the supply of this money, much as the Federal Reserve controls the supply of dollars in the U.S. economy.

Why did these countries adopt a common currency? One benefit of a common currency is that it makes trade eas-ier. Imagine that each of the 50 U.S. states had a different currency. Every time you crossed a state border you would need to change your money and perform the kind of exchange-rate calculations discussed in the text. This would be inconvenient, and it might deter you from buying goods and services outside your own state. The countries of Europe decided that as their economies became more integrated, it would be better to avoid this inconvenience.

To some extent, the adoption of a common currency in Europe was a political decision based on concerns beyond the scope of standard economics. Some advocates of the euro wanted to reduce nationalistic feelings and to make Europeans appreciate more fully their shared history and destiny. A single money for most of the continent, they argued, would help achieve this goal.

There are, however, costs of choosing a common currency. If the nations of Europe have only one money, they can have only one monetary policy. If they disagree about what monetary policy is best, they will have to reach some kind of agreement, rather than each going its own way. Because adopting a single money has both benefits and costs, there is debate among economists about whether Europe's recent adoption of the euro was a good decision. Only time will tell what effects the decision will have.

QuickQuiz Define *nominal exchange rate* and *real exchange rate*, and explain how they are related. • If the nominal exchange rate goes from 100 to 120 yen per dollar, has the dollar appreciated or depreciated?

A FIRST THEORY OF EXCHANGE-RATE DETERMINATION: PURCHASING-POWER PARITY

Exchange rates vary substantially over time. In 1970, a U.S. dollar could be used to buy 3.65 German marks or 627 Italian lira. In 1998, as both Germany and Italy were getting ready to adopt the euro as their common currency, a U.S. dollar bought 1.76 German marks or 1,737 Italian lira. In other words, over this period the value of the dollar fell by more than half compared to the mark, while it more than doubled compared to the lira.

What explains these large and opposite changes? Economists have developed many models to explain how exchange rates are determined, each emphasizing just some of the many forces at work. Here we develop the simplest theory of exchange rates, called **purchasing-power parity.** This theory states that a unit of any given currency should be able to buy the same quantity of goods in all countries.

purchasing-power parity
a theory of exchange rates whereby a unit of any given currency should be able to buy the same quantity of goods in all countries

Many economists believe that purchasing-power parity describes the forces that determine exchange rates in the long run. We now consider the logic on which this long-run theory of exchange rates is based, as well as the theory's implications and limitations.

The Basic Logic of Purchasing-Power Parity

The theory of purchasing-power parity is based on a principle called the *law of one price*. This law asserts that a good must sell for the same price in all locations. Otherwise, there would be opportunities for profit left unexploited. For example, suppose that coffee beans sold for less in Seattle than in Boston. A person could buy coffee in Seattle for, say, $4 a pound and then sell it in Boston for $5 a pound, making a profit of $1 per pound from the difference in price. The process of taking advantage of differences in prices in different markets is called *arbitrage*. In our example, as people took advantage of this arbitrage opportunity, they would increase the demand for coffee in Seattle and increase the supply in Boston. The price of coffee would rise in Seattle (in response to greater demand) and fall in Boston (in response to greater supply). This process would continue until, eventually, the prices were the same in the two markets.

Now consider how the law of one price applies to the international marketplace. If a dollar (or any other currency) could buy more coffee in the United States than in Japan, international traders could profit by buying coffee in the United States and selling it in Japan. This export of coffee from the United States to Japan would drive up the U.S. price of coffee and drive down the Japanese price. Conversely, if a dollar could buy more coffee in Japan than in the United States, traders could buy coffee in Japan and sell it in the United States. This import of coffee into the United States from Japan would drive down the U.S. price of coffee and drive up the Japanese price. In the end, the law of one price tells us that a dollar must buy the same amount of coffee in all countries.

This logic leads us to the theory of purchasing-power parity. According to this theory, a currency must have the same purchasing power in all countries. That is, a U.S. dollar must buy the same quantity of goods in the United States and Japan, and a Japanese yen must buy the same quantity of goods in Japan and the United States. Indeed, the name of this theory describes it well. *Parity* means equality, and *purchasing power* refers to the value of money. *Purchasing-power parity* states that a unit of all currencies must have the same real value in every country.

Implications of Purchasing-Power Parity

What does the theory of purchasing-power parity say about exchange rates? It tells us that the nominal exchange rate between the currencies of two countries depends on the price levels in those countries. If a dollar buys the same quantity of goods in the United States (where prices are measured in dollars) as in Japan (where prices are measured in yen), then the number of yen per dollar must reflect the prices of goods in the United States and Japan. For example, if a pound of coffee costs 500 yen in Japan and $5 in the United States, then the nominal exchange rate must be 100 yen per dollar (500 yen/$5 = 100 yen per dollar). Otherwise, the purchasing power of the dollar would not be the same in the two countries.

To see more fully how this works, it is helpful to use just a bit of mathematics. Suppose that P is the price of a basket of goods in the United States (measured in dollars), P^* is the price of a basket of goods in Japan (measured in yen), and e is the nominal exchange rate (the number of yen a dollar can buy). Now consider the quantity of goods a dollar can buy at home and abroad. At home, the price level is P, so the purchasing power of $1 at home is $1/P$. Abroad, a dollar can be exchanged into e units of foreign currency, which in turn have purchasing power e/P^*. For the purchasing power of a dollar to be the same in the two countries, it must be the case that

$$1/P = e/P^*.$$

With rearrangement, this equation becomes

$$1 = eP/P^*.$$

Notice that the left-hand side of this equation is a constant, and the right-hand side is the real exchange rate. Thus, *if the purchasing power of the dollar is always the same at home and abroad, then the real exchange rate—the relative price of domestic and foreign goods—cannot change.*

To see the implication of this analysis for the nominal exchange rate, we can rearrange the last equation to solve for the nominal exchange rate:

$$e = P^*/P.$$

That is, the nominal exchange rate equals the ratio of the foreign price level (measured in units of the foreign currency) to the domestic price level (measured in units of the domestic currency). *According to the theory of purchasing-power parity, the nominal exchange rate between the currencies of two countries must reflect the different price levels in those countries.*

A key implication of this theory is that nominal exchange rates change when price levels change. As we saw in the preceding chapter, the price level in any country adjusts to bring the quantity of money supplied and the quantity of money demanded into balance. Because the nominal exchange rate depends on the price levels, it also depends on the money supply and money demand in each country. When a central bank in any country increases the money supply and causes the price level to rise, it also causes that country's currency to depreciate relative to other currencies in the world. In other words, *when the central bank prints large quantities of money, that money loses value both in terms of the goods and services it can buy and in terms of the amount of other currencies it can buy.*

We can now answer the question that began this section: Why did the U.S. dollar lose value compared to the German mark and gain value compared to the Italian lira? The answer is that Germany pursued a less inflationary monetary policy than the United States, and Italy pursued a more inflationary monetary policy. From 1970 to 1998, inflation in the United States was 5.3 percent per year. By contrast, inflation was 3.5 percent in Germany, and 9.6 percent in Italy. As U.S. prices rose relative to German prices, the value of the dollar fell relative to the mark. Similarly, as U.S. prices fell relative to Italian prices, the value of the dollar rose relative to the lira.

Germany and Italy now have a common currency—the euro. This means that the two countries share a single monetary policy and that the inflation rates in the two countries will be closely linked. But the historical lessons of the lira and the mark will apply to the euro as well. Whether the U.S. dollar buys more or fewer euros 20 years from now than it does today depends on whether the European

Central Bank produces more or less inflation in Europe than the Federal Reserve does in the United States.

Case Study

THE NOMINAL EXCHANGE RATE DURING A HYPERINFLATION

Macroeconomists can only rarely conduct controlled experiments. Most often, they must glean what they can from the natural experiments that history gives them. One natural experiment is hyperinflation—the high inflation that arises when a government turns to the printing press to pay for large amounts of government spending. Because hyperinflations are so extreme, they illustrate some basic economic principles with clarity.

Consider the German hyperinflation of the early 1920s. Figure 3 shows the German money supply, the German price level, and the nominal exchange rate (measured as U.S. cents per German mark) for that period. Notice that these series move closely together. When the supply of money starts growing quickly, the price level also takes off, and the German mark depreciates. When the money supply stabilizes, so does the price level and the exchange rate.

The pattern shown in this figure appears during every hyperinflation. It leaves no doubt that there is a fundamental link among money, prices, and the nominal exchange rate. The quantity theory of money discussed in the previous chapter

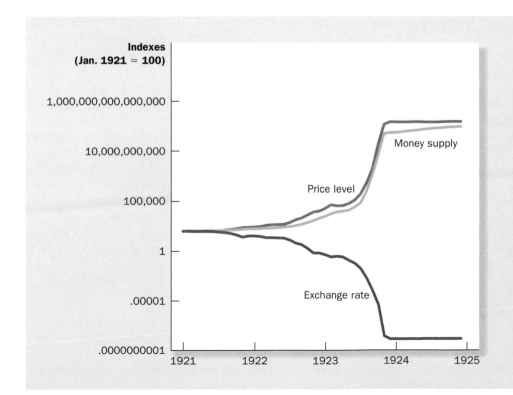

FIGURE 3

Money, Prices, and the Nominal Exchange Rate during the German Hyperinflation

This figure shows the money supply, the price level, and the exchange rate (measured as U.S. cents per mark) for the German hyperinflation from January 1921 to December 1924. Notice how similarly these three variables move. When the quantity of money started growing quickly, the price level followed, and the mark depreciated relative to the dollar. When the German central bank stabilized the money supply, the price level and exchange rate stabilized as well.

Source: Adapted from Thomas J. Sargent, "The End of Four Big Inflations," in Robert Hall, ed., *Inflation* (Chicago: University of Chicago Press, 1983), pp. 41–93. Reprinted with permission.

explains how the money supply affects the price level. The theory of purchasing-power parity discussed here explains how the price level affects the nominal exchange rate. ●

Limitations of Purchasing-Power Parity

Purchasing-power parity provides a simple model of how exchange rates are determined. For understanding many economic phenomena, the theory works well. In particular, it can explain many long-term trends, such as the depreciation of the U.S. dollar against the German mark and the appreciation of the U.S. dollar against the Italian lira discussed earlier. It can also explain the major changes in exchange rates that occur during hyperinflations.

Yet the theory of purchasing-power parity is not completely accurate. That is, exchange rates do not always move to ensure that a dollar has the same real value in all countries all the time. There are two reasons why the theory of purchasing-power parity does not always hold in practice.

The first reason is that many goods are not easily traded. Imagine, for instance, that haircuts are more expensive in Paris than in New York. International travelers might avoid getting their haircuts in Paris, and some haircutters might move from New York to Paris. Yet such arbitrage would probably be too limited to eliminate the differences in prices. Thus, the deviation from purchasing-power parity might persist, and a dollar (or euro) would continue to buy less of a haircut in Paris than in New York.

The second reason that purchasing-power parity does not always hold is that even tradable goods are not always perfect substitutes when they are produced in different countries. For example, some consumers prefer German cars, and others prefer American cars. Moreover, consumer tastes can change over time. If German cars suddenly become more popular, the increase in demand will drive up the price of German cars compared to American cars. But despite this difference in prices in the two markets, there might be no opportunity for profitable arbitrage because consumers do not view the two cars as equivalent.

Thus, both because some goods are not tradable and because some tradable goods are not perfect substitutes with their foreign counterparts, purchasing-power parity is not a perfect theory of exchange-rate determination. For these reasons, real exchange rates fluctuate over time. Nonetheless, the theory of purchasing-power parity does provide a useful first step in understanding exchange rates. The basic logic is persuasive: As the real exchange rate drifts from the level predicted by purchasing-power parity, people have greater incentive to move goods across national borders. Even if the forces of purchasing-power parity do not completely fix the real exchange rate, they provide a reason to expect that changes in the real exchange rate are most often small or temporary. As a result, large and persistent movements in nominal exchange rates typically reflect changes in price levels at home and abroad.

Case Study
THE HAMBURGER STANDARD

When economists apply the theory of purchasing-power parity to explain exchange rates, they need data on the prices of a basket of goods available in different countries.

One analysis of this sort is conducted by *The Economist,* an international news-magazine. The magazine occasionally collects data on a basket of goods consisting of "two all-beef patties, special sauce, lettuce, cheese, pickles, onions, on a sesame seed bun." It's called the "Big Mac" and is sold by McDonald's around the world.

Once we have the prices of Big Macs in two countries denominated in the local currencies, we can compute the exchange rate predicted by the theory of purchasing-power parity. The predicted exchange rate is the one that makes the cost of the Big Mac the same in the two countries. For instance, if the price of a Big Mac is $2 in the United States and 200 yen in Japan, purchasing-power parity would predict an exchange rate of 100 yen per dollar.

How well does purchasing-power parity work when applied using Big Mac prices? Here are some examples from an *Economist* article published on April 25, 2002, when the price of a Big Mac was $2.49 in the United States:

Country	Price of a Big Mac	Predicted Exchange Rate	Actual Exchange Rate
South Korea	3,100 won	1,245 won/$	1,304 won/$
Japan	262 yen	105 yen/$	130 yen/$
Sweden	26 kronor	10.4 kronor/$	10.3 kronor/$
Mexico	21.90 pesos	8.80 pesos/$	9.28 pesos/$
Euro area	2.67 euros	1.07 euros/$	1.12 euros/$
Britain	1.99 pounds	0.80 pound/$	0.69 pound/$

In the United States the price of a Big Mac is $2.49; in Japan it is 262 yen.

You can see that the predicted and actual exchange rates are not exactly the same. After all, international arbitrage in Big Macs is not easy. Yet the two exchange rates are usually in the same ballpark. Purchasing-power parity is not a precise theory of exchange rates, but it often provides a reasonable first approximation. ●

QuickQuiz Over the past 20 years, Spain has had high inflation, and Japan has had low inflation. What do you predict has happened to the number of Spanish pesetas a person can buy with a Japanese yen?

CONCLUSION

The purpose of this chapter has been to develop some basic concepts that macroeconomists use to study open economies. You should now understand why a nation's net exports must equal its net capital outflow, and why national saving must equal domestic investment plus net capital outflow. You should also understand the meaning of the nominal and real exchange rates, as well as the implications and limitations of purchasing-power parity as a theory of how exchange rates are determined.

The macroeconomic variables defined here offer a starting point for analyzing an open economy's interactions with the rest of the world. In the next chapter we develop a model that can explain what determines these variables. We can then discuss how various events and policies affect a country's trade balance and the rate at which nations make exchanges in world markets.

SUMMARY

- Net exports are the value of domestic goods and services sold abroad minus the value of foreign goods and services sold domestically. Net capital outflow is the acquisition of foreign assets by domestic residents minus the acquisition of domestic assets by foreigners. Because every international transaction involves an exchange of an asset for a good or service, an economy's net capital outflow always equals its net exports.

- An economy's saving can be used either to finance investment at home or to buy assets abroad. Thus, national saving equals domestic investment plus net capital outflow.

- The nominal exchange rate is the relative price of the currency of two countries, and the real exchange rate is the relative price of the goods and services of two countries. When the nominal

exchange rate changes so that each dollar buys more foreign currency, the dollar is said to *appreciate* or *strengthen*. When the nominal exchange rate changes so that each dollar buys less foreign currency, the dollar is said to *depreciate* or *weaken*.

- According to the theory of purchasing-power parity, a dollar (or a unit of any other currency) should be able to buy the same quantity of goods in all countries. This theory implies that the nominal exchange rate between the currencies of two countries should reflect the price levels in those countries. As a result, countries with relatively high inflation should have depreciating currencies, and countries with relatively low inflation should have appreciating currencies.

KEY CONCEPTS

closed economy, p. 380
open economy, p. 380
exports, p. 380
imports, p. 380
net exports, p. 380

trade balance, p. 380
trade surplus, p. 380
trade deficit, p. 380
balanced trade, p. 380
net capital outflow, p. 382

nominal exchange rate, p. 389
appreciation, p. 390
depreciation, p. 390
real exchange rate, p. 390
purchasing-power parity, p. 392

QUESTIONS FOR REVIEW

1. Define net exports and net capital outflow. Explain how and why they are related.

2. Explain the relationship among saving, investment, and net capital outflow.

3. If a Japanese car costs 500,000 yen, a similar American car costs $10,000, and a dollar can buy 100 yen, what are the nominal and real exchange rates?

4. Describe the economic logic behind the theory of purchasing-power parity.

5. If the Fed started printing large quantities of U.S. dollars, what would happen to the number of Japanese yen a dollar could buy?

PROBLEMS AND APPLICATIONS

1. How would the following transactions affect U.S. exports, imports, and net exports?
   a. An American art professor spends the summer touring museums in Europe.

   b. Students in Paris flock to see the latest Arnold Schwarzenegger movie.
   c. Your uncle buys a new Volvo.
   d. The student bookstore at Oxford University sells a pair of Levi's 501 jeans.

e. A Canadian citizen shops at a store in northern Vermont to avoid Canadian sales taxes.

2. International trade in each of the following products has increased over time. Suggest some reasons why this might be so.
   a. wheat
   b. banking services
   c. computer software
   d. automobiles

3. Describe the difference between foreign direct investment and foreign portfolio investment. Who is more likely to engage in foreign direct investment—a corporation or an individual investor? Who is more likely to engage in foreign portfolio investment?

4. How would the following transactions affect U.S. net capital outflow? Also, state whether each involves direct investment or portfolio investment.
   a. An American cellular phone company establishes an office in the Czech Republic.
   b. Harrod's of London sells stock to the General Electric pension fund.
   c. Honda expands its factory in Marysville, Ohio.
   d. A Fidelity mutual fund sells its Volkswagen stock to a French investor.

5. Holding national saving constant, does an increase in net capital outflow increase, decrease, or have no effect on a country's accumulation of domestic capital?

6. The business section of most major newspapers contains a table showing U.S. exchange rates. Find such a table and use it to answer the following questions.
   a. Does this table show nominal or real exchange rates? Explain.
   b. What are the exchange rates between the United States and Canada and between the United States and Japan? Calculate the exchange rate between Canada and Japan.
   c. If U.S. inflation exceeds Japanese inflation over the next year, would you expect the U.S. dollar to appreciate or depreciate relative to the Japanese yen?

7. Would each of the following groups be happy or unhappy if the U.S. dollar appreciated? Explain.
   a. Dutch pension funds holding U.S. government bonds
   b. U.S. manufacturing industries
   c. Australian tourists planning a trip to the United States
   d. An American firm trying to purchase property overseas

8. What is happening to the U.S. real exchange rate in each of the following situations? Explain.
   a. The U.S. nominal exchange rate is unchanged, but prices rise faster in the United States than abroad.
   b. The U.S. nominal exchange rate is unchanged, but prices rise faster abroad than in the United States.
   c. The U.S. nominal exchange rate declines, and prices are unchanged in the United States and abroad.
   d. The U.S. nominal exchange rate declines, and prices rise faster abroad than in the United States.

9. List three goods for which the law of one price is likely to hold, and three goods for which it is not. Justify your choices.

10. A can of soda costs $0.75 in the United States and 12 pesos in Mexico. What would the peso–dollar exchange rate be if purchasing-power parity holds? If a monetary expansion caused all prices in Mexico to double, so that soda rose to 24 pesos, what would happen to the peso–dollar exchange rate?

11. Assume that American rice sells for $100 per bushel, Japanese rice sells for 16,000 yen per bushel, and the nominal exchange rate is 80 yen per dollar.
    a. Explain how you could make a profit from this situation. What would be your profit per bushel of rice? If other people exploit the same opportunity, what would happen to the price of rice in Japan and the price of rice in the United States?
    b. Suppose that rice is the only commodity in the world. What would happen to the real exchange rate between the United States and Japan?

12. A case study in the chapter analyzed purchasing-power parity for several countries using the price of Big Macs. Here are data for a few more countries:

Country	Price of a Big Mac	Predicted Exchange Rate	Actual Exchange Rate
Indonesia	16,000 rupiah	_____ rupiah/$	9,430 rupiah/$
Hungary	459 forints	_____ forints/$	272 forints/$
Czech Republic	56.28 korunas	_____ korunas/$	34.0 korunas/$
Israel	12 shekels	_____ shekels/$	4.79 shekels/$
Canada	3.33 C$	_____ C$/$	1.57 C$/$

a. For each country, compute the predicted exchange rate of the local currency per U.S. dollar. (Recall that the U.S. price of a Big Mac was $2.49.) How well does the theory of purchasing-power parity explain exchange rates?

b. According to purchasing-power parity, what is the predicted exchange rate between the Israeli shekel and the Canadian dollar? What is the actual exchange rate?

http://

For more study tools, please visit http://mankiwXtra.swlearning.com.

A MACROECONOMIC THEORY
OF THE OPEN ECONOMY

Over the past two decades, the United States has persistently imported more goods and services than it has exported. That is, U.S. net exports have been negative. Although economists debate whether these trade deficits are a problem for the U.S. economy, the nation's business community has a strong opinion. Many business leaders claim that the trade deficits reflect unfair competition: Foreign firms are allowed to sell their products in U.S. markets, they contend, while foreign governments impede U.S. firms from selling U.S. products abroad.

Imagine that you are the president and you want to end these trade deficits. What should you do? Should you try to limit imports, perhaps by imposing a quota on the import of cars from Japan? Or should you try to influence the nation's trade deficit in some other way?

To understand what factors determine a country's trade balance and how government policies can affect it, we need a macroeconomic theory of the open economy. The preceding chapter introduced some of the key macroeconomic variables that describe an economy's relationship with other economies—including net exports, net capital outflow, and the real and nominal exchange rates. This chapter develops a model that identifies the forces that determine these variables and shows how these variables are related to one another.

To develop this macroeconomic model of an open economy, we build on our previous analysis in two important ways. First, the model takes the economy's GDP as given. We assume that the economy's output of goods and services, as measured by real GDP, is determined by the supplies of the factors of production and by the available production technology that turns these inputs into output. Second, the model takes the economy's price level as given. We assume that the price level adjusts to bring the supply and demand for money into balance. In other words, this chapter takes as a starting point the lessons learned in Chapters 25 and 30 about the determination of the economy's output and price level.

The goal of the model in this chapter is to highlight the forces that determine the economy's trade balance and exchange rate. In one sense, the model is simple: It applies the tools of supply and demand to an open economy. Yet the model is also more complicated than others we have seen because it involves looking simultaneously at two related markets—the market for loanable funds and the market for foreign-currency exchange. After we develop this model of the open economy, we use it to examine how various events and policies affect the economy's trade balance and exchange rate. We will then be able to determine the government policies that are most likely to reverse the trade deficits that the U.S. economy has experienced over the past two decades.

SUPPLY AND DEMAND FOR LOANABLE FUNDS AND FOR FOREIGN-CURRENCY EXCHANGE

To understand the forces at work in an open economy, we focus on supply and demand in two markets. The first is the market for loanable funds, which coordinates the economy's saving, investment, and the flow of loanable funds abroad (called the net capital outflow). The second is the market for foreign-currency exchange, which coordinates people who want to exchange the domestic currency for the currency of other countries. In this section we discuss supply and demand in each of these markets. In the next section we put these markets together to explain the overall equilibrium for an open economy.

The Market for Loanable Funds

When we first analyzed the role of the financial system in Chapter 26, we made the simplifying assumption that the financial system consists of only one market, called the *market for loanable funds*. All savers go to this market to deposit their saving, and all borrowers go to this market to get their loans. In this market, there is one interest rate, which is both the return to saving and the cost of borrowing.

To understand the market for loanable funds in an open economy, the place to start is the identity discussed in the preceding chapter:

$$S \quad = \quad I \quad + \quad NCO$$

$$\text{Saving} \quad = \quad \begin{array}{c}\text{Domestic}\\\text{investment}\end{array} \quad + \quad \begin{array}{c}\text{Net capital}\\\text{outflow.}\end{array}$$

Whenever a nation saves a dollar of its income, it can use that dollar to finance the purchase of domestic capital or to finance the purchase of an asset abroad. The two sides of this identity represent the two sides of the market for loanable funds. The supply of loanable funds comes from national saving (S). The demand for loanable funds comes from domestic investment (I) and net capital outflow (NCO). Note that the purchase of a capital asset adds to the demand for loanable funds, regardless of whether that asset is located at home or abroad. Because net capital outflow can be either positive or negative, it can either add to or subtract from the demand for loanable funds that arises from domestic investment.

As we learned in our earlier discussion of the market for loanable funds, the quantity of loanable funds supplied and the quantity of loanable funds demanded depend on the real interest rate. A higher real interest rate encourages people to save and, therefore, raises the quantity of loanable funds supplied. A higher interest rate also makes borrowing to finance capital projects more costly; thus, it discourages investment and reduces the quantity of loanable funds demanded.

In addition to influencing national saving and domestic investment, the real interest rate in a country affects that country's net capital outflow. To see why, consider two mutual funds—one in the United States and one in Germany—deciding whether to buy a U.S. government bond or a German government bond. The mutual funds would make this decision in part by comparing the real interest rates in the United States and Germany. When the U.S. real interest rate rises, the U.S. bond becomes more attractive to both mutual funds. Thus, an increase in the U.S. real interest rate discourages Americans from buying foreign assets and encourages foreigners to buy U.S. assets. For both reasons, a high U.S. real interest rate reduces U.S. net capital outflow.

We represent the market for loanable funds on the familiar supply-and-demand diagram in Figure 1. As in our earlier analysis of the financial system, the sup-

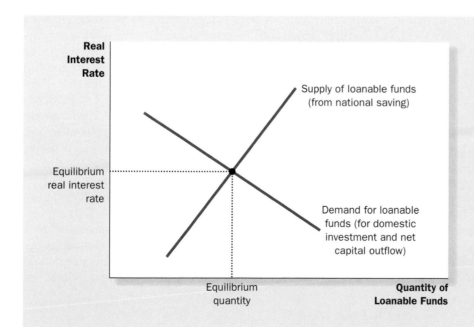

FIGURE 1

The Market for Loanable Funds

The interest rate in an open economy, as in a closed economy, is determined by the supply and demand for loanable funds. National saving is the source of the supply of loanable funds. Domestic investment and net capital outflow are the sources of the demand for loanable funds. At the equilibrium interest rate, the amount that people want to save exactly balances the amount that people want to borrow for the purpose of buying domestic capital and foreign assets.

ply curve slopes upward because a higher interest rate increases the quantity of loanable funds supplied, and the demand curve slopes downward because a higher interest rate decreases the quantity of loanable funds demanded. Unlike the situation in our previous discussion, however, the demand side of the market now represents the behavior of both domestic investment and net capital outflow. That is, in an open economy, the demand for loanable funds comes not only from those who want loanable funds to buy domestic capital goods but also from those who want loanable funds to buy foreign assets.

The interest rate adjusts to bring the supply and demand for loanable funds into balance. If the interest rate were below the equilibrium level, the quantity of loanable funds supplied would be less than the quantity demanded. The resulting shortage of loanable funds would push the interest rate upward. Conversely, if the interest rate were above the equilibrium level, the quantity of loanable funds supplied would exceed the quantity demanded. The surplus of loanable funds would drive the interest rate downward. At the equilibrium interest rate, the supply of loanable funds exactly balances the demand. That is, *at the equilibrium interest rate, the amount that people want to save exactly balances the desired quantities of domestic investment and net capital outflow.*

The Market for Foreign-Currency Exchange

The second market in our model of the open economy is the market for foreign-currency exchange. Participants in this market trade U.S. dollars in exchange for foreign currencies. To understand the market for foreign-currency exchange, we begin with another identity from the last chapter:

$$NCO = NX$$

Net capital outflow = Net exports.

This identity states that the imbalance between the purchase and sale of capital assets abroad (NCO) equals the imbalance between exports and imports of goods and services (NX). For example, when the U.S. economy is running a trade surplus ($NX > 0$), foreigners are buying more U.S. goods and services than Americans are buying foreign goods and services. What are Americans doing with the foreign currency they are getting from this net sale of goods and services abroad? They must be buying foreign assets, so U.S. capital is flowing abroad ($NCO > 0$). Conversely, if the United States is running a trade deficit ($NX < 0$), Americans are spending more on foreign goods and services than they are earning from selling abroad. Some of this spending must be financed by selling American assets abroad, so foreign capital is flowing into the United States ($NCO < 0$).

Our model of the open economy treats the two sides of this identity as representing the two sides of the market for foreign-currency exchange. Net capital outflow represents the quantity of dollars supplied for the purpose of buying foreign assets. For example, when a U.S. mutual fund wants to buy a Japanese government bond, it needs to change dollars into yen, so it supplies dollars in the market for foreign-currency exchange. Net exports represent the quantity of dollars demanded for the purpose of buying U.S. net exports of goods and services. For example, when a Japanese airline wants to buy a plane made by Boeing, it needs to change its yen into dollars, so it demands dollars in the market for foreign-currency exchange.

What price balances the supply and demand in the market for foreign-currency exchange? The answer is the real exchange rate. As we saw in the preceding chapter, the real exchange rate is the relative price of domestic and foreign goods and, therefore, is a key determinant of net exports. When the U.S. real exchange rate appreciates, U.S. goods become more expensive relative to foreign goods, making U.S. goods less attractive to consumers both at home and abroad. As a result, exports from the United States fall, and imports into the United States rise. For both reasons, net exports fall. Hence, an appreciation of the real exchange rate reduces the quantity of dollars demanded in the market for foreign-currency exchange.

Figure 2 shows supply and demand in the market for foreign-currency exchange. The demand curve slopes downward for the reason we just discussed: A higher real exchange rate makes U.S. goods more expensive and reduces the

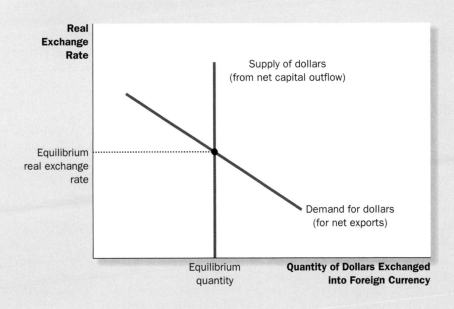

FIGURE 2

The Market for Foreign-Currency Exchange

The real exchange rate is determined by the supply and demand for foreign-currency exchange. The supply of dollars to be exchanged into foreign currency comes from net capital outflow. Because net capital outflow does not depend on the real exchange rate, the supply curve is vertical. The demand for dollars comes from net exports. Because a lower real exchange rate stimulates net exports (and thus increases the quantity of dollars demanded to pay for these net exports), the demand curve is downward sloping. At the equilibrium real exchange rate, the number of dollars people supply to buy foreign assets exactly balances the number of dollars people demand to buy net exports.

quantity of dollars demanded to buy those goods. The supply curve is vertical because the quantity of dollars supplied for net capital outflow does not depend on the real exchange rate. (As discussed earlier, net capital outflow depends on the real interest rate. When discussing the market for foreign-currency exchange, we take the real interest rate and net capital outflow as given.)

The real exchange rate adjusts to balance the supply and demand for dollars just as the price of any good adjusts to balance supply and demand for that good. If the real exchange rate were below the equilibrium level, the quantity of dollars supplied would be less than the quantity demanded. The resulting shortage of dollars would push the value of the dollar upward. Conversely, if the real exchange rate were above the equilibrium level, the quantity of dollars supplied would exceed the quantity demanded. The surplus of dollars would drive the value of the dollar downward. *At the equilibrium real exchange rate, the demand for dollars by foreigners arising from the U.S. net exports of goods and services exactly balances the supply of dollars from Americans arising from U.S. net capital outflow.*

At this point, it is worth noting that the division of transactions between "supply" and "demand" in this model is somewhat artificial. In our model, net exports are the source of the demand for dollars, and net capital outflow is the source of the supply. Thus, when a U.S. resident imports a car made in Japan, our model treats that transaction as a decrease in the quantity of dollars demanded (because net exports fall) rather than an increase in the quantity of dollars supplied. Similarly, when a Japanese citizen buys a U.S. government bond, our model treats that

PURCHASING-POWER PARITY AS A SPECIAL CASE

An alert reader of this book might ask: Why are we developing a theory of the exchange rate here? Didn't we already do that in the preceding chapter?

As you may recall, the preceding chapter developed a theory of the exchange rate called *purchasing-power parity.* This theory asserts that a dollar (or any other currency) must buy the same quantity of goods and services in every country. As a result, the real exchange rate is fixed, and all changes in the nominal exchange rate between two currencies reflect changes in the price levels in the two countries.

The model of the exchange rate developed here is related to the theory of purchasing-power parity. According to the theory of

purchasing-power parity, international trade responds quickly to international price differences. If goods were cheaper in one country than in another, they would be exported from the first country and imported into the second until the price difference disappeared. In other words, the theory of purchasing-power parity assumes that net exports are highly responsive to small changes in the real exchange rate. If net exports were in fact so responsive, the demand curve in Figure 2 would be horizontal.

Thus, the theory of purchasing-power parity can be viewed as a special case of the model considered here. In that special case, the demand curve for foreign-currency exchange, rather than being downward sloping, is horizontal at the level of the real exchange rate that ensures parity of purchasing power at home and abroad. That special case is a good place to start when studying exchange rates, but it is far from the end of the story.

This chapter, therefore, concentrates on the more realistic case in which the demand curve for foreign-currency exchange is downward sloping. This allows for the possibility that the real exchange rate changes over time, as in fact it sometimes does in the real world.

transaction as a decrease in the quantity of dollars supplied (because net capital outflow falls) rather than an increase in the quantity of dollars demanded. This use of language may seem somewhat unnatural at first, but it will prove useful when analyzing the effects of various policies.

QuickQuiz Describe the sources of supply and demand in the market for loanable funds and the market for foreign-currency exchange.

EQUILIBRIUM IN THE OPEN ECONOMY

So far we have discussed supply and demand in two markets—the market for loanable funds and the market for foreign-currency exchange. Let's now consider how these markets are related to each other.

Net Capital Outflow: The Link between the Two Markets

We begin by recapping what we've learned so far in this chapter. We have been discussing how the economy coordinates four important macroeconomic variables: national saving (S), domestic investment (I), net capital outflow (NCO), and net exports (NX). Keep in mind the following identities:

$$S = I + NCO$$

and

$$NCO = NX.$$

In the market for loanable funds, supply comes from national saving, demand comes from domestic investment and net capital outflow, and the real interest rate balances supply and demand. In the market for foreign-currency exchange, supply comes from net capital outflow, demand comes from net exports, and the real exchange rate balances supply and demand.

Net capital outflow is the variable that links these two markets. In the market for loanable funds, net capital outflow is a piece of demand. A person who wants to buy an asset abroad must finance this purchase by obtaining resources in the market for loanable funds. In the market for foreign-currency exchange, net capital outflow is the source of supply. A person who wants to buy an asset in another country must supply dollars in order to exchange them for the currency of that country.

The key determinant of net capital outflow, as we have discussed, is the real interest rate. When the U.S. interest rate is high, owning U.S. assets is more attractive, and U.S. net capital outflow is low. Figure 3 (p. 408) shows this negative relationship between the interest rate and net capital outflow. This net-capital-outflow curve is the link between the market for loanable funds and the market for foreign-currency exchange.

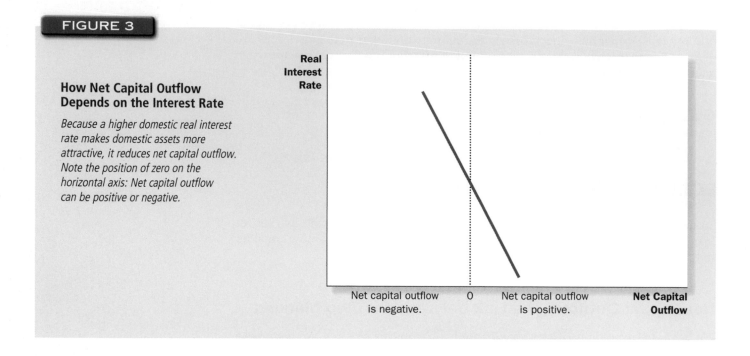

FIGURE 3

How Net Capital Outflow Depends on the Interest Rate

Because a higher domestic real interest rate makes domestic assets more attractive, it reduces net capital outflow. Note the position of zero on the horizontal axis: Net capital outflow can be positive or negative.

Simultaneous Equilibrium in Two Markets

We can now put all the pieces of our model together in Figure 4. This figure shows how the market for loanable funds and the market for foreign-currency exchange jointly determine the important macroeconomic variables of an open economy.

Panel (a) of the figure shows the market for loanable funds (taken from Figure 1). As before, national saving is the source of the supply of loanable funds. Domestic investment and net capital outflow are the source of the demand for loanable funds. The equilibrium real interest rate (r_1) brings the quantity of loanable funds supplied and the quantity of loanable funds demanded into balance.

Panel (b) of the figure shows net capital outflow (taken from Figure 3). It shows how the interest rate from panel (a) determines net capital outflow. A higher interest rate at home makes domestic assets more attractive, and this in turn reduces net capital outflow. Therefore, the net-capital-outflow curve in panel (b) slopes downward.

Panel (c) of the figure shows the market for foreign-currency exchange (taken from Figure 2). Because foreign assets must be purchased with foreign currency, the quantity of net capital outflow from panel (b) determines the supply of dollars to be exchanged into foreign currencies. The real exchange rate does not affect net capital outflow, so the supply curve is vertical. The demand for dollars comes from net exports. Because a depreciation of the real exchange rate increases net exports, the demand curve for foreign-currency exchange slopes downward. The equilibrium real exchange rate (E_1) brings into balance the quantity of dollars supplied and the quantity of dollars demanded in the market for foreign-currency exchange.

The two markets shown in Figure 4 determine two relative prices—the real interest rate and the real exchange rate. The real interest rate determined in panel (a) is the price of goods and services in the present relative to goods and services in the future. The real exchange rate determined in panel (c) is the price of domestic

FIGURE 4

The Real Equilibrium in an Open Economy

In panel (a), the supply and demand for loanable funds determine the real interest rate. In panel (b), the interest rate determines net capital outflow, which provides the supply of dollars in the market for foreign-currency exchange. In panel (c), the supply and demand for dollars in the market for foreign-currency exchange determine the real exchange rate.

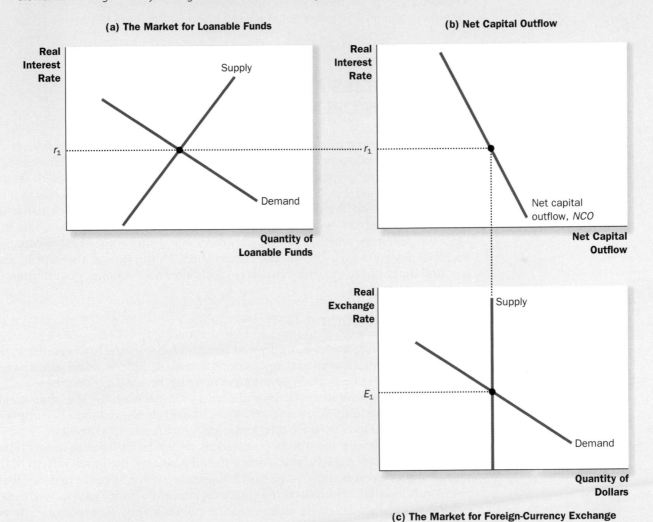

(a) The Market for Loanable Funds

(b) Net Capital Outflow

(c) The Market for Foreign-Currency Exchange

goods and services relative to foreign goods and services. These two relative prices adjust simultaneously to balance supply and demand in these two markets. As they do so, they determine national saving, domestic investment, net capital outflow, and net exports. In a moment, we will use this model to see how all these variables change when some policy or event causes one of these curves to shift.

QuickQuiz In the model of the open economy just developed, two markets determine two relative prices. What are the markets? What are the two relative prices?

HOW POLICIES AND EVENTS AFFECT AN OPEN ECONOMY

Having developed a model to explain how key macroeconomic variables are determined in an open economy, we can now use the model to analyze how changes in policy and other events alter the economy's equilibrium. As we proceed, keep in mind that our model is just supply and demand in two markets—the market for loanable funds and the market for foreign-currency exchange. When using the model to analyze any event, we can apply the three steps outlined in Chapter 4. First, we determine which of the supply and demand curves the event affects. Second, we determine which way the curves shift. Third, we use the supply-and-demand diagrams to examine how these shifts alter the economy's equilibrium.

Government Budget Deficits

When we first discussed the supply and demand for loanable funds earlier in the book, we examined the effects of government budget deficits, which occur when government spending exceeds government revenue. Because a government budget deficit represents *negative* public saving, it reduces national saving (the sum of public and private saving). Thus, a government budget deficit reduces the supply of loanable funds, drives up the interest rate, and crowds out investment.

Now let's consider the effects of a budget deficit in an open economy. First, which curve in our model shifts? As in a closed economy, the initial impact of the budget deficit is on national saving and, therefore, on the supply curve for loanable funds. Second, which way does this supply curve shift? Again as in a closed economy, a budget deficit represents *negative* public saving, so it reduces national saving and shifts the supply curve for loanable funds to the left. This is shown as the shift from S_1 to S_2 in panel (a) of Figure 5.

Our third and final step is to compare the old and new equilibria. Panel (a) shows the impact of a U.S. budget deficit on the U.S. market for loanable funds. With fewer funds available for borrowers in U.S. financial markets, the interest rate rises from r_1 to r_2 to balance supply and demand. Faced with a higher interest rate, borrowers in the market for loanable funds choose to borrow less. This change is represented in the figure as the movement from point A to point B along the demand curve for loanable funds. In particular, households and firms reduce their purchases of capital goods. As in a closed economy, budget deficits crowd out domestic investment.

FIGURE 5

The Effects of a Government Budget Deficit

When the government runs a budget deficit, it reduces the supply of loanable funds from S_1 to S_2 in panel (a). The interest rate rises from r_1 to r_2 to balance the supply and demand for loanable funds. In panel (b), the higher interest rate reduces net capital outflow. Reduced net capital outflow, in turn, reduces the supply of dollars in the market for foreign-currency exchange from S_1 to S_2 in panel (c). This fall in the supply of dollars causes the real exchange rate to appreciate from E_1 to E_2. The appreciation of the exchange rate pushes the trade balance toward deficit.

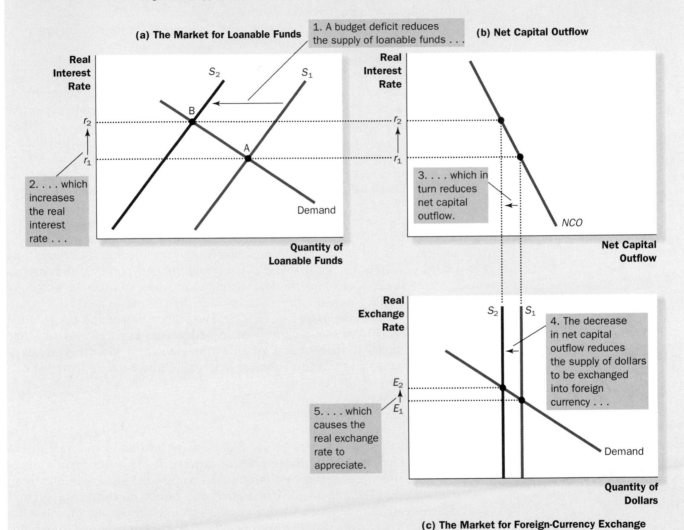

In an open economy, however, the reduced supply of loanable funds has additional effects. Panel (b) shows that the increase in the interest rate from r_1 to r_2 reduces net capital outflow. [This fall in net capital outflow is also part of the decrease in the quantity of loanable funds demanded in the movement from point A to point B in panel (a).] Because saving kept at home now earns higher rates of return, investing abroad is less attractive, and domestic residents buy fewer foreign assets. Higher interest rates also attract foreign investors, who want to earn the higher returns on U.S. assets. Thus, when budget deficits raise interest rates, both domestic and foreign behavior cause U.S. net capital outflow to fall.

Panel (c) shows how budget deficits affect the market for foreign-currency exchange. Because net capital outflow is reduced, people need less foreign currency to buy foreign assets, and this induces a leftward shift in the supply curve for dollars from S_1 to S_2. The reduced supply of dollars causes the real exchange rate to appreciate from E_1 to E_2. That is, the dollar becomes more valuable compared to foreign currencies. This appreciation, in turn, makes U.S. goods more expensive compared to foreign goods. Because people both at home and abroad switch their purchases away from the more expensive U.S. goods, exports from the United States fall, and imports into the United States rise. For both reasons, U.S. net exports fall. Hence, *in an open economy, government budget deficits raise real interest rates, crowd out domestic investment, cause the currency to appreciate, and push the trade balance toward deficit.*

An important example of this lesson occurred in the United States in the 1980s. Shortly after Ronald Reagan was elected president in 1980, the fiscal policy of the U.S. federal government changed dramatically. The president and Congress enacted large cuts in taxes, but they did not cut government spending by nearly as much, so the result was a large budget deficit. Our model of the open economy predicts that such a policy should lead to a trade deficit, and in fact it did, as we saw in a case study in the preceding chapter. The budget deficit and trade deficit during this period were so closely related in both theory and practice that they earned the nickname the *twin deficits*. We should not, however, view these twins as identical, for many factors beyond fiscal policy can influence the trade deficit.

Trade Policy

trade policy
a government policy that directly influences the quantity of goods and services that a country imports or exports

A **trade policy** is a government policy that directly influences the quantity of goods and services that a country imports or exports. Trade policy takes various forms. One common trade policy is a *tariff,* a tax on imported goods. Another is an *import quota,* a limit on the quantity of a good that can be produced abroad and sold domestically. Trade policies are common throughout the world, although sometimes they are disguised. For example, the U.S. government has sometimes pressured Japanese automakers to reduce the number of cars they sell in the United States. These so-called "voluntary export restrictions" are not really voluntary and, in essence, are a form of import quota.

Let's consider the macroeconomic impact of trade policy. Suppose that the U.S. auto industry, concerned about competition from Japanese automakers, convinces the U.S. government to impose a quota on the number of cars that can be imported from Japan. In making their case, lobbyists for the auto industry assert that the trade restriction would shrink the size of the U.S. trade deficit. Are they right? Our model, as illustrated in Figure 6, offers an answer.

FIGURE 6

The Effects of an Import Quota

When the U.S. government imposes a quota on the import of Japanese cars, nothing happens in the market for loanable funds in panel (a) or to net capital outflow in panel (b). The only effect is a rise in net exports (exports minus imports) for any given real exchange rate. As a result, the demand for dollars in the market for foreign-currency exchange rises, as shown by the shift from D_1 to D_2 in panel (c). This increase in the demand for dollars causes the value of the dollar to appreciate from E_1 to E_2. This appreciation of the dollar tends to reduce net exports, offsetting the direct effect of the import quota on the trade balance.

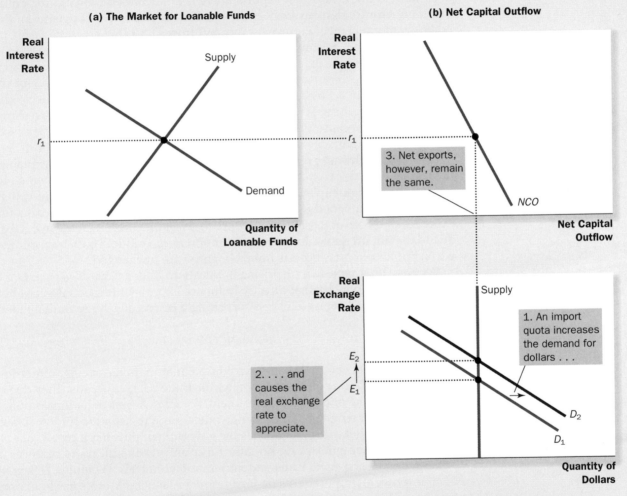

(a) The Market for Loanable Funds

Real Interest Rate

Supply

r_1

Demand

Quantity of Loanable Funds

(b) Net Capital Outflow

Real Interest Rate

r_1

3. Net exports, however, remain the same.

NCO

Net Capital Outflow

Real Exchange Rate

Supply

1. An import quota increases the demand for dollars . . .

E_2

E_1

2. . . . and causes the real exchange rate to appreciate.

D_2

D_1

Quantity of Dollars

(c) The Market for Foreign-Currency Exchange

The first step in analyzing the trade policy is to determine which curve shifts. The initial impact of the import restriction is, not surprisingly, on imports. Because net exports equal exports minus imports, the policy also affects net exports. And because net exports are the source of demand for dollars in the market for foreign-currency exchange, the policy affects the demand curve in this market.

The second step is to determine which way this demand curve shifts. Because the quota restricts the number of Japanese cars sold in the United States, it reduces imports at any given real exchange rate. Net exports, which equal exports minus imports, will therefore *rise* for any given real exchange rate. Because foreigners need dollars to buy U.S. net exports, there is an increased demand for dollars in the market for foreign-currency exchange. This increase in the demand for dollars is shown in panel (c) of Figure 6 as the shift from D_1 to D_2.

The third step is to compare the old and new equilibria. As we can see in panel (c), the increase in the demand for dollars causes the real exchange rate to appreciate from E_1 to E_2. Because nothing has happened in the market for loanable funds in panel (a), there is no change in the real interest rate. Because there is no change in the real interest rate, there is also no change in net capital outflow, shown in panel (b). And because there is no change in net capital outflow, there can be no change in net exports, even though the import quota has reduced imports.

The reason why net exports can stay the same while imports fall is explained by the change in the real exchange rate: When the dollar appreciates in value in the market for foreign-currency exchange, domestic goods become more expensive relative to foreign goods. This appreciation encourages imports and discourages exports—and both of these changes work to offset the direct increase in net exports due to the import quota. In the end, an import quota reduces both imports and exports, but net exports (exports minus imports) are unchanged.

We have thus come to a surprising implication: *Trade policies do not affect the trade balance.* That is, policies that directly influence exports or imports do not alter net exports. This conclusion seems less surprising if one recalls the accounting identity:

$$NX = NCO = S - I.$$

Net exports equal net capital outflow, which equals national saving minus domestic investment. Trade policies do not alter the trade balance because they do not alter national saving or domestic investment. For given levels of national saving and domestic investment, the real exchange rate adjusts to keep the trade balance the same, regardless of the trade policies the government puts in place.

Although trade policies do not affect a country's overall trade balance, these policies do affect specific firms, industries, and countries. When the U.S. government imposes an import quota on Japanese cars, General Motors has less competition from abroad and will sell more cars. At the same time, because the dollar has appreciated in value, Boeing, the U.S. aircraft maker, will find it harder to compete with Airbus, the European aircraft maker. U.S. exports of aircraft will fall, and U.S. imports of aircraft will rise. In this case, the import quota on Japanese cars will increase net exports of cars and decrease net exports of planes. In addition, it will increase net exports from the United States to Japan and decrease net exports from the United States to Europe. The overall trade balance of the U.S. economy, however, stays the same.

IN THE NEWS

THE U.S. TRADE DEFICIT

How should a country deal with a large trade deficit? Economists Martin and Kathleen Feldstein offer an answer.

Closing Our $1-Billion-a-Day Gap

By Martin and Kathleen Feldstein

In sharp contrast to the growing surplus in the federal budget, the U.S. trade deficit continues to surge, raising risks for the U.S. economy. By importing more than we are exporting and by selling American assets, Americans are able to consume more than we can really afford.

Borrowing from abroad has helped Americans increase their standard of living, but it also has made our economy vulnerable if foreigners decide to reduce the flow of loans and investments to the United States. An important goal for the next president should be to develop effective policies to reduce this danger by increasing national saving in order to cut our dependence on funds from abroad.

While the United States has been a net borrower from abroad for the last two decades, the numbers have become really big in the last eight years. In 1992, the United States imported $28 billion more than we exported. By the first quarter of 2000, net imports—or the excess of imports over exports—were running at a rate of more than $330 billion annually. . . .

Why have foreigners been willing to extend so much credit to the United States? Dollar bonds have been attractive to foreigners because interest rates have been higher here than in Europe and Japan (where they have been close to zero). And companies such as Daimler, Vivendi, and AXA have bought businesses here because the United States is a better place to grow their business than their home countries or other places in Europe. It is only in the area of portfolio equity investments that U.S. purchases abroad have matched foreign purchases in this country.

An important consequence of this net flow of investment to the United States has been the increase in the value of the dollar. Since 1992, the dollar has risen by nearly 14 percent, relative to a broad index of other currencies and adjusted for national differences in inflation. The strong dollar has made foreign products relatively cheap for American buyers and has made U.S. exports more expensive abroad. So it is no wonder that foreigners have slowed their purchases of U.S. goods, while Americans have been eager to buy foreign goods of all types, from cars to children's toys. The lower prices of imports also have helped to keep infla-

tion down in the United States. All of this seems quite benign. But how long will foreigners be willing to lend and invest so much in the United States? And what are the consequences if and when they pull back? . . .

In short, the rapid increase in borrowing from abroad over the last decade has left the U.S. economy in a precarious position. If—or when—foreigners decide that they don't want to lend so much to the United States, the dollar will decline, interest rates will rise, and inflation will increase.

Those are not circumstances under which Americans are likely to save more to replace the lost foreign investment inflows. To become less vulnerable, it is important for Americans to increase their saving now. That will mean reversing a long-term decline in U.S. household saving. Developing policies to encourage higher household saving should be a key priority for the next administration and Congress.

The effects of trade policies are, therefore, more microeconomic than macroeconomic. Although advocates of trade policies sometimes claim (incorrectly) that these policies can alter a country's trade balance, they are usually more motivated by concerns about particular firms or industries. One should not be surprised, for instance, to hear an executive from General Motors advocating import quotas for Japanese cars. Economists almost always oppose such trade policies. Free trade allows economies to specialize in doing what they do best, making residents of all countries better off. Trade restrictions interfere with these gains from trade and, thus, reduce overall economic well-being.

Political Instability and Capital Flight

In 1994 political instability in Mexico, including the assassination of a prominent political leader, made world financial markets nervous. People began to view Mexico as a much less stable country than they had previously thought. They decided to pull some of their assets out of Mexico in order to move these funds to the United States and other "safe havens." Such a large and sudden movement of funds out of a country is called **capital flight.** To see the implications of capital flight for the Mexican economy, we again follow our three steps for analyzing a change in equilibrium, but this time we apply our model of the open economy from the perspective of Mexico rather than the United States.

Consider first which curves in our model capital flight affects. When investors around the world observe political problems in Mexico, they decide to sell some of their Mexican assets and use the proceeds to buy U.S. assets. This act increases Mexican net capital outflow and, therefore, affects both markets in our model. Most obviously, it affects the net-capital-outflow curve, and this in turn influences the supply of pesos in the market for foreign-currency exchange. In addition, because the demand for loanable funds comes from both domestic investment and net capital outflow, capital flight affects the demand curve in the market for loanable funds.

Now consider which way these curves shift. When net capital outflow increases, there is greater demand for loanable funds to finance these purchases of capital assets abroad. Thus, as panel (a) of Figure 7 shows, the demand curve for loanable funds shifts to the right from D_1 to D_2. In addition, because net capital outflow is higher for any interest rate, the net-capital-outflow curve also shifts to the right from NCO_1 to NCO_2, as in panel (b).

To see the effects of capital flight on the economy, we compare the old and new equilibria. Panel (a) of Figure 7 shows that the increased demand for loanable funds causes the interest rate in Mexico to rise from r_1 to r_2. Panel (b) shows that Mexican net capital outflow increases. (Although the rise in the interest rate does make Mexican assets more attractive, this only partly offsets the impact of capital flight on net capital outflow.) Panel (c) shows that the increase in net capital outflow raises the supply of pesos in the market for foreign-currency exchange from S_1 to S_2. That is, as people try to get out of Mexican assets, there is a large supply of pesos to be converted into dollars. This increase in supply causes the peso to depreciate from E_1 to E_2. Thus, *capital flight from Mexico increases Mexican interest rates and decreases the value of the Mexican peso in the market for foreign-currency exchange.* This is exactly what was observed in 1994. From November 1994 to March 1995,

capital flight
a large and sudden reduction in the demand for assets located in a country

FIGURE 7

The Effects of Capital Flight

If people decide that Mexico is a risky place to keep their savings, they will move their capital to safer havens such as the United States, resulting in an increase in Mexican net capital outflow. Consequently, the demand for loanable funds in Mexico rises from D_1 to D_2, as shown in panel (a), and this drives up the Mexican real interest rate from r_1 to r_2. Because net capital outflow is higher for any interest rate, that curve also shifts to the right from NCO_1 to NCO_2 in panel (b). At the same time, in the market for foreign-currency exchange, the supply of pesos rises from S_1 to S_2, as shown in panel (c). This increase in the supply of pesos causes the peso to depreciate from E_1 to E_2, so the peso becomes less valuable compared to other currencies.

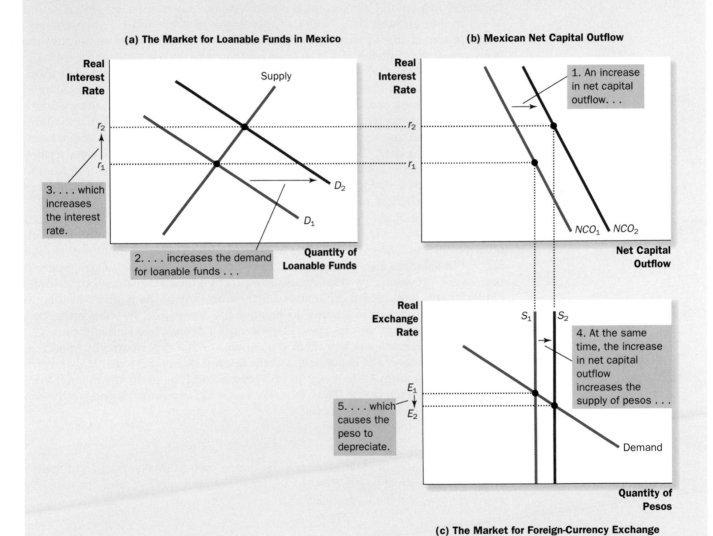

the interest rate on short-term Mexican government bonds rose from 14 percent to 70 percent, and the peso depreciated in value from 29 to 15 U.S. cents per peso.

These price changes that result from capital flight influence some key macroeconomic quantities. The depreciation of the currency makes exports cheaper and imports more expensive, pushing the trade balance toward surplus. At the same time, the increase in the interest rate reduces domestic investment, which slows capital accumulation and economic growth.

Although capital flight has its largest impact on the country from which capital is fleeing, it also affects other countries. When capital flows out of Mexico into the United States, for instance, it has the opposite effect on the U.S. economy as it has on the Mexican economy. In particular, the rise in Mexican net capital outflow coincides with a fall in U.S. net capital outflow. As the peso depreciates in value and Mexican interest rates rise, the dollar appreciates in value and U.S. interest rates fall. The size of this impact on the U.S. economy is small, however, because the economy of the United States is so large compared to that of Mexico.

The events that we have been describing in Mexico could happen to any economy in the world, and in fact they do from time to time. In 1997, the world learned that the banking systems of several Asian economies, including Thailand, South Korea, and Indonesia, were at or near the point of bankruptcy, and this news induced capital to flee from these nations. In 1998, the Russian government defaulted on its debt, inducing international investors to take whatever money they could and run. A similar (but more complicated) set of events unfolded in Argentina in 2002. In each of these cases of capital flight, the results were much as our model predicts: rising interest rates and a falling currency.

Could capital flight ever happen in the United States? Although the U.S. economy has long been viewed as a safe economy in which to invest, political developments in the United States have at times induced small amounts of capital flight. For example, the September 22, 1995, issue of *The New York Times* reported that on the previous day, "House Speaker Newt Gingrich threatened to send the United States into default on its debt for the first time in the nation's history, to force the Clinton administration to balance the budget on Republican terms" (p. A1). Even though most people believed such a default was unlikely, the effect of the announcement was, in a small way, similar to that experienced by Mexico in 1994. Over the course of that single day, the interest rate on a 30-year U.S. government bond rose from 6.46 percent to 6.55 percent, and the exchange rate fell from 102.7 to 99.0 yen per dollar. Thus, even the stable U.S. economy is potentially susceptible to the effects of capital flight.

QuickQuiz Suppose that Americans decided to spend a smaller fraction of their incomes. What would be the effect on saving, investment, interest rates, the real exchange rate, and the trade balance?

CONCLUSION

International economics is a topic of increasing importance. More and more, American citizens are buying goods produced abroad and producing goods to be sold overseas. Through mutual funds and other financial institutions, they borrow and lend in world financial markets. As a result, a full analysis of the U.S. economy requires an understanding of how the U.S. economy interacts with other economies in the world. This chapter has provided a basic model for thinking about the macroeconomics of open economies.

Although the study of international economics is valuable, we should be careful not to exaggerate its importance. Policymakers and commentators are often quick to blame foreigners for problems facing the U.S. economy. By contrast, economists more often view these problems as homegrown. For example, politicians often discuss foreign competition as a threat to American living standards. Economists are more likely to lament the low level of national saving. Low saving impedes growth in capital, productivity, and living standards, regardless of whether the economy is open or closed. Foreigners are a convenient target for politicians because blaming foreigners provides a way to avoid responsibility without insulting any domestic constituency. Whenever you hear popular discussions of international trade and finance, therefore, it is especially important to try to separate myth from reality. The tools you have learned in the past two chapters should help in that endeavor.

SUMMARY

- To analyze the macroeconomics of open economies, two markets are central—the market for loanable funds and the market for foreign-currency exchange. In the market for loanable funds, the interest rate adjusts to balance the supply of loanable funds (from national saving) and the demand for loanable funds (from domestic investment and net capital outflow).

In the market for foreign-currency exchange, the real exchange rate adjusts to balance the supply of dollars (for net capital outflow) and the demand for dollars (for net exports). Because net capital outflow is part of the demand for loanable funds and provides the supply of dollars for foreign-currency exchange, it is the variable that connects these two markets.

- A policy that reduces national saving, such as a government budget deficit, reduces the supply of loanable funds and drives up the interest rate. The higher interest rate reduces net capital outflow, which reduces the supply of dollars in the market for foreign-currency exchange. The dollar appreciates, and net exports fall.

- Although restrictive trade policies, such as tariffs or quotas on imports, are sometimes advocated as a way to alter the trade balance, they do not necessarily have that effect. A trade restriction increases net exports for a given exchange rate and, therefore, increases the demand for dollars in the market for foreign-currency exchange. As a result, the dollar appreciates in value, making domestic goods more expensive relative to foreign goods. This appreciation offsets the initial impact of the trade restriction on net exports.

- When investors change their attitudes about holding assets of a country, the ramifications for the country's economy can be profound. In particular, political instability can lead to capital flight, which tends to increase interest rates and cause the currency to depreciate.

KEY CONCEPTS

trade policy, p. 412   capital flight, p. 416

QUESTIONS FOR REVIEW

1. Describe supply and demand in the market for loanable funds and the market for foreign-currency exchange. How are these markets linked?

2. Why are budget deficits and trade deficits sometimes called the twin deficits?

3. Suppose that a textile workers' union encourages people to buy only American-made clothes. What would this policy do to the trade balance and the real exchange rate? What is the impact on the textile industry? What is the impact on the auto industry?

4. What is capital flight? When a country experiences capital flight, what is the effect on its interest rate and exchange rate?

PROBLEMS AND APPLICATIONS

1. Japan generally runs a significant trade surplus. Do you think this is most related to high foreign demand for Japanese goods, low Japanese demand for foreign goods, a high Japanese saving rate relative to Japanese investment, or structural barriers against imports into Japan? Explain your answer.

2. An article in *The New York Times* (Apr. 14, 1995) regarding a decline in the value of the dollar reported that "the president was clearly determined to signal that the United States remains solidly on a course of deficit reduction, which should make the dollar more attractive to investors." Would deficit reduction in fact raise the value of the dollar? Explain.

3. Suppose that Congress passes an investment tax credit, which subsidizes domestic investment. How does this policy affect national saving, domestic investment, net capital outflow, the interest rate, the exchange rate, and the trade balance?

4. The chapter notes that the rise in the U.S. trade deficit during the 1980s was due largely to the rise in the U.S. budget deficit. On the other hand, the popular press sometimes claims that the increased trade deficit resulted from a decline in the quality of U.S. products relative to foreign products.
   a. Assume that U.S. products did decline in relative quality during the 1980s. How did this affect net exports *at any given exchange rate?*
   b. Use a three-panel diagram to show the effect of this shift in net exports on the U.S. real exchange rate and trade balance.
   c. Is the claim in the popular press consistent with the model in this chapter? Does a decline in the quality of U.S. products have any effect on our standard of living? (Hint: When we sell our goods to foreigners, what do we receive in return?)

5. An economist discussing trade policy in *The New Republic* wrote: "One of the benefits of the United States removing its trade restrictions [is] the gain to U.S. industries that produce goods for export. Export industries would find it easier to sell their goods abroad—even if other countries didn't follow our example and reduce their trade barriers." Explain in words why U.S. *export* industries would benefit from a reduction in restrictions on *imports* to the United States.

6. Suppose the French suddenly develop a strong taste for California wines. Answer the following questions in words and using a diagram.
   a. What happens to the demand for dollars in the market for foreign-currency exchange?
   b. What happens to the value of dollars in the market for foreign-currency exchange?
   c. What happens to the quantity of net exports?

7. A senator renounces her past support for protectionism: "The U.S. trade deficit must be reduced, but import quotas only annoy our trading partners. If we subsidize U.S. exports instead, we can reduce the deficit by increasing our competitiveness." Using a three-panel diagram, show the effect of an export subsidy on net exports and the real exchange rate. Do you agree with the senator?

8. Suppose that real interest rates increase across Europe. Explain how this development will affect U.S. net capital outflow. Then explain how it will affect U.S. net exports by using a formula from the chapter and by using a diagram. What will happen to the U.S. real interest rate and real exchange rate?

9. Suppose that Americans decide to increase their saving.
   a. If the elasticity of U.S. net capital outflow with respect to the real interest rate is very high, will this increase in private saving have a large or small effect on U.S. domestic investment?
   b. If the elasticity of U.S. exports with respect to the real exchange rate is very low, will this increase in private saving have a large or small effect on the U.S. real exchange rate?

10. Over the past decade, some of Japanese saving has been used to finance American investment. That is, the Japanese have been buying American capital assets.
   a. If the Japanese decided they no longer wanted to buy U.S. assets, what would happen in the U.S. market for loanable funds? In particular, what would happen to U.S. interest rates, U.S. saving, and U.S. investment?
   b. What would happen in the market for foreign-currency exchange? In particular, what would happen to the value of the dollar and the U.S. trade balance?

11. In 1998 the Russian government defaulted on its debt payments, leading investors worldwide to raise their preference for U.S. government bonds, which are considered very safe. What effect do you think this "flight to safety" had on the U.S. economy? Be sure to note the impact on national saving, domestic investment, net capital outflow, the interest rate, the exchange rate, and the trade balance.

12. Suppose that U.S. mutual funds suddenly decide to invest more in Canada.
    a. What happens to Canadian net capital outflow, Canadian saving, and Canadian domestic investment?
    b. What is the long-run effect on the Canadian capital stock?
    c. How will this change in the capital stock affect the Canadian labor market? Does this U.S. investment in Canada make Canadian workers better off or worse off?
    d. Do you think this will make U.S. workers better off or worse off? Can you think of any reason why the impact on U.S. citizens generally may be different from the impact on U.S. workers?

http://

For more study tools, please visit http://mankiwXtra.swlearning.com.

8

SHORT-RUN ECONOMIC FLUCTUATIONS

AGGREGATE DEMAND
AND AGGREGATE SUPPLY

Economic activity fluctuates from year to year. In most years, the production of goods and services rises. Because of increases in the labor force, increases in the capital stock, and advances in technological knowledge, the economy can produce more and more over time. This growth allows everyone to enjoy a higher standard of living. On average over the past 50 years, the production of the U.S. economy as measured by real GDP has grown by about 3 percent per year.

In some years, however, this normal growth does not occur. Firms find themselves unable to sell all of the goods and services they have to offer, so they cut back on production. Workers are laid off, unemployment rises, and factories are left idle. With the economy producing fewer goods and services, real GDP and other measures of income fall. Such a period of falling incomes and rising unemployment is called a **recession** if it is relatively mild and a **depression** if it is more severe.

What causes short-run fluctuations in economic activity? What, if anything, can public policy do to prevent periods of falling incomes and rising unemployment? When recessions and depressions occur, how can policymakers reduce their length and severity? These are the questions that we take up now.

recession
a period of declining real incomes and rising unemployment

depression
a severe recession

427

The variables that we study are largely those we have already seen in previous chapters. They include GDP, unemployment, interest rates, and the price level. Also familiar are the policy instruments of government spending, taxes, and the money supply. What differs from our earlier analysis is the time horizon. So far, our focus has been on the behavior of the economy in the long run. Our focus now is on the economy's short-run fluctuations around its long-run trend.

Although there remains some debate among economists about how to analyze short-run fluctuations, most economists use the *model of aggregate demand and aggregate supply*. Learning how to use this model for analyzing the short-run effects of various events and policies is the primary task ahead. This chapter introduces the model's two key pieces—the aggregate-demand curve and the aggregate-supply curve. But before turning to the model, let's look at the facts.

THREE KEY FACTS ABOUT ECONOMIC FLUCTUATIONS

Short-run fluctuations in economic activity occur in all countries and in all times throughout history. As a starting point for understanding these year-to-year fluctuations, let's discuss some of their most important properties.

Fact 1: Economic Fluctuations Are Irregular and Unpredictable

Fluctuations in the economy are often called *the business cycle*. As this term suggests, economic fluctuations correspond to changes in business conditions. When real GDP grows rapidly, business is good. During such periods of economic expansion, firms find that customers are plentiful and that profits are growing. On the other hand, when real GDP falls during recessions, businesses have trouble. During such periods of economic contraction, most firms experience declining sales and dwindling profits.

The term *business cycle* is somewhat misleading, however, because it seems to suggest that economic fluctuations follow a regular, predictable pattern. In fact, economic fluctuations are not at all regular, and they are almost impossible to predict with much accuracy. Panel (a) of Figure 1 shows the real GDP of the U.S. economy since 1965. The shaded areas represent times of recession. As the figure shows, recessions do not come at regular intervals. Sometimes recessions are close together, such as the recessions of 1980 and 1982. Sometimes the economy goes many years without a recession. The longest period in history without a recession was the economic expansion from 1991 to 2001.

Fact 2: Most Macroeconomic Quantities Fluctuate Together

Real GDP is the variable that is most commonly used to monitor short-run changes in the economy because it is the most comprehensive measure of economic activity. Real GDP measures the value of all final goods and services produced within a

FIGURE 1

(a) Real GDP

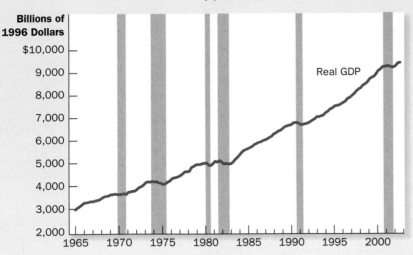

(b) Investment Spending

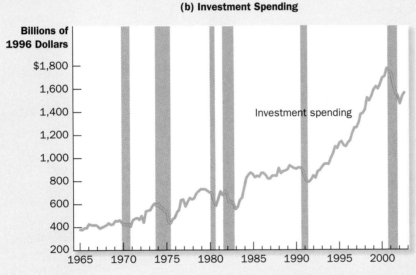

(c) Unemployment Rate

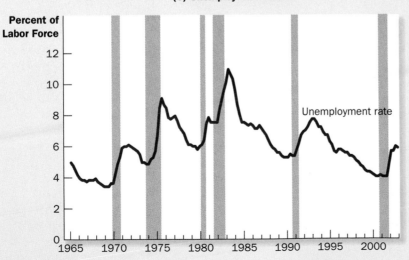

A Look at Short-Run Economic Fluctuations

This figure shows real GDP in panel (a), investment spending in panel (b), and unemployment in panel (c) for the U.S. economy using quarterly data since 1965. Recessions are shown as the shaded areas. Notice that real GDP and investment spending decline during recessions, while unemployment rises.

Source: U.S. Department of Commerce; U.S. Department of Labor.

"You're fired. Pass it on."

given period of time. It also measures the total income (adjusted for inflation) of everyone in the economy.

It turns out, however, that for monitoring short-run fluctuations, it does not really matter which measure of economic activity one looks at. Most macroeconomic variables that measure some type of income, spending, or production fluctuate closely together. When real GDP falls in a recession, so do personal income, corporate profits, consumer spending, investment spending, industrial production, retail sales, home sales, auto sales, and so on. Because recessions are economywide phenomena, they show up in many sources of macroeconomic data.

Although many macroeconomic variables fluctuate together, they fluctuate by different amounts. In particular, as panel (b) of Figure 1 shows, investment spending varies greatly over the business cycle. Even though investment averages about one-seventh of GDP, declines in investment account for about two-thirds of the declines in GDP during recessions. In other words, when economic conditions deteriorate, much of the decline is attributable to reductions in spending on new factories, housing, and inventories.

IN THE NEWS

THE TRASH INDICATOR

When the economy goes into a recession, many economic variables fall together. Here's an offbeat example from the recession of 2001.

Economy Is in the Dumper— That's Not a Lot of Garbage

By John Keilman

When people say the economy is in the trash can, they're not exaggerating.

The stalling fortunes of many businesses and families in the Chicago area show up in the smaller volume of garbage they are throwing away, according to refuse collectors and experts.

Trash as an economic indicator is not exactly an established science. But recent statistics have the unmistakable whiff of a downward trend. In Chicago, the total

waste stream dropped 6 percent from 1999 to 2000. Across 23 northwestern suburbs, annual 2 to 10 percent increases in household trash during the bull market have been replaced by a yearlong slide approaching 1 percent. . . .

"It doesn't sound like a lot, but in this business, it's a lot," said C. Brooke Beal, executive director of the Solid Waste Agency of Northern Cook County. "The increase and decrease is directly tied to how the economy is going. . . ."

Residential trash goes up notably when the economy is good, thanks mostly to purchases of furniture or items

such as televisions or computers that come with lots of packaging.

Kathy Cisco, co-director of the University of Arizona's Garbage Project, a think tank that explores what trash says about culture, said the flip side comes when times are hard. We can expect to see less big-purchase debris—large cardboard boxes, hunks of Styrofoam and tangles of cellophane—enter the waste stream.

Source: *The Chicago Tribune*, November 10, 2001, p. 1. Reprinted by permission.

Fact 3: As Output Falls, Unemployment Rises

Changes in the economy's output of goods and services are strongly correlated with changes in the economy's utilization of its labor force. In other words, when real GDP declines, the rate of unemployment rises. This fact is hardly surprising: When firms choose to produce a smaller quantity of goods and services, they lay off workers, expanding the pool of unemployed.

Panel (c) of Figure 1 shows the unemployment rate in the U.S. economy since 1965. Once again, recessions are shown as the shaded areas in the figure. The figure shows clearly the impact of recessions on unemployment. In each of the recessions, the unemployment rate rises substantially. When the recession ends and real GDP starts to expand, the unemployment rate gradually declines. The unemployment rate never approaches zero; instead, it fluctuates around its natural rate of about 5 or 6 percent.

QuickQuiz List and discuss three key facts about economic fluctuations.

EXPLAINING SHORT-RUN ECONOMIC FLUCTUATIONS

Describing the patterns that economies experience as they fluctuate over time is easy. Explaining what causes these fluctuations is more difficult. Indeed, compared to the topics we have studied in previous chapters, the theory of economic fluctuations remains controversial. In this chapter and the next two chapters, we develop the model that most economists use to explain short-run fluctuations in economic activity.

How the Short Run Differs from the Long Run

In previous chapters we developed theories to explain what determines most important macroeconomic variables in the long run. Chapter 12 explained the level and growth of productivity and real GDP. Chapters 13 and 14 explained how the financial system works and how the real interest rate adjusts to balance saving and investment. Chapter 15 explained why there is always some unemployment in the economy. Chapters 16 and 17 explained the monetary system and how changes in the money supply affect the price level, the inflation rate, and the nominal interest rate. Chapters 18 and 19 extended this analysis to open economies in order to explain the trade balance and the exchange rate.

All of this previous analysis was based on two related ideas—the classical dichotomy and monetary neutrality. Recall that the classical dichotomy is the separation of variables into real variables (those that measure quantities or relative prices) and nominal variables (those measured in terms of money). According to classical macroeconomic theory, changes in the money supply affect nominal variables but not real variables. As a result of this monetary neutrality, Chapters 12 through 15 were able to examine the determinants of real variables (real GDP, the real interest rate, and unemployment) without introducing nominal variables (the money supply and the price level).

Do these assumptions of classical macroeconomic theory apply to the world in which we live? The answer to this question is of central importance to understanding how the economy works: *Most economists believe that classical theory describes the world in the long run but not in the short run.* Beyond a period of several years, changes in the money supply affect prices and other nominal variables but do not affect real GDP, unemployment, or other real variables. When studying year-to-year changes in the economy, however, the assumption of monetary neutrality is no longer appropriate. Most economists believe that, in the short run, real and nominal variables are highly intertwined. In particular, changes in the money supply can temporarily push output away from its long-run trend.

To understand the economy in the short run, therefore, we need a new model. To build this new model, we rely on many of the tools we have developed in previous chapters, but we have to abandon the classical dichotomy and the neutrality of money.

The Basic Model of Economic Fluctuations

model of aggregate demand and aggregate supply
the model that most economists use to explain short-run fluctuations in economic activity around its long-run trend

Our model of short-run economic fluctuations focuses on the behavior of two variables. The first variable is the economy's output of goods and services, as measured by real GDP. The second variable is the overall price level, as measured by the CPI or the GDP deflator. Notice that output is a real variable, whereas the price level is a nominal variable. Hence, by focusing on the relationship between these two variables, we are highlighting the breakdown of the classical dichotomy.

We analyze fluctuations in the economy as a whole with the **model of aggregate demand and aggregate supply,** which is illustrated in Figure 2. On the vertical axis is the overall price level in the economy. On the horizontal axis is the overall

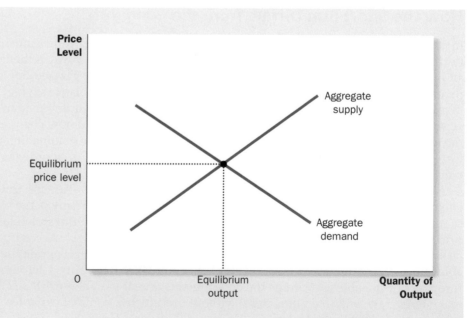

FIGURE 2

Aggregate Demand and Aggregate Supply

Economists use the model of aggregate demand and aggregate supply to analyze economic fluctuations. On the vertical axis is the overall level of prices. On the horizontal axis is the economy's total output of goods and services. Output and the price level adjust to the point at which the aggregate-supply and aggregate-demand curves intersect.

quantity of goods and services. The **aggregate-demand curve** shows the quantity of goods and services that households, firms, and the government want to buy at each price level. The **aggregate-supply curve** shows the quantity of goods and services that firms produce and sell at each price level. According to this model, the price level and the quantity of output adjust to bring aggregate demand and aggregate supply into balance.

It may be tempting to view the model of aggregate demand and aggregate supply as nothing more than a large version of the model of market demand and market supply, which we introduced in Chapter 4. Yet in fact this model is quite different. When we consider demand and supply in a particular market—ice cream, for instance—the behavior of buyers and sellers depends on the ability of resources to move from one market to another. When the price of ice cream rises, the quantity demanded falls because buyers will use their incomes to buy products other than ice cream. Similarly, a higher price of ice cream raises the quantity supplied because firms that produce ice cream can increase production by hiring workers away from other parts of the economy. This *microeconomic* substitution from one market to another is impossible when we are analyzing the economy as a whole. After all, the quantity that our model is trying to explain—real GDP—measures the total quantity produced in all of the economy's markets. To understand why the aggregate-demand curve is downward sloping and why the aggregate-supply curve is upward sloping, we need a *macroeconomic* theory. Developing such a theory is our next task.

QuickQuiz How does the economy's behavior in the short run differ from its behavior in the long run? • Draw the model of aggregate demand and aggregate supply. What variables are on the two axes?

aggregate-demand curve
a curve that shows the quantity of goods and services that households, firms, and the government want to buy at each price level

aggregate-supply curve
a curve that shows the quantity of goods and services that firms choose to produce and sell at each price level

THE AGGREGATE-DEMAND CURVE

The aggregate-demand curve tells us the quantity of all goods and services demanded in the economy at any given price level. As Figure 3 (p. 434) illustrates, the aggregate-demand curve is downward sloping. This means that, other things equal, a fall in the economy's overall level of prices (from, say, P_1 to P_2) tends to raise the quantity of goods and services demanded (from Y_1 to Y_2).

Why the Aggregate-Demand Curve Slopes Downward

Why does a fall in the price level raise the quantity of goods and services demanded? To answer this question, it is useful to recall that GDP (which we denote as Y) is the sum of consumption (C), investment (I), government purchases (G), and net exports (NX):

$$Y = C + I + G + NX.$$

Each of these four components contributes to the aggregate demand for goods and services. For now, we assume that government spending is fixed by policy. The other three components of spending—consumption, investment, and net exports—

FIGURE 3

The Aggregate-Demand Curve

A fall in the price level from P_1 to P_2 increases the quantity of goods and services demanded from Y_1 to Y_2. There are three reasons for this negative relationship. As the price level falls, real wealth rises, interest rates fall, and the exchange rate depreciates. These effects stimulate spending on consumption, investment, and net exports. Increased spending on these components of output means a larger quantity of goods and services demanded.

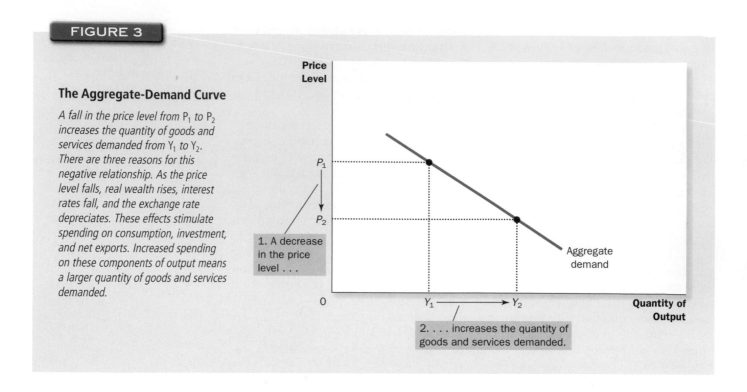

1. A decrease in the price level . . .

2. . . . increases the quantity of goods and services demanded.

depend on economic conditions and, in particular, on the price level. To understand the downward slope of the aggregate-demand curve, therefore, we must examine how the price level affects the quantity of goods and services demanded for consumption, investment, and net exports.

The Price Level and Consumption: The Wealth Effect   Consider the money that you hold in your wallet and your bank account. The nominal value of this money is fixed, but its real value is not. When prices fall, these dollars are more valuable because then they can be used to buy more goods and services. Thus, *a decrease in the price level makes consumers wealthier, which in turn encourages them to spend more. The increase in consumer spending means a larger quantity of goods and services demanded.*

The Price Level and Investment: The Interest-Rate Effect   As we discussed in Chapter 17, the price level is one determinant of the quantity of money demanded. The lower the price level, the less money households need to hold to buy the goods and services they want. When the price level falls, therefore, households try to reduce their holdings of money by lending some of it out. For instance, a household might use its excess money to buy interest-bearing bonds. Or it might deposit its excess money in an interest-bearing savings account, and the bank would use these funds to make more loans. In either case, as households try to convert some of their money into interest-bearing assets, they drive down interest rates. Lower interest rates, in turn, encourage borrowing by firms that want to invest in new plants and equipment and by households who want to invest in new housing. Thus, *a lower price level reduces the interest rate, encourages greater spending on investment goods, and thereby increases the quantity of goods and services demanded.*

The Price Level and Net Exports: The Exchange-Rate Effect As we have just discussed, a lower price level in the United States lowers the U.S. interest rate. In response, some U.S. investors will seek higher returns by investing abroad. For instance, as the interest rate on U.S. government bonds falls, a mutual fund might sell U.S. government bonds in order to buy German government bonds. As the mutual fund tries to convert its dollars into euros to buy the German bonds, it increases the supply of dollars in the market for foreign-currency exchange. The increased supply of dollars causes the dollar to depreciate relative to other currencies. Because each dollar buys fewer units of foreign currencies, foreign goods become more expensive relative to domestic goods. This change in the real exchange rate (the relative price of domestic and foreign goods) increases U.S. exports of goods and services and decreases U.S. imports of goods and services. Net exports, which equal exports minus imports, also increase. Thus, *when a fall in the U.S. price level causes U.S. interest rates to fall, the real exchange rate depreciates, and this depreciation stimulates U.S. net exports and thereby increases the quantity of goods and services demanded.*

Summary There are, therefore, three distinct but related reasons why a fall in the price level increases the quantity of goods and services demanded: (1) Consumers are wealthier, which stimulates the demand for consumption goods. (2) Interest rates fall, which stimulates the demand for investment goods. (3) The exchange rate depreciates, which stimulates the demand for net exports. For all three reasons, the aggregate-demand curve slopes downward.

It is important to keep in mind that the aggregate-demand curve (like all demand curves) is drawn holding "other things equal." In particular, our three explanations of the downward-sloping aggregate-demand curve assume that the money supply is fixed. That is, we have been considering how a change in the price level affects the demand for goods and services, holding the amount of money in the economy constant. As we will see, a change in the quantity of money shifts the aggregate-demand curve. At this point, just keep in mind that the aggregate-demand curve is drawn for a given quantity of money.

Why the Aggregate-Demand Curve Might Shift

The downward slope of the aggregate-demand curve shows that a fall in the price level raises the overall quantity of goods and services demanded. Many other factors, however, affect the quantity of goods and services demanded at a given price level. When one of these other factors changes, the aggregate-demand curve shifts.

Let's consider some examples of events that shift aggregate demand. We can categorize them according to which component of spending is most directly affected.

Shifts Arising from Consumption Suppose Americans suddenly become more concerned about saving for retirement and, as a result, reduce their current consumption. Because the quantity of goods and services demanded at any price level is lower, the aggregate-demand curve shifts to the left. Conversely, imagine that a stock market boom makes people wealthier and less concerned about saving. The resulting increase in consumer spending means a greater quantity of goods and services demanded at any given price level, so the aggregate-demand curve shifts to the right.

Thus, any event that changes how much people want to consume at a given price level shifts the aggregate-demand curve. One policy variable that has this effect is the level of taxation. When the government cuts taxes, it encourages people to spend more, so the aggregate-demand curve shifts to the right. When the government raises taxes, people cut back on their spending, and the aggregate-demand curve shifts to the left.

Shifts Arising from Investment Any event that changes how much firms want to invest at a given price level also shifts the aggregate-demand curve. For instance, imagine that the computer industry introduces a faster line of computers, and many firms decide to invest in new computer systems. Because the quantity of goods and services demanded at any price level is higher, the aggregate-demand curve shifts to the right. Conversely, if firms become pessimistic about future business conditions, they may cut back on investment spending, shifting the aggregate-demand curve to the left.

Tax policy can also influence aggregate demand through investment. As we saw in Chapter 13, an investment tax credit (a tax rebate tied to a firm's investment spending) increases the quantity of investment goods that firms demand at any given interest rate. It therefore shifts the aggregate-demand curve to the right. The repeal of an investment tax credit reduces investment and shifts the aggregate-demand curve to the left.

Another policy variable that can influence investment and aggregate demand is the money supply. As we discuss more fully in the next chapter, an increase in the money supply lowers the interest rate in the short run. This makes borrowing less costly, which stimulates investment spending and thereby shifts the aggregate-demand curve to the right. Conversely, a decrease in the money supply raises the interest rate, discourages investment spending, and thereby shifts the aggregate-demand curve to the left. Many economists believe that throughout U.S. history changes in monetary policy have been an important source of shifts in aggregate demand.

Shifts Arising from Government Purchases The most direct way that policymakers shift the aggregate-demand curve is through government purchases. For example, suppose Congress decides to reduce purchases of new weapons systems. Because the quantity of goods and services demanded at any price level is lower, the aggregate-demand curve shifts to the left. Conversely, if state governments start building more highways, the result is a greater quantity of goods and services demanded at any price level, so the aggregate-demand curve shifts to the right.

Shifts Arising from Net Exports Any event that changes net exports for a given price level also shifts aggregate demand. For instance, when Europe experiences a recession, it buys fewer goods from the United States. This reduces U.S. net exports and shifts the aggregate-demand curve for the U.S. economy to the left. When Europe recovers from its recession, it starts buying U.S. goods again, shifting the aggregate-demand curve to the right.

Net exports sometimes change because of movements in the exchange rate. Suppose, for instance, that international speculators bid up the value of the U.S. dollar in the market for foreign-currency exchange. This appreciation of the dollar would make U.S. goods more expensive compared to foreign goods, which would depress net exports and shift the aggregate-demand curve to the left. Conversely, a depreciation of the dollar stimulates net exports and shifts the aggregate-demand curve to the right.

Summary In the next chapter we analyze the aggregate-demand curve in more detail. There we examine more precisely how the tools of monetary and fiscal policy can shift aggregate demand and whether policymakers should use these tools for that purpose. At this point, however, you should have some idea about why the aggregate-demand curve slopes downward and what kinds of events and policies can shift this curve. Table 1 summarizes what we have learned so far.

QuickQuiz Explain the three reasons why the aggregate-demand curve slopes downward. • Give an example of an event that would shift the aggregate-demand curve. Which way would this event shift the curve?

TABLE 1

The Aggregate-Demand Curve: Summary

Why Does the Aggregate-Demand Curve Slope Downward?

1. *The Wealth Effect:* A lower price level increases real wealth, which encourages spending on consumption.
2. *The Interest-Rate Effect:* A lower price level reduces the interest rate, which encourages spending on investment.
3. *The Exchange-Rate Effect:* A lower price level causes the real exchange rate to depreciate, which encourages spending on net exports.

Why Might the Aggregate-Demand Curve Shift?

1. *Shifts Arising from Consumption:* An event that makes consumers spend more at a given price level (a tax cut, a stock market boom) shifts the aggregate-demand curve to the right. An event that makes consumers spend less at a given price level (a tax hike, a stock market decline) shifts the aggregate-demand curve to the left.
2. *Shifts Arising from Investment:* An event that makes firms invest more at a given price level (optimism about the future, a fall in interest rates due to an increase in the money supply) shifts the aggregate-demand curve to the right. An event that makes firms invest less at a given price level (pessimism about the future, a rise in interest rates due to a decrease in the money supply) shifts the aggregate-demand curve to the left.
3. *Shifts Arising from Government Purchases:* An increase in government purchases of goods and services (greater spending on defense or highway construction) shifts the aggregate-demand curve to the right. A decrease in government purchases on goods and services (a cutback in defense or highway spending) shifts the aggregate-demand curve to the left.
4. *Shifts Arising from Net Exports:* An event that raises spending on net exports at a given price level (a boom overseas, an exchange-rate depreciation) shifts the aggregate-demand curve to the right. An event that reduces spending on net exports at a given price level (a recession overseas, an exchange-rate appreciation) shifts the aggregate-demand curve to the left.

THE AGGREGATE-SUPPLY CURVE

The aggregate-supply curve tells us the total quantity of goods and services that firms produce and sell at any given price level. Unlike the aggregate-demand curve, which is always downward sloping, the aggregate-supply curve shows a relationship that depends crucially on the time horizon being examined. *In the long run, the aggregate-supply curve is vertical, whereas in the short run, the aggregate-supply curve is upward sloping.* To understand short-run economic fluctuations, and how the short-run behavior of the economy deviates from its long-run behavior, we need to examine both the long-run aggregate-supply curve and the short-run aggregate-supply curve.

Why the Aggregate-Supply Curve Is Vertical in the Long Run

What determines the quantity of goods and services supplied in the long run? We implicitly answered this question earlier in the book when we analyzed the process of economic growth. *In the long run, an economy's production of goods and services (its real GDP) depends on its supplies of labor, capital, and natural resources and on the available technology used to turn these factors of production into goods and services.* Because the price level does not affect these long-run determinants of real GDP, the long-run aggregate-supply curve is vertical, as in Figure 4. In other words, in the long run, the economy's labor, capital, natural resources, and technology determine the total quantity of goods and services supplied, and this quantity supplied is the same regardless of what the price level happens to be.

FIGURE 4

The Long-Run Aggregate-Supply Curve

In the long run, the quantity of output supplied depends on the economy's quantities of labor, capital, and natural resources and on the technology for turning these inputs into output. The quantity supplied does not depend on the overall price level. As a result, the long-run aggregate-supply curve is vertical at the natural rate of output.

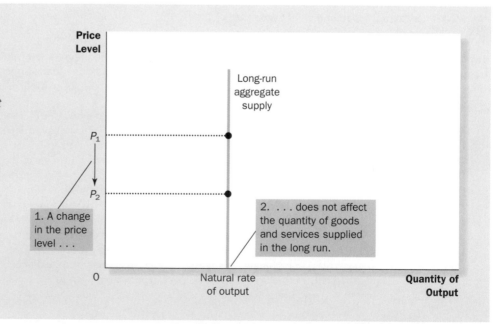

The vertical long-run aggregate-supply curve is, in essence, just an application of the classical dichotomy and monetary neutrality. As we have already discussed, classical macroeconomic theory is based on the assumption that real variables do not depend on nominal variables. The long-run aggregate-supply curve is consistent with this idea because it implies that the quantity of output (a real variable) does not depend on the level of prices (a nominal variable). As noted earlier, most economists believe that this principle works well when studying the economy over a period of many years, but not when studying year-to-year changes. Thus, the aggregate-supply curve is vertical only in the long run.

One might wonder why supply curves for specific goods and services can be upward sloping if the long-run aggregate-supply curve is vertical. The reason is that the supply of specific goods and services depends on *relative prices*—the prices of those goods and services compared to other prices in the economy. For example, when the price of ice cream rises, holding other prices in the economy constant, suppliers of ice cream can increase their production by taking labor, milk, chocolate, and other inputs away from the production of other goods, such as frozen yogurt. By contrast, the economy's overall production of goods and services is limited by its labor, capital, natural resources, and technology. Thus, when all prices in the economy rise together, there is no change in the overall quantity of goods and services supplied.

Why the Long-Run Aggregate-Supply Curve Might Shift

The position of the long-run aggregate-supply curve shows the quantity of goods and services predicted by classical macroeconomic theory. This level of production is sometimes called *potential output* or *full-employment output*. To be more accurate, we call it the *natural rate of output* because it shows what the economy produces when unemployment is at its natural, or normal, rate. The natural rate of output is the level of production toward which the economy gravitates in the long run.

Any change in the economy that alters the natural rate of output shifts the long-run aggregate-supply curve. Because output in the classical model depends on labor, capital, natural resources, and technological knowledge, we can categorize shifts in the long-run aggregate-supply curve as arising from these sources.

Shifts Arising from Labor   Imagine that an economy experiences an increase in immigration from abroad. Because there would be a greater number of workers, the quantity of goods and services supplied would increase. As a result, the long-run aggregate-supply curve would shift to the right. Conversely, if many workers left the economy to go abroad, the long-run aggregate-supply curve would shift to the left.

The position of the long-run aggregate-supply curve also depends on the natural rate of unemployment, so any change in the natural rate of unemployment shifts the long-run aggregate-supply curve. For example, if Congress were to raise the minimum wage substantially, the natural rate of unemployment would rise, and the economy would produce a smaller quantity of goods and services. As a result, the long-run aggregate-supply curve would shift to the left. Conversely, if a reform of the unemployment insurance system were to encourage unemployed workers to search harder for new jobs, the natural rate of unemployment would fall, and the long-run aggregate-supply curve would shift to the right.

Shifts Arising from Capital

An increase in the economy's capital stock increases productivity and, thereby, the quantity of goods and services supplied. As a result, the long-run aggregate-supply curve shifts to the right. Conversely, a decrease in the economy's capital stock decreases productivity and the quantity of goods and services supplied, shifting the long-run aggregate-supply curve to the left.

Notice that the same logic applies regardless of whether we are discussing physical capital or human capital. An increase either in the number of machines or in the number of college degrees will raise the economy's ability to produce goods and services. Thus, either would shift the long-run aggregate-supply curve to the right.

Shifts Arising from Natural Resources

An economy's production depends on its natural resources, including its land, minerals, and weather. A discovery of a new mineral deposit shifts the long-run aggregate-supply curve to the right. A change in weather patterns that makes farming more difficult shifts the long-run aggregate-supply curve to the left.

In many countries, important natural resources are imported from abroad. A change in the availability of these resources can also shift the aggregate-supply curve. As we discuss later in this chapter, events occurring in the world oil market have historically been an important source of shifts in aggregate supply.

Shifts Arising from Technological Knowledge

Perhaps the most important reason that the economy today produces more than it did a generation ago is that our technological knowledge has advanced. The invention of the computer, for instance, has allowed us to produce more goods and services from any given amounts of labor, capital, and natural resources. As a result, it has shifted the long-run aggregate-supply curve to the right.

Although not literally technological, there are many other events that act like changes in technology. As Chapter 9 explains, opening up international trade has effects similar to inventing new production processes, so it also shifts the long-run aggregate-supply curve to the right. Conversely, if the government passed new regulations preventing firms from using some production methods, perhaps because they were too dangerous for workers, the result would be a leftward shift in the long-run aggregate-supply curve.

Summary

The long-run aggregate-supply curve reflects the classical model of the economy we developed in previous chapters. Any policy or event that raised real GDP in previous chapters can now be viewed as increasing the quantity of goods and services supplied and shifting the long-run aggregate-supply curve to the right. Any policy or event that lowered real GDP in previous chapters can now be viewed as decreasing the quantity of goods and services supplied and shifting the long-run aggregate-supply curve to the left.

A New Way to Depict Long-Run Growth and Inflation

Having introduced the economy's aggregate-demand curve and the long-run aggregate-supply curve, we now have a new way to describe the economy's long-run trends. Figure 5 illustrates the changes that occur in the economy from decade to decade. Notice that both curves are shifting. Although there are many forces that govern the economy in the long run and can in principle cause such shifts, the two most important in practice are technology and monetary policy. Technological progress enhances the economy's ability to produce goods and services, and this continually shifts the long-run aggregate-supply curve to the right. At the same

FIGURE 5

Long-Run Growth and Inflation in the Model of Aggregate Demand and Aggregate Supply

As the economy becomes better able to produce goods and services over time, primarily because of technological progress, the long-run aggregate-supply curve shifts to the right. At the same time, as the Fed increases the money supply, the aggregate-demand curve also shifts to the right. In this figure, output grows from Y_{1980} to Y_{1990} and then to Y_{2000}, and the price level rises from P_{1980} to P_{1990} and then to P_{2000}. Thus, the model of aggregate demand and aggregate supply offers a new way to describe the classical analysis of growth and inflation.

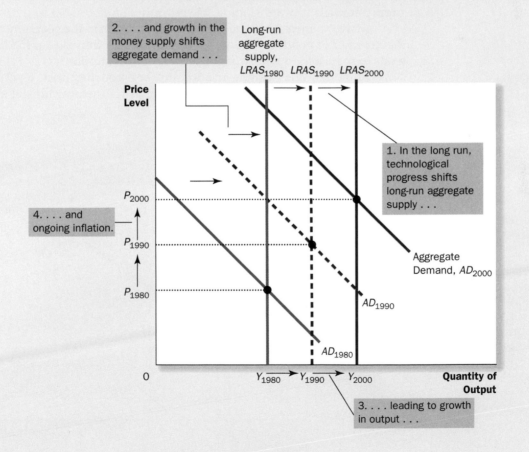

time, because the Fed increases the money supply over time, the aggregate-demand curve also shifts to the right. As the figure illustrates, the result is trend growth in output (as shown by increasing *Y*) and continuing inflation (as shown by increasing *P*). This is just another way of representing the classical analysis of growth and inflation we conducted in Chapters 12 and 17.

The purpose of developing the model of aggregate demand and aggregate supply, however, is not to dress our long-run conclusions in new clothing. Instead, it is to provide a framework for short-run analysis, as we will see in a moment. As we develop the short-run model, we keep the analysis simple by not showing the continuing growth and inflation depicted in Figure 5. But always remember that long-run trends provide the background for short-run fluctuations. *Short-run fluctuations in output and the price level should be viewed as deviations from the continuing long-run trends.*

Why the Aggregate-Supply Curve Slopes Upward in the Short Run

We now come to the key difference between the economy in the short run and in the long run: the behavior of aggregate supply. As we have already discussed, the long-run aggregate-supply curve is vertical. By contrast, in the short run, the aggregate-supply curve is upward sloping, as shown in Figure 6. That is, over a period of a year or two, an increase in the overall level of prices in the economy tends to raise the quantity of goods and services supplied, and a decrease in the level of prices tends to reduce the quantity of goods and services supplied.

What causes this positive relationship between the price level and output? Macroeconomists have proposed three theories for the upward slope of the short-

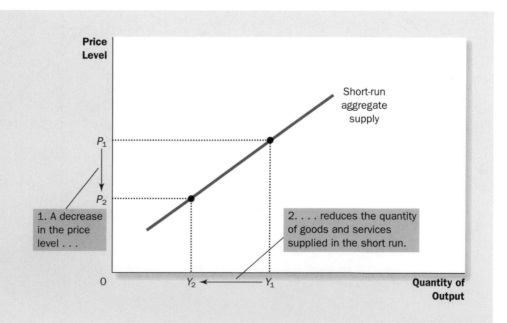

FIGURE 6

The Short-Run Aggregate-Supply Curve

In the short run, a fall in the price level from P₁ to P₂ reduces the quantity of output supplied from Y₁ to Y₂. This positive relationship could be due to sticky wages, sticky prices, or misperceptions. Over time, wages, prices, and perceptions adjust, so this positive relationship is only temporary.

1. A decrease in the price level . . .

2. . . . reduces the quantity of goods and services supplied in the short run.

run aggregate-supply curve. In each theory, a specific market imperfection causes the supply side of the economy to behave differently in the short run than it does in the long run. Although each of the following theories will differ in detail, they share a common theme: *The quantity of output supplied deviates from its long-run, or "natural," level when the price level deviates from the price level that people expected to prevail.* When the price level rises above the expected level, output rises above its natural rate, and when the price level falls below the expected level, output falls below its natural rate.

The Sticky-Wage Theory   The first and simplest explanation of the upward slope of the short-run aggregate-supply curve is the sticky-wage theory. According to this theory, the short-run aggregate-supply curve slopes upward because nominal wages are slow to adjust, or are "sticky," in the short run. To some extent, the slow adjustment of nominal wages is attributable to long-term contracts between workers and firms that fix nominal wages, sometimes for as long as three years. In addition, this slow adjustment may be attributable to social norms and notions of fairness that influence wage setting and that change only slowly over time.

To see what sticky nominal wages mean for aggregate supply, imagine that a firm has agreed in advance to pay its workers a certain nominal wage based on what it expected the price level to be. If the price level P falls below the level that was expected and the nominal wage remains stuck at W, then the real wage W/P rises above the level the firm planned to pay. Because wages are a large part of a firm's production costs, a higher real wage means that the firm's real costs have risen. The firm responds to these higher costs by hiring less labor and producing a smaller quantity of goods and services. In other words, *because wages do not adjust immediately to the price level, a lower price level makes employment and production less profitable, so firms reduce the quantity of goods and services they supply.*

The Sticky-Price Theory   Some economists have advocated another approach to the short-run aggregate-supply curve, called the sticky-price theory. As we just discussed, the sticky-wage theory emphasizes that nominal wages adjust slowly over time. The sticky-price theory emphasizes that the prices of some goods and services also adjust sluggishly in response to changing economic conditions. This slow adjustment of prices occurs in part because there are costs to adjusting prices, called *menu costs*. These menu costs include the cost of printing and distributing catalogs and the time required to change price tags. As a result of these costs, prices as well as wages may be sticky in the short run.

To see the implications of sticky prices for aggregate supply, suppose that each firm in the economy announces its prices in advance based on the economic conditions it expects to prevail. Then, after prices are announced, the economy experiences an unexpected contraction in the money supply, which (as we have learned) will reduce the overall price level in the long run. Although some firms reduce their prices immediately in response to changing economic conditions, other firms may not want to incur additional menu costs and, therefore, may temporarily lag behind. Because these lagging firms have prices that are too high, their sales decline. Declining sales, in turn, cause these firms to cut back on production and employment. In other words, *because not all prices adjust instantly to changing conditions, an unexpected fall in the price level leaves some firms with higher-than-desired prices, and these higher-than-desired prices depress sales and induce firms to reduce the quantity of goods and services they produce.*

The Misperceptions Theory   A third approach to the short-run aggregate-supply curve is the misperceptions theory. According to this theory, changes in the overall price level can temporarily mislead suppliers about what is happening in the individual markets in which they sell their output. As a result of these short-run misperceptions, suppliers respond to changes in the level of prices, and this response leads to an upward-sloping aggregate-supply curve.

To see how this might work, suppose the overall price level falls below the level that people expected. When suppliers see the prices of their products fall, they may mistakenly believe that their *relative* prices have fallen. For example, wheat farmers may notice a fall in the price of wheat before they notice a fall in the prices of the many items they buy as consumers. They may infer from this observation that the reward to producing wheat is temporarily low, and they may respond by reducing the quantity of wheat they supply. Similarly, workers may notice a fall in their nominal wages before they notice a fall in the prices of the goods they buy. They may infer that the reward to working is temporarily low and respond by reducing the quantity of labor they supply. In both cases, *a lower price level causes misperceptions about relative prices, and these misperceptions induce suppliers to respond to the lower price level by decreasing the quantity of goods and services supplied.*

Summary   There are three alternative explanations for the upward slope of the short-run aggregate-supply curve: (1) sticky wages, (2) sticky prices, and (3) misperceptions. Economists debate which of these theories is correct, and it is very possible each contains an element of truth. For our purposes in this book, the similarities of the theories are more important than the differences. All three theories suggest that output deviates from its natural rate when the price level deviates from the price level that people expected. We can express this mathematically as follows:

$$\text{Quantity of output supplied} = \text{Natural rate of output} + a\left(\text{Actual price level} - \text{Expected price level}\right)$$

where a is a number that determines how much output responds to unexpected changes in the price level.

Notice that each of the three theories of short-run aggregate supply emphasizes a problem that is likely to be only temporary. Whether the upward slope of the aggregate-supply curve is attributable to sticky wages, sticky prices, or misperceptions, these conditions will not persist forever. Eventually, as people adjust their expectations, nominal wages adjust, prices become unstuck, and misperceptions are corrected. In other words, the expected and actual price levels are equal in the long run, and the aggregate-supply curve is vertical rather than upward sloping.

Why the Short-Run Aggregate-Supply Curve Might Shift

The short-run aggregate-supply curve tells us the quantity of goods and services supplied in the short run for any given level of prices. We can think of this curve

FIGURE 7

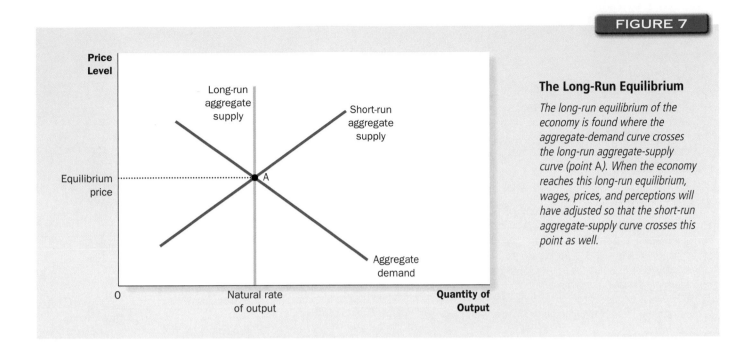

The Long-Run Equilibrium

The long-run equilibrium of the economy is found where the aggregate-demand curve crosses the long-run aggregate-supply curve (point A). When the economy reaches this long-run equilibrium, wages, prices, and perceptions will have adjusted so that the short-run aggregate-supply curve crosses this point as well.

or the outbreak of war overseas. Because of this event, many people lose confidence in the future and alter their plans. Households cut back on their spending and delay major purchases, and firms put off buying new equipment.

What is the impact of such a wave of pessimism on the economy? Such an event reduces the aggregate demand for goods and services. That is, for any given price level, households and firms now want to buy a smaller quantity of goods and services. As Figure 8 (p. 448) shows, the aggregate-demand curve shifts to the left from AD_1 to AD_2.

In this figure we can examine the effects of the fall in aggregate demand. In the short run, the economy moves along the initial short-run aggregate-supply curve AS_1, going from point A to point B. As the economy moves from point A to point B, output falls from Y_1 to Y_2, and the price level falls from P_1 to P_2. The falling level of output indicates that the economy is in a recession. Although not shown in the figure, firms respond to lower sales and production by reducing employment. Thus, the pessimism that caused the shift in aggregate demand is, to some extent, self-fulfilling: Pessimism about the future leads to falling incomes and rising unemployment.

What should policymakers do when faced with such a recession? One possibility is to take action to increase aggregate demand. As we noted earlier, an increase in government spending or an increase in the money supply would increase the quantity of goods and services demanded at any price and, therefore, would shift the aggregate-demand curve to the right. If policymakers can act with sufficient speed and precision, they can offset the initial shift in aggregate demand, return the aggregate-demand curve back to AD_1, and bring the economy back to point A. (The next chapter discusses in more detail the ways in which monetary and fiscal policy influence aggregate demand, as well as some of the practical difficulties in using these policy instruments.)

FIGURE 8

A Contraction in Aggregate Demand

A fall in aggregate demand, which might be due to a wave of pessimism in the economy, is represented with a leftward shift in the aggregate-demand curve from AD₁ to AD₂. The economy moves from point A to point B. Output falls from Y₁ to Y₂, and the price level falls from P₁ to P₂. Over time, as wages, prices, and perceptions adjust, the short-run aggregate-supply curve shifts to the right from AS₁ to AS₂, and the economy reaches point C, where the new aggregate-demand curve crosses the long-run aggregate-supply curve. The price level falls to P₃, and output returns to its natural rate, Y₁.

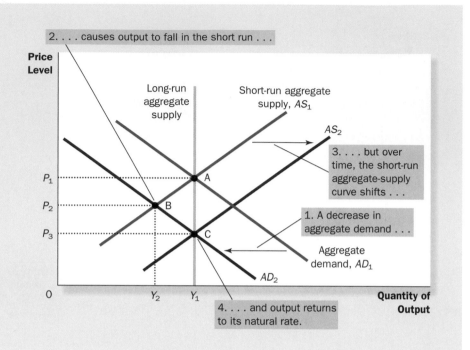

2. . . . causes output to fall in the short run . . .

3. . . . but over time, the short-run aggregate-supply curve shifts . . .

1. A decrease in aggregate demand . . .

4. . . . and output returns to its natural rate.

Even without action by policymakers, the recession will remedy itself over a period of time. Because of the reduction in aggregate demand, the price level falls. Eventually, expectations catch up with this new reality, and the expected price level falls as well. Because the fall in the expected price level alters wages, prices, and perceptions it shifts the short-run aggregate-supply curve to the right from AS_1 to AS_2 in Figure 8. This adjustment of expectations allows the economy over time to approach point C, where the new aggregate-demand curve (AD_2) crosses the long-run aggregate-supply curve.

In the new long-run equilibrium, point C, output is back to its natural rate. Even though the wave of pessimism has reduced aggregate demand, the price level has fallen sufficiently (to P_3) to offset the shift in the aggregate-demand curve. Thus, in the long run, the shift in aggregate demand is reflected fully in the price level and not at all in the level of output. In other words, the long-run effect of a shift in aggregate demand is a nominal change (the price level is lower) but not a real change (output is the same).

To sum up, this story about shifts in aggregate demand has two important lessons:

- In the short run, shifts in aggregate demand cause fluctuations in the economy's output of goods and services.
- In the long run, shifts in aggregate demand affect the overall price level but do not affect output.

Case Study

TWO BIG SHIFTS IN AGGREGATE DEMAND: THE GREAT DEPRESSION AND WORLD WAR II

At the beginning of this chapter we established three key facts about economic fluctuations by looking at data since 1965. Let's now take a longer look at U.S. economic history. Figure 9 shows data since 1900 on the percentage change in real GDP over the previous three years. In an average three-year period, real GDP grows about 10 percent—a bit more than 3 percent per year. The business cycle, however, causes fluctuations around this average. Two episodes jump out as being particularly significant—the large drop in real GDP in the early 1930s and the large increase in real GDP in the early 1940s. Both of these events are attributable to shifts in aggregate demand.

The economic calamity of the early 1930s is called the *Great Depression*, and it is by far the largest economic downturn in U.S. history. Real GDP fell by 27 percent from 1929 to 1933, and unemployment rose from 3 percent to 25 percent. At the same time, the price level fell by 22 percent over these four years. Many other countries experienced similar declines in output and prices during this period.

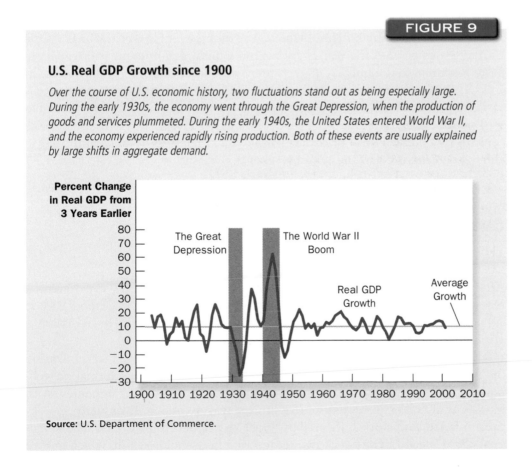

FIGURE 9

U.S. Real GDP Growth since 1900

Over the course of U.S. economic history, two fluctuations stand out as being especially large. During the early 1930s, the economy went through the Great Depression, when the production of goods and services plummeted. During the early 1940s, the United States entered World War II, and the economy experienced rapidly rising production. Both of these events are usually explained by large shifts in aggregate demand.

Source: U.S. Department of Commerce.

Economic historians continue to debate the causes of the Great Depression, but most explanations center on a large decline in aggregate demand. What caused aggregate demand to contract? Here is where the disagreement arises.

Many economists place primary blame on the decline in the money supply: From 1929 to 1933, the money supply fell by 28 percent. As you may recall from our discussion of the monetary system, this decline in the money supply was due to problems in the banking system. As households withdrew their money from financially shaky banks and bankers became more cautious and started holding greater reserves, the process of money creation under fractional-reserve banking went into reverse. The Fed, meanwhile, failed to offset this fall in the money multiplier with expansionary open-market operations. As a result, the money supply declined. Many economists blame the Fed's failure to act for the Great Depression's severity.

Other economists have suggested alternative reasons for the collapse in aggregate demand. For example, stock prices fell about 90 percent during this period, depressing household wealth and thereby consumer spending. In addition, the banking problems may have prevented some firms from obtaining the financing they wanted for investment projects, and this would have depressed investment spending. Of course, all of these forces may have acted together to contract aggregate demand during the Great Depression.

The second significant episode in Figure 9—the economic boom of the early 1940s—is easier to explain. The obvious cause of this event is World War II. As the United States entered the war overseas, the federal government had to devote more resources to the military. Government purchases of goods and services increased almost fivefold from 1939 to 1944. This huge expansion in aggregate demand almost doubled the economy's production of goods and services and led to a 20 percent increase in the price level (although widespread government price controls limited the rise in prices). Unemployment fell from 17 percent in 1939 to about 1 percent in 1944—the lowest level in U.S. history. ●

Case Study
THE RECESSION OF 2001

After the longest economic expansion in history, the U.S. economy experienced a recession in 2001. The unemployment rate rose from 3.9 percent in October 2000 to 4.9 percent in August 2001, and then to 6.0 percent in April 2002. This recession is attributable to three shocks to aggregate demand.

The first shock was the end of the dot-com bubble in the stock market. During the 1990s, many stock-market investors became optimistic about information technology, and they bid up stock prices, particularly of high-tech companies. With hindsight, it is fair to say that this optimism was excessive. Eventually, the optimism faded, and stock prices fell by about 25 percent from August 2000 to August 2001. The fall in the stock market reduced household wealth, which in turn reduced consumer spending. In addition, when the new technologies started to appear less profitable than they had originally seemed, investment spending fell. The aggregate demand curve shifted to the left.

The second shock to the economy was the terrorist attacks on New York and Washington on September 11, 2001. In the week after the attacks, the stock market fell another 12 percent, its biggest weekly loss since the Great Depression of the 1930s. Moreover, the attacks increased uncertainty about what the future would hold. Uncertainty can reduce spending, as households and firms postpone plans, waiting for the uncertainty to be resolved. Thus, the terrorist attacks also shifted the aggregate demand further to the left.

The third shock was a series of corporate accounting scandals. During 2001 and 2002, several major corporations, including Enron and WorldCom, were found to have misled the public about their profitability. When the truth became known, the value of their stock plummeted. Even honest companies experienced stock declines, as stock-market investors became less trustful of all accounting data. This fall in the stock market further depressed aggregate demand.

Policymakers were quick to respond to these events. With the president's urging, Congress passed a tax cut in 2001, including an immediate tax rebate. One goal of the tax cut was to stimulate consumer spending. After the terrorist attacks, Congress increased government spending with funds to rebuild New York and to help the troubled airline industry. Both of these fiscal measures aimed to shift the aggregate demand curve to the right, offsetting the three contractionary shocks the economy had experienced.

The Fed also helped to expand aggregate demand by pursuing expansionary monetary policy. Money growth accelerated, and interest rates fell. The interest rate on three-month Treasury bills fell from 6.4 percent in November 2000 to 1.7 percent in December 2001. Lower interest rates stimulated spending by reducing the cost of borrowing.

As this book was going to press in 2002, the recession appeared to be over. Unemployment had fallen a bit, and the economy's production of goods and services was growing once again. But the recession of 2001 is a reminder of the many kinds of events that can influence aggregate demand and, thus, the direction of the economy. ●

The Effects of a Shift in Aggregate Supply

Imagine once again an economy in its long-run equilibrium. Now suppose that suddenly some firms experience an increase in their costs of production. For example, bad weather in farm states might destroy some crops, driving up the cost of producing food products. Or a war in the Middle East might interrupt the shipping of crude oil, driving up the cost of producing oil products.

What is the macroeconomic impact of such an increase in production costs? For any given price level, firms now want to supply a smaller quantity of goods and services. Thus, as Figure 10 (p. 452) shows, the short-run aggregate-supply curve

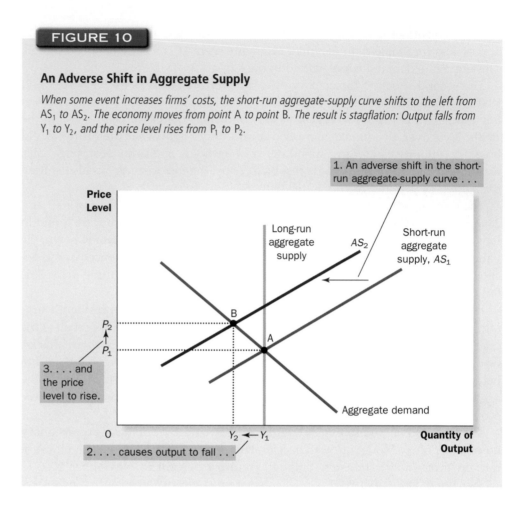

FIGURE 10

An Adverse Shift in Aggregate Supply

When some event increases firms' costs, the short-run aggregate-supply curve shifts to the left from AS₁ to AS₂. The economy moves from point A to point B. The result is stagflation: Output falls from Y₁ to Y₂, and the price level rises from P₁ to P₂.

shifts to the left from AS_1 to AS_2. (Depending on the event, the long-run aggregate-supply curve might also shift. To keep things simple, however, we will assume that it does not.)

In this figure we can trace the effects of the leftward shift in aggregate supply. In the short run, the economy moves along the existing aggregate-demand curve, going from point A to point B. The output of the economy falls from Y_1 to Y_2, and the price level rises from P_1 to P_2. Because the economy is experiencing both *stagnation* (falling output) and *inflation* (rising prices), such an event is sometimes called **stagflation.**

What should policymakers do when faced with stagflation? There are no easy choices. One possibility is to do nothing. In this case, the output of goods and services remains depressed at Y_2 for a while. Eventually, however, the recession will remedy itself as wages, prices, and perceptions adjust to the higher production costs. A period of low output and high unemployment, for instance, puts downward pressure on workers' wages. Lower wages, in turn, increase the quantity of output supplied. Over time, as the short-run aggregate-supply curve shifts back toward AS_1, the price level falls, and the quantity of output approaches its natural rate. In the long run, the economy returns to point A, where the aggregate-demand curve crosses the long-run aggregate-supply curve.

stagflation
a period of falling output and rising prices

FIGURE 11

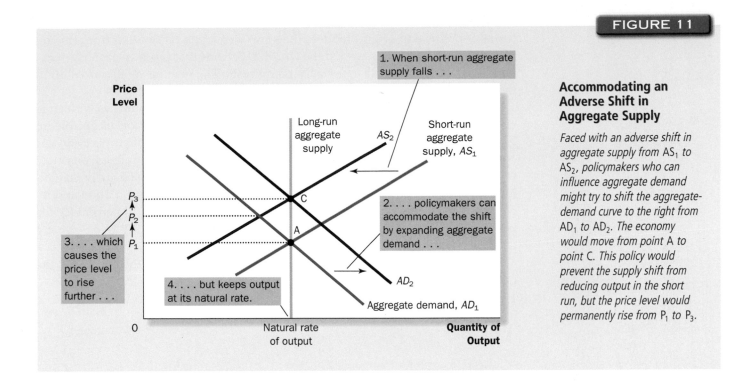

1. When short-run aggregate supply falls . . .

Price Level

Long-run aggregate supply

AS_2

Short-run aggregate supply, AS_1

P_3

P_2

3. . . . which causes the price level to rise further . . .

P_1

C

A

2. . . . policymakers can accommodate the shift by expanding aggregate demand . . .

4. . . . but keeps output at its natural rate.

AD_2

Aggregate demand, AD_1

0

Natural rate of output

Quantity of Output

Accommodating an Adverse Shift in Aggregate Supply

Faced with an adverse shift in aggregate supply from AS_1 to AS_2, policymakers who can influence aggregate demand might try to shift the aggregate-demand curve to the right from AD_1 to AD_2. The economy would move from point A to point C. This policy would prevent the supply shift from reducing output in the short run, but the price level would permanently rise from P_1 to P_3.

Alternatively, policymakers who control monetary and fiscal policy might attempt to offset some of the effects of the shift in the short-run aggregate-supply curve by shifting the aggregate-demand curve. This possibility is shown in Figure 11. In this case, changes in policy shift the aggregate-demand curve to the right from AD_1 to AD_2—exactly enough to prevent the shift in aggregate supply from affecting output. The economy moves directly from point A to point C. Output remains at its natural rate, and the price level rises from P_1 to P_3. In this case, policymakers are said to *accommodate* the shift in aggregate supply because they allow the increase in costs to permanently affect the level of prices.

To sum up, this story about shifts in aggregate supply has two important lessons:

- Shifts in aggregate supply can cause stagflation—a combination of recession (falling output) and inflation (rising prices).
- Policymakers who can influence aggregate demand cannot offset both of these adverse effects simultaneously.

Case Study

OIL AND THE ECONOMY

Some of the largest economic fluctuations in the U.S. economy since 1970 have originated in the oil fields of the Middle East. Crude oil is a key input into the production of many goods and services, and much of the world's oil comes from

Saudi Arabia, Kuwait, and other Middle Eastern countries. When some event (usually political in origin) reduces the supply of crude oil flowing from this region, the price of oil rises around the world. U.S. firms that produce gasoline, tires, and many other products experience rising costs. The result is a leftward shift in the aggregate-supply curve, which in turn leads to stagflation.

The first episode of this sort occurred in the mid-1970s. The countries with large oil reserves got together as members of OPEC, the Organization of Petroleum Exporting Countries. OPEC was a *cartel*—a group of sellers that attempts to thwart competition and reduce production in order to raise prices. And, indeed, oil prices rose substantially. From 1973 to 1975, oil approximately doubled in price. Oil-importing countries around the world experienced simultaneous inflation and recession. The U.S. inflation rate as measured by the CPI exceeded 10 percent for the first time in decades. Unemployment rose from 4.9 percent in 1973 to 8.5 percent in 1975.

Almost the same thing happened again a few years later. In the late 1970s, the OPEC countries again restricted the supply of oil to raise the price. From 1978 to 1981, the price of oil more than doubled. Once again, the result was stagflation.

FYI

THE ORIGINS OF AGGREGATE DEMAND AND AGGREGATE SUPPLY

Now that we have a preliminary understanding of the model of aggregate demand and aggregate supply, it is worthwhile to step back from it and consider its history. How did this model of short-run fluctuations develop? The answer is that this model, to a large extent, is a by-product of the Great Depression of the 1930s. Economists and policymakers at the time were puzzled about what had caused this calamity and were uncertain about how to deal with it.

In 1936, economist John Maynard Keynes published a book titled *The General Theory of Employment, Interest, and Money,* which attempted to explain short-run economic fluctuations in general and the Great Depression in

John Maynard Keynes

particular. Keynes's primary message was that recessions and depressions can occur because of inadequate aggregate demand for goods and services.

Keynes had long been a critic of classical economic theory—the theory we examined earlier in the book—because it could explain only the long-run effects of policies. A few years before offering *The General Theory,* Keynes had written the following about classical economics:

The long run is a misleading guide to current affairs. In the long run we are all dead. Economists set themselves too easy, too useless a task if in tempestuous seasons they can only tell us when the storm is long past, the ocean will be flat.

Keynes's message was aimed at policymakers as well as economists. As the world's economies suffered with high unemployment, Keynes advocated policies to increase aggregate demand, including government spending on public works.

In the next chapter we examine in detail how policymakers can try to use the tools of monetary and fiscal policy to influence aggregate demand. The analysis in the next chapter, as well as in this one, owes much to the legacy of John Maynard Keynes.

Inflation, which had subsided somewhat after the first OPEC event, again rose above 10 percent per year. But because the Fed was not willing to accommodate such a large rise in inflation, a recession was soon to follow. Unemployment rose from about 6 percent in 1978 and 1979 to about 10 percent a few years later.

The world market for oil can also be a source of favorable shifts in aggregate supply. In 1986 squabbling broke out among members of OPEC. Member countries reneged on their agreements to restrict oil production. In the world market for crude oil, prices fell by about half. This fall in oil prices reduced costs to U.S. firms, which shifted the aggregate-supply curve to the right. As a result, the U.S. economy experienced the opposite of stagflation: Output grew rapidly, unemployment fell, and the inflation rate reached its lowest level in many years.

In recent years, the world market for oil has not been as important a source of economic fluctuations. Part of the reason is that OPEC has been less effective as a cartel: The real price of oil has never again come close to the levels reached in the early 1980s. In addition, conservation efforts and changes in technology have reduced the economy's dependence on oil. The amount of oil used to produce a unit of real GDP has declined about 40 percent since the OPEC shocks of the 1970s. Nonetheless, it would be premature to conclude that the United States no longer needs to worry about oil prices. Political troubles in the Middle East (or greater cooperation among the members of OPEC) could always send oil prices higher. If the rise in oil prices were large enough, the macroeconomic result would most likely resemble the stagflation of the 1970s. ●

Changes in Middle East oil production are one source of U.S. economic fluctuations.

QuickQuiz Suppose that the election of a popular presidential candidate suddenly increases people's confidence in the future. Use the model of aggregate demand and aggregate supply to analyze the effect on the economy.

CONCLUSION

This chapter has achieved two goals. First, we have discussed some of the important facts about short-run fluctuations in economic activity. Second, we have introduced a basic model to explain those fluctuations, called the model of aggregate demand and aggregate supply. We continue our study of this model in the next chapter in order to understand more fully what causes fluctuations in the economy and how policymakers might respond to these fluctuations.

SUMMARY

- All societies experience short-run economic fluctuations around long-run trends. These fluctuations are irregular and largely unpredictable. When recessions do occur, real

GDP and other measures of income, spending, and production fall, and unemployment rises.

- Economists analyze short-run economic fluctuations using the model of aggregate demand and aggregate supply. According to this model, the output of goods and services and the overall level of prices adjust to balance aggregate demand and aggregate supply.

- The aggregate-demand curve slopes downward for three reasons. First, a lower price level raises the real value of households' money holdings, which stimulates consumer spending. Second, a lower price level reduces the quantity of money households demand; as households try to convert money into interest-bearing assets, interest rates fall, which stimulates investment spending. Third, as a lower price level reduces interest rates, the dollar depreciates in the market for foreign-currency exchange, which stimulates net exports.

- Any event or policy that raises consumption, investment, government purchases, or net exports at a given price level increases aggregate demand. Any event or policy that reduces consumption, investment, government purchases, or net exports at a given price level decreases aggregate demand.

- The long-run aggregate-supply curve is vertical. In the long run, the quantity of goods and services supplied depends on the economy's labor, capital, natural resources, and technology, but not on the overall level of prices.

- Three theories have been proposed to explain the upward slope of the short-run aggregate-supply curve. According to the sticky-wage theory, an unexpected fall in the price level temporarily raises real wages, which induces firms to reduce employment and production. According to the sticky-price theory, an unexpected fall in the price level leaves some firms with prices that are temporarily too high, which reduces their sales and causes them to cut back production. According to the misperceptions theory, an unexpected fall in the price level leads suppliers to mistakenly believe that their relative prices have fallen, which induces them to reduce production. All three theories imply that output deviates from its natural rate when the price level deviates from the price level that people expected.

- Events that alter the economy's ability to produce output, such as changes in labor, capital, natural resources, or technology, shift the short-run aggregate-supply curve (and may shift the long-run aggregate-supply curve as well). In addition, the position of the short-run aggregate-supply curve depends on the expected price level.

- One possible cause of economic fluctuations is a shift in aggregate demand. When the aggregate-demand curve shifts to the left, for instance, output and prices fall in the short run. Over time, as a change in the expected price level causes wages, prices, and perceptions to adjust, the short-run aggregate-supply curve shifts to the right, and the economy returns to its natural rate of output at a new, lower price level.

- A second possible cause of economic fluctuations is a shift in aggregate supply. When the aggregate-supply curve shifts to the left, the short-run effect is falling output and rising prices—a combination called stagflation. Over time, as wages, prices, and perceptions adjust, the price level falls back to its original level, and output recovers.

KEY CONCEPTS

recession, p. 427
depression, p. 427

model of aggregate demand and aggregate supply, p. 432

aggregate-demand curve, p. 433
aggregate-supply curve, p. 433
stagflation, p. 452

QUESTIONS FOR REVIEW

1. Name two macroeconomic variables that decline when the economy goes into a recession. Name one macroeconomic variable that rises during a recession.

2. Draw a diagram with aggregate demand, short-run aggregate supply, and long-run aggregate supply. Be careful to label the axes correctly.

3. List and explain the three reasons why the aggregate-demand curve is downward sloping.

4. Explain why the long-run aggregate-supply curve is vertical.

5. List and explain the three theories for why the short-run aggregate-supply curve is upward sloping.

6. What might shift the aggregate-demand curve to the left? Use the model of aggregate demand and aggregate supply to trace through the effects of such a shift.

7. What might shift the aggregate-supply curve to the left? Use the model of aggregate demand and aggregate supply to trace through the effects of such a shift.

PROBLEMS AND APPLICATIONS

1. Why do you think that investment is more variable over the business cycle than consumer spending? Which category of consumer spending do you think would be most volatile: durable goods (such as furniture and car purchases), nondurable goods (such as food and clothing), or services (such as haircuts and medical care)? Why?

2. Suppose that the economy is in a long-run equilibrium.
   a. Use a diagram to illustrate the state of the economy. Be sure to show aggregate demand, short-run aggregate supply, and long-run aggregate supply.
   b. Now suppose that a stock market crash causes aggregate demand to fall. Use your diagram to show what happens to output and the price level in the short run. What happens to the unemployment rate?
   c. Use the sticky-wage theory of aggregate supply to explain what will happen to output and the price level in the long run (assuming there is no change in policy). What role does the expected price level play in this adjustment? Be sure to illustrate your analysis in a graph.

3. Explain whether each of the following events will increase, decrease, or have no effect on long-run aggregate supply.
   a. The United States experiences a wave of immigration.
   b. Congress raises the minimum wage to $10 per hour.
   c. Intel invents a new and more powerful computer chip.

   d. A severe hurricane damages factories along the east coast.

4. In Figure 8, how does the unemployment rate at points B and C compare to the unemployment rate at point A? Under the sticky-wage explanation of the short-run aggregate-supply curve, how does the real wage at points B and C compare to the real wage at point A?

5. Explain why the following statements are false.
   a. "The aggregate-demand curve slopes downward because it is the horizontal sum of the demand curves for individual goods."
   b. "The long-run aggregate-supply curve is vertical because economic forces do not affect long-run aggregate supply."
   c. "If firms adjusted their prices every day, then the short-run aggregate-supply curve would be horizontal."
   d. "Whenever the economy enters a recession, its long-run aggregate-supply curve shifts to the left."

6. For each of the three theories for the upward slope of the short-run aggregate-supply curve, carefully explain the following.
   a. how the economy recovers from a recession and returns to its long-run equilibrium without any policy intervention
   b. what determines the speed of that recovery

7. Suppose the Fed expands the money supply, but because the public expects this Fed action, it simultaneously raises its expectation of the price level. What will happen to output and the price level in the short run? Compare this result to the outcome if the Fed expanded the money

supply but the public didn't change its expectation of the price level.

8. Suppose that the economy is currently in a recession. If policymakers take no action, how will the economy evolve over time? Explain in words and using an aggregate-demand/aggregate-supply diagram.

9. Suppose workers and firms suddenly believe that inflation will be quite high over the coming year. Suppose also that the economy begins in long-run equilibrium, and the aggregate-demand curve does not shift.
   a. What happens to nominal wages? What happens to real wages?
   b. Using an aggregate-demand/aggregate-supply diagram, show the effect of the change in expectations on both the short-run and long-run levels of prices and output.
   c. Were the expectations of high inflation accurate? Explain.

10. Explain whether each of the following events shifts the short-run aggregate-supply curve, the aggregate-demand curve, both, or neither. For each event that does shift a curve, use a diagram to illustrate the effect on the economy.
    a. Households decide to save a larger share of their income.
    b. Florida orange groves suffer a prolonged period of below-freezing temperatures.
    c. Increased job opportunities overseas cause many people to leave the country.

11. For each of the following events, explain the short-run and long-run effects on output and the price level, assuming policymakers take no action.
    a. The stock market declines sharply, reducing consumers' wealth.
    b. The federal government increases spending on national defense.
    c. A technological improvement raises productivity.
    d. A recession overseas causes foreigners to buy fewer U.S. goods.

12. Suppose that firms become very optimistic about future business conditions and invest heavily in new capital equipment.
    a. Use an aggregate-demand/aggregate-supply diagram to show the short-run effect of this optimism on the economy. Label the new levels of prices and real output. Explain in words why the aggregate quantity of output *supplied* changes.
    b. Now use the diagram from part (a) to show the new long-run equilibrium of the economy. (For now, assume there is no change in the long-run aggregate-supply curve.) Explain in words why the aggregate quantity of output *demanded* changes between the short run and the long run.
    c. How might the investment boom affect the long-run aggregate-supply curve? Explain.

13. In 1939, with the U.S. economy not yet fully recovered from the Great Depression, President Roosevelt proclaimed that Thanksgiving would fall a week earlier than usual so that the shopping period before Christmas would be longer. Explain this decision, using the model of aggregate demand and aggregate supply.

14. The National Bureau of Economic Research is a nonprofit economic research group that sets the official dates for the beginning and end of recessions in the United States. Go to its Web site, http://www.nber.org, and find information about business cycle dating. Notice that the NBER often uses the term "contraction" for a recession and the term "expansion" for the period of growth between recessions.
    a. What was the U.S. economy's most recent turning point? Is the U.S. economy now in an expansion or a contraction?
    b. When was the most recent completed recession? How long was it? By historical standards, was this recession short or long?
    c. When was the most recent completed expansion? How long was it? By historical standards, was this expansion short or long?

http://   For more study tools, please visit http://mankiwXtra.swlearning.com.

21

THE INFLUENCE OF MONETARY AND FISCAL POLICY ON AGGREGATE DEMAND

Imagine that you are a member of the Federal Open Market Committee, which sets monetary policy. You observe that the president and Congress have agreed to cut government spending. How should the Fed respond to this change in fiscal policy? Should it expand the money supply, contract the money supply, or leave the money supply the same?

To answer this question, you need to consider the impact of monetary and fiscal policy on the economy. In the preceding chapter we saw how to explain short-run economic fluctuations using the model of aggregate demand and aggregate supply. When the aggregate-demand curve or the aggregate-supply curve shifts, the result is fluctuations in the economy's overall output of goods and services and in its overall level of prices. As we noted in the previous chapter, monetary and fiscal policy can each influence aggregate demand. Thus, a change in one of these policies can lead to short-run fluctuations in output and prices. Policymakers will want to anticipate this effect and, perhaps, adjust the other policy in response.

In this chapter we examine in more detail how the government's tools of monetary and fiscal policy influence the position of the aggregate-demand curve. We have previously discussed the long-run effects of these policies. In Chapters 12 and

13 we saw how fiscal policy affects saving, investment, and long-run economic growth. In Chapters 16 and 17 we saw how the Fed controls the money supply and how the money supply affects the price level in the long run. We now see how these policy tools can shift the aggregate-demand curve and, in doing so, affect short-run economic fluctuations.

As we have already learned, many factors influence aggregate demand besides monetary and fiscal policy. In particular, desired spending by households and firms determines the overall demand for goods and services. When desired spending changes, aggregate demand shifts. If policymakers do not respond, such shifts in aggregate demand cause short-run fluctuations in output and employment. As a result, monetary and fiscal policymakers sometimes use the policy levers at their disposal to try to offset these shifts in aggregate demand and thereby stabilize the economy. Here we discuss the theory behind these policy actions and some of the difficulties that arise in using this theory in practice.

HOW MONETARY POLICY INFLUENCES AGGREGATE DEMAND

The aggregate-demand curve shows the total quantity of goods and services demanded in the economy for any price level. As you may recall from the preceding chapter, the aggregate-demand curve slopes downward for three reasons:

- *The wealth effect:* A lower price level raises the real value of households' money holdings, and higher real wealth stimulates consumer spending.
- *The interest-rate effect:* A lower price level lowers the interest rate as people try to lend out their excess money holdings, and the lower interest rate stimulates investment spending.
- *The exchange-rate effect:* When a lower price level lowers the interest rate, investors move some of their funds overseas and cause the domestic currency to depreciate relative to foreign currencies. This depreciation makes domestic goods cheaper compared to foreign goods and, therefore, stimulates spending on net exports.

These three effects should not be viewed as alternative theories. Instead, they occur simultaneously to increase the quantity of goods and services demanded when the price level falls and to decrease it when the price level rises.

Although all three effects work together in explaining the downward slope of the aggregate-demand curve, they are not of equal importance. Because money holdings are a small part of household wealth, the wealth effect is the least important of the three. In addition, because exports and imports represent only a small fraction of U.S. GDP, the exchange-rate effect is not very large for the U.S. economy. (This effect is much more important for smaller countries because smaller countries typically export and import a higher fraction of their GDP.) *For the U.S. economy, the most important reason for the downward slope of the aggregate-demand curve is the interest-rate effect.*

To understand how policy influences aggregate demand, therefore, we examine the interest-rate effect in more detail. Here we develop a theory of how the interest rate is determined, called the **theory of liquidity preference.** After we develop this

theory of liquidity preference
Keynes's theory that the interest rate adjusts to bring money supply and money demand into balance

theory, we use it to understand the downward slope of the aggregate-demand curve and how monetary policy shifts this curve. By shedding new light on the aggregate-demand curve, the theory of liquidity preference expands our understanding of short-run economic fluctuations.

The Theory of Liquidity Preference

In his classic book *The General Theory of Employment, Interest, and Money,* John Maynard Keynes proposed the theory of liquidity preference to explain what factors determine the economy's interest rate. The theory is, in essence, just an application of supply and demand. According to Keynes, the interest rate adjusts to balance the supply and demand for money.

You may recall that economists distinguish between two interest rates: The *nominal interest rate* is the interest rate as usually reported, and the *real interest rate* is the interest rate corrected for the effects of inflation. Which interest rate are we now trying to explain? The answer is both. In the analysis that follows, we hold constant the expected rate of inflation. (This assumption is reasonable for studying the economy in the short run, as we are now doing.) Thus, when the nominal interest rate rises or falls, the real interest rate that people expect to earn rises or falls as well. For the rest of this chapter, when we refer to changes in the interest rate, you should envision the real and nominal interest rates moving in the same direction.

Let's now develop the theory of liquidity preference by considering the supply and demand for money and how each depends on the interest rate.

Money Supply   The first piece of the theory of liquidity preference is the supply of money. As we first discussed in Chapter 16, the money supply in the U.S. economy is controlled by the Federal Reserve. The Fed alters the money supply primarily by changing the quantity of reserves in the banking system through the purchase and sale of government bonds in open-market operations. When the Fed buys government bonds, the dollars it pays for the bonds are typically deposited in banks, and these dollars are added to bank reserves. When the Fed sells government bonds, the dollars it receives for the bonds are withdrawn from the banking system, and bank reserves fall. These changes in bank reserves, in turn, lead to changes in banks' ability to make loans and create money. In addition to these open-market operations, the Fed can alter the money supply by changing reserve requirements (the amount of reserves banks must hold against deposits) or the discount rate (the interest rate at which banks can borrow reserves from the Fed).

These details of monetary control are important for the implementation of Fed policy, but they are not crucial in this chapter. Our goal here is to examine how changes in the money supply affect the aggregate demand for goods and services. For this purpose, we can ignore the details of how Fed policy is implemented and simply assume that the Fed controls the money supply directly. In other words, the quantity of money supplied in the economy is fixed at whatever level the Fed decides to set it.

Because the quantity of money supplied is fixed by Fed policy, it does not depend on other economic variables. In particular, it does not depend on the interest rate. Once the Fed has made its policy decision, the quantity of money supplied is the same, regardless of the prevailing interest rate. We represent a fixed money supply with a vertical supply curve, as in Figure 1 (p. 462).

FIGURE 1

Equilibrium in the Money Market

According to the theory of liquidity preference, the interest rate adjusts to bring the quantity of money supplied and the quantity of money demanded into balance. If the interest rate is above the equilibrium level (such as at r_1), the quantity of money people want to hold (M_1^d) is less than the quantity the Fed has created, and this surplus of money puts downward pressure on the interest rate. Conversely, if the interest rate is below the equilibrium level (such as at r_2), the quantity of money people want to hold (M_2^d) is greater than the quantity the Fed has created, and this shortage of money puts upward pressure on the interest rate. Thus, the forces of supply and demand in the market for money push the interest rate toward the equilibrium interest rate, at which people are content holding the quantity of money the Fed has created.

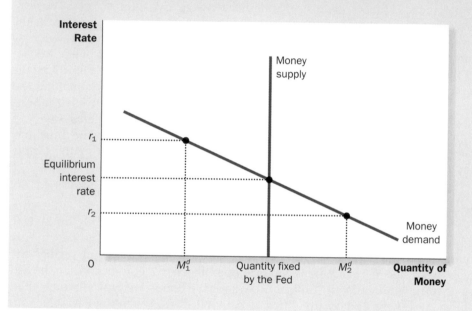

Money Demand The second piece of the theory of liquidity preference is the demand for money. As a starting point for understanding money demand, recall that any asset's *liquidity* refers to the ease with which that asset is converted into the economy's medium of exchange. Money is the economy's medium of exchange, so it is by definition the most liquid asset available. The liquidity of money explains the demand for it: People choose to hold money instead of other assets that offer higher rates of return because money can be used to buy goods and services.

Although many factors determine the quantity of money demanded, the one emphasized by the theory of liquidity preference is the interest rate. The reason is that the interest rate is the opportunity cost of holding money. That is, when you hold wealth as cash in your wallet, instead of as an interest-bearing bond, you lose the interest you could have earned. An increase in the interest rate raises the cost of holding money and, as a result, reduces the quantity of money demanded. A decrease in the interest rate reduces the cost of holding money and raises the quantity demanded. Thus, as shown in Figure 1, the money-demand curve slopes downward.

Equilibrium in the Money Market   According to the theory of liquidity preference, the interest rate adjusts to balance the supply and demand for money. There is one interest rate, called the *equilibrium interest rate*, at which the quantity of money demanded exactly balances the quantity of money supplied. If the interest rate is at any other level, people will try to adjust their portfolios of assets and, as a result, drive the interest rate toward the equilibrium.

For example, suppose that the interest rate is above the equilibrium level, such as r_1 in Figure 1. In this case, the quantity of money that people want to hold, M_1^d, is less than the quantity of money that the Fed has supplied. Those people who are

FYI

INTEREST RATES IN THE LONG RUN AND THE SHORT RUN

At this point, we should pause and reflect on a seemingly awkward embarrassment of riches. It might appear as if we now have two theories for how interest rates are determined. Chapter 13 said that the interest rate adjusts to balance the supply and demand for loanable funds (that is, national saving and desired investment). By contrast, we just established here that the interest rate adjusts to balance the supply and demand for money. How can we reconcile these two theories?

To answer this question, we must again consider the differences between the long-run and short-run behavior of the economy. Three macroeconomic variables are of central importance: the economy's output of goods and services, the interest rate, and the price level. According to the classical macroeconomic theory we developed in Chapters 12, 13, and 17, these variables are determined as follows:

1. *Output* is determined by the supplies of capital and labor and the available production technology for turning capital and labor into output. (We call this the natural rate of output.)
2. For any given level of output, the *interest rate* adjusts to balance the supply and demand for loanable funds.
3. The *price level* adjusts to balance the supply and demand for money. Changes in the supply of money lead to proportionate changes in the price level.

These are three of the essential propositions of classical economic theory. Most economists believe that these propositions do a good job of describing how the economy works *in the long run.*

Yet these propositions do not hold in the short run. As we discussed in the preceding chapter, many prices are slow to adjust to changes in the money supply; this is reflected in a short-run aggregate-supply curve that is upward sloping rather than vertical. As a result, the overall price level cannot, by itself, balance the supply and demand for money in the short run. This stickiness of the price level forces the interest rate to move in order to bring the money market into equilibrium. These changes in the interest rate, in turn, affect the aggregate demand for goods and services. As aggregate demand fluctuates, the economy's output of goods and services moves away from the level determined by factor supplies and technology.

For issues concerning the short run, then, it is best to think about the economy as follows:

1. The *price level* is stuck at some level (based on previously formed expectations) and, in the short run, is relatively unresponsive to changing economic conditions.
2. For any given price level, the *interest rate* adjusts to balance the supply and demand for money.
3. The level of *output* responds to the aggregate demand for goods and services, which is in part determined by the interest rate that balances the money market.

Notice that this precisely reverses the order of analysis used to study the economy in the long run.

Thus, the different theories of the interest rate are useful for different purposes. When thinking about the long-run determinants of interest rates, it is best to keep in mind the loanable-funds theory. This approach highlights the importance of an economy's saving propensities and investment opportunities. By contrast, when thinking about the short-run determinants of interest rates, it is best to keep in mind the liquidity-preference theory. This theory highlights the importance of monetary policy.

holding the surplus of money will try to get rid of it by buying interest-bearing bonds or by depositing it in an interest-bearing bank account. Because bond issuers and banks prefer to pay lower interest rates, they respond to this surplus of money by lowering the interest rates they offer. As the interest rate falls, people become more willing to hold money until, at the equilibrium interest rate, people are happy to hold exactly the amount of money the Fed has supplied.

Conversely, at interest rates below the equilibrium level, such as r_2 in Figure 1, the quantity of money that people want to hold, M_2^d, is greater than the quantity of money that the Fed has supplied. As a result, people try to increase their holdings of money by reducing their holdings of bonds and other interest-bearing assets. As people cut back on their holdings of bonds, bond issuers find that they have to offer higher interest rates to attract buyers. Thus, the interest rate rises and approaches the equilibrium level.

The Downward Slope of the Aggregate-Demand Curve

Having seen how the theory of liquidity preference explains the economy's equilibrium interest rate, we now consider its implications for the aggregate demand for goods and services. As a warm-up exercise, let's begin by using the theory to reexamine a topic we already understand—the interest-rate effect and the downward slope of the aggregate-demand curve. In particular, suppose that the overall level of prices in the economy rises. What happens to the interest rate that balances the supply and demand for money, and how does that change affect the quantity of goods and services demanded?

As we discussed in Chapter 17, the price level is one determinant of the quantity of money demanded. At higher prices, more money is exchanged every time a good or service is sold. As a result, people will choose to hold a larger quantity of money. That is, a higher price level increases the quantity of money demanded for any given interest rate. Thus, an increase in the price level from P_1 to P_2 shifts the money-demand curve to the right from MD_1 to MD_2, as shown in panel (a) of Figure 2.

Notice how this shift in money demand affects the equilibrium in the money market. For a fixed money supply, the interest rate must rise to balance money supply and money demand. The higher price level has increased the amount of money people want to hold and has shifted the money demand curve to the right. Yet the quantity of money supplied is unchanged, so the interest rate must rise from r_1 to r_2 to discourage the additional demand.

This increase in the interest rate has ramifications not only for the money market but also for the quantity of goods and services demanded, as shown in panel (b). At a higher interest rate, the cost of borrowing and the return to saving are greater. Fewer households choose to borrow to buy a new house, and those who do buy smaller houses, so the demand for residential investment falls. Fewer firms choose to borrow to build new factories and buy new equipment, so business investment falls. Thus, when the price level rises from P_1 to P_2, increasing money demand from MD_1 to MD_2 and raising the interest rate from r_1 to r_2, the quantity of goods and services demanded falls from Y_1 to Y_2.

Hence, this analysis of the interest-rate effect can be summarized in three steps: (1) A higher price level raises money demand. (2) Higher money demand leads to a higher interest rate. (3) A higher interest rate reduces the quantity of goods and services demanded. Of course, the same logic works in reverse as well: A lower

FIGURE 2

The Money Market and the Slope of the Aggregate-Demand Curve

An increase in the price level from P_1 to P_2 shifts the money-demand curve to the right, as in panel (a). This increase in money demand causes the interest rate to rise from r_1 to r_2. Because the interest rate is the cost of borrowing, the increase in the interest rate reduces the quantity of goods and services demanded from Y_1 to Y_2. This negative relationship between the price level and quantity demanded is represented with a downward-sloping aggregate-demand curve, as in panel (b).

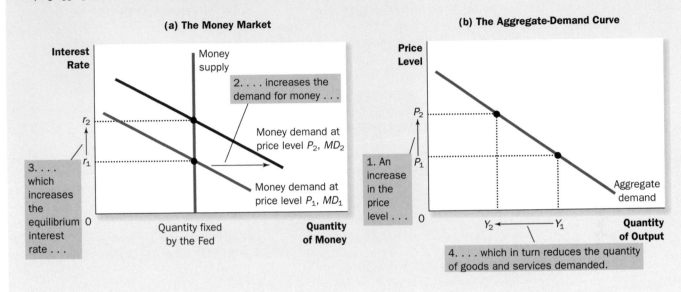

price level reduces money demand, which leads to a lower interest rate, and this in turn increases the quantity of goods and services demanded. The end result of this analysis is a negative relationship between the price level and the quantity of goods and services demanded, which is illustrated with a downward-sloping aggregate-demand curve.

Changes in the Money Supply

So far we have used the theory of liquidity preference to explain more fully how the total quantity demanded of goods and services in the economy changes as the price level changes. That is, we have examined movements along the downward-sloping aggregate-demand curve. The theory also sheds light, however, on some of the other events that alter the quantity of goods and services demanded. Whenever the quantity of goods and services demanded changes *for a given price level*, the aggregate-demand curve shifts.

One important variable that shifts the aggregate-demand curve is monetary policy. To see how monetary policy affects the economy in the short run, suppose that the Fed increases the money supply by buying government bonds in open-market operations. (Why the Fed might do this will become clear later after we understand the effects of such a move.) Let's consider how this monetary injection

FIGURE 3

A Monetary Injection

In panel (a), an increase in the money supply from MS₁ to MS₂ reduces the equilibrium interest rate from r₁ to r₂. Because the interest rate is the cost of borrowing, the fall in the interest rate raises the quantity of goods and services demanded at a given price level from Y₁ to Y₂. Thus, in panel (b), the aggregate-demand curve shifts to the right from AD₁ to AD₂.

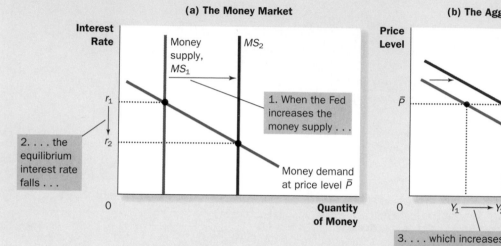

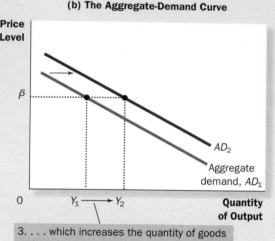

influences the equilibrium interest rate for a given price level. This will tell us what the injection does to the position of the aggregate-demand curve.

As panel (a) of Figure 3 shows, an increase in the money supply shifts the money-supply curve to the right from MS_1 to MS_2. Because the money-demand curve has not changed, the interest rate falls from r_1 to r_2 to balance money supply and money demand. That is, the interest rate must fall to induce people to hold the additional money the Fed has created.

Once again, the interest rate influences the quantity of goods and services demanded, as shown in panel (b) of Figure 3. The lower interest rate reduces the cost of borrowing and the return to saving. Households buy more and larger houses, stimulating the demand for residential investment. Firms spend more on new factories and new equipment, stimulating business investment. As a result, the quantity of goods and services demanded at a given price level, $\bar{P}$, rises from Y_1 to Y_2. Of course, there is nothing special about $\bar{P}$: The monetary injection raises the quantity of goods and services demanded rises at every price level. Thus, the entire aggregate-demand curve shifts to the right.

To sum up: *When the Fed increases the money supply, it lowers the interest rate and increases the quantity of goods and services demanded for any given price level, shifting the aggregate-demand curve to the right. Conversely, when the Fed contracts the money supply, it raises the interest rate and reduces the quantity of goods and services demanded for any given price level, shifting the aggregate-demand curve to the left.*

The Role of Interest-Rate Targets in Fed Policy

How does the Federal Reserve affect the economy? Our discussion here and earlier in the book has treated the money supply as the Fed's policy instrument. When the Fed buys government bonds in open-market operations, it increases the money supply and expands aggregate demand. When the Fed sells government bonds in open-market operations, it decreases the money supply and contracts aggregate demand.

Often discussions of Fed policy treat the interest rate, rather than the money supply, as the Fed's policy instrument. Indeed, in recent years, the Federal Reserve has conducted policy by setting a target for the *federal funds rate*—the interest rate that banks charge one another for short-term loans. This target is reevaluated every six weeks at meetings of the Federal Open Market Committee (FOMC). The FOMC has chosen to set a target for the federal funds rate (rather than for the money supply, as it has done at times in the past) in part because the money supply is hard to measure with sufficient precision.

The Fed's decision to target an interest rate does not fundamentally alter our analysis of monetary policy. The theory of liquidity preference illustrates an important principle: *Monetary policy can be described either in terms of the money supply or in terms of the interest rate.* When the FOMC sets a target for the federal funds rate of, say, 6 percent, the Fed's bond traders are told: "Conduct whatever open-market operations are necessary to ensure that the equilibrium interest rate equals 6 percent." In other words, when the Fed sets a target for the interest rate, it commits itself to adjusting the money supply in order to make the equilibrium in the money market hit that target.

As a result, changes in monetary policy can be viewed either in terms of a changing target for the interest rate or in terms of a change in the money supply. When you read in the newspaper that "the Fed has lowered the federal funds rate from 6 to 5 percent," you should understand that this occurs only because the Fed's bond traders are doing what it takes to make it happen. To lower the federal funds rate, the Fed's bond traders buy government bonds, and this purchase increases the money supply and lowers the equilibrium interest rate (just as in Figure 3). Similarly, when the FOMC raises the target for the federal funds rate, the bond traders sell government bonds, and this sale decreases the money supply and raises the equilibrium interest rate.

The lessons from all this are quite simple: Changes in monetary policy that aim to expand aggregate demand can be described either as increasing the money supply or as lowering the interest rate. Changes in monetary policy that aim to contract aggregate demand can be described either as decreasing the money supply or as raising the interest rate.

"Ray Brown on bass, Elvin Jones on drums, and Alan Greenspan on interest rates."

Case Study

WHY THE FED WATCHES THE STOCK MARKET (AND VICE VERSA)

"Irrational exuberance." That was how Federal Reserve Chairman Alan Greenspan once described the booming stock market of the late 1990s. He was right that the market was exuberant: Average stock prices increased about fourfold during this decade. And perhaps it was even irrational: In 2001 and 2002, the stock market took back some of these large gains, as stock prices experienced a pronounced decline.

Regardless of how we view the booming market, it does raise an important question: How should the Fed respond to stock-market fluctuations? The Fed has no reason to care about stock prices in themselves, but it does have the job of monitoring and responding to developments in the overall economy, and the stock market is a piece of that puzzle. When the stock market booms, households become wealthier, and this increased wealth stimulates consumer spending. In addition, a rise in stock prices makes it more attractive for firms to sell new shares of stock, and this stimulates investment spending. For both reasons, a booming stock market expands the aggregate demand for goods and services.

As we discuss more fully later in the chapter, one of the Fed's goals is to stabilize aggregate demand, for greater stability in aggregate demand means greater stability in output and the price level. To do this, the Fed might respond to a stock-market boom by keeping the money supply lower and interest rates higher than it otherwise would. The contractionary effects of higher interest rates would offset the expansionary effects of higher stock prices. In fact, this analysis does describe Fed behavior: Real interest rates were kept high by historical standards during the "irrationally exuberant" stock-market boom of the late 1990s.

The opposite occurs when the stock market falls. Spending on consumption and investment declines, depressing aggregate demand and pushing the economy toward recession. To stabilize aggregate demand, the Fed needs to increase the money supply and lower interest rates. And, indeed, that is what it typically does. For example, on October 19, 1987, the stock market fell by 22.6 percent—its biggest one-day drop in history. The Fed responded to the market crash by increasing the money supply and lowering interest rates. The federal funds rate fell from 7.7 percent at the beginning of October to 6.6 percent at the end of the month. In part because of the Fed's quick action, the economy avoided a recession. Similarly, as we discussed in a case study in the preceding chapter, the Fed also reduced interest rates during the stock market declines of 2001 and 2002, although this time monetary policy was not quick enough to avert a recession.

While the Fed keeps an eye on the stock market, stock-market participants also keep an eye on the Fed. Because the Fed can influence interest rates and economic activity, it can alter the value of stocks. For example, when the Fed raises interest rates by reducing the money supply, it makes owning stocks less attractive for two reasons. First, a higher interest rate means that bonds, the alternative to stocks, are earning a higher return. Second, the Fed's tightening of monetary policy risks pushing the economy into a recession, which reduces profits. As a result, stock prices often fall when the Fed raises interest rates. ●

QuickQuiz   Use the theory of liquidity preference to explain how a decrease in the money supply affects the equilibrium interest rate. How does this change in monetary policy affect the aggregate-demand curve?

HOW FISCAL POLICY INFLUENCES AGGREGATE DEMAND

The government can influence the behavior of the economy not only with monetary policy but also with fiscal policy. Fiscal policy refers to the government's choices regarding the overall level of government purchases or taxes. Earlier in the book we examined how fiscal policy influences saving, investment, and growth in the long run. In the short run, however, the primary effect of fiscal policy is on the aggregate demand for goods and services.

Changes in Government Purchases

When policymakers change the money supply or the level of taxes, they shift the aggregate-demand curve by influencing the spending decisions of firms or households. By contrast, when the government alters its own purchases of goods and services, it shifts the aggregate-demand curve directly.

Suppose, for instance, that the U.S. Department of Defense places a $20 billion order for new fighter planes with Boeing, the large aircraft manufacturer. This order raises the demand for the output produced by Boeing, which induces the company to hire more workers and increase production. Because Boeing is part of the economy, the increase in the demand for Boeing planes means an increase in the total quantity of goods and services demanded at each price level. As a result, the aggregate-demand curve shifts to the right.

By how much does this $20 billion order from the government shift the aggregate-demand curve? At first, one might guess that the aggregate-demand curve shifts to the right by exactly $20 billion. It turns out, however, that this is not right. There are two macroeconomic effects that make the size of the shift in aggregate demand differ from the change in government purchases. The first—the multiplier effect—suggests that the shift in aggregate demand could be *larger* than $20 billion. The second—the crowding-out effect—suggests that the shift in aggregate demand could be *smaller* than $20 billion. We now discuss each of these effects in turn.

The Multiplier Effect

When the government buys $20 billion of goods from Boeing, that purchase has repercussions. The immediate impact of the higher demand from the government is to raise employment and profits at Boeing. Then, as the workers see higher earnings and the firm owners see higher profits, they respond to this increase in income by raising their own spending on consumer goods. As a result, the government purchase from Boeing raises the demand for the products of many other firms in the economy. Because each dollar spent by the government can raise the aggregate demand for goods and services by more than a dollar, government purchases are said to have a **multiplier effect** on aggregate demand.

This multiplier effect continues even after this first round. When consumer spending rises, the firms that produce these consumer goods hire more people and experience higher profits. Higher earnings and profits stimulate consumer spending once again, and so on. Thus, there is positive feedback as higher demand leads

multiplier effect
the additional shifts in aggregate demand that result when expansionary fiscal policy increases income and thereby increases consumer spending

FIGURE 4

The Multiplier Effect

An increase in government purchases of $20 billion can shift the aggregate-demand curve to the right by more than $20 billion. This multiplier effect arises because increases in aggregate income stimulate additional spending by consumers.

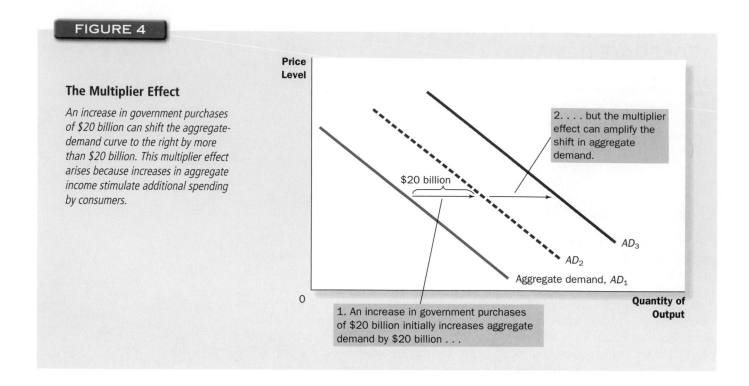

2. . . . but the multiplier effect can amplify the shift in aggregate demand.

$20 billion

AD_3

AD_2

Aggregate demand, AD_1

Price Level

Quantity of Output

0

1. An increase in government purchases of $20 billion initially increases aggregate demand by $20 billion . . .

to higher income, which in turn leads to even higher demand. Once all these effects are added together, the total impact on the quantity of goods and services demanded can be much larger than the initial impulse from higher government spending.

Figure 4 illustrates the multiplier effect. The increase in government purchases of $20 billion initially shifts the aggregate-demand curve to the right from AD_1 to AD_2 by exactly $20 billion. But when consumers respond by increasing their spending, the aggregate-demand curve shifts still further to AD_3.

This multiplier effect arising from the response of consumer spending can be strengthened by the response of investment to higher levels of demand. For instance, Boeing might respond to the higher demand for planes by deciding to buy more equipment or build another plant. In this case, higher government demand spurs higher demand for investment goods. This positive feedback from demand to investment is sometimes called the *investment accelerator*.

A Formula for the Spending Multiplier

A little high school algebra permits us to derive a formula for the size of the multiplier effect that arises from consumer spending. An important number in this formula is the *marginal propensity to consume (MPC)*—the fraction of extra income that a household consumes rather than saves. For example, suppose that the marginal propensity to consume is 3/4. This means that for every extra dollar that a household earns, the household spends $0.75 (3/4 of the dollar) and saves $0.25. With an *MPC* of 3/4, when the workers and owners of Boeing earn $20 billion from the government contract, they increase their consumer spending by $3/4 \times \$20$ billion, or $15 billion.

To gauge the impact on aggregate demand of a change in government purchases, we follow the effects step-by-step. The process begins when the government spends $20 billion, which implies that national income (earnings and profits) also rises by this amount. This increase in income in turn raises consumer spending by $MPC \times \$20$ billion, which in turn raises the income for the workers and owners of the firms that produce the consumption goods. This second increase in income again raises consumer spending, this time by $MPC \times (MPC \times \$20$ billion). These feedback effects go on and on.

To find the total impact on the demand for goods and services, we add up all these effects:

Change in government purchases =	$20 billion
First change in consumption	= MPC × $20 billion
Second change in consumption	= MPC^2 × $20 billion
Third change in consumption	= MPC^3 × $20 billion
•	•
•	•
•	•

Total change in demand =
$(1 + MPC + MPC^2 + MPC^3 + \ldots) \times \$20$ billion.

Here, "..." represents an infinite number of similar terms. Thus, we can write the multiplier as follows:

$$\text{Multiplier} = 1 + MPC + MPC^2 + MPC^3 + \ldots.$$

This multiplier tells us the demand for goods and services that each dollar of government purchases generates.

To simplify this equation for the multiplier, recall from math class that this expression is an infinite geometric series. For x between -1 and $+1$,

$$1 + x + x^2 + x^3 + \ldots = 1/(1-x).$$

In our case, $x = MPC$. Thus,

$$\text{Multiplier} = 1/(1 - MPC).$$

For example, if MPC is $3/4$, the multiplier is $1/(1 - 3/4)$, which is 4. In this case, the $20 billion of government spending generates $80 billion of demand for goods and services.

This formula for the multiplier shows an important conclusion: The size of the multiplier depends on the marginal propensity to consume. While an MPC of $3/4$ leads to a multiplier of 4, an MPC of $1/2$ leads to a multiplier of only 2. Thus, a larger MPC means a larger multiplier. To see why this is true, remember that the multiplier arises because higher income induces greater spending on consumption. The larger the MPC is, the greater is this induced effect on consumption, and the larger is the multiplier.

Other Applications of the Multiplier Effect

Because of the multiplier effect, a dollar of government purchases can generate more than a dollar of aggregate demand. The logic of the multiplier effect, however, is not restricted to changes in government purchases. Instead, it applies to any event that alters spending on any component of GDP—consumption, investment, government purchases, or net exports.

For example, suppose that a recession overseas reduces the demand for U.S. net exports by $10 billion. This reduced spending on U.S. goods and services depresses U.S. national income, which reduces spending by U.S. consumers. If the marginal propensity to consume is 3/4 and the multiplier is 4, then the $10 billion fall in net exports means a $40 billion contraction in aggregate demand.

As another example, suppose that a stock-market boom increases households' wealth and stimulates their spending on goods and services by $20 billion. This extra consumer spending increases national income, which in turn generates even more consumer spending. If the marginal propensity to consume is 3/4 and the multiplier is 4, then the initial impulse of $20 billion in consumer spending translates into an $80 billion increase in aggregate demand.

The multiplier is an important concept in macroeconomics because it shows how the economy can amplify the impact of changes in spending. A small initial change in consumption, investment, government purchases, or net exports can end up having a large effect on aggregate demand and, therefore, the economy's production of goods and services.

The Crowding-Out Effect

The multiplier effect seems to suggest that when the government buys $20 billion of planes from Boeing, the resulting expansion in aggregate demand is necessarily larger than $20 billion. Yet another effect is working in the opposite direction. While an increase in government purchases stimulates the aggregate demand for goods and services, it also causes the interest rate to rise, and a higher interest rate reduces investment spending and chokes off aggregate demand. The reduction in aggregate demand that results when a fiscal expansion raises the interest rate is called the **crowding-out effect.**

crowding-out effect
the offset in aggregate demand that results when expansionary fiscal policy raises the interest rate and thereby reduces investment spending

To see why crowding out occurs, let's consider what happens in the money market when the government buys planes from Boeing. As we have discussed, this increase in demand raises the incomes of the workers and owners of this firm (and, because of the multiplier effect, of other firms as well). As incomes rise, households plan to buy more goods and services and, as a result, choose to hold more of their wealth in liquid form. That is, the increase in income caused by the fiscal expansion raises the demand for money.

The effect of the increase in money demand is shown in panel (a) of Figure 5. Because the Fed has not changed the money supply, the vertical supply curve remains the same. When the higher level of income shifts the money-demand curve to the right from MD_1 to MD_2, the interest rate must rise from r_1 to r_2 to keep supply and demand in balance.

The increase in the interest rate, in turn, reduces the quantity of goods and services demanded. In particular, because borrowing is more expensive, the demand for residential and business investment goods declines. That is, as the increase in

FIGURE 5

The Crowding-Out Effect

Panel (a) shows the money market. When the government increases its purchases of goods and services, the resulting increase in income raises the demand for money from MD_1 to MD_2, and this causes the equilibrium interest rate to rise from r_1 to r_2. Panel (b) shows the effects on aggregate demand. The initial impact of the increase in government purchases shifts the aggregate-demand curve from AD_1 to AD_2. Yet, because the interest rate is the cost of borrowing, the increase in the interest rate tends to reduce the quantity of goods and services demanded, particularly for investment goods. This crowding out of investment partially offsets the impact of the fiscal expansion on aggregate demand. In the end, the aggregate-demand curve shifts only to AD_3.

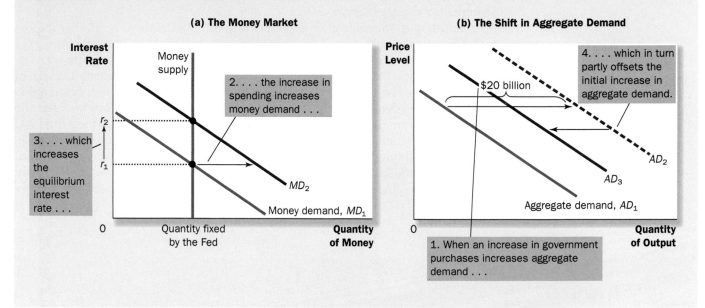

government purchases increases the demand for goods and services, it may also crowd out investment. This crowding-out effect partially offsets the impact of government purchases on aggregate demand, as illustrated in panel (b) of Figure 5. The initial impact of the increase in government purchases is to shift the aggregate-demand curve from AD_1 to AD_2, but once crowding out takes place, the aggregate-demand curve drops back to AD_3.

To sum up: *When the government increases its purchases by $20 billion, the aggregate demand for goods and services could rise by more or less than $20 billion, depending on whether the multiplier effect or the crowding-out effect is larger.*

Changes in Taxes

The other important instrument of fiscal policy, besides the level of government purchases, is the level of taxation. When the government cuts personal income taxes, for instance, it increases households' take-home pay. Households will save some of this additional income, but they will also spend some of it on consumer goods. Because it increases consumer spending, the tax cut shifts the aggregate-demand curve to the right. Similarly, a tax increase depresses consumer spending and shifts the aggregate-demand curve to the left.

The size of the shift in aggregate demand resulting from a tax change is also affected by the multiplier and crowding-out effects. When the government cuts taxes and stimulates consumer spending, earnings and profits rise, which further stimulates consumer spending. This is the multiplier effect. At the same time, higher income leads to higher money demand, which tends to raise interest rates. Higher interest rates make borrowing more costly, which reduces investment spending. This is the crowding-out effect. Depending on the size of the multiplier and crowding-out effects, the shift in aggregate demand could be larger or smaller than the tax change that causes it.

In addition to the multiplier and crowding-out effects, there is another important determinant of the size of the shift in aggregate demand that results from a tax change: households' perceptions about whether the tax change is permanent or temporary. For example, suppose that the government announces a tax cut of $1,000 per household. In deciding how much of this $1,000 to spend, households must ask themselves how long this extra income will last. If households expect the tax cut to be permanent, they will view it as adding substantially to their financial resources and, therefore, increase their spending by a large amount. In this case, the tax cut will have a large impact on aggregate demand. By contrast, if households expect the tax change to be temporary, they will view it as adding only slightly to their financial resources and, therefore, will increase their spending by

HOW FISCAL POLICY MIGHT AFFECT AGGREGATE SUPPLY

So far our discussion of fiscal policy has stressed how changes in government purchases and changes in taxes influence the quantity of goods and services demanded. Most economists believe that the short-run macroeconomic effects of fiscal policy work primarily through aggregate demand. Yet fiscal policy can potentially also influence the quantity of goods and services supplied.

For instance, consider the effects of tax changes on aggregate supply. One of the *Ten Principles of Economics* in Chapter 1 is that people respond to incentives. When government policymakers cut tax rates, workers get to keep more of each dollar they earn, so they have a greater incentive to work and produce goods and services. If they respond to this incentive, the quantity of goods and services supplied will be greater at each price level, and the aggregate-supply curve will shift to the right. Some economists, called *supply-siders,* have argued that the influence of tax cuts on aggregate supply is very large. Indeed, some supply-siders claim the influence is so large that a cut in tax rates will actually increase tax revenue by increasing worker effort. Most economists, however, believe that the supply-side effects of tax cuts are much smaller.

Like changes in taxes, changes in government purchases can also potentially affect aggregate supply. Suppose, for instance, that the government increases expenditure on a form of government-provided capital, such as roads. Roads are used by private businesses to make deliveries to their customers; an increase in the quantity of roads increases these businesses' productivity. Hence, when the government spends more on roads, it increases the quantity of goods and services supplied at any given price level and, thus, shifts the aggregate-supply curve to the right. This effect on aggregate supply is probably more important in the long run than in the short run, however, because it would take some time for the government to build the new roads and put them into use.

only a small amount. In this case, the tax cut will have a small impact on aggregate demand.

An extreme example of a temporary tax cut was the one announced in 1992. In that year, President George H. W. Bush faced a lingering recession and an upcoming reelection campaign. He responded to these circumstances by announcing a reduction in the amount of income tax that the federal government was withholding from workers' paychecks. Because legislated income tax rates did not change, however, every dollar of reduced withholding in 1992 meant an extra dollar of taxes due on April 15, 1993, when income tax returns for 1992 were to be filed. Thus, this "tax cut" actually represented only a short-term loan from the government. Not surprisingly, the impact of the policy on consumer spending and aggregate demand was relatively small.

QuickQuiz Suppose that the government reduces spending on highway construction by $10 billion. Which way does the aggregate-demand curve shift? Explain why the shift might be larger than $10 billion. Explain why the shift might be smaller than $10 billion.

USING POLICY TO STABILIZE THE ECONOMY

We have seen how monetary and fiscal policy can affect the economy's aggregate demand for goods and services. These theoretical insights raise some important policy questions: Should policymakers use these instruments to control aggregate demand and stabilize the economy? If so, when? If not, why not?

The Case for Active Stabilization Policy

Let's return to the question that began this chapter: When the president and Congress cut government spending, how should the Federal Reserve respond? As we have seen, government spending is one determinant of the position of the aggregate-demand curve. When the government cuts spending, aggregate demand will fall, which will depress production and employment in the short run. If the Federal Reserve wants to prevent this adverse effect of the fiscal policy, it can act to expand aggregate demand by increasing the money supply. A monetary expansion would reduce interest rates, stimulate investment spending, and expand aggregate demand. If monetary policy responds appropriately, the combined changes in monetary and fiscal policy could leave the aggregate demand for goods and services unaffected.

This analysis is exactly the sort followed by members of the Federal Open Market Committee. They know that monetary policy is an important determinant of aggregate demand. They also know that there are other important determinants as well, including fiscal policy set by the president and Congress. As a result, the Fed's Open Market Committee watches the debates over fiscal policy with a keen eye.

This response of monetary policy to the change in fiscal policy is an example of a more general phenomenon: the use of policy instruments to stabilize aggregate demand and, as a result, production and employment. Economic stabilization has been an explicit goal of U.S. policy since the Employment Act of 1946. This act states that "it is the continuing policy and responsibility of the federal government to . . . promote full employment and production." In essence, the government has chosen to hold itself accountable for short-run macroeconomic performance.

The Employment Act has two implications. The first, more modest, implication is that the government should avoid being a cause of economic fluctuations. Thus, most economists advise against large and sudden changes in monetary and fiscal policy, for such changes are likely to cause fluctuations in aggregate demand. Moreover, when large changes do occur, it is important that monetary and fiscal policymakers be aware of and respond to the other's actions.

The second, more ambitious, implication of the Employment Act is that the government should respond to changes in the private economy in order to stabilize aggregate demand. The act was passed not long after the publication of Keynes's *The General Theory of Employment, Interest, and Money,* which has been one of the most influential books ever written about economics. In it, Keynes emphasized the key role of aggregate demand in explaining short-run economic fluctuations. Keynes claimed that the government should actively stimulate aggregate demand when aggregate demand appeared insufficient to maintain production at its full-employment level.

Keynes (and his many followers) argued that aggregate demand fluctuates because of largely irrational waves of pessimism and optimism. He used the term "animal spirits" to refer to these arbitrary changes in attitude. When pessimism reigns, households reduce consumption spending, and firms reduce investment spending. The result is reduced aggregate demand, lower production, and higher unemployment. Conversely, when optimism reigns, households and firms increase spending. The result is higher aggregate demand, higher production, and inflationary pressure. Notice that these changes in attitude are, to some extent, self-fulfilling.

In principle, the government can adjust its monetary and fiscal policy in response to these waves of optimism and pessimism and, thereby, stabilize the economy. For example, when people are excessively pessimistic, the Fed can expand the money supply to lower interest rates and expand aggregate demand. When they are excessively optimistic, it can contract the money supply to raise interest rates and dampen aggregate demand. Former Fed chairman William McChesney Martin described this view of monetary policy very simply: "The Federal Reserve's job is to take away the punch bowl just as the party gets going."

Case Study
KEYNESIANS IN THE WHITE HOUSE

When a reporter in 1961 asked President John F. Kennedy why he advocated a tax cut, Kennedy replied, "To stimulate the economy. Don't you remember your Economics 101?" Kennedy's policy was, in fact, based on the analysis of fiscal policy we have developed in this chapter. His goal was to enact a tax cut, which would raise consumer spending, expand aggregate demand, and increase the economy's production and employment.

In choosing this policy, Kennedy was relying on his team of economic advisers. This team included such prominent economists as James Tobin and Robert Solow, who later would win Nobel prizes for their contributions to economics. As students in the 1940s, these economists had closely studied John Maynard Keynes's *General Theory*, which then was only a few years old. When the Kennedy advisers proposed cutting taxes, they were putting Keynes's ideas into action.

Although tax changes can have a potent influence on aggregate demand, they have other effects as well. In particular, by changing the incentives that people face, taxes can alter the aggregate supply of goods and services. Part of the Kennedy proposal was an investment tax credit, which gives a tax break to firms that invest in new capital. Higher investment would not only stimulate aggregate demand immediately but would also increase the economy's productive capacity over time. Thus, the short-run goal of increasing production through higher aggregate demand was coupled with a long-run goal of increasing production through higher aggregate supply. And, indeed, when the tax cut Kennedy proposed was finally enacted in 1964, it helped usher in a period of robust economic growth.

Since the 1964 tax cut, policymakers have from time to time proposed using fiscal policy as a tool for controlling aggregate demand. As we discussed earlier, the first President Bush attempted to speed recovery from a recession by reducing tax withholding. Similarly, when the second President Bush moved into the Oval Office in 2001, one of his first proposals was a more substantial and permanent tax cut, including an immediate tax rebate. One goal of the tax cut was to help the U.S. economy recover more quickly from the recession that had just begun. ●

The Case against Active Stabilization Policy

Some economists argue that the government should avoid active use of monetary and fiscal policy to try to stabilize the economy. They claim that these policy instruments should be set to achieve long-run goals, such as rapid economic growth and low inflation, and that the economy should be left to deal with short-run fluctuations on its own. Although these economists may admit that monetary and fiscal policy can stabilize the economy in theory, they doubt whether it can do so in practice.

The primary argument against active monetary and fiscal policy is that these policies affect the economy with a long lag. As we have seen, monetary policy works by changing interest rates, which in turn influence investment spending. But many firms make investment plans far in advance. Thus, most economists believe that it takes at least six months for changes in monetary policy to have much effect on output and employment. Moreover, once these effects occur, they can last for several years. Critics of stabilization policy argue that because of this lag, the Fed should not try to fine-tune the economy. They claim that the Fed often reacts too late to changing economic conditions and, as a result, ends up being a cause of rather than a cure for economic fluctuations. These critics advocate a passive monetary policy, such as slow and steady growth in the money supply.

Fiscal policy also works with a lag, but unlike the lag in monetary policy, the lag in fiscal policy is largely attributable to the political process. In the United States, most changes in government spending and taxes must go through congressional committees in both the House and the Senate, be passed by both legislative bodies, and then be signed by the president. Completing this process can take months and, in some cases, years. By the time the change in fiscal policy is passed and ready to implement, the condition of the economy may well have changed.

These lags in monetary and fiscal policy are a problem in part because economic forecasting is so imprecise. If forecasters could accurately predict the condition of the economy a year in advance, then monetary and fiscal policymakers could look ahead when making policy decisions. In this case, policymakers could stabilize the economy, despite the lags they face. In practice, however, major recessions and depressions arrive without much advance warning. The best policymakers can do at any time is to respond to economic changes as they occur.

Automatic Stabilizers

All economists—both advocates and critics of stabilization policy—agree that the lags in implementation render policy less useful as a tool for short-run stabiliza-

IN THE NEWS

THE INDEPENDENCE OF THE FEDERAL RESERVE

Closely related to the question of whether monetary and fiscal policy should be used to stabilize the economy is the question of who should set monetary and fiscal policy. In the United States, monetary policy is made by a central bank that operates free of most political pressures. As this opinion column discusses, some members of Congress want to reduce the Fed's independence.

Don't Tread on the Fed

By Martin and Kathleen Feldstein

We and most other economists give very high marks to the Federal Reserve for the way it has managed monetary policy in recent years. Fed officials have very successfully carried out their responsibility to reduce the rate of inflation and have done so without interrupting the economic expansion that began back in 1991.

Despite that excellent record, there are influential figures in Congress who are planning to introduce legislation that

would weaken the Federal Reserve's ability to continue to make sound monetary policy decisions. That legislation would give Congress and the president more influence over Federal Reserve policy, making monetary policy responsive to political pressures. If that happened, the risk of higher inflation and of increased cyclical volatility would become much greater.

To achieve the good economic performance of the past five years, the Fed had to raise interest rates several times in 1994 and, more recently, has had to avoid political calls for easier money to

speed up the pace of economic activity. Looking ahead, the economy may slow in the next year. If it does, you can expect to hear members of Congress and maybe the White House urging the Fed to lower interest rates in order to maintain economic momentum. But we're betting that, even if the economy does slow, the inflationary pressures are building and will force the Fed to raise interest rates by early in the new year.

If the Fed does raise interest rates in order to prevent a rise in inflation, the increased political pressure on the Fed may find popular support. There is always tion. The economy would be more stable, therefore, if policymakers could find a way to avoid some of these lags. In fact, they have. **Automatic stabilizers** are changes in fiscal policy that stimulate aggregate demand when the economy goes into a recession without policymakers having to take any deliberate action.

The most important automatic stabilizer is the tax system. When the economy goes into a recession, the amount of taxes collected by the government falls automatically because almost all taxes are closely tied to economic activity. The personal income tax depends on households' incomes, the payroll tax depends on workers' earnings, and the corporate income tax depends on firms' profits. Because incomes, earnings, and profits all fall in a recession, the government's tax revenue falls as well. This automatic tax cut stimulates aggregate demand and, thereby, reduces the magnitude of economic fluctuations.

Government spending also acts as an automatic stabilizer. In particular, when the economy goes into a recession and workers are laid off, more people apply for

automatic stabilizers
changes in fiscal policy that stimulate aggregate demand when the economy goes into a recession without policymakers having to take any deliberate action

public resistance to higher interest rates, which make borrowing more expensive for both businesses and homeowners. Moreover, the purpose of higher interest rates would be to slow the growth of spending in order to prevent an overheating of demand. That too will meet popular opposition. It is, in part, because good economic policy is not always popular in the short run that it is important for the Fed to be sheltered from short-run political pressures.

The Fed is an independent agency that reports to Congress but doesn't take orders from anyone. Monetary policy and short-term interest rates are determined by the Federal Open Market Committee (the FOMC), which consists of the 7 governors of the Fed plus the 12 presidents of the regional Federal Reserve Banks. The regional presidents vote on an alternating basis but all participate in the deliberations.

A key to the independence of the Fed's actions lies in the manner that appointments are made within the system. Although the 7 Federal Reserve governors are appointed by the president and confirmed by the Senate, each of the 12 Federal Reserve presidents is selected by the local board of a regional Federal Reserve Bank rather than being responsive to Washington. These regional presidents often serve for many years. Frequently they are long-term employees of the Federal Reserve system who have risen through the ranks. And many are professional economists with expertise in monetary economics. But whatever their backgrounds, they are not political appointees or friends of elected politicians. Their allegiance is to the goal of sound monetary policy, including both macroeconomic performance and supervision of the banking system.

The latest challenge to Fed independence would be to deny these Federal Reserve presidents the power to vote on monetary policy. This bad idea, explicitly proposed by Senator Paul Sarbanes, a powerful Democrat on the Senate Banking Committee, would mean shifting all of the authority to the 7 governors. Because at least one governor's term ends every two years, a president who spends eight years in the White House would be able to appoint a majority of the Board of Governors and could thus control monetary policy. An alternative bad idea, proposed by Representative Henry Gonzalez, a key Democrat on the House Banking Committee, would take away the independence of the Fed by having the regional Fed presidents appointed by the president subject to Senate confirmation.

Either approach would inevitably mean more politicalization of Federal Reserve policy. In an economy that is starting to overheat, the temptation would be to resist raising interest rates and to risk an acceleration of inflation. In the long run, that would mean volatile interest rates and less stability in the overall economy.

Ironically, such a move toward cutting the independence of the Federal Reserve is just counter to developments in other countries. Experience around the world has confirmed that the independence of central banks such as our Fed is the key to sound monetary policy. It would be a serious mistake for the United States to move in the opposite direction.

Source: *The Boston Globe*, November 12, 1996, p. D4. Copyright 1996 by GLOBE NEWSPAPER CO (MA). Reproduced with permission of GLOBE NEWSPAPER CO (MA) in the format Textbook via Copyright Clearance Center.

unemployment insurance benefits, welfare benefits, and other forms of income support. This automatic increase in government spending stimulates aggregate demand at exactly the time when aggregate demand is insufficient to maintain full employment. Indeed, when the unemployment insurance system was first enacted in the 1930s, economists who advocated this policy did so in part because of its power as an automatic stabilizer.

The automatic stabilizers in the U.S. economy are not sufficiently strong to prevent recessions completely. Nonetheless, without these automatic stabilizers, output and employment would probably be more volatile than they are. For this reason, many economists oppose a constitutional amendment that would require the federal government always to run a balanced budget, as some politicians have proposed. When the economy goes into a recession, taxes fall, government spending rises, and the government's budget moves toward deficit. If the government faced a strict balanced-budget rule, it would be forced to look for ways to raise taxes or cut spending in a recession. In other words, a strict balanced-budget rule would eliminate the automatic stabilizers inherent in our current system of taxes and government spending.

QuickQuiz Suppose a wave of negative "animal spirits" overruns the economy, and people become pessimistic about the future. What happens to aggregate demand? If the Fed wants to stabilize aggregate demand, how should it alter the money supply? If it does this, what happens to the interest rate? Why might the Fed choose not to respond in this way?

CONCLUSION

Before policymakers make any change in policy, they need to consider all the effects of their decisions. Earlier in the book we examined classical models of the economy, which describe the long-run effects of monetary and fiscal policy. There we saw how fiscal policy influences saving, investment, and long-run growth, and how monetary policy influences the price level and the inflation rate.

In this chapter we examined the short-run effects of monetary and fiscal policy. We saw how these policy instruments can change the aggregate demand for goods and services and, thereby, alter the economy's production and employment in the short run. When Congress reduces government spending in order to balance the budget, it needs to consider both the long-run effects on saving and growth and the short-run effects on aggregate demand and employment. When the Fed reduces the growth rate of the money supply, it must take into account the long-run effect on inflation as well as the short-run effect on production. In the next chapter we discuss the transition between the short run and the long run more fully, and we see that policymakers often face a tradeoff between long-run and short-run goals.

SUMMARY

- In developing a theory of short-run economic fluctuations, Keynes proposed the theory of liquidity preference to explain the determinants of the interest rate. According to this theory, the interest rate adjusts to balance the supply and demand for money.

- An increase in the price level raises money demand and increases the interest rate that brings the money market into equilibrium. Because the interest rate represents the cost of borrowing, a higher interest rate reduces investment and, thereby, the quantity of goods and services demanded. The downward-sloping aggregate-demand curve expresses this negative relationship between the price level and the quantity demanded.

- Policymakers can influence aggregate demand with monetary policy. An increase in the money supply reduces the equilibrium interest rate for any given price level. Because a lower interest rate stimulates investment spending, the aggregate-demand curve shifts to the right. Conversely, a decrease in the money supply raises the equilibrium interest rate for any given price level and shifts the aggregate-demand curve to the left.

- Policymakers can also influence aggregate demand with fiscal policy. An increase in government purchases or a cut in taxes shifts the aggregate-demand curve to the right. A decrease in government purchases or an increase in taxes shifts the aggregate-demand curve to the left.

- When the government alters spending or taxes, the resulting shift in aggregate demand can be larger or smaller than the fiscal change. The multiplier effect tends to amplify the effects of fiscal policy on aggregate demand. The crowding-out effect tends to dampen the effects of fiscal policy on aggregate demand.

- Because monetary and fiscal policy can influence aggregate demand, the government sometimes uses these policy instruments in an attempt to stabilize the economy. Economists disagree about how active the government should be in this effort. According to advocates of active stabilization policy, changes in attitudes by households and firms shift aggregate demand; if the government does not respond, the result is undesirable and unnecessary fluctuations in output and employment. According to critics of active stabilization policy, monetary and fiscal policy work with such long lags that attempts at stabilizing the economy often end up being destabilizing.

KEY CONCEPTS

theory of liquidity
preference, p. 460

multiplier effect, p. 469
crowding-out effect, p. 472

automatic stabilizers, p. 479

QUESTIONS FOR REVIEW

1. What is the theory of liquidity preference? How does it help explain the downward slope of the aggregate-demand curve?

2. Use the theory of liquidity preference to explain how a decrease in the money supply affects the aggregate-demand curve.

3. The government spends $3 billion to buy police cars. Explain why aggregate demand might increase by more than $3 billion. Explain why aggregate demand might increase by less than $3 billion.

4. Suppose that survey measures of consumer confidence indicate a wave of pessimism is sweeping the country. If policymakers do nothing, what will happen to aggregate demand? What should the Fed do if it wants to stabilize aggregate demand? If the Fed does nothing, what might Congress do to stabilize aggregate demand?

5. Give an example of a government policy that acts as an automatic stabilizer. Explain why this policy has this effect.

PROBLEMS AND APPLICATIONS

1. Explain how each of the following developments would affect the supply of money, the demand for money, and the interest rate. Illustrate your answers with diagrams.
   a. The Fed's bond traders buy bonds in open-market operations.
   b. An increase in credit card availability reduces the cash people hold.
   c. The Federal Reserve reduces banks' reserve requirements.
   d. Households decide to hold more money to use for holiday shopping.
   e. A wave of optimism boosts business investment and expands aggregate demand.
   f. An increase in oil prices shifts the short-run aggregate-supply curve to the left.

2. Suppose banks install automatic teller machines on every block and, by making cash readily available, reduce the amount of money people want to hold.
   a. Assume the Fed does not change the money supply. According to the theory of liquidity preference, what happens to the interest rate? What happens to aggregate demand?
   b. If the Fed wants to stabilize aggregate demand, how should it respond?

3. Consider two policies—a tax cut that will last for only one year, and a tax cut that is expected to be permanent. Which policy will stimulate greater spending by consumers? Which policy will have the greater impact on aggregate demand? Explain.

4. The economy is in a recession with high unemployment and low output.
   a. Use a graph of aggregate demand and aggregate supply to illustrate the current situation. Be sure to include the aggregate-demand curve, the short-run aggregate-supply curve, and the long-run aggregate-supply curve.
   b. Identify an open-market operation that would restore the economy to its natural rate.
   c. Use a graph of the money market to illustrate the effect of this open-market operation. Show the resulting change in the interest rate.
   d. Use a graph similar to the one in part (a) to show the effect of the open-market operation on output and the price level. Explain in words why the policy has the effect that you have shown in the graph.

5. In the early 1980s, new legislation allowed banks to pay interest on checking deposits, which they could not do previously.
   a. If we define money to include checking deposits, what effect did this legislation have on money demand? Explain.
   b. If the Federal Reserve had maintained a constant money supply in the face of this change, what would have happened

to the interest rate? What would have happened to aggregate demand and aggregate output?

c. If the Federal Reserve had maintained a constant market interest rate (the interest rate on nonmonetary assets) in the face of this change, what change in the money supply would have been necessary? What would have happened to aggregate demand and aggregate output?

6. This chapter explains that expansionary monetary policy reduces the interest rate and thus stimulates demand for investment goods. Explain how such a policy also stimulates the demand for net exports.

7. Suppose economists observe that an increase in government spending of $10 billion raises the total demand for goods and services by $30 billion.
   a. If these economists ignore the possibility of crowding out, what would they estimate the marginal propensity to consume (*MPC*) to be?
   b. Now suppose the economists allow for crowding out. Would their new estimate of the *MPC* be larger or smaller than their initial one?

8. Suppose the government reduces taxes by $20 billion, that there is no crowding out, and that the marginal propensity to consume is 3/4.
   a. What is the initial effect of the tax reduction on aggregate demand?
   b. What additional effects follow this initial effect? What is the total effect of the tax cut on aggregate demand?
   c. How does the total effect of this $20 billion tax cut compare to the total effect of a $20 billion increase in government purchases? Why?

9. Suppose government spending increases. Would the effect on aggregate demand be larger if the Federal Reserve took no action in response, or if the Fed were committed to maintaining a fixed interest rate? Explain.

10. In which of the following circumstances is expansionary fiscal policy more likely to lead to a short-run increase in investment? Explain.
    a. when the investment accelerator is large, or when it is small?
    b. when the interest sensitivity of investment is large, or when it is small?

11. Assume the economy is in a recession. Explain how each of the following policies would affect consumption and investment. In each case, indicate any direct effects, any effects resulting from changes in total output, any effects resulting from changes in the interest rate, and the overall effect. If there are conflicting effects making the answer ambiguous, say so.
    a. an increase in government spending
    b. a reduction in taxes
    c. an expansion of the money supply

12. For various reasons, fiscal policy changes automatically when output and employment fluctuate.
    a. Explain why tax revenue changes when the economy goes into a recession.
    b. Explain why government spending changes when the economy goes into a recession.
    c. If the government were to operate under a strict balanced-budget rule, what would it have to do in a recession? Would that make the recession more or less severe?

13. Recently, some members of Congress have proposed a law that would make price stability the sole goal of monetary policy. Suppose such a law were passed.
    a. How would the Fed respond to an event that contracted aggregate demand?
    b. How would the Fed respond to an event that caused an adverse shift in short-run aggregate supply?

In each case, is there another monetary policy that would lead to greater stability in output?

14. Go to the Web site of the Federal Reserve, http://www.federalreserve.gov, to learn more about monetary policy. Find a recent report, speech, or testimony by the Fed chairman or another Fed governor. What does it say about the state of the economy and recent decisions about monetary policy?

For more study tools, please visit http://mankiwXtra.swlearning.com.

THE SHORT-RUN TRADEOFF BETWEEN INFLATION AND UNEMPLOYMENT

Two closely watched indicators of economic performance are inflation and unemployment. When the Bureau of Labor Statistics releases data on these variables each month, policymakers are eager to hear the news. Some commentators have added together the inflation rate and the unemployment rate to produce a *misery index,* which purports to measure the health of the economy.

How are these two measures of economic performance related to each other? Earlier in the book we discussed the long-run determinants of unemployment and the long-run determinants of inflation. We saw that the natural rate of unemployment depends on various features of the labor market, such as minimum-wage laws, the market power of unions, the role of efficiency wages, and the effectiveness of job search. By contrast, the inflation rate depends primarily on growth in the money supply, which a nation's central bank controls. In the long run, therefore, inflation and unemployment are largely unrelated problems.

In the short run, just the opposite is true. One of the *Ten Principles of Economics* discussed in Chapter 1 is that society faces a short-run tradeoff between inflation and unemployment. If monetary and fiscal policymakers expand aggregate demand and move the economy up along the short-run aggregate-supply curve, they can lower unemployment for a while, but only at the cost of higher inflation. If policymakers contract aggregate demand and move the economy down the short-run aggregate-supply curve, they can lower inflation, but only at the cost of temporarily higher unemployment.

In this chapter we examine this tradeoff more closely. The relationship between inflation and unemployment is a topic that has attracted the attention of some of the most important economists of the last half century. The best way to understand this relationship is to see how thinking about it has evolved over time. As we will see, the history of thought regarding inflation and unemployment since the 1950s is inextricably connected to the history of the U.S. economy. These two histories will show why the tradeoff between inflation and unemployment holds in the short run, why it does not hold in the long run, and what issues it raises for economic policymakers.

THE PHILLIPS CURVE

"Probably the single most important macroeconomic relationship is the Phillips curve." These are the words of economist George Akerlof from the lecture he gave when he received the Nobel Prize in 2001. The *Phillips curve* is the short-run relationship between inflation and unemployment. We begin our story with the discovery of the Phillips curve and its migration to America.

Origins of the Phillips Curve

In 1958, economist A. W. Phillips published an article in the British journal *Economica* that would make him famous. The article was titled "The Relationship between Unemployment and the Rate of Change of Money Wages in the United Kingdom, 1861–1957." In it, Phillips showed a negative correlation between the rate of unemployment and the rate of inflation. That is, Phillips showed that years with low unemployment tend to have high inflation, and years with high unemployment tend to have low inflation. (Phillips examined inflation in nominal wages rather than inflation in prices, but for our purposes that distinction is not important. These two measures of inflation usually move together.) Phillips concluded that two important macroeconomic variables—inflation and unemployment—were linked in a way that economists had not previously appreciated.

Although Phillips's discovery was based on data for the United Kingdom, researchers quickly extended his finding to other countries. Two years after Phillips published his article, economists Paul Samuelson and Robert Solow published an article in the *American Economic Review* called "Analytics of Anti-Inflation Policy" in which they showed a similar negative correlation between inflation and unemployment in data for the United States. They reasoned that this correlation arose because low unemployment was associated with high aggregate demand, which in turn puts upward pressure on wages and prices throughout the economy. Samuelson and Solow dubbed the negative association between inflation and unemployment the **Phillips curve.** Figure 1 shows an example of a Phillips curve like the one found by Samuelson and Solow.

As the title of their paper suggests, Samuelson and Solow were interested in the Phillips curve because they believed that it held important lessons for policymakers.

Phillips curve
a curve that shows the short-run tradeoff between inflation and unemployment

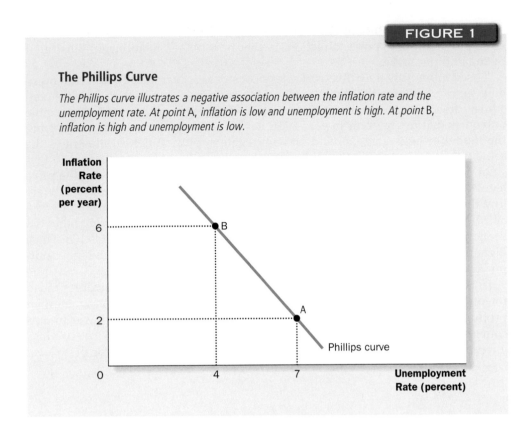

FIGURE 1

The Phillips Curve

The Phillips curve illustrates a negative association between the inflation rate and the unemployment rate. At point A, inflation is low and unemployment is high. At point B, inflation is high and unemployment is low.

In particular, they suggested that the Phillips curve offers policymakers a menu of possible economic outcomes. By altering monetary and fiscal policy to influence aggregate demand, policymakers could choose any point on this curve. Point A offers high unemployment and low inflation. Point B offers low unemployment and high inflation. Policymakers might prefer both low inflation and low unemployment, but the historical data as summarized by the Phillips curve indicate that this combination is impossible. According to Samuelson and Solow, policymakers face a tradeoff between inflation and unemployment, and the Phillips curve illustrates that tradeoff.

Aggregate Demand, Aggregate Supply, and the Phillips Curve

The model of aggregate demand and aggregate supply provides an easy explanation for the menu of possible outcomes described by the Phillips curve. *The Phillips curve simply shows the combinations of inflation and unemployment that arise in the short run as shifts in the aggregate-demand curve move the economy along the short-run aggregate-supply curve.* As we saw in Chapter 20, an increase in the aggregate demand for goods and services leads, in the short run, to a larger output of goods and services and a higher price level. Larger output means greater employment and, thus, a lower rate of unemployment. In addition, whatever the previous year's price level happens to be, the higher the price level in the current year, the higher the rate of inflation. Thus, shifts in aggregate demand push inflation and unemployment in opposite directions in the short run—a relationship illustrated by the Phillips curve.

To see more fully how this works, let's consider an example. To keep the numbers simple, imagine that the price level (as measured, for instance, by the consumer price index) equals 100 in the year 2000. Figure 2 shows two possible outcomes that might occur in year 2001. Panel (a) shows the two outcomes using the model of aggregate demand and aggregate supply. Panel (b) illustrates the same two outcomes using the Phillips curve.

In panel (a) of the figure, we can see the implications for output and the price level in the year 2001. If the aggregate demand for goods and services is relatively low, the economy experiences outcome A. The economy produces output of 7,500, and the price level is 102. By contrast, if aggregate demand is relatively high, the economy experiences outcome B. Output is 8,000, and the price level is 106. Thus, higher aggregate demand moves the economy to an equilibrium with higher output and a higher price level.

In panel (b) of the figure, we can see what these two possible outcomes mean for unemployment and inflation. Because firms need more workers when they produce a greater output of goods and services, unemployment is lower in outcome B than in outcome A. In this example, when output rises from 7,500 to 8,000, unemployment falls from 7 percent to 4 percent. Moreover, because the price level

FIGURE 2

How the Phillips Curve Is Related to the Model of Aggregate Demand and Aggregate Supply

This figure assumes a price level of 100 for the year 2000 and charts possible outcomes for the year 2001. Panel (a) shows the model of aggregate demand and aggregate supply. If aggregate demand is low, the economy is at point A; output is low (7,500), and the price level is low (102). If aggregate demand is high, the economy is at point B; output is high (8,000), and the price level is high (106). Panel (b) shows the implications for the Phillips curve. Point A, which arises when aggregate demand is low, has high unemployment (7 percent) and low inflation (2 percent). Point B, which arises when aggregate demand is high, has low unemployment (4 percent) and high inflation (6 percent).

(a) The Model of Aggregate Demand and Aggregate Supply

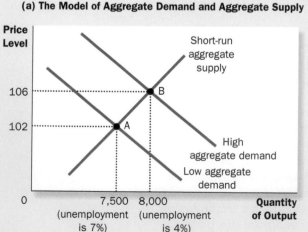

(b) The Phillips Curve

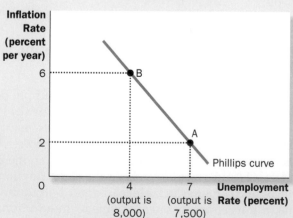

is higher at outcome B than at outcome A, the inflation rate (the percentage change in the price level from the previous year) is also higher. In particular, since the price level was 100 in year 2000, outcome A has an inflation rate of 2 percent, and outcome B has an inflation rate of 6 percent. Thus, we can compare the two possible outcomes for the economy either in terms of output and the price level (using the model of aggregate demand and aggregate supply) or in terms of unemployment and inflation (using the Phillips curve).

As we saw in the preceding chapter, monetary and fiscal policy can shift the aggregate-demand curve. Therefore, monetary and fiscal policy can move the economy along the Phillips curve. Increases in the money supply, increases in government spending, or cuts in taxes expand aggregate demand and move the economy to a point on the Phillips curve with lower unemployment and higher inflation. Decreases in the money supply, cuts in government spending, or increases in taxes contract aggregate demand and move the economy to a point on the Phillips curve with lower inflation and higher unemployment. In this sense, the Phillips curve offers policymakers a menu of combinations of inflation and unemployment.

QuickQuiz Draw the Phillips curve. Use the model of aggregate demand and aggregate supply to show how policy can move the economy from a point on this curve with high inflation to a point with low inflation.

SHIFTS IN THE PHILLIPS CURVE: THE ROLE OF EXPECTATIONS

The Phillips curve seems to offer policymakers a menu of possible inflation–unemployment outcomes. But does this menu remain stable over time? Is the Phillips curve a relationship on which policymakers can rely? Economists took up these questions in the late 1960s, shortly after Samuelson and Solow had introduced the Phillips curve into the macroeconomic policy debate.

The Long-Run Phillips Curve

In 1968 economist Milton Friedman published a paper in the *American Economic Review*, based on an address he had recently given as president of the American Economic Association. The paper, titled "The Role of Monetary Policy," contained sections on "What Monetary Policy Can Do" and "What Monetary Policy Cannot Do." Friedman argued that one thing monetary policy cannot do, other than for only a short time, is pick a combination of inflation and unemployment on the Phillips curve. At about the same time, another economist, Edmund Phelps, also published a paper denying the existence of a long-run tradeoff between inflation and unemployment.

Friedman and Phelps based their conclusions on classical principles of macroeconomics, which we discussed in Chapters 12 through 19. Recall that classical theory points to growth in the money supply as the primary determinant of inflation. But classical theory also states that monetary growth does not have real effects—it merely alters all prices and nominal incomes proportionately. In particular, monetary growth does not influence those factors that determine the economy's unemployment rate, such as the market power of unions, the role of efficiency wages, or the process of job search. Friedman and Phelps concluded that there is no reason to think the rate of inflation would, *in the long run*, be related to the rate of unemployment.

Here, in his own words, is Friedman's view about what the Fed can hope to accomplish in the long run:

> The monetary authority controls nominal quantities—directly, the quantity of its own liabilities [currency plus bank reserves]. In principle, it can use this control to peg a nominal quantity—an exchange rate, the price level, the nominal level of national income, the quantity of money by one definition or another— or to peg the change in a nominal quantity—the rate of inflation or deflation, the rate of growth or decline in nominal national income, the rate of growth of the quantity of money. It cannot use its control over nominal quantities to peg a real quantity—the real rate of interest, the rate of unemployment, the level of real national income, the real quantity of money, the rate of growth of real national income, or the rate of growth of the real quantity of money.

These views have important implications for the Phillips curve. In particular, they imply that monetary policymakers face a long-run Phillips curve that is vertical, as in Figure 3. If the Fed increases the money supply slowly, the inflation rate is low, and the economy finds itself at point A. If the Fed increases the money supply quickly, the inflation rate is high, and the economy finds itself at point B. In either case, the unemployment rate tends toward its normal level, called the *natural rate of unemployment*. The vertical long-run Phillips curve illustrates the conclusion that unemployment does not depend on money growth and inflation in the long run.

The vertical long-run Phillips curve is, in essence, one expression of the classical idea of monetary neutrality. As you may recall, we expressed this idea in Chapter 20 with a vertical long-run aggregate-supply curve. Indeed, as Figure 4 illustrates, the vertical long-run Phillips curve and the vertical long-run aggregate-supply

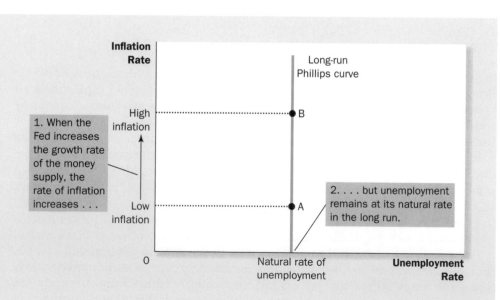

FIGURE 3

The Long-Run Phillips Curve

According to Friedman and Phelps, there is no tradeoff between inflation and unemployment in the long run. Growth in the money supply determines the inflation rate. Regardless of the inflation rate, the unemployment rate gravitates toward its natural rate. As a result, the long-run Phillips curve is vertical.

1. When the Fed increases the growth rate of the money supply, the rate of inflation increases . . .

2. . . . but unemployment remains at its natural rate in the long run.

FIGURE 4

How the Long-Run Phillips Curve Is Related to the Model of Aggregate Demand and Aggregate Supply

Panel (a) shows the model of aggregate demand and aggregate supply with a vertical aggregate-supply curve. When expansionary monetary policy shifts the aggregate-demand curve to the right from AD$_1$ to AD$_2$, the equilibrium moves from point A to point B. The price level rises from P$_1$ to P$_2$, while output remains the same. Panel (b) shows the long-run Phillips curve, which is vertical at the natural rate of unemployment. Expansionary monetary policy moves the economy from lower inflation (point A) to higher inflation (point B) without changing the rate of unemployment.

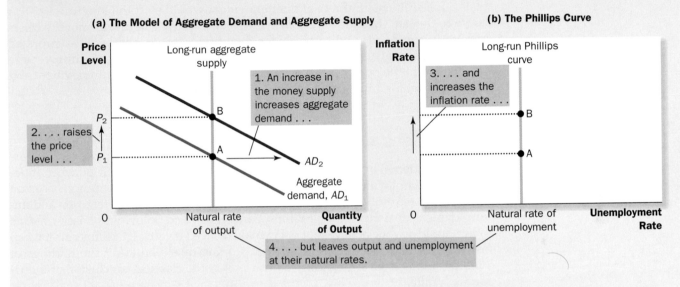

(a) The Model of Aggregate Demand and Aggregate Supply

(b) The Phillips Curve

curve are two sides of the same coin. In panel (a) of this figure, an increase in the money supply shifts the aggregate-demand curve to the right from AD_1 to AD_2. As a result of this shift, the long-run equilibrium moves from point A to point B. The price level rises from P_1 to P_2, but because the aggregate-supply curve is vertical, output remains the same. In panel (b), more rapid growth in the money supply raises the inflation rate by moving the economy from point A to point B. But because the Phillips curve is vertical, the rate of unemployment is the same at these two points. Thus, the vertical long-run aggregate-supply curve and the vertical long-run Phillips curve both imply that monetary policy influences nominal variables (the price level and the inflation rate) but not real variables (output and unemployment). Regardless of the monetary policy pursued by the Fed, output and unemployment are, in the long run, at their natural rates.

What is so "natural" about the natural rate of unemployment? Friedman and Phelps used this adjective to describe the unemployment rate toward which the economy tends to gravitate in the long run. Yet the natural rate of unemployment is not necessarily the socially desirable rate of unemployment. Nor is the natural rate of unemployment constant over time. For example, suppose that a newly formed union uses its market power to raise the real wages of some workers above the equilibrium level. The result is an excess supply of workers and, therefore, a higher natural rate of unemployment. This unemployment is "natural" not because it is good but because it is beyond the influence of monetary policy. More rapid money growth would not reduce the market power of the union or the level of unemployment; it would lead only to more inflation.

Although monetary policy cannot influence the natural rate of unemployment, other types of policy can. To reduce the natural rate of unemployment, policy-makers should look to policies that improve the functioning of the labor market. Earlier in the book we discussed how various labor-market policies, such as minimum-wage laws, collective-bargaining laws, unemployment insurance, and job-training programs, affect the natural rate of unemployment. A policy change that reduced the natural rate of unemployment would shift the long-run Phillips curve to the left. In addition, because lower unemployment means more workers are producing goods and services, the quantity of goods and services supplied would be larger at any given price level, and the long-run aggregate-supply curve would shift to the right. The economy could then enjoy lower unemployment and higher output for any given rate of money growth and inflation.

Expectations and the Short-Run Phillips Curve

At first, the denial by Friedman and Phelps of a long-run tradeoff between infla-tion and unemployment might not seem persuasive. Their argument was based on an appeal to *theory*. By contrast, the negative correlation between inflation and un-employment documented by Phillips, Samuelson, and Solow was based on *data*. Why should anyone believe that policymakers faced a vertical Phillips curve when the world seemed to offer a downward-sloping one? Shouldn't the findings of Phillips, Samuelson, and Solow lead us to reject the classical conclusion of mone-tary neutrality?

Friedman and Phelps were well aware of these questions, and they offered a way to reconcile classical macroeconomic theory with the finding of a downward-sloping Phillips curve in data from the United Kingdom and the United States. They claimed that a negative relationship between inflation and unemployment holds in the short run but that it cannot be used by policymakers in the long run. In other words, policymakers can pursue expansionary monetary policy to achieve lower unemployment for a while, but eventually unemployment returns to its nat-ural rate, and more expansionary monetary policy leads only to higher inflation.

Friedman and Phelps reasoned as we did in Chapter 20 when we explained the difference between the short-run and long-run aggregate-supply curves. (In fact, the discussion in that chapter drew heavily on the legacy of Friedman and Phelps.) As you may recall, the short-run aggregate-supply curve is upward sloping, indi-cating that an increase in the price level raises the quantity of goods and services that firms supply. By contrast, the long-run aggregate-supply curve is vertical, in-dicating that the price level does not influence quantity supplied in the long run. Chapter 20 presented three theories to explain the upward slope of the short-run aggregate-supply curve: sticky wages, sticky prices, and misperceptions about rel-ative prices. Because wages, prices, and perceptions adjust to changing economic conditions over time, the positive relationship between the price level and quan-tity supplied applies in the short run but not in the long run. Friedman and Phelps applied this same logic to the Phillips curve. Just as the aggregate-supply curve slopes upward only in the short run, the tradeoff between inflation and unem-ployment holds only in the short run. And just as the long-run aggregate-supply curve is vertical, the long-run Phillips curve is also vertical.

To help explain the short-run and long-run relationship between inflation and unemployment, Friedman and Phelps introduced a new variable into the analysis: *expected inflation.* Expected inflation measures how much people expect the overall price level to change. As we discussed in Chapter 20, the expected price level affects the wages and prices that people set and the perceptions of relative prices that they form. As a result, expected inflation is one factor that determines the position of the short-run aggregate-supply curve. In the short run, the Fed can take expected inflation (and thus the short-run aggregate-supply curve) as already determined. When the money supply changes, the aggregate-demand curve shifts, and the economy moves along a given short-run aggregate-supply curve. In the short run, therefore, monetary changes lead to unexpected fluctuations in output, prices, unemployment, and inflation. In this way, Friedman and Phelps explained the Phillips curve that Phillips, Samuelson, and Solow had documented.

Yet the Fed's ability to create unexpected inflation by increasing the money supply exists only in the short run. In the long run, people come to expect whatever inflation rate the Fed chooses to produce. Because wages, prices, and perceptions will eventually adjust to the inflation rate, the long-run aggregate-supply curve is vertical. In this case, changes in aggregate demand, such as those due to changes in the money supply, do not affect the economy's output of goods and services. Thus, Friedman and Phelps concluded that unemployment returns to its natural rate in the long run.

The analysis of Friedman and Phelps can be summarized in the following equation (which is, in essence, another expression of the aggregate-supply equation we saw in Chapter 20):

$$\begin{array}{c}\text{Unemployment}\\\text{rate}\end{array} = \begin{array}{c}\text{Natural rate of}\\\text{unemployment}\end{array} - a\left(\begin{array}{c}\text{Actual}\\\text{inflation}\end{array} - \begin{array}{c}\text{Expected}\\\text{inflation}\end{array}\right)$$

This equation relates the unemployment rate to the natural rate of unemployment, actual inflation, and expected inflation. In the short run, expected inflation is given. As a result, higher actual inflation is associated with lower unemployment. (How much unemployment responds to unexpected inflation is determined by the size of a, a number that in turn depends on the slope of the short-run aggregate-supply curve.) In the long run, however, people come to expect whatever inflation the Fed produces. Thus, actual inflation equals expected inflation, and unemployment is at its natural rate.

This equation implies there is no stable short-run Phillips curve. Each short-run Phillips curve reflects a particular expected rate of inflation. (To be precise, if you graph the equation, you'll find that the short-run Phillips curve intersects the long-run Phillips curve at the expected rate of inflation.) Whenever expected inflation changes, the short-run Phillips curve shifts.

According to Friedman and Phelps, it is dangerous to view the Phillips curve as a menu of options available to policymakers. To see why, imagine an economy at its natural rate of unemployment with low inflation and low expected inflation, shown in Figure 5 (p. 494) as point A. Now suppose that policymakers try to take advantage of the tradeoff between inflation and unemployment by using monetary or fiscal policy to expand aggregate demand. In the short run when expected inflation is given, the economy goes from point A to point B. Unemployment falls below its natural rate, and inflation rises above expected inflation. Over time, people get used to this higher inflation rate, and they raise their expectations of inflation. When expected inflation rises, firms and workers start taking higher inflation

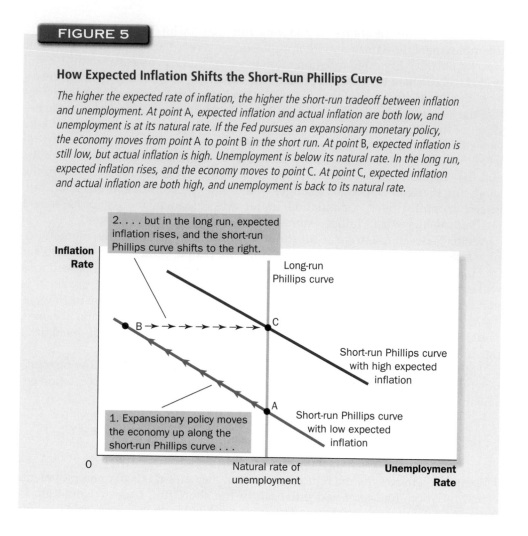

FIGURE 5

How Expected Inflation Shifts the Short-Run Phillips Curve

The higher the expected rate of inflation, the higher the short-run tradeoff between inflation and unemployment. At point A, expected inflation and actual inflation are both low, and unemployment is at its natural rate. If the Fed pursues an expansionary monetary policy, the economy moves from point A to point B in the short run. At point B, expected inflation is still low, but actual inflation is high. Unemployment is below its natural rate. In the long run, expected inflation rises, and the economy moves to point C. At point C, expected inflation and actual inflation are both high, and unemployment is back to its natural rate.

2. . . . but in the long run, expected inflation rises, and the short-run Phillips curve shifts to the right.

Inflation Rate

Long-run Phillips curve

B

C

Short-run Phillips curve with high expected inflation

A

1. Expansionary policy moves the economy up along the short-run Phillips curve . . .

Short-run Phillips curve with low expected inflation

0

Natural rate of unemployment

Unemployment Rate

into account when setting wages and prices. The short-run Phillips curve then shifts to the right, as shown in the figure. The economy ends up at point C, with higher inflation than at point A but with the same level of unemployment.

Thus, Friedman and Phelps concluded that policymakers do face a tradeoff between inflation and unemployment, but only a temporary one. If policymakers use this tradeoff, they lose it.

The Natural Experiment for the Natural-Rate Hypothesis

Friedman and Phelps had made a bold prediction in 1968: If policymakers try to take advantage of the Phillips curve by choosing higher inflation in order to reduce unemployment, they will succeed at reducing unemployment only temporarily. This view—that unemployment eventually returns to its natural rate, regardless of the rate of inflation—is called the **natural-rate hypothesis.** A few years after Friedman and Phelps proposed this hypothesis, monetary and fiscal policymakers inadvertently created a natural experiment to test it. Their laboratory was the U.S. economy.

natural-rate hypothesis
the claim that unemployment eventually returns to its normal, or natural, rate, regardless of the rate of inflation

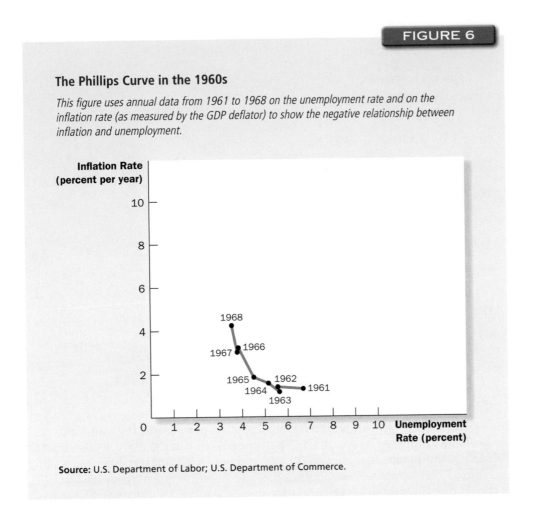

FIGURE 6

The Phillips Curve in the 1960s

This figure uses annual data from 1961 to 1968 on the unemployment rate and on the inflation rate (as measured by the GDP deflator) to show the negative relationship between inflation and unemployment.

Source: U.S. Department of Labor; U.S. Department of Commerce.

Before we see the outcome of this test, however, let's look at the data that Friedman and Phelps had when they made their prediction in 1968. Figure 6 shows the unemployment rate and the inflation rate for the period from 1961 to 1968. These data trace out a Phillips curve. As inflation rose over these eight years, unemployment fell. The economic data from this era seemed to confirm the tradeoff between inflation and unemployment.

The apparent success of the Phillips curve in the 1960s made the prediction of Friedman and Phelps all the more bold. In 1958 Phillips had suggested a negative association between inflation and unemployment. In 1960 Samuelson and Solow had showed it existed in U.S. data. Another decade of data had confirmed the relationship. To some economists at the time, it seemed ridiculous to claim that the Phillips curve would break down once policymakers tried to use it.

But, in fact, that is exactly what happened. Beginning in the late 1960s, the government followed policies that expanded the aggregate demand for goods and services. In part, this expansion was due to fiscal policy: Government spending rose as the Vietnam War heated up. In part, it was due to monetary policy: Because the Fed was trying to hold down interest rates in the face of expansionary fiscal policy, the money supply (as measured by M2) rose about 13 percent per year during the period from 1970 to 1972, compared to 7 percent per year in the early 1960s. As a

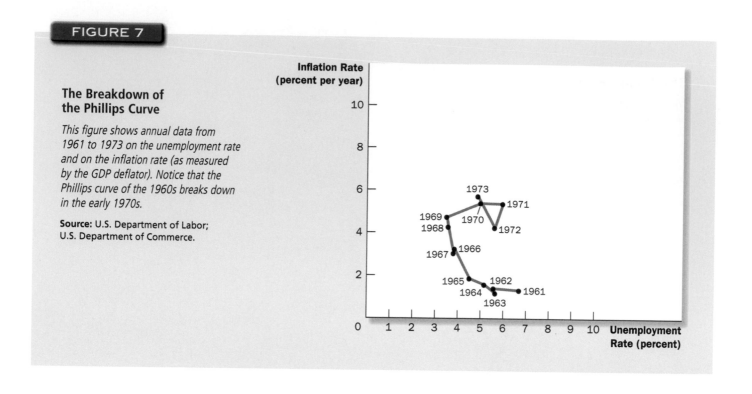

FIGURE 7

The Breakdown of the Phillips Curve

This figure shows annual data from 1961 to 1973 on the unemployment rate and on the inflation rate (as measured by the GDP deflator). Notice that the Phillips curve of the 1960s breaks down in the early 1970s.

Source: U.S. Department of Labor; U.S. Department of Commerce.

result, inflation stayed high (about 5 to 6 percent per year in the late 1960s and early 1970s, compared to about 1 to 2 percent per year in the early 1960s). But, as Friedman and Phelps had predicted, unemployment did not stay low.

Figure 7 displays the history of inflation and unemployment from 1961 to 1973. It shows that the simple negative relationship between these two variables started to break down around 1970. In particular, as inflation remained high in the early 1970s, people's expectations of inflation caught up with reality, and the unemployment rate reverted to the 5 percent to 6 percent range that had prevailed in the early 1960s. Notice that the history illustrated in Figure 7 closely resembles the theory of a shifting short-run Phillips curve shown in Figure 5. By 1973, policymakers had learned that Friedman and Phelps were right: There is no tradeoff between inflation and unemployment in the long run.

QuickQuiz   Draw the short-run Phillips curve and the long-run Phillips curve. Explain why they are different.

SHIFTS IN THE PHILLIPS CURVE: THE ROLE OF SUPPLY SHOCKS

Friedman and Phelps had suggested in 1968 that changes in expected inflation shift the short-run Phillips curve, and the experience of the early 1970s convinced most economists that Friedman and Phelps were right. Within a few years, however, the economics profession would turn its attention to a different source of shifts in the short-run Phillips curve: shocks to aggregate supply.

IN THE NEWS

THE BENEFITS OF LOW EXPECTED INFLATION

In the 1960s and 1970s, policymakers learned that high expected inflation shifts the short-run Phillips curve outward, making actual inflation more likely. In the 1990s, the opposite occurred, as expected inflation fell and helped keep actual inflation low.

The Virtuous Circle of Low Inflation

By Jacob M. Schlesinger

Why does inflation remain so low?

Some experts credit greater corporate efficiency. Others cite a growing labor force. Luck, in the form of cheap oil and a strong dollar, helps. But the raging economic debate often overlooks one simple answer: because inflation remains so low. In other words, it isn't just a matter of mathematical formulas such as a Phillips-curve tradeoff between inflation and jobs; it also is the nebulous matter of mass psychology. The economy may be entering a phase in which low inflation is no longer considered a lucky, transitory phenomenon but an integral part of its fabric. And if enough executives, suppliers, consumers and workers believe it will last, they will act in ways that help make it last.

"For the past couple of years, people were expecting inflation to rise, but it hasn't," says Janet Yellen, the chief White House economist and former Federal Reserve governor. "Slowly, people are being convinced that inflation is down and it's

going to stay down, [which] is helpful in keeping inflation down. Inflationary expectations feed directly into wage bargaining and price setting."

This substantial exorcising of the inflationary specter flows partly from the Fed's new credibility: a widespread belief that it is committed to keeping prices relatively stable and knows how to do so. . . .

A widely cited measure of public attitudes, the University of Michigan's Survey of Consumers, is reflecting two significant changes this year, says Richard Curtin, its director. First, long-term inflation expectations—the predicted annual inflation rate for the next five to 10 years—have slipped below 3% for the first time since the survey began asking the question nearly two decades ago. Second, long-term inflation expectations now nearly equal short-term expectations. . . .

This outlook eases inflationary pressures in many ways. Recall the 1970s, Ms. Yellen says, "when expectations of future inflation led workers to demand wage increases that would compensate them for expected inflation, and firms to

give wage increases believing they could pass on price increases." . . .

"In the 1970s and 1980s, we had price increases baked into our projections," says Warren L. Batts, chairman of both Premark International Inc. and Tupperware Corp. and head of the National Association of Manufacturers. "We thought we could charge our customers [more], and therefore we could pay our suppliers. [Now], you know you can't charge, so you don't pay."

Of course, inflationary fears aren't completely cured, as last week's stock and bond market jitters show. Rampant inflation in the 1970s shattered the notion that America was immune to the problem. Remaining traces of apprehension may not be all bad. "The moment we become complacent about inflation," says Deputy Treasury Secretary Lawrence Summers, "is the moment we will start to have an inflation problem."

This time, the shift in focus came not from two American economics professors but from a group of Arab sheiks. In 1974, the Organization of Petroleum Exporting Countries (OPEC) began to exert its market power as a cartel in the world oil market in order to increase its members' profits. The countries of OPEC, such as Saudi

Arabia, Kuwait, and Iraq, restricted the amount of crude oil they pumped and sold on world markets. Within a few years, this reduction in supply caused the price of oil to almost double.

A large increase in the world price of oil is an example of a supply shock. A **supply shock** is an event that directly affects firms' costs of production and thus the prices they charge; it shifts the economy's aggregate-supply curve and, as a result, the Phillips curve. For example, when an oil price increase raises the cost of producing gasoline, heating oil, tires, and many other products, it reduces the quantity of goods and services supplied at any given price level. As panel (a) of Figure 8 shows, this reduction in supply is represented by the leftward shift in the aggregate-supply curve from AS_1 to AS_2. The price level rises from P_1 to P_2, and output falls from Y_1 to Y_2. The combination of rising prices and falling output is sometimes called *stagflation*.

supply shock
an event that directly alters firms' costs and prices, shifting the economy's aggregate-supply curve and thus the Phillips curve

This shift in aggregate supply is associated with a similar shift in the short-run Phillips curve, shown in panel (b). Because firms need fewer workers to produce the smaller output, employment falls and unemployment rises. Because the price level is higher, the inflation rate—the percentage change in the price level from the previous year—is also higher. Thus, the shift in aggregate supply leads to higher unemployment and higher inflation. The short-run tradeoff between inflation and unemployment shifts to the right from PC_1 to PC_2.

Confronted with an adverse shift in aggregate supply, policymakers face a difficult choice between fighting inflation and fighting unemployment. If they con-

FIGURE 8

An Adverse Shock to Aggregate Supply

Panel (a) shows the model of aggregate demand and aggregate supply. When the aggregate-supply curve shifts to the left from AS_1 to AS_2, the equilibrium moves from point A to point B. Output falls from Y_1 to Y_2, and the price level rises from P_1 to P_2. Panel (b) shows the short-run tradeoff between inflation and unemployment. The adverse shift in aggregate supply moves the economy from a point with lower unemployment and lower inflation (point A) to a point with higher unemployment and higher inflation (point B). The short-run Phillips curve shifts to the right from PC_1 to PC_2. Policymakers now face a worse tradeoff between inflation and unemployment.

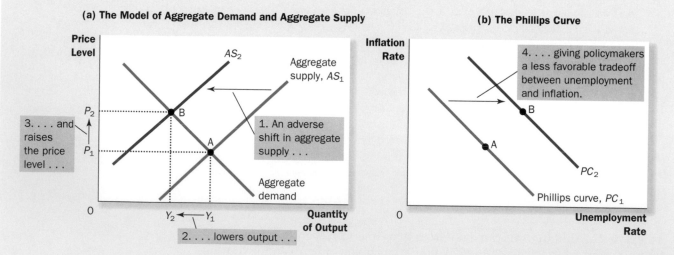

tract aggregate demand to fight inflation, they will raise unemployment further. If they expand aggregate demand to fight unemployment, they will raise inflation further. In other words, policymakers face a less favorable tradeoff between inflation and unemployment than they did before the shift in aggregate supply: They have to live with a higher rate of inflation for a given rate of unemployment, a higher rate of unemployment for a given rate of inflation, or some combination of higher unemployment and higher inflation.

An important question is whether this adverse shift in the Phillips curve is temporary or permanent. The answer depends on how people adjust their expectations of inflation. If people view the rise in inflation due to the supply shock as a temporary aberration, expected inflation does not change, and the Phillips curve will soon revert to its former position. But if people believe the shock will lead to a new era of higher inflation, then expected inflation rises, and the Phillips curve remains at its new, less desirable position.

In the United States during the 1970s, expected inflation did rise substantially. This rise in expected inflation is partly attributable to the decision of the Fed to accommodate the supply shock with higher money growth. (As we saw in Chapter 20, policymakers are said to *accommodate* an adverse supply shock when they respond to it by increasing aggregate demand.) Because of this policy decision, the recession that resulted from the supply shock was smaller than it otherwise might have been, but the U.S. economy faced an unfavorable tradeoff between inflation and unemployment for many years. The problem was compounded in 1979, when OPEC once again started to exert its market power, more than doubling the price of oil. Figure 9 shows inflation and unemployment in the U.S. economy during this period.

In 1980, after two OPEC supply shocks, the U.S. economy had an inflation rate of more than 9 percent and an unemployment rate of about 7 percent. This combination

"*Remember the good old days when all the economy needed was a little fine-tuning?*"

FIGURE 9

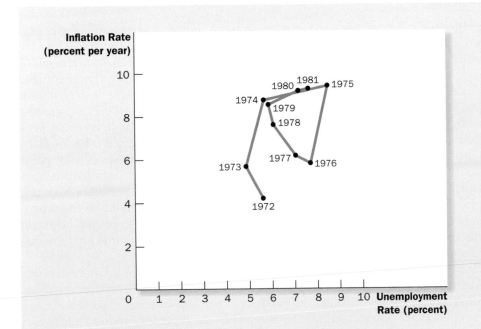

The Supply Shocks of the 1970s

This figure shows annual data from 1972 to 1981 on the unemployment rate and on the inflation rate (as measured by the GDP deflator). In the periods 1973–1975 and 1978–1981, increases in world oil prices led to higher inflation and higher unemployment.

Source: U.S. Department of Labor; U.S. Department of Commerce.

of inflation and unemployment was not at all near the tradeoff that seemed possible in the 1960s. (In the 1960s, the Phillips curve suggested that an unemployment rate of 7 percent would be associated with an inflation rate of only 1 percent. Inflation of more than 9 percent was unthinkable.) With the misery index in 1980 near an historic high, the public was widely dissatisfied with the performance of the economy. Largely because of this dissatisfaction, President Jimmy Carter lost his bid for re-election in November 1980 and was replaced by Ronald Reagan. Something had to be done, and soon it would be.

QuickQuiz Give an example of a favorable shock to aggregate supply. Use the model of aggregate demand and aggregate supply to explain the effects of such a shock. How does it affect the Phillips curve?

THE COST OF REDUCING INFLATION

In October 1979, as OPEC was imposing adverse supply shocks on the world's economies for the second time in a decade, Fed Chairman Paul Volcker decided that the time for action had come. Volcker had been appointed chairman by President Carter only two months earlier, and he had taken the job knowing that inflation had reached unacceptable levels. As guardian of the nation's monetary system, he felt he had little choice but to pursue a policy of *disinflation*—a reduction in the rate of inflation. Volcker had no doubt that the Fed could reduce inflation through its ability to control the quantity of money. But what would be the short-run cost of disinflation? The answer to this question was much less certain.

The Sacrifice Ratio

To reduce the inflation rate, the Fed has to pursue contractionary monetary policy. Figure 10 shows some of the effects of such a decision. When the Fed slows the rate at which the money supply is growing, it contracts aggregate demand. The fall in aggregate demand, in turn, reduces the quantity of goods and services that firms produce, and this fall in production leads to a fall in employment. The economy begins at point A in the figure and moves along the short-run Phillips curve to point B, which has lower inflation and higher unemployment. Over time, as people come to understand that prices are rising more slowly, expected inflation falls, and the short-run Phillips curve shifts downward. The economy moves from point B to point C. Inflation is lower, and unemployment is back at its natural rate.

   Thus, if a nation wants to reduce inflation, it must endure a period of high unemployment and low output. In Figure 10, this cost is represented by the movement of the economy through point B as it travels from point A to point C. The size of this cost depends on the slope of the Phillips curve and how quickly expectations of inflation adjust to the new monetary policy.

   Many studies have examined the data on inflation and unemployment in order to estimate the cost of reducing inflation. The findings of these studies are often summarized in a statistic called the **sacrifice ratio.** The sacrifice ratio is the number of percentage points of annual output lost in the process of reducing inflation by 1 percentage point. A typical estimate of the sacrifice ratio is 5. That is, for each

sacrifice ratio
the number of percentage points of annual output lost in the process of reducing inflation by 1 percentage point

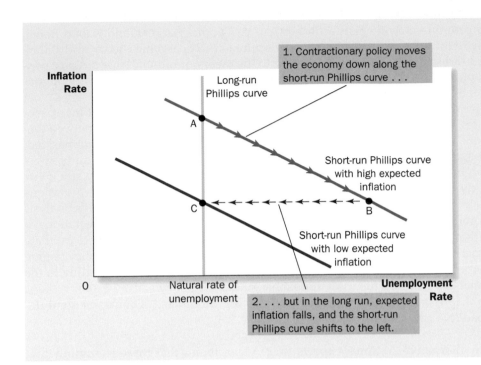

FIGURE 10

Disinflationary Monetary Policy in the Short Run and Long Run

When the Fed pursues contractionary monetary policy to reduce inflation, the economy moves along a short-run Phillips curve from point A to point B. Over time, expected inflation falls, and the short-run Phillips curve shifts downward. When the economy reaches point C, unemployment is back at its natural rate.

percentage point that inflation is reduced, 5 percent of annual output must be sacrificed in the transition.

Such estimates surely must have made Paul Volcker apprehensive as he confronted the task of reducing inflation. Inflation was running at almost 10 percent per year. To reach moderate inflation of, say, 4 percent per year would mean reducing inflation by 6 percentage points. If each percentage point cost 5 percent of the economy's annual output, then reducing inflation by 6 percentage points would require sacrificing 30 percent of annual output.

According to studies of the Phillips curve and the cost of disinflation, this sacrifice could be paid in various ways. An immediate reduction in inflation would depress output by 30 percent for a single year, but that outcome was surely too harsh even for an inflation hawk like Paul Volcker. It would be better, many argued, to spread out the cost over several years. If the reduction in inflation took place over 5 years, for instance, then output would have to average only 6 percent below trend during that period to add up to a sacrifice of 30 percent. An even more gradual approach would be to reduce inflation slowly over a decade, so that output would have to be only 3 percent below trend. Whatever path was chosen, however, it seemed that reducing inflation would not be easy.

Rational Expectations and the Possibility of Costless Disinflation

Just as Paul Volcker was pondering how costly reducing inflation might be, a group of economics professors was leading an intellectual revolution that would

rational expectations
the theory according to which people optimally use all the information they have, including information about government policies, when forecasting the future

challenge the conventional wisdom on the sacrifice ratio. This group included such prominent economists as Robert Lucas, Thomas Sargent, and Robert Barro. Their revolution was based on a new approach to economic theory and policy called **rational expectations.** According to the theory of rational expectations, people optimally use all the information they have, including information about government policies, when forecasting the future.

This new approach has had profound implications for many areas of macroeconomics, but none is more important than its application to the tradeoff between inflation and unemployment. As Friedman and Phelps had first emphasized, expected inflation is an important variable that explains why there is a tradeoff between inflation and unemployment in the short run but not in the long run. How quickly the short-run tradeoff disappears depends on how quickly expectations adjust. Proponents of rational expectations built on the Friedman–Phelps analysis to argue that when economic policies change, people adjust their expectations of inflation accordingly. Studies of inflation and unemployment that tried to estimate the sacrifice ratio had failed to take account of the direct effect of the policy regime on expectations. As a result, estimates of the sacrifice ratio were, according to the rational-expectations theorists, unreliable guides for policy.

In a 1981 paper titled "The End of Four Big Inflations," Thomas Sargent described this new view as follows:

> An alternative "rational expectations" view denies that there is any inherent momentum to the present process of inflation. This view maintains that firms and workers have now come to expect high rates of inflation in the future and that they strike inflationary bargains in light of these expectations. However, it is held that people expect high rates of inflation in the future precisely because the government's current and prospective monetary and fiscal policies warrant those expectations. . . . An implication of this view is that inflation can be stopped much more quickly than advocates of the "momentum" view have indicated and that their estimates of the length of time and the costs of stopping inflation in terms of forgone output are erroneous. . . . This is not to say that it would be easy to eradicate inflation. On the contrary, it would require more than a few temporary restrictive fiscal and monetary actions. It would require a change in the policy regime. . . . How costly such a move would be in terms of forgone output and how long it would be in taking effect would depend partly on how resolute and evident the government's commitment was.

According to Sargent, the sacrifice ratio could be much smaller than suggested by previous estimates. Indeed, in the most extreme case, it could be zero. If the government made a credible commitment to a policy of low inflation, people would be rational enough to lower their expectations of inflation immediately. The short-run Phillips curve would shift downward, and the economy would reach low inflation quickly without the cost of temporarily high unemployment and low output.

The Volcker Disinflation

As we have seen, when Paul Volcker faced the prospect of reducing inflation from its peak of about 10 percent, the economics profession offered two conflicting predictions. One group of economists offered estimates of the sacrifice ratio and

FIGURE 11

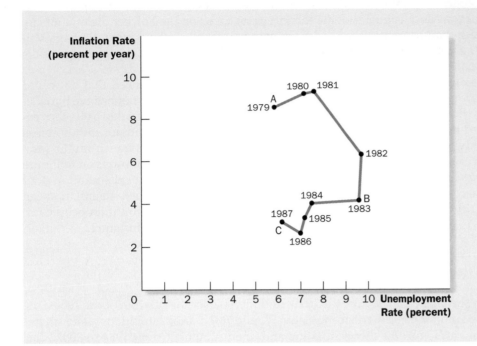

The Volcker Disinflation

This figure shows annual data from 1979 to 1987 on the unemployment rate and on the inflation rate (as measured by the GDP deflator). The reduction in inflation during this period came at the cost of very high unemployment in 1982 and 1983. Note that the points labeled A, B, and C in this figure correspond roughly to the points in Figure 10.

Source: U.S. Department of Labor; U.S. Department of Commerce.

concluded that reducing inflation would have great cost in terms of lost output and high unemployment. Another group offered the theory of rational expectations and concluded that reducing inflation could be much less costly and, perhaps, could even have no cost at all. Who was right?

Figure 11 shows inflation and unemployment from 1979 to 1987. As you can see, Volcker did succeed at reducing inflation. Inflation came down from almost 10 percent in 1981 and 1982 to about 4 percent in 1983 and 1984. Credit for this reduction in inflation goes completely to monetary policy. Fiscal policy at this time was acting in the opposite direction: The increases in the budget deficit during the Reagan administration were expanding aggregate demand, which tends to raise inflation. The fall in inflation from 1981 to 1984 is attributable to the tough anti-inflation policies of Fed Chairman Paul Volcker.

The figure shows that the Volcker disinflation did come at the cost of high unemployment. In 1982 and 1983, the unemployment rate was about 10 percent—almost twice its level when Paul Volcker was appointed Fed chairman. At the same time, the production of goods and services as measured by real GDP was well below its trend level. (See Figure 1 in Chapter 20.) The Volcker disinflation produced the deepest recession in the United States since the Great Depression of the 1930s.

Does this experience refute the possibility of costless disinflation as suggested by the rational-expectations theorists? Some economists have argued that the answer to this question is a resounding yes. Indeed, the pattern of disinflation shown in Figure 11 is very similar to the pattern predicted in Figure 10. To make the transition from high inflation (point A in both figures) to low inflation (point C), the economy had to experience a painful period of high unemployment (point B).

Yet there are two reasons not to reject the conclusions of the rational-expectations theorists so quickly. First, even though the Volcker disinflation did impose a cost of temporarily high unemployment, the cost was not as large as many economists had predicted. Most estimates of the sacrifice ratio based on the Volcker disinflation are smaller than estimates that had been obtained from previous data. Perhaps Volcker's tough stand on inflation did have some direct effect on expectations, as the rational-expectations theorists claimed.

Second, and more important, even though Volcker announced that he would aim monetary policy to lower inflation, much of the public did not believe him. Because few people thought Volcker would reduce inflation as quickly as he did, expected inflation did not fall, and the short-run Phillips curve did not shift down as quickly as it might have. Some evidence for this hypothesis comes from the forecasts made by commercial forecasting firms: Their forecasts of inflation fell more slowly in the 1980s than did actual inflation. Thus, the Volcker disinflation does not necessarily refute the rational-expectations view that credible disinflation can be costless. It does show, however, that policymakers cannot count on people immediately believing them when they announce a policy of disinflation.

The Greenspan Era

Since the OPEC inflation of the 1970s and the Volcker disinflation of the 1980s, the U.S. economy has experienced relatively mild fluctuations in inflation and unemployment. Figure 12 shows inflation and unemployment from 1984 to 2002. This period is called the Greenspan era, after Alan Greenspan who in 1987 followed Paul Volcker as chairman of the Federal Reserve.

This period began with a favorable supply shock. In 1986, OPEC members started arguing over production levels, and their long-standing agreement to restrict supply broke down. Oil prices fell by about half. As the figure shows, this

FIGURE 12

The Greenspan Era

This figure shows annual data from 1984 to 2002 on the unemployment rate and on the inflation rate (as measured by the GDP deflator). During most of this period, Alan Greenspan has been chairman of the Federal Reserve. Fluctuations in inflation and unemployment have been relatively small.

Source: U.S. Department of Labor; U.S. Department of Commerce.

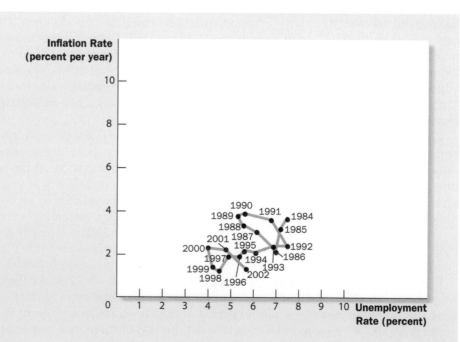

favorable supply shock led to falling inflation and falling unemployment.

Since then, the Fed has been careful to avoid repeating the policy mistakes of the 1960s, when excessive aggregate demand pushed unemployment below the natural rate and raised inflation. When unemployment fell and inflation rose in 1989 and 1990, the Fed raised interest rates and contracted aggregate demand, leading to a small recession in 1991 and 1992. Unemployment then rose above most estimates of the natural rate, and inflation fell once again.

The rest of the 1990s witnessed a period of economic prosperity. Inflation gradually drifted downward, approaching zero by the end of the decade. Unemployment also drifted downward, leading many observers to believe that the natural rate of unemployment had fallen. Part of the credit for this good economic performance goes to Alan Greenspan and his colleagues at the Federal Reserve, for low inflation can be achieved only with prudent monetary policy. But as the following case study discusses, good luck in the form of favorable supply shocks is also part of the story.

The economy, however, ran into problems in 2001, as a case study in Chapter 20 described. The end of the dot-com stock-market bubble, the 9/11 terrorist attacks, and corporate accounting scandals all depressed aggregate demand. Unemployment rose as the economy experienced its first recession in a decade.

Fed Chairman Alan Greenspan: A hard act to follow?

Case Study

WHY WERE INFLATION AND UNEMPLOYMENT SO LOW AT THE END OF THE 1990s?

As the twentieth century drew to a close, the U.S. economy was experiencing some of the lowest rates of inflation and unemployment in many years. In 1999, for instance, unemployment had fallen to 4.2 percent, while inflation was running a mere 1.3 percent per year. As measured by these two important macroeconomic variables, the United States was enjoying a period of unusual prosperity.

Some observers argued that this experience cast doubt on the theory of the Phillips curve. Indeed, the combination of low inflation and low unemployment might seem to suggest that there was no longer a tradeoff between these two variables. Yet most economists took a less radical view of events. As we have discussed throughout this chapter, the short-run tradeoff between inflation and unemployment shifts over time. In the 1990s, this tradeoff shifted leftward, allowing the economy to enjoy low unemployment and low inflation simultaneously.

What caused this favorable shift in the short-run Phillips curve? Part of the answer lies in a fall in expected inflation. Under Paul Volcker and Alan Greenspan, the Fed pursued a policy aimed at reducing inflation and keeping it low. Over time, as this policy succeeded, the Fed gained credibility with the public that it would continue to fight inflation as necessary. The increased credibility lowered inflation expectations, which shifted the short-run Phillips curve to the left.

In addition to this shift from reduced expected inflation, many economists believe that the U.S. economy experienced some favorable supply shocks during this period. (Recall that a favorable supply shock shifts the short-run aggregate-supply curve to the right, raising output and reducing prices. It therefore reduces both unemployment and inflation and shifts the short-run Phillips curve to the left.) Here are three events that may get credit for the favorable shift to aggregate supply:

- *Declining commodity prices:* In the late 1990s, the prices of many basic commodities, including oil, fell on world markets. This fall in commodity prices, in turn, was partly due to a deep recession in Japan and other Asian economies, which reduced the demand for these products. Because commodities are an important input into production, the fall in their prices reduced producers' costs and acted as a favorable supply shock for the U.S. economy.
- *Labor-market changes:* Some economists believe that the aging of the large baby-boom generation born after World War II has caused fundamental changes in the labor market. Because older workers are typically in more stable jobs than younger workers, an increase in the average age of the labor force may reduce the economy's natural rate of unemployment.
- *Technological advance:* Some economists think the U.S. economy has entered a period of more rapid technological progress. Advances in information technology,

IN THE NEWS

THE CASE FOR INFLATION TARGETING

In 2002 President George W. Bush appointed Ben Bernanke to be a governor of the Federal Reserve. Here is some advice Bernanke and his coauthors offered to monetary policymakers two years earlier.

What Happens When Greenspan Is Gone?

By Ben S. Bernanke, Frederic S. Mishkin, and Adam S. Posen

U.S. monetary policy has been remarkably successful during Alan Greenspan's 12 1/2 years as Federal Reserve chairman. But although President Clinton yesterday reappointed the 73-year-old Mr. Greenspan to a new term ending in 2004, the chairman will not be around forever. To ensure that monetary policy stays on track after Mr. Greenspan, the Fed should be thinking through its ap-

proach to monetary policy now. The Fed needs an approach that consolidates the gains of the Greenspan years and ensures that those successful policies will continue—even if future Fed chairmen are less skillful or less committed to price stability than Mr. Greenspan has been.

We think the best bet lies in a framework known as inflation targeting, which has been employed with great success in recent years by most of the world's biggest economies, except for Japan. Inflation targeting is a monetary-policy framework that commits the central bank to a forward-looking pursuit of low

inflation—the source of the Fed's current great performance—but also promotes a more open and accountable policy-making process. More transparency and accountability would help keep the Fed on track, and a more open Fed would be good for financial markets and more consistent with our democratic political system. . . .

Successful inflation targeting requires that the central bank and elected officials make a public commitment to an explicit numerical target level for inflation (usually around 2%), to be achieved over a specified horizon (usually two years).

such as the Internet, have been profound and have influenced many parts of the economy. Such technological advance increases productivity and, therefore, is a type of favorable supply shock.

Economists debate which of these explanations of the shifting Phillips curve is most plausible. In the end, the complete story may contain elements of each.

Keep in mind that none of these hypotheses denies the fundamental lesson of the Phillips curve—that policymakers who control aggregate demand always face a short-run tradeoff between inflation and unemployment. Yet the 1990s remind us that this short-run tradeoff changes over time, sometimes in ways that are hard to predict. ●

QuickQuiz What is the sacrifice ratio? How might the credibility of the Fed's commitment to reduce inflation affect the sacrifice ratio?

Equally important, the central bank must agree to provide the markets and the public with enough information to evaluate its performance, and to understand its reasoning when policy and inflation deviate from the long-run goal—as they inevitably will at times. . . .

Adoption of inflation targeting by the Federal Reserve would bring several major advantages over the current, less structured approach. First, it would transform the commitment to price stability—which has served us so well under Mr. Greenspan and his predecessor, Paul Volcker—from a personal preference of the chairman into an official policy. By depersonalizing and institutionalizing the Greenspan policy approach, the Fed would increase the likelihood that future U.S. monetary policy will look like the 1980s and 1990s rather than the 1930s or the 1970s.

Second, the transparency of the inflation-targeting approach would encourage politicians and the public to focus on what monetary policy can do (namely, maintain long-run price stability), rather than on what it can't do (create perma-

nent increases in growth through expansionary policies). In place of politically expedient demands and scapegoating by politicians—a particular danger in election years—public oversight of the Fed would be directed toward discussion of the appropriate level for the inflation target and evaluation of the Fed's effectiveness in meeting that target. The Fed would retain the sole authority for specific policy actions—such as setting the federal-funds rate—in pursuit of its target. This allocation of responsibility for monetary policy between elected officials and technocrats would serve both democratic principles and good policy. . . .

Third, increased transparency would diminish financial and economic uncertainty. More information from the Fed about its plans and expectations would reduce the perpetual, and wasteful, attempts by financial market participants to guess what the Fed will do next. An inflation target would also make it easier for businesses and consumers to plan.

Fourth, inflation targeting is particularly good insurance against the threat of falling prices. Deflation has been associ-

ated with deep recessions or even depressions, as in the 1930s and recently in Japan. Targeting an annual inflation rate a couple of percentage points above zero, as all inflation targeters have done, commits the central bank to maintaining a floor under price level movements (as well as a ceiling over them). . . .

Mr. Greenspan's reappointment should not make us complacent about the future of Fed policy. On the principle that it is better to fix the roof when skies are sunny, the Fed should announce its intentions to establish a more open policy framework now, rather than waiting to be confronted by difficult policy decisions. An explicit commitment to inflation targeting would increase the odds that those decisions would be the right ones, and that they would receive public support—whether or not Alan Greenspan is chairman of the Fed.

Source: *The Wall Street Journal,* January 5, 2000, p. A22. © 2000 by Dow Jones & Co. Inc. Reproduced with permission of DOW JONES & CO INC in the format Textbook via Copyright Clearance Center.

CONCLUSION

This chapter has examined how economists' thinking about inflation and unemployment has evolved over time. We have discussed the ideas of many of the best economists of the twentieth century: from the Phillips curve of Phillips, Samuelson, and Solow, to the natural-rate hypothesis of Friedman and Phelps, to the rational-expectations theory of Lucas, Sargent, and Barro. Four of this group have already won Nobel prizes for their work in economics, and more are likely to be so honored in the years to come.

Although the tradeoff between inflation and unemployment has generated much intellectual turmoil over the past 40 years, certain principles have developed that today command consensus. Here is how Milton Friedman expressed the relationship between inflation and unemployment in 1968:

> There is always a temporary tradeoff between inflation and unemployment; there is no permanent tradeoff. The temporary tradeoff comes not from inflation per se, but from unanticipated inflation, which generally means, from a rising rate of inflation. The widespread belief that there is a permanent tradeoff is a sophisticated version of the confusion between "high" and "rising" that we all recognize in simpler forms. A rising rate of inflation may reduce unemployment, a high rate will not.
>
> But how long, you will say, is "temporary"? . . . I can at most venture a personal judgment, based on some examination of the historical evidence, that the initial effects of a higher and unanticipated rate of inflation last for something like two to five years.

Today, more than 30 years later, this statement still summarizes the view of most macroeconomists.

SUMMARY

- The Phillips curve describes a negative relationship between inflation and unemployment. By expanding aggregate demand, policymakers can choose a point on the Phillips curve with higher inflation and lower unemployment. By contracting aggregate demand, policymakers can choose a point on the Phillips curve with lower inflation and higher unemployment.

- The tradeoff between inflation and unemployment described by the Phillips curve holds only in the short run. In the long run, expected inflation adjusts to changes in actual inflation, and the short-run Phillips curve shifts.

As a result, the long-run Phillips curve is vertical at the natural rate of unemployment.

- The short-run Phillips curve also shifts because of shocks to aggregate supply. An adverse supply shock, such as the increase in world oil prices during the 1970s, gives policymakers a less favorable tradeoff between inflation and unemployment. That is, after an adverse supply shock, policymakers have to accept a higher rate of inflation for any given rate of unemployment, or a higher rate of unemployment for any given rate of inflation.

- When the Fed contracts growth in the money supply to reduce inflation, it moves the economy along the short-run Phillips curve, which results in temporarily high unemployment. The cost of disinflation depends on how quickly expectations of inflation fall. Some economists argue that a credible commitment to low inflation can reduce the cost of disinflation by inducing a quick adjustment of expectations.

KEY CONCEPTS

Phillips curve, p. 486
natural-rate hypothesis, p. 494

supply shock, p. 498
sacrifice ratio, p. 500

rational expectations, p. 502

QUESTIONS FOR REVIEW

1. Draw the short-run tradeoff between inflation and unemployment. How might the Fed move the economy from one point on this curve to another?

2. Draw the long-run tradeoff between inflation and unemployment. Explain how the short-run and long-run tradeoffs are related.

3. What's so natural about the natural rate of unemployment? Why might the natural rate of unemployment differ across countries?

4. Suppose a drought destroys farm crops and drives up the price of food. What is the effect on the short-run tradeoff between inflation and unemployment?

5. The Fed decides to reduce inflation. Use the Phillips curve to show the short-run and long-run effects of this policy. How might the short-run costs be reduced?

PROBLEMS AND APPLICATIONS

1. Suppose the natural rate of unemployment is 6 percent. On one graph, draw two Phillips curves that can be used to describe the four situations listed here. Label the point that shows the position of the economy in each case.
   a. Actual inflation is 5 percent and expected inflation is 3 percent.
   b. Actual inflation is 3 percent and expected inflation is 5 percent.
   c. Actual inflation is 5 percent and expected inflation is 5 percent.
   d. Actual inflation is 3 percent and expected inflation is 3 percent.

2. Illustrate the effects of the following developments on both the short-run and long-run Phillips curves. Give the economic reasoning underlying your answers.

   a. a rise in the natural rate of unemployment
   b. a decline in the price of imported oil
   c. a rise in government spending
   d. a decline in expected inflation

3. Suppose that a fall in consumer spending causes a recession.
   a. Illustrate the changes in the economy using both an aggregate-supply/aggregate-demand diagram and a Phillips-curve diagram. What happens to inflation and unemployment in the short run?
   b. Now suppose that over time expected inflation changes in the same direction that actual inflation changes. What happens to the position of the short-run Phillips curve? After the recession is over, does

the economy face a better or worse set of inflation–unemployment combinations?

4. Suppose the economy is in a long-run equilibrium.
   a. Draw the economy's short-run and long-run Phillips curves.
   b. Suppose a wave of business pessimism reduces aggregate demand. Show the effect of this shock on your diagram from part (a). If the Fed undertakes expansionary monetary policy, can it return the economy to its original inflation rate and original unemployment rate?
   c. Now suppose the economy is back in long-run equilibrium, and then the price of imported oil rises. Show the effect of this shock with a new diagram like that in part (a). If the Fed undertakes expansionary monetary policy, can it return the economy to its original inflation rate and original unemployment rate? If the Fed undertakes contractionary monetary policy, can it return the economy to its original inflation rate and original unemployment rate? Explain why this situation differs from that in part (b).

5. Suppose the Federal Reserve believed that the natural rate of unemployment was 6 percent when the actual natural rate was 5.5 percent. If the Fed based its policy decisions on its belief, what would happen to the economy?

6. The price of oil fell sharply in 1986 and again in 1998.
   a. Show the impact of such a change in both the aggregate-demand/aggregate-supply diagram and in the Phillips-curve diagram. What happens to inflation and unemployment in the short run?
   b. Do the effects of this event mean there is no short-run tradeoff between inflation and unemployment? Why or why not?

7. Suppose the Federal Reserve announced that it would pursue contractionary monetary policy in order to reduce the inflation rate. Would the following conditions make the ensuing recession more or less severe? Explain.
   a. Wage contracts have short durations.
   b. There is little confidence in the Fed's determination to reduce inflation.
   c. Expectations of inflation adjust quickly to actual inflation.

8. Some economists believe that the short-run Phillips curve is relatively steep and shifts quickly in response to changes in the economy. Would these economists be more or less likely to favor contractionary policy in order to reduce inflation than economists who had the opposite views?

9. Imagine an economy in which all wages are set in three-year contracts. In this world, the Fed announces a disinflationary change in monetary

policy to begin immediately. Everyone in the economy believes the Fed's announcement. Would this disinflation be costless? Why or why not? What might the Fed do to reduce the cost of disinflation?

10. Given the unpopularity of inflation, why don't elected leaders always support efforts to reduce inflation? Economists believe that countries can reduce the cost of disinflation by letting their central banks make decisions about monetary policy without interference from politicians. Why might this be so?

11. Suppose Federal Reserve policymakers accept the theory of the short-run Phillips curve and the natural-rate hypothesis and want to keep unemployment close to its natural rate. Unfortunately, because the natural rate of unemployment can change over time, they aren't certain about the value of the natural rate. What macroeconomic variables do you think they should look at when conducting monetary policy?

http://   For more study tools, please visit http://mankiwXtra.swlearning.com.

9

FINAL THOUGHTS

FIVE DEBATES OVER
MACROECONOMIC POLICY

It is hard to open up the newspaper without finding some politician or editorial writer advocating a change in economic policy. The president should raise taxes to reduce the budget deficit, or he should stop worrying about the budget deficit. The Federal Reserve should cut interest rates to stimulate a flagging economy, or it should avoid such moves in order not to risk higher inflation. Congress should reform the tax system to promote faster economic growth, or it should reform the tax system to achieve a more equal distribution of income. Such economic issues are central to the continuing political debate in the United States and other countries around the world.

Previous chapters have developed the tools that economists use when analyzing the behavior of the economy as a whole and the impact of policies on the economy. This final chapter presents both sides in five leading debates over macroeconomic policy. The knowledge you have accumulated in this course provides the background with which we can discuss these important, unsettled issues. It should help you choose a side in these debates or, at least, help you see why choosing a side is so difficult.

23

SHOULD MONETARY AND FISCAL POLICYMAKERS TRY TO STABILIZE THE ECONOMY?

In the preceding three chapters, we saw how changes in aggregate demand and aggregate supply can lead to short-run fluctuations in production and employment. We also saw how monetary and fiscal policy can shift aggregate demand and, thereby, influence these fluctuations. But even if policymakers *can* influence short-run economic fluctuations, does that mean they *should*? Our first debate concerns whether monetary and fiscal policymakers should use the tools at their disposal in an attempt to smooth the ups and downs of the business cycle.

Pro: Policymakers Should Try to Stabilize the Economy

Left on their own, economies tend to fluctuate. When households and firms become pessimistic, for instance, they cut back on spending, and this reduces the aggregate demand for goods and services. The fall in aggregate demand, in turn, reduces the production of goods and services. Firms lay off workers, and the unemployment rate rises. Real GDP and other measures of income fall. Rising unemployment and falling income help confirm the pessimism that initially generated the economic downturn.

Such a recession has no benefit for society—it represents a sheer waste of resources. Workers who become unemployed because of inadequate aggregate demand would rather be working. Business owners whose factories are left idle during a recession would rather be producing valuable goods and services and selling them at a profit.

There is no reason for society to suffer through the booms and busts of the business cycle. The development of macroeconomic theory has shown policymakers how to reduce the severity of economic fluctuations. By "leaning against the wind" of economic change, monetary and fiscal policy can stabilize aggregate demand and, thereby, production and employment. When aggregate demand is inadequate to ensure full employment, policymakers should boost government spending, cut taxes, and expand the money supply. When aggregate demand is excessive, risking higher inflation, policymakers should cut government spending, raise taxes, and reduce the money supply. Such policy actions put macroeconomic theory to its best use by leading to a more stable economy, which benefits everyone.

Con: Policymakers Should Not Try to Stabilize the Economy

Although monetary and fiscal policy can be used to stabilize the economy in theory, there are substantial obstacles to the use of such policies in practice.

One problem is that monetary and fiscal policy do not affect the economy immediately but instead work with a long lag. Monetary policy affects aggregate demand by changing interest rates, which in turn affect spending, especially residential and business investment. But many households and firms set their spending plans in advance. As a result, it takes time for changes in interest rates to alter the aggregate demand for goods and services. Many studies indicate that changes in monetary policy have little effect on aggregate demand until about six months after the change is made.

Fiscal policy works with a lag because of the long political process that governs changes in spending and taxes. To make any change in fiscal policy, a bill must go through congressional committees, pass both the House and the Senate, and be signed by the president. It can take years to propose, pass, and implement a major change in fiscal policy.

Because of these long lags, policymakers who want to stabilize the economy need to look ahead to economic conditions that are likely to prevail when their actions will take effect. Unfortunately, economic forecasting is highly imprecise, in part because macroeconomics is such a primitive science and in part because the shocks that cause economic fluctuations are intrinsically unpredictable. Thus, when policymakers change monetary or fiscal policy, they must rely on educated guesses about future economic conditions.

All too often, policymakers trying to stabilize the economy do just the opposite. Economic conditions can easily change between the time when a policy action begins and when it takes effect. Because of this, policymakers can inadvertently exacerbate rather than mitigate the magnitude of economic fluctuations. Some economists have claimed that many of the major economic fluctuations in history, including the Great Depression of the 1930s, can be traced to destabilizing policy actions.

One of the first rules taught to physicians is "do no harm." The human body has natural restorative powers. Confronted with a sick patient and an uncertain diagnosis, often a doctor should do nothing but leave the patient's body to its own devices. Intervening in the absence of reliable knowledge merely risks making matters worse.

The same can be said about treating an ailing economy. It might be desirable if policymakers could eliminate all economic fluctuations, but that is not a realistic goal given the limits of macroeconomic knowledge and the inherent unpredictability of world events. Economic policymakers should refrain from intervening often with monetary and fiscal policy and be content if they do no harm.

QuickQuiz Explain why monetary and fiscal policy work with a lag. Why do these lags matter in the choice between active and passive policy?

SHOULD MONETARY POLICY BE MADE BY RULE RATHER THAN BY DISCRETION?

As we first discussed in Chapter 16, the Federal Open Market Committee sets monetary policy in the United States. The committee meets about every six weeks to evaluate the state of the economy. Based on this evaluation and forecasts of future economic conditions, it chooses whether to raise, lower, or leave unchanged the level of short-term interest rates. The Fed then adjusts the money supply to reach that interest-rate target until the next meeting, when the target is reevaluated.

The Federal Open Market Committee operates with almost complete discretion over how to conduct monetary policy. The laws that created the Fed give the institution only vague recommendations about what goals it should pursue. And they do not tell the Fed how to pursue whatever goals it might choose. Once members are appointed to the Federal Open Market Committee, they have little mandate but to "do the right thing."

Some economists are critical of this institutional design. Our second debate over macroeconomic policy, therefore, focuses on whether the Federal Reserve should have its discretionary powers reduced and, instead, be committed to following a rule for how it conducts monetary policy.

Pro: Monetary Policy Should Be Made by Rule

Discretion in the conduct of monetary policy has two problems. The first is that it does not limit incompetence and abuse of power. When the government sends police into a community to maintain civic order, it gives them strict guidelines about how to carry out their job. Because police have great power, allowing them to exercise that power in whatever way they want would be dangerous. Yet when the government gives central bankers the authority to maintain economic order, it gives them no guidelines. Monetary policymakers are allowed undisciplined discretion.

As an example of abuse of power, central bankers are sometimes tempted to use monetary policy to affect the outcome of elections. Suppose that the vote for the incumbent president is based on economic conditions at the time he is up for reelection. A central banker sympathetic to the incumbent might be tempted to pursue expansionary policies just before the election to stimulate production and employment, knowing that the resulting inflation will not show up until after the election. Thus, to the extent that central bankers ally themselves with politicians, discretionary policy can lead to economic fluctuations that reflect the electoral calendar. Economists call such fluctuations the *political business cycle.*

The second, more subtle, problem with discretionary monetary policy is that it might lead to more inflation than is desirable. Central bankers, knowing that there is no long-run tradeoff between inflation and unemployment, often announce that their goal is zero inflation. Yet they rarely achieve price stability. Why? Perhaps it is because, once the public forms expectations of inflation, policymakers face a short-run tradeoff between inflation and unemployment. They are tempted to renege on

IN THE NEWS

ALAN GREENSPAN VERSUS THE PC

In this opinion column, the chief executive of Cypress Semiconductor suggests replacing the Fed chairman with a policy rule run by a computer.

A Computer Would Do Better Than the Fed

By T. J. Rodgers

The Federal Reserve's power to stave off economic decline is now under attack by those who were certain of the Fed's vaunted magic just months ago. The economy here in Silicon Valley is a train wreck. And some of our suffering may be attributed to the ill-timed discount rate hikes in 2000 that the Fed is now desperately trying to reverse.

To be fair, no one—not even here in Silicon Valley—would have predicted that the dot-com crash would have spread so quickly to Internet infrastructure builders and to the technology sector in general. What the Fed did not know was that the economy it was trying to slow down was about to come to an abrupt halt on its own. And that's the point: There is a fundamental flaw in the Fed's operational assumption that it can know enough about the future to fine-tune the economy without continually making mistakes.

Events likely to alter the economy—wars, severe winters, technology breakthroughs, and so on—are not predictable by even the most complete set of economic metrics. And because surprise events often trump normal economic trends, Fed action is just as likely to exac-erbate an economic problem as it is to mitigate it.

Years ago, in a seminar on statistical process control, the math of quality control in manufacturing, I learned in a simple exercise the futility of trying to control random events. The Fed should learn the same math.

The exercise involved dropping gumballs, one at a time, through a plastic funnel held above a large piece of paper on the floor, where the point of impact was then marked. Random "noise" in the system—caused by misshapen gumballs or the unsteadiness of the person holding the funnel—caused the gumballs to land in a circle whose diameter showed the combined random variation of the entire system.

The challenge was to drop the gumballs into the tightest circle possible. It turns out that the secret is never to move the funnel, no matter how far the last gumball landed from the center of the circle. Why? Reaiming the funnel to correct for a miss amplified the error in the next drop. The probability that the "correction" would be in the right direction was only 50 percent. In other words, trying to tune random noise out actually destabilizes and adds more variation to the system.

This problem becomes even more pronounced when time delays exist in the system. When the Fed changes the discount rate, the economy responds weeks or months later. During the time delay, if an important, unexpected economic event occurs, the Fed's prior action is just as likely to exacerbate that unanticipated problem as it is to fix it. At the same time, the Fed's micromanagement of the discount rate also promotes speculative stock trading.

That's why we should use a computer to control the discount rate. The computer program should calculate the discount rate based on economic data like the consumer price index, unemployment, and the index of leading economic indicators; there would be no need to depend on Alan Greenspan's or any other individual's interpretation of the data.

Publishing the rules governing the program would allow everyone to anticipate changes rationally, eliminating stock trading based on speculation about surprise Fed rate changes. If the rules needed to change due to a radical shift in economic conditions, they could be openly debated and readjusted. This wouldn't prevent economic downturns, but at the very least, the discount rate might cease to be an extra source of economic uncertainty.

Source: *The New York Times,*
April 7, 2001, p. A25. Copyright © 2001 by The New York Times Co.
Reprinted by permission.

their announcement of price stability in order to achieve lower unemployment. This discrepancy between announcements (what policymakers *say* they are going to do) and actions (what they subsequently in fact do) is called the *time inconsistency of policy.* Because policymakers are so often time inconsistent, people are skeptical when central bankers announce their intentions to reduce the rate of inflation. As a result, people always expect more inflation than monetary policymakers claim they are trying to achieve. Higher expectations of inflation, in turn, shift the short-run Phillips curve upward, making the short-run tradeoff between inflation and unemployment less favorable than it otherwise might be.

One way to avoid these two problems with discretionary policy is to commit the central bank to a policy rule. For example, suppose that Congress passed a law requiring the Fed to increase the money supply by exactly 3 percent per year. (Why 3 percent? Because real GDP grows on average about 3 percent per year and because money demand grows with real GDP, 3 percent growth in the money supply is roughly the rate necessary to produce long-run price stability.) Such a law would eliminate incompetence and abuse of power on the part of the Fed, and it would make the political business cycle impossible. In addition, policy could no longer be time inconsistent. People would now believe the Fed's announcement of low inflation because the Fed would be legally required to pursue a low-inflation monetary policy. With low expected inflation, the economy would face a more favorable short-run tradeoff between inflation and unemployment.

Other rules for monetary policy are also possible. A more active rule might allow some feedback from the state of the economy to changes in monetary policy. For example, a more active rule might require the Fed to increase monetary growth by 1 percentage point for every percentage point that unemployment rises above its natural rate. Regardless of the precise form of the rule, committing the Fed to some rule would yield advantages by limiting incompetence, abuse of power, and time inconsistency in the conduct of monetary policy.

Con: Monetary Policy Should Not Be Made by Rule

Although there may be pitfalls with discretionary monetary policy, there is also an important advantage to it: flexibility. The Fed has to confront various circumstances, not all of which can be foreseen. In the 1930s banks failed in record numbers. In the 1970s the price of oil skyrocketed around the world. In October 1987 the stock market fell by 22 percent in a single day. The Fed must decide how to respond to these shocks to the economy. A designer of a policy rule could not possibly consider all the contingencies and specify in advance the right policy response. It is better to appoint good people to conduct monetary policy and then give them the freedom to do the best they can.

Moreover, the alleged problems with discretion are largely hypothetical. The practical importance of the political business cycle, for instance, is far from clear. In some cases, just the opposite seems to occur. For example, President Jimmy Carter appointed Paul Volcker to head the Federal Reserve in 1979. Nonetheless, in October of that year Volcker moved to contract monetary policy to combat the high rate of inflation that he had inherited from his predecessor. The predictable result of Volcker's decision was a recession, and the predictable result of the recession was a decline in Carter's popularity. Rather than using monetary policy to help the president who had appointed him, Volcker took actions he thought were in the national interest, even though they helped to ensure Carter's defeat by Ronald Reagan in the November 1980 election.

The practical importance of time inconsistency is also far from clear. Although most people are skeptical of central-bank announcements, central bankers can achieve credibility over time by backing up their words with actions. In the 1990s, the Fed has achieved and maintained a low rate of inflation, despite the ever present temptation to take advantage of the short-run tradeoff between inflation and unemployment. This experience shows that low inflation does not require that the Fed be committed to a policy rule.

Any attempt to replace discretion with a rule must confront the difficult task of specifying a precise rule. Despite much research examining the costs and benefits of alternative rules, economists have not reached a consensus about what a good rule would be. Until there is a consensus, society has little choice but to give central bankers discretion to conduct monetary policy as they see fit.

QuickQuiz Give an example of a monetary policy rule. Why might your rule be better than discretionary policy? Why might it be worse?

SHOULD THE CENTRAL BANK AIM FOR ZERO INFLATION?

One of the *Ten Principles of Economics* discussed in Chapter 1, and developed more fully in Chapter 17, is that prices rise when the government prints too much money. Another of the *Ten Principles of Economics* discussed in Chapter 1, and developed more fully in Chapter 22, is that society faces a short-run tradeoff between inflation and unemployment. Put together, these two principles raise a question for policymakers: How much inflation should the central bank be willing to tolerate? Our third debate is whether zero is the right target for the inflation rate.

Pro: The Central Bank Should Aim for Zero Inflation

Inflation confers no benefit on society, but it imposes several real costs. As we discussed in Chapter 17, economists have identified six costs of inflation:

- Shoeleather costs associated with reduced money holdings
- Menu costs associated with more frequent adjustment of prices
- Increased variability of relative prices
- Unintended changes in tax liabilities due to nonindexation of the tax code
- Confusion and inconvenience resulting from a changing unit of account
- Arbitrary redistributions of wealth associated with dollar-denominated debts

Some economists argue that these costs are small, at least for moderate rates of inflation, such as the 3 percent inflation experienced in the United States during the 1990s. But other economists claim these costs can be substantial, even for moderate inflation. Moreover, there is no doubt that the public dislikes inflation. When inflation heats up, opinion polls identify inflation as one of the nation's leading problems.

Of course, the benefits of zero inflation have to be weighed against the costs of achieving it. Reducing inflation usually requires a period of high unemployment and low output, as illustrated by the short-run Phillips curve. But this disinflationary recession is only temporary. Once people come to understand that policymakers are aiming for zero inflation, expectations of inflation will fall, and the short-run tradeoff will improve. Because expectations adjust, there is no tradeoff between inflation and unemployment in the long run.

Reducing inflation is, therefore, a policy with temporary costs and permanent benefits. That is, once the disinflationary recession is over, the benefits of zero inflation would persist into the future. If policymakers are farsighted, they should be willing to incur the temporary costs for the permanent benefits. This is precisely the calculation made by Paul Volcker in the early 1980s, when he tightened monetary policy and reduced inflation from about 10 percent in 1980 to about 4 percent in 1983. Although in 1982 unemployment reached its highest level since the Great Depression, the economy eventually recovered from the recession, leaving a legacy of low inflation. Today Volcker is considered a hero among central bankers.

Moreover, the costs of reducing inflation need not be as large as some economists claim. If the Fed announces a credible commitment to zero inflation, it can directly influence expectations of inflation. Such a change in expectations can improve the short-run tradeoff between inflation and unemployment, allowing the economy to reach lower inflation at a reduced cost. The key to this strategy is credibility: People must believe that the Fed is actually going to carry through on its announced policy. Congress could help in this regard by passing legislation that made price stability the Fed's primary goal. Such a law would make it less costly to achieve zero inflation without reducing any of the resulting benefits.

One advantage of a zero-inflation target is that zero provides a more natural focal point for policymakers than any other number. Suppose, for instance, that the Fed were to announce that it would keep inflation at 3 percent—the rate experienced during the 1990s. Would the Fed really stick to that 3 percent target? If events inadvertently pushed inflation up to 4 or 5 percent, why wouldn't they just raise the target? There is, after all, nothing special about the number 3. By contrast, zero is the only number for the inflation rate at which the Fed can claim that it achieved price stability and fully eliminated the costs of inflation.

Con: The Central Bank Should Not Aim for Zero Inflation

Although price stability may be desirable, the benefits of zero inflation compared to moderate inflation are small, whereas the costs of reaching zero inflation are large. Estimates of the sacrifice ratio suggest that reducing inflation by 1 percentage point requires giving up about 5 percent of one year's output. Reducing inflation from, say, 4 percent to zero requires a loss of 20 percent of a year's output. Although people might dislike inflation of 4 percent, it is not at all clear that they would (or should) be willing to pay 20 percent of a year's income to get rid of it.

The social costs of disinflation are even larger than this 20 percent figure suggests, for the lost income is not spread equitably over the population. When the economy goes into recession, all incomes do not fall proportionately. Instead, the fall in aggregate income is concentrated on those workers who lose their jobs. The vulnerable workers are often those with the least skills and experience. Hence, much of the cost of reducing inflation is borne by those who can least afford to pay it.

Although economists can list several costs of inflation, there is no professional consensus that these costs are substantial. The shoeleather costs, menu costs, and others that economists have identified do not seem great, at least for moderate rates of inflation. It is true that the public dislikes inflation, but the public may be misled into believing the inflation fallacy—the view that inflation erodes living standards. Economists understand that living standards depend on productivity, not monetary policy. Because inflation in nominal incomes goes hand in hand with inflation in prices, reducing inflation would not cause real incomes to rise more rapidly.

Moreover, policymakers can reduce many of the costs of inflation without actually reducing inflation. They can eliminate the problems associated with the non-indexed tax system by rewriting the tax laws to take account of the effects of inflation. They can also reduce the arbitrary redistributions of wealth between creditors and debtors caused by unexpected inflation by issuing indexed government bonds, as in fact the Clinton administration did in 1997. Such an act insulates holders of government debt from inflation. In addition, by setting an example, it might encourage private borrowers and lenders to write debt contracts indexed for inflation.

Reducing inflation might be desirable if it could be done at no cost, as some economists argue is possible. Yet this trick seems hard to carry out in practice. When economies reduce their rate of inflation, they almost always experience a period of high unemployment and low output. It is risky to believe that the central bank could achieve credibility so quickly as to make disinflation painless.

Indeed, a disinflationary recession can potentially leave permanent scars on the economy. Firms in all industries reduce their spending on new plants and equipment substantially during recessions, making investment the most volatile component of GDP. Even after the recession is over, the smaller stock of capital reduces productivity, incomes, and living standards below the levels they otherwise would have achieved. In addition, when workers become unemployed in recessions, they lose valuable job skills, permanently reducing their value as workers. Some economists have argued that the high unemployment in many European economies during the past decade is the aftermath of the disinflations of the 1980s.

Why should policymakers put the economy through a costly, inequitable disinflationary recession to achieve zero inflation, which may have only modest benefits? Economist Alan Blinder, who was once vice chairman of the Federal Reserve, argued in his book *Hard Heads, Soft Hearts* that policymakers should not make this choice:

> The costs that attend the low and moderate inflation rates experienced in the United States and in other industrial countries appear to be quite modest— more like a bad cold than a cancer on society. . . . As rational individuals, we do not volunteer for a lobotomy to cure a head cold. Yet, as a collectivity, we routinely prescribe the economic equivalent of lobotomy (high unemployment) as a cure for the inflationary cold.

Blinder concludes that it is better to learn to live with moderate inflation.

QuickQuiz Explain the costs and benefits of reducing inflation to zero. Which are temporary and which are permanent?

SHOULD THE GOVERNMENT BALANCE ITS BUDGET?

A persistent macroeconomic debate concerns the government's finances. Whenever the government spends more than it collects in tax revenue, it covers this budget deficit by issuing government debt. In 2002, for example, the U.S. federal government was expected to run a budget deficit of $157 billion.

When we studied financial markets in Chapter 13, we saw how budget deficits affect saving, investment, and interest rates. But how big a problem are budget deficits? Our fourth debate concerns whether fiscal policymakers should make balancing the government's budget a high priority.

Pro: The Government Should Balance Its Budget

The U.S. federal government is far more indebted today than it was two decades ago. In 1980, the federal debt was $710 billion; in 2002, it was $3.5 trillion. If we divide today's debt by the size of the population, we learn that each person's share of the government debt is about $13,000.

The most direct effect of the government debt is to place a burden on future generations of taxpayers. When these debts and accumulated interest come due, future taxpayers will face a difficult choice. They can pay higher taxes, enjoy less government spending, or both, in order to make resources available to pay off the debt and accumulated interest. Or they can delay the day of reckoning and put the government into even deeper debt by borrowing once again to pay off the old debt and interest. In essence, when the government runs a budget deficit and issues government debt, it allows current taxpayers to pass the bill for some of their government spending on to future taxpayers. Inheriting such a large debt cannot help but lower the living standard of future generations.

In addition to this direct effect, budget deficits also have various macroeconomic effects. Because budget deficits represent *negative* public saving, they lower national saving (the sum of private and public saving). Reduced national saving causes real interest rates to rise and investment to fall. Reduced investment leads over time to a smaller stock of capital. A lower capital stock reduces labor productivity, real wages, and the economy's production of goods and services. Thus, when the government increases its debt, future generations are born into an economy with lower incomes as well as higher taxes.

There are, nevertheless, situations in which running a budget deficit is justifiable. Throughout history, the most common cause of increased government debt is war. When a military conflict raises government spending temporarily, it is reasonable to finance this extra spending by borrowing. Otherwise, taxes during wartime would have to rise precipitously. Such high tax rates would greatly distort the incentives faced by those who are taxed, leading to large deadweight losses. In addition, such high tax rates would be unfair to current generations of taxpayers, who already have to make the sacrifice of fighting the war.

Similarly, it is reasonable to allow a budget deficit during a temporary downturn in economic activity. When the economy goes into a recession, tax revenue falls automatically, because the income tax and the payroll tax are levied on measures of income. If the government tried to balance its budget during a recession, it would have to raise taxes or cut spending at a time of high unemployment. Such a policy would tend to depress aggregate demand at precisely the time it needed to be stimulated and, therefore, would tend to increase the magnitude of economic fluctuations.

Yet not all budget deficits can be justified by appealing to war or recession. U.S. government debt as a percentage of GDP increased from 26 percent in 1980 to 50 percent in 1995. During this period, the United States avoided major military conflict and major economic downturn. Nonetheless, the government consistently ran a large budget deficit, largely because the president and Congress found it easier to increase government spending than to increase taxes.

The budget deficit of 2002 can, perhaps, be rationalized by the lingering effects of the recession of 2001 and by the war on terrorism. But it is imperative that this deficit not signal a return to the unsustainable fiscal policy of an earlier era. Compared to the alternative of ongoing budget deficits, a balanced budget means greater national saving, investment, and economic growth. It means that future college graduates will enter a more prosperous economy.

"My share of the government debt is $13,000."

Con: The Government Should Not Balance Its Budget

The problem of government debt is often exaggerated. Although the government debt does represent a tax burden on younger generations, it is not large compared to the average person's lifetime income. The debt of the U.S. federal government is about $13,000 per person. A person who works 40 years for $25,000 a year will earn $1 million over his lifetime. His share of the government debt represents less than 2 percent of his lifetime resources.

Moreover, it is misleading to view the effects of budget deficits in isolation. The budget deficit is just one piece of a large picture of how the government chooses to raise and spend money. In making these decisions over fiscal policy, policymakers affect different generations of taxpayers in many ways. The government's budget deficit or surplus should be considered together with these other policies.

For example, suppose the government reduces the budget deficit by cutting spending on public investments, such as education. Does this policy make young generations better off? The government debt will be smaller when they enter the labor force, which means a smaller tax burden. Yet if they are less well educated than they could be, their productivity and incomes will be lower. Many estimates of the return to schooling (the increase in a worker's wage that results from an additional year in school) find that it is quite large. Reducing the budget deficit rather than funding more education spending could, all things considered, make future generations worse off.

Single-minded concern about the budget deficit is also dangerous because it draws attention away from various other policies that redistribute income across generations. For example, in the 1960s and 1970s, the U.S. federal government raised Social Security benefits for the elderly. It financed this higher spending by increasing the payroll tax on the working-age population. This policy redistributed income away from younger generations toward older generations, even though it did not affect the government debt. Thus, the budget deficit is only a small part of the larger issue of how government policy affects the welfare of different generations.

To some extent, the adverse effects of government debt can be reversed by forward-looking parents. Suppose a parent is worried about the impact of the government debt on his children. The parent can offset the impact simply by saving and leaving a larger bequest. The bequest would enhance the children's ability to bear the burden of future taxes. Some economists claim that people do in fact behave this way. If this were true, higher private saving by parents would offset the public dissaving of budget deficits, and deficits would not affect the economy. Most economists doubt that parents are so farsighted, but some people probably do act this way, and anyone could. Deficits give people the opportunity to consume at the expense of their children, but deficits do not require them to do so. If the government debt were actually a great problem facing future generations, some parents would help to solve it.

Critics of budget deficits sometimes assert that the government debt cannot continue to rise forever, but in fact it can. Just as a bank evaluating a loan application would compare a person's debts to his income, we should judge the burden of the government debt relative to the size of the nation's income. Population growth and technological progress cause the total income of the U.S. economy to grow over time. As a result, the nation's ability to pay the interest on the government debt grows over time as well. As long as the government debt grows more slowly than the nation's income, there is nothing to prevent the government debt from growing forever.

Some numbers can put this into perspective. The real output of the U.S. economy grows on average about 3 percent per year. If the inflation rate is 2 percent per year, then nominal income grows at a rate of 5 percent per year. The government debt, therefore, can rise by 5 percent per year without increasing the ratio of debt to income. In 2002 the federal government debt was $3.5 trillion; 5 percent of this figure is $175 billion. As long as the federal budget deficit is smaller than $175 billion, the policy is sustainable. There will never be any day of reckoning that forces the budget deficits to end or the economy to collapse.

QuickQuiz Explain how reducing a government budget deficit makes future generations better off. What fiscal policy might improve the lives of future generations more than reducing a government budget deficit?

SHOULD THE TAX LAWS BE REFORMED TO ENCOURAGE SAVING?

A nation's standard of living depends on its ability to produce goods and services. This was one of the *Ten Principles of Economics* in Chapter 1. As we saw in Chapter 12, a nation's productive capability, in turn, is determined largely by how much it saves and invests for the future. Our fifth debate is whether policymakers should reform the tax laws to encourage greater saving and investment.

Pro: The Tax Laws Should Be Reformed to Encourage Saving

A nation's saving rate is a key determinant of its long-run economic prosperity. When the saving rate is higher, more resources are available for investment in new plant and equipment. A larger stock of plant and equipment, in turn, raises labor productivity, wages, and incomes. It is, therefore, no surprise that international data show a strong correlation between national saving rates and measures of economic well-being.

Another of the *Ten Principles of Economics* presented in Chapter 1 is that people respond to incentives. This lesson should apply to people's decisions about how much to save. If a nation's laws make saving attractive, people will save a higher fraction of their incomes, and this higher saving will lead to a more prosperous future.

Unfortunately, the U.S. tax system discourages saving by taxing the return to saving quite heavily. For example, consider a 25-year-old worker who saves $1,000 of her income to have a more comfortable retirement at the age of 70. If she buys a bond that pays an interest rate of 10 percent, the $1,000 will accumulate at the end of 45 years to $72,900 in the absence of taxes on interest. But suppose she faces a marginal tax rate on interest income of 40 percent, which is typical of many workers once federal and state income taxes are added together. In this case, her after-tax interest rate is only 6 percent, and the $1,000 will accumulate at the end of 45 years to only $13,800. That is, accumulated over this long span of time, the tax rate on interest income reduces the benefit of saving $1,000 from $72,900 to $13,800— or by about 80 percent.

The tax code further discourages saving by taxing some forms of capital income twice. Suppose a person uses some of his saving to buy stock in a corporation. When the corporation earns a profit from its capital investments, it first pays tax on this profit in the form of the corporate income tax. If the corporation pays out the rest of the profit to the stockholder in the form of dividends, the stockholder pays tax on this income a second time in the form of the individual income tax. This double taxation substantially reduces the return to the stockholder, thereby reducing the incentive to save.

The tax laws again discourage saving if a person wants to leave his accumulated wealth to his children (or anyone else) rather than consuming it during his lifetime. Parents can bequeath some money to their children without tax, but if the bequest becomes large, the inheritance tax rate can be as high as 55 percent. To a large extent, concern about national saving is motivated by a desire to ensure economic prosperity for future generations. It is odd, therefore, that the tax laws discourage the most direct way in which one generation can help the next.

In addition to the tax code, many other policies and institutions in our society reduce the incentive for households to save. Some government benefits, such as welfare and Medicaid, are means-tested; that is, the benefits are reduced for those who in the past have been prudent enough to save some of their income. Colleges and universities grant financial aid as a function of the wealth of the students and their parents. Such a policy is like a tax on wealth and, as such, discourages students and parents from saving.

There are various ways in which the tax code could provide an incentive to save, or at least reduce the disincentive that households now face. Already the tax laws give preferential treatment to some types of retirement saving. When a tax-payer puts income into an Individual Retirement Account (IRA), for instance, that income and the interest it earns are not taxed until the funds are withdrawn at re-tirement. The tax code gives a similar tax advantage to retirement accounts that go by other names, such as 401(k), 403(b), Keogh, and profit-sharing plans. There are, however, limits to who is eligible to use these plans and, for those who are eligible, limits on the amount that can be put in them. Moreover, because there are penal-ties for withdrawal before retirement age, these retirement plans provide little in-centive for other types of saving, such as saving to buy a house or pay for college. A small step to encourage greater saving would be to expand the ability of house-holds to use such tax-advantaged savings accounts.

A more comprehensive approach would be to reconsider the entire basis by which the government collects revenue. The centerpiece of the U.S. tax system is the income tax. A dollar earned is taxed the same whether it is spent or saved. An alternative advocated by many economists is a consumption tax. Under a con-sumption tax, a household pays taxes only on the basis of what it spends. Income that is saved is exempt from taxation until the saving is later withdrawn and spent on consumption goods. In essence, a consumption tax puts all saving automati-cally into a tax-advantaged savings account, much like an IRA. A switch from in-come to consumption taxation would greatly increase the incentive to save.

Con: The Tax Laws Should Not Be Reformed to Encourage Saving

Increasing saving may be desirable, but it is not the only goal of tax policy. Policy-makers also must be sure to distribute the tax burden fairly. The problem with pro-posals to increase the incentive to save is that they increase the tax burden on those who can least afford it.

It is an undeniable fact that high-income households save a greater fraction of their income than low-income households. As a result, any tax change that favors people who save will also tend to favor people with high income. Policies such as tax-advantaged retirement accounts may seem appealing, but they lead to a less egalitarian society. By reducing the tax burden on the wealthy who can take advantage of these accounts, they force the government to raise the tax burden on the poor.

Moreover, tax policies designed to encourage saving may not be effective at achieving that goal. Many studies have found that saving is relatively inelastic—that is, the amount of saving is not very sensitive to the rate of return on saving. If this is indeed the case, then tax provisions that raise the effective return by reduc-ing the taxation of capital income will further enrich the wealthy without inducing them to save more than they otherwise would.

Economic theory does not give a clear prediction about whether a higher rate of return would increase saving. The outcome depends on the relative size of two conflicting effects, called the *substitution effect* and the *income effect*. On the one hand, a higher rate of return raises the benefit of saving: Each dollar saved today produces more consumption in the future. This substitution effect tends to raise saving. On the other hand, a higher rate of return lowers the need for saving: A household has to save less to achieve any target level of consumption in the future. This income effect tends to reduce saving. If the substitution and income effects approximately cancel each other, as some studies suggest, then saving will not change when lower taxation of capital income raises the rate of return.

There are other ways to raise national saving than by giving tax breaks to the rich. National saving is the sum of private and public saving. Instead of trying to alter the tax code to encourage greater private saving, policymakers can simply raise public saving by reducing the budget deficit, perhaps by raising taxes on the wealthy. This offers a direct way of raising national saving and increasing prosperity for future generations.

Indeed, once public saving is taken into account, tax provisions to encourage saving might backfire. Tax changes that reduce the taxation of capital income reduce government revenue and, thereby, lead to a budget deficit. To increase national saving, such a change in the tax code must stimulate private saving by more than the decline in public saving. If this is not the case, so-called saving incentives can potentially make matters worse.

QuickQuiz Give three examples of how our society discourages saving. What are the drawbacks of eliminating these disincentives?

CONCLUSION

This chapter has considered five debates over macroeconomic policy. For each, it began with a controversial proposition and then offered the arguments pro and con. If you find it hard to choose a side in these debates, you may find some comfort in the fact that you are not alone. The study of economics does not always make it easy to choose among alternative policies. Indeed, by clarifying the inevitable tradeoffs that policymakers face, it can make the choice more difficult.

Difficult choices, however, have no right to seem easy. When you hear politicians or commentators proposing something that sounds too good to be true, it probably is. If they sound like they are offering you a free lunch, you should look for the hidden price tag. Few if any policies come with benefits but no costs. By helping you see through the fog of rhetoric so common in political discourse, the study of economics should make you a better participant in our national debates.

SUMMARY

- Advocates of active monetary and fiscal policy view the economy as inherently unstable and believe that policy can manage aggregate demand to offset the inherent instability. Critics of active monetary and fiscal policy emphasize that policy affects the economy with a lag and that our ability to forecast future economic conditions is poor. As a result, attempts to stabilize the economy can end up being destabilizing.

- Advocates of rules for monetary policy argue that discretionary policy can suffer from

incompetence, abuse of power, and time inconsistency. Critics of rules for monetary policy argue that discretionary policy is more flexible in responding to changing economic circumstances.

- Advocates of a zero-inflation target emphasize that inflation has many costs and few if any benefits. Moreover, the cost of eliminating inflation—depressed output and employment— is only temporary. Even this cost can be reduced if the central bank announces a credible plan to reduce inflation, thereby directly lowering expectations of inflation. Critics of a zero-inflation target claim that moderate inflation imposes only small costs on society, whereas the recession necessary to reduce inflation is quite costly.

- Advocates of a balanced government budget argue that budget deficits impose an unjustifiable burden on future generations by raising their taxes and lowering their incomes. Critics of a balanced government budget argue that the deficit is only one small piece of fiscal policy. Single-minded concern about the budget deficit can obscure the many ways in which policy, including various spending programs, affects different generations.

- Advocates of tax incentives for saving point out that our society discourages saving in many ways, such as by heavily taxing the income from capital and by reducing benefits for those who have accumulated wealth. They endorse reforming the tax laws to encourage saving, perhaps by switching from an income tax to a consumption tax. Critics of tax incentives for saving argue that many proposed changes to stimulate saving would primarily benefit the wealthy, who do not need a tax break. They also argue that such changes might have only a small effect on private saving. Raising public saving by decreasing the government's budget deficit would provide a more direct and equitable way to increase national saving.

QUESTIONS FOR REVIEW

1. What causes the lags in the effect of monetary and fiscal policy on aggregate demand? What are the implications of these lags for the debate over active versus passive policy?

2. What might motivate a central banker to cause a political business cycle? What does the political business cycle imply for the debate over policy rules?

3. Explain how credibility might affect the cost of reducing inflation.

4. Why are some economists against a target of zero inflation?

5. Explain two ways in which a government budget deficit hurts a future worker.

6. What are two situations in which most economists view a budget deficit as justifiable?

7. Give an example of how the government might hurt young generations, even while reducing the government debt they inherit.

8. Some economists say that the government can continue running a budget deficit forever. How is that possible?

9. Some income from capital is taxed twice. Explain.

10. Give an example, other than tax policy, of how our society discourages saving.

11. What adverse effect might be caused by tax incentives to raise saving?

PROBLEMS AND APPLICATIONS

1. The chapter suggests that the economy, like the human body, has "natural restorative powers."
   a. Illustrate the short-run effect of a fall in aggregate demand using an aggregate-demand/aggregate-supply diagram. What happens to total output, income, and employment?
   b. If the government does not use stabilization policy, what happens to the economy over time? Illustrate on your diagram. Does this adjustment generally occur in a matter of months or a matter of years?
   c. Do you think the "natural restorative powers" of the economy mean that policymakers should be passive in response to the business cycle?

2. Policymakers who want to stabilize the economy must decide how much to change the money supply, government spending, or taxes. Why is it difficult for policymakers to choose the appropriate strength of their actions?

3. Suppose that people suddenly wanted to hold more money balances.
   a. What would be the effect of this change on the economy if the Federal Reserve followed a rule of increasing the money supply by 3 percent per year? Illustrate your answer with a money-market diagram and an aggregate-demand/aggregate-supply diagram.
   b. What would be the effect of this change on the economy if the Fed followed a rule of increasing the money supply by 3 percent per year *plus* 1 percentage point for every percentage point that unemployment rises

above its normal level? Illustrate your answer.
   c. Which of the foregoing rules better stabilizes the economy? Would it help to allow the Fed to respond to predicted unemployment instead of current unemployment? Explain.

4. Some economists have proposed that the Fed use the following rule for choosing its target for the federal funds interest rate (r):

$$r = 2\% + \pi + 1/2\,(y - y^*)/y^* + 1/2\,(\pi - \pi^*),$$

where π is the average of the inflation rate over the past year, y is real GDP as recently measured, y^* is an estimate of the natural rate of output, and π^* is the Fed's goal for inflation.
   a. Explain the logic that might lie behind this rule for setting interest rates. Would you support the Fed's use of this rule?
   b. Some economists advocate such a rule for monetary policy but believe π and y should be the *forecasts* of future values of inflation and output. What are the advantages of using forecasts instead of actual values? What are the disadvantages?

5. The problem of time inconsistency applies to fiscal policy as well as to monetary policy. Suppose the government announced a reduction in taxes on income from capital investments, like new factories.
   a. If investors believed that capital taxes would remain low, how would the government's action affect the level of investment?
   b. After investors have responded to the announced tax reduction, does the

government have an incentive to renege on its policy? Explain.

c. Given your answer to part (b), would investors believe the government's announcement? What can the government do to increase the credibility of announced policy changes?

d. Explain why this situation is similar to the time inconsistency problem faced by monetary policymakers.

6. Chapter 2 explains the difference between positive analysis and normative analysis. In the debate about whether the central bank should aim for zero inflation, which areas of disagreement involve positive statements and which involve normative judgments?

7. Why are the benefits of reducing inflation permanent and the costs temporary? Why are the costs of increasing inflation permanent and the benefits temporary? Use Phillips-curve diagrams in your answer.

8. Suppose the federal government cuts taxes and increases spending, raising the budget deficit to 12 percent of GDP. If nominal GDP is rising 7 percent per year, are such budget deficits sustainable forever? Explain. If budget deficits of this size are maintained for 20 years, what is likely to happen to your taxes and your children's taxes in the future? Can you do something today to offset this future effect?

9. Explain how each of the following policies redistributes income across generations. Is the redistribution from young to old, or from old to young?

a. an increase in the budget deficit
b. more generous subsidies for education loans
c. greater investments in highways and bridges
d. indexation of Social Security benefits to inflation

10. Surveys suggest that most people are opposed to budget deficits, but these same people elected representatives who in the 1980s and 1990s passed budgets with significant deficits. Why might the opposition to budget deficits be stronger in principle than in practice?

11. The chapter says that budget deficits reduce the income of future generations, but can boost output and income during a recession. Explain how both of these statements can be true.

12. What is the fundamental tradeoff that society faces if it chooses to save more?

13. Suppose the government reduced the tax rate on income from savings.

a. Who would benefit from this tax reduction most directly?

b. What would happen to the capital stock over time? What would happen to the capital available to each worker? What would happen to productivity? What would happen to wages?

c. In light of your answer to part (b), who might benefit from this tax reduction in the long run?

http://   For more study tools, please visit http://mankiwXtra.swlearning.com.

GLOSSARY

absolute advantage the comparison among producers of a good according to their productivity

aggregate-demand curve a curve that shows the quantity of goods and services that households, firms, and the government want to buy at each price level

aggregate risk risk that affects all economic actors at once

aggregate-supply curve a curve that shows the quantity of goods and services that firms choose to produce and sell at each price level

appreciation an increase in the value of a currency as measured by the amount of foreign currency it can buy

automatic stabilizers changes in fiscal policy that stimulate aggregate demand when the economy goes into a recession without policymakers having to take any deliberate action

balanced trade a situation in which exports equal imports

bond a certificate of indebtedness

budget deficit a shortfall of tax revenue from government spending

budget surplus an excess of tax revenue over government spending

business cycle fluctuations in economic activity, such as employment and production

capital flight a large and sudden reduction in the demand for assets located in a country

catch-up effect the property whereby countries that start off poor tend to grow more rapidly than countries that start off rich

central bank an institution designed to oversee the banking system and regulate the quantity of money in the economy

circular-flow diagram a visual model of the economy that shows how dollars flow through markets among households and firms

classical dichotomy the theoretical separation of nominal and real variables

closed economy an economy that does not interact with other economies in the world

collective bargaining the process by which unions and firms agree on the terms of employment

commodity money money that takes the form of a commodity with intrinsic value

comparative advantage the comparison among producers of a good according to their opportunity cost

competitive market a market in which there are many buyers and many sellers so that each has a negligible impact on the market price

complements two goods for which an increase in the price of one leads to a decrease in the demand for the other

compounding the accumulation of a sum of money in, say, a bank account, where the interest earned remains in the account to earn additional interest in the future

consumer price index (CPI) a measure of the overall cost of the goods and services bought by a typical consumer

consumer surplus a buyer's willingness to pay minus the amount the buyer actually pays

consumption spending by households on goods and services, with the exception of purchases of new housing

cost the value of everything a seller must give up to produce a good

cross-price elasticity of demand a measure of how much the quantity demanded of one good responds to a change in the price of another good, computed as the percentage change in quantity demanded of the first good divided by the percentage change in the price of the second good

crowding out a decrease in investment that results from government borrowing

crowding-out effect the offset in aggregate demand that results when expansionary fiscal policy raises the interest rate and thereby reduces investment spending

currency the paper bills and coins in the hands of the public

cyclical unemployment the deviation of unemployment from its natural rate

deadweight loss the fall in total surplus that results from a market distortion, such as a tax

demand curve a graph of the relationship between the price of a good and the quantity demanded

demand deposits balances in bank accounts that depositors can access on demand by writing a check

demand schedule a table that shows the relationship between the price of a good and the quantity demanded

depreciation a decrease in the value of a currency as measured by the amount of foreign currency it can buy

depression a severe recession

diminishing returns the property whereby the benefit from an extra unit of an input declines as the quantity of the input increases

discount rate the interest rate on the loans that the Fed makes to banks

discouraged workers individuals who would like to work but have given up looking for a job

diversification the reduction of risk achieved by replacing a single risk with a large number of smaller unrelated risks

economics the study of how society manages its scarce resources

efficiency the property of a resource allocation of maximizing the total surplus received by all members of society

efficiency the property of society getting the most it can from its scarce resources

efficiency wages above-equilibrium wages paid by firms in order to increase worker productivity

efficient markets hypothesis the theory that asset prices reflect all publicly available information about the value of an asset

elasticity a measure of the responsiveness of quantity demanded or quantity supplied to one of its determinants

equilibrium a situation in which the price has reached the level where quantity supplied equals quantity demanded

equilibrium price the price that balances quantity supplied and quantity demanded

equilibrium quantity the quantity supplied and the quantity demanded at the equilibrium price

equity the property of distributing economic prosperity fairly among the members of society

exports goods and services that are produced domestically and sold abroad

externality the impact of one person's actions on the well-being of a bystander

Federal Reserve (Fed) the central bank of the United States

fiat money money without intrinsic value that is used as money because of government decree

finance the field that studies how people make decisions regarding the allocation of resources over time and the handling of risk

financial intermediaries financial institutions through which savers can indirectly provide funds to borrowers

financial markets financial institutions through which savers can directly provide funds to borrowers

financial system the group of institutions in the economy that help to match one person's saving with another person's investment

Fisher effect the one-for-one adjustment of the nominal interest rate to the inflation rate

fractional-reserve banking a banking system in which banks hold only a fraction of deposits as reserves

frictional unemployment unemployment that results because it takes time for workers to search for the jobs that best suit their tastes and skills

fundamental analysis the study of a company's accounting statements and future prospects to determine its value

future value the amount of money in the future that an amount of money today will yield, given prevailing interest rates

GDP deflator a measure of the price level calculated as the ratio of nominal GDP to real GDP times 100

government purchases spending on goods and services by local, state, and federal governments

gross domestic product (GDP) the market value of all final goods and services produced within a country in a given period of time

human capital the knowledge and skills that workers acquire through education, training, and experience

idiosyncratic risk risk that affects only a single economic actor

import quota a limit on the quantity of a good that can be produced abroad and sold domestically

imports goods and services that are produced abroad and sold domestically

income elasticity of demand a measure of how much the quantity demanded of a good responds to a change in consumers' income, computed as the percentage change in quantity demanded divided by the percentage change in income

indexation the automatic correction of a dollar amount for the effects of inflation by law or contract

inferior good a good for which, other things equal, an increase in income leads to a decrease in demand

inflation an increase in the overall level of prices in the economy

inflation rate the percentage change in the price index from the preceding period

inflation tax the revenue the government raises by creating money

informationally efficient reflecting all available information in a rational way

investment spending on capital equipment, inventories, and structures, including household purchases of new housing

job search the process by which workers find appropriate jobs given their tastes and skills

labor force the total number of workers, including both the employed and the unemployed

labor-force participation rate the percentage of the adult population that is in the labor force

law of demand the claim that, other things equal, the quantity demanded of a good falls when the price of the good rises

law of supply the claim that, other things equal, the quantity supplied of a good rises when the price of the good rises

law of supply and demand the claim that the price of any good adjusts to bring the quantity supplied and the quantity demanded for that good into balance

liquidity the ease with which an asset can be converted into the economy's medium of exchange

macroeconomics the study of economy-wide phenomena, including inflation, unemployment, and economic growth

marginal changes small incremental adjustments to a plan of action

market a group of buyers and sellers of a particular good or service

market economy an economy that allocates resources through the decentralized decisions of many firms and households as they interact in markets for goods and services

market failure a situation in which a market left on its own fails to allocate resources efficiently

market for loanable funds the market in which those who want to save supply funds and those who want to borrow to invest demand funds

market power the ability of a single economic actor (or small group of actors) to have a substantial influence on market prices

medium of exchange an item that buyers give to sellers when they want to purchase goods and services

menu costs the costs of changing prices

microeconomics the study of how households and firms make decisions and how they interact in markets

model of aggregate demand and aggregate supply the model that most economists use to explain short-run fluctuations in economic activity around its long-run trend

monetary neutrality the proposition that changes in the money supply do not affect real variables

monetary policy the setting of the money supply by policymakers in the central bank

money the set of assets in an economy that people regularly use to buy goods and services from other people

money multiplier the amount of money the banking system generates with each dollar of reserves

money supply the quantity of money available in the economy

multiplier effect the additional shifts in aggregate demand that result when expansionary fiscal policy increases income and thereby increases consumer spending

mutual fund an institution that sells shares to the public and uses the proceeds to buy a portfolio of stocks and bonds

national saving (saving) the total income in the economy that remains after paying for consumption and government purchases

natural-rate hypothesis the claim that unemployment eventually returns to its normal, or natural, rate, regardless of the rate of inflation

natural rate of unemployment the normal rate of unemployment around which the unemployment rate fluctuates

natural resources the inputs into the production of goods and services that are provided by nature, such as land, rivers, and mineral deposits

net capital outflow the purchase of foreign assets by domestic residents minus the purchase of domestic assets by foreigners

net exports the value of a nation's exports minus the value of its imports; also called the trade balance

nominal exchange rate the rate at which a person can trade the currency of one country for the currency of another

nominal GDP the production of goods and services valued at current prices

nominal interest rate the interest rate as usually reported without a correction for the effects of inflation

nominal variables variables measured in monetary units

normal good a good for which, other things equal, an increase in income leads to an increase in demand

normative statements claims that attempt to prescribe how the world should be

open economy an economy that interacts freely with other economies around the world

open-market operations the purchase and sale of U.S. government bonds by the Fed

opportunity cost whatever must be given up to obtain some item

Phillips curve a curve that shows the short-run tradeoff between inflation and unemployment

physical capital the stock of equipment and structures that are used to produce goods and services

positive statements claims that attempt to describe the world as it is

present value the amount of money today that would be needed to produce, using

prevailing interest rates, a given future amount of money

price ceiling a legal maximum on the price at which a good can be sold

price elasticity of demand a measure of how much the quantity demanded of a good responds to a change in the price of that good, computed as the percentage change in quantity demanded divided by the percentage change in price

price elasticity of supply a measure of how much the quantity supplied of a good responds to a change in the price of that good, computed as the percentage change in quantity supplied divided by the percentage change in price

price floor a legal minimum on the price at which a good can be sold

private saving the income that households have left after paying for taxes and consumption

producer price index a measure of the cost of a basket of goods and services bought by firms

producer surplus the amount a seller is paid for a good minus the seller's cost

production possibilities frontier a graph that shows the combinations of output that the economy can possibly produce given the available factors of production and the available production technology

productivity the amount of goods and services produced from each hour of a worker's time

public saving the tax revenue that the government has left after paying for its spending

purchasing-power parity a theory of exchange rates whereby a unit of any given currency should be able to buy the same quantity of goods in all countries

quantity demanded the amount of a good that buyers are willing and able to purchase

quantity equation the equation $M \times V = P \times Y$, which relates the quantity of money, the velocity of money, and the dollar value of the economy's output of goods and services

quantity supplied the amount of a good that sellers are willing and able to sell

quantity theory of money a theory asserting that the quantity of money available determines the price level and that the growth rate in the quantity of money available determines the inflation rate

random walk the path of a variable whose changes are impossible to predict

rational expectations the theory according to which people optimally use all the information they have, including information about government policies, when forecasting the future

real exchange rate the rate at which a person can trade the goods and services of one country for the goods and services of another

real GDP the production of goods and services valued at constant prices

real interest rate the interest rate corrected for the effects of inflation

real variables variables measured in physical units

recession a period of declining real incomes and rising unemployment

reserve ratio the fraction of deposits that banks hold as reserves

reserve requirements regulations on the minimum amount of reserves that banks must hold against deposits

reserves deposits that banks have received but have not loaned out

risk averse exhibiting a dislike of uncertainty

sacrifice ratio the number of percentage points of annual output lost in the process of reducing inflation by 1 percentage point

scarcity the limited nature of society's resources

shoeleather costs the resources wasted when inflation encourages people to reduce their money holdings

shortage a situation in which quantity demanded is greater than quantity supplied

stagflation a period of falling output and rising prices

stock a claim to partial ownership in a firm

store of value an item that people can use to transfer purchasing power from the present to the future

strike the organized withdrawal of labor from a firm by a union

structural unemployment unemployment that results because the number of jobs available in some labor markets is insufficient to provide a job for everyone who wants one

substitutes two goods for which an increase in the price of one leads to an increase in the demand for the other

supply curve a graph of the relationship between the price of a good and the quantity supplied

supply schedule a table that shows the relationship between the price of a good and the quantity supplied

supply shock an event that directly alters firms' costs and prices, shifting the economy's aggregate-supply curve and thus the Phillips curve

surplus a situation in which quantity supplied is greater than quantity demanded

tariff a tax on goods produced abroad and sold domestically

tax incidence the manner in which the burden of a tax is shared among participants in a market

technological knowledge society's understanding of the best ways to produce goods and services

theory of liquidity preference Keynes's theory that the interest rate adjusts to bring money supply and money demand into balance

total revenue the amount paid by buyers and received by sellers of a good, computed as the price of the good times the quantity sold

trade balance the value of a nation's exports minus the value of its imports; also called net exports

trade deficit an excess of imports over exports

trade policy a government policy that directly influences the quantity of goods and services that a country imports or exports

trade surplus an excess of exports over imports

unemployment insurance a government program that partially protects workers' incomes when they become unemployed

unemployment rate the percentage of the labor force that is unemployed

union a worker association that bargains with employers over wages and working conditions

unit of account the yardstick people use to post prices and record debts

velocity of money the rate at which money changes hands

welfare economics the study of how the allocation of resources affects economic well-being

willingness to pay the maximum amount that a buyer will pay for a good

world price the price of a good that prevails in the world market for that good

INDEX

SUGGESTIONS FOR SUMMER READING

IF YOU ENJOYED THE ECONOMICS COURSE THAT YOU HAVE JUST FINISHED, YOU MIGHT LIKE READING MORE ABOUT ECONOMIC ISSUES IN THE FOLLOWING BOOKS.

ROBERT J. BARRO

Nothing Is Sacred:
Economic Ideas for the New Millennium
Cambridge, Mass.: MIT Press, 2002

In this collection of essays, economist Robert Barro offers his views about economists, the economy, and the proper scope of public policy.

ALAN S. BLINDER AND JANET L. YELLEN

The Fabulous Decade:
Macroeconomic Lessons from the 1990s
Twentieth Century Fund, 2001

Two economic advisers to President Bill Clinton look back at a prosperous decade for the U.S. economy.

TODD G. BUCHHOLZ

New Ideas from Dead Economists
New York: Penguin Books, 1989

This amusing book provides an overview of the history of economic thought.

COUNCIL OF ECONOMIC ADVISERS

Economic Report of the President
U.S. Government Printing Office, released every year

The annual report of the CEA surveys the state of economy and presents the case for the president's economic program.

AVINASH DIXIT AND BARRY NALEBUFF

Thinking Strategically: A Competitive Edge in Business, Politics, and Everyday Life
New York: Norton, 1991

This introduction to game theory discusses how all people – from corporate executives to criminals under arrest – should and do make strategic decisions.

WILLIAM EASTERLY

The Elusive Quest for Growth: Economists' Adventures and Misadventures in the Tropics
Cambridge, Mass.: MIT Press, 2001

A World Bank economist examines the many attempts to help the world's poorest nations and why they have so often failed.